D1198942

E DUE

CLYMER

ARCTIC CAT
SNOWMOBILE SHOP MANUAL
1990-1998

The world's finest publisher of mechanical how-to manuals

PRIMEDIA
Information Data Products

P.O. Box 12901, Overland Park, KS 66282-2901

Copyright © 1999 PRIMEDIA Business Magazines & Media Inc.

FIRST EDITION
First Printing December, 1999
Second Printing December, 2001
Third Printing September, 2003
Fourth Printing November, 2004

Printed in U.S.A.

CLYMER and colophon are registered trademarks of PRIMEDIA Business Magazines & Media Inc.

ISBN: 0-89287-701-4

Library of Congress: 99-69126

TECHNICAL PHOTOGRAPHY: Mark Jacobs and Ron Wright.

TECHNICAL ILLUSTRATIONS: Michael St. Clair.

TECHNICAL ASSISTANCE:
Don Anderson, Instructor/Technical Supervisor and Coordinator, Trade and Industrial Development
Northwest Technical College
Outdoor Power Equipment & Snowmobile Technology Department
Detroit Lakes, MN 56501

Russ Seaburg
Seaburg Power Sports
Highway 59 North RR. 3
Detroit Lakes, MN 56501

Dale Fett, Technical Advisor
Fett Brothers Performance, Inc.
Route 4, Box 316
Frazee, MN 56544

Snowmobile Code of Ethics provided by the International Snowmobile Industry Association, Fairfax, Virginia.

COVER: Courtesy of Snow Goer Magazine, Maple Grove, MN 55369.

PRODUCTION: Shara Pierceall.

CLYMER®

Publisher Shawn Etheridge

EDITORIAL

Managing Editor
James Grooms

Associate Editor
Lee Buell

Technical Writers
Jay Bogart
Michael Morlan
George Parise
Mark Rolling
Ed Scott
Ron Wright

Editorial Production Manager
Dylan Goodwin

Senior Production Editor
Greg Araujo

Production Editors
Holly Messinger
Darin Watson

Associate Production Editors
Susan Hartington
Julie Jantzer-Ward
Justin Marciniak

Technical Illustrators
Steve Amos
Errol McCarthy
Mitzi McCarthy
Bob Meyer

MARKETING/SALES AND ADMINISTRATION

Associate Publisher
Vickie Martin

Advertising & Promotions Manager
Elda Starke

Advertising & Promotions Coordinators
Melissa Abbott

Art Director
Chris Paxton

Associate Art Director
Jennifer Knight

Sales Managers
Ted Metzger, Manuals
Dutch Sadler, Marine
Matt Tusken, Motorcycles

Business Manager
Ron Rogers

Customer Service Manager
Terri Cannon

Customer Service Representatives
Shawna Davis
Courtney Hollars
Susan Kohlmeyer
April LeBlond
Jennifer Lassiter

Warehouse & Inventory Manager
Leah Hicks

PRIMEDIA
Business Magazines & Media
P.O. Box 12901, Overland Park, KS 66282-2901 • 800-262-1954 • 913-967-1719

The following books and guides are published by PRIMEDIA Business Directories & Books.

More information available at *primediabooks.com*

Contents

Quick Reference Data

RECOMMENDED LUBRICANTS AND FUEL

Engine oil	Arctic Cat 50:1 Injection Oil
Coolant	Glycol-based automotive type antifreeze compounded for aluminum engines
Chaincase	Arctic Cat Chain Lube
Grease	Low-temperature grease
Fuel	87 minimum octane
Brake fluid	Arctic Cat Hi-Temp Brake Fluid

FLUID CAPACITIES

Chaincase		
Without reverse	236 cc	8 oz.
1993-1995	345 cc	12 oz.
Cooling system		
1990-1991	–	–
1992	2.4 L	2.5 qt.
1993	2.9 L	3.0 qt.
1994		
Cougar	2.4 L	2.5 qt.
EXT 580	3.3 L	3.5 qt.
ZR440, ZR580	2.9 L	3.0 qt.
1995		
Z 440	air-cooled	
ZR 440	2.9 L	3.0 qt.
Cougar, Cougar Mtn. Cat	3.3 L	3.5 qt.
Prowler 2-Up	3.3 L	3.5 qt.
EXT 580 (all models)	2.9 L	3.0 qt.
ZR 580, ZR 580 EFI	2.9 L	3.0 qt.
1996		
Z 440	air-cooled	
ZR 440	2.9 L	3.0 qt.
Cougar	3.3 L	3.5 qt.
Cougar Mtn. Cat, Cougar 2-Up	3.3 L	3.5 qt.
EXT 580 (all models)	2.9 L	3.0 qt.
ZR 580	2.9 L	3.0 qt.
ZRT 600	4.2 L	4.4 qt.

(continued)

Cooling system

  1997

Z 440	air-cooled	
Panther 440	air-cooled	
ZL 440, ZR 440	2.9 L	3.0 qt.
Cougar	2.9 L	3.0 qt.
Cougar Mtn. Cat	2.9 L	3.0 qt.
Panther 550	2.9 L	3.0 qt.
Pantera EFI	3.1 L	3.3 qt.
Powder Special (with carburetors)	4.2 L	4.4 qt.
EXT 580 EFI	3.1 L	3.3 qt.
EXT 580 EFI DLX	3.1 L	3.3 qt.
Powder Special EFI	3.1 L	3.3 qt.
ZR 580	3.1 L	3.3 qt.
EXT 600, ZRT 600	4.2 L	4.4 qt.
Powder Extreme	4.2 L	4.4 qt.

  1998

Z 440	air-cooled	
Panther 440	air-cooled	
ZL 440, ZR 440	2.9 L	3.0 qt.
ZL 500, ZR 500	3.1 L	3.3 qt.
Cougar, Cougar DLX	2.9 L	3.0 qt.
Cougar Mtn. Cat	2.9 L	3.0 qt.
Panther 550	2.9 L	3.0 qt.
Pantera EFI	2.9 L	3.0 qt.
Powder Special (with carburetors)	4.2 L	4.5 qt.
EXT 580 EFI	2.9 L	3.0 qt.
EXT 580 EFI DLX	2.9 L	3.0 qt.
Powder Special EFI	-	-
ZR 600 (with carburetors)	3.1 L	3.3 qt.
EXT 600, ZRT 600	4.2 L	4.4 qt.
Powder Extreme	4.2 L	4.4 qt.

Fuel tank

1990	29.5 L	7.8 gal.
1992		
Prowler	27.3 L	7.2 gal.
1993		
440 ZR	34 L	9 gal.
580 ZR	34 L	9 gal.
1994		
Cougar	41.6 L	11 gal.
ZR 440	38 L	10 gal.
EXT 580	42 L	11 gal.
ZR 580	38 L	10 gal.
1995		
Z 440	37.5 L	9.9 gal.
ZR 440	38 L	10 gal.
Cougar	41.7 L	11 gal.
ZR 580, ZR 580 EFI	37.5 L	9.9 gal.
1996		
Z 440	37.5 L	9.9 gal.
ZR 440	37.5 L	9.9 gal.
ZRT 600	33.7 L	8.9 gal.

(continued)

FLUID CAPACITIES (continued)

Fuel tank
1997

Z 440	39.7 L	10.5 gal.
Panther 440	39.7 L	10.5 gal.
ZL 440, ZR 440	37.5 L	9.9 gal.
ZR 580 EFI	35.9 L	9.5 gal.
Cougar, Cougar Mountain Cat	34.1 L	9 gal.
Panther 550	34.1 L	9 gal.
EXT 580 EFI	39.7 L	10.5 gal.
EXT 580 DLX	39.7 L	10.5 gal.
Pantera	39.7 L	10.5 gal.
Powder Special EFI	39.7 L	10.5 gal.
EXT 600	37.5 L	9.9 gal.
ZRT 600	37.5 L	9.9 gal.
Powder Extreme	35.9 L	9.5 gal.

1998

Z 440	39.7 L	10.5 gal.
Panther 440	39.7 L	10.5 gal.
ZL 440, ZR 440	35.7 L	9.4 gal.
ZL 500	35.7 L	9.4 gal.
Cougar, Cougar Deluxe	37.1 L	9.8 gal.
Cougar Mountain Cat	35.4 L	9.4 gal.
Panther 550	35.4 L	9.4 gal.
EXT 580 EFI	40.1 L	10.6 gal.
EXT 580 EFI DLX	40.1 L	10.6 gal.
Pantera	39.7 L	10.5 gal.
Powder Special EFI	39.7 L	10.5 gal.
EXT 600	41.3 L	10.9 gal.
EXT 600 Touring	35.4 L	9.4 gal.
ZRT 600	37.1 L	9.8 gal.
Powder Extreme	35.9 L	9.5 gal.

SPARK PLUGS

	Plug type	Gap (mm [in.])
1998 models	NGK BR9EYA	0.7 (0.028)
1997 Powder Special EFI	NGK BR9EYA	0.7 (0.028)
1997 ZR 580 EFI	NGK BR9EYA	0.7 (0.028)
All other models	NGK BR9ES	0.7 (0.028)

CARBURETOR PILOT AIR SCREW AND IDLE SPEED

	Pilot air screw turns out*	Idle speed rpm
1990		
Prowler, El Tigre EXT	1	2000-2500
1991-1992		
Cougar, Prowler, El Tigre EXT	1	2000-2500

(continued)

CARBURETOR PILOT AIR SCREW AND IDLE SPEED (continued)

	Pilot air screw turns out*	Idle speed rpm
1993		
440 ZR	1-1 1/2	1500
Cougar, Prowler	1	2000-2500
EXT 550	1	1500-2000
580 ZR, EXT 580 Z	1-1 1/2	1500
1994		
Cougar, Prowler	1	1500-2000
ZR 440, ZR 580	1	1500-2000
EXT 580	1-1 1/2	1500-2000
1995		
Z 440, ZR 440	1	1500-2000
Cougar, Prowler 2-Up	1	1500-2000
EXT 580, ZR 580	1-1 1/2	1500-2000
1996		
Z 440	1	1500-2000
ZR 440	1	1500-2000
Cougar, Cougar 2-Up	1	1500-2000
EXT 580, ZR 580	1-1 1/2	1500-2000
ZRT 600	1 1/2	1500-2000
1997		
Z 440	1	1500-2000
ZL 440, ZR 440	1	1500-2000
Panther 440 and 550	1	1500-2000
Cougar	1	1500-2000
Powder Special	1-1 1/2	1500-2000
EXT 600, ZRT 600, Powder Extreme	1 1/2	1500-2000
1998		
Z 440	3/4	1500-2000
Panther 440	3/4	1500-2000
ZL 440	1 1/2	1500-2000
ZR 440	1 1/4	1500-2000
ZL 500	1	1500-2000
Panther 550	1	1500-2000
Cougar	1	1500-2000
Powder Special	1 1/4	1500-2000
EXT 600, ZRT 600	1 1/2	1500-2000
Powder Extreme	1	1500-2000

*The listed number indicates the recommended initial setting (turns out from lightly seated) and is usually correct within ±1/8 turn.

DRIVE BELT SPECIFICATIONS

Model	Part No.	Width mm (in.)	Circumference cm (in.)
1990			
Prowler, El Tigre EXT	0227-032	34.1-35.7 (1.344-1.406)	110.5-111.1 (43.50-43.74)

(continued)

DRIVE BELT SPECIFICATIONS (continued)

Model	Part No.	Width mm (in.)	Circumference cm (in.)
1991-1992			
Prowler, Cougar, El Tigre EXT	0227-032	34.1-35.7 (1.344-1.406)	110.5-111.1 (43.50-43.74)
1993			
Prowler, Cougar	0227-032	34.1-35.7 (1.344-1.406)	110.5-111.1 (43.50-43.74)
440 ZR	0627-009	34-36 (1.339-1.417)	120-121 (47.24-47.64)
EXT 550, EXT 580	0627-012	34-36 (1.339-1.417)	120-121 (47.24-47.64)
580 ZR	0627-009	34-36 (1.339-1.417)	120-121 (47.24-47.64)
1994			
Cougar, Prowler	0227-103	34-36 (1.339-1.417)	110.3-111.1 (43.43-43.74)
ZR 440, EXT 580, ZR 580	0627-012	34-36 (1.339-1.417)	120-121 (47.24-47.64)
1995			
Cougar, Prowler 2-Up	0627-012	34-36 (1.339-1.417)	120.8-121.3 (47.56-47.76)
Z 440	0627-012	34-36 (1.339-1.417)	120.8-121.7 (47.56-47.91)
ZR 440, EXT 580, EXT 580 EFI, ZR 580, ZR 580 EFI	0627-012	34-36 (1.339-1.417)	120-121 (47.24-47.64)
1996			
Cougar	0627-012	34-36 (1.339-1.417)	120-121 (47.24-47.64)
Z 440	0627-012	34-36 (1.339-1.417)	120.8-121.7 (47.56-47.91)
ZR 440, ZRT 600	0627-010	34-36 (1.339-1.417)	120-121 (47.24-47.64)
EXT 580, EXT 580 EFI, ZR 580	0627-012	34-36 (1.339-1.417)	120-121 (47.24-47.64)
1997			
Z 440	0627-012	34-36 (1.339-1.417)	120-121 (47.24-47.64)
ZL 440	0627-012	34-36 (1.339-1.417)	120-121 (47.24-47.64)
ZR 440	0627-010	34-36 (1.339-1.417)	120-121 (47.24-47.64)
Panther 440	0627-012	34-36 (1.339-1.417)	120-121 (47.24-47.64)
Cougar	0627-012	34-36 (1.339-1.417)	120-121 (47.24-47.64)
Panther 550	0627-012	34-36 (1.339-1.417)	120-121 (47.24-47.64)
Pantera	0627-012	34-36 (1.339-1.417)	120-121 (47.24-47.64)

(continued)

DRIVE BELT SPECIFICATIONS (continued)

Model	Part No.	Width mm (in.)	Circumference cm (in.)
1997			
EXT 580 EFI	0627-012	34-36 (1.339-1.417)	120-121 (47.24-47.64)
Powder Special EFI	0627-012	34-36 (1.339-1.417)	120-121 (47.24-47.64)
ZR 580 EFI	0627-010	34-36 (1.339-1.417)	120-121 (47.24-47.64)
EXT 600	0627-010	34-36 (1.339-1.417)	120-121 (47.24-47.64)
ZRT 600	0627-010	34-36 (1.339-1.417)	120-121 (47.24-47.64)
Powder Extreme	0627-010	34-36 (1.339-1.417)	120-121 (47.24-47.64)
1998			
Z 440	0627-012	34-36 (1.339-1.417)	120-121 (47.24-47.64)
ZL 440	0627-021	34-36 (1.339-1.417)	120-121 (47.24-47.64)
ZR 440	0627-020	34-36 (1.339-1.417)	120-121 (47.24-47.64)
Panther 440	0627-021	34-36 (1.339-1.417)	120-121 (47.24-47.64)
ZL 500	0627-020	34-36 (1.339-1.417)	120-121 (47.24-47.64)
Cougar	0627-021	34-36 (1.339-1.417)	120-121 (47.24-47.64)
Panther 550	0627-021	34-36 (1.339-1.417)	120-121 (47.24-47.64)
Pantera	0627-021	34-36 (1.339-1.417)	120-121 (47.24-47.64)
EXT 580 EFI	0627-021	34-36 (1.339-1.417)	120-121 (47.24-47.64)
Powder Special EFI	0627-020	34-36 (1.339-1.417)	120-121 (47.24-47.64)
ZR 600	0627-020	34-36 (1.339-1.417)	120-121 (47.24-47.64)
EXT 600	0627-020	34-36 (1.339-1.417)	120-121 (47.24-47.64)
ZRT 600	0627-020	34-36 (1.339-1.417)	120-121 (47.24-47.64)
Powder Extreme	0627-020	34-36 (1.339-1.417)	120-121 (47.24-47.64)

Chapter One

General Information

This Clymer shop manual covers the 1990-1998 Arctic Cat Prowler, Cougar, Panther 440, Panther 550, EXT 550, EXT 580, EXT 600, Z 440, ZL 440, ZR 440, ZR 580, ZR 600, ZRT 600, Powder Special and Powder Extreme models.

Troubleshooting, tune-up, maintenance and repair are not difficult if you know what tools and equipment to use, as well as the proper procedures. Step-by-step instructions guide you through jobs ranging from simple maintenance to complete engine and suspension overhaul.

This manual can be used by anyone from a first time do-it-yourselfer to a professional mechanic. Detailed drawings and clear photographs give you all the information you need to do the work right.

Some of the procedures in this manual require the use of special tools. The resourceful mechanic can, in many cases, think of acceptable substitutes for special tools. This can be as simple as using a few pieces of threaded rod, washers and nuts to remove a bearing or fabricating a tool from scrap material. However, using a substitute for a special tool is not recommended as it could damage the part. If you find that a tool can be designed and safely made, but will require some type of machine work, you may want to search out a local community college or high school that has a machine shop curriculum. Industrial arts instructors sometimes welcome outside work that can be used as practical shop applications for advanced students.

Tables appearing at the end of this chapter provide useful general information for service. **Tables 1-8** are at the end of the chapter.

Table 1 lists model number coverage and engine displacement.

General dimensions are listed in **Table 2**. **Table 3** lists vehicle weight.

Metric and U.S. standards are used throughout this manual. U.S. to metric conversion is given in **Table 4**.

Critical torque specifications are found in table form at the end of each chapter (as required). The general torque specifications listed in **Table 5** can be used when a torque specification is not listed for a specific component or assembly.

A list of technical abbreviations are given in **Table 6**.

Metric tap drill sizes can be found in **Table 7**. **Table 8** lists wind chill factors.

MANUAL ORGANIZATION

This chapter provides general information useful to snowmobile owners and mechanics. In addition, information in this chapter discusses the tools and techniques for preventive maintenance, troubleshooting and repair.

Chapter Two contains methods and suggestions for quick and accurate diagnosis and repair of problems. Troubleshooting procedures discuss typical symptoms and logical methods to pinpoint the trouble.

Chapter Three explains all the periodic lubrication and routine maintenance necessary to keep your snowmobile operating well. Chapter Three also includes recommended tune-up procedures, eliminating the need to frequently consult other chapters on the various assemblies.

Subsequent chapters describe specific systems, providing disassembly, repair, assembly and adjustment procedures in simple step-by-step form. If a repair is impractical for a home mechanic, it is indicated. It is usually faster and less expensive to take such repairs to a dealership or competent repair shop. Specifications concerning a specific system are included at the end of the appropriate chapter.

NOTES, CAUTIONS AND WARNINGS

The terms NOTE, CAUTION and WARNING have specific meanings in this manual. A NOTE provides additional information to make a step or procedure easier or clearer. Disregarding a NOTE could cause inconvenience, but it would not cause damage or personal injury.

A CAUTION emphasizes an area where equipment damage could occur. Disregarding a CAUTION could cause permanent mechanical damage; however, personal injury is unlikely.

A WARNING emphasizes an area where personal injury or even death could result from negligence. Mechanical damage may also occur. WARNINGS *are to be taken seriously*. In some cases, serious injury and death have resulted from disregarding similar warnings.

SAFETY FIRST

Professional mechanics can work for years and never sustain a serious injury. If you observe a few rules of common sense and safety, you can enjoy many safe hours servicing your own machine. If you ignore these rules you can hurt yourself or damage the equipment.

1. Never use gasoline as a cleaning solvent.
2. Never smoke or use a torch in the vicinity of flammable liquids, such as cleaning solvent, in open containers.
3. If welding or brazing is required on the snowmobile, remove the fuel tank to a safe distance, at least 50 feet away.
4. Use the properly sized wrenches to avoid damage to fasteners and injury to yourself.
5. When loosening a tight or stuck nut, be guided by what would happen if the wrench should slip. Be careful and protect yourself accordingly.

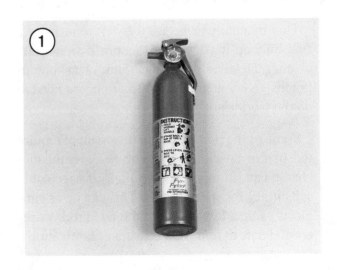

6. When replacing a fastener, make sure you use one with the same measurements and strength as the old one. Incorrect or mismatched fasteners can result in damage to the snowmobile and possible personal injury. Beware of fastener kits that are filled with inexpensive and poorly made nuts, bolts, washers and cotter pins. Refer to *Fasteners* in this chapter for additional information.

7. Keep all hand and power tools in good condition. Wipe greasy and oily tools after using

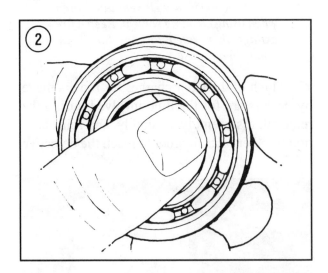

them. They are difficult to hold and can cause injury. Replace or repair worn or damaged tools.

8. Keep your work area clean and uncluttered.

9. Wear safety goggles during all operations involving drilling, grinding, using a cold chisel or anytime you feel unsure about the safety of your eyes. Wear safety goggles anytime you clean parts using solvent or compressed air.

10. Keep an approved fire extinguisher (**Figure 1**) nearby. Be sure it is rated for gasoline (Class B) and electrical (Class C) fires.

11. If drying bearings or other rotating parts with compressed air, never allow the air jet to rotate the bearing or part. The air jet is capable of rotating them at speeds far in excess of those for which they were designed. The bearing or rotating part is very likely to disintegrate and cause serious injury and damage. To prevent bearing damage when using compressed air, hold the inner bearing race (**Figure 2**) with your hand.

SERVICE HINTS

Most of the service procedures covered in this book are straightforward and can be performed by anyone reasonably handy with tools. It is suggested, however, that you consider your own capabilities carefully before attempting any operation involving major disassembly.

1. Front, as used in this manual, refers to the front of the snowmobile; the front of any component is the end closest to the front of the snowmobile. The left and right sides refer to the position of the parts as viewed by a rider sitting and facing forward. For example, the throttle control is on the right side. These rules are simple, but confusion can cause a major inconvenience during service (**Figure 3**).

2. When disassembling any engine or drive component, mark the parts for location and mark all parts that mate together. Small parts, such as bolts, can be identified by placing them in plastic

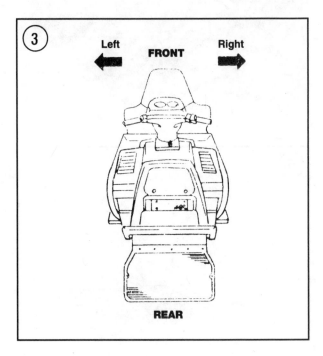

sandwich bags (**Figure 4**). Seal the bags and label them with masking tape and a marking pen.

3. Finished surfaces should be protected from physical damage or corrosion. Keep fuel off painted surfaces.

4. Use penetrating oil on frozen or tight bolts to help loosen them, then strike the bolt head a few times with a hammer and punch (use a screwdriver on screws). Avoid the use of heat where possible, as it can warp, melt or affect the temper of parts. Heat also ruins finishes, especially paint and plastics.

5. No parts removed or installed, other than bushings and bearings, in the procedures given in this manual should require unusual force during disassembly or assembly. If a part is difficult to remove or install, find out why before proceeding.

6. Cover all openings after removing parts or components to prevent the entrance of debris or small objects.

7. Read each procedure completely while looking at the actual parts before starting a job. Make sure you thoroughly understand what is to be done and then carefully follow the procedure, step by step.

8. Recommendations are occasionally made to refer service or maintenance to a snowmobile dealer or a specialist in a particular field. In these cases, the work will be done more quickly and economically than if you performed the job yourself.

9. In procedural steps, the term replace means to discard a defective part and replace it with a new or exchange unit. Overhaul means to remove, disassemble, inspect, measure, repair or replace defective parts, reassemble and install major systems or parts.

10. Some operations require the use of a hydraulic press. It is wiser to have these operations performed by a shop equipped for such work, than to try to do the job yourself with makeshift equipment that may damage your machine.

11. Repairs go much faster and easier if your machine is clean before you begin work. There are many special cleaners on the market, like Bel-Ray Degreaser, for washing the engine and related parts. Follow the manufacturer's directions on the container for the best results. Clean all oily or greasy parts with cleaning solvent as you remove them.

> *WARNING*
> *Never use gasoline as a cleaning agent. It presents an extreme fire hazard. Be sure to work in a well-ventilated area when using cleaning solvent. Keep a fire extinguisher, rated for gasoline fires, handy in any case.*

12. Much of the labor charges for repairs made by dealers are for the time involved during the removal, disassembly, assembly, and reinstallation of other parts in order to reach the defective

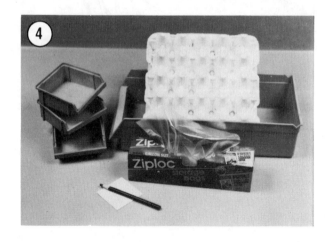

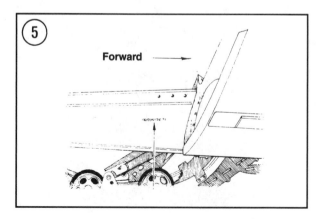

part. It is frequently possible to perform the preliminary operations yourself and then take the defective unit to the dealer for repair at considerable savings.

13. If special tools are required, make arrangements to get them before you start. It is frustrating and time-consuming to get partly into a job and then be unable to complete it.

14. Make diagrams (take a video or Polaroid picture) wherever similar-appearing parts are found or parts must be installed in a certain order or location. For instance, crankcase bolts may have differing lengths. A faulty memory can result in costly mistakes. Laying out parts in their proper order is a good practice, but if the parts are disturbed the exercise is a waste of time.

15. When assembling parts, be sure all shims and washers are replaced exactly as they came out.

16. Whenever a rotating part butts against a stationary part, look for a shim or washer. Use new gaskets if there is any doubt about the condition of the old ones. A thin coat of silicone sealant on non-pressure type gaskets may help them seal more effectively.

17. If it is necessary to make a cover gasket and you do not have a suitable old gasket to use as a guide, you can use the outline of the cover and gasket material to make a new gasket. Apply engine oil to the cover gasket surface. Then place the cover on the new gasket material and apply

pressure with your hands. The oil will leave a very accurate outline on the gasket material that can be cut around.

CAUTION
If purchasing gasket material, measure the thickness of the old gasket (at an uncompressed point) and purchase gasket material with the same approximate thickness.

18. Heavy grease can be used to hold small parts in place if they tend to fall out during assembly. Be sure to keep grease and oil away from electrical components.

19. A carburetor is best cleaned by disassembling it and cleaning the parts in hot soap and water. Never soak gaskets and rubber parts in commercial carburetor cleaners. Never use wire to clean out jets and air passages because that will damage them easily. Use compressed air to blow out the carburetor only if the float has been removed first.

20. Take your time and do the job right. Do not forget that a newly rebuilt engine must be broken in just like a new one.

ENGINE AND CHASSIS SERIAL NUMBERS

Arctic Cat snowmobiles are identified by frame and engine identification numbers. The frame or Vehicle Identification Number (VIN) is stamped on the right side of the tunnel just below the front of the seat (**Figure 5**). The engine number is stamped on the side of the crankcase as shown in **Figure 6**. The engine model number is also listed on a decal located on the fan or magneto housing as shown in **Figure 7**.

Write all the serial numbers and model numbers applicable to your machine in the front of this book. Take the serial numbers and model numbers with you when you order parts from the dealer. Always order parts by year and engine and machine numbers. If possible, compare the

old parts with the new ones before purchasing them. If the parts are not alike, have the parts manager explain the reason for the difference and insist on assurance that the new parts will fit and will be correct.

ENGINE OPERATION

The following is a general discussion of a typical two-stroke piston-ported engine. The same principles apply to engines with reed type intake valves, except that during the intake cycle, the fuel/air mixture passes through the open reed valve assembly into the crankcase. During this discussion, assume the crankshaft is rotating counterclockwise as in **Figure 8**. As the piston travels downward, a transfer port (A) between the crankcase and the cylinder is uncovered. The exhaust gases leave the cylinder through the exhaust port (B), which is also opened by the downward movement of the piston. A fresh fuel/air charge, which has been previously compressed slightly, travels from the crankcase (C) to the cylinder through the transfer port (A) as the port opens. Since the incoming charge is under pressure, it rushes into the cylinder quickly and helps to expel the exhaust gases from the previous cycle.

Figure 9 illustrates the next phase of the cycle. As the crankshaft continues to rotate, the piston moves upward, closing the exhaust and transfer ports. As the piston continues upward, the air/fuel mixture in the cylinder is compressed. Notice also that a vacuum is created in the crankcase at the same time. Further upward movement of the piston uncovers the intake port (D). A fresh fuel-air charge is then drawn into the crankcase through the intake port because of the vacuum created by the upward piston movement.

The third phase is shown in **Figure 10**. As the piston approaches top dead center, the spark plug fires, igniting the compressed mixture. The piston is then driven downward by the expanding

gases. Every downward stroke of the piston is a power stroke.

When the top of the piston uncovers the exhaust port, the fourth phase begins, as shown in **Figure 11**. The exhaust gases leave the cylinder

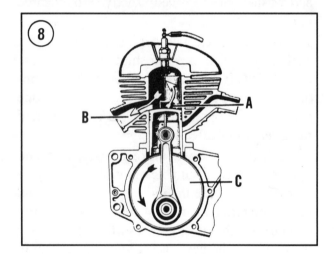

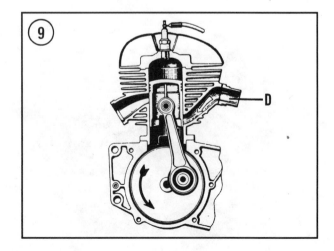

through the exhaust port. As the piston continues downward, the intake port (or reed valves) are closed and the mixture in the crankcase is compressed in preparation for the next cycle.

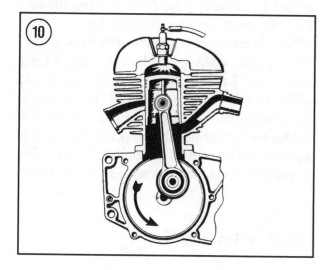

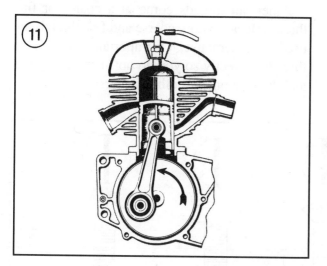

TORQUE SPECIFICATIONS

Torque specifications throughout this manual are given in Newton-meters (N.m) and foot-pounds (ft.-lb.). **Table 5** lists general torque specifications for nuts and bolts that are not listed in the respective chapters. To use the table, first determine the size of the nut or bolt by measuring it with a vernier caliper. **Figures 12** and **13** show how to do this.

FASTENERS

The materials and designs of the various fasteners used on your snowmobile are not determined by pure chance or accident. Fastener material, size, and thread type are carefully selected to decrease the possibility of physical failure. Fastener design determines the type of tool required to move the fastener (**Figure 14**).

Nuts, bolts and screws are manufactured in a wide range of thread patterns. To join a nut and bolt, the diameters of the bolt and the hole in the nut must be the same and the threads on both parts must also be the same.

The best way to tell if the threads on two fasteners are matched is to turn the nut on the bolt (or the bolt into the threaded hole in a piece of equipment) with fingers only. Be sure both pieces are clean. If much force is required, check the thread condition on each fastener. If the condition of threads on both parts is good but the

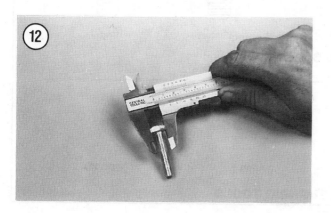

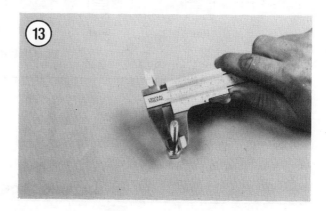

fasteners jam, the threads are not compatible. A thread pitch gauge (**Figure 15**) can also be used to determine pitch. Arctic Cat snowmobiles are manufactured with ISO metric fasteners. ISO metric threads are cut differently than those of standard American fasteners (**Figure 16**).

Most threads are cut so that the fastener must be turned clockwise to tighten it. These are called right-hand threads. Some fasteners have left-hand threads and must be turned counterclockwise to be tightened. Left-hand threads are used in locations where normal rotation of the equipment would tend to loosen a right-hand threaded fastener.

ISO Metric Screw Threads

ISO (International Organization for Standardization) metric threads come in coarse, fine and constant pitch threads. The ISO coarse pitch is used for most common fastener applications. The fine pitch thread is used on certain precision tools and instruments. The constant pitch thread is used mainly on machine parts and not for fasteners. It is also used on all metric thread spark plugs.

ISO metric threads are specified by the capital letter M followed by the diameter in millimeters and the pitch (or the distance between each thread) in millimeters separated by the sign "×". For example a M8 × 1.25 bolt is one that has a diameter of 8 millimeters with a distance of 1.25 millimeters between each thread. The measurement across two flats on the head of the bolt (**Figure 11**) indicates the proper wrench size to be used, but it is not an indication of thread size. **Figure 13** shows how to determine bolt diameter.

American Threads

American threads come in a coarse or fine thread. Because both coarse and fine threads are used for general use, it is important to match the threads correctly so you do not strip the threads and damage one or both fasteners.

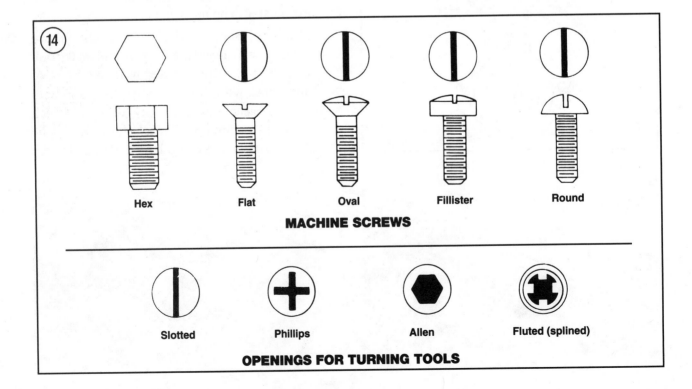

Hex   Flat   Oval   Fillister   Round

MACHINE SCREWS

Slotted   Phillips   Allen   Fluted (splined)

OPENINGS FOR TURNING TOOLS

American fasteners are normally described by diameter, threads per inch and length. For example, 3/8-16 × 2 indicates a bolt 3/8 inch in diameter with 16 threads per inch, 2 inches long. The measurement across two flats on the head of the bolt or screw indicates the proper wrench size to be used. **Figure 13** shows how to determine bolt diameter.

NOTE
*If purchasing a bolt from a dealer or parts store, you must know how to specify bolt length. Correctly measure bolt length by measuring the length starting from underneath the bolt head to the end of the bolt (**Figure 17**).*

Machine Screws

There are many different types of machine screws. **Figure 18** shows a number of screw heads requiring different types of turning tools. Heads are also designed to protrude above the metal (round) or to be slightly recessed in the metal (flat). See **Figure 19**.

Bolts

Commonly called bolts, the technical name for these types of fasteners is cap screw. Metric

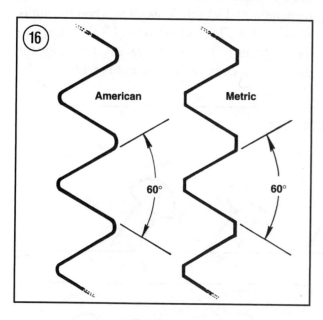

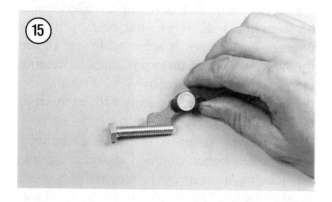

American   Metric

60°   60°

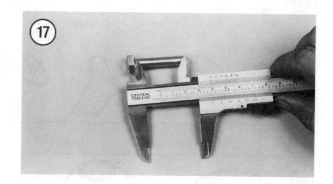

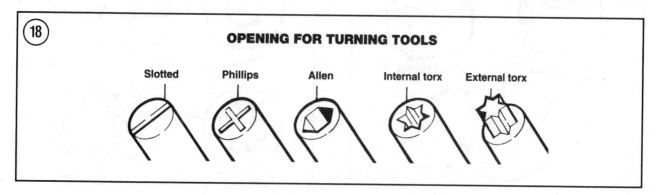

OPENING FOR TURNING TOOLS

Slotted   Phillips   Allen   Internal torx   External torx

bolts are described by the diameter and pitch (the distance between each thread).

Nuts

Nuts are manufactured in a variety of types and sizes. Most are hexagonal (six-sided) and fit on bolts, screws and studs with the same diameter and pitch.

Figure 20 shows several types of nuts. The common nut is generally used with a lockwasher. A self-locking nut usually has a nylon insert that prevents the nut from loosening and no lockwasher is required. Wing nuts are designed for fast removal by hand and are used for convenience in noncritical locations.

To indicate the size of a metric nut, manufacturers specify the diameter of the opening and the thread pitch. This is similar to bolt specifications, but without the length dimension. The

measurement across two flats on the nut indicates the proper wrench size to be used.

Self-Locking Fasteners

Several types of bolts, screws and nuts incorporate a system that develops an interference between the bolt, screw, nut or tapped hole threads. Interference is achieved in one of the following ways: by distorting threads, coating threads with dry adhesive or nylon, distorting the top of an all-metal nut or using a nylon insert in the center or at the top of a nut.

Self-locking fasteners offer greater holding strength and better vibration resistance. Some self-locking fasteners can be reused if they are in good condition. Others, like the nylon insert nut, form an initial locking condition when the nut is first installed. The nylon forms closely to the bolt thread pattern, thus reducing any tendency for the nut to loosen. When the nut is removed, the

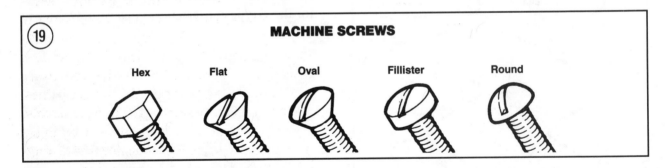

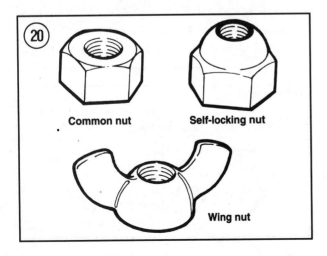

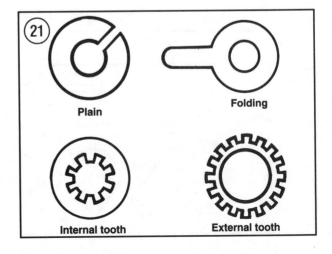

locking efficiency is greatly reduced. For the best safety, self-locking fasteners should be discarded and new ones installed whenever components are removed or disassembled.

Washers

There are two basic types of washers: flat washers and lockwashers. Flat washers are simple discs with a hole to fit a screw or bolt. Lockwashers are designed to prevent a fastener from working loose due to vibration, expansion and contraction. **Figure 21** shows several types of washers. Washers are also used in the following functions:

a. as spacers.

b. to prevent galling or damage to the equipment by the fastener.

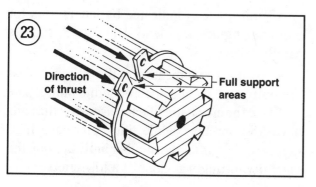

c. to help distribute fastener load during torquing.

d. as seals.

Note that flat washers are often used between a lockwasher and a fastener to provide a smooth bearing surface. This allows the fastener to be turned easily with a tool.

Cotter Pins

Cotter pins (**Figure 22**) are used to secure special kinds of fasteners. The threaded stud must have a hole in it; the nut or nut lock piece has castellations around which the cotter pin ends wrap. Cotter pins should not be reused after removal.

Snap Rings (Circlips)

Snap rings, sometimes called circlips, can be internal or external design. The external type is used to retain items on shafts and the internal type is used within tubes or bores of housings. In some applications, snap rings of varying thicknesses are used to control the end play of parts assemblies. These are often called selective snap rings. Removal weakens and deforms snap rings. Always install new snap rings during assembly.

Snap rings may be manufactured by either machining or stamping. Machined snap rings (**Figure 23**) can be installed in either direction, on the shaft or in the housing, because both faces are machined, thus creating two sharp edges. Stamped snap rings (**Figure 24**) are manufac-

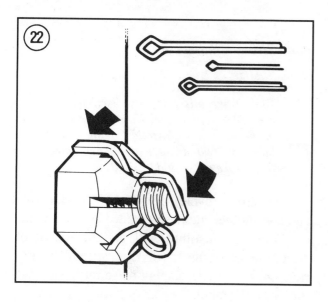

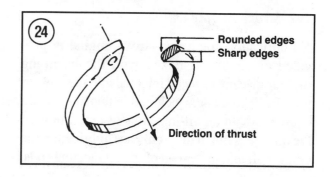

tured with one sharp edge and one rounded edge. When installing stamped snap rings in a thrust situation, the sharp edge must face away from the part producing the thrust unless the text directs otherwise. When installing snap rings, observe the following:

    a. Snap rings should be removed and installed with snap ring pliers. See *Snap Ring Pliers* in this chapter.

    b. Compress or expand snap rings only enough to install them.

    c. After the snap ring is installed, make sure it is completely seated in its groove.

LUBRICANTS

Periodic lubrication assures long life for any type of equipment. The type of lubricant used is just as important as the lubrication service itself. The following paragraphs describe the types of lubricants most often used on snowmobiles. Be sure to follow the manufacturer's recommendations for lubricant types.

Generally, all liquid lubricants are called oil. They may be mineral-based (including petroleum bases), natural-based (vegetable and animal bases), synthetic-based or emulsions (mixtures). Grease is an oil to which a thickening base has been added so that the end product is semi-solid. Grease is often classified by the type of thickener added. Lithium soap is a commonly used thickener.

Engine Oil

Two-Stroke Engine Oil

Lubrication for a two-stroke engine is provided either by oil mixed with the incoming fuel-air mixture or by oil injected into the fuel-air mixture. The models included in this manual are equipped with an oil-injection system. Some of the oil settles out in the crankcase, lubricating the crankshaft and lower end of the connecting rods.

The rest of the oil enters the combustion chamber to lubricate the piston rings and cylinder walls. This oil is burned during the combustion process, then expelled with the engine's exhaust.

Engine oil must have several special qualities to work well in a two-stroke snowmobile engine. The oil must function properly in the high operating temperature associated with two-stroke engines, as well as flow freely in cold temperatures. The oil must lubricate the engine sufficiently and burn easily during combustion. The oil cannot leave behind excessive deposits. Refer to Engine Lubrication in Chapter Three.

> *NOTE*
> *The injection oil used by Arctic Cat snowmobile engines must also be able to flow at temperatures of -40° C (-40° F). See Chapter Three under Lubrication for additional information.*

Four-Stroke Engine Oil

> *CAUTION*
> *Four-stroke oils are only discussed to provide a comparison. The engines used in these models of Arctic Cat snowmobiles are two-stroke engines and only two-stroke oil should be used.*

Four-stroke (cycle) oil for ATV, motorcycle and automotive engines is graded by the American Petroleum Institute (API) and the Society of Automotive Engineers (SAE) in several categories. Oil containers display these ratings on the top or on the label.

API oil grade is indicated by letters; oils for gasoline engines are identified by an S, such as SE, SF, SG or SH.

Viscosity is an indication of the oil's thickness or ability to flow at a specific temperature. The SAE uses numbers to indicate viscosity; thin oils have low numbers while thick oils have high numbers. A W after the number indicates that the viscosity testing was done at a low temperature to simulate cold-weather operation. Engine oils fall into the 5 to 50 range.

Multigrade oils (for example 5W-20) have been changed by additives that modify the oil to be less viscous (thinner) at low temperatures and more viscous (thicker) at high temperatures. This allows the oil to perform efficiently across a wide range of engine operating conditions. The lower the number, the easier the engine will start in cold climates. Higher numbers are usually recommended for engines running in hot weather conditions.

Grease

Greases are graded by the National Lubricating Grease Institute (NLGI). Greases are graded by number according to the consistency of the grease; these range from No. 000 to No. 6, with No. 6 being the most solid. A typical multipurpose grease is NLGI No. 2. For specific applications, equipment manufacturers may require grease with an additive such as molybdenum disulfide (MoS2).

NOTE
A low temperature grease should be used wherever grease is required on the snowmobile. Chapter Three lists low temperature grease recommended by Arctco.

RTV GASKET SEALANT

Room temperature vulcanizing (RTV) sealant is used on some preformed gaskets and to seal some components. RTV is a silicone gel supplied in tubes and can be purchased in a number of different colors. For most snowmobile use, the clear color is preferable.

Moisture in the air causes RTV to cure. Always place the cap on the tube as soon as possible when using RTV. RTV has a shelf life of one year and will not cure properly when the shelf life has expired. Check the expiration date on RTV tubes before using and keep partially used tubes tightly sealed.

Applying RTV Sealant

Clean all gasket residue from mating surfaces. Surfaces should be clean and free of oil and dirt. Remove all RTV gasket material from blind attaching holes, as it can affect bolt torque.

Apply RTV sealant in a continuous bead 2-3 mm (0.08-0.12 in.) thick. Circle all mounting holes unless otherwise specified. Torque mating parts within ten minutes after application.

THREADLOCK

Because of the snowmobile's operating conditions, a threadlock (**Figure 25**) is required to help secure many of the fasteners. A threadlock will lock fasteners against vibration loosening and seal against leaks. Loctite 242, which is blue, and 271, which is red, are recommended for many threadlock requirements described in this manual.

Loctite 242 (blue) is a medium strength threadlock for general purpose use. Component disassembly can be performed with normal hand tools. Loctite 271 (red) is a high-strength threadlock that is normally used on studs or critical fasteners. Heat or special tools, such as a press or puller, may be required for component disassembly.

Applying Threadlock

Surfaces should be clean and free of oil and dirt. If a threadlock was previously applied to the component, this residue should also be removed.

Shake the Loctite container thoroughly and apply to both parts. Assemble the parts and/or tighten the fasteners.

GASKET REMOVER

Stubborn gaskets can present a problem during engine service as they can take a long time to remove. Consequently, there is the added problem of secondary damage occurring to the gasket mating surfaces from the incorrect or accidental use of a gasket scraping tool. To quickly and safely remove stubborn gaskets, use a spray gasket remover. Spray gasket remover can be purchased through Arctic Cat dealers and automotive parts supplies. Follow the manufacturer's directions for use.

EXPENDABLE SUPPLIES

Certain expendable supplies are required during maintenance and repair work. These include grease, oil, gasket cement, shop rags and cleaning solvents. Ask your dealer for the special locking compounds, silicone lubricants and lube products which make vehicle maintenance simpler and easier. Cleaning solvent is available at some service stations.

> *WARNING*
> *Have a stack of clean shop rags on hand when performing engine and suspension service work. Clean shop rags present less danger than solvent and lubricant soaked rags. Most local fire codes require that used rags be stored in a sealed metal container with a self-closing lid until they can be washed or discarded.*

> *WARNING*
> *Even mild solvents and other chemicals can be absorbed into your skin while cleaning parts. Wear petroleum-resistant gloves when working with solvents or chemicals to prevent possible hand-related problems ranging from mild discomfort to major infections. Gloves can be purchased from industrial supply houses or hardware stores.*

BASIC HAND TOOLS

Many of the procedures in this manual can be carried out with simple hand tools and test equipment familiar to the mechanic. Keep your tools clean, organized and in a tool box. After using a tool, wipe off dirt and grease with a clean cloth and return the tool to its correct place.

Top quality tools are essential; they are also more economical in the long run. If you are just starting to build your tool collection, stay away from the "advertised specials" featured at some parts retailers, discount stores, and chain drug stores. These are usually cheap tools, both in price and quality. They are usually made of inferior material and are thick, heavy and clumsy. Their rough finish makes them difficult to clean and they usually do not last very long. If it is ever your misfortune to use such tools, you will probably find out that the wrenches do not fit the

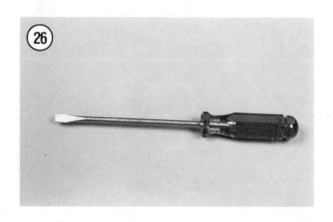

(26)

heads of bolts and nuts correctly and often will damage the fastener.

Quality tools are made of alloy steel and are heat-treated for greater strength. They are lighter and better balanced than cheap tools. Their surface is smooth, making them a pleasure to work with and easy to clean. The initial cost of good quality tools may be more, but they are less expensive in the long run. Do not try to buy everything in all sizes in the beginning. Purchase tools a little at a time until you have the necessary ones.

The following tools are required to perform virtually any repair job. Each tool is described and the recommended size is given for starting a tool collection. Additional tools and some duplicates may be added as you become familiar with the vehicle. Arctic Cat snowmobiles are built with metric and U.S. standard fasteners.

Screwdrivers

The basic screwdriver, if it is used improperly, will do more damage than good. The slot on a screw has a definite dimension and shape. A screwdriver must be selected to conform with that shape. Use a small screwdriver for small screws and a large one for large screws or the screw head will be damaged.

Two basic types of screwdrivers are required: common (flat-blade) screwdrivers (**Figure 26**) and Phillips screwdrivers (**Figure 27**).

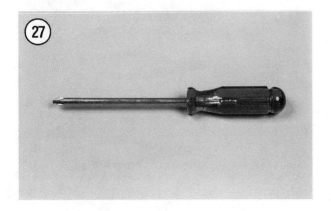

Screwdrivers are available in sets which often include an assortment of common and Phillips blades. If you buy them individually, buy at least the following:

a. common screwdriver—5/16 × 6 in. blade.

b. common screwdriver—3/8 × 12 in. blade.

c. Phillips screwdriver—size 2 tip, 6 in. blade.

Use screwdrivers only for driving screws. Never use a screwdriver for prying or chiseling metal. Do not try to remove a Phillips or Allen head screw with a common screwdriver (unless the screw has a combination head that will accept either type). If you use the improper screwdriver, you may damage the head so that the proper tool will be unable to remove it.

Keep screwdrivers in good condition and they will last longer and perform better. Always keep the tip of a common screwdriver in good condition. **Figure 28** shows how to grind the tip to the proper shape if it becomes damaged. Note the symmetrical sides of the tip.

Pliers

Pliers come in a wide range of types and sizes. Pliers are useful for holding, cutting, bending and crimping. They should never be used to cut hardened objects or to turn bolts or nuts. **Figure 29** shows several pliers useful in snowmobile repair.

Each type of pliers has a specialized function. Slip-joint pliers are used mainly for holding things and bending. Needlenose pliers are used to hold or bend small objects. Groove-joint pliers known by the brand name Channelock can be adjusted to hold various sizes of objects such as pipe or tubing. There are many more types of pliers, but the ones described are the most suitable for snowmobile repair.

> *CAUTION*
> *Pliers should not be used for loosening or tightening nuts or bolts. The sharp teeth on the pliers will grind off the cor-*

ners of the nut or bolt and damage the fastener.

CAUTION
If it is necessary to use slip-joint pliers to grasp the finished surface on an object that can be easily damaged, wrap the object with tape or cardboard for protection.

Locking Pliers

Locking pliers (**Figure 30**) hold objects very tightly like a vise. Because locking pliers exert more force than regular pliers, their sharp jaws can permanently scar any object that is held. In addition, when locking pliers are locked in position, they can crush or deform thin wall material. Locking pliers are available in many types for specific tasks.

Snap Ring (Circlip) Pliers

Snap ring pliers (**Figure 31**) are made for removing and installing snap rings and should not be used for any other purpose. External pliers (spreading or expanding) are used for removing snap rings from the outside of a shaft or other similar part. Internal snap rings are located inside a tube, gear or housing, and require pliers that squeeze the ends of the snap ring together so that the snap ring can be removed.

Box-end, Open-end and Combination Wrenches

Box-end and open-end wrenches (**Figure 32**) are available in sets or separately in a variety of sizes. The number stamped on open- and box-end wrenches refers to the distance between two parallel flats of a nut or bolt head. Combination wrenches have a box-end wrench on one end and an open-end wrench of the same size on the other end. The wrench size is stamped near the center of combination wrenches.

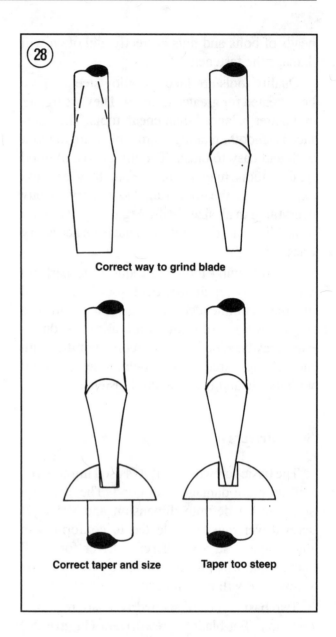

Correct way to grind blade

Correct taper and size   Taper too steep

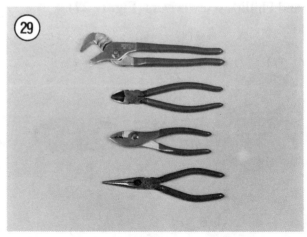

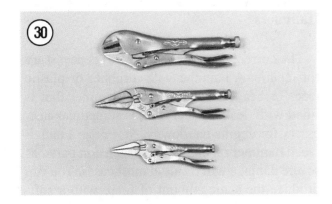

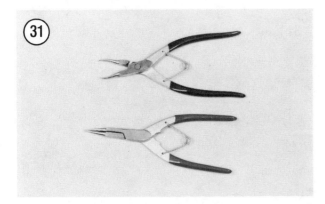

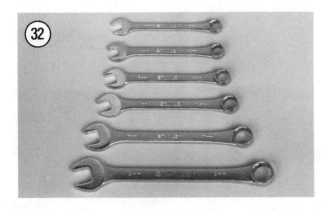

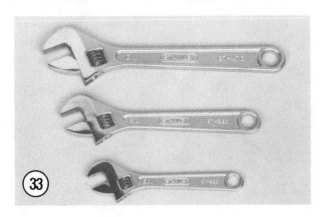

Open-end wrenches are speedy and work best in areas with limited overhead access. Their wide jaws make them unsuitable for situations where the bolt or nut is sunken in a well or close to the edge of a casting. These wrenches only grip on two flats of a fastener so if either the fastener head or wrench jaws are worn, the wrench may slip off.

The fastener must have overhead access to use box-end wrenches, but they grip all six corners of a fastener for a very secure grip. Box-end wrenches may be either 6-point or 12-point. The 12-point box-end wrench permits operation in situations where there is only a small amount of room to turn or move the wrench. The 6-point gives superior holding power and durability, but it requires a greater swinging radius.

No matter what style of wrench you choose, proper use is important to prevent personal injury. When using any wrench, get in the habit of pulling the wrench toward you. This reduces the risk of injuring your hand if the wrench should slip. If you have to push the wrench away from you to loosen or tighten a fastener, open and push with the palm of your hand. This technique gets your fingers and knuckles out of the way should the wrench slip. Before using a wrench, always consider what could happen if the wrench should slip, if the bolt were to slip, or if the bolt were to break.

Adjustable Wrenches

An adjustable wrench (sometimes called a Crescent wrench) can be adjusted to fit nearly any nut or bolt head that has clear access around its entire perimeter. An adjustable wrench (**Figure 33**) is best used as a backup wrench to keep a large nut or bolt from turning while the other end is being loosened or tightened with a proper wrench.

Adjustable wrenches have only two gripping surfaces, and one is designed to be moveable. The usually large physical size and the adjustable feature make this type of wrench more apt to slip off the fastener, damaging the part and possibly injuring your hand.

These wrenches are directional; the solid jaw must be the one transmitting the force. If you use the adjustable jaw to transmit the force, it may loosen, allowing the wrench to slip off.

Adjustable wrenches come in several sizes but a 6- or 8-inch size is recommended as an all-purpose wrench.

Socket Wrenches

This type is undoubtedly the fastest, safest and most convenient to use. Sockets which attach to a ratchet handle are available with 6-point or 12-point openings and 1/4, 3/8 and 3/4 in. drives (**Figure 34**). The drive size indicates the size of the square hole which mates with the ratchet handle.

Torque Wrench

A torque wrench (**Figure 35**) is used with a socket to measure how tightly a nut or bolt is installed. They come in a wide price range and with a 1/4, 3/8, or 1/2 in. square drive. The drive size indicates the size of the square drive which mates with the socket.

Impact Driver

This tool makes the removal of tight fasteners easy and reduces the chance for damage to bolts and screw slots. Impact drivers and interchangeable bits (**Figure 36**) are available at most large hardware, snowmobile and motorcycle dealerships. Sockets can also be used with a hand impact driver; however, make sure the socket is designed for impact use (B, **Figure 37**). Regular hand type sockets (A, **Figure 37**) may shatter if used to loosen a tight fastener.

Hammers

The correct hammer (**Figure 38**) is necessary for repairs. A hammer with a rubber or plastic face (or head), or a soft-faced hammer that is filled with lead or steel shot, is sometimes necessary for engine teardowns. Never use a metal-faced hammer on engine or suspension parts, as severe damage will result in most cases. You can produce the same amount of force with a soft-

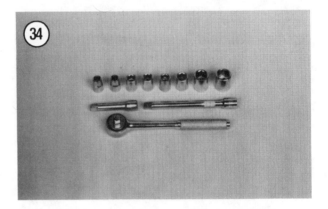

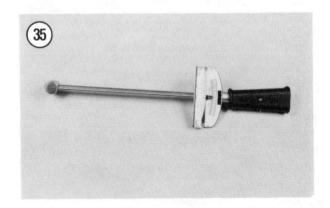

faced hammer. A metal-faced hammer, however, is required when using a hand impact driver.

PRECISION MEASURING TOOLS

Measurement is an important part of snowmobile service. When performing many of the service procedures in this manual, you will be required to make a number of measurements.

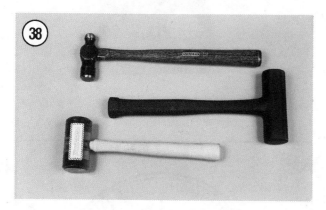

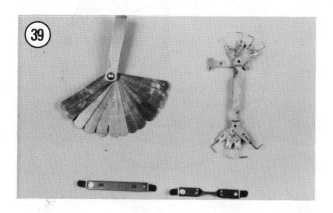

These include basic checks such as engine compression and spark-plug gap. As you get deeper into engine disassembly and service, measurements will be required to determine the condition of the piston and cylinder bore, crankshaft runout and so on. When making these measurements, the degree of accuracy will dictate which tool is required. Precision measuring tools are expensive. If this is your first experience at engine service, it may be more worthwhile to have the checks made at a dealership. However, as your skills and enthusiasm increase for doing your own service work, you may want to begin purchasing some of these specialized tools. The following paragraphs describe the measuring tools required to perform service procedures described in this manual.

Feeler Gauge

Feeler gauges are available in sets of various sizes (**Figure 39**). Each gauge is a specified thickness. The gauge is made of either a piece of flat or round hardened steel. Wire gauges are used to measure spark plug gap. Flat gauges are used for most other measurements.

Vernier Caliper

A vernier caliper (**Figure 40**) is invaluable when reading inside, outside and depth measurements with close precision. Common uses of a

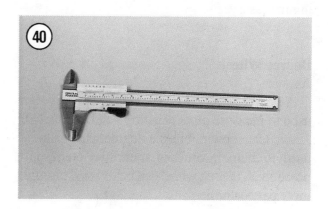

vernier caliper are measuring the length of springs, the thickness of shims and thrust washers or the height of the reed valve stops.

Outside Micrometers

One of the most reliable tools used for precision measurement is the outside micrometer. Outside micrometers will be required to measure piston diameter. Outside micrometers are also used with other tools to measure cylinder bore. Micrometers can be purchased individually or as a set (**Figure 41**).

Dial Indicator

Dial indicators (**Figure 42**) are precision tools used to check differences in machined surfaces, such as the runout of a crankshaft or brake disc. A dial indicator may also be used to locate the piston at a specific position when checking ignition timing. For snowmobile repair, select a dial indicator with a continuous dial (**Figure 43**). Several different mounting types are available, including a magnetic stand that attaches to iron surfaces, a clamp that can be attached to various components, and a spark plug adapter that locates the probe of the dial indicator through the spark plug hole of the cylinder head. See *Magnetic Stand* in this chapter. The various mounts are required for specific measuring requirements. The text will indicate the type of mounting necessary.

Degree Wheel

A degree wheel (**Figure 44**) is a specific tool used to measure parts of a circle and angles. For Arctic Cat snowmobiles, a degree wheel can be used to help locate and mark the crankshaft position. A degree wheel can be ordered through most parts suppliers.

Cylinder Bore Gauge

The cylinder bore gauge is a very specialized precision tool. The gauge set shown in **Figure 45**

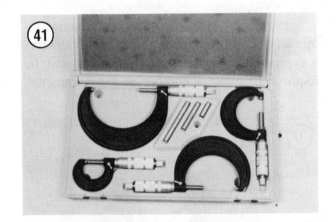

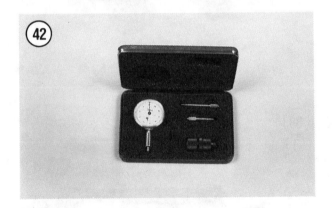

is comprised of a dial indicator, handle and a number of length adapters to adapt the gauge to different bore sizes. The bore gauge can be used to make cylinder bore measurements such as bore size, taper and out-of-round. An outside micrometer must be used to calibrate the bore gauge to a specific bore diameter.

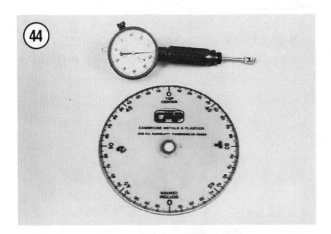

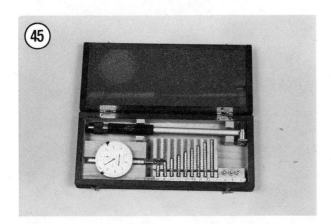

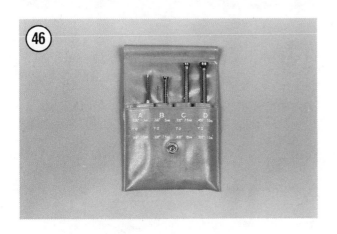

Small Hole Gauges

A set of small hole gauges (**Figure 46**) allows you to measure a hole, groove or slot ranging in size up to 13 mm (0.500 in.). An outside micrometer must be used together with the small hole gauge to determine bore dimensions.

Telescoping Gauges

Telescoping gauges (**Figure 47**) can be used to measure hole diameters from approximately 8 mm (5/16 in.) to 150 mm (6 in.). Like the small hole gauge, the telescoping gauge does not have a scale gauge for direct readings. An outside micrometer must be used together with the telescoping gauge to determine bore dimensions.

Compression Gauge

An engine with low compression cannot be properly tuned and will not develop full power. A compression gauge (**Figure 48**) measures engine compression. The one shown has a flexible stem with an extension that can allow you to hold it while starting the engine. Open the throttle all the way when checking engine compression. See Chapter Three.

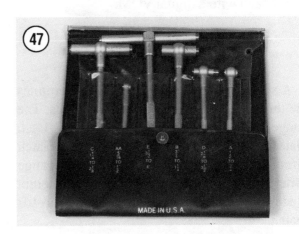

Two-stroke Pressure Tester

Refer to Chapter Two for *Two-Stroke Engine Pressure Testing*.

Strobe Timing Light

This instrument is useful for checking ignition timing. By flashing a light at the precise instant the spark plug fires, the position of the timing mark can be seen. The flashing light makes the moving mark appear to stand still so that it can be viewed in relation to the stationary mark.

Suitable lights range from inexpensive neon bulb types to powerful xenon strobe lights. See **Figure 49**. A light with an inductive pickup is recommended to eliminate any possible damage to ignition wiring. The timing light should be attached and used according to the instructions provided by the manufacturer.

Multimeter or VOM

A VOM (Volt and Ohm Meter) is a valuable tool for all electrical system troubleshooting (**Figure 50**). The voltmeter can be used to indicate the voltage applied or available to various components. The ohmmeter can be used to check for continuity and to measure resistance. Some tests are easily accomplished using a meter with sweeping needle, but other components should be checked with a digital VOM.

Screw Pitch Gauge

A screw pitch gauge (**Figure 51**) determines the thread pitch of bolts, screws and studs. The gauge is made up of a number of thin plates. Each plate has a thread shape cut on one edge to match one thread pitch. When using a screw pitch gauge to determine a thread pitch size, try to fit different blade sizes onto the bolt thread until both threads match.

Magnetic Stand

A magnetic stand (**Figure 52**) can often be used to securely hold a dial indicator when checking the runout of a round object or when checking the end play of a shaft.

V-Blocks

V-blocks (**Figure 53**) are precision ground blocks that can sometimes be used to hold a

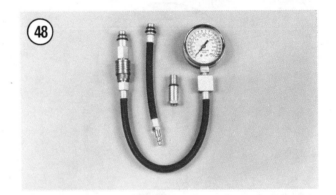

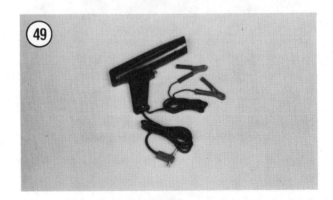

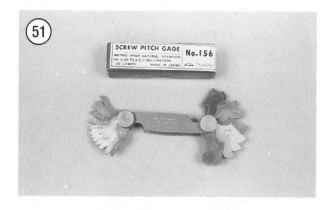

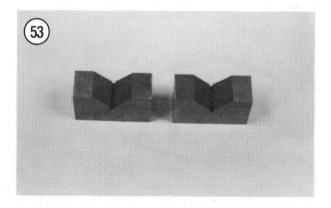

round object when checking its runout or condition.

Surface Plate

A surface plate is used to check the flatness of parts. While industrial-grade surface plates are quite expensive, the home mechanic can improvise. A piece of thick, flat metal or plate glass can sometimes be used as a surface plate. The quality of the surface plate will affect the accuracy of the measurement. The metal surface plate shown in **Figure 54** has a piece of fine grit paper on its surface to assist cleaning and smoothing a flat surface. The machined surfaces of the cylinder head, crankcase and other closely fitting parts may require a very good quality surface plate to smooth nicked or damaged surfaces.

NOTE
Check with a local machine shop, fabricating shop or a school offering a machine shop course for the availability of a metal plate that can be resurfaced and used as a surface plate.

SPECIAL TOOLS

This section describes special tools that may be unique to Arctic Cat snowmobile service and repair. These tools are often a valuable asset even if used infrequently. Most special tools can be ordered through your Arctic Cat dealer. It is often necessary to know the specific snowmobile or engine model for selecting the correct special tools.

Flywheel Puller

A flywheel puller (**Figure 55**) is required whenever it is necessary to remove the flywheel and service the stator plate assembly or when adjusting the ignition timing. In addition, when disassembling the engine, the flywheel must be

removed before the crankcases can be split.
There is no satisfactory substitute for this tool.
Because the flywheel is a taper fit on the crankshaft, makeshift removal often results in crankshaft and flywheel damage. Do not attempt
removal of the flywheel without this tool. A
puller can be ordered through Arctic Cat dealers.

Strap Wrench

A strap wrench (**Figure 56**) can be used to
hold the flywheel when loosening the flywheel
retaining nut.

Starter Pulley Holder

A universal type holder (**Figure 57**) or the
universal Grabbit (**Figure 58**) can be used to
hold the recoil starter pulley during removal and
installation.

Bearing Pullers

A bearing puller set with long arms (**Figure
59**) is valuable help for removing bearings from
suspension wheels and other locations.

Track Clip Installer

A track clip installer (**Figure 60**) is required
to install track clips.

Spring Scale

A spring scale (**Figure 61**) is required to check
track tension.

Clutch Tools

A number of special tools are required for
clutch service. These are described in Chapter
Thirteen.

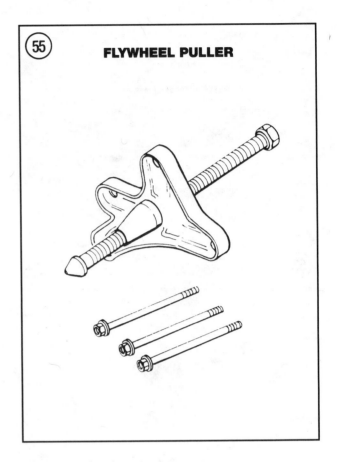

FLYWHEEL PULLER

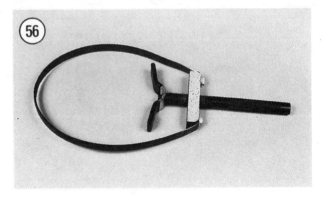

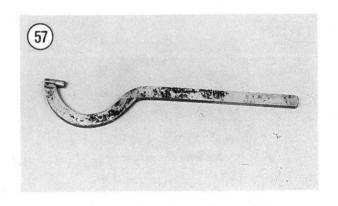

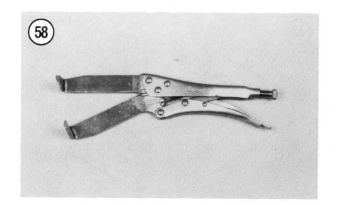

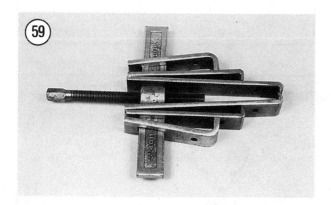

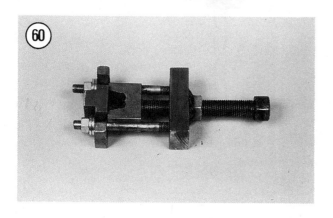

MECHANIC'S TIPS

Removing Frozen Nuts and Screws

If a fastener rusts and cannot be removed, several methods may be used to loosen it. First, apply penetrating oil such as Liquid Wrench or WD-40 which is available at hardware or auto supply stores. Apply it liberally and let it penetrate for 10-15 minutes, then tap the fastener several times with a small hammer. Do not hit it hard enough to cause damage. Reapply the penetrating oil if necessary. Using an impact driver as described in this chapter will often loosen a stuck bolt or screw.

> *CAUTION*
> *Do not pound on screwdrivers unless the steel shank of the tool extends all the way through the handle. Pounding on a plastic-handled screwdriver is a sure way to destroy the tool.*

For frozen screws, apply additional penetrating oil as described, insert a screwdriver in the slot and tap the top of the screwdriver with a hammer. This loosens the rust so the screw can be removed in the normal way. If the screw head is too chewed up to use this method, grip the head with vise-grip pliers and twist the screw out.

Avoid applying heat unless specifically instructed, as it may melt, warp or remove the temper from parts.

Removing Broken Screws or Bolts

If the head breaks off a screw or bolt, several methods are available for removing the remaining portion.

If a large portion of the remainder projects out, try gripping it with vise-grips. If the projecting portion is too small, file it to fit a wrench or cut a slot in it to fit a screwdriver. See **Figure 62**.

If the head breaks off flush, use a screw extractor. To do this, center punch as close as possible to the exact center of the remaining part of the screw or bolt. Drill a small hole in the screw and tap the extractor into the hole. Back the screw out with a wrench on the extractor. See **Figure 63**.

Remedying Stripped Threads

Occasionally, threads are damaged. Sometimes the threads can be cleaned by running a tap, for internal threads on nuts, or die, for external threads on bolts, through the threads. See **Figure 64**. To clean or repair spark plug threads, a spark plug tap can be used.

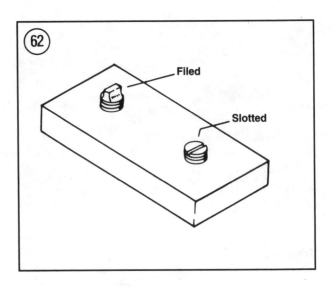

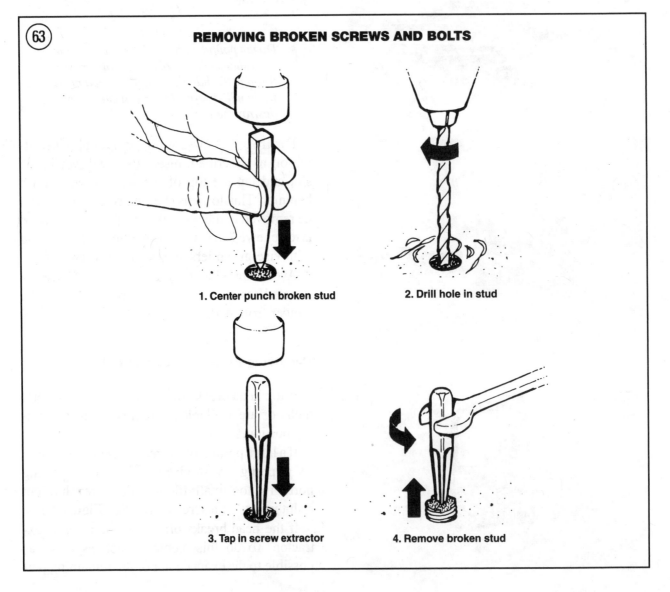

REMOVING BROKEN SCREWS AND BOLTS

1. Center punch broken stud

2. Drill hole in stud

3. Tap in screw extractor

4. Remove broken stud

NOTE
*Taps and dies can be purchased individually or in a set as shown in **Figure 65**.*

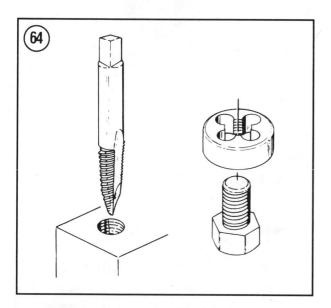

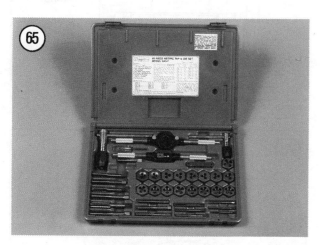

If an internal thread is damaged, it may be necessary to install a Helicoil (**Figure 66**) or some other type of thread insert. Follow the manufacturer's instructions when installing their insert.

If it is necessary to drill and tap a hole, refer to **Table 7** for metric tap drill sizes.

Removing Broken or Damaged Studs

If some threads of a stud are damaged, but some threads remain, the old stud can be removed as follows. A tube of Loctite 271 (red), two nuts, two wrenches and a new stud will be required during this procedure (**Figure 67**).

1. Thread two nuts onto the damaged stud. Then tighten the two nuts against each other so that they are locked.

NOTE
If the threads on the damaged stud do not allow installation of the two nuts, you will have to remove the stud with a pair of locking pliers.

2. Turn the bottom nut counterclockwise and unscrew the stud.

3. Clean the threads with solvent or electrical contact cleaner and allow them to thoroughly dry.

4. Install two nuts on the top half of the new stud as discussed in Step 1. Make sure they are locked securely.

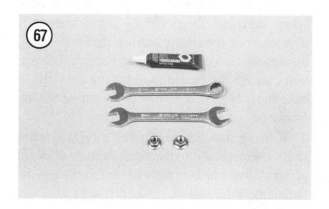

5. Coat the bottom half of a new stud with Loctite 271 (red).

6. Turn the top nut clockwise and thread the new stud securely.

7. Remove the nuts and repeat for each stud as required.

8. Follow Loctite's directions on cure time before assembling the component.

BALL BEARING REPLACEMENT

Ball bearings (**Figure 68**) are used throughout the snowmobile engine and chassis to reduce power loss, heat and noise resulting from friction. Because ball bearings are precision made parts, they must be maintained by proper lubrication and maintenance. Replace damaged bearings. Using a damaged bearing can result in additional damage to an adjacent shaft or case. If installing a new bearing, exercise care to prevent damage to the new bearing. While bearing replacement is described in the individual chapters where applicable, the following should be used as a guideline.

> *NOTE*
> *Unless otherwise specified, install bearings with the manufacturer's mark or number facing outward.*

Bearing Removal

While bearings are normally removed only when damaged, there may be times when it is necessary to remove a bearing that is in good condition. However, improper bearing removal will damage the bearing and maybe the shaft or case half. Note the following when removing bearings:

1. If using a puller to remove a bearing on a shaft, exercise care so that shaft damage does not occur. Always place a piece of metal between the end of the shaft and the puller screw. In addition,

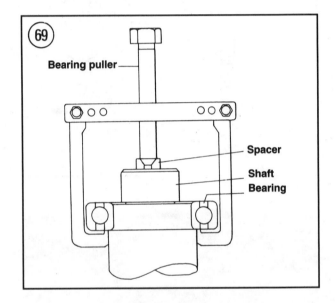

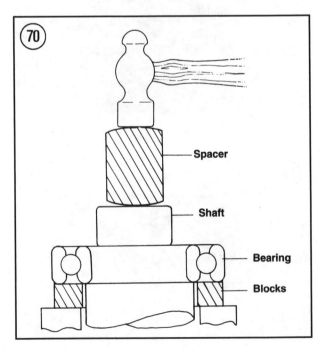

place the puller arms next to the inner bearing race. See **Figure 69**.

2. If using a hammer to remove a bearing on a shaft, do not strike the hammer directly against

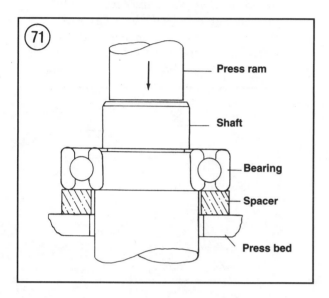

the shaft. Use a brass or aluminum rod between the hammer and shaft (**Figure 70**).

Make sure to support both bearing races with wood blocks.

3. The most ideal method of bearing removal is with a hydraulic hand press. However, certain procedures must be followed or damage may occur to the bearing, shaft or case half. Note the following when using a press:

    a. Always support the inner and outer bearing races with a suitably sized wood or aluminum ring (**Figure 71**). If only the outer race is supported, the balls and/or the inner race will be damaged.

    b. Always make sure the press ram (**Figure 71**) aligns with the center of the shaft. If the ram is not centered, it may damage the bearing and/or shaft.

    c. The moment the shaft is free of the bearing, it will drop to the floor. Secure or hold the shaft to prevent it from falling.

Bearing Installation

1. If installing a bearing in a housing, pressure must be applied to the outer bearing race (**Figure 72**). If installing a bearing on a shaft, pressure must be applied to the inner bearing race (**Figure 73**).

2. If installing a bearing as described in Step 1, some type of driver will be required. Never strike the bearing directly with a hammer or the bearing will be damaged. If installing a bearing, a piece of pipe or a socket with an outer diameter that matches the bearing race will be required. **Figure 74** shows the correct way to use a socket and hammer when installing a bearing.

3. Step 1 describes how to install a bearing in a case half and over a shaft. However, when installing over a shaft and into a housing at the same time, a snug fit will be required for both outer and inner bearing races. In this situation, a spacer must be installed underneath the driver tool so that pressure is applied evenly across both races.

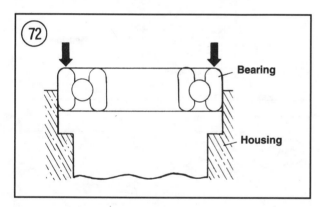

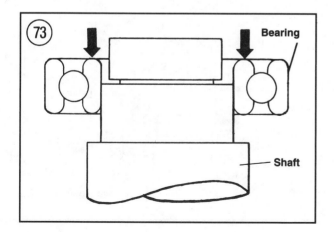

See **Figure 75**. If the outer race is not supported as shown in **Figure 75**, the balls will push against the outer bearing track and damage it.

Shrink Fit

1. Installing a bearing over a shaft: When a tight fit is required, the bearing inside diameter will be smaller than the shaft. In this case, driving the bearing on the shaft using normal methods may cause bearing damage. Instead, the bearing should be heated before installation. Note the following:

   a. Secure the shaft so that it can be ready for bearing installation.

   b. Clean the bearing surface on the shaft of all residue. Remove burrs with a file or sand-paper.

   c. Fill a suitable pot or beaker with clean mineral oil. Place a thermometer rated higher than 120° C (248° F) in the oil. Support the thermometer so that it does not rest on the bottom or side of the pot.

   d. Remove the bearing from its wrapper and secure it with a piece of heavy wire bent to hold it in the pot. Hang the bearing in the pot so that it does not touch the bottom or sides of the pot.

   e. Turn the heat on and monitor the thermome-ter. When the oil temperature rises to ap-proximately 120° C (248° F), remove the bearing from the pot and quickly install it. If necessary, place a socket on the inner bearing race and tap the bearing into place. As the bearing chills, it will tighten on the shaft so you must work quickly when in-stalling it. Make sure the bearing is installed all the way.

2. Installing a bearing in a housing: Bearings are generally installed in a housing with a slight interference fit. Driving the bearing into the housing using normal methods may damage the housing or cause bearing damage. Instead, the

housing should be heated before the bearing is installed. Note the following:

CAUTION
Before heating the crankcases in this procedure to remove the bearings, wash the cases thoroughly with detergent and water. Rinse and rewash the cases as

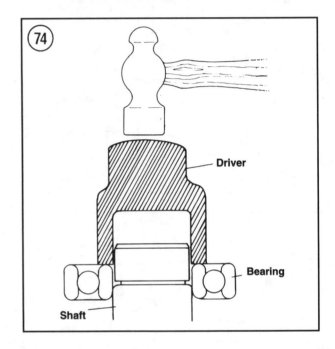

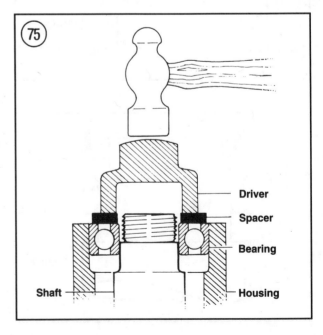

required to remove all traces of oil and other chemical deposits.

a. The housing must be heated to a temperature of about 100° C (212° F) in an oven or on a hot plate. An easy way to check to see that it is at the proper temperature is to drop tiny drops of water on the case. If they sizzle and evaporate immediately, the temperature is correct. Heat only one housing at a time.

CAUTION
Do not heat the housing with a propane or acetlyene torch. Never bring a flame into contact with the bearing or housing. The direct heat will destroy the case hardening of the bearing and will likely warp the housing.

b. Remove the housing from the oven or hot plate and hold onto the housing with a kitchen pot holder, heavy gloves or heavy shop cloths—it is hot.

NOTE
A suitably sized socket and extension works well for removing and installing bearings.

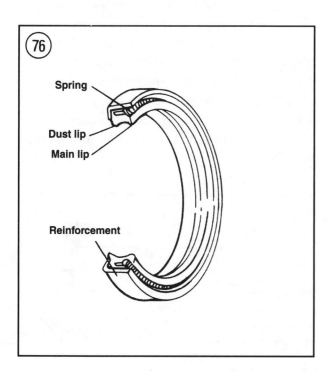
Spring
Dust lip
Main lip
Reinforcement

c. Hold the housing with the bearing side down and tap the bearing out. Repeat for all bearings in the housing.

d. While heating up the housing halves, place the new bearings in a freezer if possible. Chilling them will slightly reduce their overall diameter while the hot housing assembly is slightly larger due to heat expansion. This will make installation much easier.

NOTE
Always install bearings with the manufacturer's mark or number facing outward, unless the text directs otherwise.

e. While the housing is still hot, install the new bearing(s) into the housing. Install the bearings by hand, if possible. If necessary, lightly tap the bearing(s) into the housing with a socket placed on the outer bearing race. Do not install new bearings by driving on the inner bearing race. Install the bearing(s) until it seats completely.

SEALS

Seals (**Figure 76**) are used to prevent leakage of oil, grease or combustion gasses from a housing and a shaft. Improper procedures to remove a seal can damage the housing or the shaft. Improper installation can damage the seal. Note the following:

a. Prying is generally the easiest and most effective method of removing a seal from a housing. However, always place a rag underneath the pry tool to prevent damage to the housing.

b. A low temperature grease should be packed in the seal lips before the seal is installed.

c. Oil seals should always be installed so that the manufacturer's numbers or marks face out.

NOTE
A socket of the correct size can often be used as a seal driver. Select a socket that fits the seal's outer diameter properly and clears any protruding shafts.

d. Oil seals should be installed with a seal driver placed on the outside of the seal as shown in **Figure 77**. Make sure the seal is driven squarely into the housing. Never install a seal by hitting against the top of the seal with a hammer.

SNOWMOBILE OPERATION

Snowmobiles are ideal machines for travelling through otherwise inaccessible areas during winter months. However, because snowmobiles are often operated in extreme weather conditions, over rough terrain, and in remote areas, they should be checked before each ride and maintained on a periodic basis.

WARNING
Never lean into a snowmobile's engine compartment while wearing a scarf or other loose clothing when the engine is running or when the driver is attempting to start the engine. If the scarf or clothing should catch in the drive belt or clutch, severe injury or death could result.

Prestart Inspection

A prestart inspection should always be performed before heading out on your snowmobile. While the following list may look exhaustive, it can be performed rather quickly after you become familiar with it.

1. Familiarize yourself with your snowmobile.
2. Clean the windshield with a clean, damp cloth. Do not use gasoline, solvents or abrasive cleaners.
3. Check track tension (Chapter Three) and adjust if necessary.

4. Check the tether switch and the emergency stop switch for proper operation. If your machine is new or if you are using a friend's machine, practice using the tether or stop switch a few times so that its use will be automatic during an emergency.
5. Check brake operation. Be sure the brake system is correctly adjusted and operates properly.
6. Check the fuel level and fill as needed.
7. Check the oil injection tank. Make sure it is full.
8. Check the coolant level.
9. Operate the throttle lever. It should open and close smoothly.
10. Open the belt guard and visually inspect the drive belt. If the belt appears worn or damaged, replace it. Chapter Fourteen lists drive belt wear limit specifications. Close the belt guard after inspecting the belt. Make sure the belt guard mounts are not loose or damaged.
11. While the engine shroud is open, visually inspect all hoses, fittings and parts for looseness or damage. Check the tightness of all bolts and nuts. Tighten as required.
12. Check the handlebar and steering components for looseness or damage. Do not ride the vehicle if any steering component is damaged. Tighten loose fasteners as required.
13. After closing the shroud, make sure the shroud latches are fastened securely.
14. Check the skis for proper alignment (Chapter Three). Check the ski pivot bolt for tightness or damage.

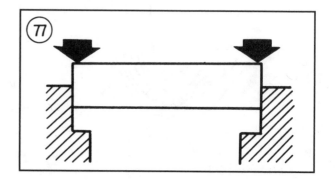

WARNING
When starting the engine, be sure that no bystanders are in front or behind the snowmobile. A sudden lurch of the machine could cause serious injury.

15. Make sure all lights are working.

NOTE
If abnormal noises are detected after starting the engine, locate and repair the problem before starting out.

NOTE
Refer to the appropriate chapter for tightening torques and service procedures.

Tools and Spare Parts

Before leaving on a trip, make sure that you carry tools and spare parts in case of emergency. A tool kit should include the following:
   a. Flashlight
   b. Rope
   c. Tools
   d. Tape
   A Spare parts kit should include the following:
   a. Drive belt
   b. Emergency starter rope
   c. Light bulbs
   d. Spark plugs
   e. Main jets
   f. Throttle cable
   g. Brake cable
   h. This book . . . just in case
   If you are going out on a long trip, you should carry extra oil and fuel.

Emergency Starting

If your recoil starter rope should break and the electric starter does not work, the engine can be started with an emergency starting strap stored in your snowmobile's tool kit.

WARNING
*The drive belt guard must be removed when starting the engine with the emergency starting strap. **Never** lean into the snowmobile's engine compartment while wearing a scarf or other loose clothing while the engine is running or when attempting to start the engine. If the scarf or clothing should catch in the drive belt or clutch, severe injury or death could result.*

1. Open the shroud.
2. Remove the belt guard pin and rotate the belt guard forward.
3. Remove the emergency starting strap from your tool kit.
4. Set all switches to ON.

WARNING
The emergency strap must be used as described in Step 5 only. Do not wrap the strap around the clutch tower or personal injury may occur when attempting to start the engine.

5. Wrap the emergency starting strap counterclockwise around the primary sheave so that the end of the strap is on the outside of the clutch tower.
6. Pull the strap upward and start the engine.

WARNING
Do not casually hold the emergency starting strap over the clutch assembly after it disengages from the primary sheave. If the end of the strap should fall into and engage with the rotating clutch or drive belt, personal injury to yourself or damage to the clutch or drive belt assembly may result.

7. Reinstall the drive belt guard after starting the engine.
8. Close and secure the shroud.
9. Store the emergency starting strap in your tool kit.
10. Repair the recoil starter assembly as soon as possible.

Clearing the Track

If the snowmobile has been operated in deep or slushy snow, clear the track after stopping to prevent the track from freezing. This condition would make starting and running difficult.

WARNING
Make sure no one is behind the machine when clearing the track. Ice and rocks thrown from the track can cause injury.

Tip the snowmobile on its side until the track clears the ground completely. Run the track at a moderate speed until all the ice and snow is thrown clear.

CAUTION
If the track does freeze, it must be broken loose manually with the engine turned OFF. Attempting to force a frozen track with the engine will burn and damage the drive belt.

SNOWMOBILE SAFETY

Proper Clothing

Warm and comfortable clothing are a must to provide protection from frostbite. Even mild temperatures can be very uncomfortable and dangerous when combined with a strong wind or when traveling at high speeds. See **Table 8** for wind chill factors. Always dress according to what the wind chill factor is, not the temperature. Check with an authorized dealer for suggested types of snowmobile clothing.

WARNING
To provide additional warmth as well as protection against head injury, always wear an approved helmet when snowmobiling.

Emergency Survival Techniques

1. Do not panic in the event of an emergency. Relax, think the situation over, then decide on a course of action. You may be within a short distance of help. If possible, repair your snowmobile so you can drive to safety. Conserve your energy and stay warm.

2. Keep hands and feet active to promote circulation and avoid frostbite while servicing your machine.

3. Mentally retrace your route. Where was the last point where help could be located? Do not attempt to walk long distances in deep snow. Make yourself comfortable until help arrives.

4. If you are properly equipped for your trip, you can turn any undesirable area into a suitable campsite.

5. If necessary, build a small shelter with tree branches or evergreen boughs. Look for a sheltered area against a hill or cliff. Even burrowing in snow offers protection from the cold and wind.

6. Prepare a signal fire using evergreen boughs and snowmobile oil. If you cannot build a fire, make an S-O-S in the snow.

7. Use a policeman's whistle or beat cooking utensils to attract attention.

8. When your camp is established, climb the nearest hill and determine your whereabouts. Observe landmarks on the way, so you can find your way back to your campsite. Do not rely on your footprints. They may be covered by blowing snow.

SNOWMOBILE CODE OF ETHICS

1. I will be a good sportsman and conservationist. I recognize that people judge all snowmobilers by my actions. I will use my influence with other snowmobile owners and operators to promote sportsmanlike conduct.

2. I will not litter any trails or areas, nor will I pollute streams or lakes. I will carry out what I carry in.

3. I will not damage living trees, shrubs or other natural features.

4. I will respect other people's properties and rights.

5. I will lend a helping hand when I see someone in need.

6. I will make myself and my vehicle available to assist in search and rescue operations.

7. I will not interfere with the activities of other winter sportsmen. I will respect their right to enjoy their recreational activity.

8. I will know and obey all federal, state or provincial and local rules regulating the operation of snowmobiles in areas where I use my vehicle.

9. I will not harass wildlife.

10. I will not operate my snowmobile where prohibited.

Table 1 ARCTIC CAT MODEL LISTING

Year and model	Engine displacement
1990	
Prowler	435.8 cc (26.6 cu. in.)
El Tigre EXT	529 cc (32.3 cu. in.)
1991	
Cougar, Prowler, Prowler Special	435.8 cc (26.6 cu. in.)
El Tigre EXT	529 cc (32.3cu. in.)
1992	
Cougar, Prowler, Prowler Special	435.8 cc (26.6 cu. in.)
El Tigre EXT	550 cc (33.6cu. in.)
1993	
440 ZR	435.8 cc (26.6 cu. in.)
Cougar, Prowler, Prowler II	435.8 cc (26.6 cu. in.)
EXT 550	550 cc (33.6 cu. in.)
580 ZR, EXT 580Z, EXT 580 Mountain Cat	580 cc (35.4 cu. in.)
1994	
Cougar, Cougar Mountain Cat, Prowler, Prowler II	435.8 cc (26.6 cu. in.)
ZR 440	435.8 cc (26.6 cu. in.)
EXT 580, EXT 580 Mountain Cat, ZR 580	580 cc (35.4 cu. in.)
1995	
Z 440	431 cc (26.3 cu. in.)
ZR 440	435.8 cc (26.6 cu. in.)
Cougar, Cougar Mountain Cat, Prowler 2-Up	550 cc (33.6 cu. in.)
EXT 580, EXT 580 EFI, EXT 580 EFI Mountain Cat	580 cc (35.4 cu. in.)
ZR 580, ZR 580 EFI	580 cc (35.4 cu. in.)
1996	
Z 440	431 cc (26.3 cu. in.)
ZR 440	437.4 cc (26.7 cu. in.)
Cougar, Cougar Mountain Cat, Cougar 2-Up	550 cc (33.6 cu. in.)
EXT 580, EXT 580 EFI, EXT 580 EFI Mountain Cat	580 cc (35.4 cu. in.)
EXT 580 Powder Special, EXT 580 EFI Deluxe	580 cc (35.4 cu. in.)
ZR 580, ZR 580 EFI	580 cc (35.4 cu. in.)
ZRT 600	594 cc (36.3 cu. in.)
1997	
Z 440	431 cc (26.3 cu. in.)
ZL 440	435.8 cc (26.6 cu. in.)
ZR 440	437.4 cc (26.7 cu. in.)
Panther 440	431 cc (26.3 cu. in.)
Cougar, Cougar Mountain Cat	550 cc (33.6 cu. in.)
Panther 550	550 cc (33.6 cu. in.)
EXT 580, Powder Special (with carburetors)	580 cc (35.4 cu. in.)

(continued)

Table 1 ARCTIC CAT MODEL LISTING (continued)

Year and model	Engine displacement
1997	
EXT 580 EFI, EXT 580 EFI Deluxe, Powder Special EFI	580 cc (35.4 cu. in.)
ZR 580	580 cc (35.4 cu. in.)
Pantera EFI 580	580 cc (35.4 cu. in.)
EXT 600, ZRT 600, Powder Extreme	594 cc (36.3 cu. in.)
1998	
Z 440	431 cc (26.3 cu. in.)
ZL 440	435.8 cc (26.6 cu. in.)
ZR 440	437.4 cc (26.7 cu. in.)
Panther 440	431 cc (26.3 cu. in.)
Cougar, Cougar Deluxe, Cougar Mountain Cat	550 cc (33.6 cu. in.)
Panther 550	550 cc (33.6 cu. in.)
EXT 580 EFI, EXT 580 EFI Deluxe	580 cc (35.4 cu. in.)
Pantera EFI 580	580 cc (35.4 cu. in.)
EXT 600, EXT 600 Touring, ZRT 600, 600 Powder Extreme	594 cc (36.3cu. in.)

Table 2 GENERAL DIMENSIONS

Model and dimension	cm	in.
Overall length		
1990		
Prowler	275.6	108.5
Cougar, El Tigre EXT	269	106
1991		
Cougar, El Tigre EXT	269	106
Prowler, Prowler Special	275.6	108.5
1992		
Cougar	269	106
Prowler, Prowler Special	275.6	108.5
El Tigre EXT	275.6	108.5
1993		
440 ZR, 580 ZR	282	111
Cougar, Prowler	274	108
EXT 580 Z	274	108
EXT 580 Mountain Cat	294	115.7
1994		
Cougar, Prowler	274	108
Cougar Mountain Cat	294	115.7
Prowler II	311	122.5
ZR 440, EXT 580, ZR 580	282	111
EXT 580 Mtn. Cat	301	118.5
1995		
Z 440	294	115.7
ZR 440, Cougar, ZR 580, ZR 580 EFI	282	111
Cougar Mountain Cat	301	118.5
Prowler 2-Up	311	122.5
EXT 580, EXT 580 EFI	282	111
EXT 580 EFI Mtn. Cat	301	118.5
ZR 580, ZR 580 EFI	282	111
1996		
Z 440, Cougar	282	111
ZR 440	291	114.5

(continued)

Table 2 GENERAL DIMENSIONS (continued)

Model and dimension	cm	in.
Overall length		
1996		
Cougar Mountain Cat	301	118.5
Cougar 2-Up	311	122.5
EXT 580, EXT 580 EFI	282	111
EXT 580 EFI Mtn. Cat, Powder Spl.	301	118.5
EXT 580 EFI Deluxe	282	111
ZR 580, ZR 580 EFI, ZRT 600	282	111
1997		
Z 440	282	111
ZL 440	282	111
ZR 440	284	112
Panther 440	301	118.5
ZR 580 EFI	282	111
Cougar	282	111
Cougar Mountain Cat	301	118.5
Panther 550	301	118.5
EXT 580 carburetor	282	111
EXT 580 EFI	282	111
EXT 580 EFI Deluxe	282	111
Pantera EFI	301	118.5
Powder Special	301	118.5
Powder Special EFI	301	118.5
EXT 600	282	111
ZRT 600	282	111
Powder Extreme	301	118.5
1998		
Z 440	284	112
ZL 440	284	112
ZR 440	284	112
Panther 440	301	118.5
Cougar	282	111
Cougar Deluxe	282	111
Cougar Mountain Cat	301	118.5
Panther 550	315	124
EXT 580 EFI	282	111
EXT 580 EFI Deluxe	282	111
Pantera EFI	320	126
EXT 600	282	111
EXT 600 Touring	284	112
ZRT 600	284	112
Powder Extreme	301	118.5
Overall width		
1990		
Prowler	106	41.5
Cougar, Cougar Mtn. Cat, El Tigre EXT	108	42.5
1991		
Cougar, El Tigre EXT	108	42.5
Prowler	106	41.5
Prowler Special	113	44.5
1992		
Cougar	108	42.5

(continued)

Table 2 GENERAL DIMENSIONS (continued)

Model and dimension	cm	in.
Overall width		
1992		
Prowler, Prowler Special	109	43
El Tigre EXT	114	45
1993		
440 ZR, Cougar, Prowler, Prowler II	114	45
580 ZR, EXT 550, EXT 580 Z	114	45
EXT 580 Mountain Cat	114	45
1994		
Cougar, Cougar Mountain Cat	114	45
Prowler, Prowler II	114	45
ZR 440, ZR 580	114	45
EXT 580, EXT 580 Mtn. Cat	116	46
1995		
Z 440	117	46
ZR 440	114	45
Cougar, Cougar Mountain Cat,		
Prowler 2-Up	117	46
EXT 580	117	46
EXT 580 EFI	117	46
EXT 580 EFI Mtn. Cat	117	46
ZR 580	117	46
ZR 580 EFI	117	46
1996		
Z 440	117	46
ZR 440	116	45.7
Cougar, Cougar Mountain Cat,		
Cougar 2-Up	117	46
EXT 580, EXT 580 EFI,		
EXT 580 EFI Mtn. Cat	117	46
EXT 580 Powder Spl.	109	43
EXT 580 EFI Deluxe, ZR 580,		
ZR 580 EFI	117	46
ZRT 600	114	45
1997		
Z 440	114	45
ZL 440	114	45
ZR 440	114	45
Panther 440, 550	114	45
ZR 580 EFI	114	45
Cougar	114	45
Cougar Mountain Cat	114	45
EXT 580 EFI	117	46
EXT 580 Deluxe	117	46
Pantera EFI	114	45
Powder Special	114	45
Powder Special EFI	114	45
EXT 600	114	45
ZRT 600	114	45
Powder Extreme	114	45
1998		
Z 440	117	46
ZL 440	117	46

(continued)

GENERAL DIMENSIONS (continued)

	cm	in.
	117	46
	114	45
	114	45
	114	45
	114	45
	114	45
	114	45
	114	45
	117	46
	114	45
	117	46
	117	46
	121	47.5
Prowler	122	48
Cougar, El Tigre EXT	107	42
1991		
Cougar	117	46
Prowler, Prowler Special	122	48
El Tigre EXT	107	42
1992		
Cougar	117	46
Prowler, Prowler Special	120.7	47
El Tigre EXT	120	47
1993		
440 ZR, Cougar	111	43.5
Prowler, Prowler II	118	46.5
580 ZR	111	43.5
EXT 580 Z, EXT 550, EXT 580 Mountain Cat	110	43
1994		
Cougar, Cougar Mountain Cat	109	43
Prowler, Prowler II	118	46.5
ZR 440, EXT 580, ZR 580	111	43.5
EXT 580 Mtn. Cat	112	44
1995		
Z 440, ZR 580, ZR 580 EFI	94	37
ZR 440	111	43.5
Cougar, Cougar Mountain Cat	112	44
Prowler 2-Up	117	46
EXT 580, EXT 580 EFI, EXT 580 EFI Mtn. Cat	112	44
1996		
Z 440, ZR 440	113	44.5
Cougar, Cougar Mountain Cat	112	44
Cougar 2-Up	117	46
EXT 580, EXT 580 EFI, EXT 580 EFI Mtn. Cat	112	44

(continued)

Table 2 GENERAL DIMENSIONS (continued)

Model and dimension	cm	in.
Overall height		
1996		
EXT 580 Powder Special,		
EXT 580 EFI Deluxe	112	44
ZR 580, ZRT 600	94	37
1997		
Z 440	94	37
ZL 440	94	37
ZR 440	94	37
Panther 440, 550	112	44
ZR 580 EFI	94	37
Cougar	112	44
Cougar Mountain Cat	112	44
EXT 580 EFI	112	44
EXT 580 EFI Deluxe	114	37
Powder Special	109	43
Powder Special EFI	109	43
EXT 600	94	37
ZRT 600	94	37
Powder Extreme	94	37
1998		
Z 440	94	37
ZL 440	94	37
ZR 440	94	37
Panther 440, 550	112	44
Cougar	112	44
Cougar Deluxe	112	44
Cougar Mountain Cat	112	44
EXT 580 EFI	112	44
EXT 580 EFI Deluxe	114	37
Pantera EFI	122	48
EXT 600	94	37
EXT 600 Touring	122	48
ZRT 600	94	37
Powder Extreme	94	37

Table 3 VEHICLE WEIGHT

Model	kg	lb.
1990		
Prowler, Cougar	198	437
El Tigre EXT	212	467
1991		
Cougar, Prowler Special	202	445
Prowler	198	437
El Tigre EXT	212	467
1992		
Cougar	250	551
Prowler	198	437
Prowler Special	–	–
El Tigre EXT	227	500

(continued)

Table 3 VEHICLE WEIGHT (continued)

Model	kg	lb.
1993		
440 ZR, 580 ZR	216	476
Cougar, Prowler	198	437
Prowler II	–	–
EXT 580 Z	204	450
EXT 580 Mountain Cat	214	472
1994		
Cougar	212	467
Cougar Mountain Cat	218	481
Prowler	198	437
Prowler II	–	–
ZR 440, ZR 580	218	481
EXT 580	223	492
EXT 580 Mtn. Cat	234	516
1995		
Z 440	182	401
ZR 440	215	474
Cougar	231	509
Cougar Mountain Cat	243	536
Prowler 2-Up	249	549
EXT 580	214	472
EXT 580 EFI	216	476
EXT 580 EFI Mtn. Cat	227	500
ZR 580	204	450
ZR 580 EFI	219	483
1996		
Z 440	188	414
ZR 440	215	474
Cougar	197	434
Cougar Mountain Cat	243	536
Cougar 2-Up	249	549
EXT 580	204	450
EXT 580 EFI	214	472
EXT 580 EFI Mtn. Cat	223	492
EXT 580 Powder Spl.	218	481
EXT 580 EFI Deluxe	–	–
ZR 580	207	456
ZR 580 EFI	219	483
ZRT 600	240	529
1997		
Z 440	188	414
ZL 440	212	467
ZR 440	218	481
Panther 440	211	465
ZR 580 EFI	224	494
Cougar	197	434
Cougar Mountain Cat	204	450
EXT 580 EFI	214	471
EXT 580 EFI Deluxe	–	–
Pantera EFI	234	516
Powder Special	218	481
Powder Special EFI	232	511
EXT 600	243	536

(continued)

Table 3 VEHICLE WEIGHT (continued)

Model	kg	lb.
1997		
ZRT 600	241	531
Powder Extreme	249	549
1998		
Z 440	213	470
ZL 440	216	476
ZR 440	211	465
Cougar	197	434
Cougar Deluxe	223	492
Cougar Mountain Cat	231	509
Panther 550	251	553
EXT 580 EFI	232	511
EXT 580 EFI Deluxe	244	540
Pantera EFI	264	582
EXT 600	244	538
EXT 600 Touring	269	593
ZRT 600	262	578
Powder Extreme	250	551

Table 4 DECIMAL AND METRIC EQUIVALENTS

Fractions	Decimal in.	Metric mm	Fractions	Decimal in.	Metric mm
1/64	0.015625	0.39688	33/64	0.515625	13.09687
1/32	0.03125	0.79375	17/32	0.53125	13.49375
3/64	0.046875	1.19062	35/64	0.546875	13.89062
1/16	0.0625	1.58750	9/16	0.5625	14.28750
5/64	0.078125	1.98437	37/64	0.578125	14.68437
3/32	0.09375	2.38125	19/32	0.59375	15.08125
7/64	0.109375	2.77812	39/64	0.609375	15.47812
1/8	0.125	3.1750	5/8	0.625	15.87500
9/64	0.140625	3.57187	41/64	0.640625	16.27187
5/32	0.15625	3.96875	21/32	0.65625	16.66875
11/64	0.171875	4.36562	43/64	0.671875	17.06562
3/16	0.1875	4.76250	11/16	0.6875	17.46250
13/64	0.203125	5.15937	45/64	0.703125	17.85937
7/32	0.21875	5.55625	23/32	0.71875	18.25625
15/64	0.234375	5.95312	47/64	0.734375	18.65312
1/4	0.250	6.35000	3/4	0.750	19.05000
17/64	0.265625	6.74687	49/64	0.765625	19.44687
9/32	0.28125	7.14375	25/32	0.78125	19.84375
19/64	0.296875	7.54062	51/64	0.796875	20.24062
5/16	0.3125	7.93750	13/16	0.8125	20.63750
21/64	0.328125	8.33437	53/64	0.828125	21.03437
11/32	0.34375	8.73125	27/32	0.84375	21.43125
23/64	0.359375	9.12812	55/64	0.859375	21.82812
3/8	0.375	9.52500	7/8	0.875	22.22500
25/64	0.390625	9.92187	57/64	0.890625	22.62187
13/32	0.40625	10.31875	29/32	0.90625	23.01875
27/64	0.421875	10.71562	59/64	0.921875	23.41562

(continued)

Table 4 DECIMAL AND METRIC EQUIVALENTS (continued)

Fractions	Decimal in.	Metric mm	Fractions	Decimal in.	Metric mm
7/16	0.4375	11.11250	15/16	0.9375	23.81250
29/64	0.453125	11.50937	61/64	0.953125	24.20937
15/32	0.46875	11.90625	31/32	0.96875	24.60625
31/64	0.484375	12.30312	63/64	0.984375	25.00312
1/2	0.500	12.70000	1	1.00	25.40000

Table 5 GENERAL TORQUE SPECIFICATIONS

Item	N·m	ft.-lb.
Bolt		
6 mm	6	4.4
8 mm	15	11
10 mm	30	22
12 mm	55	41
14 mm	85	63
16 mm	130	96
Nut		
6 mm	6	4.4
8 mm	15	11
10 mm	30	22
12 mm	55	41
14 mm	85	63
16 mm	130	96

Table 6 TECHNICAL ABBREVIATIONS

ABDC	After bottom dead center
ATDC	After top dead center
BBDC	Before bottom dead center
BDC	Bottom dead center
BTDC	Before top dead center
C	Celsius (Centigrade)
cc	Cubic centimeters
CDI	Capacitor discharge ignition
cu. in.	Cubic inches
EFI	Electronic fuel injection
F	Fahrenheit
ft.-lb.	Foot-pounds
gal.	Gallons
H/A	High altitude
hp	Horsepower
in.	Inches
kg	Kilogram
kg/cm^2	Kilograms per square centimeter
kgm	Kilogram meters
km	Kilometer
l	Liter
m	Meter
MAG	Magneto
ml	Milliliter
mm	Millimeter

(continued)

Table 6 TECHNICAL ABBREVIATIONS (continued)

N·m	Newton-meters
oz.	Ounce
psi	Pounds per square inch
PTO	Power take off
pts.	Pints
qt.	Quarts
rpm	Revolutions per minute

Table 7 METRIC TAP DRILL SIZES

Metric tap (mm)	Drill size	Decimal equivalent	Nearest fraction
3 × 0.50	No. 39	0.0995	3/32
3 × 0.60	3/32	0.0937	3/32
4 × 0.70	No. 30	0.1285	1/8
4 × 0.75	1/8	0.125	1/8
5 × 0.80	No. 19	0.166	11/64
5 × 0.90	No. 20	0.161	5/32
6 × 1.00	No. 9	0.196	13/64
7 × 1.00	16/64	0.234	15/64
8 × 1.00	J	0.277	9/32
8 × 1.25	17/64	0.265	17/64
9 × 1.00	5/16	0.3125	5/16
9 × 1.25	5/16	0.3125	5/16
10 × 1.25	11/32	0.3437	11/32
10 × 1.50	R	0.339	11/32
11 × 1.50	3/8	0.375	3/8
12 × 1.50	13/32	0.406	13/32
12 × 1.75	13/32	0.406	13/32

Table 8 WINDCHILL FACTORS

Estimated wind speed in mph	Actual thermometer reading (°F)											
	50	40	30	20	10	0	−10	−20	−30	−40	−50	−60
	Equivalent temperature (°F)											
Calm	50	40	30	20	10	0	−10	−20	−30	−40	−50	−60
5	48	37	27	16	6	−5	−15	−26	−36	−47	−57	−68
10	40	28	16	4	−9	−21	−33	−46	−58	−70	−83	−95
15	36	22	9	−5	−18	−36	−45	−58	−72	−85	−99	−112
20	32	18	4	−10	−25	−39	−53	−67	−82	−96	−110	−124
25	30	16	0	−15	−29	−44	−59	−74	−88	−104	−118	−133
30	28	13	−2	−18	−33	−48	−63	−79	−94	−109	−125	−140
35	27	11	−4	−20	−35	−49	−67	−82	−98	−113	−129	−145
40	26	10	−6	−21	−37	−53	−69	−85	−100	−116	−132	−148
*		Little danger (for properly clothed person)			Increasing danger				Great danger			
					• Danger from freezing of exposed flesh •							

*Wind speeds greater than 40 mph have little additional effect.

Chapter Two

Troubleshooting

Diagnosing mechanical problems is relatively simple if you use orderly procedures and keep a few basic principles in mind. The first step in any troubleshooting procedure is to define the symptoms as closely as possible and then localize the problem. Subsequent steps involve testing and analyzing those areas which could cause the symptoms. A haphazard approach may eventually solve the problem, but it can be very costly in terms of wasted time and unnecessary parts replacements.

Proper lubrication, maintenance and periodic tune-ups as described in Chapter Three will reduce the necessity for troubleshooting. Even with the best of care, however, all snowmobiles are prone to problems which will require troubleshooting.

Never assume anything. Do not overlook the obvious. If the engine will not start, check the position of the emergency cut-out switch and the tether switch. Is the engine flooded with fuel from using the primer too much?

If the engine suddenly quits, check the easiest, most accessible problem first. Is there gasoline in the tank? Has a spark plug wire broken or fallen off?

If nothing obvious turns up in a quick check, look a little further. Learning to recognize and describe symptoms will make repairs easier for you or a mechanic at the shop. Describe problems accurately and fully.

Gather as many symptoms as possible to aid in diagnosis. For instance, note whether the engine lost power gradually or all at once. If smoke comes out of the exhaust pipe, note the color of the smoke. After the symptoms are defined, areas which could cause problems can be tested and analyzed. Guessing at the cause of a problem may provide the solution, but it usually leads to frustration, wasted time and a series of expensive, unnecessary parts replacements.

You do not need fancy equipment or complicated test gear to determine whether you should attempt repairs at home. A few simple checks could save a large repair bill and lost time while your snowmobile sits in a dealer's service department. On the other hand, be realistic and do not attempt repairs that are beyond your abilities.

Service departments tend to charge heavily for putting together an engine that someone else has disassembled. Some will not even take such a job, so use common sense and do not get in over your head.

Electrical specifications are listed in **Tables 1-7** at the end of this chapter.

OPERATING REQUIREMENTS

An engine needs three basic requirements to run properly: correct fuel/air mixture, sufficient compression and a spark at the right time (**Figure 1**). If one basic requirement is missing, the engine will not run. Two-stroke engine operating principles are described in Chapter One under Engine Principles. Ignition problems are a frequent cause of breakdowns and the ignition system can be quickly and easily checked. Keep that in mind before you begin tampering with carburetor adjustments.

If the snowmobile has been sitting for any length of time and refuses to start, check and clean the spark plugs. Then check the condition of the battery, if so equipped, to make sure it is fully charged. If the spark plugs and the battery are okay, then check the fuel delivery system. This includes the tank, fuel shutoff valve, fuel pump and fuel line to the carburetor. Gasoline deposits may have gummed up the carburetor's fuel inlet needle, jets and small air passages. Gasoline tends to lose its potency after standing for long periods and condensation may contaminate it with water. Drain the old gas and try starting with a fresh tankful.

TROUBLESHOOTING INSTRUMENTS

Chapter One lists the instruments needed and detailed instruction on their use.

TESTING ELECTRICAL COMPONENTS

Most dealerships and parts houses will not accept returns of any electrical parts. When testing electrical components, make sure you perform the test procedures as described in this chapter and your test equipment is working properly. If a test result shows the component is defective, it is still a good idea to have the component retested by an Arctic Cat dealership to verify the test result before purchasing a new component.

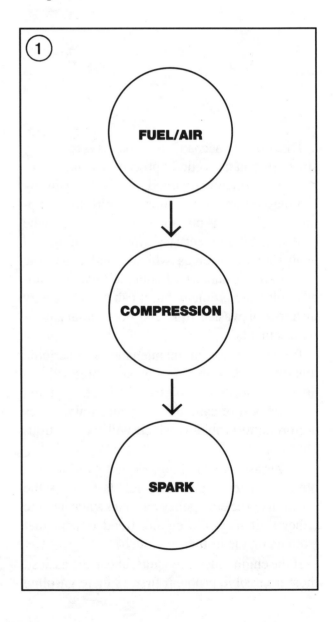

ENGINE ELECTRICAL SYSTEM TROUBLESHOOTING

All models are equipped with a capacitor discharge ignition system. This section describes complete ignition and charging system troubleshooting.

This solid state system uses no contact breaker points or other moving parts. Because of the solid state design, problems with the capacitor discharge system are relatively few. Problems are usually limited to no spark. In some instances, a lack of spark may be intermittent and occur only when the engine is subjected to certain temperatures, loads or vibrations. It is often easier to find the cause of no spark than those with intermittent problems. If the ignition has no spark, first check for broken or damaged wires.

General troubleshooting procedures are provided in **Figure 2**.

Test Equipment

Complete testing of the engine ignition and electrical system will require an Electro Specialties Model 1L, Arctco Ignition Analyzer (part No. 0644-052), or similar tester. You can purchase the Arctco Ignition Analyzer and the necessary attaching cable through Arctic Cat dealers. Information and instructions for use are included with the tester. You can perform basic testing of the electrical system with an accurate ohmmeter and voltmeter.

If you do not have access to the special tester shown in **Figure 3** or **4**, you can use visual inspection and an ohmmeter to pinpoint electrical problems caused by dirty or damaged connectors, faulty or damaged wiring or electrical components that may have cracked or broken. If basic checks fail to locate the problem, take your snowmobile to an Arctic Cat dealership and have them troubleshoot the electrical system.

Precautions

Certain measures must be taken to protect the capacitor discharge system. Instantaneous damage to semiconductors in the system will occur if the following is not observed:
1. Do not crank the engine if the CDI unit is not grounded to the engine.
2. Do not touch or disconnect any ignition components when the engine is running or while the battery cables are connected.
3. Keep all connections between the various units clean and tight. Be sure that the wiring connectors are pushed together firmly.

Troubleshooting Preparation

NOTE
To test the wiring harness for poor connections in Step 1, bend the molded rubber connector while checking each wire for resistance.

Refer to the wiring diagram for your model at the end of this book when performing the following:
1. Check the wiring harness for visible signs of damage.
2. Make sure all of the connectors are properly connected as follows:

NOTE
*Never pull on the electrical wires when separating an electrical connector. Pull only on the plastic housing of the connector. See **Figure 5**.*

a. Disconnect each electrical connector in the ignition circuit. Check for bent or damaged male connector pins (**Figure 6**). A bent pin will not connect properly and will cause an open circuit.
b. Check each female connector end. Make sure the metal connector at the end of each wire (**Figure 7**) is pushed all the way into the plastic connector. If not, use a small,

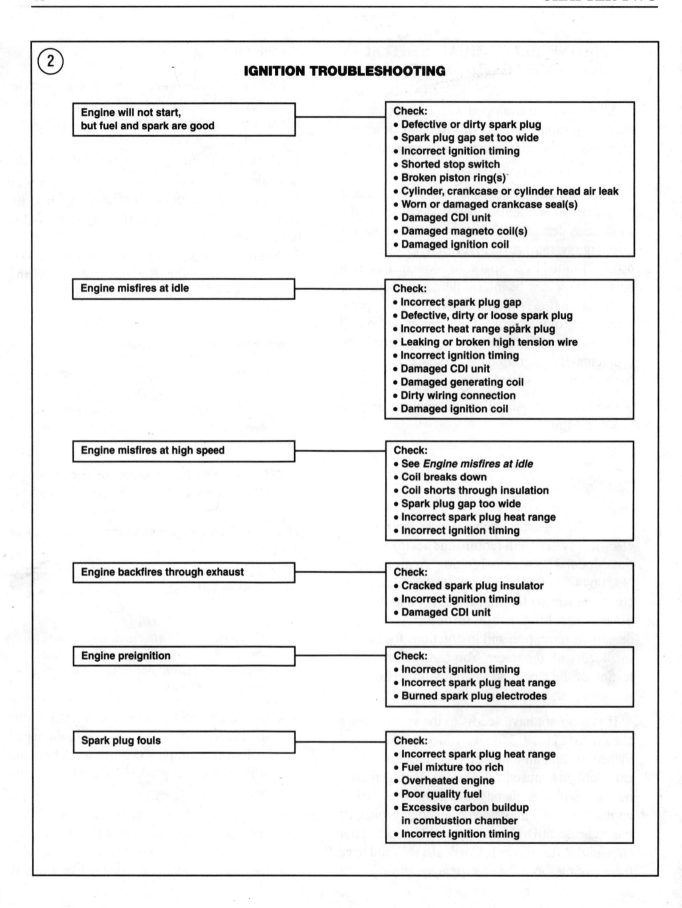

② **IGNITION TROUBLESHOOTING**

Engine will not start, but fuel and spark are good

Check:
- Defective or dirty spark plug
- Spark plug gap set too wide
- Incorrect ignition timing
- Shorted stop switch
- Broken piston ring(s)
- Cylinder, crankcase or cylinder head air leak
- Worn or damaged crankcase seal(s)
- Damaged CDI unit
- Damaged magneto coil(s)
- Damaged ignition coil

Engine misfires at idle

Check:
- Incorrect spark plug gap
- Defective, dirty or loose spark plug
- Incorrect heat range spark plug
- Leaking or broken high tension wire
- Incorrect ignition timing
- Damaged CDI unit
- Damaged generating coil
- Dirty wiring connection
- Damaged ignition coil

Engine misfires at high speed

Check:
- See *Engine misfires at idle*
- Coil breaks down
- Coil shorts through insulation
- Spark plug gap too wide
- Incorrect spark plug heat range
- Incorrect ignition timing

Engine backfires through exhaust

Check:
- Cracked spark plug insulator
- Incorrect ignition timing
- Damaged CDI unit

Engine preignition

Check:
- Incorrect ignition timing
- Incorrect spark plug heat range
- Burned spark plug electrodes

Spark plug fouls

Check:
- Incorrect spark plug heat range
- Fuel mixture too rich
- Overheated engine
- Poor quality fuel
- Excessive carbon buildup in combustion chamber
- Incorrect ignition timing

narrow blade screwdriver to carefully push them in. Make sure you do not pinch or cut the wire. Also, make sure that you do not spread the connector.

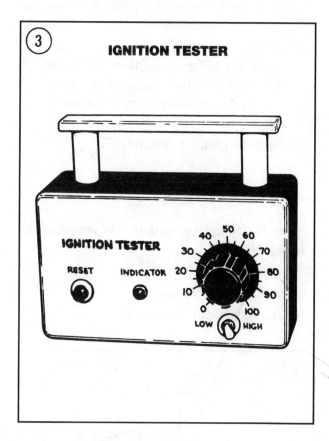

c. Check the wires to make sure that each one is properly attached to a metal connector inside the plastic connector.

d. Make sure all electrical connectors are clean and free of corrosion. If necessary, clean the connectors with an electrical contact cleaner.

e. After making sure that all of the individual connectors are alright, push the connectors

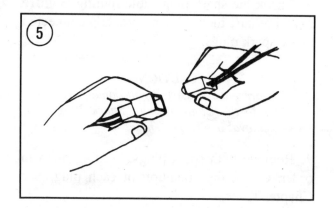

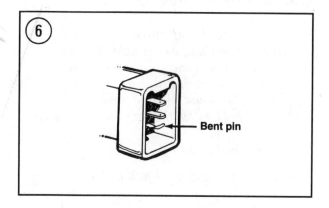

Bent pin

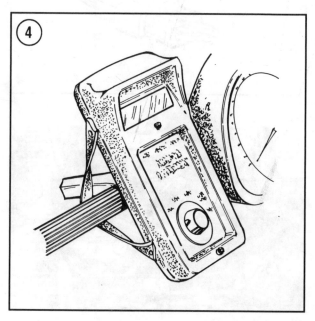

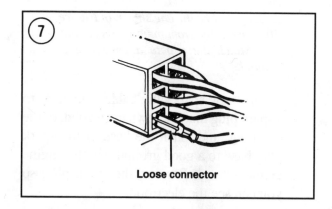

Loose connector

together until they click. Make sure they are fully engaged and locked together (**Figure 8**).

3. Check all electrical components for a good ground to the engine.

4. Check all wiring for short circuits or open circuits.

5. Make sure the fuel tank has an adequate supply of fresh gasoline and that the oil tank is properly filled.

6. Check the spark plug cable routing (**Figure 9**) and be sure the cables are properly connected to the spark plugs.

> *CAUTION*
> *To prevent expensive engine damage, refer to the Caution under **Spark Plug Removal** in Chapter Three.*

7. Remove both spark plugs, keeping them in order. Check the condition of each plug. See Chapter Three.

8. Perform the following spark test:

> *WARNING*
> *During this test, do not hold the spark plug, wire or connector with your fingers or a serious electrical shock may result. If necessary, use a pair of insulated pliers to hold the spark plug wire.*

a. Open the hood.

b. Remove one of the spark plugs.

> *NOTE*
> *A test plug like the one shown in **Figure 10** is available from many parts suppliers. Attach the clip to a good engine ground.*

c. Connect the spark plug cable connector to a spark plug that is known to be good, or the test plug, and touch the base of the spark plug base to a good ground like the engine cylinder head. Position the spark plug so you can see the electrode.

d. Turn the ignition switch ON and set the tether and cut-out switches to the ON position.

e. Crank the engine over with the starter. A fat blue spark should be evident across the spark plug electrode.

f. If there is no spark or only a weak one, check for loose connections at the coil. If all external wiring connections are good, check the remaining components of the ignition system.

g. Turn the ignition switch OFF.

Switch Tests

Test the following switches as described in Chapter Nine:

a. ignition switch.

b. tether cut-out switch.

c. emergency cut-out switch.

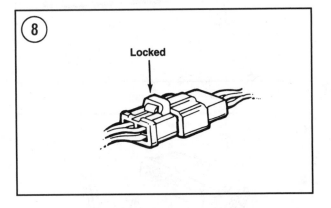

Ignition Testing with the Electro-Specialties Model 1L Ignition Tester or Arctco Ignition Analyzer

An ignition tester (**Figure 3** or **4**) designed for this system is required for complete testing of the ignition system. The Arctco Ignition Analyzer (part no. 0644-052) and the necessary attaching cable can purchased through Arctic Cat dealers. Information and instructions are included with the tester. Refer to **Table 1** for ignition test specifications. If you do not have access to this test instrument, have the tests performed by an Arctic Cat dealer.

Prior to testing the ignition system, note the following:

a. Perform the Troubleshooting Preparation procedures in this section.

b. Tests are similar for all models, but it is important to follow the instructions for the particular model that is being tested.

c. The following tests must be made at cranking speed. This means that while it is not necessary to have the engine running, it is important to pull vigorously on the starter rope while checking the ignition.

d. Each test should be performed three times to reduce the chance for an erronous reading.

e. The ignition tester should be reset after each test by depressing the reset button on the front of the tester.

f. Have the dealership recheck components to verify the unit is faulty before buying a replacement.

g. Make sure that the replacement part is correct. Units are very similar, but similar parts may not be interchangeable.

> *WARNING*
> *Do not touch any ignition component when cranking the engine for the following tests. A powerful electric shock may occur if you do so.*

Ignition Component Resistance Test

An accurate ohmmeter will be required to perform the following tests. Only the coils, wiring and connections can be checked with an ohmmeter. The CDI unit cannot be tested adequately by only making resistance tests.

Ignition high-tension coil

1. Open the hood and locate the ignition high-tension coil(s). Refer to **Figure 11** or **12** for typical coil installation.

2. Disconnect the two primary connectors from the high-tension coil.

3. Check ignition coil primary resistance as follows:

a. If necessary, switch the ohmmeter to the R × 1 scale.

b. Measure resistance between the two primary terminals using an accurate ohmmeter. Refer to **Figures 13** and **14**.

c. Compare the measured resistance with the specifications listed in **Table 3**.

d. Disconnect the meter leads.

4. Check ignition coil secondary resistance as follows:

    a. Remove the spark plug cap from the end of each high-tension cable.

    b. If necessary, switch the ohmmeter to the R × 1000 scale.

    c. On coils with two spark plug wires, measure the resistance between the ends of the two high-tension (spark plug) cables. Refer to **Figure 13**.

    d. On the single coil of three cylinder models, measure the resistance between the end of the high-tension (spark plug) cable and the primary lead. Refer to **Figure 14**.

    e. Compare the measured resistance with the specifications listed in **Table 3**.

    f. Disconnect the meter leads.

5. Check ignition coil insulation as follows:

    a. If necessary, switch the ohmmeter to the R × 1 scale.

    b. On coils with two spark plug cables, measure resistance between the primary lead terminals and each high-tension (spark plug) cable. The meter should read infinity.

    c. Measure resistance between the primary lead terminals and the ignition coil core (mounting). The meter should read infinity.

6. If resistance tests of the coil are not as specified in Steps 3-5, the coil is probably faulty. Have a dealership recheck the coil to verify that the unit is faulty before buying a replacement. See Chapter Nine.

> *NOTE*
> *Normal resistance in both the primary and secondary (high-tension) coil windings is not a guarantee that the unit is working properly. Only an operational spark test can indicate whether or not a*

coil is producing an adequate spark from the input voltage. An Arctic Cat dealership may have the equipment to test the coil's output. If not, substitute a known good coil to determine whether or not the problem is fixed.

Ignition charge coil

The ignition charge coil is mounted on the stator plate under the flywheel.

1. Open the hood.

2. Disconnect the three-prong connector between the CDI (ignition module) and magneto. This connector has three wires. The black/white wire is the ground connection.

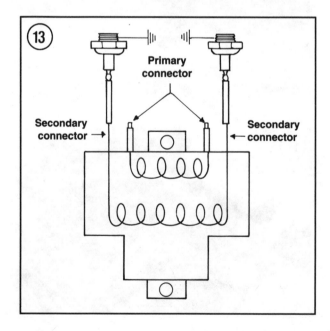

3. Connect an ohmmeter between the black/white and black/red (or green) wires to check the ignition charging coil.

4. Compare the reading to the specification in **Table 4**. If the reading is not within specifications, replace the charge coil assembly as described in Chapter Nine.

5. Reconnect the three-prong connector.

6. Close the hood.

Ignition trigger coil (coil under flywheel)

The ignition trigger coil is mounted on the stator plate under the flywheel of some models.

1. Open the hood.

2. Disconnect the three-prong connector between the CDI (ignition module) and magneto. This connector has three wires that may be black/white, black/red and red/white or black/white, green and white/red. The black/white wire is the ground connection.

3. Connect an ohmmeter between the black/white and red/white wires to check the trigger coil.

4. Compare the reading to the specification in **Table 5**. If the reading is not within specification,

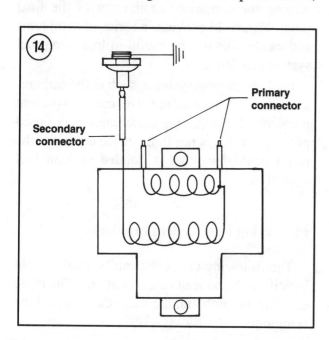

replace the trigger coil assembly as described in Chapter Nine.

5. Reconnect the three-prong connector.

6. Close the hood.

Ignition trigger coil (coil outside flywheel)

On fuel-injected and three-cylinder models, a separate ignition trigger coil is located just outside the flywheel. The wires from the trigger coil are green/white and brown. Models with EFI are equipped with a second sensor that is similarly located.

1. Open the hood.

2. Disconnect the black two-prong connector located between the CDI control unit and the ignition trigger coil. Wires to the CDI control unit may have one white wire and one black or one green/white and one brown wire.

3. Connect an ohmmeter between the green/white and brown wires from the ignition trigger coil.

4. Compare the reading to the specification in **Table 5**. If the reading is not within specification, replace the trigger coil assembly as described in Chapter Nine.

5. Reattach the two-prong connector.

6. Close the hood.

Lighting coil

The lighting coil of all models is mounted on the stator plate behind the flywheel.

1. Open the hood.

2. Locate the four-plug connector which contains the two yellow wires or the yellow, yellow/red and brown wires.

3. Separate the connector and attach an ohmmeter to the engine wires as listed in **Table 6**.

4. Switch the ohmmeter to the R × 1 scale.

5. Compare the reading to the specification in **Table 6**. If the reading is not within specification, replace the lighting coil assembly as described in Chapter Nine.

6. Reattach the wire connector.

7. Close the hood.

VOLTAGE REGULATOR

Some models are equipped with a voltage regulator. If you are experiencing blown bulbs or if all of the lights are dim, test the voltage regulator as follows. In addition, check the bulb filament. An overcharged condition will usually melt the filament rather than break it.

1. Position the snowmobile so that the ski tips are placed against a stationary object. Then raise the rear of the snowmobile so that the track is clear of the ground.

2. Open the hood and secure it so that it cannot fall.

3. Set the voltmeter to the 25-volt DC scale, then connect one of the voltmeter leads to a good ground.

NOTE
Do not disconnect the voltmeter leads when testing voltage output.

4. Connect the other voltmeter lead to the voltage regulator yellow wire.

WARNING
When performing the following steps, ensure that the track area is clear and that no one walks behind the track or serious injuries may result.

WARNING
Do not lean into the snowmobile's engine compartment while wearing a scarf or other loose clothing when the engine is running or when attempting to start the engine. If any clothing should catch in the drive belt or clutch, severe injury or death could occur. Be sure the pulley guard is in place.

5. Have an assistant start the engine. When starting the engine, do not use the throttle to increase the engine speed more than necessary.

6. Observe the voltmeter while the engine is at idle speed. The voltmeter should indicate 11-13 volts DC.

7. Slowly increase the engine rpm to 2,500-2,700 rpm and observe the voltmeter reading. If the voltmeter indicates less than 11 volts or more than 13 volts, replace the voltage regulator. See Chapter Nine.

8. Turn the engine off and disconnect the voltmeter.

9. Close the hood and lower the snowmobile track to the ground.

FUEL SYSTEM

Many snowmobile owners automatically assume that the carburetor or Electronic Fuel Injection (EFI) is at fault when the engine does not run properly. Fuel system problems are not uncommon, but most are caused by an empty tank, a plugged fuel filter, a malfunctioning fuel pump or bad fuel. Changing the carburetor or EFI adjustments will not correct these problems and will only compound the problem.

Fuel system troubleshooting should start at the fuel tank and progress through the system, reserving the carburetor or injector as the final point. **Figure 15** provides a series of symptoms and causes that can be useful in localizing fuel system problems.

Fuel enrichment systems, such as the carburetor's starting enrichment valve, can also present problems. If the starting enrichment is not used properly or if it is not functioning correctly, the result could be either a flooded or lean fuel condition.

Identifying Fuel System Problems

The following check list can be used to help identify rich and lean fuel conditions. The more extreme the problem, the more exaggerated the symptoms.

If the engine is running rich, one or more of the following conditions may be noticed:

a. The spark plug(s) foul often. Sometimes this condition has been masked by installing spark plugs of a hotter heat range.

b. The engine misses and runs rough when operating under a load.

c. Exhaust smoke is excessive when the throttle is depressed.

d. When the throttle is open, the exhaust will sound choked or dull. Stopping the snowmobile and trying to clear the exhaust by holding the throttle open does not change the sound.

If the engine is running lean, one or more of the following conditions may be noticed:

a. The firing end of the spark plugs become very white or blistered in appearance. Sometimes spark plugs of a colder heat range have been installed which masks the problem.

b. The engine overheats.

c. Acceleration is slower.

d. Performance flat spots are felt during operation. These feel like the engine is trying to run out of gas.

e. Engine power is reduced.

f. At full throttle, engine rpm will not hold steady.

ELECTRONIC FUEL INJECTION

Refer to Chapter Seven for troubleshooting information on the fuel injection system.

ENGINE

Engine problems are generally symptoms of something wrong in another system, such as ignition, fuel or starting. If properly maintained and serviced, the engine should experience no problems other than those caused by age and wear.

Overheating and Lack of Lubrication

Overheating and lack of lubrication will cause major engine mechanical damage. Make sure the cooling system is not damaged and the oil injection tank is always filled. Make sure that the cooling fluid has antifreeze that is properly mixed and in the proper ratio to protect at the temperatures encountered. Check to be sure that the thermostat is opening correctly. Incorrect ignition timing, a faulty cooling system or an excessively lean fuel mixture can also cause the engine to overheat. The wrong spark plug may cause preignition and overheating.

Preignition

Preignition is the premature burning of fuel and is caused by hot spots in the combustion chamber (**Figure 16**). The fuel actually ignites before it should. Glowing deposits in the combustion chamber, inadequate cooling or overheated spark plugs can all cause preignition. This is first noticed in the form of a power loss but will eventually result in extended damage to the internal parts of the engine because of higher combustion chamber temperatures.

Detonation

Commonly called spark knock or fuel knock, detonation is the violent explosion of fuel in the combustion chamber instead of a controlled burning and expansion (**Figure 17**). The excessive combustion pressure can cause severe mechanical damage. Use of low octane gasoline is a common cause of detonation, but detonation can still occur when high octane gasoline is used.

Some causes of detonation are improper ignition timing, lean fuel mixture, inadequate engine cooling, cross-firing of spark plugs or the excessive accumulation of deposits in the combustion

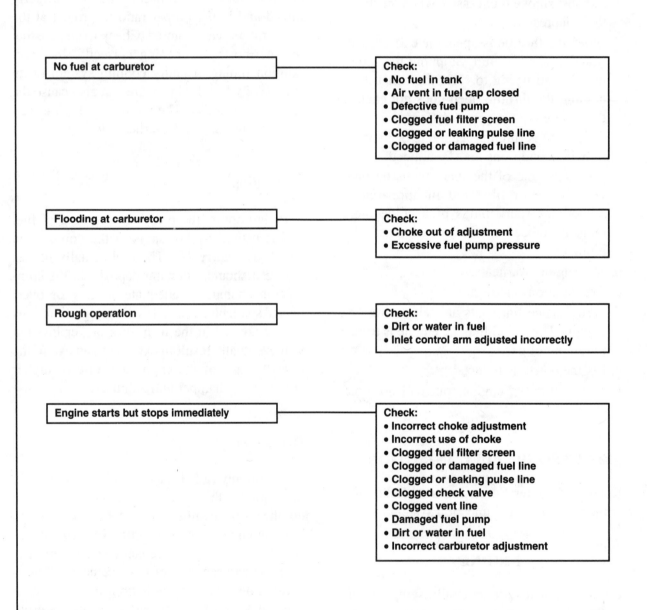

(15)

FUEL SYSTEM TROUBLESHOOTING

No fuel at carburetor

Check:
- No fuel in tank
- Air vent in fuel cap closed
- Defective fuel pump
- Clogged fuel filter screen
- Clogged or leaking pulse line
- Clogged or damaged fuel line

Flooding at carburetor

Check:
- Choke out of adjustment
- Excessive fuel pump pressure

Rough operation

Check:
- Dirt or water in fuel
- Inlet control arm adjusted incorrectly

Engine starts but stops immediately

Check:
- Incorrect choke adjustment
- Incorrect use of choke
- Clogged fuel filter screen
- Clogged or damaged fuel line
- Clogged or leaking pulse line
- Clogged check valve
- Clogged vent line
- Damaged fuel pump
- Dirt or water in fuel
- Incorrect carburetor adjustment

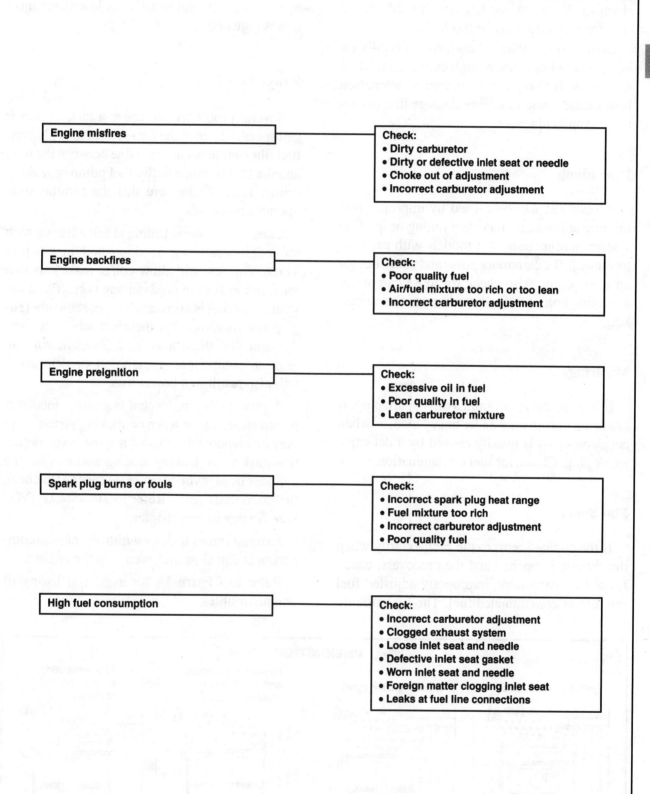

Engine misfires

Check:
- Dirty carburetor
- Dirty or defective inlet seat or needle
- Choke out of adjustment
- Incorrect carburetor adjustment

Engine backfires

Check:
- Poor quality fuel
- Air/fuel mixture too rich or too lean
- Incorrect carburetor adjustment

Engine preignition

Check:
- Excessive oil in fuel
- Poor quality in fuel
- Lean carburetor mixture

Spark plug burns or fouls

Check:
- Incorrect spark plug heat range
- Fuel mixture too rich
- Incorrect carburetor adjustment
- Poor quality fuel

High fuel consumption

Check:
- Incorrect carburetor adjustment
- Clogged exhaust system
- Loose inlet seat and needle
- Defective inlet seat gasket
- Worn inlet seat and needle
- Foreign matter clogging inlet seat
- Leaks at fuel line connections

2

chamber. If the engine has been modified, the compression ratio may be too high.

Detonation may not be noticed, especially on liquid-cooled engines, at high engine rpm when wind noise is also present. Unnoticed detonation is often the cause of engine damage that occurs for no apparent reason.

Poor Idling

A poor idle can be caused by improper fuel mixture adjustment, incorrect timing or ignition system malfunctions. On models with carburetors, check the carburetor pulse and vent lines for an obstruction. Also check for loose carburetor mounting bolts or a faulty carburetor flange gasket.

Misfiring

Misfiring can result from a dirty spark plug. If misfiring occurs only under heavy load, as when accelerating, it is usually caused by a defective spark plug. Check for fuel contamination.

Flat Spots

If the engine seems to die momentarily when the throttle is opened and then recovers, check for a dirty carburetor, improperly adjusted fuel mixture or contaminated fuel. The fuel mixture may be too rich, but usually the low speed mixture is adjusted too lean.

Power Loss

Several problems can cause a lack of power and speed. Check in the fuel system for a plugged fuel filter, air leaks in a fuel line between the tank and the fuel pump, a faulty fuel pump or leaking primer lines. Make sure that the throttle slide operates properly.

Check the ignition timing at full advance with the engine running as described in Chapter Three. This test will allow you to make sure that the ignition system is advancing correctly. If the ignition timing is correct when set statically (engine not running), but incorrect when checked dynamically, there may be a problem with an ignition component. Preignition or detonation will also result in a power loss.

A piston or cylinder that is galling, incorrect piston clearance or worn or sticking piston rings may be responsible. Look for loose bolts, defective gaskets or leaking mating surfaces on the cylinder head, cylinder or crankcase. Also check the crankshaft seals. Refer to *Two-Stroke Pressure Testing* in this chapter.

Exhaust fumes leaking within the engine compartment can slow and even stop the engine.

Refer to **Figure 18** for a general listing of engine troubles.

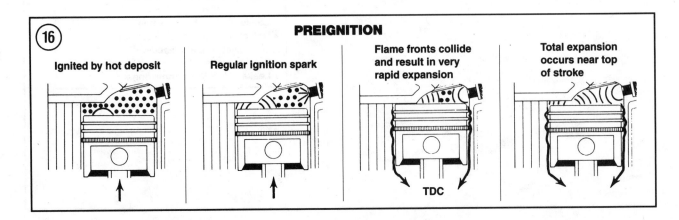

PREIGNITION

(16)

Ignited by hot deposit | Regular ignition spark | Flame fronts collide and result in very rapid expansion | Total expansion occurs near top of stroke

TDC

Piston Seizure

Piston seizure or galling is the transfer of metal from the piston to the cylinder bore. Friction and the heat causes piston seizure. Some causes may be pistons with incorrect bore clearances, piston rings with an improper end gap or a compression leak. Other causes are incorrect type of oil, lack of oil or an incorrectly operating oil injection pump. A spark plug with a wrong heat range, incorrect ignition timing or overheating may result in piston seizure.

A noticeable reduction of speed may be your first sign of seizure, while immediate stoppage indicates a full lockup. A top end rattle is often an early sign of seizure.

When diagnosing piston seizure, the pistons themselves can be used to troubleshoot and determine the failure cause. High cylinder temperatures normally cause seizure above the piston rings while seizure below the piston rings is usually caused by a lack of proper lubrication.

See **Figures 19** and **20** for examples of piston seizure.

Excessive Vibrations

Excessive vibrations may be caused by loose engine, suspension or steering mount bolts.

Engine Noises

A change in the sound of the engine is often the first clue that an engine problem exists. Noises are difficult to differentiate and even harder to describe. Experience is needed to accurately diagnose problems using engine sounds (**Figure 21**).

TWO-STROKE PRESSURE TESTING

Hard to start and generally poor performing two-stroke engines may be suffering from leaking crankcase compression. Fuel delivery, either carburetor or EFI, and ignition systems may be good, and a compression test may indicate that the engine's upper end is okay. A conventional compression test does *not* show a lack of primary (crankcase) compression. In a two-stroke engine, the crankcase must be alternately under pressure and vacuum. After the piston closes the intake port, further downward movement of the piston causes the trapped mixture to be pressurized so that it can rush quickly into the cylinder when the scavenging ports are opened. Upward piston movement lowers the pressure (creates a vacuum) in the crankcase, drawing the air-fuel mixture in from the carburetor or EFI.

NOTE
The operational sequence of a two-stroke engine is illustrated in Chapter One under **Engine Principles**.

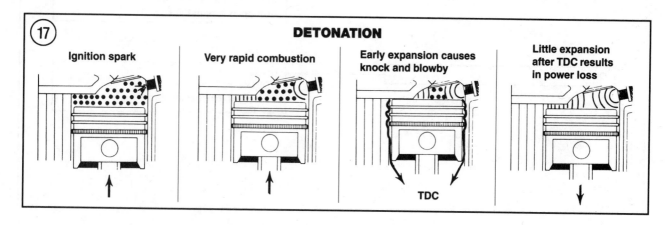

(17) **DETONATION**

| Ignition spark | Very rapid combustion | Early expansion causes knock and blowby | Little expansion after TDC results in power loss |

TDC

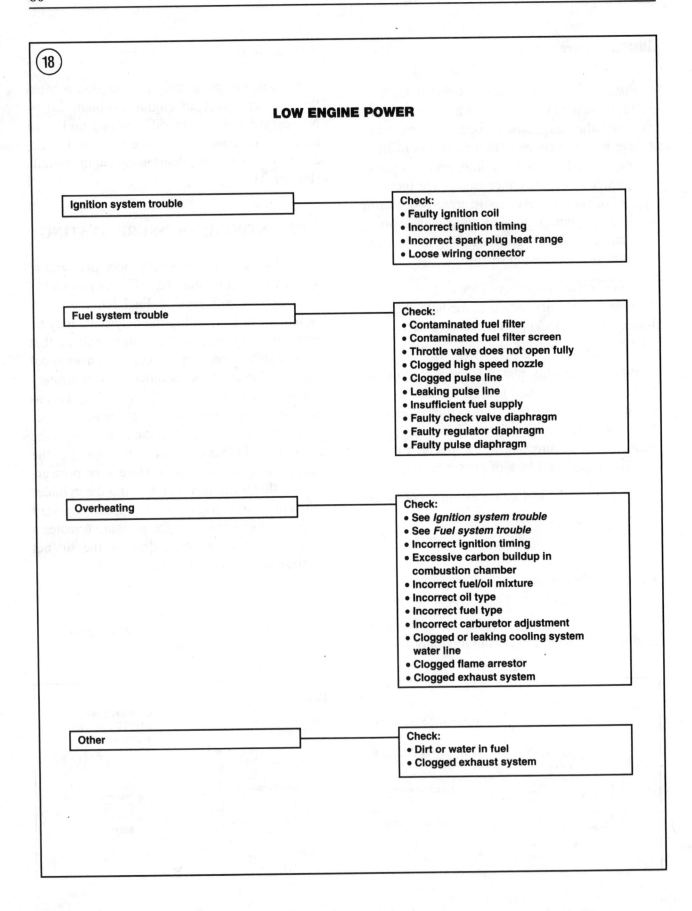

LOW ENGINE POWER

Ignition system trouble

Check:
- **Faulty ignition coil**
- **Incorrect ignition timing**
- **Incorrect spark plug heat range**
- **Loose wiring connector**

Fuel system trouble

Check:
- **Contaminated fuel filter**
- **Contaminated fuel filter screen**
- **Throttle valve does not open fully**
- **Clogged high speed nozzle**
- **Clogged pulse line**
- **Leaking pulse line**
- **Insufficient fuel supply**
- **Faulty check valve diaphragm**
- **Faulty regulator diaphragm**
- **Faulty pulse diaphragm**

Overheating

Check:
- **See *Ignition system trouble***
- **See *Fuel system trouble***
- **Incorrect ignition timing**
- **Excessive carbon buildup in combustion chamber**
- **Incorrect fuel/oil mixture**
- **Incorrect oil type**
- **Incorrect fuel type**
- **Incorrect carburetor adjustment**
- **Clogged or leaking cooling system water line**
- **Clogged flame arrestor**
- **Clogged exhaust system**

Other

Check:
- **Dirt or water in fuel**
- **Clogged exhaust system**

If crankcase seals or cylinder base gaskets leak, the crankcase cannot hold either pressure or vacuum and proper engine operation is impossible. Any other source of leakage such as porous or cracked crankcase castings will result in the same conditions.

It is possible to test for and isolate engine crankcase leaks. The test is simple but requires special equipment. A typical two-stroke pressure test kit is shown in **Figure 22**. Pressure testing requires plugging all engine openings, then applying air pressure. If the engine does not hold air, a leak is present that must be located and repaired.

The following procedure describes a typical pressure test:

CAUTION
Do not exceed 8 psi (55.2 kPa) during the pressure test. Damage to the engine seals will occur.

NOTE
The labyrinth seal at the center of the crankshaft prevents the cylinders from being checked individually. When one cylinder is pressurized, the other cylinder(s) is also pressurized. All cylinders must be blocked before applying pressure during testing.

1. Remove the carburetors or EFI fuel system as described in Chapter Six or Chapter Seven.
2. Insert a plug tightly in the intake manifold.
3. Remove the exhaust pipes and block off the exhaust ports using suitable adapters and fittings.
4. Remove one spark plug and install the pressure gauge adaptor into the spark plug hole. Connect the tester pump and gauge to the spark plug adaptor, then pressurize the crankcase to 8 psi (55.2 kPa).
5. Observe the pressure gauge. The pressure must not drop at a rate of more than 1 psi (6.9 kPa) per minute.
6. If the pressure drops faster than specified, first be sure that there are no leaks in the test equipment or sealing plugs. If the equipment shows no signs of leakage, inspect the entire engine carefully. Large leaks can be heard. To find smaller leaks, apply a soapy solution with a small brush to all possible sources of leakage. Possible leakage points are listed below:

   a. Crankshaft seals.

   b. Spark plug(s).

   c. Cylinder head joint.

   d. Cylinder base joint.

   e. Carburetor base joint.

   f. Crankcase joint.

   g. Reed valve housing gasket.

POWER TRAIN

The following items provide a starting point from which to troubleshoot power train malfunctions. The possible causes for each malfunction are listed in a logical sequence.

Drive Belt Not Operating Smoothly in Primary Sheave

a. Rough, grooved, pitted or scored drive sheave face.
b. Defective drive belt.

Uneven Drive Belt Wear

a. Misaligned primary and secondary sheaves.
b. Loose engine mounts.

Glazed Drive Belt

a. Excessive slippage caused by stuck or frozen track.
b. Engine idle speed too high.

Drive Belt Too Tight at Idle

a. Engine idle speed too high.
b. Incorrect sheave distance.
c. Incorrect belt length.

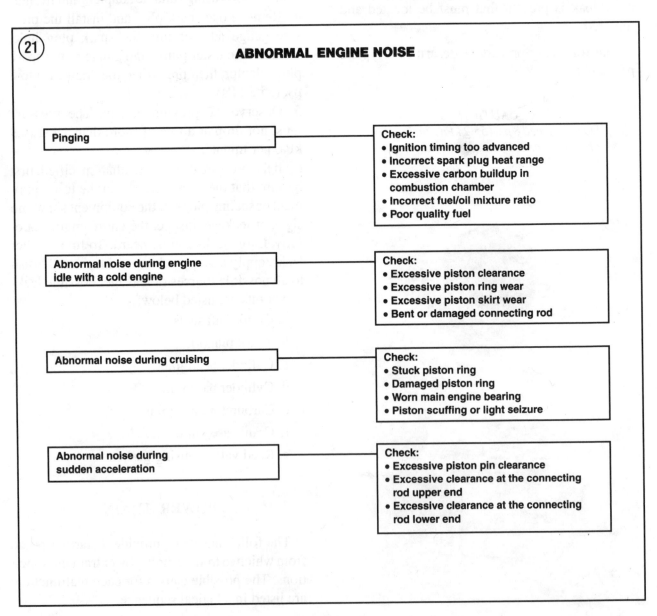

21

ABNORMAL ENGINE NOISE

Pinging
Check:
• Ignition timing too advanced
• Incorrect spark plug heat range
• Excessive carbon buildup in combustion chamber
• Incorrect fuel/oil mixture ratio
• Poor quality fuel

Abnormal noise during engine idle with a cold engine
Check:
• Excessive piston clearance
• Excessive piston ring wear
• Excessive piston skirt wear
• Bent or damaged connecting rod

Abnormal noise during cruising
Check:
• Stuck piston ring
• Damaged piston ring
• Worn main engine bearing
• Piston scuffing or light seizure

Abnormal noise during sudden acceleration
Check:
• Excessive piston pin clearance
• Excessive clearance at the connecting rod upper end
• Excessive clearance at the connecting rod lower end

Drive Belt Edge Cord Failure

a. Misaligned primary and secondary sheaves.
b. Loose engine mounts.

Brake Not Holding Properly

a. Incorrect brake cable adjustment.
b. Worn brake pads.
c. Worn brake disc.
d. Oil-saturated brake pads.
e. Sheared key on brake disc.
f. Incorrect brake adjustment.
g. Air in hydraulic lines of models with hydraulic brakes.

Brake Not Releasing Properly

a. Weak or broken return spring.
b. Bent or damaged brake lever.
c. Incorrect brake adjustment.

Excessive Chaincase Noise

a. Incorrect chain tension.
b. Excessive chain stretch.
c. Worn sprocket teeth.
d. Damaged chain and/or sprockets.

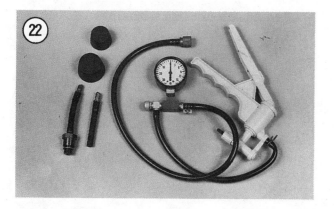

Chain Slippage

a. Incorrect chain tension.
b. Excessive chain stretch.
c. Worn sprocket teeth.

Leaking Chaincase

a. Loose chaincase cover mounting bolts.
b. Damaged chaincase cover gasket.
c. Damaged chaincase oil seal(s).
d. Cracked or broken chaincase.

Rapid Chain and Sprocket Wear

a. Insufficient chaincase oil level.
b. Broken chain tensioner.
c. Misaligned sprockets.

Drive Clutch Engages Before Engagement Speed

a. Worn spring.
b. Incorrect clutch weights.

Drive Clutch Engages After Engagement Speed

a. Incorrect spring.
b. Worn or damaged secondary sheave buttons.

Erratic Shifting

a. Worn rollers and bushings.
b. Scuffed or damaged weights.
c. Dirty primary sheave assembly.
d. Worn or damaged secondary sheave buttons.

Engine Bogs During Engagement

a. Incorrect secondary sheave width adjustment.
b. Drive belt worn too thin.
c. Incorrect sheave distance.

Primary or Secondary Sheave Sticks

a. Damaged sheave assembly.
b. Moveable sheave damaged.
c. Dirty sheave assembly.

SKIS AND STEERING

Refer to the following list when troubleshooting ski and steering problems. Some possible causes are listed below each malfunction.

Loose Steering

a. Loose steering post bushing.
b. Loose steering post or steering column fasteners.
c. Loose tie rod ends.
d. Worn spindle bushings.
e. Stripped spindle splines.

Unequal Steering

a. Improperly adjusted tie rods.
b. Improperly installed steering arms.
c. Damaged steering components.

Rapid Ski Wear

a. Skis misaligned.
b. Worn out ski wear rods (skags).

TRACK ASSEMBLY

The following items provide a starting point from which to troubleshoot track assembly malfunctions. Also refer to track inspection in Chapter Sixteen.

Frayed Track Edge

a. Incorrect track alignment.
b. Track contacts rivets in tunnel area because of incorrect rivets previously installed.

Track Grooved on Inner Surface

a. Track too tight.
b. Frozen rear idler shaft bearing.

Track Drive Ratcheting

a. Track too loose.
b. Drive sprockets misaligned.
c. Damaged drive sprockets.

Rear Idlers Turning on Shaft

Frozen rear idler shaft bearings.

Table 1 ELECTRO SPECIALTIES MODEL 1L SETTINGS

1990
  Lighting coil: yellow to yellow   80 LOW

1991
  Cougar   –
  Prowler, Prowler Special   –
  El Tigre EXT   –

1992
  Cougar   –
  Prowler, Prowler Special
    Ignition coil: Spark plug lead to engine ground   85 HIGH
    CDI unit: (+)white/black to orange(–)   72 HIGH
    Ignition charge coil: (+)green to engine ground(–)   80 LOW
    Trigger coil: (+)white/red to black/white(–)   80 LOW
    Lighting coil: yellow to yellow   80 LOW
  El Tigre EXT   –

1993
  440 ZR   –
  Cougar   –
  Prowler, Prowler II   –
  EXT 550   –
  580 ZR   –
  EXT 580 Z   –
  EXT 580 Mountain Cat   –

1994
  Cougar, Prowler
    Ignition coil: Spark plug lead to engine ground   85 HIGH
    CDI unit: (+)white/black to orange(–)   72 HIGH
    Ignition charge coil: (+)green to engine ground(–)   80 LOW
    Trigger coil: (+)white/red to black/white(–)   80 LOW
    Lighting coil: yellow to yellow   80 LOW

1995
  Z 440
    Ignition coil: Spark plug lead to engine ground   75 HIGH
    CDI unit: (+)white/blue to black/white(–)   75 HIGH
    Ignition charge coil: (+)red/white to black/white(–)   50 HIGH
    Trigger coil: (+)white/red to black/red(–)   80 LOW
    Lighting coil: yellow to yellow   80 LOW

Table 2 ARCTCO IGNITION ANALYZER PEAK VOLTAGES

Model	Peak voltage at 2,000 rpm	Peak voltage at 3,000 rpm	Peak voltage at 4,000 rpm
1992			
Cougar	–	–	–
Prowler, Prowler Special			
Ignition charge coil	188	184	123
Trigger coil	33	54	75
CDI unit	176	173	163
Lighting coil	32	50	67
El Tigre EXT	–	–	–

(continued)

Table 2 ARCTCO IGNITION ANALYZER PEAK VOLTAGES (continued)

Model	Peak voltage at 2,000 rpm	Peak voltage at 3,000 rpm	Peak voltage at 4,000 rpm
1993			
440 ZR			
Ignition charge coil	169	159	153
Trigger coil	167	157	153
CDI unit	162	153	147
Lighting coil	32	50	67
Cougar	–	–	–
Prowler, Prowler II	–	–	–
580 ZR, EXT 580 Z, EXT 580 Mountain Cat			
Ignition charge coil	169	159	153
Trigger coil	167	157	153
CDI unit	162	153	147
Lighting coil	32	50	67
1994			
Cougar, Cougar Mountain Cat			
Ignition charge coil	188	184	123
Trigger coil	33	54	75
CDI unit	176	173	163
Lighting coil	25	37	50
Prowler, Prowler II	–	–	–
ZR 440, EXT 580, EXT 580 Mountain Cat			
Ignition charge coil	169	159	153
Trigger coil	167	157	153
CDI unit	162	153	147
Lighting coil	32	50	67
1995			
Z 440			
Ignition charge coil	216	205	200
Trigger coil	213	203	198
CDI unit	208	198	193
Lighting coil	32	50	67
ZR 440, Cougar, Cougar Mountain Cat, Prowler 2-Up			
Ignition charge coil	169	159	153
Trigger coil	167	157	153
CDI unit	162	153	147
Lighting coil	32	50	67
EXT 580			
Ignition charge coil	216	205	200
Trigger coil	213	203	198
CDI unit	208	198	193
Lighting coil	32	50	67
EXT 580 EFI, EXT 580 EFI Mountain Cat			
Ignition charge coil	–	–	–
Trigger coil	–	–	–
CDI unit	–	–	–
Lighting coil	–	–	–
ZR 580			
Ignition charge coil	169	159	153
Trigger coil	167	157	153
CDI unit	162	153	147
Lighting coil	32	50	67
ZR 580 EFI	–	–	–

(continued)

Table 2 ARCTCO IGNITION ANALYZER PEAK VOLTAGES (continued)

Model	Peak voltage at 2,000 rpm	Peak voltage at 3,000 rpm	Peak voltage at 4,000 rpm
1996			
Z 440			
Ignition charge coil	216	205	200
Trigger coil	213	203	198
CDI unit	208	198	193
Lighting coil	32	50	67
ZR 440	–	–	–
Cougar, Cougar Mountain Cat, Prowler 2-Up			
Ignition charge coil	169	159	153
Trigger coil	167	157	153
CDI unit	162	153	147
Lighting coil	32	50	67
EXT 580, EXT 580 Powder Special			
Ignition charge coil	216	205	200
Trigger coil	213	203	198
CDI unit	208	198	193
Lighting coil	32	50	67
EXT 580 EFI, EXT 580 EFI Mountain Cat, EXT 580 EFI Deluxe			
Ignition charge coil	169	159	153
Trigger coil	167	157	153
CDI unit	162	153	147
Lighting coil	32	50	67
ZR 580			
Ignition charge coil	169	159	153
Trigger coil	167	157	153
CDI unit	162	153	147
Lighting coil	32	50	67
ZRT 600			
Ignition charge coil	–	–	–
Trigger coil	–	–	–
CDI unit	–	–	–
Lighting coil	–	–	–
1997			
Z 440, ZL 440, ZR 440			
Ignition charge coil	169	159	153
Trigger coil	167	157	153
CDI unit	162	153	147
Lighting coil	32	50	67
Cougar, Cougar Mountain Cat	–	–	–
EXT 580 Carburetor, Powder Special			
Ignition charge coil	216	205	200
Trigger coil	213	203	198
CDI unit	208	198	193
Lighting coil	32	50	67
ZR 580 EFI, EXT 580 EFI, EXT 580 DLX			
Ignition charge coil	–	–	–
Trigger coil	–	–	–
CDI unit	–	–	–
Lighting coil	–	–	–
EXT 600	–	–	–
ZRT 600	–	–	–
Powder Extreme	–	–	–

2

Table 3 IGNITION HIGH TENSION COIL

Model	Primary resistance ohms	Secondary resistance ohms*
1990		
Prowler	0.092***	4,100***
El Tigre EXT	0.30**	6,300***
1991		
Cougar	0.092***	4,100***
Prowler, Prowler Special	0.092***	4,100***
El Tigre EXT	0.30**	6,300***
1992		
Cougar	0.092***	4,100***
Prowler, Prowler Special	0.092***	4,100***
El Tigre EXT	0.30**	6,300***
1993		
Cougar, Prowler, Prowler II	0.092***	4,100***
440 ZR, 580 ZR	0.30***	6,300**
EXT 580 Z, EXT 580 Mtn. Cat	0.30***	6,300**
1994		
Cougar, Cougar Mountain Cat	0.092***	4,100***
Prowler, Prowler II, ZR 440, EXT 580,		
EXT 580 Mtn. Cat and ZR 580	0.30***	6,300**
1995	0.30***	6,300**
1996		
2-Cylinder models	0.30***	6,300**
ZRT 600	0.34***	7,900**
1997		
Z 440, ZL 440, ZR 440	0.30***	6,300**
ZR 580 EFI	0.255-0.345	5040-7560
Cougar, Cougar Mountain Cat	0.30***	6,300**
EXT 580 Carburetor	0.30***	6,300**
EXT 580 EFI	0.255-0.345	5040-7560
EXT 580 DLX	0.255-0.345	5040-7560
Powder Special	0.30***	6,300**
3-Cylinder models	0.34***	7,900**

*Spark Plug cap removed. Resistance of the spark plug cap should be about 5,000 ohms.
** ± 20%
*** ± 15%

Table 4 IGNITION CHARGE COIL

Model	Resistance ohms
1990	
Prowler: (+)green to black/white(−)	1,260*
El Tigre EXT: (+)red/white to black/white(−)	127.5**
1991-1992	
Cougar, Prowler: (+)green to black/white(−)	1,260*
El Tigre EXT: (+)red/white to black/white(−)	127.5**

(continued)

Table 4 IGNITION CHARGE COIL (continued)

Model	Resistance ohms
1993	
Cougar, Prowler, Prowler II: (+)green to black/white(–)	1,260*
440 ZR, 580 ZR, EXT 580 Z, EXT 580 Mountain Cat:	
(+)red/white to black/white(–)	160**
1994	
Cougar, Cougar Mountain Cat, Prowler,	
Prowler II: (+)green to black/white(–)	1,260*
ZR 440, EXT 580, EXT 580 Mountain Cat,	
ZR 580: (+)red/white to black/white(–)	160**
1995	
Cougar, Cougar Mountain Cat, Prowler 2-Up,	
Z 440, ZR 440: (+)red/white to black/white(–)	160**
EXT 580, ZR 580 (carburetor):	
(+)red/white to black/white(–)	160**
EXT 580 EFI, EXT 580 EFI Mountain Cat	
Coil (1): (+)green to brown(–)	450**
Coil (2): (+)black to green(–)	45**
ZR 580 EFI	
Coil (1): (+)green to brown(–)	450**
Coil (2): (+)black to green(–)	45**
1996	
Cougar, Cougar Mountain Cat, Cougar 2-Up,	
Z 440, ZR 440: (+)red/white to black/white(–)	160**
EXT 580, EXT 580 Powder Special (carburetor):	
(+)red/white to black/white(–)	160**
EXT 580 EFI, EXT 580 EFI Mtn. Cat,	
EXT 580 EFI Deluxe, ZR 580	
Coil (1): (+)green to brown(–)	450**
Coil (2): (+)black to green(–)	45**
ZRT 600	
Coil (1): (+)green to white(–)	450**
Coil (2): (+)green to black/red(–)	25.7**
1997	
Cougar, Cougar Mountain Cat, Z 440, ZL 440:	
(+)red/white to black/white(–)	160**
ZR 440, EXT 580 (carburetor):	
(+)red/white to black/white(–)	160**
ZR 580 EFI	
Low speed: (+)brown to green(–)	360-540
High speed: (+)black to green(–)	36.8-55.2
EXT 580 EFI, EXT 580 DLX, Powder Special	
Low speed: (+)brown to green(–)	360-540
High speed: (+)black to green(–)	36.8-55.2
EXT 600, ZRT 600, Powder Extreme	
Coil (1): (+)green to white(–)	450** ohms
Coil (2): (+)green to black/red(–)	25.7** ohms

* ± 10%
** ± 20%

Table 5 IGNITION TRIGGER COIL (SENSOR)

Model	Resistance ohms
1990	
Prowler: (+)red/white to black/white(−)	15.9*
El Tigre EXT: (+)red/white to black/red(−)	46.5**
1991	
Cougar, Prowler, Prowler Special:	
(+)red/white to black/white(−)	15.9*
El Tigre EXT: (+)red/white to black/red(−)	46.5**
1992	
Cougar, Prowler, Prowler Special:	
(+)red/white to black/white(−)	15.9*
El Tigre EXT: (+)red/white to black/red(−)	46.5**
1993	
Cougar, Prowler, Prowler II:	
(+)red/white to black/white(−)	15.9*
440 ZR, 580 ZR, EXT 580 Z, EXT 580 Mountain Cat:	
(+)red/white to black/red(−)	17**
1994	
Cougar, Cougar Mountain Cat, Prowler, Prowler II:	
(+)red/white to black/white(−)	15.9*
ZR 440, EXT 580, EXT 580 Mountain Cat, ZR 580:	
(+)red/white to black/red(−)	17**
1995	
Z 440, ZR 440, Cougar, Cougar Mountain Cat,	
Prowler 2-Up: (+)red/white to black/red(−)	17**
EXT 580, ZR 580 (carburetor):	
(+)red/white to black/red(−)	17**
EXT 580 EFI, EXT 580 EFI Mountain Cat:	
(+)green/white to brown(-)	190**
ZR 580 EFI: (+)green/white to brown(−)	190**
1996	
Z 440, ZR 440, Cougar, Cougar Mountain Cat,	
Cougar 2-Up: (+)red/white to black/red(−)	17**
EXT 580, ZR 580, EXT 580 Powder Special (carburetor):	
(+)red/white to black/red(−)	17**
EXT 580 EFI, EXT 580 EFI Deluxe,	
EXT 580 EFI Mtn. Cat: (+)green/white to brown(−)	190**
ZRT 600: (+)green/white to brown(−)	100**
1997	
Z 440, ZL 440, ZR 440, Cougar, Cougar Mountain Cat:	
(+)red/white to black/red(−)	17**
ZR 580 EFI, EXT 580 EFI, EXT 580 DLX,	
Powder Special EFI: (+)green/white to brown(−)	152-228
EXT 580, Powder Special (carburetor models):	
(+)red/white to black/red(−)	17**
EXT 600, ZRT 600, Powder Extreme	100**

* ± 10%
** ± 20%

Table 6 LIGHTING COIL

Model	Resistance ohms
1990-1992: yellow to yellow	0.11*
1993	
440 ZR, 580 ZR, EXT 580 Z,	
EXT 580 Mountain Cat: yellow to yellow	0.22**
Cougar, Prowler, Prowler II: yellow to yellow	0.11*
1994	
Cougar, Cougar Mountain Cat, Prowler,	
Prowler II: yellow to yellow	0.11*
ZR 440, EXT 580, EXT 580 Mountain Cat, ZR 580:	
yellow to yellow	0.22**
1995	
Models with carburetors: yellow to yellow	0.22**
Models with Electronic Fuel Injection	
Lighting: (+)yellow to brown(−)	0.14**
Battery charging: (+)yellow/red to yellow/red(−)	0.20**
1996	
Two cylinder models with carburetors:	
yellow to yellow	0.22**
Two cylinder models with Electronic Fuel Injection	
Lighting: (+)yellow to brown(−)	0.14**
Battery charging: (+)yellow/red to yellow/red(−)	0.20**
EXT 600, ZRT 600, Powder Extreme: yellow to yellow	0.21**
1997	
Two cylinder models with carburetors:	
yellow to yellow	0.22**
Two cylinder models with Electronic Fuel Injection:	
yellow to yellow	0.072-0.108
EXT 600, ZRT 600, Powder Extreme: yellow to yellow	0.21**

* ± 10%
** ± 20%

Table 7 INJECTION TRIGGER COIL (SENSOR)

Model	Resistance ohms
Models with battery EFI: (+)white/black to brown(−)	190 ± 20%

Chapter Three

Lubrication, Maintenance and Tune-up

This chapter covers the regular maintenance required to keep your snowmobile in top shape. Regular, careful maintenance is the best guarantee for a trouble-free, long-lasting vehicle. Snowmobiles are high-performance vehicles that demand proper lubrication, maintenance and tune-ups to maintain a high level of performance, extend engine life and extract the maximum economy of operation.

You can do your own lubrication, maintenance and tune-ups if you follow the correct procedures and use common sense. Always remember that engine damage can result from improper tuning and adjustment. In addition, if special tools or testers are identified in a particular maintenance or adjustment procedure, that tool should be used or you should refer service to a qualified dealer or repair shop.

The following information, based on recommendations from Arctic Cat, will help you keep your snowmobile operating at its peak level.

Tables 1-11 are at the end of the chapter.

NOTE
Be sure to follow the correct procedure and specifications for your model. Also use the correct quantity and type of fluid as indicated in the tables.

PRE-RIDE CHECKS

You should check the machine before each ride. Refer to Chapter One.

FLUID CHECKS

Check vital fluids daily or before each ride to ensure proper operation and prevent severe component damage. Refer to **Table 1**.

BREAK-IN PROCEDURE

Following cylinder service (boring, honing or installing new rings) and major lower end work, break in the engine just as if it were new. The performance and service life of the engine depends greatly on a careful and sensible break-in.

For the first 10-15 hours of operation, apply no more than 3/4 throttle and vary the speed as much as possible. Avoid prolonged steady running at one speed, no matter how moderate. Avoid hard acceleration. Also avoid wet snow conditions during break-in.

To ensure adequate protection to the engine during break-in, pre-mix the first tank of fuel at a 50:1 ratio with the same oil used in the injection system. Arctic Extreme 50:1 Injection Oil or equivalent is recommended. This oil will be used *together* with the oil supplied by the injection system. Throughout the break-in period, check the oil injection reservoir tank to make sure the injection system is working. The oil level will diminish.

NOTE
*Do not continue to use a 50:1 pre-mix after the first tank unless the snowmobile is operating in weather conditions where the ambient temperature is -26° C (-15° F) or colder. Under these conditions, the 50:1 pre-mix will help to ensure sufficient engine lubrication. Refer to **Correct Fuel Mixing** in this chapter for additional information.*

After the initial 10-15 hours, all engine and chassis fasteners should be checked for tightness. If the snowmobile is going to be used in extreme conditions, you may want to increase the break-in a few hours. After break-in, tighten the cylinder head nuts as described in this chapter.

NOTE
After break-in is complete, install new spark plugs as described in this chapter.

Correct Fuel Mixing

Oil can be mixed with the fuel to ensure sufficient lubrication for the first tank after re-building the engine, when running the engine while bleeding the oil injection pump, when removing the snowmobile from storage or when operating the snowmobile under extreme weather conditions. The use of the additional oil under normal conditions will lead to spark plug fouling and rapid carbon buildup. Refer to the following when mixing oil with the fuel:

WARNING
Gasoline is an extreme fire hazard. Never open a container containing gasoline near sparks, heat or flame. Do not smoke while mixing fuel.

a. Mix the oil with the gasoline in a well-ventilated location. The oil temperature should be at least 20° C (68° F) before attempting to mix the oil and gasoline.

b. Mix the oil and gasoline thoroughly in a separate, clean, sealable container that is larger than the quantity being mixed to allow for agitation.

c. Always measure quantities exactly. For a 50:1 gasoline-to-oil mixture, mix 7 3/4 fl. oz. (229 mL) of oil with 3 U.S. gallons (11.4 L) of gasoline.

d. Always use fresh gasoline with an octane rating of 87 or higher.

e. Pour approximately 1/2 the required amount of gasoline into the mixing container, add the correct full amount of oil, then agitate the mixture thoroughly.

f. Add the remaining fuel to complete the mixture, then agitate the mixture to completely mix the fuel and oil.

g. Use a funnel with a filter when pouring the pre-mixed gasoline and oil into the snowmobile's fuel tank.

MAINTENANCE SCHEDULES

Arctic Cat divides its maintenance schedules into three parts: daily, weekly and monthly. All schedules should be performed on time during the snowmobiling season. Refer to **Table 1** for the daily schedule, **Table 2** for the weekly schedule and **Table 3** for the monthly schedule.

NOTE
Repeat the engine inspection checks every time you overhaul the engine top end or bottom end or remove the engine from the frame for other service. Likewise, perform the chassis and steering inspection procedures after you have performed major service to these components.

LUBRICATION

WARNING
Serious fire hazards always exist around gasoline. Do not allow any smoking in areas where fuel is being mixed or while refueling your machine. Always have a fire extinguisher, rated for gasoline and electrical fires, within reach when refueling or servicing any part of the fuel system.

Proper Fuel Selection

The Suzuki two-stroke engines used in Arctic Cat snowmobiles are lubricated by oil that circulates through the crankcase and eventually into the combustion chamber with the fuel. The oil is eventually burned with the fuel and expelled through the exhaust. The various components of the engine are lubricated by the oil as it clings to the various parts as it passes through the crankcase and cylinders. All models are equipped with an oil injection system. Pre-mixing oil with the fuel is not required on any of the models covered in this manual except during engine break-in. See *Break-In* in this chapter.

Arctic Cat recommends the use of gasoline with a minimum octane rating of 87. Most regular, unleaded gasolines are acceptable. If oxygenates are added to the gasoline, ethanol content should not exceed 10 percent and MTBE

should not exceed 15 percent. If oxygenated gasoline is used, install a main jet one size larger than standard in the carburetor. It is not necessary to add antifreeze to the fuel if gasoline blended with ethanol is used.

Engine Oil Tank

An oil injection system is used on all models. During engine operation, oil is automatically injected into the engine at a variable ratio depending on engine rpm.

Check the oil level in the reservoir tank (**Figure 1**, typical) daily and each time the snowmobile is filled with fuel.

The oil tank is equipped with an oil level sensor that is connected to the injection oil level pilot lamp on the instrument panel. When the oil level in the tank reaches a specified low point, the pilot lamp will light. Add oil as soon as possible when the low oil pilot light comes on.

When the oil level is low, perform the following:

1. Open the hood.

2. Remove the oil tank fill cap (**Figure 1**) and pour in the required amount of Arctic Extreme 50:1 Injection Oil or equivalent. Fill the tank until the oil level is up to the full mark on the transparent tank.

3. Reinstall the fill cap and close the hood.

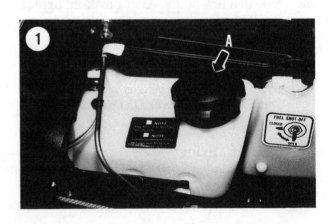

Chaincase Oil

Oil in the chain housing lubricates the chain and sprockets. Transmission Lube (part No. 0636-817) is available from Arctic Cat dealers. Different types or brands will often vary slightly in their composition and a mixture of the two may not lubricate as well as either alone. Always try to use one type and brand of oil.

Oil level check

The chain housing oil level is checked with the dipstick (**Figure 2**).

1. Park the snowmobile on a level surface. Open the hood.

2. Unscrew and remove the dipstick (**Figure 2**) from the chaincase cover. Wipe the dipstick off and insert it back into the chaincase. Do not screw the dipstick back into the cover.

3. Lift the dipstick out of the chaincase and check the oil level on the dipstick. The oil level should be between the upper and lower marks on the dipstick.

4. If the oil level is low, top off with chaincase oil. Do not overfill. Recheck the oil level.

5. Reinstall the dipstick. Tighten it securely.

Changing oil

Oil in the chaincase should be changed once each year or every 1,000 miles. The manufacturer suggests draining and filling with new oil when preparing the machine for summer storage.

1. Park the snowmobile on a level surface.

2. Open the hood.

3. Remove the exhaust pipe and muffler as described in Chapter Eight.

4. Place an old carpet scrap or several shop cloths under the chaincase cover to absorb spilled oil.

> *NOTE*
> *Oil can be drained from late models by removing the drain plug (**Figure 3**) from the back of the chaincase. However, it is necessary to remove the chaincase cover from models not equipped with a drain plug. Try to catch as much of the spilled oil as possible in shop cloths.*

5A. On later models, remove the drain plug (**Figure 3**) and drain oil from the chaincase. The cover can be removed from the chaincase for inspection and cleaning if desired.

5B. To remove the chaincase cover, proceed as follows:

    a. Remove the screws and washers attaching the cover (**Figure 2**) to the chaincase.

    b. Remove the cover and O-ring (**Figure 4**).

    c. Clean the chaincase cover thoroughly. Remove as much oil from the bottom of the chaincase as possible.

    d. Inspect the chaincase cover O-ring and replace if necessary. See **Figure 4**.

6. Clean up as much oil as possible with the shop cloths.

> *NOTE*
> *Store the oil-soaked shop cloths in a suitable container until they can be cleaned.*

7A. If the drain plug was removed, proceed as follows:

    a. Inspect magnet in drain plug.

    b. Clean and reinstall plug.

7B. If the cover was removed, proceed as follows:

    a. Install the sealing O-ring (**Figure 4**).

    b. Reinstall the chaincase cover, attaching screws and washers.

    c. Tighten screws securely.

8. Remove the filler plug from the chaincase (**Figure 5**).

9. Insert a funnel into the filler plug hole and fill the chain housing with the correct type (**Table 4**) and quantity (**Table 5**) of chaincase oil.

10. Check the oil level as described in the previous procedure.

Steering Spindle Lubrication

The steering spindles should be lubricated monthly with a low-temperature grease. If the snowmobile is operated under conditions or in wet snow, lubrication should be performed more frequently. Locate the grease fitting on the spindle housing (**Figure 6**). Wipe the grease fitting with a clean shop cloth to remove all traces of dirt. Fit the end of a hand-operated grease gun onto the grease fitting and pump grease into the spindle until it is forced from the top and/or bottom of the spindle housing. Remove the grease gun from the nipple and wipe the excess grease from the fitting and spindle. Repeat the procedure for the spindle on the other side of the snowmobile.

Slide Suspension Lubrication

The slide suspension should be lubricated monthly or every 40 hours with a low-temperature grease at each of the grease fittings shown in **Figure 7**. If the snowmobile is operated under severe conditions or in wet snow, lubricate the fittings more often.

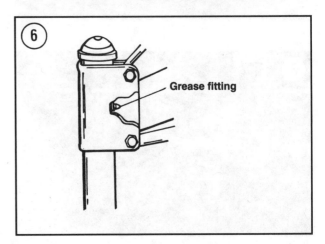

NOTE
It is not necessary to remove the slide suspension when performing this procedure.

WARNING
Before laying the snowmobile on its side in Step 1, the fuel tank should be less than 1/4 full.

1. Place a piece of cardboard beside the snowmobile and turn it on its side.
2. Locate the grease fittings on the slide suspension (**Figure 7**).
3. Wipe each of the grease fittings with a clean shop cloth to remove all traces of dirt.
4. Fit the end of a hand-operated grease gun onto the grease fitting and pump grease into the fitting.
5. Remove the grease gun from the fitting and wipe the excess grease from the fitting and from any point where grease has come out.

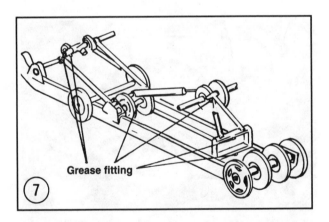

Grease fitting

(7)

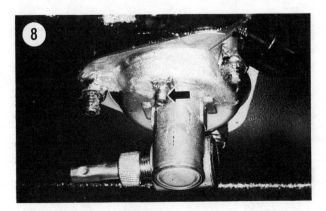

(8)

6. Repeat the procedure for each grease fitting (**Figure 7**).
7. Roll the snowmobile back onto its track.

Speedometer Drive Adaptor

The speedometer drive adaptor (**Figure 8**) should be lubricated twice a year with low-temperature grease.
1. Open and secure the hood.
2. Locate the grease fitting on the speedometer drive adaptor (**Figure 8**).

NOTE
It should not be necessary to remove the secondary sheave to gain access to the grease fitting.

3. Wipe the fitting with a clean shop cloth to remove all traces of dirt.
4. Fit the end of a hand-operated grease gun onto the grease fitting and pump one or two strokes of grease into the fitting.
5. Remove the grease gun from the fitting and wipe away any excess grease.
6. Close and secure the hood.

AIR COOLING SYSTEM

The Z440 is equipped with a 431 cc air-cooled engine. This is the only air cooled engine used on these models.

Checking/Adjusting Fan Belt Tension

1. Unbolt and remove the fan intake cover (**Figure 9**).

NOTE
Check the condition of the fan drive belt. If it is frayed or otherwise damaged, install a new belt.

2. Press the belt (A, **Figure 10**) with your finger at about midpoint and observe the amount of deflection.

3

3. Adjust the belt tension as follows if the belt can be depressed more than 6 mm (1/4 in.).

   a. Remove the nut (B, **Figure 10**) and washers. Some of the flat washers may be adjusting shims.

> *NOTE*
> *Shims should be located between the pulley halves. If none are found when the outer pulley half is removed in substep 3c, the belt may be worn, stretched or the incorrect size. Replace the belt if needed.*

   b. Withdraw the outer pulley half.

   c. To tighten the belt tension, remove a shim from between the pulley halves. If the belt is too tight, it will be necessary to add shims between the pulley halves.

   d. Make sure the belt and shims are properly positioned, then install the outer pulley half.

> *NOTE*
> *Any shims not needed between the pulley halves for adjustment should be installed outside the pulley. These shims are needed between the pulley halves when a new belt is installed.*

   e. Position any shims not installed between the pulley halves outside the outer pulley, then install the thicker flat washer.

   f. Install the lockwasher and nut (B, **Figure 10**). Tighten the nut to 25-40 N·m (18-30 ft.-lb.) torque. Turn the pulleys while tightening to prevent pinching the belt between the pulley halves.

4. Install the fan intake cover.

Fan Belt Removal/Installation

1. Remove the fan intake cover (**Figure 9**).

2. Remove the recoil starter assembly (C, **Figure 10**).

3. Remove the nut (B, **Figure 10**) and washers. Some of the flat washers may be adjusting shims.

4. Withdraw the outer pulley half. Do not lose shims which may be located between the pulley halves.

5. Lift the belt from the lower pulley (**Figure 11**).

6. Inspect the belt carefully. Install a new belt if its condition is questionable.

7. When installing, install the belt in the groove of the lower pulley and position the belt against the upper pulley inner half.

> *NOTE*
> *If a new belt is installed, position all of the shims between the pulley halves. If the old belt is installed, position the shims in the same place they were originally installed. Shims not needed between the pulley halves should be located outside the pulley under the flat washer for later adjustment.*

8. Install the outer pulley half.

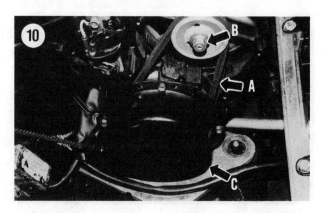

9. Install any shims not needed between the pulley halves for adjustment outside the pulley. These shims may be required for later adjustment. Refer to *Checking/Adjusting Fan Belt Tension.*

10. Install the flat washer, lockwasher and the pulley retaining nut. Tighten the nut to 25-40 N•m (18-29 ft.-lb.).

NOTE
Turn the pulleys while tightening the retaining nut to prevent pinching the belt between the pulley halves.

11. Install the recoil starter and fan intake cover.

LIQUID COOLING SYSTEM

Refer to the following for servicing the liquid cooling system used on all models except those equipped with an air-cooled 431 cc engine.

Cooling System Inspection

WARNING
*When performing any service work to the engine or cooling system, never remove the radiator cap (**Figure 12**, typical), drain coolant or disconnect any hose while the engine is hot. Scalding fluid and steam may be blown out under pressure and cause serious injury.*

Once a year, or whenever troubleshooting the cooling system, check the following items. If you do not have the proper equipment, tests can be performed by an Arctic Cat dealer or radiator shop.

1. Park the snowmobile on level ground.

2A. On 1994 and earlier models, elevate the front of the snowmobile 15-20 cm (6-8 in.).

2B. On 1995 and later models, elevate the front of the snowmobile 30-36 cm (12-14 in.).

3. Loosen then remove the reservoir cap (A, **Figure 12**).

4. Check the cap seals for tears or cracks. Check for a bent or distorted cap. Rinse the cap under warm tap water to flush away any loose rust or dirt particles.

5. Inspect the cap neck seat for dents, distortion or contamination. Wipe the sealing surface with a clean cloth to remove any rust or dirt.

6. Check the fluid level and fill the system, if necessary, as described in *Check/Fill Coolant* paragraphs in this chapter.

NOTE
*The original reservoir cap (A, **Figure 12**) is special and must be used during normal operation of the closed cooling*

system; however, a different cap is used for some tests. Be sure to install the original equipment cap or its replacement when tests are finished.

7. Check all cooling system hoses for damage or deterioration. Replace any hose that is questionable. Make sure all hose clamps are tight.

8. Check the heat exchangers (**Figure 13**) for cracks or damage. If necessary, replace as described in Chapter Eleven.

Check/Fill Coolant

WARNING
*Do not remove the cap (A, **Figure 12**) from the pressurized cooling system when the engine is hot.*

1. Park the snowmobile on level ground.

2A. On 1994 and earlier models, elevate the front of the snowmobile 15-20 cm (6-8 in.).

2B. On 1995 and later models, elevate the front of the snowmobile 30-36 cm (12-14 in.).

3. Loosen then remove the reservoir cap (A, **Figure 12**).

4. Check the level of fluid in the system. It should be full.

5. If the cooling system is not full, add fluid as follows:

    a. Fill the system with a mixture of antifreeze and water that will provide protection to -36° C (-34° F). Refer to the *Coolant* paragraphs in this chapter for mixing the water and antifreeze.

NOTE
*The original reservoir cap (A, **Figure 12**) is special and must be used during normal operation of the closed cooling system. However, for the following filling procedure a different (non-pressurized) cap must be used. Be sure to install*

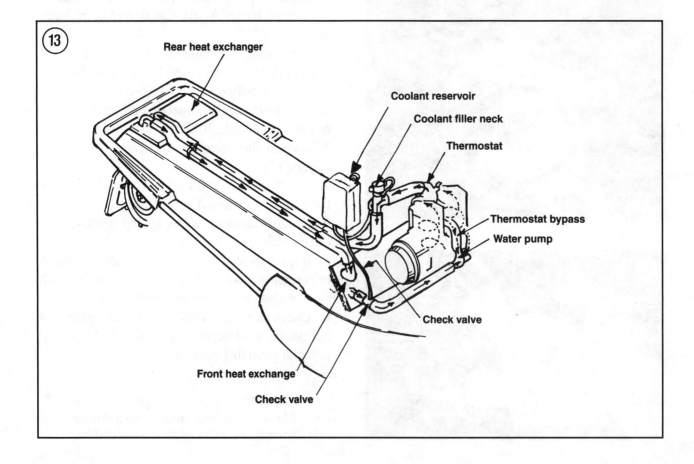

Figure 13
- Rear heat exchanger
- Coolant reservoir
- Coolant filler neck
- Thermostat
- Thermostat bypass
- Water pump
- Check valve
- Front heat exchange
- Check valve

the original equipment cap or its replacement when finished.

b. Install a non-pressurized test cap (part no.
0644-156).

c. Start the engine and run it at 3,000-3,500
rpm until the rear heat exchanger (**Figure
13**) becomes hot to the touch.

d. Stop the engine and allow the engine and
cooling system to cool.

e. Remove the test cap and check the level of
the cooling fluid. The cooling system
should still be filled completely. If not, add
the mixture of antifreeze and water; return
to substep 5b.

6. Install the original reservoir cap or a suitable
replacement.

7. Add coolant to the holding tank (B, **Figure
12**) until the tank is 3/4 full.

Coolant

Only a high-quality ethylene glycol-based
coolant designed for aluminum engines should
be used. The coolant should be mixed with water
in a 60:40 ratio. Coolant capacity is listed in
Table 5. When mixing antifreeze with water, use
only soft or distilled water. Distilled water can
be purchased at supermarkets in gallon containers. Do not use tap or salt water because it will
damage engine parts.

> *CAUTION*
> *Always mix coolant in the proper ratio
> for the coldest temperature in your area.
> Ratios of more than 60 percent antifreeze
> will reduce cooling system efficiency.*

Coolant Change

The cooling system should be completely
drained and refilled with a fresh mixture of antifreeze and water at least once each year prefer-
ably before off-season storage.

> *CAUTION*
> *Use only a high-quality ethylene glycol
> antifreeze specifically labeled for use
> with aluminum engines. Do not use an
> alcohol-based antifreeze.*

The following procedure must be performed
when the engine is *cold*:

> *CAUTION*
> *Be careful not to spill antifreeze on
> painted surfaces, as it may damage the
> surface. Wash any spilled antifreeze im-
> mediately with soapy water, then rinse
> the area thoroughly with clean water.*

1. Park the snowmobile on a level surface.
2. Open the hood.

> *WARNING*
> *Do not remove the reservoir cap (A, Fig-
> ure 12) when the engine is hot.*

3. Remove the reservoir cap (**Figure 12**).
4. Attach a hose to the drain spout (**Figure 14**),
then place the end of the hose in a small bucket.
5. Loosen the drain spout (**Figure 14**) and allow
the system to drain.
6. When the coolant stops draining, raise the
rear of the snowmobile with a jack to allow the
heat exchangers to drain. Be sure to support the
vehicle sufficiently to prevent injury.
7. Use a primer pump and a suitable length of
hose to siphon the coolant from the coolant
recovery tank into a suitable container.

WARNING
Do not siphon coolant with your mouth and a hose. The coolant mixture is poisonous and ingesting even a very small amount may cause sickness. Observe warning labels on antifreeze containers. Animals are attracted to antifreeze so make sure you discard used antifreeze in a safe and suitable manner. Do not store antifreeze in open containers.

WARNING
The EPA has classified ethylene glycol as an environmental toxic waste that cannot be legally flushed down a drain or poured on the ground. Treat antifreeze that is to be discarded as you treat motor oil. Put it in suitable containers and dispose of it according to local regulations.

WARNING
Concrete floors become very slippery when antifreeze is spilled. Wipe up spilled antifreeze as soon as possible.

8. Remove additional coolant by detaching hoses and removing components of the cooling system. Reinstall the recovery tank and hoses if they were removed.

9. Rinse spilled coolant from the engine and engine compartment with clean water.

10. Pour the coolant mixture of antifreeze and distilled water into the coolant system until the system is full. Refer to *Check/Fill Coolant* paragraphs for filling procedure.

NOTE
After draining and refilling the cooling system, the coolant level may drop as pockets of trapped air fill with coolant. To prevent operating the engine with a low coolant level, check the level at least once again before starting the engine. It may be necessary to allow the system to cool and be filled at least once again, before the system is completely filled.

11. Close and secure the hood.

DAILY MAINTENANCE

Items requiring daily maintenance are listed in **Table 1**.

Liquid Coolant Level

Check the complete cooling system for evidence of leaking, especially if the system is low on fluid. Refer to the *Liquid Cooling System* paragraphs in this chapter for checking and filling the system with the proper mixture of antifreeze and water.

Oil Injection Tank

Refer to the *Lubrication* paragraphs in this chapter for filling the oil tank. If the oil tank has been allowed to run dry, it may be necessary to bleed air from the oil injection lines.

Chaincase Oil Level

Refer to the *Lubrication* paragraphs in this chapter for checking and filling the system with oil.

Drive Belt Check

A worn or damaged drive belt (**Figure 15**) will reduce engine performance and may fail leaving you stranded when on the trail.

1. With the engine stopped, open and secure the hood.

2. Remove the drive belt cover.

3. Visually check the drive belt for cracking, fraying or unusual wear as described in Chapter Thirteen.

NOTE
The drive belt should be removed once a month and measured. Refer to Chapter Thirteen for minimum width and maximum circumference.

Stop and Tether Switch Operation

The stop and tether switches are an important part of snowmobile safety. Both switches must operate properly and should be replaced if damaged. Do not bypass a switch and operate the snowmobile.

1. Start the engine.

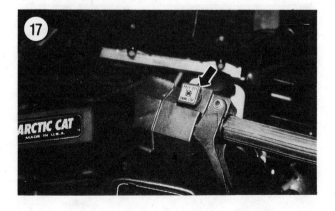

2. Check the tether switch (**Figure 16**) by pulling the cap from the switch. The engine should stop.

3. Reattach the tether switch cap.

4. Start the engine.

5. Push the emergency stop switch (**Figure 17**) on the right handlebar to the OFF position. The engine should stop.

6. If either switch fails to work as described or if the engine fails to start and a stop switch is suspected, test the switches as described in Chapter Nine.

WARNING
Do not ride the snowmobile unless both stop switches operate properly. The ability to stop the engine is important for snowmobile safety.

Headlight and Taillight Lens

Clean the headlight and taillight lenses with a clean cloth to ensure full illumination. Replace damaged lens assemblies if necessary.

Headlight and Taillight Operation

The headlight and taillight must operate correctly for safe operation on trails. Start the engine and make sure the headlight and taillight are both on. Operate the dimmer switch on the left handlebar assembly and check that the headlight operates properly on both high beam and low beam. Operate the brake lever and check that the brake light illuminates properly. Replace bulbs as required.

Steering Operation

Check the steering assembly for play and adjustment as follows:

1. Support the snowmobile so the skis are above the ground.

2. Turn the handlebars from side to side. The shaft should pivot smoothly with no signs of binding, noise or other abnormal conditions.

3. If the steering has excessive play, check the bolts for tightness as described in this chapter.

4. If the steering is tight, binding or otherwise damaged, service the assembly as described in Chapter Fifteen.

Steering Bolts Check

Steering and ski alignment cannot be maintained if the fasteners are loose or missing. Check the steering assembly as described in Chapter Fifteen.

Carburetor and Throttle Cable Inspection

Check the throttle cable for proper routing, adjustment and operation. If the throttle sticks or you question the condition of the cable, detach components from the cable and check the condition further. On models with carburetors, the throttle opens as many as three throttle slides and moves the oil injection pump control. A junction block (**Figure 18**) connects the single throttle cable to the other cables. If the condition of a cable is causing the throttle to stick, install a new cable assembly. Refer to *Carburetor Adjustment* under *Tune-up* in this chapter for adjusting and synchronizing the throttle cable.

If excessive play is felt at the carburetor, adjust the carburetor as described in the *Carburetor Adjustment* paragraphs in the *Tune-up* section.

NOTE
*On some models, a throttle/ignition safety switch (**Figure 19**) is installed in the carburetor throttle system to monitor the position of the throttle slide. If the throttle slide does not return to idle position when the throttle lever is released, the safety switch will stop the engine. Excessive throttle cable free play will cause the safety switch to override the*

ignition system and prevent the engine from starting.

Correct carburetor jetting will depend upon the altitude and temperature. It may be necessary to change the jet size in the carburetor(s) when operating at a different altitude. Refer to Chapter Four.

Battery

On models so equipped, check the battery fluid level. Inspect the electrical connections for loose connections. If corrosion is present at the terminal ends, detach the wires, clean the terminals and reattach. Make sure that wires are correctly routed and will not rub against moving parts or touch hot, especially exhaust, parts.

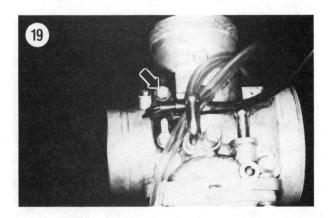

WEEKLY MAINTENANCE

Items requiring weekly maintenance are listed in **Table 2**.

Recoil Starter

Pull out the starter rope and inspect it for fraying. If its condition is questionable, replace the rope as described in Chapter Twelve.

Check the action of the starter. It should operate smoothly and should return completely when the rope is released. If the starter action is rough or if the rope does not return, service the starter as described in Chapter Twelve.

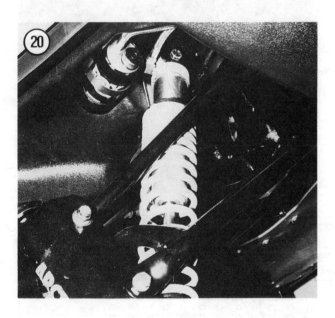

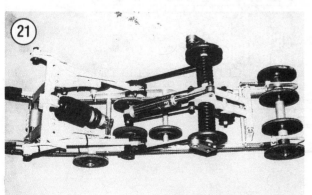

Exhaust System

The exhaust system is important to the engine's performance. Check the complete exhaust system from each cylinder's exhaust port to the muffler outlet for missing gaskets, loose or missing fasteners or damaged components. Refer to Chapter Eight.

Shock Absorbers

Check the front and rear shock absorbers (**Figures 20** and **21**) for oil leakage, a bent shaft or housing damage. Most of the shock absorber units used are not rebuildable, but some of the units can be rebuilt. If any shock absorber is damaged, either replace or rebuild it as required.

Along with a visual inspection, the dampening action of each shock absorber should be checked periodically. Remove and check the shock absorbers as described in Chapter Fifteen or Chapter Sixteen.

Ski and Ski Runner Check

Check the skis (**Figure 22**) for cracks, bending or other signs of damage. Raise the front of the snowmobile so the skis are off the ground. Check ski movement by pivoting both skis up and down. The skis should pivot smoothly with no signs of binding. If a ski is tight, refer to Chapter Fifteen for removal and installation.

Excessively worn or damaged ski runners reduce handling performance and can cause wear to the bottom of the ski. Because track and snow conditions determine runner wear, they should be inspected often. Check the ski runners for wear and replace them if they are cracked or more than half worn at any point. Refer to Chapter Fifteen.

Ski Alignment

Ski alignment should be checked at the beginning of each season, when a steering component has been replaced, or if control is a problem. Ski alignment should also be checked if a ski experiences a hard side impact. Refer to Chapter Fifteen for complete ski alignment procedures.

1. Park the snowmobile on a level surface.

2. Turn the handlebar so it faces straight ahead.

3. With the handlebar facing straight ahead, slide a long straightedge under the snowmobile against one side of the track. See **Figure 23**.

4. Make sure the straightedge is against the track, then measure the distance from the straightedge to a flat surface at the front of a ski and to a flat surface at the rear of the same ski. See **Figure 24**. Record these measurements.

5. Measure the distance from the straightedge to a flat surface at the front and at the rear of the other ski. Record these measurements.

6. The measured difference from the straightedge to the side of the skis should be either the same at the front and rear or no more than 1/8 in. (3.2 mm) greater at the front of the ski than at the rear. If the measurement at the front of the skis is more than the measurement at the rear of the skis, the skis are toed out.

NOTE
*The threads of the rod ends (A, **Figure 25**) at the outer ends of the tie rods, the matching threads of jam nuts (B, **Figure 25**) and the threads in the outer ends of the tie rods are **left-hand**. Threads of the tie rod ends, jam nuts and in the tie rods at the inner end are right-hand. The length of the tie rod can be changed after loosening the jam nuts at the ends of the tie rod by twisting the tie rod.*

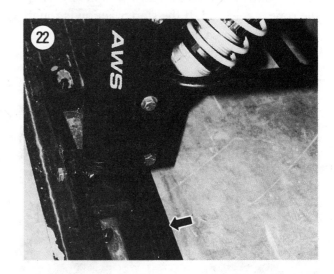

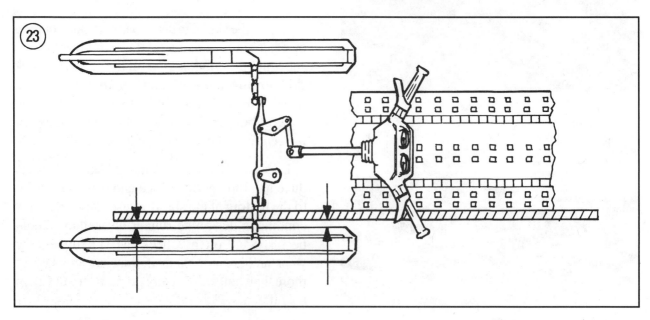

7. If the measured ski alignment is incorrect, loosen the jam nuts at each end of the tie rods, then turn the tie rod (C, **Figure 25**) as necessary to correct the alignment of the skis. Adjust the tie rods for both sides.

8. After making any changes, tighten the jam nuts securely, then measure the toe-out of both skis again as described in Steps 5 and 6.

9. When adjustment is correct, loosen each jam nut (B, **Figure 25**) in turn. Apply Loctite 242 to the threads, then tighten the nut securely. Make sure all four jam nuts are tightened.

10. Reinstall any covers that were removed and remove the straightedge.

Front Suspension Check

Check the front suspension for loose, damaged or missing components. Refer to Chapter Fifteen.

Rear Suspension Check

Check the rear suspension for loose, damaged or missing components. Refer to Chapter Sixteen.

Rear Suspension Rail Wear Strip Inspection

The wear strips (**Figure 26**) mounted on the bottom of the rear suspension rails should be checked frequently. Note the following:

1. Visually check the wear strips (**Figure 26**) for cracks, excessive wear or other damage.

2. Measure the thickness of the wear strips at 25.4 cm (10 in.) intervals with a vernier caliper. The minimum allowable thickness is 10.7 mm (0.42 in.).

3. If any one wear strip is damaged or if its thickness at any point is less than the minimum

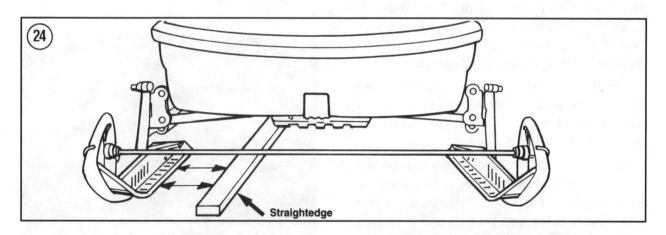

specified in Step 2, replace both wear strips as described in Chapter Sixteen.

Track Inspection

Inspect the track for wear or other damage as described in Chapter Sixteen.

Track Adjustment

The track is subject to high torque loads which may cause the track to stretch and wear. Check the track adjustment frequently as part of a routine maintenance schedule. Failure to maintain correct track tension and alignment will reduce performance and wear the track prematurely. Track adjustments include track tension and alignment.

Correct track tension is important because a loose track slaps on the bottom of the tunnel and wears the track, tunnel and heat exchangers. A loose track can also ratchet on the drive sprockets and damage both the track and sprockets.

A track that is too tight rapidly wears the slider shoe material and the idler wheels. Performance is also reduced because of increased friction and drag on the system.

Track alignment is related to track tension and should be checked and adjusted at the same time as the tension. If the track is misaligned, the rear idler wheels, drive sprocket lugs and track lugs wear rapidly. The resistance between the track and the sides of the wheels reduces snowmobile performance.

Tension adjustment

> *NOTE*
> *Arctic Cat suggests running the snowmobile in snow for approximately 15-20 minutes before measuring and adjusting track tension.*

1. Raise the snowmobile with a suitable lift so that the track is clear of the ground.

2. Clean ice, snow and dirt from the track and suspension.

3. Attach a spring scale to the track at approximately the middle of the slider shoe (**Figure 27**). Pull the scale to deflect the track away from the slider shoe until a force of 9 kg. (20 lbs.) is indicated by the scale.

4. Measure the distance between the slider shoe and the inside of the track. Refer to **Table 6** for the recommended deflection.

5. If the measured deflection is incorrect, adjust track tension as follows:

   a. Loosen the locknut (A, **Figure 28**) on each of the two adjusters. One adjuster is located on the left side and the other adjuster is located on the right side. Be careful not to disturb the setting of the adjuster screw (B, **Figure 28**).

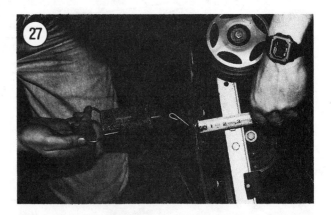

NOTE
*One adjuster (B, **Figure 28**) is located on each side of the track and the setting of the adjusters controls both track tension and track alignment. Track alignment and tension must both be checked when disturbing the adjusters.*

b. If the track is too loose, turn both adjusters (B, **Figure 28**) **in** exactly the same amount to tighten the track.

c. If the track is too tight, turn both adjusters (B, **Figure 28**) **out** exactly the same amount to loosen the track.

d. Push the underside of the track up and down vigorously to relocate the drive components, then measure track deflection again as described in Steps 3 and 4. If it is incorrect, adjust tension as required.

e. Tighten the locknuts (A, **Figure 28**) when adjustment is complete.

f. Apply the recommended amount of force and recheck the adjustment as described in Step 3 and Step 4.

6. Check track alignment as follows after setting the track tension.

Track alignment

1. Check and, if necessary, adjust the track tension as described in this chapter.

2. Position the machine on its skis so that the ski tips are against a wall or other immovable barrier.

3. Elevate and support the machine so that the track is completely clear of the ground and free to rotate.

WARNING
Do not stand behind or in front of the machine when the engine is running and take care to keep hands, feet and clothing away from the track when it is moving.

4. Start the engine and apply just enough throttle to turn the track several complete revolutions.

5. Shut off the engine and allow the track to coast to a stop. Do not stop it with the brake.

6. Check the alignment of the rear idler wheels and the track lugs.

7. If the idlers are equal distance from the lugs and the openings in the track are centered with the slider shoes (**Figure 29**), the alignment is correct.

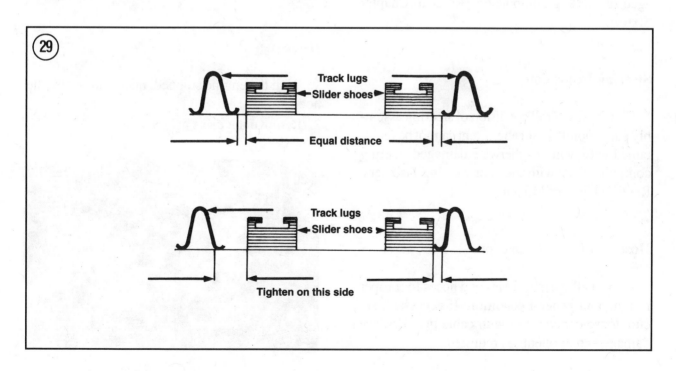

29

Track lugs
Slider shoes
Equal distance

Track lugs
Slider shoes
Tighten on this side

8. If the track is closer to the slider shoes on one side, the alignment should be adjusted as follows:

   a. Loosen locknuts (A, **Figure 28**) on adjusters of both sides.

   b. If the track is **offset to the left**, tighten the left adjuster bolt (B, **Figure 28**) and loosen the right one exactly the same amount.

   c. If the track is **offset to the right**, tighten the right adjuster bolt (B, **Figure 28**) and loosen the left one exactly the same amount.

   d. Repeat Steps 4, 5 and 6 to recheck alignment. If alignment is still not correct, repeat substep 8a-8c to adjust, then Steps 4, 5 and 6 until the track is properly aligned.

9. Recheck track tension as described in this chapter after making any changes to the adjuster bolts (B, **Figure 28**).

Slide Suspension Inspection

Check the suspension system for loose, damaged or missing components. Refer to Chapter Sixteen.

Steering Inspection

Check the overall condition of steering assembly parts monthly. Ski alignment cannot be maintained with bent or otherwise damaged steering components or with loose or missing fasteners. Refer to Chapter Fifteen.

Hose and Cable Inspection

Inspect all wiring, cables and hoses for proper routing and general condition. If necessary, secure loose components with cable ties. Replace damaged components as required.

Electrical Connectors

Inspect the high-tension electrical leads to the spark plugs (**Figure 30**) for cracks and breaks in the insulation and replace the leads if they are not perfect. Breaks in the insulation allow the spark to arc to ground and will impair engine performance.

Check primary ignition and lighting wiring for damaged insulation. Usually minor damage can be repaired by wrapping the damaged area with electrical insulating tape. If insulation damage is extensive, replace the damaged wires.

Spark Plugs

Periodically check the spark plugs for firing tip condition and gap. Refer to spark plug service under *Tune-Up* in this chapter.

MONTHLY MAINTENANCE

Items requiring monthly maintenance are listed in **Table 3**.

Drive Belt

1. With the engine stopped, open and secure the hood.
2. Remove the drive belt cover.

3. Visually check the drive belt for cracks, fraying or unusual wear as described in Chapter Thirteen.

4. Replace the drive belt if its width is less than specified in Chapter Thirteen.

Drive and Driven Clutch Inspection

The drive and driven clutch assemblies do not require periodic lubrication. If wear or damage is suspected, refer to Chapter Thirteen.

Chaincase Oil Level Check

Refer to *Chaincase Oil* under *Lubrication* in this chapter.

Suspension Lubrication

Refer to *Steering Spindle Lubrication* and *Slide Suspension Lubrication* in this chapter.

Fuel Filter

An inline filter (**Figure 31**) is located between the fuel tank, or fuel shutoff valve, and the fuel pump. To ensure adequate fuel flow, the filter should be inspected monthly or if fuel restriction

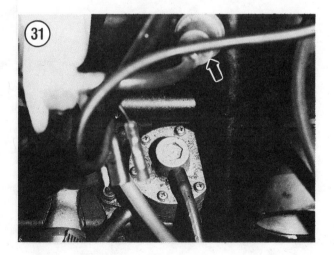

is suspected. A new filter should be installed at least once each year.

NON-SCHEDULED MAINTENANCE

Frequently check the following service items and service as required.

Engine Mounts and Fasteners

Loose engine mount bolts will cause incorrect drive belt alignment. Check the engine mounting bolts to make sure they are all tight. See **Figures 32-34**. It may be necessary to refer to Chapter Five to tighten some of the mounting fasteners. If the engine mounts are loose, check the clutch alignment as described in Chapter Thirteen.

Brake Pad Wear Check

On 1994 and earlier models with mechanically (cable) actuated brakes, the brake pads should be replaced if the thickness of either brake pad is less than 6.2 mm (0.244 in.) thick.

On 1995 and later models with mechanically (cable) actuated brakes, the brake pads should be replaced if the thickness of the fixed brake pad is less than 6.2 mm (0.244 in.) or the movable brake pad is less than 12.7 mm (0.500 in.) thick.

On models with a hydraulic brake, both pads should be replaced if either is less than 3.2 mm (0.125 in.) thick.

Refer to Chapter Fourteen for brake service to both mechanical and hydraulic units.

Brake Adjustment (Mechanical Brake)

All models with mechanically actuated brakes must be adjusted for wear periodically. Check and adjust the mechanical brake as follows:

1. Open the hood.
2. Rotate the brake disc by hand.
3. Apply the brake firmly.

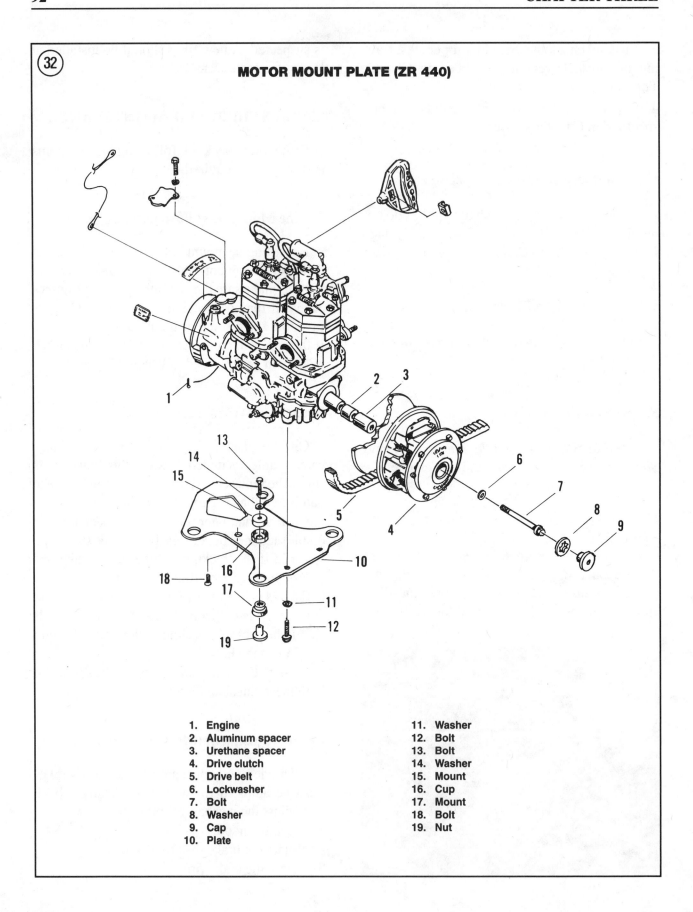

MOTOR MOUNT PLATE (ZR 440)

1. Engine
2. Aluminum spacer
3. Urethane spacer
4. Drive clutch
5. Drive belt
6. Lockwasher
7. Bolt
8. Washer
9. Cap
10. Plate
11. Washer
12. Bolt
13. Bolt
14. Washer
15. Mount
16. Cup
17. Mount
18. Bolt
19. Nut

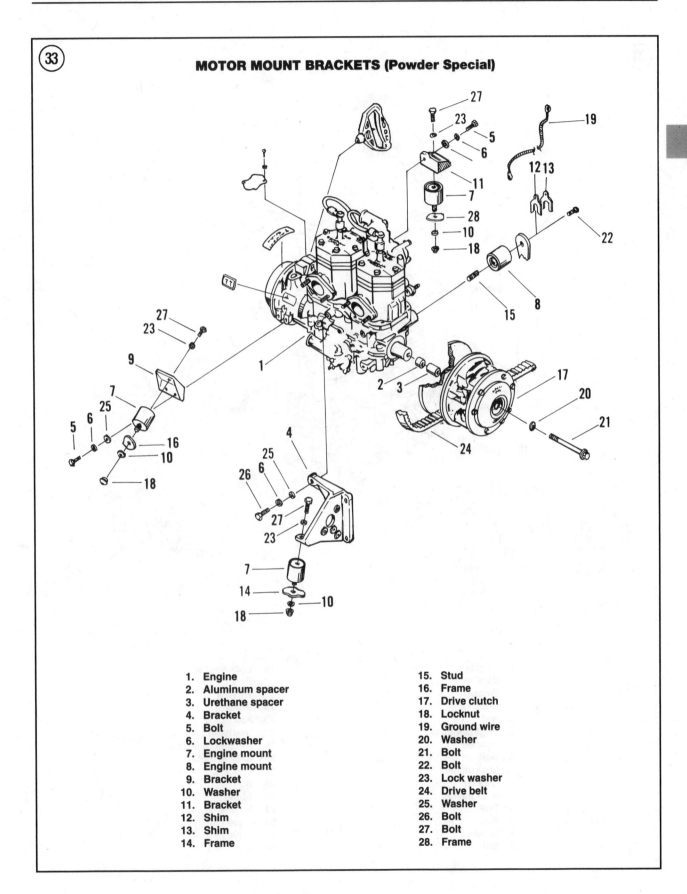

33 MOTOR MOUNT BRACKETS (Powder Special)

1. Engine	15. Stud
2. Aluminum spacer	16. Frame
3. Urethane spacer	17. Drive clutch
4. Bracket	18. Locknut
5. Bolt	19. Ground wire
6. Lockwasher	20. Washer
7. Engine mount	21. Bolt
8. Engine mount	22. Bolt
9. Bracket	23. Lock washer
10. Washer	24. Drive belt
11. Bracket	25. Washer
12. Shim	26. Bolt
13. Shim	27. Bolt
14. Frame	28. Frame

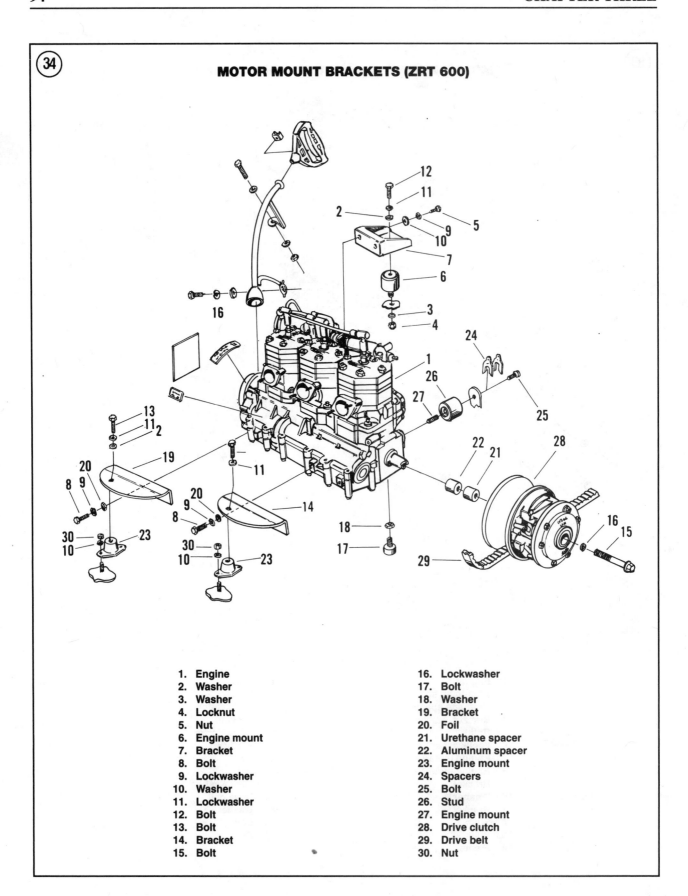

MOTOR MOUNT BRACKETS (ZRT 600)

1. Engine	16. Lockwasher
2. Washer	17. Bolt
3. Washer	18. Washer
4. Locknut	19. Bracket
5. Nut	20. Foil
6. Engine mount	21. Urethane spacer
7. Bracket	22. Aluminum spacer
8. Bolt	23. Engine mount
9. Lockwasher	24. Spacers
10. Washer	25. Bolt
11. Lockwasher	26. Stud
12. Bolt	27. Engine mount
13. Bolt	28. Drive clutch
14. Bracket	29. Drive belt
15. Bolt	30. Nut

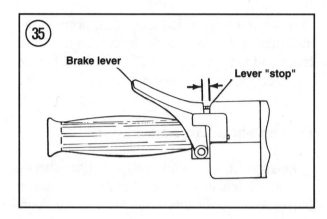

Brake lever

Lever "stop"

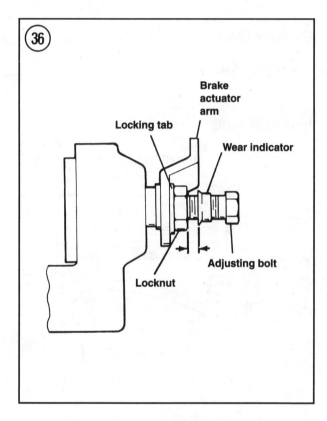

Brake
actuator
arm

Locking tab

Wear indicator

Adjusting bolt

Locknut

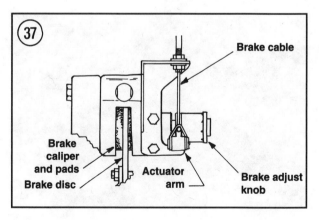

Brake cable

Brake
caliper
and pads

Brake disc

Actuator
arm

Brake adjust
knob

3

4. Measure the distance from the handlebar brake lever to the lever stop as shown in **Figure 35**. The distance should be 6-13 mm (1/4-1/2 in.).

5A. On 1994 and earlier models, adjust the brake as follows if the distance measured in Step 4 is incorrect.

NOTE
If the wear indicator has bottomed against the locknut, the brake pads are worn and should be replaced. Refer to Chapter Fourteen for pad replacement.

a. Pry the locking tab away from the adjusting bolt locknut (**Figure 36**).

b. Turn the adjusting bolt as required to correct the travel of the handlever (**Figure 35**). Turning the adjuster clockwise will adjust the brake tighter.

c. Tighten the locknut against the brake actuator arm and bend the locking tab over the locknut when the adjustment is correct.

5B. On 1995 and later models, adjust the brake as follows if the distance measured in Step 4 is incorrect.

WARNING
The adjustment knob may be hot if the snowmobile has just been operated.

a. Pull the brake adjustment knob out, then turn the knob as required to adjust the brake. Turning the knob clockwise tightens the brake. See **Figure 37**.

b. Recheck the distance from the handlebar brake lever to the stop as shown in **Figure 35**, then readjust as necessary.

6. If the distance cannot be corrected, check the brake assembly as described in Chapter Fourteen.

NOTE
If brake adjustment is difficult or if you are unsure about its operation, refer adjustment to an Arctic Cat dealer. For safe operation, it is important to have brakes that stop properly.

Hydraulic Brake Checking

The hydraulic brakes are self-adjusting in normal operation. The hydraulic brake should grip the disc firmly and should not require pumping the lever. The manufacturer recommends that only Arctic Cat Hi-Temp Brake fluid (part No. 0638-315) be used in the hydraulic brake system. Do not substitute a different fluid or mix different types of fluid.

1. Pull the handlebar brake lever and measure the distance between the end of the lever and the handlebar grip as shown in **Figure 38**. Do not pump the hand lever.

2. If the distance is less than approximately 2.54 cm (1 in.), check the following:

   a. Remove the brake reservoir cover and check the fluid level. Add fluid if the level is low.

   b. Check the thickness of the brake pads. If necessary, install new brake pads as described in Chapter Fourteen.

   c. The lever should be firm when the brake is engaged. If the brake feels soft, bleed the brakes as described in this chapter.

Before storage, Arctco recommends draining the brake fluid and filling the system with new fluid if the fluid has been contaminated, has overheated, been in use more than 1000 miles or at the end of the season.

Refer to Chapter Fourteen for the disassembling procedure of the brake system.

Drive Chain (Non-Reverse Gear)

The drive chain should not be adjusted to compensate for wear. Refer to Chapter Fourteen for inspecting and adjusting models that require initial setting. On models without reverse, chain tension is maintained by two movable tensioner blocks held against the chain by the tension of the spring (**Figure 39**). Only one spring tension roller is used on models with reverse.

If the chain noise is louder than normal, remove the cover and check the condition of the chain and tensioner assembly. Refer to Chapter Fourteen for disassembly and service.

Primary Sheave Adjustment

Refer to Chapter Thirteen for normal checking, adjustment and service. For high altitude or other special applications, refer to Chapter Four.

Cylinder Head Torque

Refer to *Tune-up* in this chapter.

Ignition Timing

Refer to *Tune-up* in this chapter.

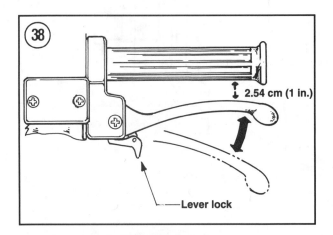

Carburetor/Fuel Injection Adjustment

Refer to *Tune-up* in this chapter.

Throttle Cable Routing

The single throttle cable that begins at the thumb control is attached to two, three or four

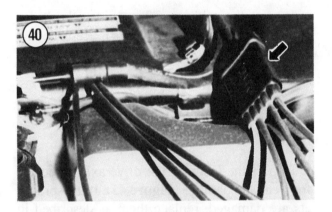

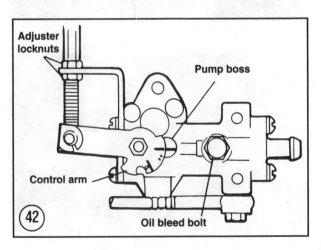

cables at a junction block (**Figure 40**). The branched cables are connected to each carburetor, or EFI throttle, and the oil-injection pump. Check the throttle cable from the thumb throttle to the carburetor (**Figure 41**) and oil pump for proper routing. Check the cable ends for fraying or splitting that could cause the cable to break or stick in the housing.

Oil Injection Pump Adjustment

The oil injection pump injects lubricating oil into the engine. Throttle position determines the amount of oil injected. Control cable adjustment is necessary because cables wear and stretch during normal use. Incorrect cable adjustment can cause too little or too much oil and result in engine seizure and poor performance.

The oil injection pump cable adjustment should be checked once a year, or whenever the throttle cable is disconnected or replaced.

1. Open the hood and secure it in the open position.

2. Adjust the carburetors as described under *Tune-up* in this chapter.

> *CAUTION*
> *If the carburetors are not adjusted before adjusting the oil pump, engine damage may occur. The oil injection pump operation must be synchronized with the carburetor opening.*

3. Make sure the engine is stopped and the key or stop switch is in proper position to prevent the engine from starting.

4. Press the thumb throttle lever until the throttle is completely open and hold the throttle control in this wide-open position.

5. Check the position of the oil injection pump control arm. The mark on the injection pump control arm must align with the mark on the pump boss (**Figure 42**).

6. If the injection pump adjustment marks are not aligned as shown in **Figure 42**:

a. Loosen the cable adjuster locknuts (**Figure 42**).

b. Reposition the cable until the two marks align.

c. Tighten the locknuts and recheck the adjustment.

7. Close and secure the hood.

Headlight Beam

Refer to Chapter Nine.

GENERAL INSPECTION AND MAINTENANCE

Recoil Starter

Pull the starter handle (**Figure 43**) out and inspect the rope for fraying. If its condition is questionable, replace the rope as described in Chapter Twelve.

Check the action of the starter. It should be smooth and, when the rope is released, it should return all the way. If the starter action is rough or if the rope does not return, service the starter as described in Chapter Twelve.

Body Inspection

Damaged body panels should be repaired or replaced.

Body Fasteners

Tighten any loose body bolts. Replace loose rivets by first drilling out the old rivet and then installing a new one. A pop-rivet tool and an assortment of rivets are available through many hardware and auto parts stores. Follow the manufacturer's instructions for installing rivets.

Welded joints should be checked for cracks and damage. Damaged welded joints should be repaired by a competent welding shop.

Drive Assembly

Refer to Chapter Four for drive assembly tuning and adjustment. Refer to Chapter Thirteen for drive assembly service.

Guide Wheel Inspection

Inspect the rubber on the guide wheels for wear and damage (**Figure 44**). Replace the wheels if they are in poor condition. Refer to Chapter Sixteen.

Drive Axle Sprockets

Inspect the teeth on the drive axle sprockets for wear and damage (**Figure 45**). If the sprockets are damaged, replace them as described in Chapter Sixteen.

Fuel Tank

Inspect the fuel tank for cracks and abrasions. If the tank is damaged or leaking, replace it. See Chapter Six or Chapter Seven.

Fuel Tank Cleaning

The fuel tank should be removed and thoroughly flushed once a season. Refer to Chapter Six or Seven.

Oil Tank

Inspect the oil tank for cracks, abrasions or leaks. Replace the tank if its condition is in doubt.

Oil and Fuel Lines

Inspect the oil and fuel lines for loose connections and damage. Tighten all connections and replace any lines that are damaged or cracked.

Electrical System

All the switches should be checked for proper operation. Refer to Chapter Nine.

Electrical Connectors

Inspect the high-tension leads to the spark plugs (**Figure 30**) for cracks and breaks in the insulation and replace the leads if they are not perfect. Breaks in the insulation allow the spark to arc to ground and impairs engine performance.

Check all wiring for damaged insulation. Usually minor damage can be repaired by wrapping the damaged area with electrical insulating tape. If insulation damage is extensive, replace the damaged wires.

Abnormal Engine Noise

> *WARNING*
> *Never lean into the snowmobile's engine compartment while wearing a scarf or other loose clothing when the engine is running or when anyone is attempting to start the engine. If the scarf or clothing should catch in the drive belt or clutch, severe injury could occur. Make sure the belt guard is in place.*

Open the hood, then start the engine and listen for abnormal noises. Often the first indication of trouble is a change in sound. An unusual rattle might indicate a loose fastener that can be easily repaired or the first warning sign of severe engine damage. With familiarity of the machine and with practice, you will be able to identify most new sounds. Periodic inspection for abnormal engine noises can prevent engine failure later on.

Pulse Hose

The pulse hose between the engine crankcase and the fuel pump should be inspected at the beginning of each season for cracks or other damage. Worn or damaged hoses cause air leaks that result in intermittent operating problems. Check the pulse hose for loose connections or damaged hose clamps. Replace the pulse hose and clamps when necessary.

ENGINE TUNE-UP

The number of definitions of the term "tune-up" is probably equal to the number of people defining it. For the purposes of this book, a tune-up is general adjustment and maintenance to ensure peak engine performance.

The following paragraphs discuss the different parts of a tune-up. Perform them in the order given. Have the new parts on hand before you begin.

To perform a tune-up on your snowmobile, you need the following tools and equipment:

   a. 14 mm spark plug wrench.

   b. Socket wrench and assorted sockets.

   c. Phillips screwdriver.

   d. Spark plug wire feeler gauge and gapper tool.

   e. Dial indicator.

   f. Flywheel puller.

   g. Compression gauge.

Cylinder and Cylinder Head Nuts

The engine must be at room temperature for this procedure.

1. Open the hood.

2. Tighten each cylinder head screw or nut in a crisscross pattern to the tightening torque in **Table 7**. Refer to **Figure 46-50**.

Cylinder Compression

A cylinder compression check is one of the quickest ways to check the condition of the engine by measuring the compression built up in the cylinder. It is a good idea to check compression at each tune-up, record the compression of each cylinder, then compare the current compression with test results from earlier tune-ups. The first step is to write the measured compression of each cylinder and the date, so it can be compared with tests recorded at the next tune-up.

A gradual change may indicate normal wear or may help you spot a developing problem.

1. Elevate and support the machine so that the track is completely off the ground and free to rotate. Start and run the engine until it warms to normal operating temperature, then turn the engine off.

> *WARNING*
> *Do not stand behind or in front of the machine when the engine is running, and take care to keep hands, feet and clothing away from the track when it is turning.*

> *CAUTION*
> *To prevent expensive engine damage, use compressed air to blow away any dirt that has accumulated next to the spark plug base. The dirt could fall into the*

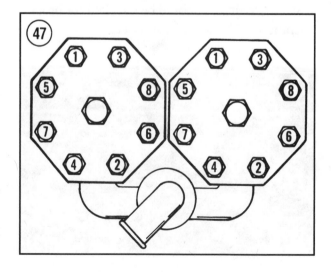

cylinder when the plug is removed, causing serious engine damage.

2. Remove all the spark plugs, then attach the plugs back to the spark plug wires and ground the plugs to the cylinder head.

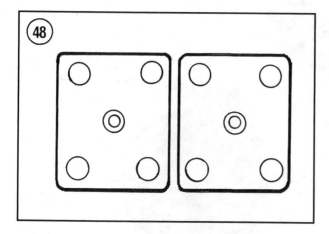

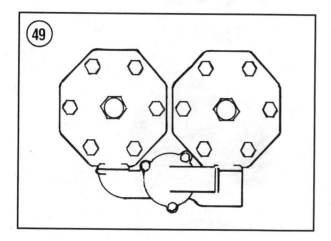

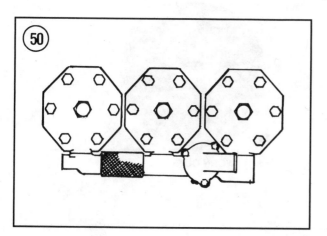

CAUTION
If the plugs are not grounded during the compression test, the CDI ignition could be damaged.

3. Screw a compression gauge into one spark plug hole, or if you have a press-in type gauge, hold it firmly in position.

4. Check that the emergency cut-out switch is in the OFF position.

5. Hold the throttle wide open and crank the engine several revolutions until the gauge gives its highest reading. Record the reading, indicating the cylinder location (MAG end, center or PTO end). Remove the pressure tester and relieve the pressure valve.

6. Repeat Steps 3, 4 and 5 for the other cylinder(s).

7. There should be no more than a 10 percent difference in compression between cylinders.

8. If the compression is very low, it is likely that a ring is broken or there is a hole in the piston.

9. Reinstall the spark plugs and reconnect the spark plug wires.

Correct Spark Plug Heat Range

The proper spark plug is very important in obtaining maximum performance and reliability. The condition of a used spark plug can tell a trained mechanic a lot about engine condition and fuel mixture.

Select plugs of the heat range designed for the loads and conditions under which the snowmobile will be operated. Use of spark plugs with incorrect heat ranges can result in a seized piston, scored cylinder wall or damaged piston crown.

In general, use a hot plug for low speeds and low temperatures. Use a cold plug for high speeds, high engine loads and high temperatures. The plug should operate hot enough to burn off unwanted deposits, but not so hot that they burn themselves or cause preignition. The insulator of a spark plug that is the correct heat range will be

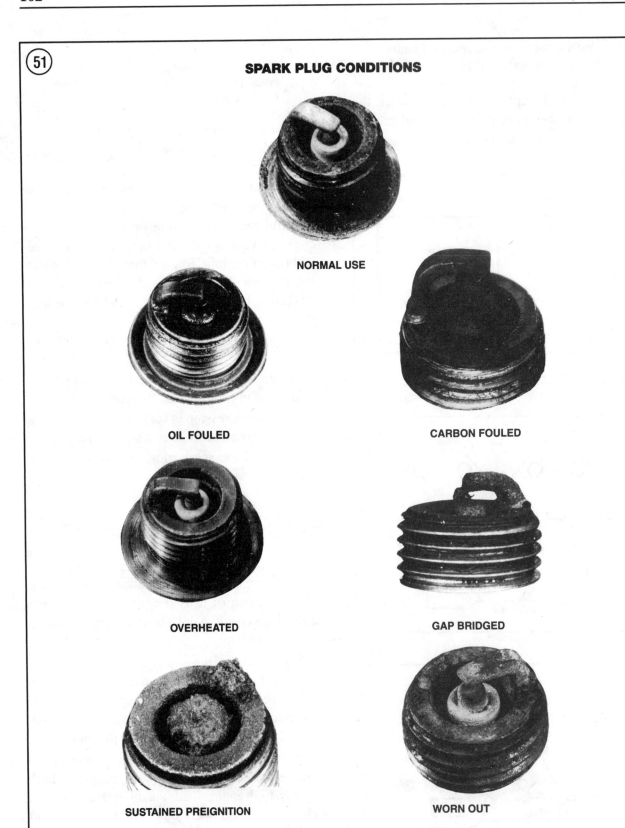

SPARK PLUG CONDITIONS

NORMAL USE

OIL FOULED

CARBON FOULED

OVERHEATED

GAP BRIDGED

SUSTAINED PREIGNITION

WORN OUT

a light tan color after the engine has operated for awhile. See **Figure 51**.

The reach, or length, of a plug is also important. A shorter than normal plug will cause hard starting, reduced engine performance and carbon buildup on the exposed cylinder head threads. A spark plug that is longer than normal could interfere with the piston or cause overheating. Physical damage to the piston or overheating often results in permanent and severe engine damage. If the spark plug extends into the combustion chamber as shown by the *too long* view in **Figure 52**, carbon built up on the exposed threads may prevent the spark plug from being removed. Forcing the spark plug out will probably damage the threads in the cylinder head.

The standard heat range spark plug is listed in **Table 8**. It may be desirable to install spark plugs of a slightly different heat range than listed to match operating conditions.

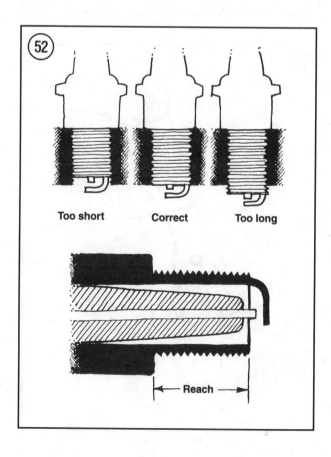

Too short   Correct   Too long

Reach

Spark Plug Removal/Cleaning

1. Grasp the spark plug lead as near the plug as possible and pull it from the plug. If the spark plug cap (**Figure 46**) is stuck to the plug, twist the cap slightly to break it loose.

CAUTION
Dirt near the spark plug could fall into the cylinder when removing the plug, causing serious engine damage.

2. Use compressed air to blow away any dirt that has accumulated next to the spark plug base.

NOTE
If the plug is difficult to remove, apply penetrating oil, like WD-40 or Liquid Wrench, around the base of the plug and let it soak. If the plug is still difficult to remove, apply penetrating oil and let it soak into the threads again.

3. Remove the spark plug with a 14 mm spark plug wrench.
4. Inspect the plug carefully. Look for a broken center porcelain, excessively eroded electrodes and excessive carbon buildup or oil fouling. See **Figure 51**.

Gapping and Installing the Plug

Carefully set the gap between the electrodes of a new spark plug before installing. A specific gap is necessary to ensure a reliable, consistent spark. Use a special spark plug gapping tool to bend the ground electrode and a wire feeler gauge to measure the gap between the electrodes.

NOTE
Never try to close the spark plug gap by tapping the spark plug ground electrode on a solid surface; this can damage the plug. Always use the special tool to bend the ground electrode when adjusting the electrode gap. Bending the electrode excessively may break or weaken it.

1. Insert a wire feeler gauge between the center and side electrode (**Figure 53**). The correct gap is listed in **Table 8**. If the gap is correct, you will feel a slight drag as you pull the wire through. If there is no drag, or the gauge will not pass through, bend the side (ground) electrode with a gapping tool (**Figure 54**) to set the proper gap.

2. Apply antiseize to the plug threads before installing the spark plug.

> *NOTE*
> *Antiseize can be purchased at most auto-motive parts stores.*

3. Screw the spark plug in by hand until it seats. Very little effort should be required. If force is necessary, the threads are dirty or the plug is cross-threaded. Unscrew the plug, clean the threads and try again.

4. Use a spark plug wrench and tighten the spark plugs to the torque specification listed in **Table 7**. If a torque wrench is not available, tighten the plug an additional 1/4 to 1/2 turn after the gasket has made contact with the head. If you are in-stalling an old, regapped plug and reusing the old gasket, only tighten an addition 1/4 turn.

> *CAUTION*
> *Do not overtighten. This will only squash the gasket and destroy its sealing ability. This could cause compression leakage around the base of the plug.*

5. Attach the spark plug wires. Make sure they snap onto the top of the plugs tightly.

> *CAUTION*
> *Be certain the spark plug wire is located away from the exhaust pipe.*

Reading Spark Plugs

Much information about engine and spark plug performance can be determined by careful examination of the spark plugs. Refer to Chapter Four.

Ignition Timing (Liquid-Cooled Engines)

All models are equipped with a capacitor dis-charge ignition (CDI), but all the systems are not alike. Some use normal open stop switches and others use normal closed ignition switches. All of the systems used are much less susceptible to

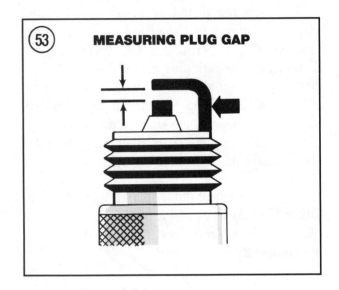

MEASURING PLUG GAP

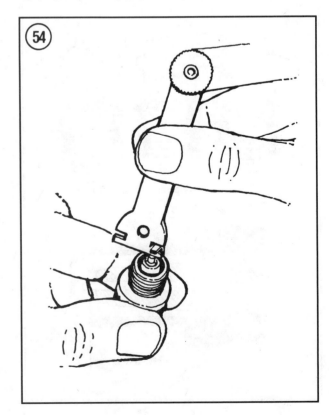

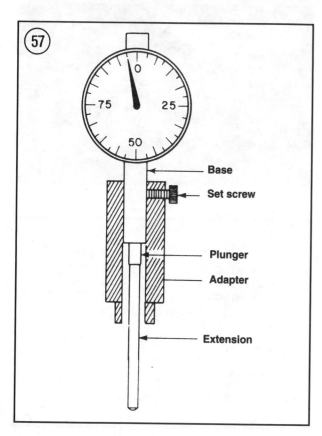

failures caused by dirt, moisture and wear than earlier breaker point systems. Different troubleshooting, testing and timing procedures may be used for the various models, so it is important to use the correct procedure for the engine being serviced.

Static timing to verify the flywheel timing marks may be necessary before using a timing light to check ignition timing. Most flywheels are marked with several lines, but the correct timing mark may not be easily distinguished from the other lines. The static timing procedure can be used for the following:

   a. to verify and identify factory timing marks.

   b. to detect a broken or missing flywheel Woodruff key.

   c. to detect a twisted crankshaft.

   d. to scribe timing marks on a new flywheel.

Dynamic engine timing uses a timing light connected to the MAG (magneto) side spark plug lead. As the engine is cranked or running, the light flashes each time the spark plug fires. When the light is pointed at the moving flywheel, the mark on the flywheel appears to stand still. The flywheel mark should align with the stationary timing pointer on the engine.

Static timing check

The static timing is used only to locate the proper position for the ignition timing when the engine is running at a specific speed. It is important to check the ignition timing using the correct mark and at the rpm listed in **Table 9**.

1. Open the hood.

2. Remove all the spark plugs as described in this chapter.

3. On some models, it is necessary to remove the crankcase inspection plug (**Figure 55**) or some other equipment (**Figure 56**).

4. Install and position a dial indicator as follows:

   a. Screw the extension onto a dial indicator and insert the dial indicator into the adapter (**Figure 57**).

b. Screw the dial indicator adaptor into the cylinder head on the MAG side. Do not lock the dial indicator in the adapter at this time.

c. Rotate the flywheel by turning the primary sheave until the dial indicator rises all the way up in its holder (piston is approaching top dead center). Then slide the indicator far enough into the holder to obtain a reading.

d. Lightly tighten the set screw on the dial indicator adaptor to secure the dial gauge.

e. Rotate the flywheel until the dial on the gauge stops and reverses direction. This is top dead center. Zero the dial guage by aligning the zero with the dial (**Figure 58**).

f. Tighten the set screw on the dial indicator adaptor securely.

5. Rotate the crankshaft counterclockwise (viewed fron the right side) until the gauge needle has made approximately three revolutions. Then carefully turn the crankshaft clockwise until the gauge indicates that the piston is the correct distance before top dead center as indicated in **Table 9**.

NOTE
There may be more than one mark on the flywheel. To identify the correct mark to use when performing dynamic timing, apply chalk or paint to the correct mark.

6. View the timing marks through the hole in the crankcase (**Figure 59**). The timing mark should line up with the pointer. If not, perform the following:

a. Scribe a new mark on the flywheel that aligns with the crankcase pointer.

b. Repeat the timing procedure to check the accuracy of the new mark.

c. This mark will be used as the reference when using the timing light. Apply paint over the scribe mark if necessary to make the mark more visible.

7. Remove the gauge and adapter. Install the spark plugs and connect the high-tension leads.

Dynamic timing check

1. Open the hood.

2. Perform the *Static Timing Check* in this chapter to make sure the flywheel is correctly installed and to identify the correct timing mark.

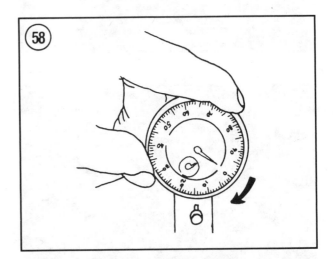

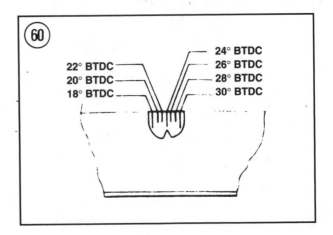

Refer to the following drawings to identify the factory timing marks:

Figure 60—Models EXT 580, ZR 440 and ZR 580; 1995-1998 Cougar, Cougar Deluxe, Cougar Mountain Cat, Panther 550 and Prowler 2-up.

Figure 61—Model ZL 440; prior to 1995 Cougar, Cougar Mountain Cat, Prowler and Prowler 2-up.

Figure 62—Models ZR 580 EFI, EXT 580 EFI, EXT 580 EFI Deluxe and Pantera 580.

Figure 63—Models Powder Special and ZL 500.

Figure 64—Models EXT 600 Triple, EXT 600 Triple Touring and ZRT 600.

3. Attach a stroboscopic timing light according to the manufacturer's instructions to the MAG side spark plug lead (**Figure 65**).

4. Connect a tachometer according to the manufacturer's instructions.

5. Position the machine, on its skis, so the tips of the skis are against a wall or other immovable barrier. Elevate and support the machine so the track is completely clear of the ground and free to rotate.

WARNING
Do not allow anyone to stand behind or in front of the machine when the engine is running. Keep hands, feet and clothing away from the track when it is running.

NOTE
Because ignition components are temperature sensitive, check ignition timing when the engine is at normal temperature.

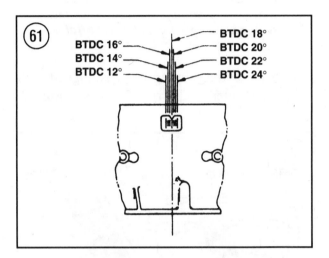

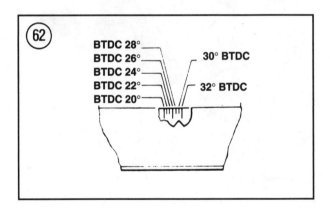

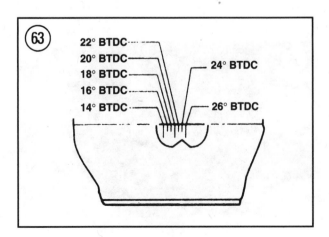

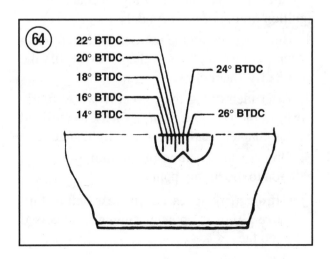

6. Start the engine and allow it to idle until it reaches normal temperature.

7. Increase engine speed until it reaches the test rpm listed in **Table 9**, then briefly point the timing light at the timing inspection hole (**Figure 59**). The timing light will flash, appearing to stop the timing mark at the instant of ignition.

8. If the ignition timing is correct, the proper flywheel timing mark will be aligned with the housing pointer on the hole.

9. Turn off the engine and lower the snowmobile to the ground. Remove the timing light and tachometer. Install any covers that were removed.

10. If the timing marks are not correctly aligned, the ignition timing may require adjustment. Refer to *Setting Ignition Timing* in this chapter.

Setting ignition timing

Ignition must occur at a specific time for the engine to perform at its optimum. The procedure for changing the ignition timing is not the same for all engine models. Refer to **Table 10** for the type of ignition installed on your specific model, then refer to the appropriate following paragraphs.

Models with trigger coil under flywheel. **Figure 66** shows the ignition typical of the type used on two-cylinder engines without electronic fuel injection. Refer to the following for changing the ignition timing of these models:

1. Before changing the ignition timing, refer to *Static Timing Check* in this chapter to identify the correct flywheel mark.

2. After identifying the correct flywheel mark, perform the *Dynamic Timing Check* as outlined in this chapter. Leave the timing light attached.

3. Observe the position of the timing mark in relation to the timing pointer.

   a. If the mark appears to the rear (left in **Figure 59**) of the pointer, timing is advanced too far.

b. If the mark is located in front (right in **Figure 59**) of the pointer, timing is retarded.

> *NOTE*
> *The flywheel may have several marks. It is important to use the correct mark as determined by the static timing procedure. It is also important to check the timing at the specific rpm listed in **Table 9**.*

c. If the correct timing mark is aligned with the pointer at the rpm listed in **Table 9**,

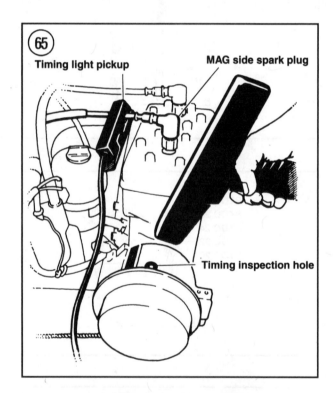

Timing light pickup   MAG side spark plug

Timing inspection hole

ignition timing can be considered correct and does not require changing.

4. If the timing mark is not aligned with the pointer, remove the recoil starter assembly as described in Chapter Twelve.

5. Remove the starter pulley and flywheel as described in Chapter Nine.

6. Change the ignition timing by moving the stator plate (A, **Figure 66**) as follows:

NOTE
*The stator may have no marks, one mark or three marks. If not marked or if marks are not aligned, scratch a reference mark that is aligned with the mark on the crankcase as shown in **Figure 67**. If the stator has three marks, the marks are located at two-degree increments to assist setting the timing.*

a. The stator plate and crankcase should be marked as shown in **Figure 67**.

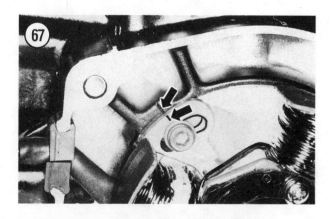

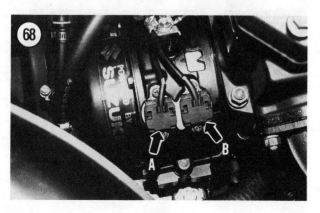

NOTE
The screws securing the stator may be coated with threadlocking compound to prevent loosening. If necessary, apply heat to the screws to facilitate removal. Use care to prevent damage to the surrounding components.

b. If the timing was too far advanced as described in substep 3a, loosen the two screws (B, **Figure 66**) retaining the stator plate. Turn the stator plate clockwise to retard the ignition timing slightly, then tighten both screws.

c. If the timing was retarded as described in substep 3b, loosen the two screws (B, **Figure 66**) retaining the stator plate. Turn the stator plate counterclockwise to advance the ignition timing slightly, then tighten both screws.

7. Install the flywheel and starter, then recheck the dynamic timing. If the timing is still incorrect, return to Step 3.

8. When the dynamic timing is correct as listed in **Table 9**, coat the threads of the screws (B, **Figure 66**) with threadlocking compound. Remove the recoil starter and flywheel, then remove one screw, apply Loctite 242 and reinstall. Remove the second screw and coat its threads with Loctite 242 after the first screw is tight.

9. Install the flywheel and lockwasher, then coat the threads of the retaining nut with Loctite 271 and tighten to the torque listed in **Table 7**.

Models with trigger coil outside flywheel. This type of ignition is used on some two-cylinder engines and on all three-cylinder engines. The separate trigger coil is attached to the engine crankcase outside the flywheel as shown in **Figure 68** (typical of some two-cylinder engines) or **Figure 69** (typical of three-cylinder engines).

The ignition timing is not adjustable on these engines, but some problems can change the ignition timing. If ignition timing is incorrect, refer to *Static Timing Check* in this chapter to identify the correct flywheel mark. After identifying the correct mark, perform the *Dynamic Timing Check* as outlined in this chapter.

If the timing is not correct at the engine speed listed in **Table 9**, refer to Chapter Two and test the resistance of the ignition timing sensor (**Figure 68** or **Figure 69**). If the resistance is incorrect, install a new sensor and recheck the timing. Other problems that may cause the timing to be incorrect are a damaged flywheel, damaged drive key or faulty electrical connections.

Ignition Timing (Air-Cooled Engines)

A capacitor discharge ignition (CDI) is used on 431 cc air-cooled engines. The system is not usually susceptible to failures caused by dirt, moisture and wear. It is important to use the correct procedure when servicing the engine.

Static timing to verify the flywheel timing marks may be necessary before using a timing light to check ignition timing. Most flywheels are marked with several lines, but the correct timing mark may not be easily distinguished from the other lines. The static timing procedure can be used for the following:

a. to verify and identify the factory timing marks.

b. to detect a broken or missing flywheel Woodruff key.

c. to detect a twisted crankshaft.

d. to scribe timing marks on a new flywheel.

NOTE
The ignition timing marks located on the engine flywheel of air-cooled engines may be very difficult to view with the engine installed. A wire, or similar, pointer can be securely attached to the engine near the drive pulley, then a temporary timing mark can be scribed on the pulley for checking the timing with the engine running. Use the following static timing check to locate the crankshaft at the correct timing position, then scribe the temporary mark on the stationary pulley in line with the pointer.

Dynamic engine timing uses a timing light connected to the MAG (magneto) side spark plug lead. As the engine is cranked or running, the light flashes each time the spark plug fires. When the light is pointed at the moving flywheel, the mark on the flywheel appears to stand still. The flywheel mark should align with the stationary timing pointer on the engine.

Static timing check

The static timing is only used to locate the proper position for the ignition timing when the engine is running at a specific speed. It is important to check the ignition timing using the correct mark and at the engine speed listed in **Table 9**.

1. Open the hood.

2. Remove all the spark plugs as described in this chapter.

3. Remove the cover from the cooling fan so that the flywheel timing mark and the crankcase mark can be seen (**Figure 70**).

4. Install and position a dial indicator as follows:

  a. Screw the extension onto a dial indicator and insert the dial indicator into the adapter (**Figure 57**).

  b. Screw the dial indicator adaptor into the cylinder head on the MAG side. Do not lock the dial indicator in the adapter at this time.

  c. Rotate the flywheel by turning the primary sheave until the dial indicator rises all the way up in its holder (piston is approaching top dead center). Slide the indicator far enough into the holder to obtain a reading.

  d. Lightly tighten the set screw on the dial indicator adaptor to secure the dial gauge.

  e. Rotate the flywheel until the dial on the gauge stops and reverses direction. This is top dead center. Zero the dial gauge by aligning the zero with the dial (**Figure 58**).

  f. Tighten the set screw on the dial indicator adaptor securely.

5. Rotate the crankshaft clockwise (viewed from the right-hand side) until the gauge needle has made approximately three revolutions. Care-

fully turn the crankshaft clockwise until the gauge indicates that the piston is the correct distance before top dead center as indicated in **Table 9**.

NOTE
There may be more than one mark on the flywheel. To identify the correct mark to use when performing dynamic timing, apply chalk or paint to the correct mark.

6. View the flywheel timing marks through the opening (**Figure 70**). The timing mark on the flywheel should line up with the arrow (A, **Figure 71**). If not, perform the following:

  a. Scribe a new mark on the flywheel that aligns with the crankcase pointer.

  b. Repeat the timing procedure to check the accuracy of the new mark.

  c. This mark will be used as the reference when using the timing light. Apply paint over the scribe mark if necessary to make the mark more visible.

7. Remove the gauge and adapter. Install the spark plugs and connect the high-tension leads.

Dynamic timing check

NOTE
The ignition timing marks located on the engine flywheel of air-cooled engines may be very difficult to view with the engine installed. A wire, or similar, pointer can be securely attached to the engine near the drive pulley, then a temporary timing mark can be scribed on the pulley for checking the timing with the engine running. Use the following dynamic timing check to locate the crankshaft at the correct timing position, then scribe the temporary mark on the stationary pulley in line with the pointer.

1. Open the hood.

2. Perform the *Static Timing Check* in this chapter to make sure the flywheel is correctly installed and to identify the correct timing mark.

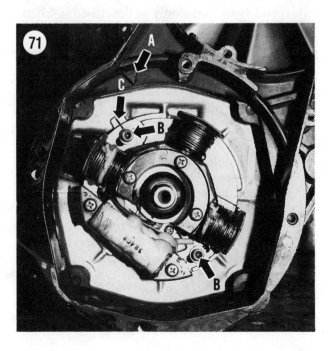

3. Attach a stroboscopic timing light according to the manufacturer's instructions to the MAG side spark plug lead (**Figure 65**).

4. Connect a tachometer according to the manufacturer's instructions.

5. Position the machine, on its skis, so the tips of the skis are against a wall or other immovable barrier. Elevate and support the machine so the track is completely clear of the ground and free to rotate.

WARNING
Do not allow anyone to stand behind or in front of the machine when the engine is running. Keep hands, feet and clothing away from the track when it is running.

NOTE
Because ignition components are temperature sensitive, ignition timing should be checked when the engine is at normal temperature.

6. Start the engine and allow it to idle for a short time until it reaches normal temperature.

7. Increase engine speed until it reaches the test rpm listed in **Table 9**, then briefly point the timing light at the timing marks. The timing light will flash, appearing to stop the timing mark on the flywheel or pulley at the instant of ignition.

8. If the ignition timing is correct, the timing mark will be aligned.

9. Turn off the engine and lower the snowmobile to the ground. Remove the timing light and tachometer. Install any covers that were removed.

10. If the timing marks are not correctly aligned, the ignition timing may require adjustment. Refer to *Setting Ignition Timing* in this chapter.

Setting ignition timing

The ignition must occur at a specific time for the engine to perform at its optimum. **Figure 71** shows the ignition system coils with the flywheel removed. Refer to the following for changing the ignition timing:

1. Before changing the ignition timing, refer to *Static Timing Check* in this chapter to identify or position the correct mark.

2. After identifying the correct marks, perform the *Dynamic Timing Check* as outlined in this chapter.

3. Observe the position of the rotating timing mark in relation to the stationary timing pointer.

 a. If the rotating mark appears to the rear of the arrow (A, **Figure 71**) or other stationary pointer, timing is advanced too far.

 b. If the flywheel mark is located in front of the arrow (A, **Figure 71**) or other stationary pointer, timing is retarded.

NOTE
*It is important to use the correct mark as determined by the static timing procedure. It is also important to check the timing at the specific engine speed listed in **Table 9**.*

 c. If the correct timing marks are aligned at the engine speed listed in **Table 9**, ignition timing is correct and does not require adjustment.

4. If the timing marks are not aligned, remove the recoil starter assembly as described in Chapter Twelve.

5. Remove the starter pulley and flywheel as described in Chapter Nine.

6. Change the ignition timing by moving the stator plate as follows:

NOTE
*The stator may have no marks, one mark or three marks. If not marked or if marks are not aligned, scratch a reference mark that is aligned with the mark on the crankcase as shown (C, **Figure 71**). If the stator has three marks, the marks are located at two-degree increments to assist setting the timing.*

 a. The stator plate and crankcase should be marked as shown (C, **Figure 71**).

NOTE
The screws attaching the stator should be coated with threadlocking compound to prevent loosening. It may be necessary to apply heat to the screws to facilitate removal. Use care to prevent damage to the surrounding components.

b. If the timing is advanced too far as described in substep 3a, loosen the two screws (B, **Figure 71**) retaining the stator plate. Turn the stator plate clockwise to retard ignition timing slightly, then tighten both screws.

c. If the timing is retarded as described in substep 3b, loosen the two screws (B, **Figure 71**) retaining the stator plate. Turn the stator plate counterclockwise to advance ignition timing slightly, then tighten both screws.

7. Install the flywheel and starter, then recheck the dynamic timing. If the timing is still incorrect, return to Step 3.

8. When the dynamic timing is correct as listed in **Table 9**, coat the threads of the screws (B, **Figure 71**) with threadlocking compound. Remove the recoil starter and flywheel, then remove one screw, apply Loctite 242 and reinstall. Remove the second screw and coat its threads with Loctite 242 after the first screw is tight.

9. Install the flywheel and lockwasher, then coat the threads of the retaining nut with Loctite 271 and tighten to the torque listed in **Table 7**.

Carburetur Adjustment

Refer to Chapter Seven for adjusting the Electronic Fuel Injection (EFI) of models so equipped.

Synchronization

For maximum engine performance, both cylinders must work equally. If one cylinder's throttle opens earlier, that cylinder will be required to work harder. This causes poor acceleration, rough engine performance and engine overheating. For proper carburetor synchronization, the throttle slides for all of the carburetors must begin to lift at exactly the same time and continue to be open the same amount throughout their operating range.

Carburetor synchronization should be checked at each tune-up or whenever the engine suffers from reduced performance.

1. With the engine stopped, open and secure the hood.

2. Loosen the locknut on the cable adjuster of each carburetor, then turn the cable adjuster in until the cable has some free play.

3. Turn the carburetor idle speed screw (**Figure 72**) of each carburetor counterclockwise so that the carburetor slides will drop all the way to the bottom. Check to be sure the cable adjuster (Step 2) is not stopping the throttle movement.

4. Turn one carburetor idle speed screw (B, **Figure 72**) clockwise until it just touches the carburetor slide. Then turn the idle speed screw 1 1/2 turns clockwise.

5. Repeat Step 4 for the other carburetor(s).

6. Check the throttle cable free play at the top of each carburetor by lifting the throttle cable by hand. Turn the cable adjusters (C, **Figure 72**) as necessary to remove almost all free play from the cable.

7. Remove the boot from between each carburetor and the intake silencer.

CAUTION
CAUTION
Running the engine with the boots or the silencers disconnected or removed will result in a lean fuel mixture and possible engine damage.

8. Feel inside each carburetor bore while moving the throttle from the idle position. Throttle slides for both (or all three) carburetors should begin to move from idle speed position at exactly the same time. Turn the cable adjuster (C, **Figure 72**) to synchronize the beginning movement of the throttle slides. Tighten the locknut on the cable adjuster when finished, then recheck to be sure that the adjustment is still correct.

9. Repeat Step 8 for the other carburetor(s).

10. Operate the throttle lever a few times, then hold the handlebar throttle lever wide open. Check each throttle cable for free play.

CAUTION
Maintaining throttle cable free play is critical to prevent throttle cable damage.

11. Pull each of the throttle cables or push the throttle valve up with your fingers to make sure the cables have some free play when controls are wide open. Each of the cables should have approximately 1.5 mm or 1/16 in. free play. If the cables are binding, readjust the cable adjusters beginning in Step 2.

12. After completing carburetor synchronization, perform the *Oil Pump Adjustment* procedure in this chapter.

13. Reinstall the air intake silencer and attach the boots to the carburetors.

14. Start the engine and run it until it reaches normal operating temperature. Check idle speed (see **Table 11**). If necessary, turn both idle speed adjustment screws (B, **Figure 72**) equal amounts to obtain specified idle speed.

CAUTION
Do not use the pilot air screw (A, Figure 72) to change the engine idle speed. Ad-

just the pilot air screw as described, otherwise, the engine may be damaged due to an excessively lean mixture.

Idle speed

1. Open the hood.

2. Attach a tachometer according to the tool manufacturer's instructions.

NOTE
When turning the throttle stop screw in Step 3, turn the screws on both carburetors the same amount.

3. Set the engine idle speed by turning the throttle stop screws (B, **Figure 72**) on both or all carburetors exactly the same amount. Turn the stop screws in to increase or out to decrease idle speed. Refer to **Table 11** for the correct idle speed for your model.

Idle mixture

The pilot air screw controls the fuel and air mixture at idle speed. Turning the pilot air screw (A, **Figure 72**) clockwise reduces the amount of air and richens the mixture.

1. Open the hood.

2. Locate the pilot air screw (A, **Figure 72**) on the side of each carburetor.

3. Turn both (all) of the pilot air screws in (clockwise) until they lightly seat.

4. Back the pilot air screw out the number of turns specified in **Table 11**.

CAUTION
Do not use the pilot air screw to attempt to set engine idle speed. Adjust the pilot air screw as specified; otherwise, the engine may be damaged due to an excessively lean mixture.

Table 1 DAILY MAINTENANCE SCHEDULE

Check coolant level
Check injection system oil level
Check chaincase oil level
Check for cooling system leaks
Check condition of the drive belt
Check the stop and tether switch operation
Check headlight and taillight operation
Check headlight and taillight lens
Check steering operation
Check steering bolts for tightness
Check throttle cable for proper routing, adjustment and operation
Check battery fluid level, if so equipped
Check and adjust carburetor as necessary

Table 2 WEEKLY MAINTENANCE SCHEDULE

Check recoil starter rope for wear of damage
Check recoil starter operation
Check exhaust system for leakage or other signs of damage
Check shock absorbers for leakage or damage
Check ski alignment
Check ski wear bar for looseness or damage
Check front suspension for loose or damaged components
Check rear suspension rail wear strips for wear and damage
Check/adjust track tension and alignment
Check for loose, damaged or missing fasteners
Check all hoses and cables for routing and damage
Check wiring for loose connections, damage or incorrect routing
Check spark plug condition and gap

Table 3 MONTHLY MAINTENANCE SCHEDULE

Check drive belt length and width for excessive wear
Check drive and driven pulley
Check drive chain condition
Check chaincase oil level
Lubricate rear suspension and spindles
Check cooling fan drive belt tension and condition (air cooled models)
Check the fuel system for leaks, damage or wear and repair as required
Check fuel filter

Table 4 RECOMMENDED LUBRICANTS AND FUEL

Item	Type
Countershaft bearing, hub bearings, bogie wheels, ski legs, idler bearings, leaf spring cushion pads	A
Oil seal interior lips	A
Engine injection oil	B
(continued)	

Table 4 RECOMMENDED LUBRICANTS AND FUEL (continued)

Item	Type
Chaincase	C
Fuel	D

Legend:
A. Multipurpose lithium base grease for use through a temperature range of -40° to 95° C (-40° to 203° F). This grease will be referred to as a low temperature grease throughout this manual.
B. Arctco 50:1 Injection Oil or equivalent. Injection oil must flow at -40° C (-40° F).
C. Arctco Transmission Lube (part No. 0636-817) chaincase oil or equivalent. Make sure equivalent oil provides lubrication at low temperatures.
D. Unleaded gasoline with octane rating of 87 or higher. If oxygenates are added to the gasoline, ethanol content should not exceed 10 % and MTBE should not exceed 15 %. If oxygenated gasoline is used, install a main jet one size larger than standard in the carburetor. It is not necessary to add antifreeze fluid to the fuel if gasoline blended with ethanol is used.

Table 5 APPROXIMATE REFILL CAPACITY

Chaincase		
1990-1998	236 cc	8 oz.
With reverse 1990-1998	354 cc	12 oz.
Cooling system		
1990-1991	–	–
1992	2.4 L	2.5 qt.
1993	2.9 L	3 qt.
1994		
Cougar	2.4 L	2.5 qt.
EXT 580	3.3 L	3.5 qt.
ZR440, ZR580	2.9 L	3 qt.
1995		
Z 440	air-cooled	
ZR 440	2.9 L	3 qt.
Cougar, Cougar Mtn. Cat	3.3 L	3.5 qt.
Prowler 2-Up	3.3 L	3.5 qt.
EXT 580 (all models)	2.9 L	3 qt.
ZR 580, ZR 580 EFI	2.9 L	3 qt.
1996		
Z 440	air-cooled	
ZR 440	2.9 L	3 qt.
Cougar	3.3 L	3.5 qt.
Cougar Mtn. Cat, Cougar 2-Up	3.3 L	3.5 qt.
EXT 580 (all models)	2.9 L	3 qt.
ZR 580	2.9 L	3 qt.
ZRT 600	4.2 L	4.4 qt.
1997		
Z 440	air-cooled	
Panther 440	air-cooled	
ZL 440, ZR 440	2.9 L	3 qt.
Cougar	2.9 L	3 qt.
Cougar Mtn. Cat	2.9 L	3 qt.
Panther 550	2.9 L	3 qt.
Pantera EFI	3.1 L	3.3 qt.

(continued)

Table 5 APPROXIMATE REFILL CAPACITY (continued)

Cooling system		
1997		
Powder Special (with carburetors)	4.2 L	4.4 qt.
EXT 580 EFI	3.1 L	3.3 qt.
EXT 580 EFI DLX	3.1 L	3.3 qt.
Powder Special EFI	3.1 L	3.3 qt.
ZR 580	3.1 L	3.3 qt.
EXT 600, ZRT 600	4.2 L	4.4 qt.
Powder Extreme	4.2 L	4.4 qt.
1998		
Z 440	air-cooled	
Panther 440	air-cooled	
ZL 440, ZR 440	2.9 L	3 qt.
ZL 500, ZR 500	3.1 L	3.3 qt.
Cougar, Cougar DLX	2.9 L	3 qt.
Cougar Mtn. Cat	2.9 L	3 qt.
Panther 550	2.9 L	3 qt.
Pantera EFI	2.9 L	3 qt.
Powder Special (with carburetors)	4.2 L	4.4 qt.
EXT 580 EFI	2.9 L	3 qt.
EXT 580 EFI DLX	2.9 L	3 qt.
Powder Special EFI	3.1 L	3.3 qt.
ZR 600	3.1 L	3.3 qt.
EXT 600, ZRT 600	4.2 L	4.4 qt.
Powder Extreme	4.2 L	4.4 qt.
Fuel tank		
1990	29.5 L	7.8 gal.
1991		
Prowler	–	–
Cougar	–	–
El Tigre EXT	–	–
1992		
Cougar	27.3 L	7.2 gal.
Prowler	27.3 L	7.2 gal.
El Tigre EXT	–	–
1993		
440 ZR	34 L	9 gal.
Cougar	–	–
Prowler	–	–
Prowler II	–	–
580 ZR	34 L	9 gal.
EXT 550	–	–
EXT 580 Z	–	–
EXT 580 Mountain Cat	–	–
1994		
Cougar	41.6 L	11 gal.
Cougar Mountain Cat	41.6 L	11 gal.
Prowler, Prowler 2-up	–	–
ZR 440	38 L	10 gal.
EXT 580	42 L	11 gal.
EXT 580 Mountain Cat	–	–
ZR 580	38 L	10 gal.

(continued)

Table 5 APPROXIMATE REFILL CAPACITY (continued)

Fuel tank		
1995		
Z 440	37.5 L	9.9 gal.
ZR 440	38 L	10 gal.
Cougar	41.7 L	11 gal.
Cougar Mountain Cat	41.7 L	11 gal.
Prowler 2-Up	41.7 L	11 gal.
EXT 580	–	–
EXT 580 EFI	42 L	11 gal.
EXT 580 EFI Mountain Cat	–	–
ZR 580, ZR 580 EFI	37.5 L	9.9 gal.
1996		
Z 440	37.5 L	9.9 gal.
ZR 440	37.5 L	9.9 gal.
Cougar	–	–
Cougar Mountain Cat	–	–
EXT 580	–	–
EXT 580 EFI	–	–
EXT 580 EFI Mountain Cat	–	–
EXT 580 Powder Special	–	–
EXT 580 EFI Deluxe	–	–
ZR 580	–	–
ZR 580 EFI	–	–
ZRT 600	33.7 L	8.9 gal.
1997		
Z 440	39.7 L	10.5 gal.
Panther 440	39.7 L	10.5 gal.
ZL 440, ZR 440	37.5 L	9.9 gal.
ZR 580 EFI	35.9 L	9.5 gal.
Cougar, Cougar Mountain Cat	34.1 L	9 gal.
Panther 550	34.1 L	9 gal.
EXT 580 EFI	39.7 L	10.5 gal.
EXT 580 DLX	39.7 L	10.5 gal.
Pantera	39.7 L	10.5 gal.
Powder Special EFI	39.7 L	10.5 gal.
EXT 600	37.5 L	9.9 gal.
ZRT 600	37.5 L	9.9 gal.
Powder Extreme	35.9 L	9.5 gal.
1998		
Z 440	39.7 L	10.5 gal.
Panther 440	39.7 L	10.5 gal.
ZL 440, ZR 440	35.7 L	9.4 gal.
ZL 500	35.7 L	9.4 gal.
Cougar, Cougar Deluxe	37.1 L	9.8 gal.
Cougar Mountain Cat	35.4 L	9.4 gal.
Panther 550	35.4 L	9.4 gal.
EXT 580 EFI	40.1 L	10.6 gal.
EXT 580 EFI DLX	40.1 L	10.6 gal.
Pantera	39.7 L	10.5 gal.
Powder Special EFI	39.7 L	10.5 gal.
EXT 600	41.3 L	10.9 gal.
EXT 600 Touring	35.4 L	9.4 gal.
ZRT 600	37.1 L	9.8 gal.
Powder Extreme	35.9 L	9.5 gal.

Table 6 TRACK TENSION

Force Kg. (lb.)	9 (20)
Deflection mm (in.)	
During break-in	19-25 (3/4-1)
After break-in except long track models	19-25 (3/4-1)
After break-in long track models	25-32 (1-1 1/4)

3

Table 7 MAINTENANCE TIGHTENING TORQUES

	N·m	ft.-lb.
Cylinder base screws or nuts		
Prowler	30-40	22-30
Cougar		
1991-1994	30-40	22-30
1995-1998	40-60	30-44
Panther	40-60	30-44
Powder Extreme, Powder Special	18-28	13-21
Z 440 (cyl./head)	18-28	13-21
ZL 440/500	30-40	22-30
ZR 440	30-40	22-30
El Tigre (529 cc)		
M8	18-22	13-16
M10	30-40	22-30
El Tigre (550 cc)	30-40	22-30
EXT 550	30-40	22-30
EXT 580		
1994	30-40	22-30
1995-1998	40-60	30-44
ZR 580		
1993-1994	30-40	22-30
1995-1997	40-60	30-44
EXT 600	18-28	13-21
ZRT 600	18-28	13-21
Cylinder head		
Prowler	18-28	13-21
Cougar	18-28	13-21
Panther	18-28	13-21
Powder Extreme, Powder Special	20-25	15-18
Z 440 (cyl./head)	18-28	13-21
ZL 440/500	18-28	13-21
ZR 440	18-28	13-21
El Tigre (529 cc)	20-25	15-18
El Tigre (550 cc)	18-28	13-21
EXT 550	18-28	13-21
EXT 580	18-28	13-21
ZR 580	18-28	13-21
ZRT 600	20-25	15-18
EXT 600	20-25	15-18
Engine mounts		
Prowler 1990-1994		
Engine mounts to frame	28-35	21-26
Mount plate to engine	76	56

(continued)

Table 7 MAINTENANCE TIGHTENING TORQUES (continued)

	N·m	ft.-lb.
Engine mounts		
Prowler 1995		
Engine mounts to frame	76	56
Mount plate to engine	28-35	21-26
Cougar 1990-1994		
Engine mounts to frame	28-35	21-26
Mount plate to engine	76	56
Cougar 1995-1998		
Engine mounts to frame	76	56
Mount plate to engine	28-35	21-26
Z 440 and Panther 440 1995-1997		
Engine mounts to frame	28-35	21-26
Mount plate to engine	76	56
Z 440 and Panther 440 1998		
Engine mounts to frame	28	21
Mount plate to engine	76	56
ZL 440 1997		
Engine mounts to frame	28	21
Mount plate to engine	76	56
ZL 440/500 1998		
Engine mounts to frame	28-35	21-26
Mount plate to engine	24	18
ZR 440 1993-1995		
Engine mounts to frame	42	31
Mount plate to engine	76	56
ZR 440 1996-1998		
Front engine mounts to frame	28-35	21-26
Right-rear engine mount to frame	28-35	21-26
Left-rear engine mount to frame	69	51
El Tigre 1990-1992		
Engine mounts to frame	28-35	21-26
Mount plate to engine	76	56
EXT 550 1993	18-28	13-21
Engine mounts to frame	28-35	21-26
Mount plate to engine	76	56
EXT 580 1994-1998		
Mounting brackets to engine	24	18
Engine mounts to frame	28-35	21-26
ZR 580 1993-1997		
Engine mounts to frame	42	31
Mount plate to engine	76	56
ZRT 600 1996-1998		
Mounting brackets to engine	24	18
PTO-side mount to engine	14	10
Engine mounts to frame	42	31
EXT 600, Powder Extreme 1998		
Mounting brackets to engine	24	18
PTO-side mount to engine	14	10
Engine mounts to frame	42	31
Exhaust manifold		
El Tigre (529 cc) 1990-1991	15-19	11-14
All other models	18-22	13-16

(continued)

Table 7 MAINTENANCE TIGHTENING TORQUES (continued)

	N·m	ft.-lb.
Water manifold (thermostat housing)		
Models so equipped	7-10	5-7
Reed block		
Models so equipped	8-12	6-9
Flywheel nut		
El Tigre	90-110	66-81
Prowler		
1990-1993	90-110	66-81
1994-1995	69-90	51-66
All other models	69-90	51-66
Starter pulley to flywheel		
El Tigre (529 cc) 1990-1991	–	–
All other models	10	7
Spark plug	25-28	18-21

Table 8 SPARK PLUGS

	Plug type	Gap mm (in.)
1998 models	NGK BR9EYA	0.7 (0.028)
1997 Powder Special EFI	NGK BR9EYA	0.7 (0.028)
1997 ZR 580 EFI	NGK BR9EYA	0.7 (0.028)
All other models	NGK BR9ES	0.7 (0.028)

Table 9 IGNITION TIMING

	mm	in.	Degrees @ RPM
1990			
Prowler	1.860	0.073	18 @ 6000
El Tigre EXT	2.725	0.107	21 @ 6000
1991			
Cougar, Prowler	1.860	0.073	18 @ 6000
El Tigre EXT	2.725	0.107	21 @ 6000
1992			
Cougar, Prowler	1.860	0.073	18 @ 6000
El Tigre EXT	3.531	0.139	24 @ 6000
1993			
440 ZR	3.240	0.128	24 @ 6000
Cougar, Prowler	1.836	0.072	18 @ 6000
EXT 550	3.531	0.128	24 @ 6000
580 ZR, EXT 580 Z	3.834	0.151	25 @ 6000
1994			
Cougar, Prowler	1.836	0.072	18 @ 6000
ZR 440	3.240	0.128	24 @ 6000
EXT 580	3.834	0.151	25 @ 6000
ZR 580	3.834	0.151	25 @ 6000
1995			
Z 440	2.032	0.080	18 @ 6000
ZR 440	3.540	0.139	25 @ 6000
Cougar, Prowler 2-Up	3.531	0.139	24 @ 6000
EXT 580, EXT 580 EFI	5.459	0.215	30 @ 4000
ZR 580, ZR 580 EFI	5.459	0.215	30 @ 4000

(continued)

3

Table 9 IGNITION TIMING (continued)

	mm	in.	Degrees @ RPM
1996			
Z 440	2.032	0.080	18 @ 6000
ZR 440	2.384	0.093	20 @ 6000
Cougar	3.540	0.139	24 @ 6000
EXT 580, EXT 580 EFI	5.459	0.215	30 @ 4000
ZR 580, ZR 580 EFI	5.459	0.215	30 @ 4000
ZRT 600	3.884	0.153	27 @ 4000
1997			
Z 440	2.032	0.080	18 @ 6000
Panther 440	2.032	0.080	18 @ 6000
ZL 440	1.860	0.073	18 @ 6000
ZR 440	2.387	0.094	20 @ 6000
Panther 550	3.540	0.139	24 @ 6000
ZR 580 EFI	5.459	0.215	30 @ 4000
Cougar, Cougar Mountain Cat	3.540	0.139	24 @ 6000
EXT 580, EXT 580 EFI	5.459	0.215	30 @ 4000
Powder Special	5.459	0.215	30 @ 4000
EXT 600, ZRT 600, Powder Extreme	3.884	0.153	27 @ 4000
1998			
Z 440	2.012	0.079	18 @ 6000
Panther 440	2.012	0.079	18 @ 6000
ZL 440	1.860	0.073	18 @ 6000
ZR 440	1.937	0.076	18 @ 6000
ZL 500	3.390	0.133	24 @ 4000
Panther 550	3.540	0.139	24 @ 6000
Pantera 580	5.459	0.215	30 @ 4000
Cougar, Cougar Mountain Cat	3.540	0.139	24 @ 6000
EXT 580 EFI	5.459	0.215	30 @ 4000
Powder Special	3.390	0.133	24 @ 3250
EXT 600, ZRT 600, Powder Extreme	3.884	0.153	27 @ 4000
EXT Triple Touring	3.884	0.153	27 @ 4000

Table 10 IGNITION TIMING TYPE

	Trigger coil
1990	
Prowler, El Tigre EXT	Under flywheel
1991	
Cougar, Prowler, El Tigre EXT	Under flywheel
1992	
Cougar, Prowler, El Tigre EXT	Under flywheel
1993	
440 ZR, 580 ZR, EXT 550, EXT 580	Under flywheel
Cougar, Prowler	Under flywheel
1994	
Cougar, Prowler, ZR 440, EXT 580, ZR 580	Under flywheel
1995	
Models with carburetor	Under flywheel
Models with Electronic Fuel Injection	Outside flywheel

(continued)

Table 10 IGNITION TIMING TYPE (continued)

	Trigger coil
1996	
Z 440, ZR 440, Cougar, Cougar 2-Up	Under flywheel
Electronic Fuel Injected 580 models	Outside flywheel
580 models with carburetor	Under flywheel
ZRT 600	Outside flywheel
1997	
Z 440, ZL 440, ZR 440	Under flywheel
ZR 580 EFI	Outside flywheel
Cougar	Under flywheel
EXT 580 EFI	Outside flywheel
EXT 600, ZRT 600, Powder Extreme	Outside flywheel
Panther 440 and 550	Under flywheel
Pantera	Outside flywheel
Powder Special	Under flywheel
Powder Special EFI	Outside flywheel
1998	
Z 440, ZL 440, ZR 440	Under flywheel
ZL 550 EFI	Outside flywheel
ZR 580 EFI	Outside flywheel
Cougar	Under flywheel
EXT 580 EFI	Outside flywheel
EXT 600, ZRT 600, Powder Extreme	Outside flywheel
Panther 440 and 550	Under flywheel
Pantera	Outside flywheel
Powder Special	Outside flywheel
Powder Special EFI	Outside flywheel

Table 11 CARBURETOR PILOT AIR SCREW AND IDLE SPEED

	Pilot air screw turns out*	Idle speed rpm
1990		
Prowler	1-1/2	2000-2500
El Tigre EXT	1	2000-2500
1991-1992		
Cougar, Prowler, El Tigre EXT	1	2000-2500
1993		
440 ZR	1-1 1/2	1500
Cougar, Prowler	1	2000-2500
EXT 550	1	1500-2000
580 ZR, EXT 580 Z	1-1 1/2	1500
1994		
Cougar, Prowler	1	1500-2000
ZR 440, ZR 580	1	1500-2000
EXT 580	1-1 1/2	1500-2000
1995		
Z 440, ZR 440	1	1500-2000
Cougar, Prowler 2-Up	1	1500-2000
EXT 580, ZR 580 (carbureted)	1-1 1/2	1500-2000

(continued)

Table 11 CARBURETOR PILOT AIR SCREW AND IDLE SPEED (continued)

	Pilot air screw turns out*	Idle speed rpm
1996		
Z 440	1	1500-2000
ZR 440	1	1500-2000
Cougar, Cougar 2-Up	1	1500-2000
EXT 580, ZR 580 (carbureted)	1-1 1/2	1500-2000
ZRT 600	1 1/2	1500-2000
1997		
Z 440	1	1500-2000
ZL 440, ZR 440	1	1500-2000
Panther 440 and 550	1	1500-2000
Cougar	1	1500-2000
Powder Special	1-1 1/2	1500-2000
EXT 600, ZRT 600, Powder Extreme	1 1/2	1500-2000
1998		
Z 440	3/4	1500-2000
Panther 440	1	1500-2000
ZL 440	1 1/2	1500-2000
ZR 440	1 1/4	1500-2000
ZL 500	1	1500-2000
Panther 550	1	1500-2000
Cougar	1	1500-2000
Powder Special	1 1/4	1500-2000
EXT 600, ZRT 600	1 1/2	1500-2000
Powder Extreme	1	1500-2000

*The listed number indicates the recommended initial setting (turns out from lightly seated) and is usually correct within ±1/8 turn.

Chapter Four

Adjustments for Special Use

If the snowmobile is to deliver its maximum efficiency and peak performance, the engine and chassis must be properly adjusted to the conditions in which it is being operated. This chapter describes carburetor changes for different altitudes and adjustments to the rear suspension for different snow conditions.

Basic tune-up procedures are described in Chapter Three. **Tables 1-5** are found at the end of the chapter.

CARBURETOR TUNING

Arctic Cat snowmobiles are tuned at the factory for sea level conditions. However, when the snowmobile is operated at a higher altitude, engine performance will drop because of a change in air density. At sea level, the air is quite a bit denser than the air at 10,000 feet. You should figure on a three percent loss of power output for every increase of 1,000 feet of elevation. This decrease in power is caused by a drop in cylinder pressure and a change in the air/fuel ratio. For example, an engine that produces 40 horsepower at sea level will produce approximately 38.8 horsepower at 1,000 feet. At 10,000 feet, the engine produces 29.5 horsepower. With sea level jetting, the engine would run extremely rich at 10,000 feet.

Conversely, if the carburetors are adjusted for proper operation at 10,000 feet altitude, the engine would run lean when operated at lower altitudes. Lean conditions reduce performance and also lead to overheating and detonation, both of which can result in severe engine damage.

Air temperature must also be considered when jetting the carburetor. For example, the carburetors are set at the factory to run at temperatures of -4 to 32° F (-20 to 0° C) at sea level. Adjust the carburetors using the following information if the snowmobile is to be operated under conditions other than those specified.

Figure 1 illustrates the different carburetor circuits and how they overlap during engine operation.

Before adjusting the carburetor, make the following adjustments as described in Chapter Three:

a. carburetor adjustment (including synchronization).
b. oil pump adjustment.

NOTE
Changes in the ports (shape or smoothness), expansion chamber or carburetor will also require jetting changes because these factors alter the engine's ability to breathe. Aftermarket equipment manufacturers or engine modifiers usually provide adjustment information so the engine will operate at peak perfomance. This information should be taken into account along with altitude and temperature conditions previously mentioned.

NOTE
It is important to note that the following jetting guidelines should be used as guidelines only. Individual adjustments will vary because of altitude, temperature and snow conditions. The condition of the spark plugs should be used as the determining factor when changing jets and adjusting the carburetor.

Carburetor Adjustment

Refer to **Table 1** for recommended standard jet size originally installed in your model. The sizes and settings listed in **Table 1** are approximate. Changes from the sizes and settings listed may be necessary even for the altitudes listed. It will probably be necessary to reduce the jet size when the snowmobile is going to be run at a high altitude. Replace jets as required. Refer to Chapter Six for carburetor removal and disassembly.

Low speed tuning

The pilot jet and pilot air screw control the fuel mixture from 0 to about 1/4 throttle (**Figure 1**).

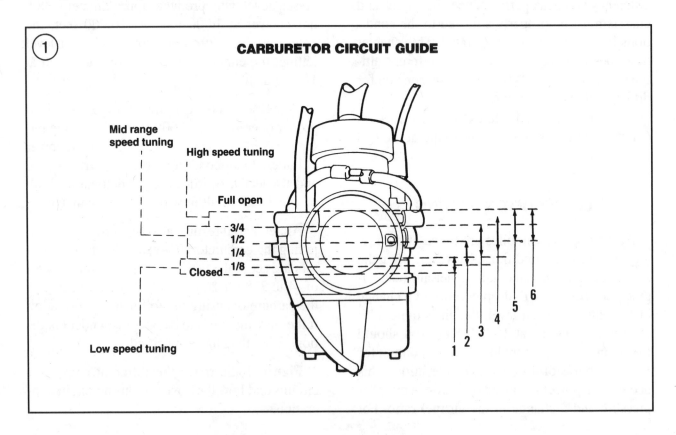

CARBURETOR CIRCUIT GUIDE

Mid range speed tuning
High speed tuning
Full open
3/4
1/2
1/4
1/8
Closed
Low speed tuning

In addition, the pilot air screw controls mixture adjustment when the throttle is opened from idle to the full open position quickly and when the engine is run at half-throttle. Note the following when adjusting the pilot air screw:

    a. Turning the pilot air screw clockwise closes the pilot air and richens the fuel mixture at idle.

    b. Turning the pilot air screw counterclockwise leans the fuel mixture.

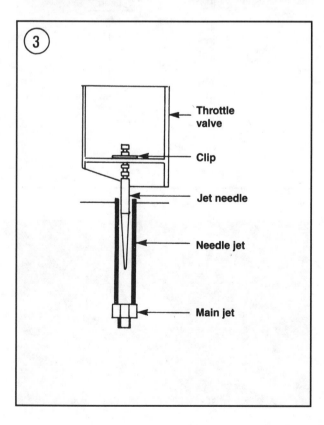

    c. Pilot jets are identified by number. Pilot jets with larger numbers will flow more fuel than jets with smaller numbers. Installing jets with larger numbers will richen the fuel mixture.

    d. When operating the snowmobile in relatively warm weather or at a higher altitude, turn the pilot air screw counterclockwise. When operating the snowmobile in excessively cold weather conditions, turn the pilot air screw clockwise to richen the mixture.

1. Open the hood.

NOTE
__Figure 2__ shows the carburetor removed for clarity.

2. Locate the pilot air screw (A, **Figure 2**) on the side of each carburetor.

3. Turn the pilot air screws in until they seat very lightly.

4. Back the screws out the number of turns specified for your model in **Table 2**.

5. Start the engine and allow it to warm to normal operating temperature.

6. Adjust the throttle stop screw (B, **Figure 2**) until the engine is idling as near as possible to the correct idle speed listed in **Table 1**.

NOTE
While adjusting the pilot air screws in Step 7, it will occasionally be necessary to turn the idle speed stop screws (B, __Figure 2__) counterclockwise to keep the idle speed at 1,500-2,000 rpm. Maintain the speed as close to the idle speed listed in __Table 2__ as possible.

7. Begin turning the pilot air screws (A, **Figure 2**) slowly counterclockwise until the engine is idling smoothly at the highest engine speed. Turning the pilot air screws counterclockwise will richen the fuel mixture.

8. To check the pilot air screw setting, proceed as follows:

a. Turn both mixture screws clockwise slightly to see if the engine's speed increases.

b. *If the speed increases*, continue turning both screws until the speed begins to slow, then turn the screws (B, **Figure 2**) counterclockwise until the engine is idling smoothly at the highest engine speed.

c. If the speed *does not increase*, turn the screws back to their original settings and continue to Step 9.

9. When the pilot air screws are set to provide the optimum mixture at idle speed, operate the snowmobile and check performance.

10. If performance is off at high altitudes or in extremely cold temperature, it may be necessary to install larger pilot jets. Refer to Chapter Six for carburetor removal and disassembly.

11. If the off-idle pickup is poor, richen the idle mixture slightly by turning the pilot air screws clockwise slightly, then repeat Step 9. If off-idle pickup is poor after readjusting the pilot air screws, it may be necessary to install smaller pilot jets. After replacing the pilot jets, repeat Steps 2-9.

Mid-range tuning

The position of the jet needle (**Figure 3**) controls the mixture at medium speeds, from approximately 1/4 to 3/4 throttle (**Figure 1**). The lower part of the jet needle is tapered and extends into the needle jet. A clip installed at the top of the jet needle positions the jet needle in the throttle valve.

When the throttle valve is lowered to the idle speed position, the jet needle is also at its lowest position, which closes most of the needle jet opening as shown in **Figure 3**. Until the throttle valve is raised to approximately 1/4 open, the opening between the needle jet and jet needle is so small that fuel cannot flow through the space. As the throttle valve is raised, the tapered portion

of the jet needle also moves up opening the needle jet.

The top of the jet needle has five evenly spaced grooves (**Figure 4**). A clip is installed in one of these grooves to attach the jet needle to the throttle valve. The position of the jet needle in relation to the throttle valve is determined by the position of the clip. Installing the clip in a higher groove will lower the needle deeper into the jet resulting in a leaner mixture. Installing the clip in a lower groove will raise the needle resulting in a richer mixture.

1. Open the hood.

NOTE
Prior to removing the top cap, thoroughly clean the area around it so that no dirt can fall into the carburetor.

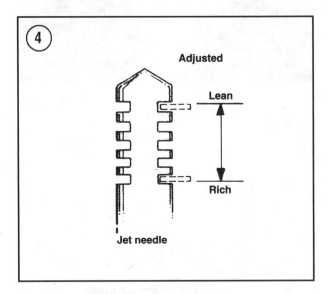

2. Unscrew and remove the carburetor top cap (**Figure 5**) and pull the throttle valve assembly (**Figure 6**) from the carburetor.

3. Remove the jet needle (**Figure 7**, typical) from the throttle valve.

NOTE
Some models have a washer installed on the jet needle. Do not lose the washer,

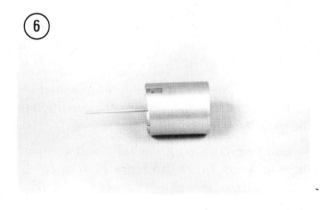

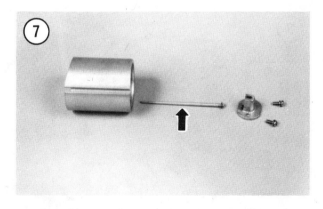

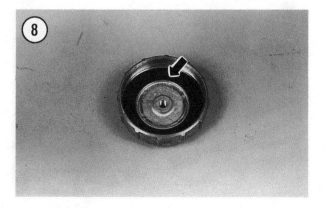

screws or any other small pieces when removing the jet needle.

4. Note the position of the clip (**Figure 4**) before removing it. Remove the clip and reposition it on the jet needle. Make sure the clip seats in the needle groove completely.

5. Reverse the procedure to assemble. Make sure the seal (**Figure 8**) in the cap is positioned correctly before installing the cap.

4

High-speed tuning

The main jet controls the mixture from 3/4 to full open throttle (**Figure 1**). The main jet also has some effect at lesser throttle openings. Each main jet is stamped with a number. Larger numbers provide a richer mixture, smaller numbers a leaner mixture. Refer to **Table 1** for the initial size of the main jet.

When operating the snowmobile in relatively warm weather or at a higher altitude, a smaller main jet should be used. When operating the snowmobile in excessively cold weather conditions and lower altitudes, install a larger main jet.

CAUTION
*The information given in **Table 1** for determining main jet sizes should be used as a guideline only. Variables may exist with each individual machine and the specific operating condition. Spark plug condition is the most reliable source of information regarding carburetor jetting, but the ability to correctly read the spark plugs is gained by experience. Incorrect changes can seriously damage the engine, therefore it is suggested that an Arctic Cat dealer in the area where you will be operating be consulted regarding approximate jetting changes. When in doubt, always select jets on the rich side.*

1. Determine the altitude and temperature range in which the snowmobile will be operated.

2. Refer to **Table 1** and find your snowmobile model and production year.

3. Check the specifications listed in **Table 1** and note if there are changes suggested for the operating altitude.

4. If changes are recommended, begin by making these changes. Refer to Chapter Six for carburetor removal and installation.

> *CAUTION*
> *The engine can be damaged by operating without the air intake silencer installed even while tuning. Always reassemble the snowmobile while testing.*

> *WARNING*
> *If you are taking spark plug readings, the engine will be HOT! Be careful whenever any fuel is spilled, such as when the main jet cover is removed from the bottom of the float bowl. Spilled fuel is an extreme fire hazard. Have a fire extinguisher and an assistant standing by when performing this procedure.*

5. Run the snowmobile at high speed and then stop the engine.

6. Open the hood and remove the spark plugs. Read the spark plugs as described in this chapter.

7. Reinstall the spark plugs.

8. If it is necessary to change the main jets, perform the following:

   a. Remove the carburetor as described in Chapter Six.

   b. Remove the float bowl (**Figure 9**) or the bowl plug.

   c. Remove and replace the main jet (**Figure 10**).

   d. Reinstall the float bowl. Make sure the float bowl gasket is in place and not torn or damaged.

   e. Repeat the procedure for the remaining carburetor(s).

   f. Reinstall the carburetors as described in Chapter Six.

   g. Make sure the throttle cables work smoothly before starting the engine.

Reading Spark Plugs

Because the firing end of a spark plug operates in the combustion chamber, it reflects the operating condition of the engine. Much information about engine and spark plug performance can be determined by careful examination of the spark plug. This information is only valid after performing the following steps.

1. Ride the snowmobile a short distance at full throttle.

2. Turn the ignition switch to the OFF position before closing the throttle, then coast and brake to a stop.

3. Remove the spark plugs. Keep the plug for each cylinder separate, because the condition of the plugs may not be alike.

4. Examine each plug carefully and compare them to those shown in **Figure 11**. The conditions of the removed plugs may not be as obvious

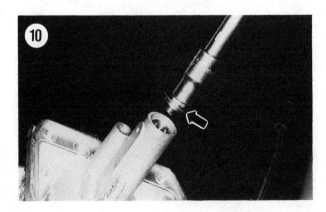

(11)

SPARK PLUG CONDITIONS

NORMAL USE

OIL FOULED

CARBON FOULED

OVERHEATED

GAP BRIDGED

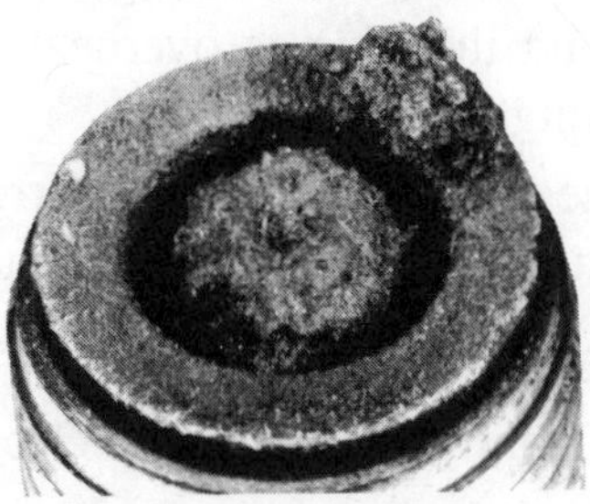

SUSTAINED PREIGNITION

WORN OUT

4

as those shown, while still exhibiting the same condition.

Normal condition

If the plug has a light tan- or gray-colored deposit and no abnormal gap wear or erosion, good engine, carburetion and ignition condition are indicated. The plug is of the proper heat range and may be serviced and returned to use.

Carbon fouled

Soft, dry, sooty deposits covering the entire firing end of the plug are evidence of incomplete combustion. Even though the firing end of the plug is dry, the plug's insulation decreases. An electrical path is formed that lowers the voltage from the ignition system. Engine misfiring is a sign of carbon fouling. Carbon fouling can be caused by one or more of the following:

  a. Too rich fuel mixture (incorrect jetting).
  b. Spark plug heat range too cold.
  c. Over-retarded ignition timing.
  d. Ignition component failure.
  e. Low engine compression.

Oil fouled

The tip of an oil fouled plug has a black insulator tip, a damp oily film over the firing end and a carbon layer over the entire nose. The electrodes will not be worn. This condition may occur following engine service. The oil used during assembly, oil added to the first tank of fuel and the oil normally injected by the injection system may foul the spark plugs. These procedures are used on a newly overhauled engine to ensure adequate initial lubrication. The condition should be corrected by cleaning or changing the spark plugs after using the first tank of gasoline/oil mix and filling the tank with gasoline. Other causes for this condition are:

  a. Too much oil in the fuel (incorrect mixture of gasoline and oil or incorrect oil pump adjustment).
  b. Wrong type of oil.
  c. Ignition component failure.
  d. Spark plug heat range too cold.
  e. Engine still being broken in.

Oil fouled spark plugs may be cleaned in an emergency, but it is better to replace them. It is important to correct the cause of fouling before the engine is returned to service.

Gap bridging

Plugs with this condition exhibit gaps shorted by combustion deposits between the electrodes. If this condition is encountered, check for an improper oil type, excessive carbon in the combustion chamber or a clogged exhaust port and pipe. Be sure to locate and correct the cause of this condition.

Overheating

Badly worn electrodes and premature gap wear are signs of overheating, along with a gray or white "blistered" porcelain insulator surface. The most common cause for this condition is using a spark plug with a heat range that is too hot. If you have not changed to a hotter spark plug and the plug is overheated, consider the following causes:

  a. Lean fuel mixture (incorrect main jet or incorrect oil pump adjustment).
  b. Ignition timing too advanced.
  c. Cooling system malfunction.
  d. Engine air leak.
  e. Improper spark plug installation (overtightening).
  f. No spark plug gasket.

Worn out

Corrosive gases formed by combustion and high voltage sparks have eroded the electrodes. Spark plugs in this condition require more voltage to fire under hard acceleration. Replace with a new spark plug.

Preignition

If the electrodes are melted, preignition is almost certainly the cause. Check for carburetor mounting or intake manifold leaks and overadvanced ignition timing. It is also possible that a plug with a heat range that is too hot is being used. Find the cause of the preignition before returning the engine into service.

HIGH-ALTITUDE CLUTCH TUNING

Standard clutch and drive specifications are listed in **Tables 3-4**. When the snowmobile is operated at an altitude of more than 4,000 feet (1,200 meters), it may be necessary to adjust the clutch to compensate for engine power loss. If the clutch is not adjusted, the engine may bog down when the belt engages. The engine may also bog when running in deep snow. Both conditions can lead to premature drive belt failure.

Refer to Chapter Thirteen for complete clutch service procedures.

GEARING

Depending upon altitude, snow and track conditions, a different gear ratio may be required. Snow conditions that offer few rough sections may require less gear reduction. Less optimum snow conditions or more rugged terrain require more gear reduction. Refer to the sprocket specifications chart in **Table 4**. Replacement sprockets and chains can be purchased through Arctic Cat dealers. Refer to Chapter Fourteen for sprocket and chain replacement procedures.

SPRING SUSPENSION ADJUSTMENT

You can adjust the suspension to accommodate rider weight and snow conditions.

Correct suspension adjustment is arrived at largely through a matter of trial-and-error tuning. There are several fundamental points that must be understood and applied before the suspension can be successfully adjusted to your needs.

Ski pressure—the load on the skis relative to the load on the track—is the primary factor controlling handling performance. If the ski pressure is too light, the front of the machine tends to float and steering control becomes vague, with the machine tending to drive straight ahead rather than turn, and wander when running straight at steady throttle.

On the other hand, if ski pressure is too heavy, the machine tends to plow during cornering and the skis dig in during straight-line running rather than stay on top of the snow.

Ski pressure for one snow condition is not necessarily good for another condition. For instance, if the surface is very hard and offers little steering traction, added ski pressure—to permit the skis to dig into the snow—is desirable. Also, the hard surface will support the skis and not allow them to penetrate when the machine is running in a straight line under power.

On the other hand, if the surface is soft and tacky, lighter ski pressure is desirable to prevent the skis from sinking into the snow. Also, the increased traction afforded by the snow will allow the skis to turn with light pressure.

It is apparent, then, that good suspension adjustment involves a thorough analysis relating to ski pressure versus conditions. The suspension has been set at the factory to work in most conditions encountered by general riding. However, when the snowmobile is operated in varying or more difficult conditions, the suspension should be adjusted. It is important to remember that suspension tuning is a compromise. An adjustment that works well in one situation may not work as well in another.

The rear suspension is equipped with a front suspension arm and a rear suspension arm. Each arm is provided with a shock absorber and a spring or springs. On some models, the springs for the front arm are located at the ends of the front arm. On other models, the front shock absorber is fitted with a spring. On all models, the rear arm of the rear suspension is fitted with springs at the ends and a shock absorber attached to the middle of the rear arm.

Refer to the following to adjust the springs at each location.

Front Suspension Spring Preload

The front suspension shock absorber spring of some models is provided with adjusting nuts to adjust spring preload. See **Figures 12** and **13**. The length of the exposed threads (**Figure 14**) is adjustable on most models. The length of the exposed threads listed in **Table 5** is the initial setting of the spring preload nut. Changes may be necessary to provide the best handling.

Make sure the setting for one side is the same as the setting for the other. On models equipped with rebuildable shock absorbers, also check the pressure of the nitrogen charge. The charge

should be 200 psi (1380 kPa). Install the screw or cap over the charge valve.

CAUTION
Use a suitable, regulated nitrogen filling tank, regulator, gauge, hose and fittings to charge the shock with gas. If suitable equipment is not available, take the shock to an Arctic Cat dealer.

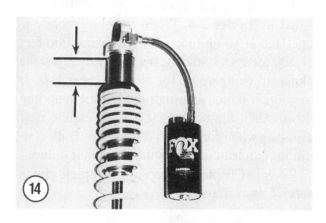

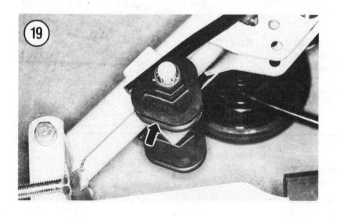

Rear Suspension
(Front Arm Spring Preload)

On some models, the spring for the front arm of the rear suspension is located at the ends of the front arm as shown in **Figure 15**. The spring tension is set at the factory for normal riding conditions. The initial setting is usually with 9 mm (3/8 in.) of threads showing behind the nut. Changes may be necessary and can be accomplished by turning the nut (**Figure 15**) to a different position on the eyebolt.

On some models, the spring for the front arm of the rear suspension is located on the shock absorber as shown in **Figures 16** or **17**. You can change the spring tension for models with the threaded setting nut (**Figure 17**) by turning the nut on the threaded body.

Rear Suspension
(Rear Arm Spring Preload)

The rear arm of the suspension system is provided with a spring located at each end as shown in **Figure 18**. You can adjust spring tension by turning the cams (**Figure 19**). Each of the three sides of the adjust cam is a different distance from the pivot bolt. The lowest spring setting is generally for riders weighing approximately 100 lb. The middle setting is for riders weighing 150-190 lb. The highest setting provides the most spring preload and is for riders weighing 200 lb. and above. Make sure the cams for both sides are set the same.

Rear Suspension Limit Straps

The front arm of the rear suspension system is equipped with limit straps. See **Figures 20** or **21**. The limit straps control weight transfer during acceleration. When the straps are longer, the track lead angle can be greater and more weight will be transferred to the track, resulting in better traction. When the straps are shortened, the track

4

lead angle will be reduced, allowing less weight transfer, but will also result in more positive steering control.

On some models, the straps are provided with several holes as shown in **Figure 20**. Make sure that both straps are adjusted the same. If the straps require replacement, replace both straps.

On some models, the limit straps are provided with adjustment at the attachment points shown in **Figure 21**. The length of the straps is adjusted by turning the self-locking nuts. Adjust both straps to the same length.

Slide Rails

The slide rails of many models have mounting holes that are not used on all models. The same

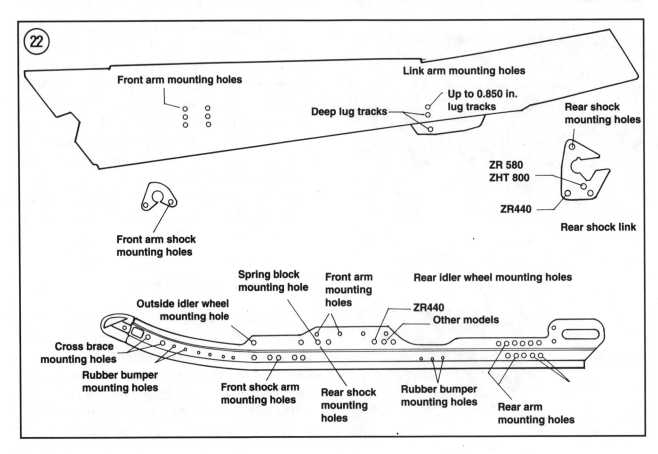

rail may be used on several models and certain holes may be used for only a few models. Refer to **Figure 22**. The holes are not intended to be used for tuning the suspension, but handling may be affected by assembly using the wrong holes.

Before unbolting parts from the slide rails, it is important to mark the original mounting locations. If the correct mounting location is unknown, contact an Arctic Cat dealer or inspect another snowmobile that is the same model.

Table 1 CARBURETOR SPECIFICATIONS

Year/Model	Main jet	Needle jet	Jet needle	Pilot jet	Idle mixture screw turns out	Idle speed
1990						
Prowler	240	Q-0(480)	6DH7-3	25	1	2000-2500
El Tigre EXT (VM34)	240	P-5(480)	6DH7-4	30	1-1 1/2	2000-2500
1991						
Prowler, Prowler Special, Cougar (VM36)	290	Q-5	6DH7-3	35	1	2000-2500
El Tigre EXT (VM34)	240	P-5(480)	6DH7-4	30	1-1 1/2	2000-2500
1992						
Prowler, Prowler Special, Cougar (VM36)	290	Q-5	6DH7-3	35	1	2000-2500
El Tigre EXT (VM38)	340	P-2(480)	6DH8-3	35	1	2000-2500
1993						
Prowler, Prowler Special, Cougar (VM36-162)	310	Q-5	6DH7-3	35	1	1500-2000
440 ZR	330	P-2(480)	6DH8-3	45	1	1500
EXT 550 (VM38)	340	P-2(480)	6DH8-3	35		1500
580 ZR (VM38)	340	P-2(480)	6DH8-3	35	1	1500
EXT 580 (VM38-269)	340	P-4(480)	6DH8-3	35	1	1500
1994						
Cougar, Cougar Mountain Cat, Prowler, Prowler II (VM36-162)	310	Q-5	6DH7-3	35	1	1500-2000
ZR 440 (VM38-271)	350	P-2(480)	6DH8-3	50	1	1500-1550
EXT 580 and EXT 580 Mountain Cat (VM38-269)	340	P-4(480)	6DH8-3	35	1	1500
ZR 580 (VM40)	400	Z-8(224)	7DJ5-2	45	1	1500-1550
1995						
Cougar, Cougar Mountain Cat, Prowler 2-Up (VM38-269)	340	P-2(480)	6DH8-3	35	1	1500
Z 440 (VM34-424)	280	P4(480)	6DH2-3	25	1	1500
ZR 440 (VM38)	290	P-4(159)	6DH2-4	35	1	1500

(continued)

Table 1 CARBURETOR SPECIFICATIONS (continued)

Year/Model	Main jet	Needle jet	Jet needle	Pilot jet	Idle mixture screw turns out	Idle speed
1995						
EXT 580, EXT 580						
Powder Special (VM38)	340	P-4(480)	6DH8-3	35	1	1500
ZR 580 (VM40)	370	AA-0(224)	7DH5-2	45	1	1500
1996						
Z 440 (VM34)	280	P4(480)	6DH2-3	25	1	1500
ZR 440 (VM38)	370	P-4(159)	6DH2-4	40	3/4-1 1/4	1500
Cougar,						
Cougar Mountain Cat,						
Cougar 2-Up (VM38-269)	340	P-2(480)	6DH8-3	35	1	1500
EXT 580, EXT 580						
Powder Special (VM38)	340	P-4(480)	6DH8-3	35	1	1500
ZRT 600 (VM36)	360	P-4(480)	6DH41-2	35	1 1/2	1500
1997						
Z 440 (VM34)	280	P-4(480)	6DH2-3	30	1	1500
ZL 440 (VM36)	310	Q-5(480)	6DH7-3	40	1	1500
ZR 440 (VM34)	340	P-4(159)	6DH7-3	35	1	1500
Panther 440 (VM34)	280	P-4(480)	6DH2-3	25	1	1500
Panther 550 (VM38)	340	P-2(480)	6DH8-3	40	1	1500
Cougar, Cougar Mountain						
Cat (VM38)	340	P-2(480)	6DH8-3	40	1	1500
Powder Special (VM38)	390	P-3(480)	6DH8-3	50	1 1/2	1500
EXT 600, ZRT 600 (VM36)	370	P-2(480)	6DH8-3	40	1 1/2	1500
1998						
Z 440 (VM34)	270	P-4(480)	6DH2-3	30	3/4	1500
ZL 440 (VM36)	250	Q-5(480)	6DH7-3	40	1 1/2	1500
ZR 440 (VM34)	330	P-7(159)	6DH7-3	40	1 1/4	1500
Panther 440 (VM34)	280	P-4(480)	6DH2-3	25	1	1500
ZL 500 (VM38)	360	Q-2(480)	6DH41-3	35	1	1500
Panther 550 (VM38)	340	P-2(480)	6DH8-3	40	1	1500
Cougar, Cougar Deluxe,						
Cougar Mountain						
Cat (VM38)	340	P-2(480)	6DH8-3	40	1 1/4	1500
Powder Special (VM38)	410	Q-3(480)	6EGJ1-3	40	1 1/4	1500
EXT 600, ZRT 600 (VM36)	370	P-2(480)	6DH8-3	40	1 1/2	1500

Table 2 DRIVEN PULLEY TORQUE BRACKET AND SPRING APPLICATION

Model	Spring part No./Color	Torque bracket part No. (angle degrees)
1990		
Prowler	0648-012/blue	0648-011 (48-44)
El Tigre EXT	–/yellow	0648-002 (53)
1991		
Prowler, Cougar	0648-012/blue	0648-011 (48-44)
El Tigre EXT	–/yellow	0648-002 (53)
1992		
Prowler, Cougar	0648-012/blue	0648-011 (48-44)
El Tigre EXT	–/yellow	0648-002 (53)

(continued)

Table 2 DRIVEN PULLEY TORQUE BRACKET AND SPRING APPLICATION (continued)

Model	Spring part No./Color	Torque bracket part No. (angle degrees)
1993		
Prowler, Cougar	0648-012/blue	0648-011 (48-44)
440 ZR	0148-227/yellow	0648-001 (52-44)
EXT 550	–	–
580 ZR	0148-227/yellow	0648-014 (49)
EXT 580	–	–
1994		
Cougar, Prowler	0648-012/blue	0648-011 (48-44)
ZR 440		
0-8000 ft.	0148-227/yellow	0648-002 (53)
8000-10,000 ft.	0148-227/yellow	0648-014 (49)
above 10,000 ft.	0148-227/yellow	0648-011 (48-44)
EXT 580, EXT 580 EFI		
0-10,000 ft.	0148-404/yellow	0648-014 (49)
10,000 ft.	0148-404/yellow	0648-011 (48-44)
ZR 580		
0-4000 ft.	0148-227/yellow	0648-002 (53)
4000-8000 ft.	0148-227/yellow	0148-222 (51)
above 8000 ft.	0148-227/yellow	0648-014 (49)
1995		
Cougar, Cougar Mountain Cat, Prowler 2-Up		
0-8000 ft.	0648-012/blue	0648-014 (49)
8000-10,000 ft.	0648-012/blue	0648-011 (48-44)
above 10,000 ft.	0148-227/yellow	0648-011 (48-44)
Z 440	0648-012/blue	0648-002 (53)
ZR 440		
0-8000 ft.	0148-227/yellow	0648-024 (55-53)
8000-10,000 ft.	0148-227/yellow	0148-222 (49)
above 10,000 ft.	0148-227/yellow	0648-011 (48-44)
EXT 580, EXT 580 EFI, EXT 580 Powder Special, ZR 580		
0-8000 ft.	0148-227/yellow	0648-002 (51)
8000-10,000 ft.	0148-227/yellow	0148-222 (49)
above 10,000 ft.	0148-227/yellow	0648-014 (47)
1996		
Z 440	0648-012/blue	0648-002 (53)
ZR 440	0148-227/yellow	0648-002 (53)
Cougar	–	–
Cougar Mountain Cat	–	–
Cougar 2-Up	–	–
EXT 580	–	–
EXT 580 EFI	–	–
EXT 580 EFI Mountain Cat	–	–
EXT 580 Powder Special	–	–
EXT 580 EFI Deluxe	–	–
ZR 580		
0-4000 ft.	0648-037/red	0648-058 (42-34)
4000-10,000 ft.	0648-060/blue	0648-058 (42-34)
above 10,000 ft.	0648-060/blue	0648-038 (34)

4

(continued)

Table 2 DRIVEN PULLEY TORQUE BRACKET AND SPRING APPLICATION (continued)

Model	Spring part No./Color	Torque bracket part No. (angle degrees)
1996		
ZRT 600		
0-4000 ft.	0148-227/yellow	0648-005 (55)
above 4000 ft.	0148-227/yellow	0648-002 (53)
1997		
Z 440	0648-012/blue	0648-002 (53)
ZL 440	0648-012/blue	0648—014 (49)
ZR 440	0148-227/yellow	0648-002 (53)
Panther 440	0648-012/blue	0648-002 (53)
Cougar	0148-227/yellow	0648-014 (49)
Panther	0148-227/yellow	0648-014 (49)
EXT 580 EFI	0148-227/yellow	0148-222 (51)
Pantera	0148-227/yellow	0148-222 (51)
Powder Special	0148-227/yellow	0648-002 (53)
ZR 580 EFI	0648-076/green	0648-058 (42-34)
EXT 600	0148-227/yellow	0648-005 (55)
ZRT 600	0148-227/yellow	0648-005 (55)
Powder Extreme	0148-227/yellow	0648-005 (55)
1998		
Z 440	0648-012/blue	0648-002 (53)
ZL 440	0148-227/yellow	0648-002 (53)
ZR 440		
0-5000 ft.	0148-227/yellow	0648-005 (55)
5000-9000 ft.	0148-227/yellow	0648-002 (53)
Above 9000 ft.	0148-227/yellow	0648-025 (47)
Panther 440	–	–
ZL 500	0148-227/yellow	0648-222 (51)
Cougar	0148-227/yellow	0648-014 (49)
Panther	0148-227/yellow	0648-014 (49)
EXT EFI	0148-227/yellow	0648-002 (53)
EXT EFI Deluxe	0148-227/yellow	0648-014 (49)
EXT Triple Touring	0148-227/yellow	0648-005 (55)
Pantera	0148-227/yellow	0648-014 (49)
Powder Special	0148-227/yellow	0648-002 (53)
ZR 580 EFI	0648-076/green	0648-058 (42-34)
EXT 600	0148-227/yellow	0648-005 (55)
ZRT 600	0148-227/yellow	0648-005 (55)
Powder Extreme	0148-227/yellow	0648-005 (55)

Table 3 CAM ARM SPECIFICATIONS

Model	Part No.	Weight (grams)
1990		
Prowler		
0-4000 ft.	0646-115	47.0
Prowler		
4000-8000 ft.	0146-530	44.5
8000-10,000 ft.	0646-018	43.5
above 10,000 ft.	0646-019	42.0
	(continued)	

Table 3 CAM ARM SPECIFICATIONS (continued)

Model	Part No.	Weight (grams)
1990		
El Tigre EXT		
0-4000 ft.	0646-098	54.5
4000-8000 ft.	0646-099	54.0
above 8000 ft.	0646-102	50.5
1991		
Prowler, Cougar		
0-4000 ft.	0646-115	47.0
4000-8000 ft.	0146-530	44.5
8000-10,000 ft.	0646-018	43.5
above 10,000 ft.	0646-019	42.0
El Tigre EXT		
0-4000 ft.	0646-098	54.5
4000-8000 ft.	0646-099	54.0
above 8000 ft.	0646-102	50.5
1992		
Prowler, Cougar		
0-4000 ft.	0646-115	47.0
4000-8000 ft.	0146-530	44.5
8000-10,000 ft.	0646-018	43.5
above 10,000 ft.	0646-019	42.0
El Tigre EXT		
0-4000 ft.	0646-098	54
4000-8000 ft.	0646-099	54
above 8000 ft.	0646-102	50.5
1993		
Prowler, Cougar		
0-4000 ft.	0646-115	47.0
4000-8000 ft.	0146-530	44.5
8000-10,000 ft.	0646-018	43.5
above 10,000 ft.	0646-019	42.0
440 ZR		
0-4000 ft.	0646-157	46.5
4000-8000 ft.	0646-156	45.0
8000-10,000 ft.	0646-018	43.5
above 10,000 ft.	0646-019	42.0
EXT 550		
0-4000 ft.	0646-102	50.5
4000-8000 ft.	0646-080	48.5
above 8000 ft.	0646-115	47.0
580 ZR		
0-4000 ft.	0646-102	50.5
4000-8000 ft.	0646-080	48.5
8000-10,000 ft.	0646-115	47.0
above 10,000 ft.	0646-027	44.5
EXT 580		
0-4000 ft.	0646-102	50.5
4000-8000 ft.	0646-080	48.5
8000-10,000 ft.	0646-115	47.0
above 10,000 ft.	0646-027	44.5

4

(continued)

Table 3 CAM ARM SPECIFICATIONS (continued)

Model	Part No.	Weight (grams)
1994		
Cougar, Prowler		
0-4000 ft.	0646-115	47.0
4000-8000 ft.	0146-530	44.5
8000-10,000 ft.	0646-018	43.5
above 10,000 ft.	0646-019	42.0
ZR 440		
0-4000 ft.	0646-102	50.5
above 4000 ft.	0646-166	39.5
EXT 580, EXT 580 EFI		
0-4000 ft.	0646-102	50.5
4000-8000 ft.	0646-080	48.5
8000-10,000 ft.	0646-115	47.0
above 10,000 ft.	0646-027	44.5
ZR 580		
0-4000 ft.	0646-157	46.5
4000-10,000 ft.	0646-156	45.0
above 10,000 ft.	0646-162	
1995		
Cougar		
0-4000 ft.	0646-102	50.5
4000-8000 ft.	0646-080	48.5
above 8000 ft.	0646-115	47.0
Z 440		
0-4000 ft.	0646-080	48.5
4000-8000 ft.	0146-530	44.5
above 8000 ft.	0646-079	43.5
ZR 440		
0-4000 ft.	0646-199	46.5
above 4000 ft.	0646-166	39.5
EXT 580		
0-4000 ft.	0646-102	50.5
4000-8000 ft.	0646-080	48.5
8000-10,000 ft.	0646-115	47.0
above 10,000 ft.	0646-027	44.5
EXT 580 EFI		
0-4000 ft.	0646-164	49.0
above 4000 ft.	0646-156	45.0
ZR 580		
0-4000 ft.	0646-164	49.0
4000-8000 ft.	0646-157	46.5
above 8000 ft.	0646-156	45.0
Powder Special		
0-4000 ft.	0646-164	49.0
4000-10,000 ft.	0646-157	46.5
above 10,000 ft.	0646-156	45.0
ZR 580 EFI		
0-4000 ft.	0646-164	49.0
above 4000 ft.	0646-156	45.0

(continued)

Table 3 CAM ARM SPECIFICATIONS (continued)

Model	Part No.	Weight (grams)
1996		
Z 440		
0-4000 ft.	0646-080	48.5
4000-8000 ft.	0146-530	44.5
above 8000 ft.	0646-079	43.5
ZR 440	0646-250	44.5
Cougar		
0-4000 ft.	0646-102	50.5
4000-8000 ft.	0646-080	48.5
above 8000 ft.	0646-115	47.0
EXT 580		
0-4000 ft.	0646-102	50.5
4000-8000 ft.	0646-080	48.5
8000-10,000 ft.	0646-115	47.0
above 10,000 ft.	0646-027	44.5
EXT 580 EFI		
0-4000 ft.	0646-164	49.0
above 4000 ft.	0646-156	45.0
EXT 580 Powder Special		
0-4000 ft.	0646-164	49.0
4000-10,000 ft.	0646-157	46.5
above 10,000 ft.	0646-156	45.0
ZR 580		
0-4000 ft.	0646-249	–
4000-10,000 ft.	0646-235	–
above 10,000 ft.	0646-234	–
ZRT 600		
0-4000 ft.	0746-500	54.0
4000-10,000 ft.	0746-547	50.0
above 10,000 ft.	0746-546	48.0
1997		
Z 440	–	–
ZL 440	–	–
ZR 440	–	–
Cougar	–	–
EXT 580 EFI	–	–
Powder Special (carbureted)	–	–
Powder Special EFI		
0-5000 ft.	0746-527	50.5
5000-9000 ft.	0746-566	48.0
above 9000 ft.	0746-567	46.0
ZR 580 EFI		
0-5000 ft.	0746-574	48.5
5000-9000 ft.	0746-564	45.0
above 9000 ft.	0746-567	46.0
EXT 600	–	–
ZRT 600	–	–
Powder Extreme	–	–
1998		
Z 440		
0-5000 ft.	0746-527	50.5
5000-9000 ft.	0746-525	44.0
Above 9000 ft.	0746-526	42.0

(continued)

Table 3 CAM ARM SPECIFICATIONS (continued)

Model	Part No.	Weight (grams)
1998		
ZL 440		
0-5000 ft.	0746-583	46.5
5000-9000 ft.	0746-594	44.5
Above 9000 ft.	0746-562	42.0
ZR 440		
0-5000 ft.	0746-576	45.0
5000-9000 ft.	0746-595	41.5
Above 9000 ft.	0746-590	40.5
ZL 500		
0-5000 ft.	0746-579	46.5
5000-9000 ft.	0746-598	44.0
Above 9000 ft.	0746-590	40.5
Panther 440		
0-4000 ft.	—	—
4000-10,000 ft.	—	—
Above 10,000 ft.	—	—
Cougar		
0-5000 ft.	0746-527	50.5
5000-9000 ft.	0746-524	48.5
Above 9000 ft.	0746-523	47.0
Panther 550		
0-5000 ft.	0746-527	50.5
5000-9000 ft.	0746-524	48.5
Above 9000 ft.	0746-523	47.0
EXT EFI		
0-5000 ft.	0746-501	48.5
5000-9000 ft.	0746-583	46.5
Above 9000 ft.	0746-591	44.0
EXT EFI DELUXE		
0-5000 ft.	0746-527	50.5
5000-9000 ft.	0746-524	48.5
Above 9000 ft.	0746-591	44.0
Pantera		
0-5000 ft.	0746-527	50.5
5000-9000 ft.	0746-524	48.5
Above 9000 ft.	0746-591	44.0
Powder Special (carbureted)		
0-5000 ft.	0746-587	50.0
5000-9000 ft.	0746-584	45
Above 9000 ft.	0746-602	42.5
Powder Special EFI		
0-5000 ft.	—	—
5000-9000 ft.	—	—
Above 9000 ft.	—	—
ZR 600 EFI		
0-5000 ft.	0746-585	
5000-9000 ft.	0746-593	
Above 9000 ft.	0746-597	
EXT 600		
0-5000 ft.	0746-582	48.5
5000-9000 ft.	0746-582	48.5
Above 9000 ft.	0746-589	45.0

(continued)

Table 3 CAM ARM SPECIFICATIONS (continued)

Model	Part No.	Weight (grams)
1998		
EXT Triple Touring		
0-5000 ft.	0746-582	48.5
5000-9000 ft.	0746-583	46.5
Above 9000 ft.	0746-591	44.0
ZRT 600		
0-5000 ft.	0746-582	48.5
5000-9000 ft.	0746-582	48.5
Above 9000 ft.	0746-589	45.0
Powder Extreme		
0-5000 ft.	0746-581	52.5
5000-9000 ft.	0746-583	46.5
Above 9000 ft.	0746-596	44.5

Table 4 SPROCKET SPECIFICATIONS

Model	Upper sprocket (number of teeth)	Lower sprocket (number of teeth)
1990		
Prowler	–	–
El Tigre EXT		
Models without reverse	20	35
Models with reverse	24	39
1991		
Prowler, Cougar		
0-4000 ft.	20	39
above 4000 ft.	18	40
El Tigre EXT		
Models without reverse	20	35
Models with reverse	24	39
1992		
Prowler, Cougar		
0-4000 ft.	20	39
above 4000 ft.	18	40
El Tigre EXT		
Models without reverse	20	35
Models with reverse	24	39
1993		
Prowler, Cougar		
0-4000 ft.	20	39
above 4000 ft.	18	40
440 ZR		
0-4000 ft.	20	39
above 4000 ft.	19	39
EXT 550	19	39
580 ZR, EXT 580	20	39

(continued)

Table 4 SPROCKET SPECIFICATIONS (continued)

Model	Upper sprocket (number of teeth)	Lower sprocket (number of teeth)
1994		
Cougar, Cougar Mountain Cat		
0-4000 ft.	20	39
above 4000 ft.	18	40
Prowler		
0-4000 ft.	20	39
above 4000 ft.	18	40
ZR 440, ZR 580	20	39
EXT 580	20	39
1995		
Cougar, Cougar Mountain Cat	20	39
Prowler 2-Up	19	39
Z 440		
0-10,000 ft.	20	39
over 10,000 ft.	18	40
ZR 440	20	39
EXT 580, EXT 580 EFI	20	39
ZR 580, ZR 580 EFI	20	39
1996		
Z 440		
0-10,000 ft.	20	39
over 10,000 ft.	18	40
ZR 440	20	39
Cougar, Cougar Mountain Cat	20	39
Cougar 2-Up	19	39
EXT 580, EXT 580 EFI	20	39
EXT 580 EFI Mountain Cat,		
EXT 580 Powder Special		
0-5000 ft.	20	39
above 5000 ft.	19	40
ZR 580	20	39
ZRT 600	23	40
1997		
Z 440		
0-5000 ft.	20	39
Above 5000 ft.	19	40
ZL 440, ZR 440	20	39
Panther 440		
0-5000 ft.	19	39
Above 5000 ft.	18	40
Cougar, Cougar Mountain Cat	20	39
Panther 550	20	39
EXT 580 EFI		
0-5000 ft.	20	39
Above 5000 ft.	19	40
ZR 580 EFI, Powder Special EFI		
0-5000 ft.	20	39
Above 5000 ft.	19	40
Pantera		
0-5000 ft.	19	39
5000-9000 ft.	19	40
Above 9000 ft.	19	39

(continued)

Table 4 SPROCKET SPECIFICATIONS (continued)

Model	Upper sprocket (number of teeth)	Lower sprocket (number of teeth)
1997		
EXT 600		
0-5000 ft.	23	40
Above 5000 ft.	20	39
ZRT 600		
0-5000 ft.	23	40
Above 5000 ft.	20	39
Powder Extreme		
0-5000 ft.	23	40
Above 5000 ft.	20	39
1998		
Z 440, ZL 440		
0-5000 ft.	20	39
Above 5000 ft.	19	40
ZR 440	19	40
Panther 440	–	–
ZL 500		
0-5000 ft.	20	39
Above 5000 ft.	19	40
Cougar, Cougar Mountain Cat	20	39
Cougar Deluxe	19	39
Panther 550	19	39
EXT EFI		
0-5000 ft.	20	39
Above 5000 ft.	19	40
EXT EFI Deluxe	19	39
ZR 600 EFI	19	39
Powder Special (carbureted)	19	40
Powder Special EFI	–	–
Pantera	19	39
EXT 600		
0-5000 ft.	23	40
Above 5000 ft.	20	39
EXT Triple Touring		
0-5000 ft.	23	40
Above 5000 ft.	19	39
ZRT 600		
0-5000 ft.	23	40
Above 5000 ft.	20	39
Powder Extreme	20	39

Table 5 SHOCK ABSORBER SPRING SETTINGS

Model	Threads exposed mm (in.)	Floating piston mm (in.)
1992		
Prowler	19-25 (3/4-1)	–
El Tigre EXT	–	–
1993		
Prowler, Cougar, 440 ZR, 580 ZR	19-25 (3/4-1)	–
	(continued)	

Table 5 SHOCK ABSORBER SPRING SETTINGS (continued)

Model	Threads exposed mm (in.)	Floating piston mm (in.)
1994		
Cougar, Prowler	19-25 (3/4-1)	–
ZR 440	31-38 (1 1/4-1 1/3)	3 (1/8) from bottom
EXT 580	19-24 (3/4-1)	–
ZR 580	31-38 (1 1/4-1 1/2)	19.4 (0.764)
1995		
Cougar, Prowler, Z 440	19-24 (3/4-1)	–
ZR 440	31-38 (1 1/4-1 1/2)	3 (1/8) from bottom
EXT 580	19-24 (3/4-1)	–
ZR 580	31-38 (1 1/4-1 1/2)	19.4 (0.764)
1996		
Z 440	31-38 (1 1/4-1 1/2)	–
ZR 440, ZR 580, ZRT 600	31-38 (1 1/4-1 1/2)	3 (1/8) from bottom
Cougar	–	–
EXT 580	19-24 (3/4-1)	–
1997		
Z 440	19-25 (3/4-1)	–
ZL 440	19-25 (3/4-1)	–
ZR 440	38-48 (1 1/2-1 7/8)	20.32 (0.800)
Cougar	19-25 (3/4-1)	–
EXT 580 EFI	19-25 (3/4-1)	–
Powder Special EFI	31-38 (1 1/4-1 1/2)	20.32 (0.800)
ZR 580 EFI	15.8 (5/8)	20.32 (0.800)
EXT 600	19-25 (3/4-1)	–
ZRT 600	15.8 (5/8)	20.32 (0.800)
1998		
Z 440	12.5-25 (1/2-1)	–
ZL 440	12.5-25 (1/2-1)	–
ZR 440	38-48 (1 1/2-1 7/8)	20.32 (0.800)
Cougar	19-25 (3/4-1)	–
Panther 550	19-25 (3/4-1)	–
EXT EFI	76-109 (3.0-4.3)*	–
EXT EFI Deluxe	12.5-25 (1/2-1)	–
Pantera	12.5-25 (1/2-1)	–
Powder Extreme	12.5-25 (1/2-1)	–
Powder Special	76-109 (3.0-4.3)*	–
EXT 600	12.5-25 (1/2-1)	–
ZRT 600	13 (1/2)	20.32 (0.800)

*Eyelet to bottom of adjuster.

Chapter Five

Engine

The Arctic Cat snowmobiles covered in this manual are equipped with an Arctic Cat/Suzuki air-cooled or water-cooled two-stroke engine with either two or three cylinders. The Arctic Cat/Suzuki engines are equipped with anti-friction ball or roller type bearings at the crankshaft main bearings and on both ends of the connecting rods. Crankshaft components are available as individual parts. However, other than replacing the outer seals, you should entrust your crankshaft work to a dealer or other competent engine specialist.

This chapter covers information that provides top-end service as well as crankcase disassembly and crankshaft service.

Work on the snowmobile engine requires considerable mechanical ability. You should carefully consider your own capabilities before attempting any operation involving major disassembly of the engine.

Much of the labor charge for dealer repairs involves the removal and disassembly of other parts to reach the defective component. Even if you decide not to tackle the entire engine overhaul after studying the text and illustrations in this chapter, it may be less expensive to perform the preliminary operations yourself and then take the engine to your dealer. Since dealers have lengthy waiting lists for service, especially during the fall and winter season, this practice can reduce the length of time your snowmobile is in the shop.

Refer to **Table 1** for engine application and general engine specifications. **Tables 1-10** are found at the end of the chapter.

ENGINE NUMBER IDENTIFICATION

The engine model number is located on a plate attached to the engine (**Figure 1**, typical). The engine model and serial number are stamped into the intake side of the engine crankcase (**Figure 2**, typical). Refer to **Table 1** for model listing and original engine application.

Record all of the serial numbers and model numbers that are applicable to your machine and have these numbers with you when you order parts. Always order parts by year, engine model and serial number. If possible, compare the old parts with the new ones before purchasing them. If the parts are not alike, have the parts manager explain the reason for the difference and insist on assurance that the new part is correct and will fit.

For convenience, write all of the frame and engine identification numbers in the front of this book.

ENGINE LUBRICATION

The engine is normally lubricated by the oil-injection system. Refer to Chapter Ten for service information covering the oil-injection pump. Lubrication of a new or rebuilt engine or an engine that has not been run for an extended time may be initially supplemented by adding oil to the gasoline used to power the engine. Refer to *Break-In Procedure* in Chapter Three.

SERVICE PRECAUTIONS

Whenever you work on your Arctic Cat, there are several precautions that you should follow to help with disassembly, inspection and reassembly.

1. In the text there is frequent mention of the left or right side of the engine. This refers to the engine as it is mounted in the frame, not as it sits on your workbench. See **Figure 3**.

2. Always replace a worn or damaged fastener with one of the same size, type and torque requirements. Make sure to identify each screw before replacing it with another. Screw threads should be lubricated with engine oil, unless otherwise specified, before torque is applied. If a tightening torque is not listed in **Table 10** at the end of this chapter, refer to the torque and fastener information in Chapter One.

3. Use special tools where noted. In some cases, it may be possible to perform the procedure with makeshift tools, but this procedure is not recommended. The use of makeshift tools can damage the components and may cause serious personal injury. If special snowmobile tools are required, purchase them through any Arctic Cat dealer. Other tools can be purchased through your dealer, from a motorcycle store or from an auto parts store. When purchasing tools from an auto parts store, remember that all threaded parts that screw into the engine must have metric threads.

4. Before removing the first screw or nut, get a number of boxes, plastic bags and containers (**Figure 4**). Use these containers to separate and organize the parts as they are removed. Also have a roll of masking tape and a permanent, waterproof marking pen to label each part or assembly. If your snowmobile was purchased second hand and it appears that some of the wiring may have

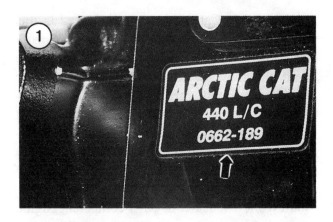

been changed or replaced, label each electrical connection before separating it.

5. Use a vise with protective jaws to hold parts. If protective jaws are not available, insert wooden blocks on either side of the part(s) before clamping it in the vise.

6. Remove and install pressed-on parts with an appropriate mandrel, support and hydraulic press. *Do not* try to pry, hammer or otherwise force them on or off.

7. Refer to **Table 10** at the end of the chapter for torque specifications. Proper torque is essential to ensure long life and satisfactory service from snowmobile components.

8. Discard all O-rings and oil seals during disassembly. Apply a small amount of heat-resistant grease to the inner lips of each oil seal to prevent damage when the engine is first started.

9. Keep a record of all shims as they are removed. As soon as the shims are removed, inspect them for damage and write down their thickness and location.

10. Work in an area where there is sufficient lighting and room for component storage.

5

SERVICING ENGINE IN FRAME

Some of the components can be serviced while the engine is mounted in the frame:

    a. Cylinder head.
    b. Cylinder.
    c. Piston.
    d. Carburetors.
    e. Magneto.
    f. Oil pump.
    g. Recoil starter.
    h. Clutch assembly.

ENGINE REMOVAL

Engine removal and crankcase separation is required for repair of the bottom end (crankshaft, connecting rod and bearings).

1. Remove the hood as follows:
    a. Open the hood.
    b. Disconnect any interfering wiring. It may be necessary to detach the wiring from the hood or speedometer cable.
    c. Disconnect the speedometer cable.
    d. Disconnect the hood restraining cable and have an assistant support the hood.
    e. Remove the screws that attach the hood hinge, then lift off the hood.
    f. Set the hood out of the way to prevent damage to it.

2. Remove the exhaust assembly as follows:

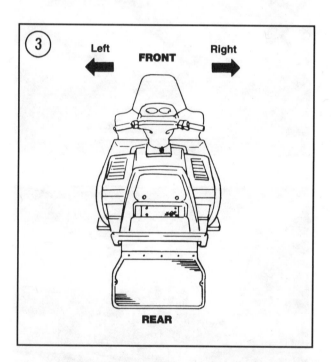

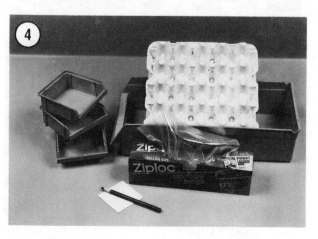

a. Disconnect the springs (**Figure 5** or **6**, typical) that hold the exhaust pipe(s) to the muffler.

b. Disconnect the springs that hold the exhaust pipe(s) to the exhaust sockets (**Figure 7**) or to the manifold (**Figure 8**).

c. Disconnect any clamps or springs that retain the exhaust pipe(s), then remove the exhaust pipe(s).

3. Remove the drive belt as described in Chapter Thirteen.

4. Remove both the drive and driven pulleys as described in Chapter Thirteen.

5. On liquid-cooled models, drain the cooling system as described under *Coolant Change* in Chapter Three.

6. Disconnect spark plug cables from the spark plugs.

7. Remove the recoil starter as described in Chapter Twelve.

8. Remove the air silencer as described in Chapter Six or Chapter Seven.

NOTE
Mark the carburetors for identification. The two or three carburetors may appear to be identical, but may have different jetting. Even if they are identical, the throttle slides and starting enrichment slides should be reinstalled in the carburetor from which they were removed.

9A. On engines equipped with carburetors, observe the following:

CAUTION
It is not necessary to remove the throttle slides (substep a) or starting enrichment valves (substep b) from the cables unless service to these parts is required. Insert each slide and valve in a plastic bag to protect them from damage, then tie the cables, caps, slides and valves out of the way.

a. Unscrew the carburetor caps (**Figure 9**) and withdraw the throttle valves (slides) from

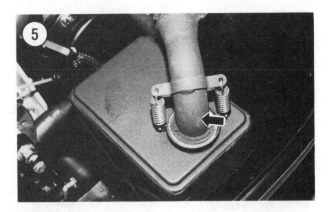

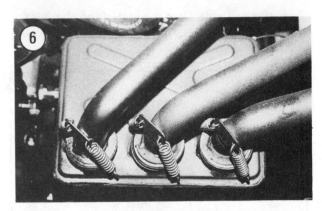

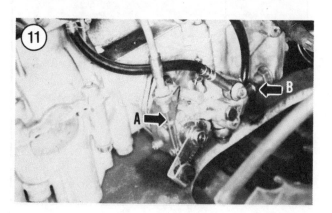

the carburetors. Be careful that you do not damage the jet needles.

   b. Unscrew the fuel enrichment (choke) valves (**Figure 10**) from the carburetors. Withdraw the valves, leaving the cables attached, then tie the valves and cables out of the way.

9B. On engines equipped with Electronic Fuel Injection, detach the vacuum lines, electrical connectors, fuel lines and throttle cable from the EFI system.

10. Disconnect the oil injection cable (A, **Figure 11**) from the oil pump.

11. Disconnect and plug the oil hose attached to fitting (B, **Figure 11**).

12A. On engines so equipped, remove the carburetors as described in Chapter Six.

12B. On engines with EFI, remove the fuel injection unit as described in Chapter Seven.

13. On liquid-cooled engines, disconnect the coolant hoses from the pump inlet and the outlet (thermostat) housing.

14. Disconnect the fuel pump impulse hose from the crankcase fitting.

15. Be sure that all wires for the CDI unit, charging system, temperature gauge sending unit or other components are detached from the engine. If any electrical connector is still attached that would interfere with engine removal, detach it.

16. Be sure all hoses and cables that would interfere with removal are removed or detached.

17. If necessary, you can remove the engine top end (cylinder heads, pistons and cylinder blocks) before removing the engine from the frame. Refer to *Cylinder* in this chapter.

NOTE
Because of the number of bushings, washers and rubber dampers used on the engine bracket assemblies, you should mark all parts so they can be reinstalled in their original position. Putting the components from each location in separate plastic bags, then marking the bags

5

with the location from which they were removed can facilitate assembly.

18. Remove bolts from the front and rear engine mounts. Remove any nuts, washers and shims from the engine mounts.

19. With at least one assistant, lift the engine up and remove it from the frame. Carry it to a workbench for further disassembly.

ENGINE MOUNTS

Removal/Installation

The engine may be supported in the snowmobile frame either by a support plate or by individual brackets. A thrust bumper may also be used to limit engine movement. Refer to the appropriate following section when servicing the engine mounts.

Models equipped with a support plate. The engine support plate and mounts (**Figure 12**) are accessible after the engine is removed. See *Engine Removal*. Refer to **Figure 13** for a drawing of a typical mount assembly. Note the following when servicing the mounts and support plate:

NOTE
To ease installation, mark location of pieces during removal. The bolts that hold the mounts and supports may have different lengths.

a. Inspect the engine mounts, rubber mounts and engine supports for damage. Install new parts if the condition of the old parts is questioned.

NOTE
You should replace all rubber mounts at the same time.

b. Inspect all engine and support mount bolts for damage. Replace damaged bolts with the same type.

c. Inspect the washers for damage.

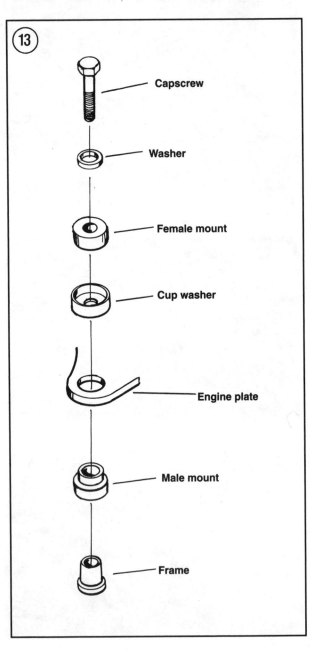

d. Inspect the threads of all tapped holes for damaged threads or debris. Clean threads with the correct sized tap. If Loctite was previously used, be sure to remove all traces of Loctite residue before reinstalling bolts.

e. Inspect the front and rear engine mount brackets in the frame for signs of damage.

NOTE
The screws securing the engine mounting plate to the engine crankcase should not be loosened or tightened unless they are removed and the threads are re-coated with Loctite. See Figure 14.

f. Attach the engine mounting plate securely to the bottom of the engine crankcase. Apply Loctite to the threads of the retaining screws and tighten them to the torque listed in **Table 10**.

g. Tighten retaining nuts to the torque specified in **Table 10**.

h. Refer to Chapter Thirteen for *Drive Belt Alignment and Distance Adjustment*. A stopper (**Figure 15**, typical) is used to adjust the center-to-center distance of the drive pulleys.

Models equipped with engine-support brackets. Some models are supported by brackets and rubber mounts. Refer to **Figure 16** for a drawing of a typical mounting system. Typical front mounts are shown in **Figures 17** and **18**. A typical rear mount is shown in **Figure 19**. Note the following when servicing the mounts:

NOTE
To ease installation, mark each of the engine mounting brackets, supports and rubber mounts for position during removal. The bolts used to hold the mounts and supports may be of different lengths.

a. Check the engine mounts, rubber mounts and engine support for damage. If required, brackets can be unbolted and removed from the engine.

b. Inspect all the engine and support mount bolts and studs for damage. Replace damaged parts with the same type. Installation of bolts that are weaker will loosen and allow the engine to slip.

c. Inspect all washers for damage.

d. Inspect the threads of all tapped holes in the crankcase for damaged threads or debris. If necessary, clean threads with the correct sized metric tap. If Loctite was previously used, make sure you remove all traces of Loctite residue before reinstalling bolts.

e. Check the front and rear engine mount brackets and the surrounding area of the frame for cracks or other signs of damage. Check any tapped holes in the bracket for thread damage or debris. Clean the threads before assembling.

f. Replace worn or damaged parts as required.

g. Be sure to reinstall spacers and tighten retaining nuts to the torque specified in **Table 10**.

h. Refer to Chapter Thirteen for *Drive Belt Alignment and Distance Adjustment*. A stopper (**Figure 20**, typical) is used to adjust the center-to-center distance of the drive pulleys.

ENGINE INSTALLATION

1. Degrease the engine compartment.
2. Clean all the exposed electrical connectors with an electrical contact cleaner.

3. Inspect components which are difficult to view when the engine is installed. Observe the following:

a. On liquid-cooled engines, check all the coolant hoses and the hose connections for looseness or damage. Make sure the hose clamps are tight. Many of the coolant hoses are preshaped and should only be replaced with duplicates of the originals. When replacing any coolant hose, make sure it is positioned correctly.

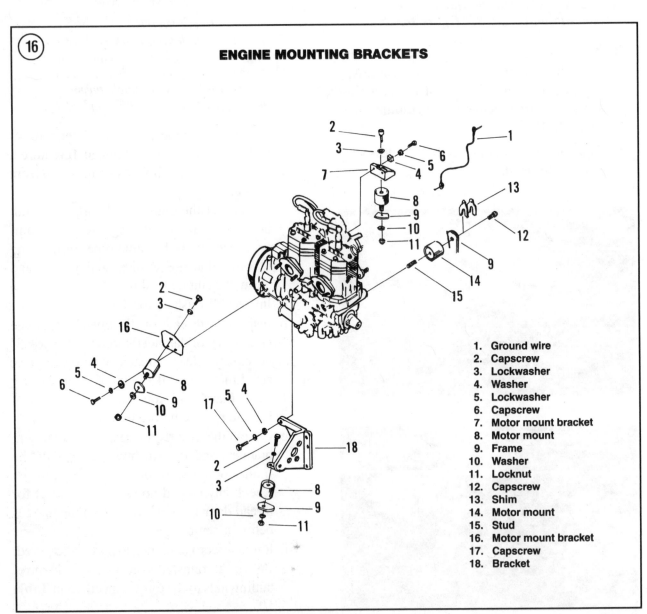

(16) ENGINE MOUNTING BRACKETS

1. Ground wire
2. Capscrew
3. Lockwasher
4. Washer
5. Lockwasher
6. Capscrew
7. Motor mount bracket
8. Motor mount
9. Frame
10. Washer
11. Locknut
12. Capscrew
13. Shim
14. Motor mount
15. Stud
16. Motor mount bracket
17. Capscrew
18. Bracket

b. Check all the steering component tightening torques as described in Chapter Fifteen. Check the steering shaft clamp (**Figure 21**, typical) for tightness.

c. Check the fuel pump mounting screws for tightness. Check the fuel pump outlet and pulse hoses for deterioration or damage. Replace hoses as required.

4. Examine the engine mounts and supports as described in this chapter.

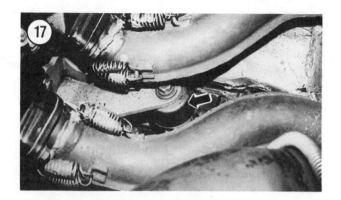

5. Check for any object that may interfere with engine installation. Make sure wiring harnesses are routed and secured properly.

6. Install the front and rear engine supports and mounts onto the engine as described in this chapter.

7. With an assistant, place the engine partway into position on the frame.

NOTE
To ease installation of the coolant hoses in the following steps, coat the inside of the hose where it slides on the mating joint with antifreeze.

8. On liquid-cooled engines, it may be easier to connect the lower coolant hose at the water pump before the engine is completely lowered onto the frame. Attach the coolant hose to the water pump. Make sure the hose is not twisted and that the clamp will not contact the frame when the engine is lowered onto the frame. Tighten the

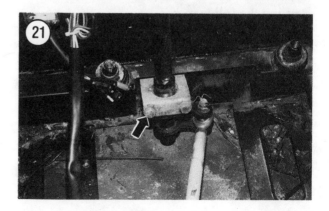

hose and lower the engine onto the frame brackets.

9. Install, but do not tighten, the engine mount bolts.

10. Install the primary sheave and drive belt as described in Chapter Thirteen.

11. Align the engine/clutch assembly as described in Chapter Thirteen.

12. Tighten the engine mount bolts to the torque specified in **Table 10**.

13. Install any remaining engine top end components.

14. Attach the spark plug cables to the spark plugs.

15. Reconnect all electrical connectors.

16. Reconnect the pulse hose to the crankcase and secure the clamp. Different fuel pumps have been used, but the pulse hose routes crankcase pulses to the center of the fuel pump.

17. On liquid-cooled engines, connect the coolant hose(s) to the coolant outlet (thermostat) housing and secure the clamp.

18. Attach the hose from the oil injection tank to the oil pump.

19. Connect the oil injection control cable to the oil pump (**Figure 11**, typical).

CAUTION
Do not adjust the oil injection control cable until after the carburetors have been synchronized as described in Chapter Three.

20A. On engines equipped with carburetors, reinstall and assemble the carburetors while observing the following:

NOTE
The carburetors may appear to be identical, but may have different jetting. Even if they are identical, the throttle slides and starting enrichment slides should be reinstalled in the carburetor from which they were removed.

   a. If the carburetors were removed, reinstall them as described in Chapter Six.

   b. Install the throttle slides and caps onto the carburetors.

   c. Install the starting enrichment slides onto the carburetors.

20B. On engines equipped with EFI, attach the vacuum lines, electrical connectors, fuel lines and throttle cable to the EFI system. Refer to Chapter Seven for installing the fuel injection unit.

21. On engines equipped with carburetors, refer to the synchronization procedure described in Chapter Three.

22. Adjust the oil injection control cable as described in Chapter Three.

23. Bleed the oil injection pump as described in Chapter Ten.

24. Install the air silencer as described in Chapter Six or Chapter Seven.

25. Install the recoil starter assembly as described in Chapter Twelve. Check starter operation.

26. On liquid-cooled engines, refill the cooling system as described in Chapter Three.

27. Install the exhaust pipe and muffler. See **Figure 5-8**. Make sure all springs are properly attached and none of the exhaust components are binding.

28. Install the engine hood. Reconnect the headlight electrical connector.

ENGINE TOP END

The engine top end consists of the cylinder head, cylinder blocks, pistons, piston rings, piston pins and the connecting rod small-end bearings. A single cylinder head covers both cylinders on engines with 497 and 599 cc displacement. Individual cylinder heads are used on each cylinder of all other engines.

The engine top end can be serviced with the engine installed in the frame; however, the following service procedures are shown with the engine removed for clarity.

Refer to the illustration for your model when servicing the engine top end.

a. **Figure 22**: Liquid-cooled 529 cc engine
b. **Figure 23**: Air-cooled 431 cc engines
c. **Figure 24**: Liquid-cooled 435.8, 437.4, 550, 580 and 594 cc engines
d. **Figure 25**: Liquid-cooled 497 and 599 cc engines

Cylinder Head Removal/Installation

CAUTION
To prevent warping and damage to any component, remove the cylinder heads only when the engine has cooled to room temperature. Never pry the cylinder head or cylinder head cover while trying to remove it.

NOTE
*If the engine is being disassembled for inspection, check the compression as described in Chapter Three **before** disassembly.*

1. If the engine is mounted in the frame, perform the following:

a. Open the engine hood. If desirable, remove the engine hood as outlined in the *Engine Removal* section.
b. On liquid-cooled engines, drain the cooling system as described in Chapter Three.
c. On liquid-cooled engines, loosen the hose clamp, then disconnect the coolant hose(s) from the thermostat and outlet housing.
d. Disconnect the spark plug cables from the spark plugs.
e. Remove the exhaust pipe(s), then unbolt the exhaust manifold from the cylinders.
f. On all two-cylinder engines except 1996-on ZR 440, refer to Chapter Six or Chapter Seven and remove the air silencer and carburetor(s) or fuel injection.

2. Loosen, but do not remove, the spark plugs so they can be removed later.

3. On air-cooled engines, unbolt and remove the top cooling shroud, then slide the front shroud off from around the exhaust studs. Remove the exhaust gaskets located between the cylinder and front shroud.

4A. On liquid-cooled engines, except 497 and 599 cc engines, unbolt and remove the outlet and thermostat housing (**Figure 26**) from the cylinder heads.

4B. On 497 and 599 cc engines, unbolt and remove the thermostat housing.

5. Loosen the fasteners retaining the cylinder head evenly to prevent warping.

6. Remove the cylinder head bolts or nuts. Loosen the cylinder head by tapping around the outer edge with a rubber or plastic mallet, then remove the cylinder head.

7. Remove and discard the cylinder head gaskets (**Figure 27**) or sealing rings (**Figure 28**).

8. Lay a rag over the open cylinders to prevent dirt from falling into the cylinders or water passages.

9. Inspect the cylinder head as described in this chapter.

NOTE
*While the cylinder head is removed, check the retaining studs (**Figure 27**) or bolts for stripped threads or other damage. Make sure the studs are tight in the crankcase. Check the condition of threads in the cylinder block. If necessary, remove the cylinder and replace damaged studs or repair damaged threads.*

10. Install the head gaskets as follows:

a. On air-cooled engines, make sure the sealing surfaces are clean and not nicked, then install the gasket over the studs (**Figure 27**).

b. On liquid-cooled engines, install the inner and outer O-rings (**Figure 28**) into the cylinder O-ring grooves. Check that each O-ring seats squarely in the groove.

5

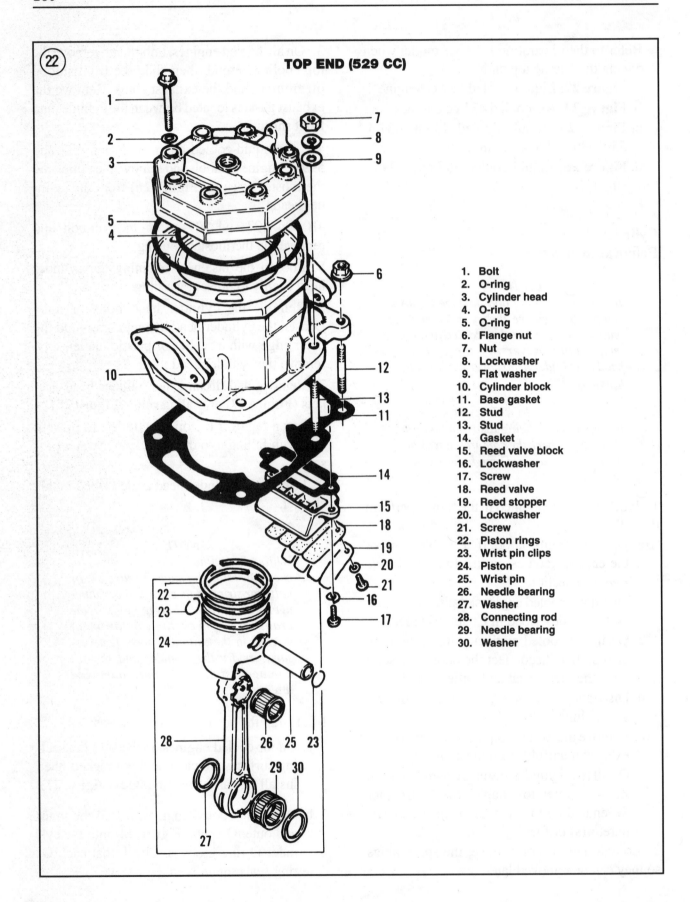

TOP END (529 CC)

1. Bolt
2. O-ring
3. Cylinder head
4. O-ring
5. O-ring
6. Flange nut
7. Nut
8. Lockwasher
9. Flat washer
10. Cylinder block
11. Base gasket
12. Stud
13. Stud
14. Gasket
15. Reed valve block
16. Lockwasher
17. Screw
18. Reed valve
19. Reed stopper
20. Lockwasher
21. Screw
22. Piston rings
23. Wrist pin clips
24. Piston
25. Wrist pin
26. Needle bearing
27. Washer
28. Connecting rod
29. Needle bearing
30. Washer

11A. On liquid-cooled engines, install the cylinder head so the coolant outlet or thermostat housing is to the rear (inlet side) of the engine.

11B. On air-cooled engines, install the cylinder head over the studs.

12. Lubricate the threads of cylinder head retaining studs or bolts and install fingertight. Observe the following:

    a. On air-cooled engines, the two longer nuts should be on studs at the right side as shown in **Figure 29**.

    b. On liquid-cooled engines, a seal ring (**Figure 30**) should be located on each of the retaining screws.

13. Tighten the retaining screws or nuts in a crisscross pattern (**Figure 31-35**) to the torque listed in **Table 10**.

14. On air-cooled engines, install the cooling shrouds. Install new gaskets between the cylinders and front shroud and between the shroud and the exhaust manifold.

15. Install the spark plugs.

5

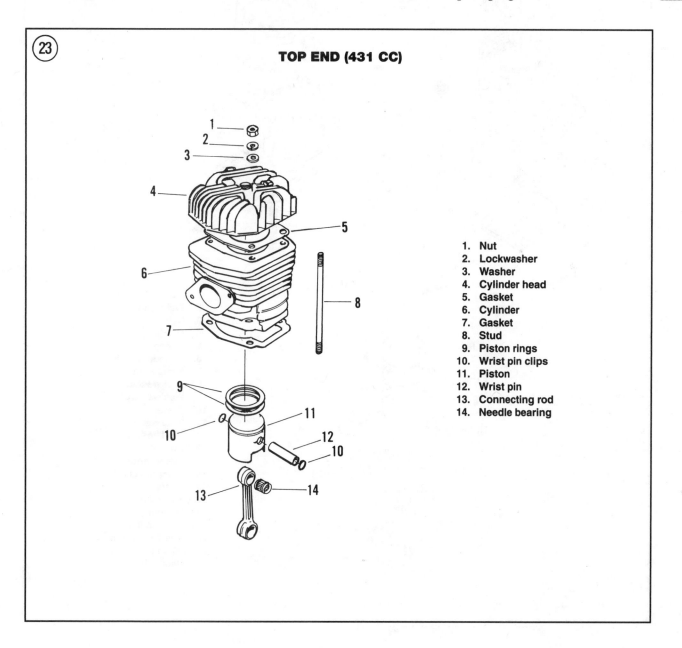

㉓ **TOP END (431 CC)**

1. Nut
2. Lockwasher
3. Washer
4. Cylinder head
5. Gasket
6. Cylinder
7. Gasket
8. Stud
9. Piston rings
10. Wrist pin clips
11. Piston
12. Wrist pin
13. Connecting rod
14. Needle bearing

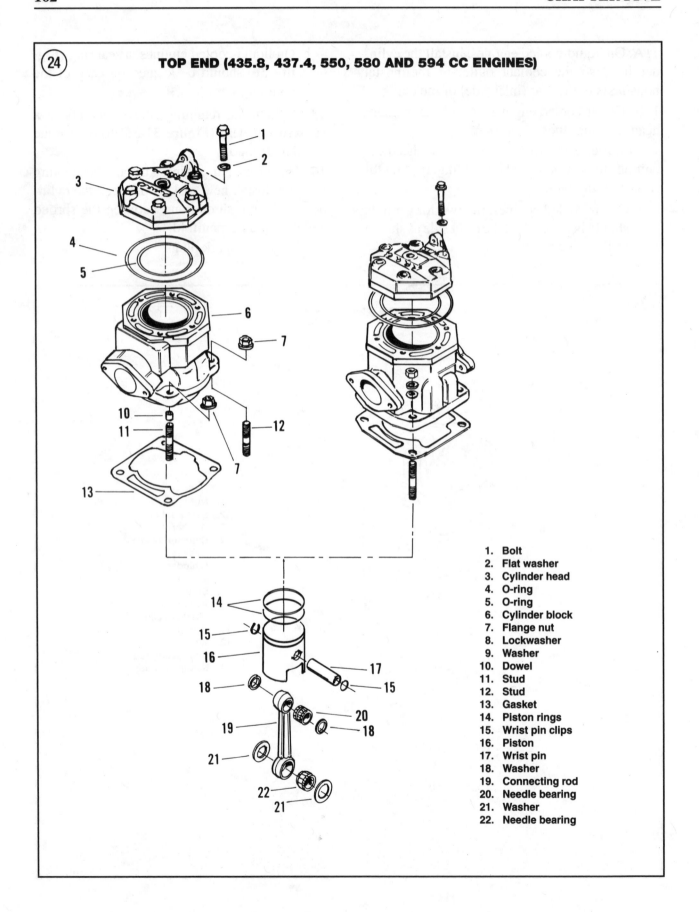

(24) **TOP END (435.8, 437.4, 550, 580 AND 594 CC ENGINES)**

1. Bolt
2. Flat washer
3. Cylinder head
4. O-ring
5. O-ring
6. Cylinder block
7. Flange nut
8. Lockwasher
9. Washer
10. Dowel
11. Stud
12. Stud
13. Gasket
14. Piston rings
15. Wrist pin clips
16. Piston
17. Wrist pin
18. Washer
19. Connecting rod
20. Needle bearing
21. Washer
22. Needle bearing

TOP END (497 AND 599 CC)

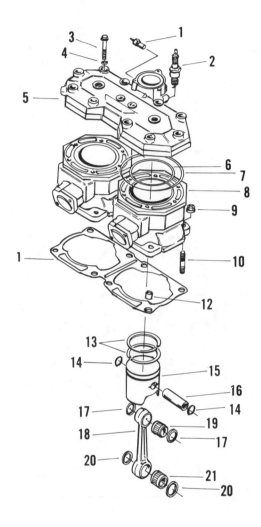

1. Temperature sensor
2. Spark plug
3. Bolt
4. Washer
5. Cylinder head
6. O-ring
7. O-ring
8. Cylinder block
9. Nut
10. Stud
11. Gasket
12. Dowel
13. Piston rings
14. Wrist pin clips
15. Piston
16. Wrist pin
17. Washer
18. Connecting rod
19. Needle bearing
20. Washer
21. Needle bearing

5

16. If the engine is installed in the frame, perform the following:

    a. Connect the spark plug cables to the spark plugs.

    b. On liquid-cooled engines, attach the coolant hoses to the coolant pump and the outlet housing.

    c. On liquid-cooled engines, refill the cooling system as described in Chapter Three.

    d. If removed, reinstall the engine hood.

Inspection

1. Wipe away any soft deposits from the cylinder head (**Figure 35**). Hard deposits should be carefully removed with a wire brush. Be careful not to damage the aluminum surfaces.

> *NOTE*
> *Always use an aluminum thread fluid or kerosene on the thread chaser and cylinder head threads when performing Step 2.*

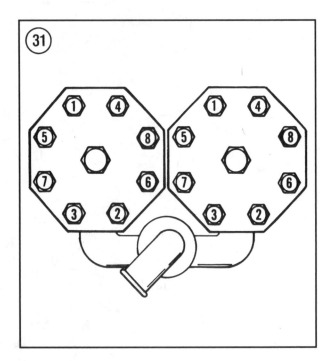

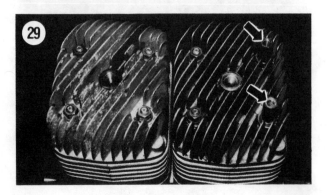

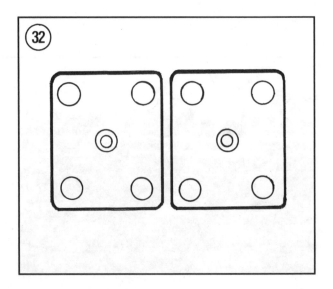

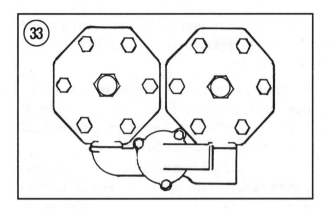

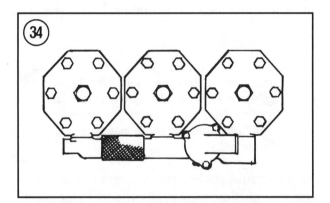

2. Inspect the spark plug threads in the cylinder head (A, **Figure 36**) for any signs of carbon buildup or damage. The carbon can be removed with a 14 mm spark plug thread chaser (**Figure 37**). Reinstall the spark plug and make sure it can be threaded into the cylinder head completely.

3. On liquid-cooled engines, inspect the recesses on top of the cylinder head around the retaining screws for damage or corrosion that would interfere with sealing.

4. Use a straightedge and feeler gauge to measure the flatness of the cylinder head. Small imperfections or slight warping can be removed by resurfacing the cylinder head as follows:

   a. Tape a piece of 400-600 grit wet emery sandpaper to a piece of thick plate glass or surface plate.

   b. Slowly resurface the head by moving it in a figure-eight pattern on the sandpaper (**Figure 38**).

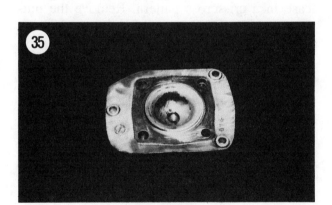

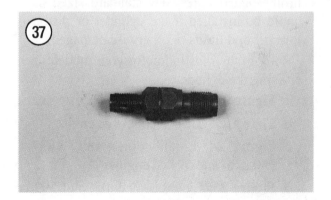

5

c. Rotate the head several times to avoid removing too much material from one side. Check progress often with the straightedge and feeler gauge (**Figure 39**).

d. If the cylinder head warpage still exceeds the service limit, it will be necessary to have the head resurfaced by a machine shop familiar with snowmobile and motorcycle service. Note that removing material from the cylinder head mating surface will change the compression ratio and clearance of the squish area around the outside edge.

5. On liquid-cooled engines, check the cylinder head water passages for coolant residue. Clean the passages thoroughly.

6. Wash the cylinder head in hot soap and water and rinse thoroughly before installation.

CYLINDER

The aluminum cylinder block has a hard chrome-plated bore. New standard sized parts should be installed if the cylinder or piston is worn beyond limits or otherwise damaged.

Refer to the illustration for your model when servicing the cylinder:

a. **Figure 22**: Liquid-cooled 529 cc engine

b. **Figure 23**: Air-cooled 431 cc engines

c. **Figure 24**: Liquid-cooled 435.8, 437.4, 550, 580 and 594 cc engines

d. **Figure 25**: Liquid-cooled 497 and 599 cc engines

Removal

1. Remove the cylinder head as described in this chapter.

2. On liquid-cooled engines, observe the following:

a. If the engine is installed in the frame, remove the muffler and exhaust pipe(s) as described in Chapter Eight.

b. On engines with a Y-type exhaust manifold, unbolt and remove the manifold from both cylinders.

3. On all engines with carburetors or fuel injection attached to the cylinders, remove the carburetors as described in Chapter Six or the EFI unit as described in Chapter Seven.

4. Detach the oil injection line near the intake port from each of the cylinders and plug the lines.

5. On 529 cc engines, remove the two flange nuts securing the cylinder on the intake side.

> *NOTE*
> *The cylinder of air-cooled engines is attached by the same four nuts as the cylinder head. If the cylinder base is loosened for any reason, the cylinder should be removed and a new base gasket installed.*

6. On liquid-cooled engines, gradually loosen the four nuts securing each cylinder to the crankcase in a crisscross pattern. Remove the nuts (**Figure 40**) and washers.

> *NOTE*
> *Mark the cylinders before removal so they can be reinstalled in the same locations.*

7. Rotate the engine until the piston is at the bottom of its stroke, then pull the cylinder straight up, away from the piston.

CAUTION
Do not rest the weight of the cylinder on the reed valve assembly located at the bottom of the cylinder on 529 cc engines.

8. Repeat the procedure to remove the other cylinder(s).

9. Remove and discard the cylinder base gasket.

10. Cover the openings in the crankcase around the connecting rods with clean rags to keep dirt and loose parts from entering the crankcase.

Inspection

Cylinder measurement requires a precision inside micrometer or bore gauge. If you do not have the right tools, have your dealer or a machine shop measure the parts.

1. On the 529 cc engine, remove the reed valve from the bottom of the cylinder.

2. Remove all gasket residue from the bottom gasket surface.

3A. On liquid-cooled engines, clean the cylinder O-ring groove (**Figure 28**) with a wooden dowel sharpened to a point.

3B. On air-cooled engines, clean the top of the cylinder carefully. Do not scratch the sealing surface.

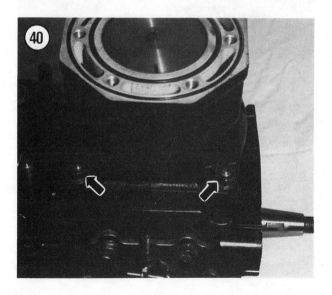

4. Clean all gasket residue from the exhaust manifold sealing area of the cylinder.

CAUTION
When cleaning the exhaust port in Step 5, do not allow the wire brush or scraper to slip inside the cylinder and damage the cylinder bore. Be especially careful when using power equipment, such as a rotating wire brush in an electric drill.

5. Use a soft scraper or a wire brush to remove all carbon deposits from the exhaust port.

6. Wash the cylinder with hot soapy water, then rinse with water to remove loose dirt and carbon particles before attempting to measure the cylinder bore. Measurements may be incorrect if the cylinder is not cleaned thoroughly.

7. Measure the cylinder bore diameter as described under *Piston/Cylinder Clearance Check* in this chapter.

NOTE
If the cylinder diameters are within specification, it is possible to buy and install new standard size pistons without reboring. New pistons will take up some of the excessive piston-to-cylinder clearance. However, do not install new standard size pistons in a cylinder that is worn past the wear limit.

8. If the cylinder bore is not worn past the service limit, check the bore carefully for scratches or gouges. The hardened surface of the cylinder bore should also be checked for flaking and bits of aluminum from the piston stuck to the cylinder bore.

9. Check all threaded holes in the cylinder block for thread damage. Minor damage can be cleaned up with a suitable metric tap. Refer to Chapter One for information pertaining to threads, fasteners and repair tools. If damage is severe, a thread insert should be installed.

10. Check the cylinder base studs for looseness, stripping or other damage. If necessary, replace studs as described in this chapter.

5

11. Check the top surface of the cylinder. If the surface appears warped, scratched or corroded, the cylinder can be resurfaced lightly as follows.

    a. Tape a piece of 400-600 grit wet emery sandpaper to a piece of thick plate glass or surface plate.

    b. Slowly resurface the top of the cylinder by moving it in a figure-eight pattern on the sandpaper (**Figure 38**, typical).

    c. Rotate the cylinder several times to avoid removing too much material and check the progress often.

12. After the cylinder has been serviced, wash the bore with hot soapy water. This is the only way to clean the fine grit material left from the bore or honing job from the cylinder wall. After washing, run a clean white cloth through the cylinder. The white cloth should show no traces of grit or other debris. If the white cloth test indicates the cylinder is still dirty, rewash the cylinder wall. After the cylinder is thoroughly cleaned, lubricate the cylinder wall with clean engine oil.

Cylinder Stud Replacement

Damaged or dirty threaded holes or studs will prevent parts from fitting together as tightly as they should, allowing combustion gases or crankcase pressure to escape. In addition to reducing engine performance, leakage can cause engine damage. The following procedure for replacing damaged cylinder base studs can also be used to replace other damaged studs.

A tube of Loctite 242 (blue), two nuts, two wrenches and a new stud is required during this procedure.

1. Thread two nuts onto the damaged cylinder stud. Then tighten the two nuts against each other so that they are locked.

NOTE
If the threads of the damaged stud do not allow installation of the two nuts, you can remove the stud by using a stud

removal tool available from many tool suppliers.

2. Turn the bottom nut and stud counterclockwise to unscrew the stud.

3. Clean the threaded hole in the crankcase with solvent cleaner and thoroughly dry with compressed air.

NOTE
Install the new stud with the shorter threads screwed into the crankcase.

4. Install two nuts on the longer threads of the new stud as in Step 1 and tighten to make sure they are locked together securely.

5. Coat the shorter threads of the new stud with Loctite 242 (blue).

6. Turn the top nut and stud clockwise to screw the new stud in securely.

7. Remove the nuts and repeat for each stud as required.

8. Follow Loctite's directions on cure time before installing the cylinder.

Threaded Holes and Screws

Damaged or dirty threaded holes, studs or bolts will prevent parts from fitting together as tightly as they should. This will reduce engine performance and cause engine damage. Be sure the studs are properly seated and that proper washers are used.

Installation

1. If the intake adapter or the carburetor mounting flange were removed from the cylinder, install them using new gaskets.
2. On the 529 cc engine, attach the reed valve assembly to the cylinder block.

3. Clean the cylinder bore as described under *Inspection* in this chapter.
4. Make sure the top surface of the crankcase and the bottom cylinder surface are clean prior to installation.
5. Install a new base gasket.

> *NOTE*
> *Check the pistons to make sure the piston pin clips (**Figure 41**) are installed and correctly positioned so that the gap is down.*

6. Make sure the end gaps of the piston rings are aligned with the locating pins in the ring grooves (**Figure 42**). Oil the piston rings and the inside of the cylinder bores lightly with injection oil.
7. Place a piston holding tool or a wooden block (**Figure 43**) under one piston and turn the crankshaft until the piston is down firmly against the tool.

> *NOTE*
> *When reinstalling the original cylinders, install them in the previously marked locations.*

8. Align the cylinder with the piston so that the exhaust port will face toward the front of the engine. Install the cylinder, compressing each piston ring with your fingers as the cylinder slides over it. When both rings are in the cylinder, slide the cylinder down and remove the piston holding tool. Slide the cylinder all the way down against the gasket and crankcase. Make sure the base of the cylinder is fully seated against the crankcase. See **Figure 44**.
9. Repeat the procedure to install the other cylinder(s).

> *NOTE*
> *On air-cooled engines, long studs are used that pass through the cylinder and the cylinder head. The cylinder is retained by the cylinder head, which is secured by nuts on the studs.*

5

10A. *On 529 cc engines*, install the cylinders as follows:

a. Install the four flat washers, four lockwashers, four standard nuts and the two flange nuts that attach the cylinder base to the crankcase. Tighten the six nuts finger-tight.

b. Make sure you clean all gasket residue from the water manifold.

c. Apply a thin coat of silicone sealer to the two manifold gaskets.

d. Install the gaskets and coolant manifold (**Figure 45**).

e. Tighten the screws securing the coolant manifold to the torque listed in **Table 10**.

f. Tighten the cylinder base retaining nuts in a crossing pattern to the torque listed in **Table 10**.

10B. *On liquid-cooled engines, except the 529 cc El Tigre*, install the cylinders as follows:

a. On engines so equipped, be sure the two dowel pins are installed and properly seated. The dowels align the cylinders in the crankcase.

b. Install the flat washers and lockwashers, if used, and nuts that secure the cylinder base to the crankcase. Tighten the nuts finger-tight.

c. Install the exhaust manifold and tighten the retaining nuts securely. It is not necessary to install the gaskets at this time; the manifold is only used to align the cylinders and can be removed after tightening the cylinder base nuts.

d. Tighten the cylinder base retaining nuts in a crossing pattern to the torque listed in **Table 10**.

11. Install the cylinder head as outlined in this chapter.

NOTE
Before installing the exhaust manifold, check the ports and passages in the manifold for carbon buildup. Clean the ports as necessary.

12. Attach the oil injection line to each of the cylinders (near the intake port).

13. If the engine is installed in the frame, perform the following:

a. Install the carburetors as described in Chapter Six or EFI as described in Chapter Seven.

b. Install the exhaust system as described in Chapter Eight.

NOTE
On air-cooled engines, gaskets are located around the intake and exhaust ports on each side of the heat deflector, or shroud.

14. If new components were installed or if the cylinders were bored or honed, the engine must be broken-in as if it were new. Refer to *Break-In Procedure* in Chapter Three.

PISTON, PISTON PIN, AND PISTON RINGS

The piston is made of an aluminum alloy. The piston pin is a precision fit and is held in place by a clip at each end. A caged needle bearing is used at the small end of the connecting rod.

Refer to the illustration for your model when servicing the piston assembly.

a. **Figure 22**: Liquid-cooled 529 cc engine

b. **Figure 23**: Air-cooled 431 cc engines

c. **Figure 24**: Liquid-cooled 435.8, 437.4, 550, 580 and 594 cc engines

d. **Figure 25**: Liquid-cooled 497 and 599 cc engines

Piston and Piston Ring Removal

1. Remove the cylinder head and cylinder as described in this chapter.

NOTE
The pistons should be marked with an arrow cast on the top or inside, under the crown pointing to the exhaust port.

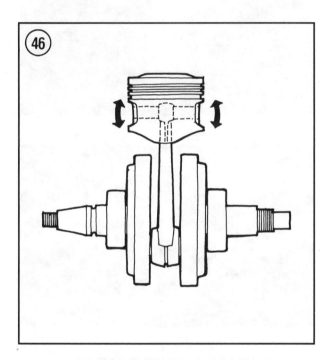

2. Identify the pistons and cylinders by marking on the tops of the pistons the letters PTO (left side), MAG (right side) or CEN (middle of three-cylinder models). In addition, keep each piston together with its pin, bearing and piston rings to avoid confusion during reassembly.

3. Before removing the piston, hold the rod tightly and rock the piston as shown in **Figure 46**. Do not confuse any rocking motion with the normal side-to-side sliding motion. Rocking indicates wear on the piston pin, needle bearing, piston pin bore or a combination of all three.

NOTE
Wrap a clean shop cloth under the piston so the clip will not fall into the crankcase.

WARNING
Wear safety glasses when performing Step 4.

4. Remove the piston pin clip from the outside of the piston (**Figure 47**) with needle nose pliers. Hold your thumb over one edge of the clip when removing it to prevent it from springing out.

5. Use a properly sized wooden dowel or socket extension and push the pin from the piston.

CAUTION
If the engine ran hot or seized, the piston pin may be difficult to remove, but do not drive the piston pin from the piston. Hammering will damage the piston, needle bearing and connecting rod. If the piston pin will not push out by hand, remove it as described in Step 6.

6. If the piston pin is tight, use a puller as shown in **Figure 48**. The tool can be fabricated as shown. Assemble the tool onto the piston and pull the piston pin from the piston. Be sure to install a pad between the piston and piece of pipe to prevent damaging the piston.

NOTE
*If the pin is left partly in the piston as shown in **Figure 49**, the pin and piston*

will remain together and not mistakenly mixed with other similar parts.

7. Lift the piston from the connecting rod.

8. Remove the needle bearing from the connecting rod (**Figure 50**).

9. Repeat the removal procedure for the other piston(s).

10. If the pistons are going to remain off for some time, cover the end of each rod with a piece of foam insulation tube or a shop cloth to protect it.

NOTE
Always remove the top piston ring first.

11. Remove the upper ring by spreading the ends with your thumbs just enough to slide it up over the piston (**Figure 51**). Repeat for the lower ring.

Piston (Wrist) Pin and Needle Bearing Inspection

1. Clean the needle bearing (**Figure 52**) in solvent and dry it thoroughly. Use a magnifying glass and inspect the bearing cage for cracks at the corners of the needle slots and inspect the needles themselves for cracking. If any cracks are found, the bearing must be replaced.

2. Check the piston pin (**Figure 53**) for severe wear, scoring or chrome flaking. Also check the wrist pin for cracks along the top and side surfaces. Replace the piston pin if necessary.

3. With a micrometer, measure the piston pin outside diameter (**Figure 54**) at several different points and compare to the service specification listed in **Table 2-9**. If the piston pin is worn, replace the pin and bearing as a set.

4. Measure the piston pin bore in the piston with a snap gauge (**Figure 55**), then measure the snap gauge with a micrometer to determine the pin bore diameter. Compare measurement with serv-

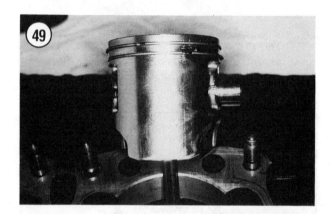

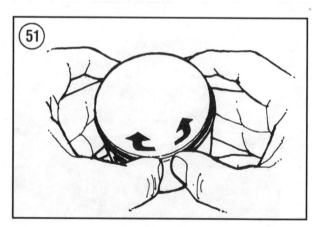

48

Pad   Nut

Pipe   Washer
Threaded rod

ice specification listed in **Table 2-9**. Replace the piston if the piston pin bore diameter is too large.

5. If you do not have access to a micrometer and snap gauge to perform Steps 3 and 4, perform the following:

   a. Oil the needle bearing and piston pin and install them in the connecting rod. Slowly rotate the piston pin and check for radial and axial play (**Figure 56**). If any play exists, the pin and bearing should be replaced, providing the rod bore is in good condition. If the condition of the rod bore is in question, the old pin and bearing can be checked with a new connecting rod.

   b. Oil the piston pin and install it in the piston pin hole (**Figure 57**). Check for up and down play between the pin and piston. There should be no noticeable play. If play is noticeable, replace the piston pin and/or piston.

CAUTION
If there are signs of piston seizure or overheating, replace the piston pins and bearings. These parts have been weakened from excessive heat and may fail later.

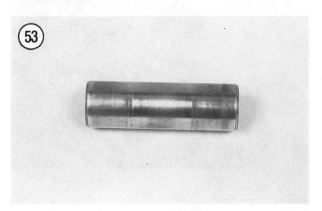

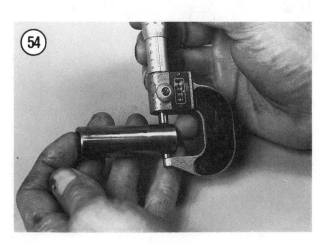

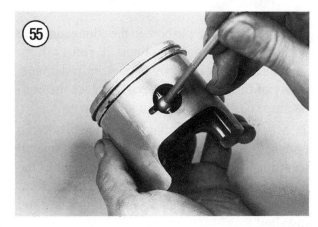

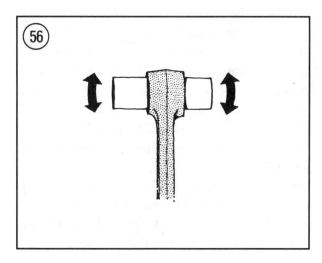

Connecting Rod Inspection

> *NOTE*
> *To replace the connecting rods, the crankshaft must be pressed apart, then pressed together and aligned using precision holding, measuring and pressing equipment. These special tools and technicians trained and experienced at rebuilding the crankshaft assembly are not available at most service shops. The manufacturer recommends replacement of the connecting rods and crankshaft if any part other than the outer seals or the main bearings at the ends of the crankshaft require replacement. Parts for the crankshaft may also not be available. If the condition of the connecting rods or the crankshaft are questioned, the assembly should be inspected by a competent dealer familiar with crankshaft repair.*

1. Wipe the piston pin bore in the connecting rod with a clean rag and check it for galling, scratches, or any other signs of wear or damage. If any of these conditions exist, replace the connecting rods as described in this chapter.

2. Measure the inside diameter of the piston pin bore in the connecting rod (**Figure 58**) at several locations. If any measurement is not within the specifications listed in **Tables 2-9**, the crankshaft will have to be rebuilt and a new connecting rod installed.

3. Check the connecting rod big end axial play. You can make a quick check by simply rocking the connecting rod back and forth (**Figure 59**). If there is more than a very slight rocking motion (some side-to-side sliding is normal), you should have an Arctic Cat dealer check the crankshaft further to see if it is satisfactory for further use.

4. Rotate the crankshaft and check the smoothness of the connecting rod as it moves around the crankpin. If the connecting rod catches, or ratchets, as the crankshaft is rotated, you should have an Arctic Cat dealer check the crankshaft further to see if it is satisfactory for further use.

5. While performing the connecting rod check in Step 4, the crankshaft main bearings should also turn smoothly. The outer bearings can be removed and replaced without disassembling the crankshaft.

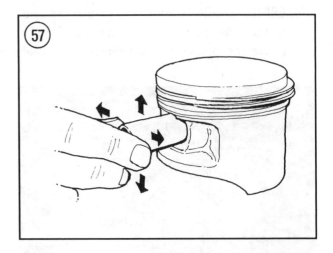

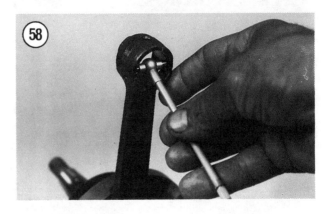

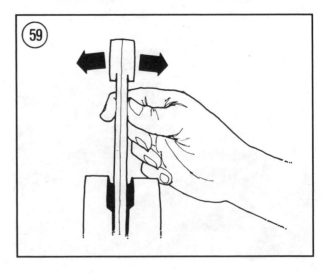

Piston and Ring Inspection

1. Carefully check the piston for cracks at the top edge of the transfer cutaways (**Figure 60**) and replace if found. Check the piston skirt for brown varnish buildup. More than a slight amount is an indication of worn or sticking rings which should be replaced. Clean the piston carefully before installing new rings.

2. Check the piston skirt for galling and abrasion (**Figure 61**) which may have resulted from piston seizure. If light galling is present, smooth the affected area with No. 400 emery paper and oil or a fine oilstone. If galling is severe or if the piston is deeply scored, replace it.

3. Check the condition of the piston crown. Normal carbon buildup can be removed with a wire wheel mounted on a drill press. If the piston is damaged, it is important to pinpoint the cause so that the failure will not repeat after engine assem-

bly. Note the following when checking damaged pistons:

  a. If the piston damage is confined to the area above the piston pin bore, the engine is probably overheating. Seizure or galling conditions confined to the area below the piston pin bore are usually caused by a lack of lubrication, rather than overheating.

  b. If the piston has seized and appears very dry with an apparent lack of oil or lubrication on the piston, a lean fuel mixture probably caused the overheating. Overheating can result from incorrect jetting, air leaks or over-advanced ignition timing.

  c. Preignition will cause a sand-blasted appearance on the piston crown. This condition is discussed in Chapter Two.

  d. If the piston damage is confined to the exhaust port area on the front of the piston, look for incorrect jetting producing a too-lean mixture or over-advanced ignition timing.

  e. If the piston has a melted pocket starting in the crown or if there is a hole in the piston crown, the engine is running too lean. This may be caused by incorrect jetting, an air leak or over-advanced ignition timing. A spark plug that is too hot can also cause this type of piston damage.

  f. If the piston is seized around the skirt but the dome color indicates proper lubrication (no signs of dryness or excessive heat), the damage may result from a condition referred to as cold seizure. This condition typically results from running the engine too hard without first properly warming it up. A lean fuel mixture can also cause skirt seizure.

4. Check the piston ring locating pins in the piston (**Figure 42**). The pins should be tight and the piston should show no signs of cracking around the pins. If a locating pin is loose, replace the piston. A loose pin will fall out and cause severe engine damage.

5

5. Inspect the piston pin retaining clip grooves in the piston (**Figure 41**) for damage that could allow a clip to come out and cause severe engine damage. Replace the piston if either groove shows signs of wear or damage.

NOTE
Maintaining proper piston ring end gap helps to ensure peak engine perform-ance. Excessive ring end gap reduces engine performance and may cause overheating. Insufficient ring end gap will cause the ring ends to butt together and break the ring, resulting in severe engine damage.

6. Measure piston ring end gap as follows:
  a. Position a ring in the bottom of the cylinder, then push it into the cylinder with the crown of the piston (**Figure 62**) until the ring is just below the transfer ports. Using the pis-ton to move the ring ensures that the ring is square in the cylinder bore.
  b. Measure the end gap with a flat feeler gauge (**Figure 63**) and compare to the wear limit in **Table 2-9**.
  c. If the gap is greater than specified, replace the rings as a set.

NOTE
When installing new rings, measure the end gap as described in Step 6. If the gap is less than specified, make sure you have the correct piston rings. If the replace-ment rings are correct but the end gap is too small, carefully file the ends with a fine-cut file until the gap is correct (Fig-ure 64). Insufficient gap may allow the ends to butt together and break the ring, which could cause severe piston and cyl-inder damage.

CAUTION
An old ring can be broken and used to clean carbon from the ring groove as shown in Figure 65. Be careful to re-move only carbon from the grooves and do not cut into the soft aluminum of the piston. Some rings and their grooves have the top tapered, so be careful when

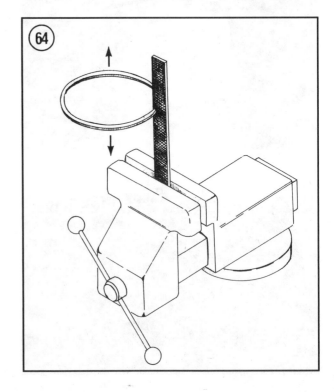

cleaning the grooves. If you damage the grooves while cleaning, a new piston must be installed.

7. Carefully remove all carbon buildup from the ring grooves. Inspect the piston for missing, broken or cracked ring lands. Inspect the grooves carefully for cleanliness and for absence of burrs or nicks. Recondition or replace the piston if necessary.

8. Check the side clearance of each ring in its groove by rolling the new ring around the piston in its groove as shown in **Figure 66**. If the ring grooves show excessive wear, install a new piston.

9. Inspect the condition of the piston crown. Normal carbon buildup can be removed with a

wire brush or scraper. If the piston shows signs of overheating, pitting or other abnormal conditions, the engine may be experiencing preignition or detonation. Both conditions are discussed in Chapter Two.

> *CAUTION*
> *Do not clean piston skirts or ring lands using a wire brush. The wire brush removes aluminum, which will increase piston clearance. The brush also rounds the corners of the ring lands which results in decreased support for the piston rings.*

10. If the piston checked out okay after performing these inspection procedures, measure the piston outside diameter as described under *Piston/Cylinder Clearance* in this chapter.

11. If new piston rings are required, the cylinders should be honed before assembling the engine. Refer to *Cylinder Honing* in this chapter.

Piston/Cylinder Clearance

The following procedure requires the use of highly specialized and expensive measuring tools. If such equipment is not readily available, have the measurements performed by a dealer or machine shop. Always replace all pistons as a set.

1. Measure the outside diameter of the piston with a micrometer approximately 1 cm (7/16 inch) above the bottom of the piston skirt, at a 90° angle to the piston pin (**Figure 67**).

2. Clean the cylinder block completely. Wash the cylinder bore with soap and water to remove oil and carbon particles. Clean the cylinder bore thoroughly before attempting any measurement to prevent inaccurate readings caused by foreign matter.

3. Measure the cylinder bore with a bore gauge or telescoping gauge (**Figure 68**). Then measure the bore gauge or telescoping gauge with a micrometer to determine the bore diameter. Measure the cylinder bore at three vertical locations

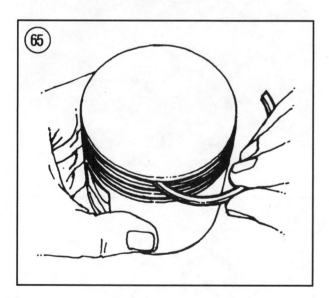
65

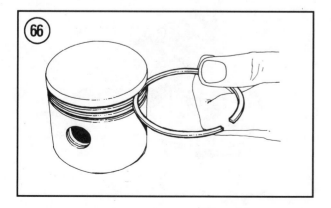
66

in the cylinder, in line with the piston pin and at 90° to the pin as shown in **Figure 69**.

4. Piston clearance is the difference between the maximum piston diameter and the minimum cylinder diameter.

> *NOTE*
> *Arctco does not list specifications for the piston outside diameter or the cylinder bore inside diameter. Wear is monitored by checking the piston-to-cylinder clearance. When the clearance is excessive, measure the clearance again using a new piston. If the clearance is still excessive with a new piston, the cylinder bore is worn. Because the cylinder bores are hard-chrome plated, resizing is not possible. If the cylinder bore is excessively worn, the cylinder must either be replaced or machined to accept a cast iron liner. Installation of a liner should be performed only by a qualified machinist familiar with these service products and the required tools.*

Cylinder Honing

The original cylinder walls are plated with a hard metal and cannot be bored oversize. However, the plated cylinder bores should be lightly honed with a fine-grit aluminum oxide ball hone to deglaze the cylinder when installing new rings. This service should be performed by an Arctic Cat dealer or repair shop familiar with plated cylinder work. The cost of having a cylinder honed by a dealer is usually minimal compared to purchasing the correct hone and doing the job yourself. If you choose to hone the cylinder yourself, follow the hone manufacturer's instructions closely and note the following:

   a. Do not make more passes through each cylinder than absolutely necessary. Usually ten passes is all that is required to provide the proper surface.

   b. Ball type hones are recommended because they will exert lighter pressure against the plated surface than bar type hones.

   c. Operate the hone slowly about 600 rpm at a rate of about 30 strokes per minute to produce a 60° cross hatch.

> *CAUTION*
> *After reconditioning a cylinder by honing, clean the cylinder bore with soap and water to remove all material left from the machining operation. Improper cleaning will result in rapid wear of the new piston and rings. After washing, run a clean white cloth through the cylinder. The cloth should show no traces of grit or other debris. If not, rewash the cylin-*

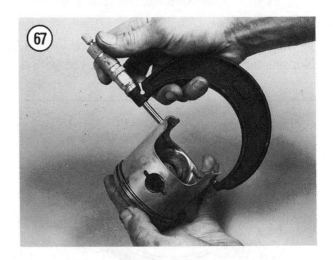

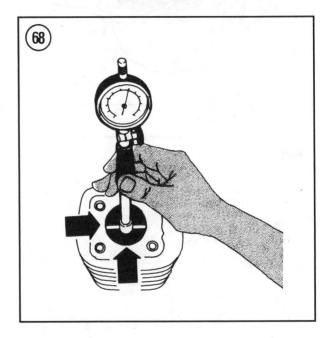

der wall. *After the cylinder is thoroughly cleaned, lubricate the cylinder wall with clean engine oil.*

Piston Installation

1. Prior to assembly, perform the inspection procedures to make sure all worn or defective parts have been cleaned or replaced. Thoroughly clean all parts before installation or assembly.

NOTE
*Most engine models have thrust washers (**Figure 52**) located at the sides of the piston pin bearing.*

2. Lubricate the piston pin needle bearing with oil and install it in the connecting rod. If so equipped, position the thrust washers against the sides as shown in **Figure 70** with the flat sides out.

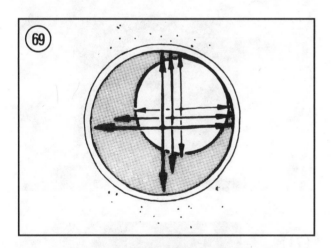

3. Oil the piston pin and install it in the piston until the end extends slightly beyond the inside of the boss (**Figure 49**).

NOTE
If you are reinstalling the original pistons, they should have been marked to indicate their original cylinder location (PTO, MAG or CEN) and the direction of the exhaust port. The arrow cast into the piston top should point to the exhaust port as described in Step 4.

4. Place the piston over the connecting rod with the arrow cast in the top of the piston, or inside the piston under the crown, pointing toward the front (exhaust side) of the engine. Refer to **Figure 71**. This is essential so the ends of the piston rings will be correctly positioned and will not catch in the ports. Line up the piston pin with the bearing and push the pin into the piston until it is even with the piston pin clip grooves.

CAUTION
*If the piston pin will not slide in the piston smoothly with hand pressure, use a tool described during **Piston Removal** to install the piston pin (**Figure 48**). The pipe is not used when installing the pin. Instead, insert the threaded rod through the piston pin, pin bearing, connecting rod and piston. A small washer and nut should be on the threaded rod at the end which extends from the piston pin. Slide a large washer onto the opposite end of the threaded rod next to the piston. Install the nut next to the large washer and*

tighten it to pull the piston pin into the piston. Do not use excessive force. If it is difficult to move the piston pin, check to make sure the pin is not catching on the needle bearing in the connecting rod.

5. Install *new* piston pin clips (**Figure 72**), making sure they are completely seated in their grooves. The manufacturer recommends the opening of clips in three-cylinder engines be toward the top. The clip opening on other models can be either up or down. If the clip gap is toward the side, it may come out while the engine is running.

> *CAUTION*
> *Always install new piston pin clips and make sure the clips snap securely into the piston grooves. A weak or improperly installed clip could disengage during engine operation and cause severe engine damage.*

6. Check the installation by rocking the piston back and forth around the pin. It should rotate freely.

7. Install the bottom piston ring first, then the top ring. Make sure that the rings are installed with the manufacturer's mark toward the top of the piston. Spread the ends of the ring carefully with your thumbs and slip the ring gently over the top of the piston.

8. Make sure the ring(s) are free to enter the groove(s) all the way around the circumference

and that the ends are aligned with the locating pins. See **Figure 73**.

9. If new components were installed, the engine must be broken in as if it were new. Refer to *Break-In Procedure* in Chapter Three.

REED VALVE ASSEMBLY (1990-1991 EL TIGRE)

The 529 cc engine used in 1990-1991 El Tigre models is equipped with crankcase reeds attached to the bottom of each cylinder as shown in **Figure 74**. Whenever you remove the cylinder from the engine, do not rest the cylinder on the reed valve. If it is necessary to stand the cylinder up, support the bottom of the cylinder with wooden blocks as shown in **Figure 75**.

Removal/Installation

1. Remove the cylinder as described in this chapter.

2. Turn the cylinder over so the reed valve faces up (**Figure 74**).

3. Remove the two Phillips screws. Screw threads may be coated with Loctite and it may be necessary to apply heat before the screws can

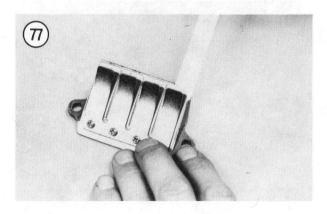

be loosened. Lift the reed valve assembly from the cylinder.

4. Remove and discard the gasket and clean any residue from the valve housing and the cylinder.

5. Check the threaded holes in the cylinder for damage and repair as necessary.

6. Inspect the reed valve assembly as described in this chapter.

7. Install a new gasket on the cylinder block and position the reed assembly onto the cylinder block.

8. Coat threads of the retaining screws with Loctite 242 (blue), then tighten the screws securely.

9. Install the cylinder as described in this chapter.

Inspection

1. Carefully examine the reed valve assembly for visible signs of wear, distortion or damage.

2. If any reed petal is chipped or broken, install new reeds.

3. Check the coating on the reed cage for separation or other damage.

> *CAUTION*
> *Do not attempt to bend the stop plate while it is mounted on the reed valve block because the reed block may be severely damaged. Replace the stop plate if it is severely bent or damaged.*

4. Use a scale or vernier caliper, to measure the height of the reed stop. Measure from the end of the reed stop to the reed valve seat (**Figure 76**, typical). Compare the measured distance with the specification listed in **Table 2**.

5. Measure the clearance between the reed valve to the seat with a feeler gauge (**Figure 77**, typical). If the clearance is 0.20 mm (0.008 in.) or more, the reed petals should be replaced.

NOTE
Screw threads may be coated with Loc-
tite and it may be necessary to apply heat
before you can loosen the screws.

6. Remove the screws (**Figure 78**) securing the reed stop and reed petals to the reed cage. Be careful that the screwdriver does not slip and damage parts.

7. Carefully examine the removed parts for cracks, fatigue marks, distortion or other damage.

8. Check the threaded holes in the reed cage. If threads are damaged, replace the reed valve assembly.

9. Assemble the unit as follows:

    a. Locate the beveled corners (**Figure 78**) on the reed petal and the stop. Align the beveled corners during assembly.

    b. Make sure all the parts are clean and free of any small dirt particles or lint.

    c. Apply Loctite 271 to the threads of the screws securing the reed valve stop and petals before installation.

    d. Assemble and align the parts of the reed valve, then install the retaining screws and tighten securely.

10. Install the reed valve assembly on the cylinder using a new gasket.

REED VALVE ASSEMBLY
(437.4, 497, 594 AND 599 CC ENGINES)

Reed valve induction is used on 437.4, 497 and 599 cc two-cylinder engines and 594 cc engines. The reed valves are located between each carburetor and the upper half of the crankcase (**Figure 79**).

Removal/Installation

1. Remove the carburetor(s) as described in Chapter Six.

2. Detach the oil injection hose from the fitting (**Figure 80**) on the carburetor adapter.

3. Remove the six retaining screws and remove the carburetor adapter.

4. Lift the reed valve assembly (**Figure 81**) from the crankcase.

5. Remove and discard the gasket and clean residue from the valve housing and the crankcase.

6. Check the threaded holes in the crankcase for damage and repair as necessary.

7. Inspect the reed valve assembly as described in this chapter.

8. Check the condition of the carburetor adapter (**Figure 82**). The adapter must seal against the

reed valve housing and seal to the carburetor. Leaks will cause that cylinder to run lean.

9. Install a new gasket against the crankcase and position the reed assembly into the crankcase opening.

10. Position the carburetor adapter against the reed valve housing and install the six retaining screws. Tighten the screws evenly to the torque listed in **Table 10**.

> *NOTE*
> *Fill the oil injection lines with oil before reconnecting them if the oil has drained from them.*

11. Attach the oil injection line to the fitting (**Figure 80**).

12. Install the carburetor(s) as described in Chapter Six.

Inspection

1. Carefully examine the removed reed valve assembly (**Figure 83**) for visible signs of wear, distortion or damage.

2. If any reed petal is chipped or broken, install new reeds.

3. Check the coating on the reed cage for separation or other damage.

> *CAUTION*
> *Do not attempt to bend the stop plate while it is mounted on the reed valve block because the reed block may be severely damaged. Replace the stop plate if it is severely bent or damaged.*

4. Use a scale or vernier caliper to measure the height of the reed stop. Measure from the end of the reed stop to the reed valve seat (**Figure 76**, typical). Compare the measured distance with the specification listed in **Table 6** or **8**.

5. Measure the clearance between the reed valve to the seat with a feeler gauge (**Figure 77**, typical). If the clearance is 0.20 mm (0.008 in.) or more, the reed petals should be replaced.

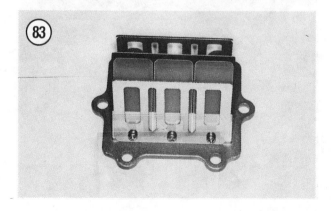

NOTE
Screw threads may be coated with Loc-tite and it may be necessary to apply heat before you can loosen the screws.

6. Remove the screws (**Figure 83**) securing the reed stop and reed petals to the reed cage. Be careful that the screwdriver does not slip and damage parts.

7. Carefully examine the removed parts for cracks, fatigue marks, distortion or other damage.

8. Check the threaded holes in the reed cage. If threads are damaged, replace the reed valve assembly.

9. Assemble the unit as follows:
   a. Locate the beveled corners of the reed petal and the stop. Align these beveled corners at the right corner during assembly.
   b. Make sure all the parts are clean and free of any small dirt particles or lint.
   c. Before installation of the screws securing the reed valve stop and petals, apply Loctite 271 to the screw threads.
   d. Assemble and align the parts of the reed valve, then install the retaining screws and tighten securely.

CRANKCASE AND CRANKSHAFT

Disassembling the crankcase for access to the crankshaft assembly requires engine removal from the frame. The cylinder head, cylinders and other attached assemblies can be removed with the engine in the frame, before removing the engine.

The diecast, thin wall aluminum alloy crankcase (**Figure 84**) is precision machined in two halves. To avoid damage to the crankcase, do not hammer or pry on any of the interior or exterior walls. The crankcase halves are sold only as a matched set and if one half of the crankcase is damaged, both must be replaced. The crankcase halves are bolted together and aligned with dowel pins. The crankcase is assembled without

a gasket, using a light coat of RTV High Temperature Silicone Sealant (part no. 0636-069).

Crankshaft service includes disassembly of the crankshaft, replacement of unsatisfactory parts and accurate crankshaft alignment. Special measuring and alignment tools, a hydraulic press and experience are necessary to disassemble, assemble and accurately align the crankshaft assembly. Components of the crankshaft may be

available as individual parts; however, entrust service only to a trained dealer or engine specialist. You can save considerable expense by disassembling the engine and taking the crankshaft to the dealer.

The procedures which follow describe a complete, step-by-step lower end overhaul.

Crankcase Disassembly

1. Remove the engine from the frame as described in this chapter.

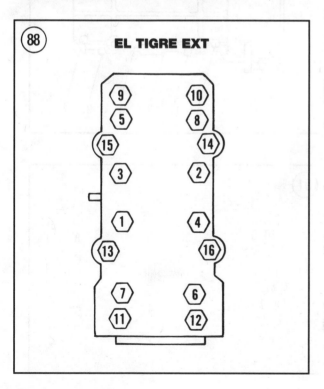

2. Remove all the engine mounts from the crankcase as described in this chapter.

3. Remove the flywheel and stator plate as described in Chapter Nine.

4. Remove the oil pump and water pump as described in this chapter.

5. Remove the cylinders and pistons as described in this chapter.

> *NOTE*
> *The four screws or bolts shown in Figures 85 or 86 are secured with Loctite. Apply heat to and/or use an impact driver to remove them.*

6. Remove the four screws or bolts securing the end plate (**Figures 85** or **86**) to the engine, then remove the end plate from the crankcase.

> *CAUTION*
> *Do not damage the crankcase studs when performing the following procedures.*

7. Turn the crankcase assembly so that it rests upside-down as shown in **Figure 87**. Support the crankcase with wooden blocks so that the connecting rods are not damaged.

> *NOTE*
> *On some engines, the tightening sequence for the crankcase bolts is embossed in the crankcase. Reverse the sequence when loosening the screws.*

> *NOTE*
> *Different size and length bolts are used to secure the crankcase halves. To ease assembly, draw the outline of the lower crankcase half on a piece of cardboard, then punch a hole in the cardboard to represent each bolt position. As the bolts are remove from the crankcase, insert them in their numbered position.*

8. Loosen the crankcase bolts in two or more stages in a crisscross pattern by reversing the sequence shown in **Figure 88-92**. Remove all the crankcase bolts.

CAUTION
Prying the cases apart with a screw-driver or any other sharp tool will damage the sealing surface. If all of the case bolts are removed, you should be able to separate the case halves with no more force other than tapping the bolt bosses as described in Step 9. Remember, damage to one case half will require replacement of both.

9. Tap on the large bolt bosses with a soft mallet to break the crankcase halves apart and then remove the bottom half (**Figure 87**).

NOTE
To reduce the damage to the long studs attached to the upper crankcase half of air-cooled models, lift the upper case half from the lower half. On liquid-cooled models, lift the bottom case half from the top half.

10. Lift the crankshaft (**Figure 93**) from the upper crankcase half and set it aside carefully so that you do not damage the connecting rods. Block the crankshaft so that it cannot roll off of the workbench.

11. If necessary, remove the coolant pump and oil injection pump driveshaft as described in this chapter.

Cleaning

1. Clean both crankcase halves with cleaning solvent. Thoroughly dry with compressed air and wipe off with a clean shop cloth. Be sure to remove all traces of old sealer from mating surfaces.

2. Clean all the oil passages in the crankcase, then blow passages out with compressed air.

CAUTION
Make sure the cleaning solvent used to clean the crankshaft is clean. If any dirt enters the close clearances of the bearings while cleaning, it will be difficult to remove and can cause bearing damage.

3. Clean the crankshaft assembly in solvent and dry with compressed air. Lubricate the bearings with injection oil to prevent rusting.

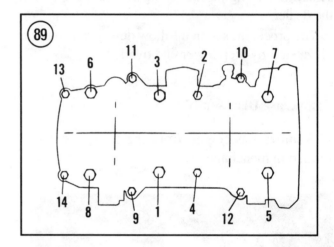

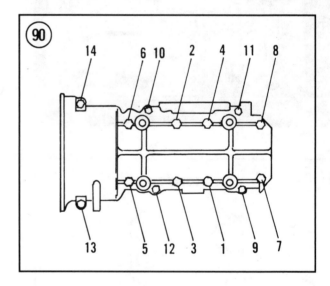

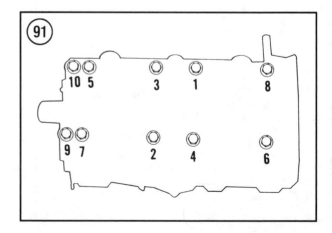

Crankcase Inspection

1. Carefully inspect the case halves for cracks and fractures. Also check the areas around the stiffening ribs, around bearing bosses and all the threaded holes. If you discover any damage, have it repaired by a shop specializing in the repair of precision aluminum castings or replace the crankcase.

2. Check the mating surfaces of the crankcase halves for high spots, burrs or any roughness that would interfere with sealing. The following procedure can be used to check the sealing surfaces and to remove small localized high spots.

    a. Tape a piece of 400-600 grit wet emery paper onto a piece of plate glass or a surface plate.

    b. Move the case half slowly in a figure-eight pattern on the sandpaper. See **Figure 94**.

    c. Check the sealing surface often and stop when the surface is flat.

    d. Rotate the case half several times to avoid removing too much material from one spot.

3. Check the bearing support area of both the upper (**Figure 95**) and lower (**Figure 96**) halves.

4. Check the threaded holes in both crankcase halves for damage or dirt buildup. If necessary, clean or repair the threads with a suitably sized metric tap. Coat the tap threads with kerosene or aluminum tap fluid before use.

5. Check the cylinder studs (**Figure 97**) in the upper crankcase for thread damage. If necessary,

replace damaged studs as described under *Cylinder Stud Replacement* in this chapter.

6. Check the upper and lower crankcase halves around the grooves for the oil seals and bearing retaining rings (**Figure 95** and **96**) for cracks or damage.

7. Inspect the seal and bearings for the coolant pump and oil injection pump as described in this chapter.

8. Check the machined surfaces of the coolant pump on the lower crankcase half (**Figure 98**). Check the surface for gouges or other damage that would indicate damage.

9. Inspect the coolant pump as described in this chapter.

10. If there is any doubt as to the condition of the crankcase halves, and they cannot be repaired, replace the crankcase halves as a set.

Crankshaft Inspection

Do not remove any bearings that are pressed onto the crankshaft unless new bearings are available. Refer to **Figure 99** for a typical crankshaft. A single roller bearing is used on some models in place of the two ball bearings (2 and 4, **Figure 99**) shown.

1. Remove the crankshaft seals from each end of the crankshaft. Even though the seals may appear okay, they should be replaced when the crankcase is disassembled to make sure the crankcase is airtight when it is assembled.

2. Support the crankshaft on V-blocks so it can be rotated while inspecting it.

3. Inspect the small end (**Figure 70**) and big end (**Figure 100**) of each connecting rod for excessive heat discoloration or bearing damage.

4. Spin each connecting rod by hand, while checking for excessive noise or roughness.

5. Carefully examine the condition of the crankshaft main bearings (**Figure 101**). Clean the bearings with solvent and dry with compressed air. Do not allow bearings to spin while drying. Oil each bearing, then check it by rolling each

bearing by hand. Make sure that it turns quietly and smoothly. There must not be any rough spots or apparent radial play. Replace defective bearings.

6. Inspect the drive gear (**Figure 102**) for cracks, deep scoring or excessive wear. Check the gear (**Figure 103**) on the coolant and injection pump driveshaft for damage. If either gear is damaged, replace *both* gears. If the drive gear is damaged, the crankshaft will have to be disassembled or replaced; refer crankshaft disassembly to a dealer or crankshaft specialist.

> *NOTE*
> *The bearings installed on the outside of the crank wheels can be replaced as described under **Crankshaft Bearing Replacement** in this chapter. To replace the bearings, seals and center gear installed between the crank wheels, the crankshaft must be disassembled. Refer*

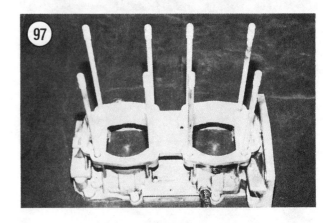

service to a qualified dealer or crank-shaft specialist.

7. Check crankshaft runout as follows:

   a. Support the crankshaft by placing the main bearings at the ends onto two precision V-blocks.

   b. Position dial indicators so that the plungers contact the crankshaft at the specific distances from the ends of the crankshaft indicated in **Tables 2-9**.

c. Turn the crankshaft slowly and observe the gauge reading. The maximum difference recorded is crankshaft runout.

d. If the runout at any position exceeds the service limit (**Tables 2-9**), the crankshaft should be serviced by a dealer or crankshaft specialist.

NOTE
Do not check crankshaft runout with the crankshaft placed between lathe centers. Use V-blocks as described in Step 7.

5

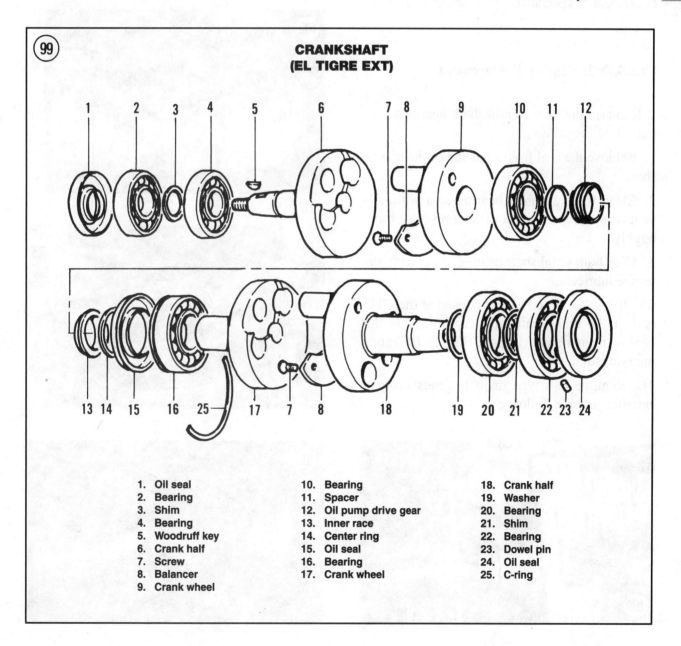

**CRANKSHAFT
(EL TIGRE EXT)**

1. Oil seal	10. Bearing	18. Crank half
2. Bearing	11. Spacer	19. Washer
3. Shim	12. Oil pump drive gear	20. Bearing
4. Bearing	13. Inner race	21. Shim
5. Woodruff key	14. Center ring	22. Bearing
6. Crank half	15. Oil seal	23. Dowel pin
7. Screw	16. Bearing	24. Oil seal
8. Balancer	17. Crank wheel	25. C-ring
9. Crank wheel		

8. Check the crankshaft threads for stripping, cross threading or other damage. Have threads repaired by a dealer or machine shop.

9. Check the woodruf key seat (**Figure 104**) in the crankshaft for cracks or other damage. If the key seat is damaged, refer service to a dealer or machine shop.

10. If the crankshaft exceeded any of the service limits or if one or more bearings are worn or damaged, have the crankshaft rebuilt by a dealer or crankshaft specialist.

Crankshaft Bearing Replacement

Replace the outer crankshaft bearings and outer seals as follows:

1. Remove the seal from each end of the crankshaft.

2. Clean the crankshaft bearing area with solvent or electrical contact cleaner and dry thoroughly.

3. Coat both crankshaft bearing areas with antiseize lubricant.

4A. If a roller type bearing is used at the PTO end of the crankshaft, you can withdraw the bearing from the shaft by hand (**Figure 105**) after the seal is removed.

4B. Remove ball type main bearings using a suitable puller as follows:

CAUTION
The procedure necessary to move the bearing far enough to install the puller may damage the crankshaft.

a. Support the crankshaft and use a chisel (**Figure 106**) or bearing splitter to move the outer bearing toward the end of the crankshaft far enough to install a bearing puller.

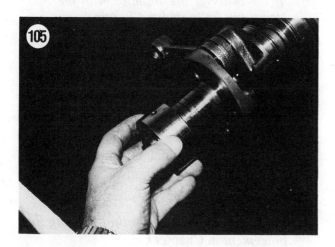

CAUTION
When using a puller to remove bearings from the ends of the crankshaft, place a protective cap over the crankshaft to prevent the puller screw from damaging the end of the crankshaft.

b. Attach a puller as shown in **Figure 107**, then use the puller to remove the bearing assemblies.

c. Check to see if shims (3, **Figure 99**) are located between the two PTO end bearings or between the bearing and the crankshaft. Record their location and thickness, then save these shims so they can be reinstalled in their original location. The shims are used to position the crankshaft when installing the new bearing.

NOTE
Different bearings are used as main bearings at specific locations on the crankshaft. When you purchase the replacement bearings, have the parts man-

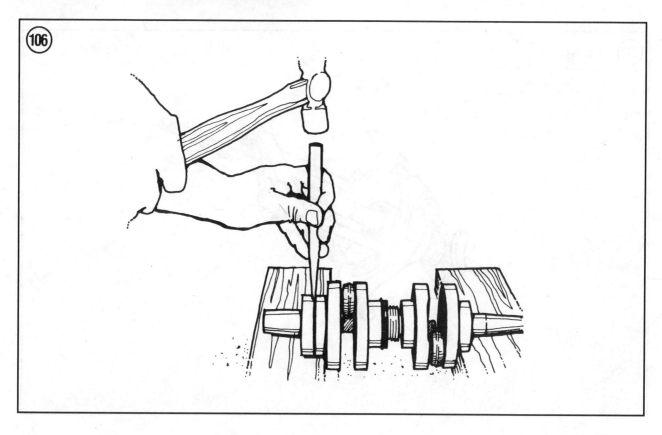

ager identify each bearing and its position on the crankshaft. It is critical that the bearings are properly installed.

5A. Install the roller bearing as follows:

a. Clean the crankshaft main journal, then coat the journal with engine oil.

b. Lubricate the bearing with engine oil.

c. Locate the two holes in the roller bearing (**Figure 108**). The blind hole that stops before going through the bearing race is for the locating dowel pin. The hole that extends through the bearing race into the bearing rollers is the lubrication hole.

d. Slide the bearing onto the main journal with the dowel pin hole in (A, **Figure 108**), toward the center of the crankshaft. The lubrication hole (B, **Figure 108**) should then align with the oil passage in the crankcase.

5B. Install ball type bearings as follows:

a. Lay the bearings and shims, if used, on a clean, lint-free surface in the order of assembly.

b. Make sure that the holes in the outer race are properly located and indexed before installing the bearings.

NOTE
If the bearings are installed with the dowel pin holes and the locating ring grooves incorrectly aligned, the lubrication holes will not line up properly with the passages in the crankcase.

c. Install any shims located between the bearing and the crankshaft. If shims were removed when disassembling, the same shims or the original thickness of shims should be installed. Shims at this location position the crankshaft.

d. Refer to *Shrink Fit* under *Ball Bearing Replacement* in Chapter One.

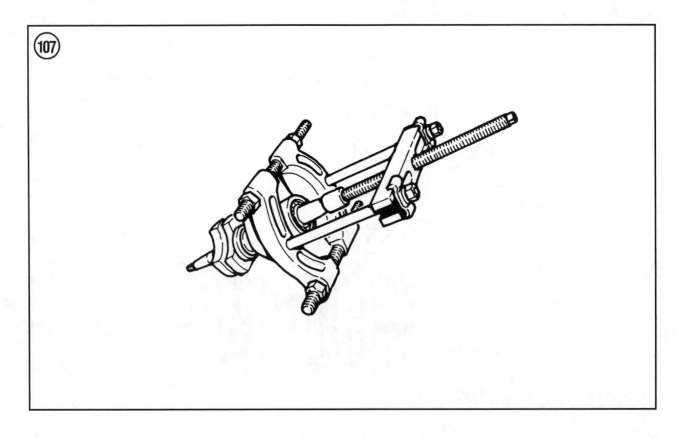
(107)

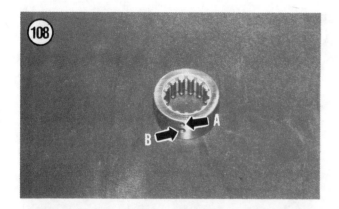

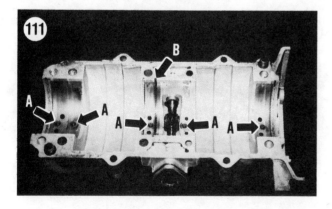

NOTE
Arctco recommends that ball type bearings be heated to 75° C (167° F) in oil before installation. Read Step 5 before heating and installing bearings. During bearing installation, support the crankshaft securely so the bearings can be installed quickly. If a bearing cools and tightens on the crankshaft before it is completely installed, remove the bearing with the puller and reheat the bearing.

e. Heat and install the bearings. Make sure the bearings are fully seated.

5

Crankshaft Installation

1. Install the coolant pump and oil injection pump driveshaft as described in this chapter.

2. Fill both of the outer crankshaft seal lip cavities with a low-temperature lithium-based grease.

3. Install the seals over the ends of the crankshaft as shown in **Figure 109**. The shield side of the seals must face out.

4A. On air-cooled Z 440, Panther 440 and 529 cc El Tigre engines, support the lower crankcase.

4B. On liquid-cooled engines, support the upper crankcase by its crankcase studs.

CAUTION
Do not install a pin in the lubrication passages.

5. If removed, make sure all the bearing locating pins (**Figure 110** or A, **Figure 111**) are installed.

6. On models so equipped, install the bearing locating C-ring in the groove as shown in B, **Figure 111** and **Figure 112**.

NOTE
Installation is easier if the holes in the main bearings' outer races for the locking dowel pins are in line and straight down when lowering the crankshaft into the crankcase lower half. It still may be necessary to move the outer races

slightly to engage the locking pins, but little movement should be required.

NOTE
Step 7A, 7B or 7C describes crankshaft installation; however, because of the number of separate procedures required during installation, read all the procedures included in Step 7A, 7B or 7C before installing the crankshaft.

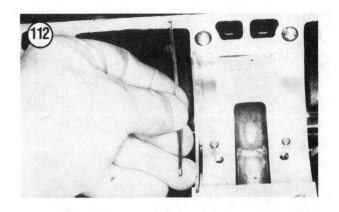

7A. On air-cooled Z 440 and Panther 440 engines, align the crankshaft with the lower crankcase half and install the crankshaft with the connecting rods up (**Figure 113**). Observe the following:

a. Make sure that the crankshaft center oil seal ring fits into the crankcase groove as shown in **Figure 114**.

b. Make sure that the crankshaft center drive gear (**Figure 102**) meshes properly with the gear on the coolant pump and oil injection pump drive shaft (**Figure 103**).

c. Be sure the groove in the center bearing fits around the C-ring (**Figure 112**).

d. Make sure the end seals fit into the crankcase properly.

e. Check that all five of the bearing locating pins properly engage the holes in the outer races of all five bearings. Try to turn each bearing's outer race to make sure the pin properly seats in the bearing.

CAUTION
It is important that the bearings and seals are properly aligned with the pins, C-ring and grooves, before continuing assembly. The upper half of the crankcase cannot be installed until the crankshaft, seals and bearings are completely seated in the lower half. Attempting to force the parts into place will only damage the parts.

7B. On 529 cc El Tigre engines, align the crankshaft with the lower crankcase half and install the crankshaft with the connecting rods down (**Figure 115**). Observe the following:

NOTE
*Installation is easier if the holes in the main bearings outer races for the locking dowel pins are in line (**Figure 116**) and straight down when lowering the crankshaft into the crankcase lower half. It still may be necessary to move the outer races slightly to engage the locking pins, but little movement should be required.*

a. Align the groove in the bearing with the C-ring (B, **Figure 111**) in the crankcase groove.

b. Align the ring on the oil seal with the crankcase groove as shown in **Figure 117**.

c. Make sure the center drive gear meshes properly with the gear on the coolant pump and oil injection pump driveshaft.

d. Make sure the end seals fit into the crankcase properly.

e. Check that all six of the bearing locating pins properly engage the holes in the outer races of all six bearings. Try to turn each bearing's outer race to make sure the pin properly seats in the bearing.

CAUTION
It is important that the bearings and seals are properly aligned with the pins, C-ring and grooves, before continuing assembly. The upper half of the crankcase cannot be installed until the crankshaft, seals and bearings are completely seated in the lower half. Attempting to force the parts into place will damage the parts.

7C. On 440 (435.8 and 437.4 cc), 500, 550, 580 and 600 (594 and 599 cc) engines, align the crankshaft with the upper crankcase half and install the crankshaft with the connecting rods down (**Figure 118**, typical). Observe the following:

a. Check that all the bearing locating pins properly engage the holes in the outer races of all main bearings. Try to turn each bearing's outer race to make sure the pin properly seats in the bearing.

b. Turn the crankshaft center seal rings (**Figure 119**) until the end gaps are 180° away from each other. On three-cylinder engines, none of the gaps should be aligned.

c. Make sure the end seals fit into the crankcase properly.

CAUTION
It is important that the bearings and seals are properly aligned with the pins and grooves, before continuing assembly. The lower half of the crankcase cannot be installed until the crankshaft, seals and bearings are completely seated in the upper half. Attempting to force the parts into place will damage the parts.

8. Recheck Steps 7A, 7B or 7C before proceeding with assembling the crankcase.

Crankcase Assembly

1. Install the crankshaft in one of the crankcase halves as described in this chapter.
2. Oil the crankshaft gear and the bottom end bearings with two-stroke oil.
3. If removed, install the two dowel pins in the crankcase.
4. Make sure the crankcase mating surfaces are completely clean and dry.
5. Apply RTV High Temperature Sealant (part no. 0636-069) to the entire mating surface of the crankcase half.
6. Position the other crankcase half onto the crankshaft and the other case half. If the lower crankcase half is being assembled onto the crankshaft and upper case half, make sure the gear on the coolant pump and oil injection pump driveshaft (**Figure 103**) meshes properly with the crankshaft center gear (**Figure 102**).

7. Make sure the case halves mate properly before installing the retaining screws. If a gap remains between the cases, make sure the bearing outer races are properly aligned with their locating pins, before continuing assembly. The crankcase halves will not fit together until the bearings are completely seated. Any attempt to force the case halves together will damage the parts.

8. Install the crankcase bolts and tighten by hand.

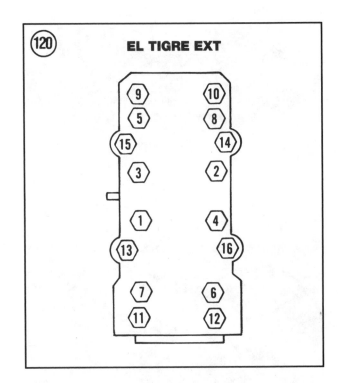

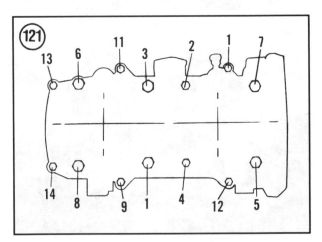

NOTE
Numbers may be located on the crank-case of some models indicating the recommended sequence for tightening the crankcase screws. If the sequence is not marked on the crankcase near the screws, use the tightening sequence shown in Figure 120-124.

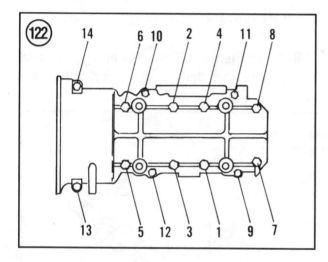

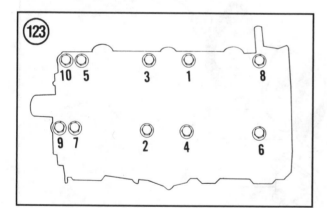

9. Refer to **Table 10** for the recommended final torque, then tighten the screws evenly in at least three steps to the torque listed. Check frequently while tightening the screws to be sure the crankshaft continues to turn freely.

CAUTION
If the crankshaft becomes difficult to turn, STOP and make sure the bearing locating rings and dowel pins are aligned properly. When correctly assembled, the crankshaft should turn freely.

10. Position the seal protector plate (**Figure 125** or **126**) around the crankshaft and against the crankcase.

11. Coat the threads of the retaining screws or bolts (**Figure 125** or **126**) with Loctite 242 and tighten securely.

12. Install the pistons and cylinders as described in this chapter.

13. Install the ignition stator plate and flywheel as described in Chapter Nine.

14. Install the oil injection pump and coolant pump as described in this chapter.

15. Install the engine mount plate or brackets and tighten the retaining screws to the torque listed in **Table 10**.

16. Install the engine in the frame as described in this chapter.

17. If new components were installed, the engine must be broken in as if it were new. Refer to *Break-In Procedure* in Chapter Three.

DRIVESHAFT FOR COOLANT PUMP AND OIL INJECTION PUMP

The illustration shown is typical of all models. However, O-rings are sometimes used in place of gaskets (3 and 5, **Figure 127**).

Shaft Removal

Refer to **Figure 127** for this procedure. You can remove the shaft without separating the

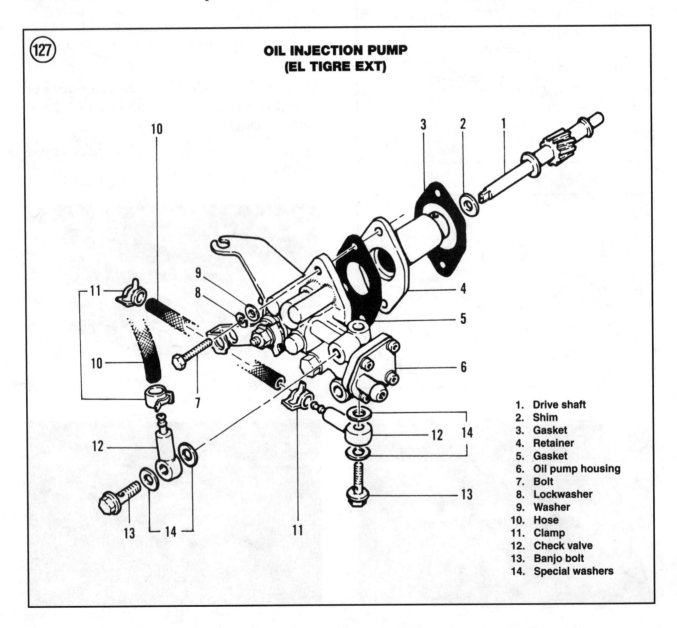

OIL INJECTION PUMP (EL TIGRE EXT)

1. Drive shaft
2. Shim
3. Gasket
4. Retainer
5. Gasket
6. Oil pump housing
7. Bolt
8. Lockwasher
9. Washer
10. Hose
11. Clamp
12. Check valve
13. Banjo bolt
14. Special washers

crankcase halves, but service is usually accomplished in conjunction with other engine service.

A kit (part No. 0644-084) is available from Arctic Cat for rebuilding the coolant pump on liquid-cooled models.

1. On liquid-cooled models, remove the cooling pump impeller as follows:

    a. Remove the screws securing the coolant pump cover to the crankcase.

    b. Carefully remove the pump cover and gasket.

    c. Remove the screw securing the impeller (**Figure 128**).

    d. Carefully pull the impeller from the driveshaft.

2. Detach oil line from the crankcase (**Figure 129**).

3. Detach the oil injection lines from the cylinders or the carburetor adapters.

4. Remove the two screws (**Figure 130**) securing the oil pump to the crankcase, then remove the pump from the engine.

NOTE
Do not lose or damage any shims (Figure 131) that may be located between the retainer (Figure 132) and the shoulder of the driveshaft (Figure 131).

5. Withdraw the retainer (**Figure 132**) from the crankcase.

CAUTION
The end of the driveshaft can be easily damaged during removal. Do not re-

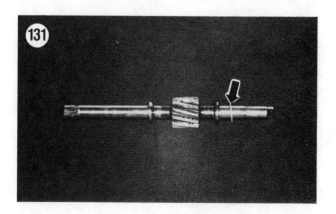

move the shaft unless new seals will be installed.

6. Carefully pull the driveshaft (**Figure 131**) toward the rear of the engine crankcase.

7. On models with liquid cooling, remove the seals at the front of the shaft as follows:

   a. Insert the seal removal tool (A, **Figure 133**) through the lower case half and pass it through the inner bearing and inner seal until the end of the tool engages the back of the outer (coolant) seal.

   b. Carefully tap the seal removal tool with a hammer to remove the coolant pump seal (**Figure 133**).

   c. Remove the circlip (**Figure 134**) securing the inner seal.

   d. Insert the seal removal tool from the front and remove the inner seal (**Figure 135**).

   e. If it is necessary to remove the bearing, insert the bearing driver (A, **Figure 136**) through the lower case half and drive the bearing (B, **Figure 136**) out toward the front.

Inspection

1. Clean the lower case half with solvent and dry with compressed air.

2. Check the condition of all bushings and bearings. Install new parts as necessary.

3. On liquid-cooled models, observe the following:

   a. Check the circlip groove in the case for damage. If you removed a circlip (C, **Figure 137**), you should install a new circlip.

   b. Check the impeller cover and housing for cracks, scoring or other damage. Repair or replace parts as necessary.

   c. Check the seal surface (A, **Figure 138**) carefully for scratches, cracks or wear.

   d. Check the impeller blades for broken blades, nicks or other damage. Check the center bore and driving flat in the center of

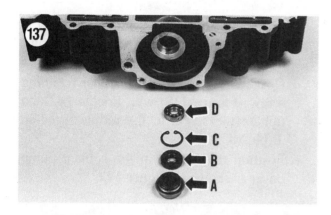

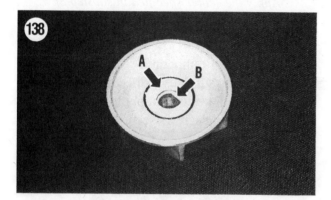

the impeller (B, **Figure 138**). Install a new impeller if damaged.

    e. Always install new seals when assembling.

4. Inspect the machined surfaces of the shaft and the gear (**Figure 131**) for any evidence of wear or damage. Replace as necessary.

Assembly

The coolant pump seal and bearing service kit (part No. 0644-084) contains the drivers and protectors necessary for assembly of liquid-cooled models.

1. Make sure the case half is free of all solvent before assembling the components of the coolant pump and oil pump drive.

2. Slip the bearing over the end of the bearing driver (**Figure 139**) and press the bearing into the case until seated.

3A. On liquid-cooled models, observe the following:

    a. Fill the inner lips of the seals with grease.

    b. Slip the inner oil seal over the driver with the spring side toward the crankshaft and press the seal into the case until seated.

    c. Install the circlip into its groove in the case. Make sure the clip is properly seated.

    d. Use the seal driver and gently tap the outer seal (**Figure 140**) into the case bore until seated.

    e. Coat the sealing surface of the driveshaft lightly with grease, then carefully insert the shaft through the bearing and seals. Twist the shaft when installing to help it pass through the seals without damaging them.

3B. On air-cooled Z 440 and Panther 440 models, install the oil pump driveshaft into the case and bearing.

4. Install shims on the pump shaft. The shims are used to limit the end play of the shaft and should not cause the shaft to bind when the retainer is installed.

5. Install the retainer (**Figure 132**) using a new gasket or sealing ring.

5

NOTE
*Make sure the drive shaft tang (**Figure 141**) and the slot in the pump shaft are aligned when installing the pump.*

6. Install the oil injection pump using a new sealing ring or gasket between the pump and the retainer. Tighten the two retaining screws to the torque listed in **Table 10**.

7. Attach the oil line to the crankcase and to each cylinder's injection fittings.

8. On liquid-cooled models, observe the following:

a. Lightly coat the seal surface (A, **Figure 138**) on the impeller with grease.

b. Install the impeller. Push the impeller onto the shaft until seated.

c. Make sure the impeller retaining screw is fitted with the special washer with the rubber side toward the impeller.

d. Coat the threads of the impeller retaining screw (**Figure 128**) with Loctite 242 and tighten the screw to the torque listed in **Table 10**.

e. Position the O-ring in the coolant pump cover as shown in **Figure 142**.

NOTE
Apply the sealer specified in substep 8f only to the mating surfaces of the case halves.

f. Apply high temperature silicone sealer to the mating surfaces of the crankcase halves and install the coolant pump cover. Tighten the retaining screws securely.

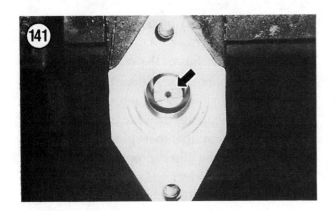

Table 1 ENGINE IDENTIFICATION

Model	Engine cooling type	Bore/stroke mm (in.)	Displacement cc (cid.)
1990			
Prowler	Liquid	68 × 60	435.8
El Tigre EXT	Liquid	72 × 65	529
El Tigre Mountain Cat	Liquid	72 × 65	529
1991			
Prowler	Air/fan	68 × 60	435.8
Prowler Mountain Cat	Liquid	68 × 60	435.8
Cougar	Liquid	73.4 × 65	550
El Tigre EXT	Liquid	72 × 65	529
El Tigre Mountain Cat	Liquid	72 × 65	529
(continued)			

Table 1 ENGINE IDENTIFICATION (continued)

Model	Engine cooling type	Bore/stroke mm (in.)	Displacement cc (cid.)
1992			
Prowler	Liquid	68 × 60	435.8
Prowler Mountain Cat	Liquid	68 × 60	435.8
Cougar	Liquid	73.4 × 65	550
El Tigre EXT	Liquid	73.4 × 65	550
El Tigre EXT Special	Liquid	73.4 × 65	550
El Tigre Mountain Cat	Liquid	73.4 × 65	550
1993			
Prowler	Liquid	68 × 60	435.8
Prowler Special	Liquid	68 × 60	435.8
Cougar	Liquid	68 × 60	435.8
440 ZR	Liquid	68 × 60	435.8
EXT 550	Liquid	73.4 × 65	550
EXT 550			
Mountain Cat	Liquid	73.4 × 65	550
Pantera	Liquid	73.4 × 65	550
580 ZR	Liquid	75.4 × 65	580
EXT 580 EFI	Liquid	75.4 × 65	580
EXT 580 EFI			
Mountain Cat	Liquid	75.4 × 65	580
1994			
Cougar	Liquid	68 × 60	435.8
Cougar Mountain Cat	Liquid	68 × 60	435.8
Prowler	Liquid	68 × 60	435.8
Prowler II	Liquid	68 × 60	435.8
ZR 440	Liquid	68 × 60	435.8
Pantera	Liquid	73.4 × 65	550
EXT 580	Liquid	75.4 × 65	580
EXT 580			
Mountain Cat	Liquid	75.4 × 65	580
EXT 580 EFI	Liquid	75.4 × 65	580
EXT 580 EFI			
Mountain Cat	Liquid	75.4 × 65	580
ZR 580	Liquid	75.4 × 65	580
1995			
Cougar	Liquid	73.4 × 65	550
Cougar Mountain Cat	Liquid	73.4 × 65	550
Prowler 2-Up	Liquid	73.4 × 65	550
440	Air/fan	65 × 65	431
ZR 440	Liquid	68 × 60	435.8
EXT 580	Liquid	75.4 × 65	580.4
EXT 580 EFI	Liquid	75.4 × 65	580
EXT 580 EFI			
Mountain Cat	Liquid	75.4 × 65	580
EXT 580			
Powder Special	Liquid	75.4 × 65	580
ZR 580	Liquid	75.4 × 65	580
ZR 580 EFI	Liquid	75.4 × 65	580

5

(continued)

Table 1 ENGINE IDENTIFICATION (continued)

Model	Engine cooling type	Bore/stroke mm (in.)	Displacement cc (cid.)
1996			
Z 440	Air/fan	65 × 65	431
ZR 440	Liquid	66.5 × 63	437.4
Cougar	Liquid	73.4 × 65	550
Cougar Mountain Cat	Liquid	73.4 × 65	550
Cougar 2-Up	Liquid	73.4 × 65	550
EXT 580	Liquid	75.4 × 65	580
EXT 580 EFI	Liquid	75.4 × 65	580
EXT 580 EFI			
Mountain Cat	Liquid	75.4 × 65	580
EXT 580			
Powder Special	Liquid	75.4 × 65	580
EXT EFI Deluxe	Liquid	75.4 × 65	580
Pantera	Liquid	75.4 × 65	580
ZR 580	Liquid	75.4 × 65	580
ZR 580 EFI	Liquid	75.4 × 65	580
ZRT 600	Liquid	66.5 × 57	594
1997			
Z 440	Air/fan	65 × 65	431
ZL 440	Liquid	68 × 60	435.8
ZR 440	Liquid	66.5 × 63	437.4
Cougar	Liquid	73.4 × 65	550
Cougar Mountain Cat	Liquid	73.4 × 65	550
Panther 550	Liquid	73.4 × 65	550
EXT 580 EFI	Liquid	75.4 × 65	580
EXT 580 DLX	Liquid	75.4 × 65	580
Pantera	Liquid	75.4 × 65	580
Powder Special	Liquid	75.4 × 65	580
Powder Special EFI	Liquid	75.4 × 65	580
ZR 580 EFI	Liquid	75.4 × 65	580
EXT 600 Triple	Liquid	66.5 × 57	594
ZRT 600	Liquid	66.5 × 57	594
Powder Extreme	Liquid	66.5 × 57	594
1998			
Z 440	Air/fan	65 × 65	431
ZL 440	Liquid	68 × 60	435.8
ZR 440	Liquid	66.5 × 63	437.4
ZL 500	Liquid	71 × 62.7	496.5
ZR 500	Liquid	71 × 62.7	496.5
Cougar	Liquid	73.4 × 65	550
Cougar Deluxe	Liquid	73.4 × 65	550
Cougar			
Mountain Cat	Liquid	73.4 × 65	550
Panther 550	Liquid	73.4 × 65	550
EXT 580 EFI	Liquid	75.4 × 65	580
EXT 580 DLX	Liquid	75.4 × 65	580
Pantera	Liquid	75.4 × 65	580
Powder Special	Liquid	78 × 62.7	599

(continued)

Table 1 ENGINE IDENTIFICATION (continued)

Model	Engine cooling type	Bore/stroke mm (in.)	Displacement cc (cid.)
1998			
Powder Special EFI	Liquid	78 × 62.7	599
ZR 580 EFI	Liquid	75.4 × 65	580
EXT 600 Triple	Liquid	66.5 × 57	594
EXT 600 Triple Touring	Liquid	66.5 × 57	594
ZR 600	Liquid	78 × 62.7	599
ZR 600 EFI	Liquid	78 × 62.7	599
ZRT 600	Liquid	66.5 × 57	594
Powder Extreme	Liquid	66.5 × 57	594

5

Table 2 529 CC ENGINE (1990-1991 EL TIGRE)

	mm (in.)
Cylinder flatness (max. limit)	0.1 (0.0039)
Piston ring end gap	0.20-0.83 (0.008-0.033)
Piston skirt clearance	0.113-0.15 (0.0044-0.0059)
Piston pin outside diameter	17.995-18.000 (0.7085-0.7087)
Pin bore diameter in piston	18.002-18.010 (0.7087-0.7091)
Connecting rod small end	
Inside diameter	23.000-23.01 (0.9056-0.9059)
Crankshaft	
Runout (maximum)	0.05 (0.002)
End play	0.05-0.10 (0.002-0.004)
Reed stop height	8.5-9.5 (0.335-0.373)

Table 3 AIR-COOLED 431 CC ENGINE (Z 440 AND PANTHER 440 1995-1998)

	mm (in.)
Piston ring end gap	0.15-0.83 (0.006-0.033)
Piston skirt clearance	0.08-0-0.150 (0.0031-0.0059)
Piston pin	
Outside diameter	15.995-16.000 (0.6297-0.6299)
Out of round (maximum)	0.02 (0.001)
Pin bore diameter in piston	15.996-16.004 (0.6298-0.6301)
Connecting rod small end	
Inside diameter	21.003-21.011 (0.8269-0.8272)
Crankshaft	
Runout (maximum)	0.05 (0.002)
Distance measured from PTO end	15 (0.590)
Distance measured from MAG end	35 (1.377)
End play	0.05-0.10 (0.002-0.004)
Cylinder bore	
Out of round (maximum)	0.1 (0.004)
Taper (maximum)	0.1 (0.004)

Table 4 435.8 CC ENGINE (EXCEPT 1993-1995 ZR 440)

	mm (in.)
Piston ring end gap	0.20-0.83 (0.008-0.033)
Piston skirt clearance	0.105-0.150 (0.0041-0.006)
Piston pin outside diameter	17.995-18.000 (0.7085-0.7087)
Pin bore diameter in piston	17.998-18.006 (0.7086-0.7089)
Connecting rod small end	
Inside diameter	23.00-23.011 (0.9056-0.9059)
Crankshaft	
Runout (maximum)	0.05 (0.002)
Distance measured from PTO end	10 (0.393)
Distance measured from MAG end	30.5 (1.200)
End play	0.05-0.10 (0.002-0.004)
Cylinder bore	
Out of round (maximum)	0.1 (0.004)
Taper (maximum)	0.1 (0.004)

Table 5 435.8 CC ENGINE (1993-1995 ZR 440)

	mm (in.)
Piston ring end gap	0.15-0.83 (0.006-0.033)
Piston skirt clearance	0.115-0.150 (0.0045-0.0059)
Piston pin outside diameter	17.995-18.000 (0.7085-0.7087)
Pin bore diameter in piston	17.998-18.006 (0.7086-0.7089)
Connecting rod small end	
Inside diameter	23.000-23.011 (0.9056-0.9059)
Crankshaft	
Runout (maximum)	0.05 (0.002)
Distance measured from PTO end	10 (0.393)
Distance measured from MAG end	30.5 (1.200)
End play	0.05-0.10 (0.002-0.004)
Cylinder bore	
Out of round (maximum)	0.1 (0.004)
Taper (maximum)	0.1 (0.004)

Table 6 437.4 CC ENGINE (1996-ON ZR 440)

	mm (in.)
Piston ring end gap	0.15-0.83 (0.006-0.033)
Piston skirt clearance	0.115-0.150 (0.0045-0.0059)
Piston pin outside diameter	17.995-18.000 (0.7085-0.7087)
Pin bore diameter in piston	18.002-18.010 (0.7087-0.7091)
Connecting rod small end	
Inside diameter	23.003-23.011 (0.9056-0.9059)
Crankshaft	
Runout (maximum)	0.05 (0.002)
Distance measured from PTO end	5 (0.197)
Distance measured from MAG end	30 (1.181)
End play	0.05-0.10 (0.002-0.004)
Cylinder bore	
Out of round (maximum)	0.1 (0.004)
Taper (maximum)	0.1 (0.004)
Reed stop height	9.58-9.8 (0.372-0.388)

Table 7 496.5 AND 599 CC ENGINE

	mm (in.)
Piston ring end gap	0.20-0.83 (0.008-0.033)
Piston skirt clearance	0.083-0.150 (0.0033-0.0059)
Piston pin outside diameter	19.995-20.000 (0.7872-0.7874)
Pin bore diameter in piston	20.002-20.010 (0.7875-0.7878)
Connecting rod small end	
Inside diameter	23.003-23.011 (0.9056-0.9059)
Crankshaft	
Runout (maximum)	0.05 (0.002)
Distance measured from PTO end	5 (0.197)
Distance measured from MAG end	30 (1.181)
End play	0.05-0.10 (0.002-0.004)
Cylinder bore	
Out of round (maximum)	0.1 (0.004)
Taper (maximum)	0.1 (0.004)
Reed stop height	9.4-9.8 (0.37-0.39)

Table 8 550 AND 580 CC ENGINES

	mm (in.)
Piston ring end gap	0.20-0.83 (0.008-0.033)
Piston skirt clearance	0.95-0.150 (0.0037-0.0059)
Piston pin outside diameter	19.995-20.000 (0.7872-0.7874)
Pin bore diameter in piston	20.002-20.010 (0.7875-0.7878)
Connecting rod small end	
Inside diameter	26.003-26.011 (1.0237-1.0241)
Crankshaft	
Runout (maximum)	0.05 (0.002)
Distance measured from PTO end	10 (0.393)
Distance measured from MAG end	30.5 (1.200)
End play	0.05-0.10 (0.002-0.004)
Cylinder bore	
Out of round (maximum)	0.1 (0.004)
Taper (maximum)	0.1 (0.004)

Table 9 THREE-CYLINDER 594 CC ENGINE

	mm (in.)
Piston ring end gap	0.20-0.83 (0.008-0.033)
Piston skirt clearance	0.085-0.095 (0.0030-0.0037)
Piston pin outside diameter	17.995-18.000 (0.7085-0.7087)
Pin bore diameter in piston	18.002-18.008 (0.7087-0.7090)
Connecting rod small end	
Inside diameter	23.003-23.011 (0.9056-0.9059)
Crankshaft	
Runout (maximum)	0.05 (0.002)
Distance measured from PTO end	15 (0.590)
Distance measured from MAG end	5 (0.197)
End play	0.05-0.10 (0.002-0.004)
Cylinder bore	
Out of round (maximum)	0.1 (0.004)
Taper (maximum)	0.1 (0.004)
Reed stop height	9.3-9.9 (0.368-0.392)

5

Table 10 ENGINE TIGHTENING TORQUES

	N·m	ft.-lb.
Coolant outlet housing	7-10	5-7
Coolant pump, Impeller	8-12	6-9
Cooling shroud		
Air-cooled 431 cc engine		
(Z 440 and Panther 440 1995-1998)	4-7	3-5
Crankcase bolts		
529 cc engine (1990-1991 El Tigre)		
6 mm	8-10	6-7
8 mm	18-22	13-16
Fan Cooled 431 cc engine		
(Z 440 and Panther 440 1995-1998)		
6 mm	8-12	6-8.5
8 mm	18-28	13-20
435.8, 550 and 580 cc engines		
6 mm	8-12	6-9
8 mm	18-28	13-20
437.4 cc engine (1996-on ZR 440)	30-40	22-29
Three-cylinder 594 cc engine	28	20
Cylinder head		
529 cc Engine (1990-1991 El Tigre)	20-25	14-18
Air-cooled 431 cc engine		
(Z 440 and Panther 440 1995-1998)	18-28	13-20
435.8 cc engine		
(except 1993-1995 ZR 440)	20-25	14.5-18
435.8 cc engine		
(1993-1995 ZR 440)	18-28	13-20
437.4 cc engine		
(1996-on ZR 440)	18-28	13-20
496.5 and 599 cc engines	18-28	13-20
550 and 580 cc engines	18-28	13-20
Three-cylinder 594 cc engine	20-25	14.5-18
Cylinder base screws or nuts		
Prowler	30-40	22-29
Cougar		
1991-1994	30-40	22-29
1995-1998	40-60	29-43
Panther	40-60	29-43
Powder Extreme, Powder Special	18-28	13-20
Z 440 and Panther 440 (cyl./head)	18-28	13-20
ZL 440/500	30-40	22-29
ZR 440	30-40	22-29
El Tigre (529 cc)		
M8	18-22	13-16
M10	30-40	22-29
El Tigre (550 cc)	30-40	22-29
EXT 550	30-40	22-29
EXT 580		
1994	30-40	22-29
1995-1998	40-60	29-43
ZR 580		
1993-1994	30-40	22-29
1995-1997	40-60	29-43
EXT 600	18-28	13-20

(continued)

Table 10 ENGINE TIGHTENING TORQUES (continued)

	N·m	ft.-lb.
Cylinder base screws or nuts		
ZRT 600	18-28	13-20
Drive clutch	69-76	50-55
Engine mounts		
Prowler 1990-1994		
Engine mounts to frame	28-35	20-25
Mount plate to engine	76	55
Prowler 1995		
Engine mounts to frame	76	55
Mount plate to engine	28-35	20-25
Cougar 1990-1994		
Engine mounts to frame	28-35	20-25
Mount plate to engine	76	55
Cougar 1995-1998		
Engine mounts to frame	76	55
Mount plate to engine	28-35	20-25
Z 440 and Panther 440 1995-1997		
Engine mounts to frame	28-35	20-25
Mount plate to engine	76	55
Z 440 and Panther 440 1998		
Engine mounts to frame	28	20
Mount plate to engine	76	55
ZL 440 1997		
Engine mounts to frame	28	20
Mount plate to engine	76	55
ZL 440/500 1998		
Engine mounts to frame	28-35	20-25
Mount plate to engine	24	17
ZR 440 1993-1995		
Engine mounts to frame	42	30
Mount plate to engine	76	55
ZR 440 1996-1998		
Front engine mounts to frame	28-35	20-25
Right-rear engine mount to frame	28-35	20-25
Left-rear engine mount to frame	69	50
El Tigre 1990-1992		
Engine mounts to frame	28-35	20-25
Mount plate to engine	76	55
EXT 550 1993	18-28	13-20
Engine mounts to frame	28-35	20-25
Mount plate to engine	76	55
EXT 580 1994-1998		
Mounting brackets to engine	24	17
Engine mounts to frame	28-35	20-25
ZR 580 1993-1997		
Engine mounts to frame	42	30
Mount plate to engine	76	55
ZRT 600 1996-1998		
Mounting brackets to engine	24	17
PTO-side mount to engine	14	10
Engine mounts to frame	42	30

(continued)

Table 10 ENGINE TIGHTENING TORQUES (continued)

	N·m	ft.-lb.
Engine mounts		
EXT 600, Powder Extreme 1998		
Mounting brackets to engine	24	17
PTO-side mount to engine	14	10
Engine mounts to frame	42	30
Exhaust manifold		
El Tigre (529 cc) 1990-1991	15-19	11-14
All other models	18-22	13-16
Fan case to engine		
Fan-cooled 431 cc engine		
(Z 440 and Panther 440 1995-1998)		
6 mm	8-12	6-9
8 mm	18-22	13-16
Fan pulley, Lower		
Fan-cooled 431 cc engine		
(Z 440 and Panther 440 1995-1998)	8-12	6-9
Fan pulley, Upper		
Fan-cooled 431 cc engine		
(Z 440 and Panther 440 1995-1998)	25-40	18-29
Flywheel housing		
529 cc engine (1990-1991 El Tigre)	18-22	13-16
Flywheel nut		
El Tigre	90-110	65-79
Prowler		
1990-1993	90-110	65-79
1994-1995	69-90	50-65
All other models	69-90	50-65
Intake manifold		
529 cc engine (1990-1991 El Tigre)	15-19	11-14
Magneto housing		
Three-cylinder 594 cc engine	18-22	13-16
Oil pump	7	5
Recoil starter housing	7	5
Recoil starter pulley		
529 cc engine (1990-1991 El Tigre)	–	–
All other models	10	7
Reed block		
437.4 cc engine (1996-on ZR 440)	8-12	6-9
Three-cylinder 594 cc engine	8-12	6-9
Spark plug	25-28	18-20
Thermostat housing	7-10	5-7

Chapter Six

Fuel System—Carbureted Models

The fuel system consists of the fuel tank, fuel pump, carburetors and air silencer. This chapter includes service procedures for all parts of the carbureted fuel system. Two-cylinder models without Electronic Fuel Injection (EFI) are equipped with two slide type carburetors. Three-cylinder models are equipped with three slide type carburetors. Refer to the *Fuel Injection System* in Chapter Seven for service information on EFI models. There are differences among the different models, which are noted in the service procedures and tables.

Carburetor application and specifications are listed in **Tables 1** and **2** at the end of the chapter.

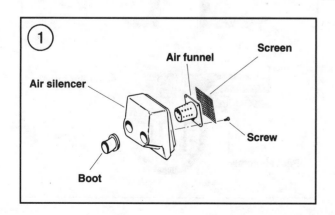

AIR SILENCER

The air silencer typical of all models is shown in **Figure 1** and **2**. The air silencer, sometimes referred to as the air box, should be inspected periodically for cleanliness and cracks.

> *CAUTION*
> *Never run the engine with the air silencer removed. Running without the air silencer or air filters can lean the fuel mixture (too much air—not enough fuel) and may result in engine seizure. The air silencer and filters must be installed during carburetor adjustments.*

Carburetor Operation

For proper operation, a gasoline engine must be supplied with fuel and air mixed in proper proportions. A mixture in which there is too much fuel is said to be rich. A lean mixture is one that has insufficient fuel. A carburetor that is operating correctly and properly adjusted will supply the proper mixture of air and fuel at various engine speeds and under a wide range of operating conditions.

The carburetors installed on these models contain several major systems. A float and float valve mechanism are used to maintain a constant fuel level in the float bowl. The idle mixture system controls the amount of fuel at low engine speeds. The main fuel system controls the amount of fuel at high speeds. At intermediate engine speeds, the fuel is controlled by the needle jet and its jet needle. A starting enrichment (choke) system is incorporated in the carburetor to supply the rich mixture necessary for starting a cold engine.

Float Mechanism

The carburetor is equipped with a float valve. The fuel inlet valve (**Figure 3**) is attached to the float and moves up and down with the float. Movement of the fuel inlet valve in relationship to the inlet valve seat opens and closes the fuel inlet valve to maintain a steady supply of fuel at a constant height in the float bowl. Fuel is supplied to the float valve by a pulse-operated fuel pump.

Idle, Intermediate and Main Fuel Systems

The purpose of the carburetor is to atomize fuel and mix it in correct proportion with air throughout the entire speed range. At small throttle openings (from idle to about 1/8 open), only a small amount of fuel is mixed with a small

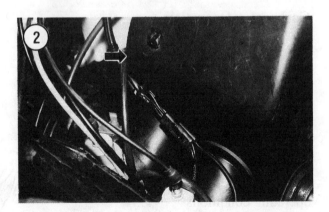

amount of air. A typical idle mixture system is shown in **Figure 4**. The pilot air screw controls a small amount of air mixed with fuel from the pilot jet. Opening the pilot air screw (sometimes called an idle mixture screw) permits more air to enter the idle mixture system and leans the mixture.

As the throttle is opened further, more air enters the engine around the throttle slide as shown in **Figures 5** and **6**. Fuel is drawn into the air stream through the needle jet. The jet needle limits the amount of fuel flowing through the needle jet.

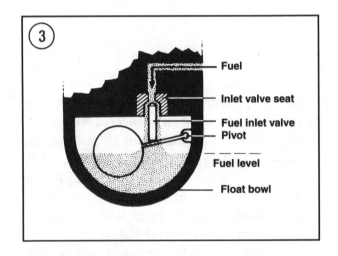

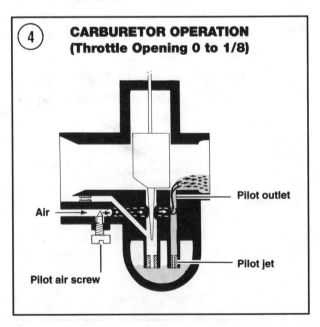

When the throttle is completely open, the amount of fuel drawn into the air stream is limited by the size of the main jet (**Figure 7**).

The changes from the idle mixture circuit to the intermediate (jet needle) range to high speed (main jet) is transitional.

Starting Enrichment

Choke lever (**Figure 8**) located on the control console operates the starting enrichment system. When the engine is cold, move the choke lever to the full choke position to enrich the air-fuel mixture for starting.

Removal/Installation

> *NOTE*
> *Carburetors are often different for the left, right or center cylinders. The carburetors should be marked to indicate the original cylinder location. Parts should be similarly marked as they are removed. A simple way is to apply a different colored mark to the the parts for each location.*

1. Open the hood.

2. Label the hoses at the carburetors before detaching them from the carburetor. Loosen the hose clamps, then pull the hoses from the fittings on the carburetors.

> *NOTE*
> *The throttle slide operates in a machined bore in the carburetor body and should always remain with that carburetor body. Mark the parts before removing to ensure correct assembly.*

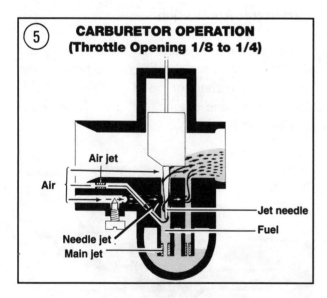

CARBURETOR OPERATION
(Throttle Opening 1/8 to 1/4)

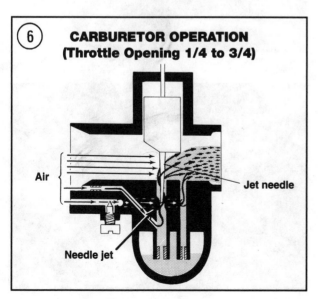

CARBURETOR OPERATION
(Throttle Opening 1/4 to 3/4)

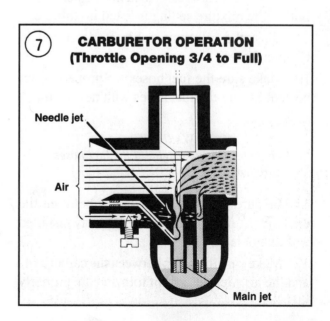

CARBURETOR OPERATION
(Throttle Opening 3/4 to Full)

3. Turn the carburetor caps (A, **Figure 9**) counterclockwise to loosen, then withdraw the throttle slide assemblies from the carburetors.

> *CAUTION*
> *Handle the slide carefully to prevent scratching or otherwise damaging the slide and needle jet. If it is not necessary to remove the throttle slide or other parts from the throttle cable, wrap the assembly in a plastic bag, mark its location and attach to the handlebar to reduce the chance of damage.*

4. Loosen the clamps (B, **Figure 9**) and pull the carburetor from its attaching hoses. On some models, a clamp may also be on the intake (C, **Figure 9**).

5. Remove the starting enrichment (choke) valve from the carburetor.

6. Installation is the reverse of these steps.

7. Install the carburetors in their original location. Slip the intake side of the carburetor into the silencer boot, then slide the carburetor forward into the mounting boot. Make sure the carburetor is straight, then tighten the attaching clamp.

8. Make initial adjustments to the carburetors and control cables as described in Chapter Three. Initial idle mixture setting is listed in **Table 2**.

9. Adjust the oil pump cable as described in Chapter Three.

10. Make sure the fuel hoses are properly connected. Secure the fuel hoses with new clamps.

> *WARNING*
> *Do not start the engine if the fuel hoses are leaking.*

11. Be sure the boots and clamps between the carburetors and the engine are properly installed and do not leak.

12. Make sure the boots between the carburetors and the air silencer are not torn and are properly installed.

13. Make final adjustments to the carburetors as described in Chapter Three. Idle speed setting is listed in **Table 2**.

Carburetor to Engine Boots

Boots between the engine and the carburetors should be inspected frequently for looseness or damage that would allow air leakage. Air leaks between the carburetor and the engine can result in a lean fuel mixture.

Carburetor Application

The carburetors used on these models are similar, but there may be differences between the two or three carburetors used on different cylinders of the same engine. Refer to **Table 1** for original application.

Disassembly

Refer to **Figure 10** for this procedure.

NOTE
Because the jetting between the carburetors may be different, store the components for each carburetor in a separate box.

1. Before removing the pilot air screw (19, **Figure 10**), count the turns while screwing it in until it seats lightly. Record the original exact position, then back the screw out and remove it and the spring from the carburetor.

2. Remove the screws attaching the float bowl to the carburetor housing. Remove the float bowl (**Figure 11**) and bowl gasket.

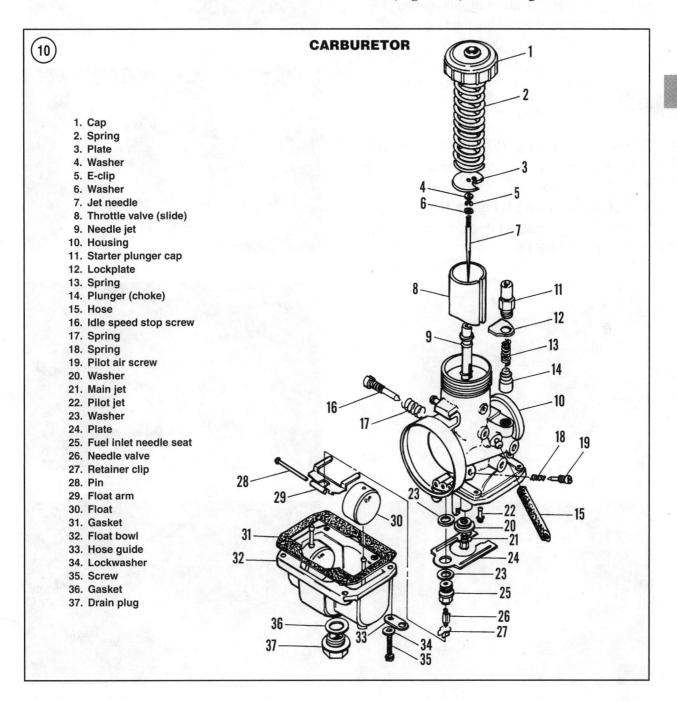

⑩ **CARBURETOR**

1. Cap
2. Spring
3. Plate
4. Washer
5. E-clip
6. Washer
7. Jet needle
8. Throttle valve (slide)
9. Needle jet
10. Housing
11. Starter plunger cap
12. Lockplate
13. Spring
14. Plunger (choke)
15. Hose
16. Idle speed stop screw
17. Spring
18. Spring
19. Pilot air screw
20. Washer
21. Main jet
22. Pilot jet
23. Washer
24. Plate
25. Fuel inlet needle seat
26. Needle valve
27. Retainer clip
28. Pin
29. Float arm
30. Float
31. Gasket
32. Float bowl
33. Hose guide
34. Lockwasher
35. Screw
36. Gasket
37. Drain plug

6

3. Remove any loose baffle rings (**Figure 12**) that may be located around the main jet.

4. Remove the pivot pin and float arm (28 and 29, **Figure 10**).

5. Remove the retainer clip from the needle valve. See **Figure 13**.

6. Lift the fuel inlet needle from the seat, then unscrew the seat. A baffle plate and gasket (**Figure 14**) are located under the inlet valve seat.

CAUTION
You can easily damage the pilot jet if you use the wrong size of screwdriver to remove or install the jet.

7. Remove the pilot jet (**Figure 15**) using a flat tip screwdriver with straight sides that fits the slot in the jet correctly.

8. Remove the main jet (**Figure 16**).

9. Remove the needle jet through the top of the carburetor (**Figure 17**).

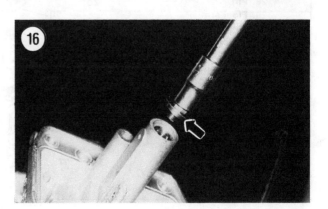

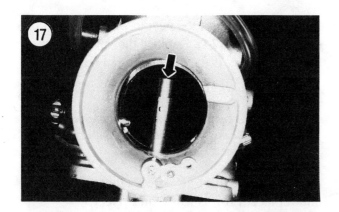

10. Clean and inspect the carburetor assembly as described in this chapter.

Assembly

Refer to **Figure 10** for this procedure.

1. Install the needle valve assembly as follows:
    a. Install the first washer (**Figure 18**).
    b. Install the baffle plate (**Figure 19**).
    c. Install the second washer.
    d. Install and tighten the inlet valve seat (**Figure 20**).
    e. Install the fuel inlet valve with the tapered end inside, against the valve seat (**Figure 21**).
    f. Install the retaining clip (**Figure 13**).
2. Install the float arm and the pivot pin. Push the pin in fully.
3. Install the needle jet so that the notch in the bottom aligns with the pin in the needle jet bore (**Figure 22**).

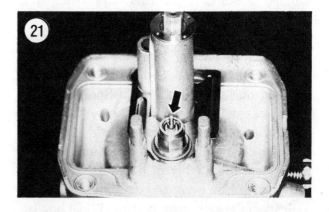

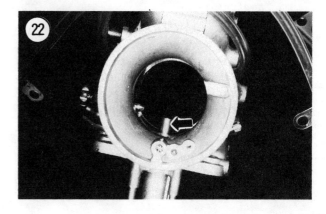

4. Install the main jet and washer (**Figure 16**).

5. Install the pilot jet (**Figure 15**).

6. Install a new float bowl gasket if the old gasket is damaged. Install the floats.

7. Install the float bowl (**Figure 23**). Tighten the attaching screws securely.

8. Slide the spring onto the pilot air screw (idle mixture needle), then install the screw and spring in the carburetor body.

9. Turn the pilot air screw (19, **Figure 10**) in until it bottoms lightly against the seat, then back the screw out the same number of turns that were recorded during disassembly. The approximate setting is listed in **Table 2**.

10. Adjust the carburetor, as described in Chapter Three, after installing the carburetors.

Cleaning/Inspection
(All Models)

Most commercial carburetor cleaners will damage rubber O-rings, seals and plastic parts. Be sure that all parts that could be damaged by the cleaner are removed before using a harsh cleaner.

1. Clean the carburetor castings and metal parts with aerosol solvent and a brush. Spray the aerosol solvent on the casting and scrub off any gum or varnish with a small bristle brush.

2. After cleaning the castings and metal parts, wash them thoroughly in hot water and soap. Rinse with clean water and dry thoroughly.

3. Inspect the carburetor body and float bowl.

CAUTION
Do not use wire or a drill bit to clean carburetor passages or jets. This can enlarge the passages and change the carburetor calibration. If a passage or jet is severely clogged, use a piece of broom straw to clean it.

4. Use a spray cleaner to remove varnish from the jets, then blow compressed air through the jets to dry and make sure that passages are open.

5. Inspect the tip of the needle valve for wear or damage (**Figure 24**). Replace the valve and needle seat as a set if they are less than perfect.

NOTE
A damaged or worn needle valve seat can cause incorrect float level, imparing performance.

6. Inspect the pilot air screw taper for scoring and replace it if it is less than perfect.

7. Inspect the jets for damage. Replace any jet that is less than perfect. Make sure replacement jets are the same size as the originals.

CAUTION
The jets must be completely clean. The residue that builds up on jets is often nearly clear and shiny. Some small holes may appear to be clean but may be completely blocked. Inspect all jets and internal passages carefully and critically. Any burring, roughness, abrasion or dis-

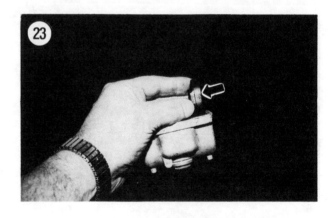

tortion could also cause a lean mixture that may result in major engine damage.

8. Check the movement of the float arm on the pivot pin. It must move freely without binding.

9. O-ring seals tend to become hardened after prolonged use and heat and therefore lose their ability to seal properly. Inspect all O-rings and replace if necessary.

10. Check the floats (**Figure 23**) for fuel saturation, deterioration or excessive wear where it contacts the float arm. If the float is in good condition, check it for leakage by filling the float bowl with water and pushing the floats down.

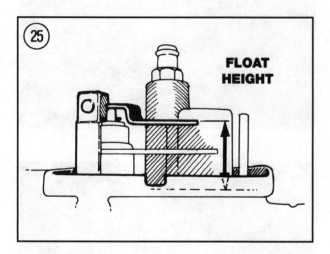

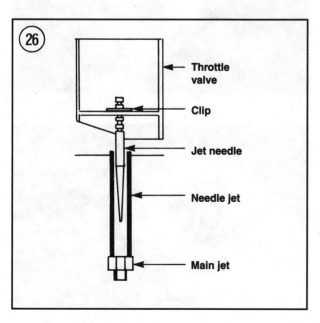

There should be no signs of bubbles. Replace the floats if necessary.

Float Height
Check and Adjustment

1. Remove the float bowl as described in this chapter.

2. Remove the float bowl gasket.

3. Invert the carburetor. Allow the float arm to contact the fuel inlet valve, but do not compress the spring-loaded plunger located in the valve.

4. Measure the distance from the float arm to the float bowl gasket surface (**Figure 25**). Refer to **Table 1** for float height.

5. If the float height is incorrect, remove the float pin and float arm (28 and 29, **Figure 10**). Bend tang on the end of the arm to adjust.

6. Reinstall float arm and pin. Recheck the adjustment.

7. Install float bowl as described in this chapter.

Jet Needle/Throttle Valve
Removal/Installation

A typical jet needle/throttle valve assembly is shown in **Figure 26**.

1. Turn the carburetor cap (A, **Figure 9**) counterclockwise to loosen, then withdraw the throttle slide from the carburetor.

2. Push the throttle valve up against the spring. Then detach the cable from the throttle valve.

NOTE
*The magnet (**Figure 27**) is used to trigger the electrical switch (**Figure 28**) located on the side of the carburetor.*

3. Remove the screw (**Figure 29**) attaching the magnet block to the throttle valve and remove the magnet block.

4. Remove the jet needle, E-clip and washers (4, 5, 6 and 7, **Figure 10**).

5. Installation is the reverse of these steps. Note the following:

6

a. Carburetor tuning is described in Chapter Four.

b. When inserting the throttle valve into the carburetor, align the groove in the throttle valve with the pin in the carburetor bore while also aligning the jet needle with the opening of the needle jet.

FUEL PUMP

Removal/Installation

Different types of fuel pumps have been used, but all are basically the same. Refer to **Figure 30** for the routing of the hoses to the crankcase (A, **Figure 30**), fuel inlet line from the tank (B, **Figure 30**) and fuel output (pressure) lines to the carburetors (C, **Figure 30**). The actual location of the pump may be different than that shown in either **Figure 30** or **31**.

1. Open the hood.

2. Label the hoses at the fuel pump (**Figure 30**).

3. Loosen the hose clamps, then detach the hoses from the pump. Plug the hoses to prevent fuel leakage or contamination.

4. Remove the screws holding the fuel pump to the air silencer frame and remove the fuel pump.

5. Replace the hose clamps as necessary.

6. Installation is the reverse of these steps. Reconnect the hoses according to the identification marks made before disassembly.

Inspection

1. Plug the four pump body fuel fittings and clean the pump in solvent. Thoroughly dry.

2. Test the pump outlet check valve by sucking and blowing through one of the outlet openings while blocking the other outlet opening(s). See **Figure 30** for typical positions of the outlet to the carburetors. You should be able to draw air though the valve, but not blow air through it.

3. Test the pump inlet check valve by sucking and blowing through the inlet opening. You

should be able to blow through the valve, but not draw air through it.

4. Install a new pump if damaged. Repair parts are not available for the fuel pumps.

ALTITUDE COMPENSATOR

Later Powder Extreme and Powder Special models are equipped with an altitude compensa-

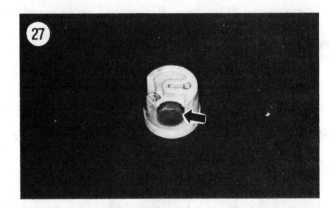

tor. The altitude compensator contains a spring-loaded bellows and piston that adjust air pressure in the carburetor float chamber according to altitude and air density. At low altitude, the compensator permits full atmospheric pressure to enter the float chamber. At high altitude, the compensator limits air pressure to the float chamber thereby leaning the air mixture. The

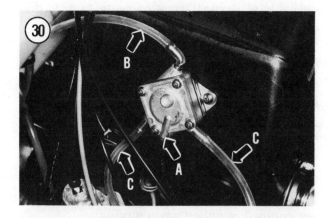

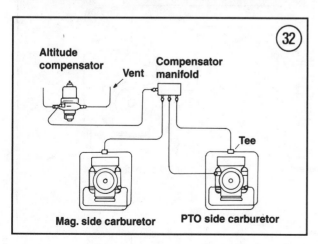

compensator must be serviced as a unit assembly.

CAUTION
Do not turn the adjustment screw on the compensator. Improper adjustment may damage the engine. Engine damage due to the improper adjustment of the compensator will void the engine warranty.

A heated elbow is located on the PTO-side carburetor. The heated elbow prevents icing in the hose. Should the heater fail and the hose become plugged by ice, the fuel mixture will be excessively rich at high altitude.

Refer to **Figures 32** and **33** for hose routing. Note that the hose wraps around the carburetor. There must be no kinks or sharp bends in the hose.

NOTE
Hose length is critical for proper operation. A replacement hose must be the same length as the original hose.

FUEL TANK

Removal/Installation

1. Remove the seat.

2. Turn the fuel off at the shut-off valve.

3. Disconnect the fuel line from the fuel tank and plug the line.

4. Open the side covers, then remove the screws attaching the console to the steering support.

5. Remove any bolts or clamps holding the fuel tank to the frame.

6. Disconnect the fuel vent hose from the tank.

7. Raise the rear of the console above the filler neck and remove the fuel tank to the rear.

8. Installation is the reverse of these steps. Check all hoses and connections for kinks or leaks.

Cleaning/Inspection

WARNING
Clean the fuel tank in an open area away
from all sources of flames or sparks.

1. Pour old gasoline from the tank into a sealable container manufactured specifically for gasoline storage.

2. Pour about 1 quart of fresh gasoline into the tank and slosh it around for several minutes to loosen sediment. Then pour the contents into a sealable container.

3. Examine the tank for cracks and abrasions, particularly at points where the tank contacts the body. Areas that rub can be protected and cushioned by coating them with a nonhardening silicone sealer and allowing it to dry before installing the tank. If the abrasion is extensive or if the tank is leaking, replace it.

THROTTLE CABLE REPLACEMENT

1. Remove the carburetor caps and detach the cables from the throttle valves as described in this chapter.
2. Detach the cable from the oil injection pump.
3. Detach the throttle cable from the throttle lever.
4. Mark or otherwise identify the routing of the old cable(s). Route the new cable the same as the original.
5. Make sure the circlip is installed at the upper (handlebar control) end of the cable.
6. Adjust the carburetors as described in Chapter Three. See *Synchronization*.
7. Adjust the oil injection cable as described in Chapter Three.
8. Operate the throttle lever to make sure the carburetor throttle slides operate correctly.
9. Check cable routing. Make sure the cable is not crimped or pulled when turning.

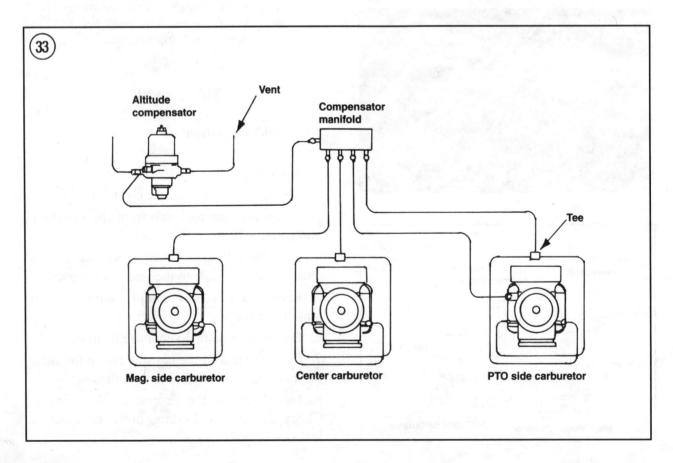

Table 1 CARBURETOR APPLICATION

Year/Model	Main jet	Needle jet	Jet needle	Pilot jet	Float setting mm (in.)
1990					
Prowler	240	Q-0(480)	6DH7-3	25	
El Tigre EXT (VM34)	240	P-5(480)	6DH7-4	30	22-24 (0.87-0.95)
1991					
Prowler, Prowler Special, Cougar (VM36)	290	Q-5	6DH7-3	35	17-19 (0.67-0.75)
El Tigre EXT (VM34)	240	P-5(480)	6DH7-4	30	22-24 (0.87-0.95)
1992					
Prowler, Prowler Special, Cougar (VM36)	290	Q-5	6DH7-3	35	17-19 (0.66-0.75)
El Tigre EXT (VM38)	340	P-2(480)	6DH8-3	35	21-23 (0.827-0.906)
1993					
Prowler, Prowler Special, Cougar (VM36-162)	310	Q-5	6DH7-3	35	17-19 (0.67-0.75)
440 ZR	330	P-2(480)	6DH8-3	45	21-23 (0.827-0.906)
EXT 550 (VM38)	340	P-2(480)	6DH8-3	35	21-23 (0.827-0.906)
580 ZR (VM38)	340	P-2(480)	6DH8-3	35	21-23 (0.827-0.906)
EXT 580 (VM38-269)	340	P-4(480)	6DH8-3	35	21-23 (0.827-0.906)
1994					
Cougar, Cougar Mountain Cat, Prowler, Prowler II (VM36-162)	310	Q-5	6DH7-3	35	17-19 (0.67-0.75)
ZR 440 (VM38-271)	350	P-2(480)	6DH8-3	50	21-23 (0.827-0.906)
EXT 580 and EXT 580 Mountain Cat (VM38-269)	340	P-4(480)	6DH8-3	35	21-23 (0.827-0.906)
ZR 580 (VM40)	400	Z-8(224)	7DJ5-2	45	21-23 (0.827-0.906)
1995					
Cougar, Cougar Mountain Cat, Prowler 2-Up (VM38-269)	340	P-2(480)	6DH8-3	35	21-23 (0.827-0.906)
Z 440 (VM34-424)	280	P4(480)	6DH2-3	25	22-24 (0.87-0.94)

(continued)

6

Table 1 CARBURETOR APPLICATION (continued)

Year/Model	Main jet	Needle jet	Jet needle	Pilot jet	Float setting mm (in.)
1995					
ZR 440 (VM38)	290	P-4(159)	6DH2-4	35	22-24 (0.86-0.94)
EXT 580, EXT 580 Powder Special (VM38)	340	P-4(480)	6DH8-3	35	21-23 (0.827-0.906)
ZR 580 (VM40)	370	AA-0(224)	7DH5-2	45	21-23 (0.827-0.906)
1996					
Z 440 (VM34)	280	P4(480)	6DH2-3	25	22-24 (0.87-0.94)
ZR 440 (VM38)	370	P-4(159)	6DH2-4	40	22-24 (0.87-0.94)
Cougar, Cougar Mountain Cat, Cougar 2-Up (VM38-269)	340	P-2(480)	6DH8-3	35	21-23 (0.827-0.906)
EXT 580, EXT 580 Powder Special (VM38)	340	P-4(480)	6DH8-3	35	21-23 (0.827-0.906)
ZRT 600 (VM36)	360	P-4(480)	6DH41-2	35	21-23 (0.827-0.906)
1997					
Z 440 (VM34)	280	P-4(480)	6DH2-3	30	22-24 (0.86-0.94)
ZL 440 (VM36)	310	Q-5(480)	6DH7-3	40	17-19 (0.66-0.74)
ZR 440 (VM34)	340	P-4(159)	6DH7-3	35	22-24 (0.86-0.94)
Panther 440 (VM34)	280	P-4(480)	6DH2-3	25	17-19 (0.66-0.74)
Panther 550 (VM38)	340	P-2(480)	6DH8-3	40	17-19 (0.66-0.74)
Cougar, Cougar Mountain Cat (VM38)	340	P-2(480)	6DH8-3	40	17-19 (0.66-0.74)
Powder Special (VM38)	390	P-3(480)	6DH8-3	50	21-23 (0.827-0.906)
EXT 600, ZRT 600 (VM36)	370	P-2(480)	6DH8-3	40	17-19 (0.66-0.74)
1998					
Z 440 (VM34)	270	P-4(480)	6DH2-3	30	22-24 (0.86-0.94)
ZL 440 (VM36)	250	Q-5(480)	6DH7-3	40	17-19 (0.66-0.74)
ZR 440 (VM34)	330	P-7(159)	6DH7-3	40	22-24 (0.86-0.94)
Panther 440 (VM34)	280	P-4(480)	6DH2-3	25	17-19 (0.66-0.74)

(continued)

Table 1 CARBURETOR APPLICATION (continued)

Year/Model	Main jet	Needle jet	Jet needle	Pilot jet	Float setting mm (in.)
1998					
ZL 500 (VM38)	360	Q-2(480)	6DH41-3	35	17-19 (0.66-0.74)
Panther 550 (VM38)	340	P-2(480)	6DH8-3	40	17-19 (0.66-0.74)
Cougar, Cougar Deluxe, Cougar Mountain Cat (VM38)	340	P-2(480)	6DH8-3	40	17-19 (0.66-0.74)
Powder Special (VM38)	410	Q-3(480)	6EGJ1-3	40	17-19 (0.66-0.74)
EXT 600, ZRT 600 (VM36)	370	P-2(480)	6DH8-3	40	17-19 (0.66-0.74)

6

Table 2 CARBURETOR PILOT AIR SCREW ADJUSTMENT

Year/Model	Turns out	Idle speed
1990		
Prowler	1-1/2	2000-2500
El Tigre EXT	1-1 1/2	2000-2500
1991		
Prowler, Prowler Special, Cougar	1	2000-2500
El Tigre EXT	1-1 1/2	2000-2500
1992		
Prowler, Prowler Special, Cougar		
El Tigre EXT	1	2000-2500
1993		
Prowler, Prowler Special, Cougar	1	1500-2000
440 ZR, EXT 580,		
EXT 580 Mountain Cat, 580 ZR	1	1500
1994		
Cougar, Cougar Mountain Cat, Prowler	1	1500-2000
Prowler II	1	1500-2000
ZR 440, ZR 580	1	1500-1550
EXT 580, EXT 580 Mountain Cat	1	1500
1995		
Cougar, Cougar Mountain Cat	1	1500
Prowler 2-Up	1	1500
Z 440, ZR 440, ZR 580	1	1500
EXT 580, EXT 580 Powder Special	1	1500
1996		
Z 440	1	1500
ZR 440	3/4-1 1/4	1500
Cougar, Cougar Mountain Cat	1	1500
Cougar 2-Up	1	1500
EXT 580, EXT 580 Powder Special	1	1500
ZRT 600	1 1/2	1500

(continued)

Table 2 CARBURETOR PILOT AIR SCREW ADJUSTMENT (continued)

Year/Model	Turns out	Idle speed
1997		
Z 440, ZL 440, ZR 440	1	1500
Panther 440, Panther 550	1	1500
Cougar, Cougar Mountain Cat	1	1500
Powder Special	1	1500
EXT 600, ZRT 600	1 1/2	1500
Powder Extreme	1 1/2	1500
1998		
Z 440	3/4	1500
ZL 440	1 1/2	1500
ZR 440	1 1/4	1500
Panther 440, Panther 550, ZL 500	1	1500
Cougar, Cougar Deluxe, Cougar Mountain Cat	1	1500
Powder Special	1 1/4	1500
EXT 600, ZRT 600	1 1/2	1500
Powder Extreme	1	1500

Chapter Seven

Fuel System—Fuel Injected Models

For optimum performance, a gasoline engine must be supplied with fuel and air mixed in proper proportions. A mixture in which there is too much fuel is said to be rich. A lean mixture has insufficient fuel for efficient combustion.

A fuel system operating correctly and properly adjusted will supply the proper mixture of air and fuel at various engine speeds and under a wide range of operating conditions.

Electronic Fuel Injection (EFI) has been used on some 1994 and later models. On all models prior to 1997, the EFI system uses a battery to power the system. In 1997 an EFI system was introduced similar to earlier models, but it does not require a battery. Both EFI systems have been used on 1997 and 1998 models.

NOTE
The type of fuel injection system—mag-neto-powered or battery-powered—can be identified by the color and location of the ECU box. On battery-powered systems the ECU is mounted next to the chaincase and the box is shiny. On bat-teryless systems the ECU is mounted on the airbox and the box is black.

The fuel injection system consists of the following subsystems: air flow system, fuel flow system, electronic control system and electrical system. This chapter includes service procedures for all parts of the fuel system. Specifications are listed in **Tables 1-4** at the end of the chapter.

WARNING
Gasoline is highly flammable. Always exercise extreme care when working around gasoline. Work in a well-venti-lated area, away from any flame, sparks or other possible ignition source. Pre-vent spills by being prepared to plug any

disconnected hoses and clean up any spills immediately. Sparks or other accidental ignition sources are possible even when care is taken, so be prepared for an emergency.

CAUTION
*The system contains components that should **NOT** be disassembled and the system should **NEVER** be modified in any way either by changing or removing of components. Refer to the following CAUTIONs whenever testing or servicing the Electronic Fuel Injection system.*

1. Be reluctant to change any adjustments to the system. Follow recommended procedures carefully after determining that adjustment is necessary. Be careful not to change any fuel system adjustments in an attempt to correct a different problem.

2. Do not disassemble the Electronic Control Unit (ECU).

3. Do not disassemble, change or substitute any of the system's sensors. Each is specifically designed to function in balance with other components on this engine and in this application.

4. Use only parts recommended by the manufacturer and available from your Arctic Cat dealer when replacing defective parts.

5. Always install new O-rings, sealing washers and gaskets when assembling. Make sure there are no air or fuel leaks after assembling.

6. Do not touch any of the terminals with your hands or attempt to clean terminals using any product except cleaners specified for electronic connectors and components.

7. Do not disconnect the battery or any electrical wires from fuel injection components with the engine running. Make sure that the main switch is OFF, then disconnect the negative (ground) cable from the battery, before disconnecting any wires from a component of the system.

8. Use approved tools and procedures when removing and installing system components. Use care to prevent damaging parts while removing or installing.

9. Make sure that fuel lines are not restricted either accidentally or deliberately. Never attempt to restrict or block a fuel line.

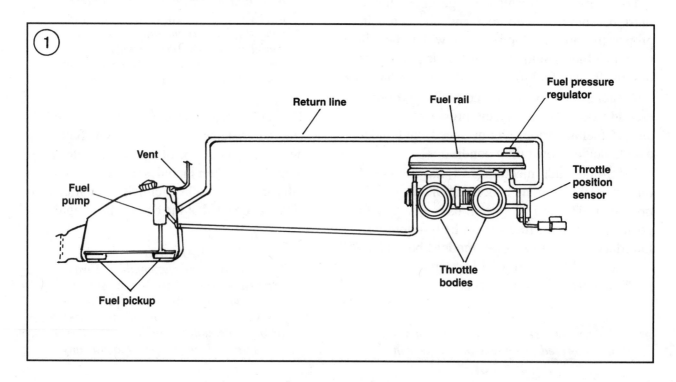

10. Bleed pressure from fuel lines slowly into an absorbant towel before removing the hose.

11. Be prepared to plug detached fuel lines before disconnecting or removing any component.

12. Be sure that all the fuel lines and other parts are connected before turning ON the main switch or operating the fuel pump.

13. Do not use compressed air to clean system components. The sensitive components can be easily damaged.

14. Do not operate the system (or fuel pump) dry. Gasoline provides both cooling and lubrication for some parts.

15. Make sure that components of the system are protected from both mechanical and electrical shocks. Impacts that might occur in an accident or while servicing may physically break printed circuits or other small components. Static electricity discharged when you touch a component can also damage parts.

FUEL INJECTION SYSTEM COMPONENTS

The fuel injection system consists of a fuel pump, fuel filters, one fuel injector per cylinder, fuel lines, fuel pressure regulator, throttle housing assembly and electronic control hardware. Refer to **Figures 1** and **2** for drawings typical of the fuel delivery system and the electronic control system.

The fuel injection system consists of the following subsystems: air flow system, fuel flow system, electronic control system and electrical system.

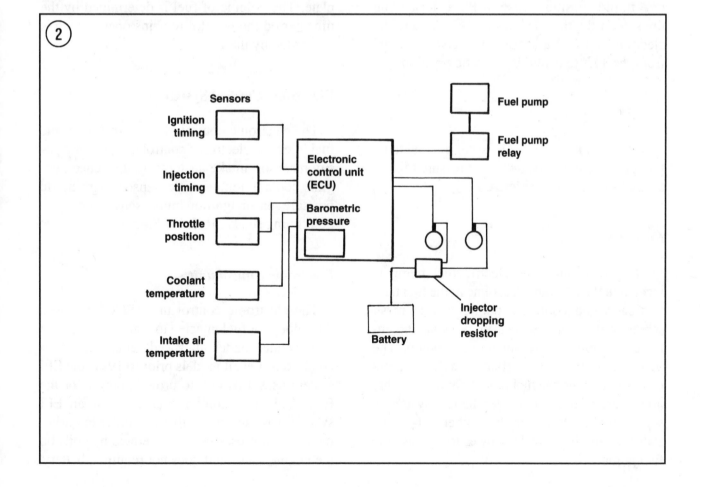

Air Flow System

Air for the air/fuel mixture is drawn into the engine by engine vacuum. The air filter removes foreign objects before the air enters the intake system. Throttle bodies control the amount of air entering each cylinder.

Throttle bodies

Individual throttle bodies (**Figure 1**) control the amount of air entering the engine. Each throttle body controls the air intake for one cylinder using a throttle plate in the throttle body bore. The throttle plates move in response to movement of the handlebar mounted speed control. Adjustment screws are used to synchronize throttle plate movement so both cylinders perform equally.

A throttle position sensor (TPS) is located on the side of the throttle housing (**Figure 1**). The electronic control unit (ECU) receives a signal from the TPS to determine throttle position.

Fuel Flow System

The fuel flow system consists of the fuel tank, fuel pump, fuel filters, fuel rail, pressure regulator and fuel injectors (**Figure 1**).

Fuel pump

The roller vane type electric fuel pump is located in the fuel tank. Gasoline in the fuel tank lubricates and cools the pump. A fine mesh screen in the fuel tank pick-up prevents the entrance of foreign material into the pump. The battery of 1996 and earlier models provides power to operate the fuel pump. On models that do not use a battery to power the EFI system, a separate coil, incorporated with other coils on the stator assembly, provides power to operate the fuel pump.

CAUTION
Running the fuel pump without gasoline supplied to the pump can damage the fuel pump.

Fuel pressure regulator assembly

The fuel pump supplies pressurized fuel to the fuel rail. The fuel pressure regulator assembly, attached to the right side of the fuel rail, controls fuel pressure. Excess fuel returns to the fuel tank through the hose connection attached to the regulator. The injector nozzles are attached to the fuel rail.

Fuel injector

A fuel injector for each cylinder directs fuel into the throttle bore just behind the throttle plate. The volume of fuel is determined by the time period the injector remains open, which is controlled by the ECU.

Electronic Control System

The electronic control system consists of the fuel injection electronic control unit, throttle position sensor, intake air temperature sensor, engine coolant temperature sensor, barometric pressure sensor, ignition timing sensor and injection timing sensor. Refer to **Figure 2**.

Electronic control unit

The electronic control unit (ECU) manages the amount of fuel injected to maintain optimum performance under all speed ranges and load conditions. On all models prior to 1997, the EFI system uses a battery to provide power for the ECU and other components. In 1997 an EFI system was introduced that is similar to earlier models, but it uses power generated by coils on the engine stator and does not require a battery.

Both EFI systems have been used on 1997 and 1998 models.

> *NOTE*
> *The type of fuel injection system—batteryless or battery-powered—can be identified by the color and location of the ECU box. On battery-powered systems, the ECU is mounted next to the chaincase and the box is shiny. On batteryless systems, the ECU is mounted on the airbox and the box is black.*

The ECU receives information from the input sensors and devices, then determines the optimum air/fuel mixture. Sensors provide information concerning engine temperature, intake air temperature and throttle position. The ECU monitors engine speed, amount of ignition advance and crankshaft position. A barometric pressure sensor located in the ECU case provides information on barometric pressure so the ECU can adjust the air/fuel mixture for different altitudes. The ECU controls the amount of fuel injected by controlling the amount of time the fuel injectors are open.

The ECU receives signals from the sensors to monitor performance while the engine is running, then compares current input data with the reference data in the computer chip. For instance, if the signal from a sensor is outside of the range for normal operation, the ECU determines a problem exists. If the ECU finds a problem, it signals the possible problem by flashing the monitor light, which is located on the ECU housing, in a coded sequence.

Throttle position sensor

The throttle position sensor (TPS) is a variable resistance device located on the end of the throttle shaft (**Figure 1**). Throttle movement changes sensor resistance. The sensor sends the position of the throttle plate to the ECU.

Intake air temperature sensor

The air temperature sensor, a variable resistance device located in the front of the air silencer, changes resistance in relation to the intake air temperature. The sensor sends a signal specifying the air temperature to the ECU.

Barometric pressure sensor

The atmospheric pressure sensor, located inside the ECU housing, cannot be removed from the housing. The sensor measures barometric pressure to determine altitude for use by the ECU.

Coolant temperature sensor

The engine coolant temperature sensor is located in the end of the coolant outlet housing. The sensor is a variable resistance type that changes resistance with temperature changes. The sensor sends a signal specifying the coolant temperature to the ECU.

Fuel pump coil

On models that do not use the battery as the power source for the EFI system, a separate coil located on the stator assembly provides power to operate the fuel pump.

Electrical System

Several electrical components make up the electrical system in the electronic fuel injection system.

Fuses

Fuses protect the EFI system on models that use the battery as the power source. On models prior to 1997, three fuses are located in the fuse

7

box shown in **Figure 3**. The 15 amp main fuse is located in the circuit between the battery and the regulator/rectifier. The 10 amp fuse protects the fuel pump relay control circuit. The 3 amp fuse protects the ECU and the control circuits.

On models after 1996, four fuses are located in the fuse box attached to the ECU mounting plate. The 5 amp fuse protects the ECU and control circuits. The 10 amp fuse protects the fuel pump and fuel injector circuits.

Fuel pump relay

On 1996 and earlier models, a relay controls power to the fuel pump. The relay is located under the console, behind the air silencer.

TESTING AND TROUBLESHOOTING (EFI POWERED BY BATTERY)

Problems with the fuel injection system can usually be isolated by following a series of logical steps to locate the faulty component. Compare the current conditions with those that are standard and note any differences. Check for obvious conditions that point to specific failure. Check to see if the diagnostic light on the ECU (A, **Figure 4**) is indicating a trouble code. Check voltages delivered to the various components, then check the resistance of individual components. If you have difficulty determining EFI faults, have an Arctic Cat dealer diagnose the machine with the special Arctco EFI Analyzer.

> *NOTE*
> *Arctco analyzer (part No. 0644-202) and diagnostic harness (part No. 0644-181) can be used to test systems that use a battery for power. Arctco analyzer (part No. 0644-212), diagnostic harness and analyzer EPROM update kit (part No. 0644-256) can be used to test systems on models 1997-on.*

A special Arctco EFI Analyzer is available which attaches to the EFI test plug located near the ECU. This special tester is able to test battery voltage, engine rpm, ignition timing, throttle valve angles in degrees, throttle valve angle in volts, intake air temperature in degrees Celsius, coolant temperature in degrees Fahrenheit and barometric pressure as determined by the installed components. The special analyzer is able to display existing problems and malfunctions stored in the ECU memory, as well as clear stored trouble codes from the ECU memory. If this analyzer is available, follow the manufacturer's instructions carefully. The analyzer is not able to test some items, including fuses, emergency stop relay, fuel pump relay, fuel pressure regulator, fuel pump, switches, connections or the main harness.

System diagnosis

Preparation and initial checks—Read through the following procedures completely before starting the tests. Some tests require special equipment and procedures.

1. Check the battery to make sure it is fully charged.

> *NOTE*
> *The ECU will not operate if battery voltage is 9 volts or less.*

NOTE
If it is necessary to charge the battery, disconnect the ground cable from the battery negative terminal before attaching a battery charger. Failure to disconnect the battery can damage the ECU.

2. Before starting the engine, turn the key switch ON and check the battery charge light. With the key ON, the light should glow.

3. If the charge light does not glow, turn all of the accessories ON and check the light again.

4. If the charge light still does not glow, the problem must be isolated and corrected before continuing.

   a. Squeeze the throttle lever. If the charge light now glows, the throttle monitor assembly is faulty.

   b. Check the fuse (**Figure 3**)—3 amp on early models, 5 amp on later models. If the fuse is blown, replace the fuse and check to be sure the new fuse corrects the problem.

   c. Check the condition of the charge light bulb.

   d. Check the DC voltage regulator assembly and replace as necessary.

   e. Check battery voltage with all the accessories switches ON. Voltage should remain above 12 volts.

   f. Some other possible causes are a faulty ignition switch, emergency shut-off switch or tether stop switch. Loose or corroded connections to these switches could cause the problem.

5. When the charge light is illuminated, check the diagnostic monitor light (**Figure 4**, later models similar) on the ECU, which should flash one time. The single flash indicates current is reaching the ECU and all the EFI components are operating properly.

6. Start the engine. Once the engine starts, the charge light should turn OFF. If the light continues to glow, the charging system is not operating correctly.

7

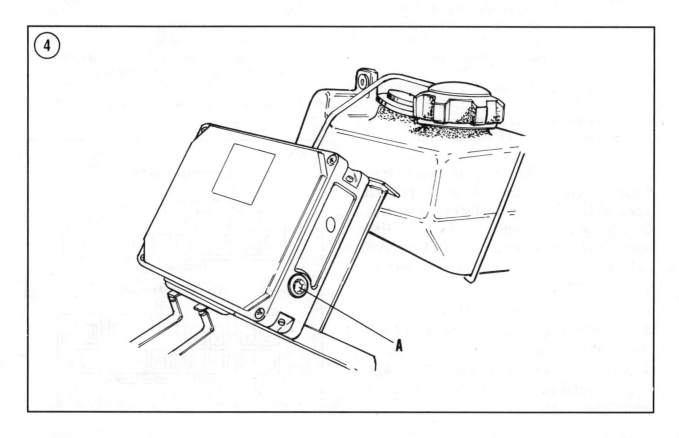

Self test—The Electronic Control Unit (ECU) contains a built-in self-diagnostic system. The diagnostic monitor light is located on the EFI housing (A, **Figure 4**) on models prior to 1997. On 1997 and 1998 models, the monitor light is located on the ECU mounting panel adjacent to the fuse. With the key switch ON and the system operating properly, the monitor light (A, **Figure 4**) should flash one time. The single flash indicates that current is reaching the ECU and all the EFI components are operating properly.

If the monitor light glows OFF and ON during normal use, a problem is indicated. The duration of the light may be either short or long. A series of illumination pulses is an error code. Each error code begins with a long pulse. The error code is repeated following a pause of about two seconds. Refer to **Table 1** for determining the possible causes of the indicated error codes.

> *NOTE*
> *The trouble codes only identify problem areas, not specific components. A problem may lie with a sensor, faulty wiring, bad connection or internal ECU circuit. The trouble codes generated by the ECU identify only electrical problems recognized by the ECU. Other problems, such as mechanical problems or fuel delivery problems, may not be recognized and will not trigger an ECU trouble code.*

Memory recall—The ECU stores the code for problems that have occurred during operation. The error codes are stored in the ECU's memory. On 1997 and 1998 models, the ECU will flash trouble codes when power is applied. On 1996 and earlier models, use the following steps to obtain the trouble codes:

1. Turn the ignition switch OFF.

2. Attach the diagnostic harness as described in this chapter.

3. Attach a jumper wire between the No. 14 pin (**Figure 5**) of the diagnostic harness and the ECU ground (housing).

4. With the No. 14 pin grounded, turn the ignition switch ON.

> *NOTE*
> *Do not break the ground connection until all of the trouble codes are determined in Step 5. Breaking the ground connection will erase the memory. There may be more than one trouble code stored.*

5. Check the diagnostic monitor light (A, **Figure 4**). If it is flashing, compare the code to those listed in **Table 1**.

Clear memory—To erase the memory on models prior to 1997, turn the ignition switch ON, then proceed as follows:

1. Touch the jumper, ground, wire to pin No. 14 (**Figure 5**).

2. Remove the wire from pin No. 14.

3. Wait about a second.

4. Repeat Steps 1, 2 and 3 several times.

5. Ground pin No. 14 with the jumper wire and check to see if the memory contains any other codes.

> *NOTE*
> *If the code(s) cannot be removed by following the procedure in Steps 1-5, it may be indicating a recurring problem.*

6. If codes are still stored, repeat Steps 1-5.

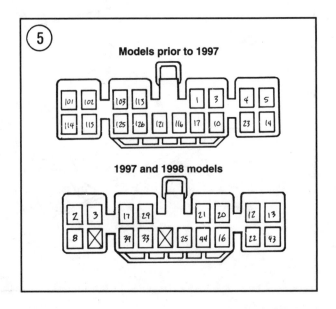

(5)

Models prior to 1997

1997 and 1998 models

Diagnostic harness—You can use the special diagnostic harness and a digital volt/ohmmeter, such as Fluke Model 73, to check operation of some components.

> *NOTE*
> *Use diagnostic harness part No. 0644-181 to test systems on 1996 and earlier models. Use harness part No. 0644-266 to test systems on 1997 and 1998 models.*

1. Disconnect the battery ground cable before attaching the diagnostic harness.

2. Separate the necessary connectors and attach the diagnostic harness.

3. Attach the battery ground to test the system or component. The pins (**Figure 5**) on the diagnostic harness test connection correspond with those on ECM connectors and are referred to in the text.

Component tests

Individual components can sometimes be isolated and tested with voltage applied. Other tests include isolating the component, then measuring its resistance and comparing the measured resistance with a specified standard. The ECU can be checked only by installing a component known to be good.

You can use the diagnostic harness and a digital volt/ohmmeter, such as Fluke Model 73, to check operation of some installed components. Disconnect the battery ground cable before attaching the diagnostic harness as described in this chapter. Attach the battery ground to test the system or component. The pins (**Figure 5**) on the diagnostic harness test connection correspond with those on the ECM connectors and are referred to in the text.

Fuel Pump—A quick check to determine if the fuel pump is receiving power is to turn the ignition ON and listen for the pump to run. The pump (A, **Figure 6**), mounted in the front of the fuel tank, should produce audible noise.

If the pump does not make any noise, proceed as follows.

1. *Check the fuse*—15 amp on models prior to 1997 or 10 amp on 1997 and 1998 models.

2. Check battery voltage, which should be at least 12.6 volts.

3. If the battery and fuse are okay, check the pump relay as described in this chapter.

4. If the battery, fuse and relay are okay, check the wiring harness and connections between pin No. 13 of the ECU and the pump relay.

5. If the pump is receiving sufficient battery voltage, but not running, install a new pump.

> *NOTE*
> *If the machine is not used for a long period, the fuel pump may stick due to residue from evaporated gasoline. The pump may free up after filling the tank with fresh gasoline and operating the pump for a short time.*

6. If insufficient volume or pressure is suspected, check the fuel pressure as described in this chapter.

Fuel Pressure—Fuel pressure of 250 kPa (36.2 psi) is controlled by the regulator unit attached to the right side of the fuel rail. Check

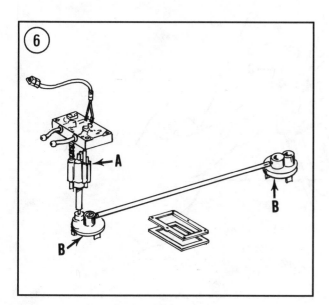

fuel pressure by attaching a fuel pressure gauge to the fuel line.

If fuel pressure is low, or insufficient volume is suspected, be sure to inspect the fuel tank pickup filters (B, **Figure 6**). Make sure the battery voltage is not low.

Excessively high pressure can be caused by a restricted return hose between the regulator and the fuel tank. Do not attempt to disassemble the regulator (**Figure 7**).

Relays—models prior to 1997. On models prior to 1997, there are two identical black relays (A and B, **Figure 8**) located on the back of the ECU mounting bracket. The pink wire in the harness is attached to the fuel pump relay. The other relay is the emergency stop relay.

NOTE
If the fuel pump relay is suspected to be faulty, a quick check is to switch the two identical black relays. If the fuel pump now works, replace the faulty relay.

To check the removed relay, proceed as follows.

1. Use an ohmmeter to measure the resistance between the two gold- colored connectors (**Figure 9**). The resistance should be 85-115 ohms.

2. Attach an ohmmeter between the two brass-colored connectors (**Figure 9**) and measure the resistance between the terminals. With no power

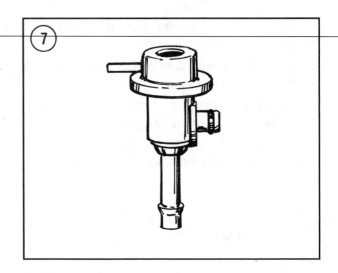

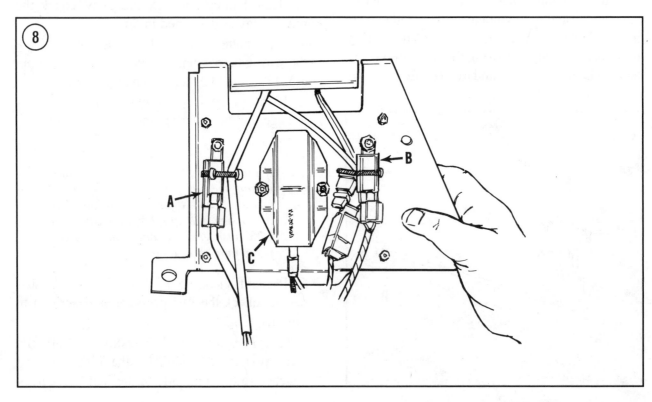

applied to the relay, resistance between the brass-colored terminals should be no continuity (open circuit).

NOTE
Make sure that voltage is applied only to the gold-colored terminals in Step 3.

3. Apply a 12 volts power source to the gold-colored terminals (**Figure 9**), then check conti-

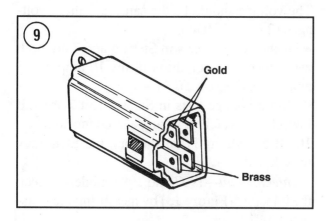

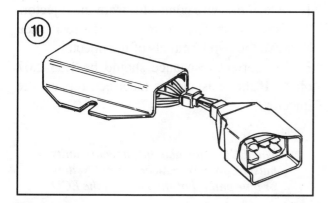

nuity between the brass terminals. Applying power to the gold terminals should close connection between brass terminals and the resistance should be near zero.

Dropping resistors—Each dropping resistor reduces the voltage to the injector. On models prior to 1997, the dropping resistor is located on the back of the ECU mounting bracket (C, **Figure 8**). On 1997 and 1998 models, the dropping resistor (**Figure 10**) is attached to a panel near the oil reservoir. Use an accurate ohmmeter to check the resistance between the white wire connector and each of the black wire connectors. Resistance of each should be 5.185-7.015 ohms.

Injector ground circuit—models prior to 1997. If one or both of the injectors fail to operate, complete the following tests to determine if the cause is the dropping resistor, 10 amp fuse, injector lead, injector or the wiring harness.

1. Turn the ignition switch off.

2. Detach the smaller of the two connectors (**Figure 11**) from the ECU.

3. Position the connector as shown in **Figure 12**.

4. Attach a jumper wire to ground and touch each wire (**Figure 12**) momentarily.

5. When the ground wire is touched to one pin, you should hear one of the injectors click open. Touching the other pin should cause the other injector to click open.

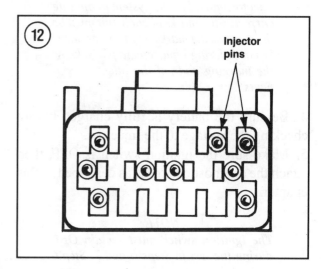

6. If the test in Step 5 fails to operate both injectors, check the following:

    a. Check the 10 amp fuse (**Figure 3**).

    b. Check the battery voltage. It should be 12.6 volts.

    c. Check the dropping resistor as described in this chapter.

    d. Check the wiring harness and connectors for proper connection and broken wires.

    e. If all else checks okay, the problem could be the ECU.

7. If the test in Step 5 checks okay, but the injector fails to operate, clean all pin connectors and make sure that all are properly connected.

8. If the system still fails to operate, check resistance of the injector unit and the injector timing sensor as described in this chapter.

Injector unit—models prior to 1997. The injectors (**Figure 13**) can be checked by measuring the resistance as follows.

1. Detach the wire connector from the injector.

2. Use an accurate ohmmeter to measure the resistance between the 2 terminals of the injector.

3. The correct resistance is 1.53-2.07 ohms. If the resistance is incorrect, replace the injector.

> *NOTE*
> *The ECU chip and the injector units must be properly matched. A red, yellow or blue paint spot should be on the ECU chip, the ECU housing and each of the injector units. For the system to operate correctly, the marks of each unit must be the same as the marks on the other parts. When ordering replacement parts, know the marking code of the other components.*

4. Be sure the battery is fully charged before checking the voltage to the injectors.

5. Make sure the ignition switch is OFF, then attach the diagnostic harness as described in this chapter.

> *NOTE*
> *The ignition switch must remain OFF during the test in Steps 6 and 7. Step 6*

checks the injector voltage to the injector on the MAG side. Step 7 checks the injector voltage to the injector on the PTO side.

6. Measure the voltage between pin No. 101 and pin No. 121 (**Figure 5**) of the diagnostic harness. The voltage should be the same as battery voltage (12.6-12.8 VDC).

7. Measure the voltage between pin No. 102 and pin No. 121 (**Figure 5**) of the diagnostic harness. The voltage should be the same as battery voltage (12.6-12.8 VDC).

8. If the voltage tests in Steps 6 and 7 are both zero, check the condition of the 10 amp and 3 amp fuses (**Figure 3**).

9. If the voltage tests in Steps 6 and 7 are still low, check switches, wiring and connectors.

10. If everything is satisfactory, the ECU may have failed.

Injector unit—1997 and 1998 models. Check the injectors (**Figure 13**) by measuring the resistance as follows.

1. Detach the wire connector from the injector.

2. Use an ohmmeter to measure the resistance between the two terminals of the injector.

3. The correct resistance should be 1.53-2.07 ohms. If the resistance is incorrect, replace the injector.

> *NOTE*
> *The ECU chip and the injector units must be properly matched. A red, yellow or blue paint spot should be on the ECU*

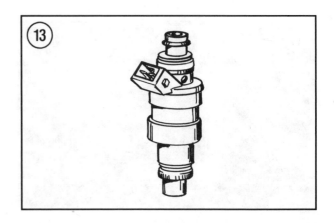

chip, the ECU housing and each of the injector units. For the system to operate correctly, the marks of each unit must be the same as the marks on the other parts. If ordering replacement parts, know the marking code of the other components.

4. Remove the spark plugs and ground the spark plugs to the engine.

5. Turn switches ON.

NOTE
Step 6 checks the injector voltage to the injector on the MAG side. Step 7 checks the injector voltage to the injector on the PTO side.

NOTE
These measurements are performed using reverse polarity to obtain an accurate reading.

6. Connect the black (negative) voltmeter lead to pin No. 2 (**Figure 5**) of the diagnostic harness. Connect the red (positive) voltmeter lead to ground.

7. Operate the recoil starter rapidly while checking the voltmeter reading. The voltmeter should indicate approximately 8-10 volts. If the reading is incorrect, repeat test. If the reading remains incorrect, check the dropping resistor.

8. Repeat test for the PTO side injector by connecting the voltmeter to pin No. 3.

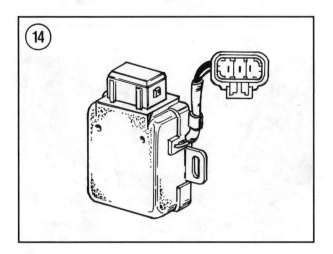

Throttle position sensor—models prior to 1997. Test the throttle position sensor (TPS), with the engine not running.

1. Disconnect the electrical plug from the TPS (**Figure 14**).

2. Use an ohmmeter to read the resistance between the terminals for the red and black wires. Resistance should be 4250-6750 ohms.

3. With the throttle at idle, measure the resistance between the black and white wires. Resistance should be 722.5-977.5 ohms.

4. Open the throttle and measure the resistance between the black and white wires again. Resistance should be 4250-6750 ohms.

5. With the ohmmeter attached to the black and white wires, move the throttle lever. The resistance should change as the control is moved.

6. Make sure the ignition switch is OFF, then connect the wiring harness to the terminal of the throttle position sensor.

7. Attach the diagnostic harness as described in this chapter.

8. Turn the ignition switch ON.

9. Measure the voltage between pin No. 1 and pin No. 17 (**Figure 5**) of the diagnostic harness. The voltage should be 5.22-5.02 VDC.

10. If the voltage measured in Step 9 is zero, continue to check as follows.

   a. Battery voltage should be 12.6-12.8 VDC.

   b. Make sure all of the switches are ON and working. The battery light on the console should glow.

   c. Check the condition of the 3 amp fuse (**Figure 3**).

   d. If the voltage is low, but the checks in substeps 10a-10c are okay, detach the wiring harness from the throttle position sensor. If the voltage in Step 9 is now within limits, the throttle position sensor is faulty.

11. Measure the voltage between pin No. 3 and pin No. 17 (**Figure 5**) of the diagnostic harness. The voltage should be 0.82-0.825 VDC. If the voltage is too high, make sure the throttle is at idle position (fully closed).

12. Press the handlebar mounted throttle control to the wide open (fast) position and measure the voltage between pin No. 3 and pin No. 17 (**Figure 5**) of the diagnostic harness. The voltage should be 3.8-4.2 VDC. If the voltage is more than in Step 11, but is too low, make sure the throttle cable is adjusted properly to permit the throttle to open fully.

Throttle position sensor—1997 and 1998 models. Test the throttle position sensor (TPS), with the engine not running.

1. Disconnect the electrical plug from the TPS (**Figure 14**).

2. Use an ohmmeter to read the resistance between the terminals for the red and black wires. Resistance should be 4250-6750 ohms.

3. With the throttle at idle, measure the resistance between the black and white wires. Resistance should be 722.5-977.5 ohms.

4. Open the throttle and measure the resistance between the black and white wires again. Resistance should be 4250-6750 ohms.

5. With the ohmmeter attached to the black and white wires, move the throttle lever. The resistance should change as the control is moved.

6. Make sure the ignition switch is OFF, then connect the wiring harness to the terminal of the throttle position sensor.

7. Attach the diagnostic harness as described in this chapter.

8. Turn the ignition switch ON.

9. Measure voltage between pin No. 20 (**Figure 5**) of the diagnostic harness and ground. The voltage should be 0.8 VDC at idle and 3.81-4.23 VDC at wide open throttle.

10. If the voltage measured at idle is incorrect, adjust the idle speed screw to obtain correct voltage reading.

11. If the voltage reading is incorrect at wide open throttle after adjusting idle setting, attempt to obtain desired voltage reading by adjusting the throttle cable. If correct voltage reading is not obtainable, replace the throttle body.

Coolant temperature sensor—To test the engine coolant temperature sensor, make sure the engine is not running and ignition is off.

1A. If the sensor is installed, detach the electrical connectors from the sensor (**Figure 15**).

1B. If the sensor is removed, put the sensor in a container filled with water and measure the temperature of the water.

2. Attach an ohmmeter to the sensor terminals and measure the resistance of the unit.

3. Compare the measured resistance with the values in **Table 2**. The temperature of the sensor should be as indicated.

4. Models prior to 1997—The condition of the coolant temperature sensor can also be checked by measuring the voltage as follows.

   a. Attach the diagnostic harness as described in this chapter.

   b. Turn the ignition switch ON.

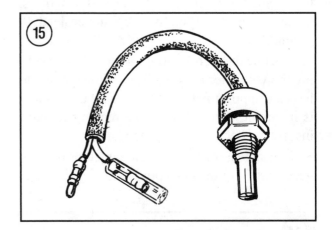

c. Measure the voltage between pin No. 4 and pin No. 17 (**Figure 5**) of the diagnostic harness.

d. Compare the measured voltage with the values in **Table 2**. The temperature of the sensor should be as indicated.

5. Install new sensor if tests are significantly different than indicated in **Table 2**.

6. Use new gaskets on sensors when reinstalling.

Air temperature sensor—To test the inlet air temperature sensor (**Figure 16**), make sure the engine is not running and ignition is off.

1. Detach the electrical connectors from the sensor.

2. Attach an ohmmeter to the sensor terminals and measure the resistance of the unit.

3. Compare the measured resistance with the values in **Table 4**. The temperature of the sensor should be as indicated.

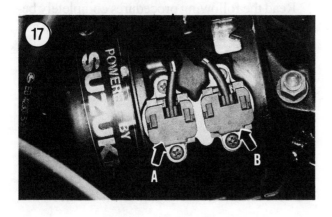

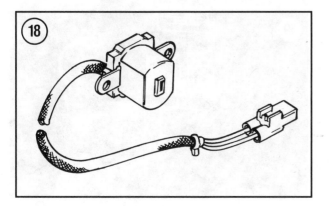

4. Models prior to 1997—Check the condition of the inlet air temperature sensor by measuring the voltage as follows.

a. Attach the diagnostic harness as described in this chapter.

b. Turn the ignition switch ON.

c. Measure the voltage between pin No. 5 and pin No. 17 (**Figure 5**) of the diagnostic harness.

d. Compare the measured voltage with the values in **Table 4**. The temperature of the sensor should be as indicated.

5. Install new sensor if tests are much different than indicated in **Table 4**.

Injector timing sensor—The injection sensor (A, **Figure 17**) is located on the magneto housing. This sensor can be identified by its white/black wire. Check the sensor (**Figure 18**) by measuring the resistance as follows.

1. Make sure the ignition switch is OFF.

2. Detach the sensor at the white two-wire connector.

3. Use an ohmmeter to measure the resistance between the 2 terminals of the sensor. Be sure the wires are white/black and brown.

4. The correct resistance is 152-228 ohms. If the resistance is incorrect, the sensor is faulty.

5. Models prior to 1997—To test the sensor voltage output, first attach the diagnostic harness as described in this chapter.

6. Attach a voltmeter that will measure low AC volts to pins No. 23 and No. 17 (**Figure 5**) of the diagnostic harness.

7. Crank the engine as hard as possible while observing the voltage output.

8. The voltage should be in the range of 0.1-3.5 VAC.

9. If the voltage measured in Step 7 is low, replace the sensor.

Ignition sensor—The ignition sensor (B, **Figure 17**) is located on the magneto housing. This sensor can be identified by its green/white wire. Check the sensor (**Figure 18**) by measuring the resistance as follows.

1. Make sure the ignition switch is OFF.

2. Detach the sensor at the black two-wire connector.

3. Use an ohmmeter to measure the resistance between the 2 terminals of the sensor. Be sure the wires are green/white and brown.

4. The correct resistance is 152-228 ohms. If the resistance is incorrect, the sensor is faulty.

5. Models prior to 1997—To test the sensor voltage output, attach the diagnostic harness as described in this chapter.

6. Attach a voltmeter that will measure low AC volts to pins No. 10 and No. 17 (**Figure 5**) of the diagnostic harness.

7. Crank the engine as hard as possible while observing the voltage output.

8. The voltage should be in the range of 0.1-0.9 VAC.

9. If the voltage measured in Step 7 is low, replace the sensor.

Atmospheric pressure sensor—The atmospheric barometric pressure sensor is located inside the waterproof case containing the ECU. The Arctco EFI Analyzer should be used to test the atmospheric pressure sensor. If the pressure displayed is significantly different than the actual barometric pressure, replace the ECU.

TESTING AND TROUBLESHOOTING (EFI SYSTEM MAGNETO-POWERED)

Problems with the fuel injection system can usually be isolated by following a series of logical steps to locate the faulty component. Compare the current conditions with those that are standard and note any differences. Check for obvious conditions that point to specific failure. If you have difficulty determining EFI faults, have an Arctic Cat dealer diagnose the machine with the special Arctco EFI analyzer.

NOTE
Arctco analyzer (part No. 0644-212), diagnostic harness and analyzer EPROM update kit (part No. 0644-256) are used

to test the batteryless systems found on 1997 and 1998 models.

A special Arctco EFI analyzer attaches to the EFI test plug located near the ECU. This special analyzer is able to test engine rpm, ignition timing, throttle valve angles in degrees, throttle valve angle, intake air temperature in degrees, coolant temperature in degrees and barometric pressure, as determined by the installed components. The special analyzer displays existing problems and malfunctions stored in the ECU memory, as well as clear stored trouble codes from the ECU memory. If this analyzer is available, follow the manufacturer's instructions carefully. The analyzer is not able to test some items, including the ECU, fuel pressure regulator, fuel pump, switches, connections or the main harness.

System diagnosis

Read the following procedures completely before starting. Tests require special equipment and procedures.

NOTE
Use Arctco analyzer (part No. 0644-212), diagnostic harness and analyzer EPROM update kit (part No. 0644-256).

1. Remove the cover from the connector (A, **Figure 19**) on the ECU. Attach the diagnostic harness and Arctco analyzer to the connector.

2. Connect the red lead from the harness to the positive (+) terminal of a 12 VDC battery and the black lead to the negative (–) terminal of the same battery.

3. Turn the analyzer switch ON and press the MENU SELECT buttons as necessary until KOKUSAN appears on the display.

4. Press the TEST button. The analyzer is now set up to begin testing the system.

Self Test—The Electronic Control Unit (ECU) contains a built in self-diagnostic system. The diagnostic monitor light is located on the EFI housing (B, **Figure 19**). Since there is no battery in the system, it is necessary to attach the diagnostic harness, analyzer and battery as described in this chapter before checking the ECU's memory for error codes.

If the monitor light glows OFF and ON, a problem is indicated. A series of illumination pulses becomes an error code. Each error code is separated from any following error codes by a pause of about two seconds. The error code is repeated following a pause of about two seconds. Refer to **Table 1** for determining the possible causes of the indicated error codes.

> *NOTE*
> *The trouble codes only identify problem areas, not specific components. A problem may lie with a sensor, faulty wiring, bad connection or internal ECU circuit. The trouble codes are generated by the ECU, so they identify only electrical problems recognized by the ECU. Other problems, such as mechanical problems or fuel delivery problems, may not be recognized and will not trigger an ECU trouble code.*

Memory recall—The ECU stores the code for problems that have occurred during operation. Proceed as follows to retrieve these stored error codes.

1. Attach the diagnostic harness and Arctco analyzer as described in this chapter.

2. Press the MENU SELECT buttons on the analyzer until the words MEMORY PROBLEM DIAGNOSIS TEST appear on the display.

3. Press the TEST button.

4. If all the sensors are okay, the words SENSORS ALL O.K. will appear on the display.

5. If a sensor has failed, it will appear on the display. Repair or replace the sensor as required.

Clear memory—To clear error codes from the memory of the ECU, proceed as follows:

1. Attach the diagnostic harness as described in this chapter.

2. Press the TEST button on the Arctco analyzer as many times as it takes to remove all the trouble codes.

3. If the code(s) cannot be removed, it may be indicating a recurring problem.

Ignition timing—The Arctco analyzer (part No. 0644-212) can be used to test the ignition timing. The timing should be 28-32° BTDC when the engine is running at 4,000 rpm. If the ignition timing is not within this range, the ignition timing sensor or the CDI unit may be faulty.

Component tests

Individual components can be isolated, then tested by measuring its resistance and comparing the measured resistance with a specified standard. The ECU can be checked only by installing a component known to be good.

> *NOTE*
> *Use diagnostic harness and EPROM update kit (part No. 0644-256) to test components used on 1997 and later models.*

A digital volt/ohmmeter, such as Fluke Model 73, can be used to check operation of some installed components. It may be necessary to attach the diagnostic harness and a battery to the diagnostic harness, as described in this chapter, to test some systems or components.

Throttle position sensor—Test the throttle position sensor (TPS) with the engine not running.

7

1. Disconnect the four-wire electrical connector from the TPS (**Figure 20**).

2. Use an ohmmeter to read the resistance between terminals No. 1 and No. 4. Resistance should be 4250-5750 ohms.

> *NOTE*
> *When testing the fully closed throttle position, note that the idle stop or throttle cable adjustment may prevent the throttles from closing completely.*

3. With the throttle at idle, measure the resistance between terminals No. 2 and No. 4. Resistance should be 723.5-977.5 ohms.

4. Open the throttle and measure the resistance between terminals No. 2 and No. 4 again. Resistance should be 4250-5750 ohms.

5. Attach the ohmmeter leads to the black and white wires of the wiring harness and move the throttle lever. The resistance should change as the control is moved.

6. The throttle valve angle can also be checked by measuring the voltage using the Arctco analyzer (part No. 0644-212).

    a. At idle, the throttle valve angle should be 7.85-8.0° and the voltage should be 8.0 volts.

    b. At full-open throttle, the angle should be 75.37-84.93° and the voltage should be 3.81-4.23 volts.

    c. If the indicated throttle angle remains at 2.25° and the voltage remains at 0.570 volts, the throttle position sensor is faulty and the ECU is in the limp home mode.

> *NOTE*
> *If the throttle position sensor is faulty on models equipped with a magneto-powered EFI system, the manufacturer recommends replacing the complete throttle body assembly.*

7. If the throttle position sensor is faulty, install a new unit and adjust as described in this chapter.

Injector unit—Check the injectors (**Figure 21**) by measuring the resistance as follows.

1. Detach the wire connector (**Figure 22**) from the injector.

2. Use an ohmmeter to measure the resistance between the two terminals of the injector.

3. The correct resistance is 2.46-3.34 ohms.

> *NOTE*
> *The ECU chip and the injector units must be properly matched with each other and with the fuel used. The injectors are marked with a square, circle or triangle. The identifying marks should be the same as the components originally installed. Know the correct identifying mark when ordering replacement parts. If you have questions about correct applications, contact your Arctic Cat dealer.*

4. If the resistance is incorrect, replace the injector.

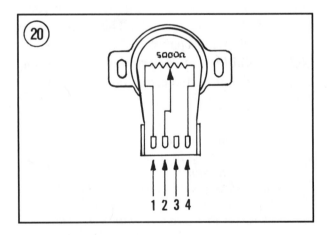

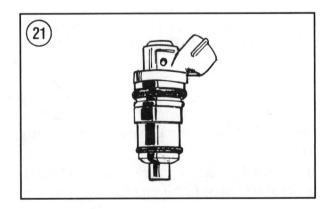

Ignition sensor—The ignition sensor (**Figure 23**) is located on the magneto housing and identified by its green/white wire. Check the ignition sensor by measuring the resistance as follows.

1. Make sure the ignition switch is OFF.

2. Detach the sensor at the black two-wire connector.

3. Use an ohmmeter to measure the resistance between the 2 terminals of the sensor. Be sure the wires are green/white and brown.

4. The correct resistance is 152-228 ohms.

5. If the resistance is incorrect, the sensor is faulty.

Fuel pump pulse coil—The coil supplies current to operate the fuel pump. It is part of the stator assembly. Check the fuel pump pulse coil by measuring the resistance as follows.

Disconnect the white connector located on the two orange wires between the fuel pump pulse coil and the ECU.

Use an ohmmeter to measure the resistance of the coil and the wires between the connector and the coil.

The correct resistance is 1.4-2.2 ohms.

If the measured resistance is incorrect, replace the pulse coil.

Fuel pump—The fuel pump is located in the fuel tank.

1. To test the pump, separate the two-wire connector located on the black and red wires between the fuel pump and the ECU.

2. Use an ohmmeter to measure the resistance of the pump. If the ohmmeter does not show continuity, the pump is faulty.

3. Before installing a new fuel pump, check the removed pump as follows:

    a. Connect 12 VDC to the pump. Observe the correct polarity when making the connection.

    b. If the pump runs, it is okay.

4. If the fuel pump and the fuel pump pulse coil both test okay, but the pump does not run, the problem may be a faulty ECU.

Coolant temperature sensor—To test the engine coolant temperature sensor, it is important to know the exact temperature of the coolant being used for the test.

1A. If the sensor is installed, detach the electrical connectors from the sensor.

1B. If the sensor is removed, put the sensor in a container filled with water. Measure the temperature of the water.

2. Attach an ohmmeter to the sensor terminals. Measure the resistance of the unit.

3. Compare the measured resistance with the values in **Table 3**. The temperature of the sensor should be as indicated.

4. The condition of the coolant temperature sensor can also be checked by measuring the voltage using the Arctco analyzer (part No. 0644-212).

    a. Compare the measured voltage with the values in **Table 3**.

    b. If the coolant temperature sensor has failed, the ECU will indicate a preset temperature

7

depending on engine speed. If the following readings are indicated, replace the sensor: 0° C (32° F) at 0-3,000 rpm; 30° C (86° F) at 3,000-5,000 rpm; 60° C (140° F) over 5,000 rpm.

5. Install a new sensor if tests are much different than indicated in **Table 3**.

6. Apply Teflon tape to the threads of the sensor before installing.

Air temperature sensor—To test the inlet air temperature sensor (**Figure 16**, typical), make sure the engine is not running and ignition is off.

1. Detach the electrical connectors from the sensor.

2. Attach an ohmmeter to the sensor terminals. Measure the resistance of the unit.

3. Compare the measured resistance with the values in **Table 4**. The temperature of the sensor should be as indicated.

4. The condition of the intake air temperature sensor can also be checked by measuring the voltage using the Arctco analyzer (part No. 0644-212).

   a. Compare the measured voltage with the values in **Table 4**.

   b. If the indicated temperature is -40° C and °F, but the temperature is much different, the sensor has failed. The ECU automatically sets the temperature to -40° C and °F if the sensor fails.

5. Install a new sensor if tests are much different than indicated in **Table 4**.

Barometric pressure sensor—The barometric pressure sensor, an integral part of the ECU assembly, cannot be replaced separately.

1. The condition of the barometric pressure sensor can be checked using the Arctco analyzer (part No. 0644-212).

2. Check with a local weather service to obtain the current barometric pressure.

3. Compare the barometric pressure indicated by the analyzer with the actual barometric pressure.

4. If the indicated and actual pressures are significantly different, the sensor has failed. The ECU will automatically set the barometric pressure to 880 mm/hg (34.65 in/hg) if the sensor fails.

COMPONENT SERVICE

Fuel Tank

Removal/installation

1. On models so equipped, detach the ground cable from the negative terminal of the battery.

2. Remove the recoil starter handle as follows.
   a. Pull out the recoil starter handle.
   b. Tie a temporary knot in the rope that will keep the starter rope from rewinding.
   c. Remove the recoil starter handle.

3. Unbolt the console from the steering support, footrest and tunnel brackets.

4. Remove the cap from the fuel tank.

5. Remove the seal from around the filler opening.

6. Remove the knurled nut from the choke cable to the console. Lable the wiring connection to aid in installation.

7. Disconnect the wiring harness from the ignition switch, battery light and warmer switch.

8. Raise the rear of the console above the fuel filler and remove the console.

9. Remove the two cap screws, washers and locknuts securing the rear of the seat to the tunnel. The screws are located in the rear compartment.

10. Disconnect the vent hose from the fuel tank.

11. Detach the electrical wiring from the fuel pump.

12. Identify and label the supply and return hoses. Detach the hoses from the fuel tank.

13. Raise the rear of the seat enough to detach the taillight wiring harness. Remove the seat and fuel tank assembly.

14. Reverse the removal procedure to install the fuel tank, seat and console. Refer to **Figure 24**,

typical, when attaching the wiring harness to the switches in the console.

NOTE
Be sure to attach the supply and return hoses to the correct fittings.

15. Check all hoses and connections for leaks.

Cleaning/inspection

You must remove the fuel tank to thoroughly clean and inspect it.

WARNING
Clean the fuel tank in an open area away from all sources of flames or sparks.

1. Pour old gasoline from the tank into a sealable container manufactured specifically for gasoline storage.

2. Pour about 1 quart of fresh gasoline into the tank and slosh it around for several minutes to loosen sediment. Pour the contents into a sealable container.

3. Examine the tank for cracks and abrasions, particularly at points where the tank contacts the body. Areas that rub can be protected and cushioned by coating them with a nonhardening silicone sealer. Allow it to dry before installing the tank. If abrasion is extensive or if the tank is leaking, replace it.

Throttle Cable

Replacement

The throttle cable uses a junction for cables branching to the throttles and the oil injection pump. When replacing the throttle cable, observe the following:

7

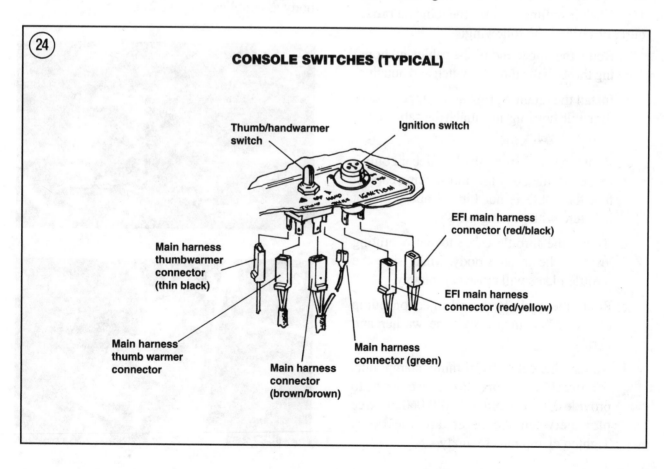

CONSOLE SWITCHES (TYPICAL)

Thumb/handwarmer switch
Ignition switch
EFI main harness connector (red/black)
Main harness thumbwarmer connector (thin black)
EFI main harness connector (red/yellow)
Main harness thumb warmer connector
Main harness connector (green)
Main harness connector (brown/brown)

1. Open the clutch cover and remove the drive belt.

2. Remove the driven pulley (Chapter Fourteen).

3. Remove the E-ring attaching the control cable to the oil injection pump control lever. Do not lose the washer.

4. Loosen the clamp nuts attaching the lower end of the oil injection pump control cable.

5. Separate the control cable from the oil injection pump control lever and the cable housing bracket.

6. Loosen the clamp nuts (**Figure 25** or **Figure 26**) attaching the cable housing to the bracket.

7. Remove the handlebar pad.

8. Remove the ties securing the throttle cable.

9. Detach the cable from the throttle lever.

10. Remove the retaining ring from the upper end of the cable housing, then withdraw the cable from the throttle switch and control assembly.

11. When installing, reverse the removal procedure, observing the following:

    a. Route the upper end of the cable and housing through the throttle switch and housing.

    b. Install the retaining ring at the upper end of the cable housing and attach the cable to the throttle lever.

    c. Route the cable from the handlebar control to the throttle body assembly, being careful that the cable is not kinked and will not interfere with moving parts.

    d. Attach the throttle cable to the operating lever of the throttle body. Make sure the throttle plates will close completely.

    e. Route the cable to the oil injection pump control lever, then install the washer and E-ring.

    f. Adjust the cable by turning clamp nuts (**Figure 25** or **Figure 26**), as necessary, to provide 0.75-1.5 mm (0.030-0.060 in.) free play between the lever and the body. Tighten clamp nuts securely.

    g. Secure the cable to the steering post with ties, then be sure the throttle plates will open and close completely.

    h. Be sure the cable is not kinked and does not bind, then install the handlebar pad.

    i. Refer to Chapter Three and adjust the oil injection pump and idle speed.

Fuel Rail, Pressure Regulator and Injectors (EFI System Powered by Battery)

The fuel pump supplies pressurized fuel to the left end of the fuel rail. The pressure regulator assembly, located at the right end of the fuel rail, controls the pressure of the fuel in the fuel rail. Fuel released by the pressure regulator is returned to the fuel tank through the hose connection attached to the regulator. The injectors are clamped between the fuel rail and the throttle body assemblies (**Figure 27**).

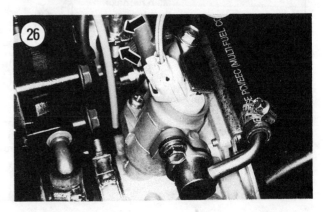

Removal/installation

Refer to **Figure 27** for this procedure.

1. Detach the ground cable from the negative terminal of the battery.

> **CAUTION**
> *Clean dirt and foreign matter from the area around the fuel injectors and fuel rail prior to removing the fuel injectors. Any dirt or foreign matter that falls into the fuel or the injector openings in the throttle body may cause engine damage.*

> **WARNING**
> *Be prepared to plug fuel lines before gasoline begins to leak from detached hoses. The gasoline may still be under pressure. Gasoline is a fire hazard.*

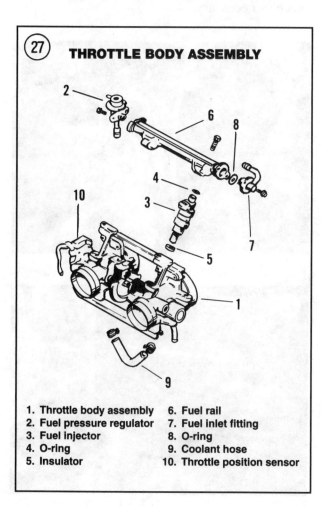

(27) THROTTLE BODY ASSEMBLY

1. Throttle body assembly	6. Fuel rail
2. Fuel pressure regulator	7. Fuel inlet fitting
3. Fuel injector	8. O-ring
4. O-ring	9. Coolant hose
5. Insulator	10. Throttle position sensor

2. Detach hose from the inlet fitting (7, **Figure 27**) and the vent and return fittings of the regulator (2, **Figure 27**).

3. Mark the original location, then detach electrical connectors from the injectors.

4. Remove the two screws attaching the fuel rail (6, **Figure 27**) to the throttle bodies (1, **Figure 27**).

5. Lift the fuel rail from the injectors and throttle body assembly.

6. The injectors can be lifted from the throttle body.

7. Remove the O-ring and insulator from each injector.

8. Reinstall by reversing the procedure. Make sure that all seals are in good condition. Lubricate O-rings and seals with oil before assembling. Tighten retaining screws securely.

9. Attach the fuel delivery hose to the inlet fitting (7, **Figure 27**) as follows.

   a. Push the fuel delivery hose onto the inlet fitting (7, **Figure 27**) until the end of the hose is 20-30 mm (0.8-1.2 in.) past the end of the fitting.

   b. Position the hose clamp 3-7 mm (0.12-0.28 in.) from the end of the hose.

   c. Tighten the clamp securely.

10. Purge air from the fuel system as described in this chapter.

> **WARNING**
> *Check for fuel system leaks before starting the engine. Any leakage is hazardous.*

Disassembly and assembly

Refer to **Figure 27** for this procedure. The injectors, fuel rail and regulator are available separately. Be sure all seals are in good condition when assembling.

> **CAUTION**
> *Most commercial carburetor cleaners will damage rubber O-rings, seals and plastic parts. Be sure all parts that could*

be damaged by the cleaner are removed before using a harsh cleaner.

1. If necessary, the fuel inlet fitting (7, **Figure 27**) can be unbolted and separated from the fuel rail for cleaning.

2. The fuel pressure regulator (2, **Figure 27**) can be unbolted and separated from the fuel rail. The regulator assembly is available for service only as a unit. Do not attempt to disassemble this unit.

NOTE
The ECU chip and each of the injector nozzles must be properly matched. A red, yellow or blue paint spot should be on the ECU chip, the ECU housing and each of the injector units. When ordering replacement parts, be sure you know the color code of the components. If you have questions about correct application, see your Arctic Cat dealer.

3. The fuel injectors (3, **Figure 27**) are available separately. Observe the following:

   a. Do not clean the red, yellow or blue color code spot from the injector nozzle.

   b. Do not attempt to disassemble or alter the injector assemblies.

   c. If a new injector is installed, make sure the color code of the replacement unit matches the code of the ECU chip in the ECU housing.

4. Make sure that seals are new or in good condition and coated with oil when assembling the fuel delivery assembly.

Fuel Rail, Pressure Regulator and Injectors (EFI System not Powered by a Battery)

The fuel pump supplies pressurized fuel to the end of the fuel rail. The pressure regulator assembly, located at the right end of the fuel rail, controls the pressure of the fuel in the fuel rail. Fuel released by the pressure regulator is returned to the fuel tank through the hose connection attached to the regulator. The injectors are held in the bores of the fuel rail by the retainer

(**Figure 28**). The fuel rail is attached to the throttle body with screws (**Figure 29**).

NOTE
It should not be necessary to separate the fuel rail from the throttle body assembly.

1. Loosen the clamp on the fuel delivery hose, then pull the hose from the inlet fitting located on the left end of the fuel rail.

2. Detach the electrical connector from the fuel injector.

3. Remove the two screws (**Figure 28**) attaching the retainer to the fuel rail.

4. Pull the injector straight up out of its bore in the fuel rail.

5. Inspect the condition of the O-rings and replace as necessary.

6. Make sure the bore in the fuel rail is clean and smooth.

7. Coat the O-rings with a light coat of oil before inserting the nozzles into the fuel rail.

8. Carefully slide the injector into its bore with the electrical connection toward the front.

9. Install the retainer and tighten the two screws securely.

10. Attach the wiring harness electrical connector to the terminals of the injector.

11. Connect the fuel delivery hose to the inlet fitting as follows:

   a. Push the fuel delivery hose onto the inlet fitting until the end of the hose is 20-30 mm (0.8-1.2 in.) past the end of the fitting.

   b. The position the hose clamp should be 3-7 mm (0.12-0.28 in.) from the end of the hose.

   c. Tighten the clamp securely.

12. Purge air from the fuel system as described in this chapter.

WARNING
*Check for fuel system leaks before start-
ing engine. Any leakage is hazardous.*

Throttle Body Assembly

Removal/installation

Individual parts of the throttle body assembly are not available separately. Be sure that all seals are in good condition when assembling.

CAUTION
*Most commercial carburetor cleaners
will damage rubber O-rings, seals and
plastic parts. Be sure all parts that could
be damaged by the cleaner are removed
before using a harsh cleaner.*

1. If equipped with a battery, detach the ground cable from the negative terminal of the battery.

CAUTION
*Clean dirt and foreign matter from the
area around the fuel injectors and fuel
rail prior to removing the fuel injectors.
Any dirt or foreign matter that falls into
the fuel or the injector openings in the
throttle body may cause engine damage.*

WARNING
*Be prepared to plug fuel lines before
gasoline begins to leak from detached
hoses. The gasoline may still be under
pressure. Gasoline is a fire hazard.*

2. Detach hoses from the inlet fitting (7, **Figure 27**) and the vent and return fittings of the regulator (2, **Figure 27**).

3. Loosen the clamp securing the engine coolant hose on the PTO side of the throttle body. Detach the hose. Plug both openings to reduce the loss of coolant.

4. Mark the original location, then detach electrical connectors from each injector, the throttle position sensor and the coolant temperature sensor.

5. Loosen the clamp nuts (**Figure 25** or **Figure 26**) attaching the cable housing to the bracket and detach the cable from the throttle lever.

6. Loosen the clamps securing the throttle body mounting flanges.

7. Lift the throttle body assembly from the mounting flanges.

NOTE
*The adjustment (**Figure 30**) is used to
synchronize the opening of the two throttle valves. Both valves must open and
close at exactly the same time. This adjustment should not be required, but the*

opening and closing should be checked. Synchronize the throttle valves if necessary.

8. When installing, reverse the removal procedure.

9. Attach the fuel delivery hose to the inlet fitting (7, **Figure 27**) as follows.

  a. Push the fuel delivery hose onto the inlet fitting (7, **Figure 27**) until the end of the hose is 20-30 mm (0.8-1.2 in.) past the end of the fitting.

  b. Position the hose clamp 3-7 mm (0.12-0.28 in.) from the end of the hose.

  c. Tighten the clamp securely.

10. Purge air from the fuel system as described in this chapter.

> *WARNING*
> *Check for fuel system leaks before starting the engine. Any leakage is hazardous.*

Purge the Fuel System

When the fuel system is serviced, air can enter the fuel passages. The following procedure will remove air from most of the passages.

1. Place the rear of the snowmobile on a safety stand.

2. For models with battery-powered EFI system, proceed as follows.

  a. Turn the ignition key ON and listen for the fuel pump. The pump should run for about 5 seconds, then stop.

  b. Turn the ignition key OFF.

  c. Repeat substeps 2a-b several times to bleed air from the system. Usually six times will be sufficient.

3. Start the engine without touching the throttle. The engine may idle slowly at first, but should increase speed to the normal idle rpm on its own, without touching the throttle.

4. If the engine dies, turn the ignition OFF, then turn the ignition ON and restart.

Fuel Pump

Removal/installation

The fuel pump is located in the fuel tank.

1. Remove the fuel tank as described in this chapter.

2. Thoroughly clean the area around the fuel pump mounting plate.

3. Remove the six screws from the pump mounting plate. Be sure the six nylon washers are also removed.

> *NOTE*
> *The fuel pump will contain gasoline. Be prepared to catch and drain gasoline from the fuel pump.*

4. Separate the fuel pump mounting plate from the top of the fuel tank, then lift the mounting plate, fuel pump and pickup assembly from the tank.

5. Remove the gasket.

6. Reinstall the fuel pump by reversing the removal steps while noting the following:

  a. Make sure all of the hoses inside the tank are fitted with suitable clamps.

  b. The front pickup has two hose connections. The rear pickup has only one hose connection.

  c. The screens of both fuel pickups should be down.

  d. Install the gasket against the tank before installing the fuel pump assembly.

  e. The long hose with the fuel pickup should be at the rear of the tank.

  f. Make sure that a nylon washer is on each of the screws attaching the plate to the top of the fuel tank. Tighten the screws to 1 N·m (12 in.-lb.) torque. Do not overtighten the screws.

> *CAUTION*
> *Check for fuel leaks before starting engine.*

7. After assembly is complete, turn the ignition switch ON, but do not start the engine. Turning on the ignition switch will energize the fuel pump for about 5 seconds.

8. Check for fuel leaks.

WARNING
Do not start the engine if there is the slightest fuel leak. Any leakage is hazardous.

9. Start the engine and check again for leaks.

Electronic Control Unit (ECU)

Removal/installation

CAUTION
Components of the ECU can be damaged by static electricity. It is important to work in an environment that prevents static electricity. When working on or around the ECU housing, ground yourself to the metal case of the housing to discharge any static electricity. If the ECU housing is opened, ground yourself and any tools before touching the EPROM chip or other electrical components located in the housing.

1. Make sure the ignition switch is OFF. Disconnect the ground cable from the negative terminal of the battery.

2. Detach the electrical connectors (**Figure 31**, typical) from the ECU.

3. Remove the fasteners attaching the ECU mounting bracket.

4. Tip the ECU mounting bracket forward, then remove the four screws attaching the ECU housing to the mounting bracket.

5. Installation is the reverse of removal.

Changing the EPROM chip

Except for the Eraseable Programable Read Only Memory (EPROM) chip, individual components of the ECU are not available separately.

1. Make sure the ignition switch is OFF. Disconnect ground cable from the negative terminal of the battery.

2. Remove the screws attaching the cover to the ECU housing. On 1996 and earlier models, see **Figure 31**. On 1997 and later models, the cover is located under the ECU housing.

NOTE
The cover may be sealed onto the housing. Do not damage the cover or housing when removing.

3. Carefully remove the cover.

CAUTION
Ground yourself and any tools to the metal frame of the housing before touching the EPROM chip or other electrical components located in the housing.

4. Observe the EPROM chip installed in the socket near the top of the circuit board. The chip and its socket have a notch at one end to indicate correct reference for installation.

NOTE
The ECU chip and each of the injectors must be properly matched. On battery-powered EFI systems, a red, yellow or blue paint spot should be on the ECU chip and each of the injector units. On magneto-powered EFI systems, each injector is marked with a square, circle or triangle. The identifying color or shape on all of the parts should be the same as

those originally installed for the system to operate correctly. When ordering replacement parts, know the identifying code of the other components. If you have questions about correct application, see your Arctic Cat dealer.

5. Use a suitable chip puller to lift the EPROM straight out of its mounting socket.

6. Pins on the EPROM are easily bent by improper assembly techniques. Observe the following when installing the chip.

   a. Start one row of pins in the socket.

   b. Align the second row of pins with the socket.

   c. Press the chip firmly into the socket when all the pins are aligned.

7. Make sure the cover gasket is in good condition. On 1996 and earlier models, apply a bead of silicone to the cover near the plastic connection.

8. Install the cover and tighten the retaining screws securely.

Throttle Position Sensor (TPS) Removal/Installation

The throttle position sensor (**Figure 14**, typical) is located on the end of the throttle shaft. On magneto-powered EFI systems, the throttle position sensor (TPS) is attached and adjusted at the factory and should not be removed or adjusted. If the TPS is faulty, the throttle body and TPS should be replaced as a unit.

Use the following procedure to replace the throttle position sensor on battery-powered EFI systems.

1. Disconnect the throttle cable from the throttle shaft.

2. Loosen the locknut and turn the idle speed stop screw (**Figure 32**) counterclockwise until the lever will not touch the stop screw.

3. Open and release the throttle several times, allowing the throttle plate to snap shut.

NOTE
Make sure the lever does not touch the stop screw. The throttle plates should be completely closed when adjusting the throttle position sensor.

4. Disconnect the TPS lead.

5. Remove the two mounting screws.

6. Carefully pull the sensor from the throttle body assembly.

7. Remove the O-ring located between the TPS and the throttle body. The O-ring fits in a groove in the throttle body.

8. Apply a light coat of silicone grease to the area around the outside of the TPS flange and in the groove for the O-ring.

9. Stick the O-ring in the groove of the throttle body.

10. Align the flat of the TPS with the matching flat of the throttle shaft and install the TPS.

11. Install the two screws, flat washers and lockwashers that attach the TPS, but do not tighten them until adjustment is complete.

12. Attach the wiring harness to the TPS.

13. After installation, refer to *Adjustments* in this chapter to synchronize TPS setting.

ADJUSTMENTS

Idle Speed and Throttle Synchronization

For maximum engine performance, both cylinders must work equally. For proper synchroni-

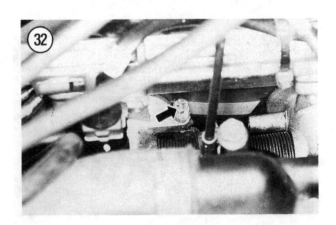

zation, both throttle plates must begin to open at exactly the same time and continue to be open the same amount throughout their operating range.

Throttle synchronization should not change during normal operation, but you should check it when the throttle body assembly is removed or if the engine suffers from reduced performance and synchronization problems are suspected.

Refer to *Throttle Body Assembly Removal/Installation* in this chapter for synchronizing the opening and closing of the two throttle valves.

> *CAUTION*
> *Maintaining throttle cable free play is critical to prevent throttle cable damage.*

TPS Setting

On magneto-powered EFI systems, the throttle position sensor (TPS) attached to the end of the throttle body assembly at the factory, should not be removed or adjusted. If the TPS is faulty, the throttle body and TPS should be replaced as a unit.

The throttle position sensor (TPS) on battery-powered EFI systems has elongated mounting holes to allow adjustment when installing. It may be necessary to synchronize the TPS with the throttle plates if the TPS has been replaced or moved during servicing. Use the following procedure to adjust the position of the throttle position sensor on battery-powered systems.

1. Open the hood and make sure the wiring harness is attached to the TPS.

2. Back out the idle speed screw (**Figure 32**) so the throttle plates will close completely.

3. Open the throttle and allow it to snap closed several times to make sure the throttle plates close completely. If not, adjust the throttle cable.

4. Make sure the ignition switch is OFF, then attach the diagnostic harness as described in this chapter.

5. Loosen the screws attaching the TPS to the throttle body.

6. Turn the ignition switch ON and measure the voltage between pin No. 3 and pin No. 17 (**Figure 5**) of the diagnostic harness.

7. Rotate TPS, as required, until the voltage is exactly 0.538 VDC, then tighten the TPS mounting screws.

> *NOTE*
> *If the voltage measured between pins No. 3 and No. 17 keeps changing, the sensor may be faulty. Before installing a new sensor, be sure the throttle cable is not sticking.*

8. Open and close the throttle several times to make sure the voltage remains the same as set in Step 7. Readjust if necessary.

> *NOTE*
> *Leave the diagnostic harness in place until the idle speed stop has been set.*

9. Set the idle speed stop as described in this chapter.

Idle Speed Stop

Use the following procedure when adjusting the idle speed stop on battery-powered EFI systems.

1. Check the TPS setting as described in this chapter. Leave the diagnostic harness in place to set the idle speed stop.

> *NOTE*
> *If the diagnostic harness is not yet installed, make sure the ignition switch is OFF before attaching the diagnostic harness as described in this chapter.*

2A. *Battery-Powered EFI Systems*—Turn the ignition switch ON and measure the voltage between pin No. 3 and pin No. 17 (**Figure 5**) of the diagnostic harness.

2B. *Magneto-powered EFI Systems*—Turn the ignition switch ON and measure the voltage between pin No. 20 (**Figure 5**) of the diagnostic harness and ground.

3. Turn the idle speed stop screw (**Figure 32**), as required, to set the measured voltage to 0.82-0.825 VDC.

4A. *Battery-Powered EFI Systems*—Open the throttle fully and observe the voltage between pin No. 3 and pin No. 17 (**Figure 5**).

4B. *Magneto-powered EFI Systems*—Open the throttle fully and measure the voltage between pin No. 20 (**Figure 5**) of the diagnostic harness and ground.

5. If the wide-open voltage is not 3.81-4.23 VDC, recheck the TPS closed setting as de-scribed in this chapter. If the closed setting is correct, the sensor is faulty.

NOTE
If the measured voltage keeps changing, the sensor may be faulty. Before install-ing a new sensor, be sure the throttle cable is not sticking.

6. Start the engine and observe the idle speed. After the engine reaches operating temperature, the engine should idle smoothly and speed should be stable at 1500 rpm.

Table 1 ELECTRONIC FUEL INJECTION ERROR CODES

Monitor light symbol	Possible cause
1996 and earlier models*	
1 long, 1 short	Open or short in Throttle Position Sensor (TPS).
1 long, 3 short	Open or short in intake air temp sensor.
1 long, 4 short	Open or short in engine coolant temp sensor.
2 long, 1 short	Faulty #1 (MAG) injector control circuit in ECU or open or short in circuit to the #1 injector.
2 long, 2 short	Faulty #2 (PTO) injector control circuit in ECU or open or short in circuit to the #2 injector.
4 long, 1 short	Open or short in the injector timing sensor.
4 long, 2 short	Open or short in the ignition timing sensor.
1997-on models**	
1 flash	Open or short in Throttle Position Sensor (TPS).
2 flashes	Open or short in engine coolant temp sensor.
3 flashes	Open or short in intake air temp sensor.
4 flashes	Open or short in the barometric pressure sensor.
5 flashes	Faulty fuel injectors.

* The EFI of 1996 and earlier models uses the vehicle battery to energize the system.
** The EFI of 1997-on models is the magneto-powered type and power must be supplied by an external source via the diagnostic harness.

Table 2 ENGINE COOLANT TEMPERATURE SENSOR SPECIFICATIONS (1996 AND EARLIER BATTERY-POWERED SYSTEMS)

| Temperature | | | Resistance |
°C	°F	Voltage	(ohms)
100	212	0.812	190
98	208	0.847	201
96	205	0.883	213
94	201	0.921	224
92	198	0.960	236
90	194	1.002	247
88	190	1.045	263
86	187	1.090	278
84	183	1.137	294
82	180	1.187	309
80	176	1.239	325
78	172	1.293	347
76	169	1.350	368
74	165	1.409	390
72	162	1.471	411
70	158	1.535	433
68	154	1.601	466
66	151	1.669	500
64	147	1.739	533
62	144	1.811	567
60	140	1.886	600
58	136	1.962	648
56	133	2.039	696
54	129	2.118	744
52	126	2.199	792
50	122	2.280	840
48	118	2.363	908
46	115	2.446	976
44	111	2.531	1,044
42	108	2.615	1,112
40	104	2.700	1,180
38	100	2.785	1,284
36	97	2.870	1,388
34	93	2.955	1,492
32	90	2.039	1,596
30	86	3.123	1,700
28	82	3.206	1,933
26	79	3.288	2,065
24	75	3.368	2,206
22	72	3.448	2,359
20	68	3.526	2,524
18	64	3.602	2,706
16	61	3.676	2,906
14	57	3.749	3,128
12	54	3.819	3,376
10	50	3.887	3,653
8	46	3.952	3,965
6	43	4.016	4,316
4	39	4.076	4,712
2	36	4.134	5,159

7

(continued)

Table 2 ENGINE COOLANT TEMPERATURE SENSOR SPECIFICATIONS (1996 AND EARLIER BATTERY-POWERED SYSTEMS) (continued)

| Temperature | | | Resistance |
°C	°F	Voltage	(ohms)
0	32	4.190	5,664
-2	28	4.242	6,234
-4	25	4.292	6,877
-6	21	4.339	7,601
-8	18	4.383	8,416
-10	14	4.425	9,330
-12	10	4.464	10,355
-14	7	4.450	11,502
-16	3	4.533	12,782
-18	-0.4	4.565	14,207
-20	-4	4.593	15,795
-22	-8	4.620	17,554
-24	-11	4.645	19,502
-26	-15	4.668	21,655
-28	-18	4.689	24,029
-30	-22	4.709	26,642
-32	-26	4.728	29,513
-34	-29	4.747	32,660
-36	-32	4.765	36,104
-38	-36	4.783	39,867
-40	-40	4.802	43,971

Table 3 ENGINE COOLANT TEMPERATURE SENSOR SPECIFICATIONS (1997 AND LATER MAGNETO-POWERED SYSTEMS)

| Temperature | | | Resistance |
°C	°F	Voltage	ohms
110	230	0.115	129
108	226	0.129	137
106	223	0.143	145
104	219	0.157	153
102	216	0.171	161
100	212	0.185	169
98	208	0.192	180
96	205	0.199	191
94	201	0.206	202
92	198	0.213	213
90	194	0.220	224
88	190	0.235	240
86	187	0.250	256
84	183	0.265	273
82	180	0.280	289
80	176	0.295	305
78	172	0.317	327
76	169	0.339	349
74	165	0.361	371
72	162	0.383	393

(continued)

**Table 3 ENGINE COOLANT TEMPERATURE SENSOR SPECIFICATIONS
(1997 AND LATER MAGNETO-POWERED SYSTEMS) (continued)**

| Temperature | | | Resistance |
°C	°F	Voltage	ohms
70	158	0.405	415
68	154	0.438	445
66	151	0.471	475
64	147	0.504	505
62	144	0.537	535
60	140	0.570	565
58	136	0.598	609
56	133	0.626	653
54	129	0.654	697
52	126	0.682	741
50	122	0.710	785
48	118	0.759	849
46	115	0.808	913
44	111	0.857	977
42	108	0.906	1,041
40	104	0.955	1,105
38	100	1.023	1,214
36	97	1.091	1,323
34	93	1.159	1,432
32	90	1.227	1,541
30	86	1.295	1,650
28	82	1.377	1,800
26	79	1.469	1,950
24	75	1.541	2,100
22	72	1.623	2,250
20	68	1.705	2,400
18	64	1.806	2,670
16	61	1.907	2,940
14	57	2.008	3,210
12	54	2.109	3,480
10	50	2.210	3,750
8	46	2.327	4,170
6	43	2.444	4,590
4	39	2.561	5,010
2	36	2.678	5,430
0	32	2.795	5,850
-2	28	2.901	6,510
-4	25	3.007	7,170
-6	21	3.113	7,830
-8	18	3.219	8,490
-10	14	3.325	9,150
-12	10	3.421	9,422
-14	7	3.517	9,694
-16	3	3.613	9,966
-18	-0.4	3.709	10,238
-20	-4	3.805	10,510
-22	-8	3.885	13,688
-24	-11	3.965	16,866
-26	-15	4.045	20,044
-28	-18	4.125	23,222
-30	-22	4.205	26,400

(continued)

Table 3 ENGINE COOLANT TEMPERATURE SENSOR SPECIFICATIONS (1997 AND LATER MAGNETO-POWERED SYSTEMS) (continued)

Temperature °C	°F	Voltage	Resistance ohms
-32	-26	4.267	30,520
-34	-29	4.329	34,640
-36	-32	4.391	38,760
-38	-36	4.453	42,880
-40	-40	4.515	47,000
-42	-44	4.553	55,100
144	-47	4.591	63,200
-46	-51	4.629	71,300
-48	-54	4.667	79,400
-50	-58	4.705	87,500

Table 4 INTAKE AIR TEMPERATURE SENSOR SPECIFICATIONS (1997 AND LATER MAGNETO-POWERED SYSTEMS)

Temperature °C	°F	Voltage	Resistance ohms
100	212	0.113	555
98	208	0.121	595
96	205	0.128	635
94	201	0.136	675
92	198	0.143	715
90	194	0.151	755
88	190	0.162	819
86	187	0.173	883
84	183	0.184	947
82	180	0.195	1,011
80	176	0.206	1,075
78	172	0.222	1,160
76	169	0.238	1,245
74	165	0.253	1,330
72	162	0.269	1,415
70	158	0.285	1,500
68	154	0.308	1,640
66	151	0.331	1,780
64	147	0.353	1,920
62	144	0.376	2,060
60	140	0.399	2,200
58	136	0.432	2,410
56	133	0.466	2,620
54	129	0.498	2,830
52	126	0.531	3,040
50	122	0.564	3,250
48	118	0.612	3,595
46	115	0.659	3,940
44	111	0.707	4,285
42	108	0.754	4,630
40	104	0.802	4,975
38	100	0.869	5,490

(continued)

Table 4 INTAKE AIR TEMPERATURE SENSOR SPECIFICATIONS (1997 AND LATER MAGNETO-POWERED SYSTEMS) (continued)

Temperature			Resistance
°C	°F	Voltage	ohms
36	97	0.937	6,005
34	93	1.004	6,520
32	90	1.072	7,035
30	86	1.139	7,550
28	82	1.230	8,540
26	79	1.322	9,530
24	75	1.413	10,520
22	72	1.505	11,510
20	68	1.596	12,500
18	64	1.716	14,020
16	61	1.836	15,540
14	57	1.955	17,060
12	54	2.075	18,580
10	50	2.195	20,100
8	46	2.323	23,060
6	43	2.452	26,020
4	39	2.580	28,980
2	36	2.709	31,940
0	32	2.837	34,900
-2	28	2.969	39,940
-4	25	3.101	44,980
-6	21	3.233	50,020
-8	18	3.365	55,060
-10	14	3.497	60,100
-12	10	3.610	76,080
-14	7	3.722	92,060
-16	3	3.835	108,040
-18	-0.4	3.947	124,020
-20	-4	4.060	140,000
-22	-8	4.142	156,000
-24	-11	4.224	172,000
-26	-15	4.306	188,000
-28	-18	4.388	204,000
-30	-22	4.470	220,000
-32	-26	4.522	261,000
-34	-29	4.574	302,000
-36	-32	4.625	343,000
-38	-36	4.677	384,000
-40	-40	4.729	425,000

7

Chapter Eight

Exhaust System

The exhaust system consists of the exhaust manifold, or individual exhaust sockets, expansion chamber(s) and a muffler.

This chapter includes service procedures for all parts of the exhaust systems.

Removal/Installation

Refer to **Figure 1** or **Figure 2** for this procedure.

1. Open the hood.

> **WARNING**
> *If the exhaust system is hot, wait until it cools before removing it.*

2. Detach the springs (**Figure 3** or **Figure 4**) that attach the expansion chamber(s) to the muffler.

> **NOTE**
> *A hooked tool can be used to pull the spring far enough to release one of the hooked ends.*

3. Disconnect the springs that attach the expansion chamber(s) to the manifold (**Figure 5**) or exhaust socket (**Figure 6**).

4. If so equipped, remove the long spring that crosses the expansion chamber(s).

5. Remove the expansion chamber(s).

6. Unbolt and remove the muffler (**Figure 7** or **Figure 8**).

7. Remove the nuts and washers holding the exhaust manifold (**Figure 9** or **Figure 10**) or exhaust socket (**Figure 11**) onto the cylinders. Remove the exhaust manifold or exhaust socket.

8. Examine the expansion chamber(s), muffler, manifold and exhaust sockets for cracks or other damage. Repair as described in this chapter.

9. Install by reversing the removal procedure, while observing the following:

   a. Install new exhaust gaskets. The metal side of the manifold gasket must be out as shown in **Figure 12**.

   b. Check the condition of all retaining springs (**Figure 13**). Replace, as necessary.

c. Attach one end of the spring, then use a hooked tool to pull the spring far enough to attach the hooked end.

d. Check the exhaust system for leaks after installation.

Cleaning

1. Clean all accessible exhaust passages with a blunt roundnose tool.

2. There are several ways to clean areas further down the pipe, including the following.

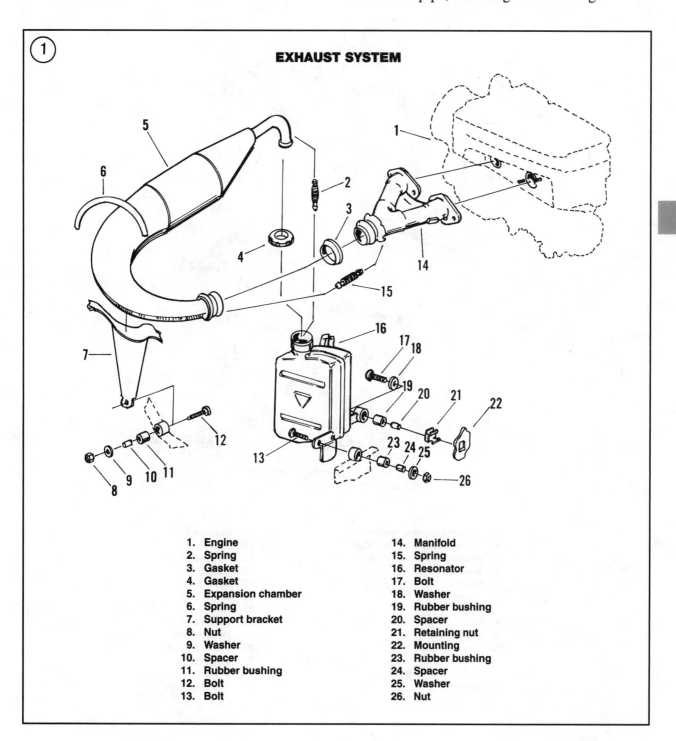

EXHAUST SYSTEM

1. Engine	14. Manifold
2. Spring	15. Spring
3. Gasket	16. Resonator
4. Gasket	17. Bolt
5. Expansion chamber	18. Washer
6. Spring	19. Rubber bushing
7. Support bracket	20. Spacer
8. Nut	21. Retaining nut
9. Washer	22. Mounting
10. Spacer	23. Rubber bushing
11. Rubber bushing	24. Spacer
12. Bolt	25. Washer
13. Bolt	26. Nut

8

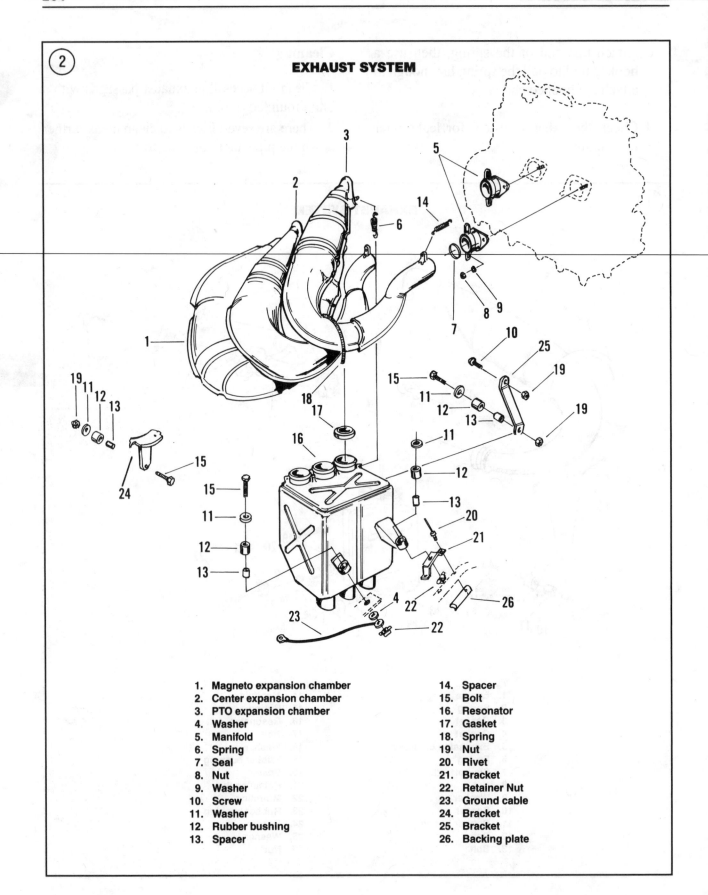

EXHAUST SYSTEM

1. Magneto expansion chamber
2. Center expansion chamber
3. PTO expansion chamber
4. Washer
5. Manifold
6. Spring
7. Seal
8. Nut
9. Washer
10. Screw
11. Washer
12. Rubber bushing
13. Spacer
14. Spacer
15. Bolt
16. Resonator
17. Gasket
18. Spring
19. Nut
20. Rivet
21. Bracket
22. Retainer Nut
23. Ground cable
24. Bracket
25. Bracket
26. Backing plate

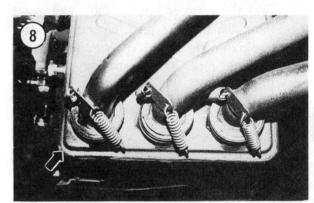

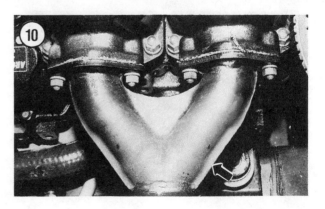

WARNING
When performing Step 2b, do not start the drill until the cable is inserted into the pipe. At no time should the drill be running when the cable is free of the pipe. The whipping action of the cable could cause serious injury. Wear heavy shop gloves and a face shield when using this equipment.

a. Insert a section of discarded speedometer cable in an electric drill chuck (**Figure 14**). Fray the loose end of the cable and insert the cable into the pipe. Operate the drill while moving the cable back and forth inside the pipe. Take your time and do a thorough job.

WARNING
Make sure all foreign objects are removed from the pipe when finished cleaning.

b. Find several large ball bearings or nuts that will just fit into the expansion chamber or muffler. Count the bearings or nuts as they are inserted, then shake the pipe violently to break loose carbon that is inside.

3. Shake the large pieces out into a trash container.

EXHAUST SYSTEM REPAIR

A dent in the expansion chamber will change the system's flow characteristics and may degrade performance. Minor damage can be easily repaired if you have welding equipment, some simple body tools and a slide hammer.

Small Dents

1. Drill a small hole in the center of the dent. Screw the end of the slide hammer into the hole.

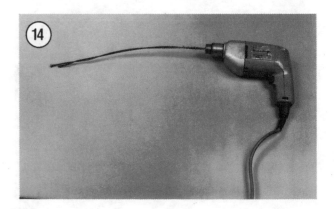

2. Heat the area around the dent evenly with a torch.

3. When the dent is heated to a uniform orange-red color, operate the slide hammer to raise the dent.

4. When the dent is removed, unscrew the slide hammer and weld the drilled hole closed.

Large Dents

Large dents that are not crimped can be removed with heat and a slide hammer as previously described. However, several holes must be drilled along the center of the dent so that it can be pulled out evenly.

If the dent is sharply crimped along the edges, the affected section should be cut out with a hacksaw, straightened with a body dolly and hammer and welded back into place.

Before cutting the exhaust pipe apart, scribe alignment marks across the area to be cut to facilitate correct alignment when rewelding the pipe.

After the welding is completed, wire brush and clean up all welds. Paint the entire pipe with a high-temperature paint to prevent rusting.

8

Table 1 TIGHTENING TORQUE

	N·m	ft.-lb.
Exhaust manifold		
1990-1992	15-19	11-14
1993-on	18-22	13-16

Chapter Nine

Electrical System

The electrical system includes the ignition, lighting, starting and other electrical accessory systems.

All models are equipped with a Capacitor Discharge Ignition (CDI) system. There are several differences between the ignition systems used on the various models (**Figure 1-7**, typical).

This chapter provides service procedures for the ignition and electrical systems. Refer to Chapter Two for ignition system troubleshooting and test procedures. Refer to Chapter Seven for troubleshooting and servicing the EFI. Wiring diagrams are at the end of the book. **Tables 1-2** are located at the end of the chapter.

Some models are equipped with a battery and electric starter system. Procedures for servicing the starter motor are included in this chapter.

FLYWHEEL AND STATOR ASSEMBLY

The stator of two-cylinder models without EFI includes an ignition generating coil, ignition trigger coil and lighting coil assembly. The ignition generating coil (10, **Figure 1** or 8, **Figure 2**) on some models includes the trigger coil assembly. On some models, the ignition generating coil (7, **Figure 3**) is separate from the ignition trigger coil (10, **Figure 3**).

The stator on two-cylinder models with battery-powered EFI includes ignition generating coil and lighting coil. The ignition timing and injection timing sensors (1 and 2, **Figure 4**) are located outside the flywheel.

The stator on two-cylinder models with magneto-powered EFI includes the ignition low and high speed coils, lighting coil, injection coil and fuel pump coil. The timing sensor (5, **Figure 5**) is located outside the flywheel.

The stator of three-cylinder models includes ignition generating coils (9, **Figure 6**) and the lighting coil. The timing sensor is located outside the flywheel.

Each system uses components that may be different from similar units and only parts de-

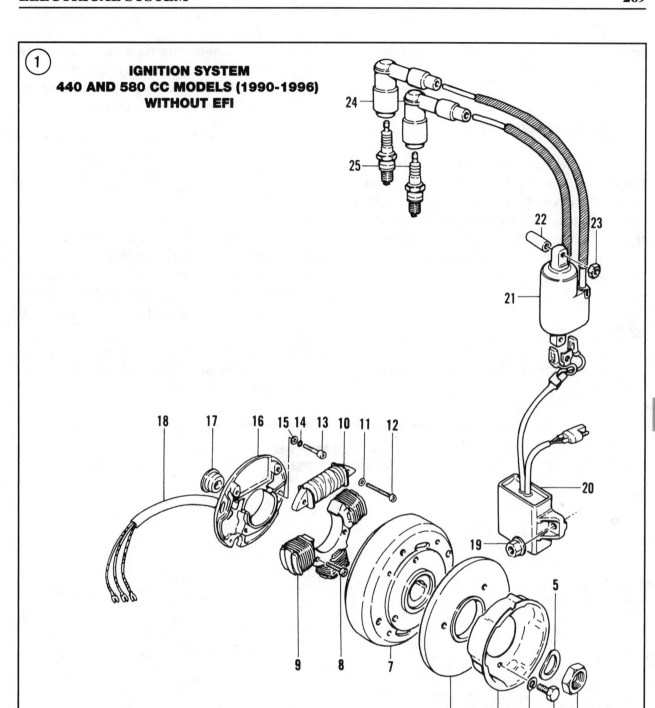

**IGNITION SYSTEM
440 AND 580 CC MODELS (1990-1996)
WITHOUT EFI**

9

1. Nut	10. Ignition generating coil	18. Wires
2. Bolt	11. Lockwasher	19. Nut
3. Lockwasher	12. Bolt	20. CDI unit
4. Starter pulley	13. Bolt	21. Ignition coil
5. Lockwasher	14. Lockwasher	22. Spacer
6. Counterweight	15. Washer	23. Nut
7. Flywheel	16. Stator plate	24. Spark plug caps
8. Bolt	17. Grommet	25. Spark plugs
9. Lighting coil		

signed for the specific system should be installed.

Flywheel Removal/Installation

The flywheel must be removed to service the stator coils. Flywheel replacement is usually necessary, only if the keyway in the flywheel is damaged, magnets have been damaged or if the flywheel is damaged by improper removal procedures. Refer to the appropriate procedure for your model.

El Tigre EXT

Refer to **Figure 1** when performing this procedure.

1. Unbolt and remove the recoil starter assembly (**Figure 8**). It is not necessary to remove the handle if the starter assembly can be located out of the way inside the engine compartment.

NOTE
You can remove the flywheel with the engine installed. The accompanying photographs show the engine removed for clarity.

2. Remove the bolts attaching the flywheel cover, then remove the cover (**Figure 9**).
3. Remove the engine coolant pump pulley or reposition the pump as described in Chapter Eleven. The flywheel will not clear the pump pulley.
4. Hold the starter pulley and loosen the flywheel retaining nut (**Figure 10**). Threads of the nut may be fixed with Loctite.

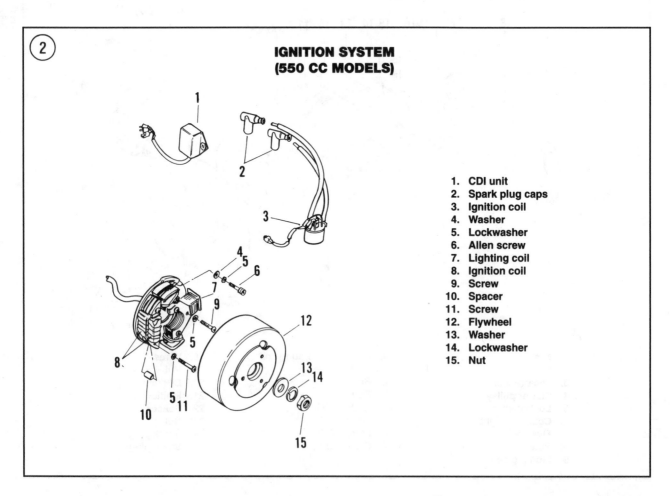

②

**IGNITION SYSTEM
(550 CC MODELS)**

1. CDI unit
2. Spark plug caps
3. Ignition coil
4. Washer
5. Lockwasher
6. Allen screw
7. Lighting coil
8. Ignition coil
9. Screw
10. Spacer
11. Screw
12. Flywheel
13. Washer
14. Lockwasher
15. Nut

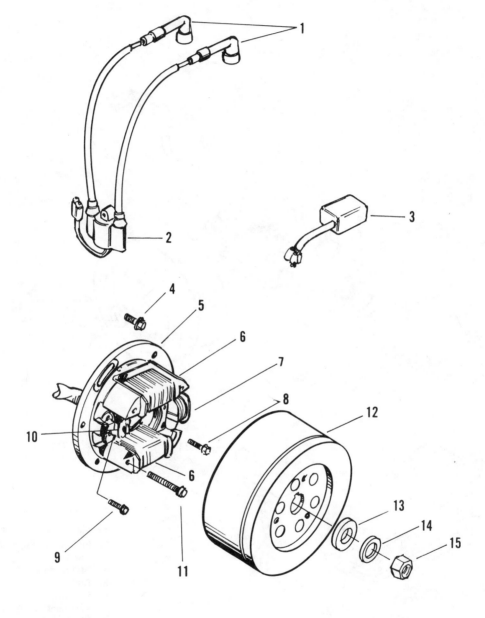

③

**IGNITION SYSTEM
(2-CYLINDER MODELS WITH BATTERY POWERED EFI)**

9

1. Spark plug caps	6. Lighting coil	11. Screw
2. Ignition coil	7. Ignition coil	12. Flywheel
3. CDI unit	8. Screw	13. Washer
4. Allen screw	9. Screw	14. Lockwasher
5. Stator plate	10. Timing coil	15. Nut

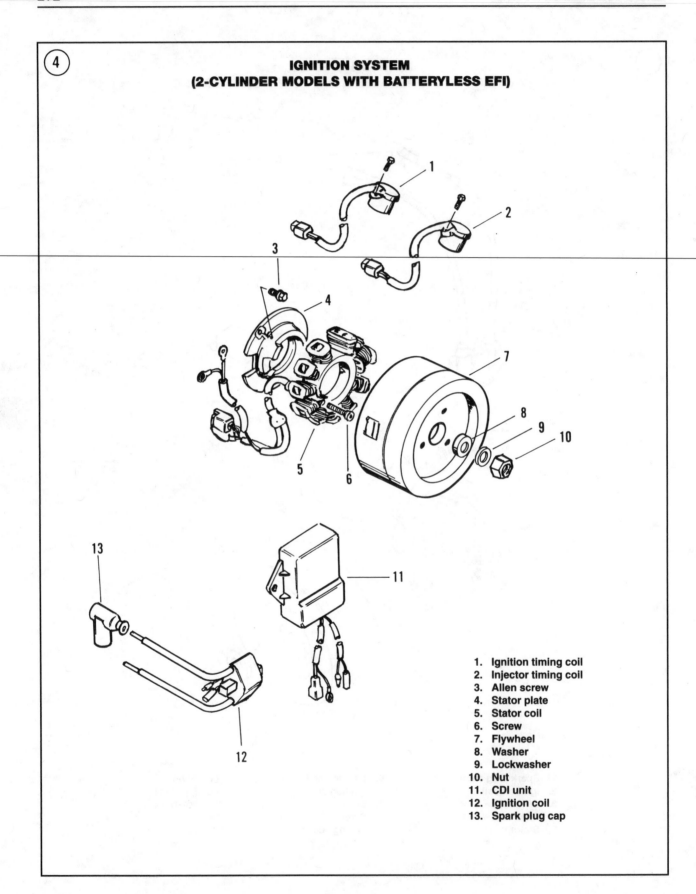

④

**IGNITION SYSTEM
(2-CYLINDER MODELS WITH BATTERYLESS EFI)**

1. Ignition timing coil
2. Injector timing coil
3. Allen screw
4. Stator plate
5. Stator coil
6. Screw
7. Flywheel
8. Washer
9. Lockwasher
10. Nut
11. CDI unit
12. Ignition coil
13. Spark plug cap

5. Unbolt and remove the starter pulley (**Figure 11**) from the flywheel.

6. Remove the coolant pump drive pulley (**Figure 12**).

7. Remove the flywheel retaining nut and washer(s).

CAUTION
Protect the crankshaft from damage while using the puller in Step 8. A protective cap can be made by welding a

small plate to the end of a stock flywheel nut.

8. Attach the Arctco flywheel puller (part No. 0144-112) or equivalent as shown in **Figure 13**.

CAUTION
Do not heat the flywheel or pound on the flywheel while attempting to remove it. Heat can cause the flywheel to seize onto the crankshaft. Hitting the flywheel can damage the flywheel, crankshaft or crankshaft bearings.

9

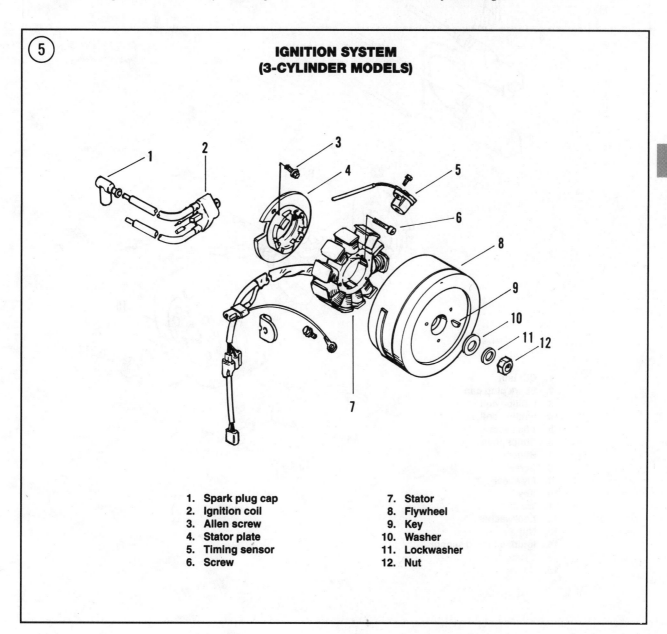

⑤ **IGNITION SYSTEM
(3-CYLINDER MODELS)**

1. Spark plug cap
2. Ignition coil
3. Allen screw
4. Stator plate
5. Timing sensor
6. Screw
7. Stator
8. Flywheel
9. Key
10. Washer
11. Lockwasher
12. Nut

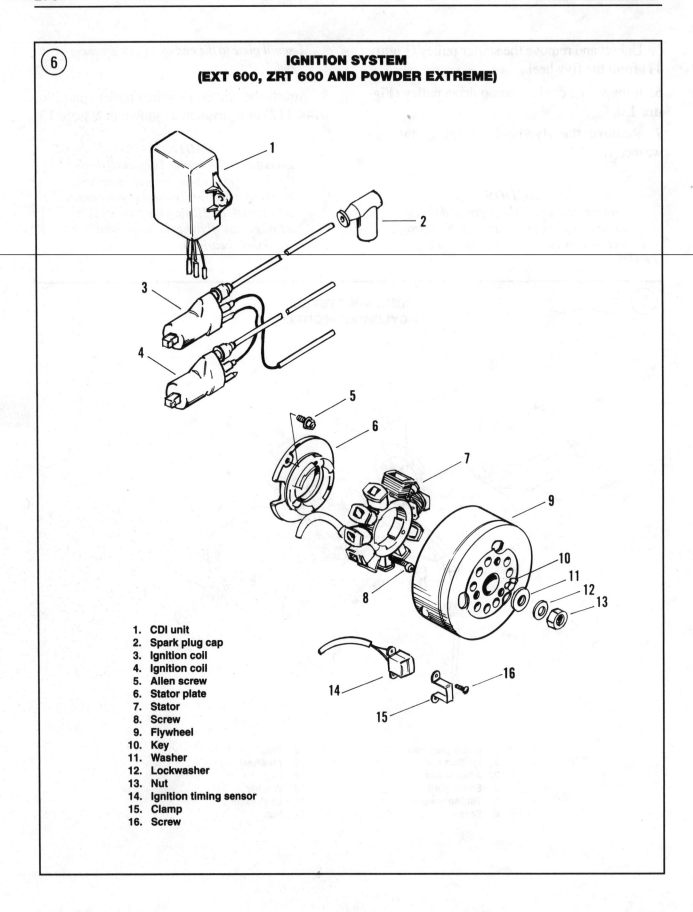

⑥

**IGNITION SYSTEM
(EXT 600, ZRT 600 AND POWDER EXTREME)**

1. CDI unit
2. Spark plug cap
3. Ignition coil
4. Ignition coil
5. Allen screw
6. Stator plate
7. Stator
8. Screw
9. Flywheel
10. Key
11. Washer
12. Lockwasher
13. Nut
14. Ignition timing sensor
15. Clamp
16. Screw

9. Tighten the puller screw and break the flywheel free of the crankshaft taper. It may be necessary to tap the center screw of the puller sharply with a hammer to jar the flywheel loose. Do not hit the flywheel.

10. Remove the flywheel and the puller assembly, then remove the puller from the flywheel.

11. Remove the Woodruff key (**Figure 14**) from the crankshaft.

12. Clean the tapered surfaces of the flywheel and crankshaft. The surfaces must be dry and clean when installing the flywheel.

13. Check the flywheel magnets (**Figure 15**) for metal that may have been attracted while the

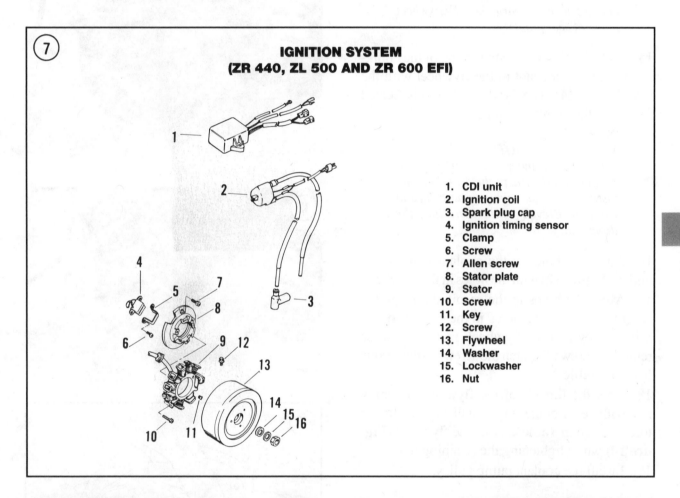

⑦

IGNITION SYSTEM
(ZR 440, ZL 500 AND ZR 600 EFI)

1. CDI unit
2. Ignition coil
3. Spark plug cap
4. Ignition timing sensor
5. Clamp
6. Screw
7. Allen screw
8. Stator plate
9. Stator
10. Screw
11. Key
12. Screw
13. Flywheel
14. Washer
15. Lockwasher
16. Nut

9

assembly is removed. Clean the flywheel, as necessary.

14. Place the Woodruff key (**Figure 14**) into the slot in the crankshaft.

> *CAUTION*
> *Be sure the key is seated properly before installing the flywheel. If the flywheel catches on the Woodruff key, the flywheel may not seat properly.*

15. Slide the flywheel onto the end of the crankshaft, aligning the slot in the flywheel with the key (**Figure 14**). The flywheel should be seated firmly on the crankshaft taper.

> *NOTE*
> *If the coolant pump was removed with the pulley attached, fit the drive belt and install the coolant pump as described in Chapter Eleven while installing the drive pulley.*

16. Align the holes in the coolant pump drive pulley (**Figure 12**) with the holes in the flywheel.

17. Align the holes in the recoil starter pulley (**Figure 11**) with the holes in the coolant pump drive pulley and the flywheel. Install the three retaining screws. Tighten the screws to the torque listed in **Table 2**.

18. Coat the threads of the flywheel retaining nut with red Loctite and install the nut to the torque listed in **Table 2**. Hold the flywheel (**Figure 10**) while tightening the retaining nut.

19. Install the coolant pump pulley.

20. Install the flywheel cover (**Figure 9**). Tighten the retaining screws securely.

21. Install the recoil starter (**Figure 8**). Tighten the retaining screws securely.

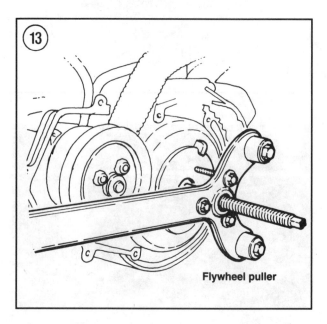

Flywheel puller

Air-cooled Z440 models

Refer to **Figure 1** when performing this procedure.

1. Unbolt and remove the recoil starter assembly (**Figure 16**). It is not necessary to remove the handle if the starter assembly can be located out of the way inside the engine compartment.

NOTE
You can remove the flywheel with the engine installed. The accompanying photographs show the engine removed for clarity.

2. Remove the fan drive belt (**Figure 17**) as described in Chapter Three.

3. Hold the starter pulley and loosen the flywheel retaining nut (**Figure 10**, typical). Threads of the nut may be fixed with Loctite.

4. Unbolt and remove the starter pulley (**Figure 11**, typical) from the flywheel.

5. Remove the fan drive pulley.

6. Remove the flywheel retaining nut and washer(s).

CAUTION
Protect the crankshaft from damage while using the puller in Step 7. A protective cap can be made by welding a small plate to the end of a stock flywheel nut.

7. Attach the flywheel puller (part No. 0144-310) available from Arctco, or equivalent, as shown in **Figure 18**.

CAUTION
Do not heat the flywheel or pound on the flywheel while attempting to remove it.

9

Heat can cause the flywheel to seize onto the crankshaft. Hitting the flywheel can damage the flywheel, crankshaft or crankshaft bearings.

8. Tighten the puller screw until the flywheel breaks free of the crankshaft taper. It may be necessary to tap the center screw of the puller sharply with a hammer to jar the flywheel loose. Do not hit the flywheel.

9. Remove the flywheel and the puller assembly, then remove the puller from the flywheel.

10. Remove the Woodruff key (**Figure 14**, typical) from the crankshaft.

11. Clean the tapered surfaces of the flywheel and crankshaft. The surfaces must be dry and clean when installing the flywheel.

12. Check the flywheel magnets for metal that may have been attracted while the assembly was removed. Clean the flywheel as necessary.

13. Place the Woodruff key (**Figure 14**, typical) into the slot in the crankshaft.

CAUTION
Be sure the key is seated properly before installing the flywheel. If the flywheel catches on the Woodruff key, the flywheel may not seat properly.

14. Slide the flywheel onto the end of the crankshaft, aligning the slot in the flywheel with the key (**Figure 14**, typical). The flywheel should be seated firmly on the crankshaft taper.

15. Align the holes in the fan drive pulley with the holes in the flywheel.

16. Align the holes in the recoil starter pulley (**Figure 19**) with the holes in the fan drive pulley and the flywheel, then install the three retaining screws. Tighten the screws to the torque listed in Table 2.

17. Coat the threads of the flywheel retaining nut with red Loctite. Install the nut to the torque listed in **Table 2**. Hold the flywheel (**Figure 10**, typical) while tightening the retaining nut.

18. Install the fan drive belt as described in Chapter Two. Adjust the tension of the belt as described.

19. Install fan covers and recoil starter.

All other liquid-cooled models

Refer to **Figures 3-7** when performing this procedure.

1. Unbolt and remove the recoil starter assembly. It is not necessary to remove the handle if the starter assembly can be located out of the way inside the engine compartment.

NOTE
The flywheel can be removed with the engine installed. The accompanying photographs show the engine removed for clarity.

2. Hold the starter pulley and loosen the flywheel retaining nut (**Figure 10**, typical). Threads of the nut may be fixed with Loctite.

3. Unbolt and remove the starter pulley (**Figure 19**) from the flywheel.

CAUTION
Protect the crankshaft from damage while using the puller in Step 4. A protective cap can be made by welding a small plate to the end of a stock flywheel nut.

4. Attach the flywheel puller (part No. 0144-310) available from Arctco, or equivalent (**Figure 18**, typical).

CAUTION
*On models so equipped, be careful not to damage the sensors (**Figure 20** or **Figure 21**) located outside the flywheel when removing the flywheel. The safer procedure is to remove the sensors before removing the flywheel.*

CAUTION
Do not heat the flywheel or pound on the flywheel while attempting to remove it. Heat can cause the flywheel to seize onto the crankshaft. Hitting the flywheel can damage the flywheel, crankshaft or crankshaft bearings.

5. Tighten the puller screw until the flywheel breaks free of the crankshaft taper. It may be necessary to tap the center screw of the puller sharply with a hammer to jar the flywheel loose. Do not hit the flywheel.

6. Remove the flywheel and the puller assembly, then remove the puller from the flywheel.

7. Remove the Woodruff key (**Figure 14**, typical) from the crankshaft.

8. Clean the tapered surfaces of the flywheel and crankshaft. The surfaces must be dry and clean when installing the flywheel.

CAUTION
*Check the condition of the keyway in the flywheel (**Figure 22**) and in the crankshaft (**Figure 14**). Some cleanup is possible, but extreme damage cannot be repaired and should be serviced by installing new parts.*

9

9. Check the flywheel magnets for metal that may have been attracted while the assembly was removed. Clean the flywheel, as necessary.

10. Place the Woodruff key (**Figure 14**, typical) into the slot in the crankshaft.

> *CAUTION*
> *Be sure the key is seated properly before installing the flywheel. If the flywheel catches on the Woodruff key, the flywheel may not seat properly.*

11. Slide the flywheel onto the end of the crankshaft, aligning the slot in the flywheel with the key (**Figure 14**, typical). The flywheel should be seated firmly on the crankshaft taper.

12. Align the holes in the recoil starter pulley (**Figure 19**) with the holes in the flywheel, then install the three retaining screws. Tighten the screws to the torque listed in **Table 2**.

13. Coat the threads of the flywheel retaining nut with red Loctite. Install the nut to the torque listed in **Table 2**. Hold the flywheel (**Figure 10**, typical) while tightening the retaining nut.

14. Install the covers and recoil starter.

Inspection

1. Check the flywheel carefully for cracks or breaks.

> *WARNING*
> *Replace a cracked or chipped flywheel. A damaged flywheel may fly apart at high rpm, causing severe engine damage. Do not attempt to repair a damaged flywheel.*

2. Check the tapered bore of the flywheel and the crankshaft taper for signs of wear.

3. Check the key slot in the flywheel (**Figure 22**) for cracks or other damage. Check the key slot in the crankshaft (**Figure 14**) for cracks or other damage.

4. Check the Woodruff key for cracks or damage.

5. Check the crankshaft and flywheel nut threads for wear or damage.

6. Replace the flywheel, flywheel nut, crankshaft half and Woodruff key, as required.

7. Check the balancer attached to the flywheel of some models.

    a. Install a new balancer if cracked or bent.

    b. Install a new balancer if it makes a metallic ring when shaken.

Stator Plate
Removal/Installation

Refer to Chapter Two for troubleshooting and test procedures. Depending on the model, refer to **Figures 1-7** for this procedure.

1. Remove the flywheel as described in this chapter.

2. If the engine is installed, disconnect the wires from the stator at the electrical connectors.

3. Make a mark on the stator plate and crankcase for alignment during reassembly (**Figure 23**, typical).

4. Remove the screws (B, **Figure 24** or **Figure 25**) that attach the stator plate to the crankcase. Remove the grommet and pull the wires through the opening while removing the stator plate.

5. Installation is the reverse of the preceding steps. Observe the following:

   a. Check the coil wires for chafing or other damage. Replace the coil harness, if necessary.

   b. Check and adjust ignition timing as described in Chapter Three.

   c. Make sure all electrical connections are tight and free from corrosion. Loose or

corroded connections often cause the failure of electronic ignition systems.

Ignition Generating Coil Replacement

The ignition generating coil (10, **Figure 1**, 8, **Figure 2** or 7, **Figure 3**) on some models can be removed and replaced individually. On other models, the ignition generating coil is incorporated in the stator assembly and the complete stator must be replaced as an assembly. Refer to Chapter Two for testing before removing the ignition coil.

1. Remove the stator plate as described in this chapter.

NOTE
*The coil retaining screws may be secured by Loctite. It may be necessary to heat the back of the stator plate near the coil attaching screws to loosen the Loctite. Do not exceed 200° F (93°C) when heating the screws and protect the wire harness at the stator plate (**Figure 16**).*

2. Remove the screws holding the generating coil(s) to the stator plate (**Figure 26**, typical).

3. If necessary, cut or unsolder the wires at the coil as close to the coil as possible.

4. Reverse the removal procedure to install the new coil. Observe the following:

   a. Resolder the wires to the new coil terminals with rosin core solder.

   b. Remove the shipping nuts from the new coil screws.

   c. Position the new generating coil onto the stator plate.

   d. Apply Loctite 242 (blue) to the new screws and install them.

Lighting Coil Replacement

The lighting coil (9, **Figure 1**, 7, **Figure 2** or 6, **Figure 3**) of some models can be removed and replaced individually. On other models, the igni-

tion generating coil is incorporated in the stator assembly and the complete stator must be replaced as an assembly. Refer to Chapter Two for testing before removing the ignition coil.

1. Remove the stator plate as described in this chapter.

NOTE
The coil retaining screws may be secured by Loctite. It may be necessary to heat the back of the stator plate near the coil attaching screws to loosen the Loctite. Do not exceed 200° F (93° C) when heating the screws and protect the wire harness at the stator plate.

2. Heat the back of the stator plate to loosen the Loctite used to secure the coil screws.

3. Remove the screws holding the lighting coil to the stator plate.

4. Observe the following to disconnect the coil wires from the main wire harness.

   a. Pull the harness tubes toward the lighting coil to uncover the soldered joint.

   b. Unsolder both coil wires.

   c. Using rosin core solder, solder the wire from the lighting coil to the appropriate wire in the harness.

5. Reverse the removal procedure to install the new coil. Observe the following:

   a. Position the new lighting coil onto the stator plate.

   b. Coat the new screws with Loctite 242 (blue) and install the screws.

IGNITION COIL

Refer to **Figures 27** and **28** when performing procedures in this section.

Removal/Installation

1. Open the hood.

2. Detach the spark plug caps from the spark plugs.

3. Detach the primary wires to the coil at the connectors near the coil.

4. Remove the nuts securing the ignition coil and remove the ignition coil.

5. Installation is the reverse of the preceding steps.

   a. Clean the primary lead connectors of the wiring harness and the coil.

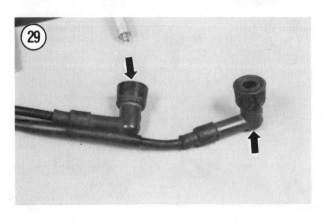

b. Coat the primary lead connectors with dielectric grease.

c. Attach the wiring harness primary leads to the coil primary leads.

d. Connect the spark plug caps to the spark plugs.

e. Make sure the connectors are tight and the insulators are in place and in good condition.

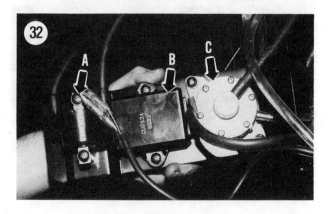

Spark Plug Caps

You can replace the spark plug caps (**Figure 29**) by pulling the old caps off the coil's high-tension wire. Reverse to install. Make sure the cap is pushed all the way onto the high-tension wire.

Testing

Refer to Chapter Two for testing and troubleshooting the ignition coils.

CDI UNIT

Removal/Installation

NOTE
*On models with electronic fuel injection (EFI), components for the capacitor discharge ignition (CDI) are incorporated in the electronic control unit (ECU) box (**Figure 30** or **Figure 31**). Refer to Chapter Seven for removal of the ECU.*

1. Open the hood and locate the CDI box in the engine compartment (B, **Figure 32** or **Figure 33**, typical).

2. Separate the connector plugs to the CDI at or near the CDI unit.

3. Remove the CDI unit. On some models, it may be necessary to unbolt the mounting bracket (**Figure 32**) before removing the CDI unit.

9

4. Install by reversing the preceding removal steps. Before attaching the electrical connectors to the unit, make sure the connectors are clean. Use electrical contact cleaner to clean the connectors.

VOLTAGE REGULATOR

The voltage regulator is attached to the vehicle frame. Refer to **Figure 34** for typical installation.

1. Disconnect voltage regulator wires.
2. Remove the nut and screw from the center of the voltage regulator.
3. Installation is the reverse of the preceding steps. Before connecting the electrical wire connectors at the unit, make sure the connectors are clean. Use electrical contact cleaner to clean the connectors.

Testing

Refer to Chapter Two for testing and troubleshooting the charging system, including the voltage regulator.

LIGHTING SYSTEM

The lighting system consists of the headlight, taillight/brakelight combination, instrument warning illumination lights and pilot lamps. In the event of trouble with any light, the first thing to check is the affected bulb itself. If the bulb is good, check all wiring and connections with a test light or ohmmeter.

Headlight Replacement
(Single-bulb Type)

> *WARNING*
> *If the headlight has just burned out or turned off, it will be **hot**. Do not touch the bulb until it cools off.*

1. Open the hood.

2. Push the retaining ring (**Figure 35**) toward the bulb. Twist the ring to release it from the housing. Slide the retaining ring down the wiring harness.

3. Pull the wiring harness and bulb from the housing.

> *CAUTION*
> *Quartz-halogen bulbs are used on most models. Do not touch the bulb glass with your fingers. Traces of oil from your hands on the bulb will reduce the life of the bulb. Clean any traces of oil from the bulb with a cloth moistened in alcohol or lacquer thinner.*

4. Pull the bulb from the connector.

5. Installation is the reverse of the preceding steps. Make sure the bulb engages the connector fully.

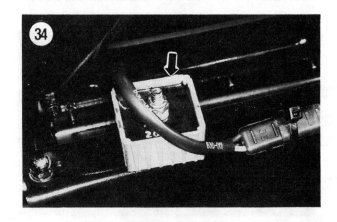

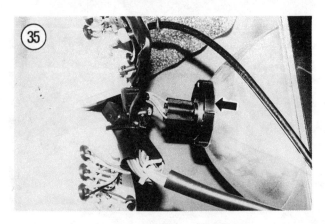

Headlight Replacement (Multiple-bulb Type)

> *WARNING*
> *If the headlight has just burned out or turned off it will be **hot**. Do not touch the bulb until it cools off.*

1. Open the hood.
2. Disconnect the wire from the headlight bulb base.
3. Rotate the headlight bulb base counterclockwise and remove the bulb.
4. Installation is the reverse of the preceding steps. Make sure the bulb engages the connector fully.

Headlight Adjustment

1. Park the snowmobile on a level surface 25 ft. (8 m) from a vertical wall (**Figure 36**).

> *NOTE*
> *A rider should be seated on the snowmobile when performing the following.*

2. Measure the distance from the floor to the center of the headlight lens (**Figure 36**). Make a mark on the wall the same distance from the floor. For instance, if the center of the headlight lens is two feet above the floor, mark "A" in

Figure 36 should also be two feet above the floor.

3. Start the engine, turn on the headlight and set the beam selector to HIGH. Do not adjust the headlight beam with the selector set on LOW.
4. The center area of the beam on the wall should be 2 in. (5 cm) below the A mark (**Figure 36**).
5. To move the beam, turn the headlight housing adjusting screws (**Figure 37**).

Taillight Bulb Replacement

1. Remove the taillight lens mounting screws (**Figure 38**) and remove the lens.
2. Turn the bulb counterclockwise and remove it.
3. Clean the lens in a mild detergent and check for cracks.
4. Installation is the reverse of the preceding steps.

INSTRUMENT ASSEMBLY

The instrument assembly may consist of a speedometer, tachometer, fuel level gauge and temperature gauge. The instruments are installed in the hood (**Figure 39**).

9

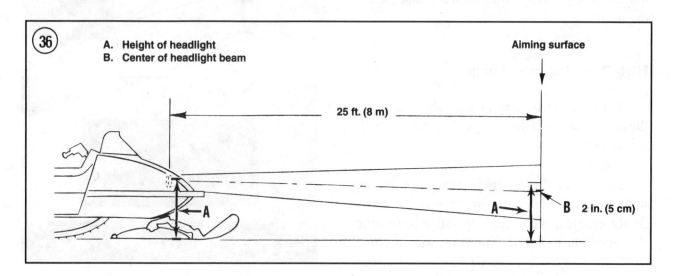

(36)
A. Height of headlight
B. Center of headlight beam

Aiming surface

25 ft. (8 m)

A

A → B 2 in. (5 cm)

Bulb Replacement

1. Open the hood.
2. Locate the bulb socket at the affected meter assembly and pull the bulb socket out of the meter assembly.
3. Replace the bulb.

Instrument Removal/Installation

1. Open the hood.
2. Disconnect the electrical connectors at the instrument.
3. Pull the bulb socket out of the instrument assembly.
4. Disconnect the speedometer cable (A, **Figure 40**) at the instrument.
5. Remove the nuts (B, **Figure 40**) securing the mounting bracket and remove the instrument.
6. Installation is the reverse of the preceding steps.

WARNING LAMPS

Several different indicator lights may be located on the dash or console. Service is similar for most of the lamps and usually limited to installing a new bulb. Some of the warning lamps may be connected to a wire from a sensor (sending unit).

High Beam Indicator Lamp

The high beam indicator lamp lights whenever the headlight is on HIGH beam. Replace the bulb if it does not light.

1. Open the hood.
2. Disconnect the electrical connector at the high beam indicator lamp and remove the lamp.
3. Reverse to install. Check operation by turning the headlight to HIGH. The lamp should come on.

Oil Level Warning Lamp

The oil tank is equipped with an oil level sensor that is wired to the injection oil level warning lamp on the instrument panel. When the oil level in the tank reaches a specified low point, the warning lamp will light.

The oil injection level warning lamp lights whenever the brake lever is operated. If the lamp does not light during brake operation, replace the lamp as follows:

1. Open the hood.
2. Disconnect the electrical connector at the oil level pilot lamp and remove the pilot lamp.

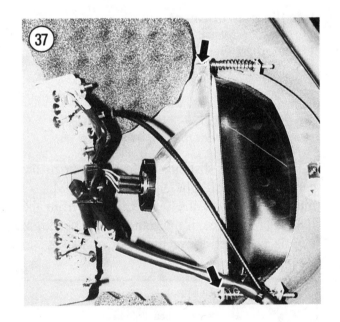

EXTRA TRAVEL TUNNEL

3. Reverse to install. Check the pilot lamp operation by applying the brake lever with the engine running. The lamp should come on.

SWITCHES

You can test switches for continuity with an ohmmeter (see Chapter One) or a test light at the switch connector plug by operating the switch in

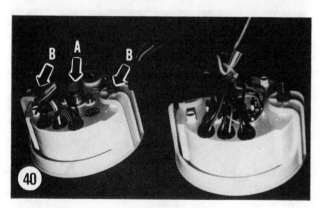

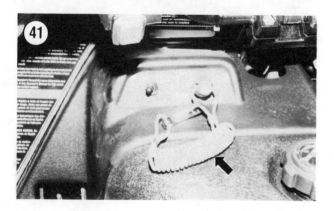

each of its operating positions and comparing results with the switch operation.

When testing switches, observe the following:

a. When separating any connector, pull on the connector housings and not the wires.

b. After locating a defective circuit, check the connectors to make sure they are clean, tight and properly joined. Check all wires going into a connector housing to make sure each wire is properly positioned and the wire is not broken and the terminal end is not loose.

c. When joining connectors, push them together until they click into place.

d. When replacing the handlebar switch assemblies, make sure the cables are routed correctly so they will not crimp when the handlebar is turned from side to side.

Safety Stop Switches

The tether switch, the emergency stop switch, the emergency kill switch and the main ignition switch can be used to stop the engine. Depending upon the ignition type, the switch may stop the ignition by either grounding the ignition circuit or opening the ignition circuit. If the ignition switch is normally open to run, grounding the circuit will stop ignition. If the ignition switch is normally closed to run, opening the circuit will stop the ignition.

Tether Switch Removal/Installation

The tether switch (**Figure 41**) should stop the engine when it is removed from the dash. To remove the tether switch, disconnect the electrical connector, then unscrew and remove the switch. Reverse procedure to reinstall.

9

Emergency Kill (Stop) Switch

The emergency stop switch (**Figure 42**) is located in the throttle housing. To replace the switch, disassemble the throttle housing. Disconnect the switch connectors and remove the switch. Reverse to install.

Headlight Dimmer Switch

The headlight dimmer switch is mounted in the brake lever housing. To replace the switch, unbolt the switch from the brake housing. Disconnect the switch connectors and remove the switch. Reverse to install.

Brake Light Switch

The brake light switch is located in the brake lever housing. To replace the switch, disassemble the brake housing. Disconnect the switch connectors and remove the switch. Reverse the removal procedure to install.

Ignition Switch

The ignition switch is mounted on the console. Depending upon the ignition type, the switch may stop the ignition by either grounding the ignition circuit or opening the ignition circuit. If the ignition switch is normally open to run, grounding the circuit will stop ignition. If the ignition switch is normally closed to run, opening the circuit will stop the ignition. Make sure the replacement switch is the correct type.

Temperature Sensor

The temperature sensor (**Figure 43**, typical) is located in the coolant outlet (thermostat) housing. Some models are equipped with an overheat warning light, while others are equipped with a gauge. Refer to Chapter Seven to test the unit on models with EFI. For models with an overheat warning light, the sensor should have no continuity until the sensor is heated above 190° F (88° C) and should indicate less than 20 ohms until the temperature exceeds 230° F (110° C). To replace the temperature sensor, proceed as follows:

> **WARNING**
> *Do not attempt to remove the temperature sensor while the engine and coolant is hot; serious burns may result. Make sure that engine and coolant have cooled before attempting to remove the sensor.*

1. Detach wires from the sensor.

2. Drain the coolant or be prepared to catch fluid that will leak when the sensor is removed.

3. Unscrew the sensor from the housing.

4. Apply Teflon tape or sealer on the threads of the sensor before installation. Reverse the procedure to install.

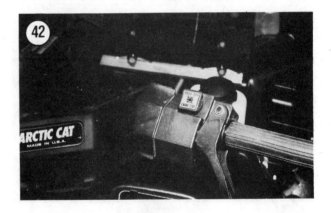

FUEL LEVEL SENSOR

Some models are equipped with an electric fuel level gauge located in the instrument console. A sensor and float assembly, mounted in the fuel tank, sends an electrical signal to the fuel gauge.

To replace the fuel level sensor, observe the following:

1. Remove and drain the fuel tank as described in Chapter Six or Chapter Seven.
2. Remove the screws and washers securing the sensor to the fuel tank.
3. Remove the sensor and gasket. Discard the gasket.
4. Reverse the removal procedure to install the fuel level sensor. Use a new gasket. Tighten the retaining screws securely and evenly.

OIL LEVEL GAUGE

All models are equipped with a warning light on the instrument console to indicate when oil in the engine lubrication reservoir reaches a dangerously low level. The sender is located in the oil tank (**Figure 44**).

To replace the low oil level sender, proceed as follows:

1. Open the hood.
2. Disconnect wires from the electrical connector.
3. Pull the sender (**Figure 44**) from the tank.

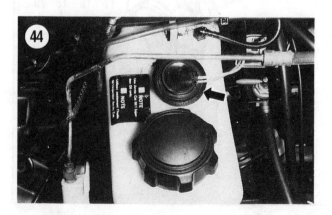

4. The sender is installed by pushing it into place. Replace the sealing grommet if it is damaged or hard.

ELECTRIC STARTING MOTOR

The starter circuit includes the battery, starter relay and the starter motor. The starter switch is incorporated in the ignition key switch and the starter relay is attached to a bracket near the battery holder. The electric starter is attached to the front of the engine and engages a ring gear attached to the drive pulley.

Removal and Installation

1. Open the hood and remove the cover from the battery.
2. Detach the ground cable from the negative terminal of the battery. Insulate the cable end so that it can not accidentally ground the battery.

> *WARNING*
> *Electrical sparks or unplanned operation of an electrical device can cause injury. One method to make sure that the ground cable can not accidentally make contact is to insulate the cable end with tape, hose or similar insulating cover. Another method is to remove the battery.*

3. Remove the drive belt guard, belt and drive pulley as described in Chapter Thirteen.
4. Remove the nut and lockwasher attaching the positive cable from the battery, then lift the cable from the starter terminal.
5. Remove the screw, washer and lockwasher attaching the rear (right) end of the starter to the support bracket. Make sure you remove the rubber bumper.
6. Remove the two locknuts attaching the nose of the starter to the bracket, then lift the starter motor from the engine compartment.
7. Reinstall by reversing the removal procedure while noting the following:

9

a. Position the starter in the bracket. Install the rubber bumper between the starter motor and the crankcase.

b. Tighten the locknuts to 17-21 N•m (12-15 ft.-lb.) torque.

c. Attach the positive cable to the starter before attaching the ground cable to the battery.

d. Install a tie wrap around the starter to hold the positive cable against the starter motor.

Disassembly

Refer to **Figure 45** for this procedure.

1. Hold the starter pinion (17, **Figure 45**) with a suitable wrench and remove nut (20, **Figure 45**).

NOTE
Check the end of the armature shaft for burrs that could damage the bore in the pinion gear. Smooth the burrs with a file,

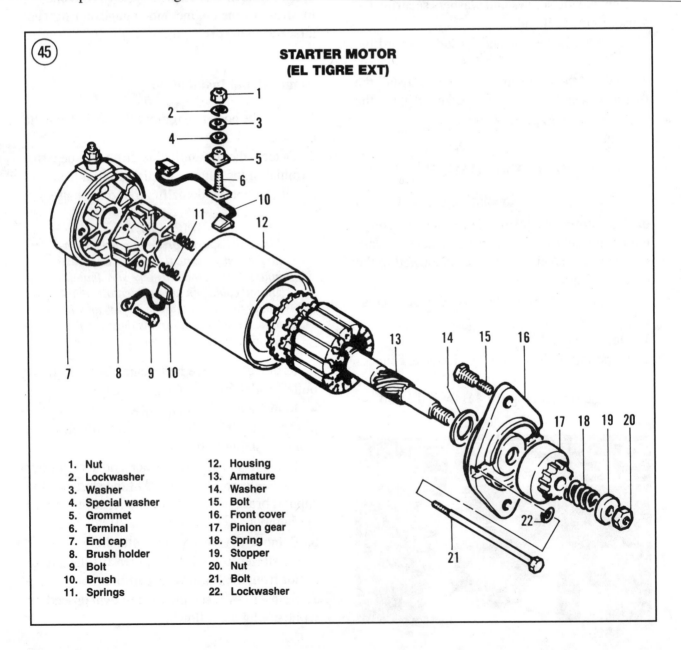

**STARTER MOTOR
(EL TIGRE EXT)**

1.	Nut	12.	Housing
2.	Lockwasher	13.	Armature
3.	Washer	14.	Washer
4.	Special washer	15.	Bolt
5.	Grommet	16.	Front cover
6.	Terminal	17.	Pinion gear
7.	End cap	18.	Spring
8.	Brush holder	19.	Stopper
9.	Bolt	20.	Nut
10.	Brush	21.	Bolt
11.	Springs	22.	Lockwasher

if necessary, before removing the bendix assembly in Step 2.

2. Remove the stopper (19, **Figure 45**), spring (18, **Figure 45**) and pinion gear (17, **Figure 45**) from the end of the starter motor.

3. Mark the end cap (7, **Figure 45**), housing (12, **Figure 45**) and front cover (16, **Figure 45**) so they can be easily aligned when assembling.

4. Support the starter on the end cap (7, **Figure 45**) in an upright position and loosen the two through bolts (21, **Figure 45**).

5. Support the starter and remove the 2 through bolts.

CAUTION
Be careful not to lose thrust washers, springs or other small parts when disassembling. Some parts may be propelled by spring pressure when parts are separated.

6. Remove the end cap (7, **Figure 45**), brush holder (8, **Figure 45**) and brushes (10, **Figure 45**). Be careful not to lose the brush springs (11, **Figure 45**).

CAUTION
One or more washers (14, Figure 45) may be located on the nose of the armature shaft. The washer(s) may stick to the front cover or may stay on the armature shaft. Account for washer(s) when disassembling.

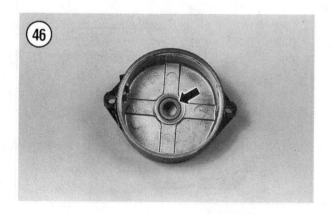
46

7. Tap the front cover (16, **Figure 45**) with a soft-faced hammer if necessary to separate it from the center housing.

Inspection

1. Clean all grease, dirt and carbon from the armature, case and end covers.

CAUTION
Do not immerse the armature in solvent that would damage its insulation. Wipe the windings with a clean, dry cloth, then blow with low pressure compressed air.

2. Check threaded parts and bushings for wear or damage. Replace as necessary.

3. Measure the inside diameter of the bushing in end cap (7, **Figure 45**). Replace the end cap if the bushing is larger than 8.6 mm (0.339 in.) (**Figure 46**).

4. Measure the inside diameter of the bushing in the front cap (16, **Figure 45**) and replace the front cap if the bushing is larger than 13.2 mm (0.520 in.).

5. Measure the length of the brushes (10, **Figure 45**). Replace all of the brushes if any of them are shorter than 7.6 mm (0.30 in.) (**Figure 47**).

6. Check the brushes for chips, cracks or frayed wires. Replace as necessary.

7. Inspect the commutator end of the armature (13, **Figure 45**). If the commutator is rough, burned or otherwise damaged, replace the armature. Do not attempt to repair the commutator.

8. Inspect the grooves in the commutator for built-up dirt. You can clean the commutator grooves using a hacksaw blade ground to the original width of the groove. Do not attempt to cut the groove deeper than the original depth.

9. Use an ohmmeter to check for continuity between the commutator bars and the armature shaft. Any evidence of continuity indicates a short to ground and that the armature should be replaced.

9

10. Clean the pinion gear in solvent and dry throroughly.

11. Check the pinion gear for cracks, chips, deep scoring, excessive wear or heat discoloration.

12. Check the armature shaft spiral gear for cracks, chips, excessive wear or heat discoloration.

13. Slide the pinion gear onto the armature shaft and work the gear back and forth by hand. The gear should move smoothly with no sign of roughness or binding.

14. Check the pinion spring for wear, damage or fatigue.

15. Replace worn or damaged parts as required.

Assembly

1. Clamp the armature in a soft-jawed vise with the drive end up.

2. Apply a small amount of grease in the bushing located in the front cover (16, **Figure 45**).

3. Place the shim washer (14, **Figure 45**) or washers that were removed over the armature shaft.

4. Install the front cover (16, **Figure 45**) over the armature shaft.

5. Apply a light coat of lubriplate to the armature shaft. Install the pinion gear (17, **Figure 45**).

6. Install the spring and stopper (18 and 19, **Figure 45**).

7. Install the nut (20, **Figure 45**) and tighten to 19-22 N•m (14-16 ft.-lb.) torque.

8. Remove the armature from the vise. Install the housing (12, **Figure 45**) over the armature.

9. Assemble the brushes in the brush holder (8, **Figure 45**) as follows.

  a. Install the positive terminal (6, **Figure 45**) through the end cover. Turn the terminal so the longer brush lead is to the right when viewing into the end cap with the stud at the top. Make sure the insulator is installed onto the terminal.

  b. Install washers onto the positive terminal in the following order: Special washer, flat washer and lockwasher.

  c. Apply a small amount of Loctite 271 (red) to the threads of the terminal, then install the nut. Tighten the nut to 7 N•m (5 ft.-lb.) torque.

  d. Insert the brush holder in the end cap.

  e. Install the ground brush to the left, as viewed into the end cap with the stud on the top, and secure the lead with the screw.

  f. Install the ground brush to the right, as viewed into the end cap with the stud on the top, and secure the lead with the screw. The longer positive brush lead should be behind, or under, the ground wire.

10. Apply a small amount of grease in the bushing located in the end cap (7, **Figure 45**).

11. Insert the four brush springs into the brush holder, then position the four brushes against the springs with the flat side against the spring.

12. Position the end cap and brushes on a bench with the brush holder side up.

13. Press the brushes into the pockets in the holder with special tool (part No. 0644-052) or equivalent, then hold the brushes in position.

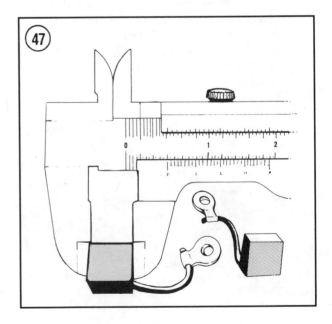

(47)

CAUTION
Do not remove the special tool too soon or the brushes will come out, which could damage the brushes or other parts.

14. Lower the housing and armature assembly into the end cap. When the end cap and housing are nearly together, remove the special tool used to hold the brushes in place.

NOTE
The housing should fit tightly between the front cover and the end cap. If the starter does not fit tightly together, remove the end cap and repeat Steps 12-14.

15. Align the marks on the end cap, housing and front cover that were made before disassembling. Install the two through bolts. Tighten the bolts to 10-14 N·m (7-10 ft.-lb.) torque.

16. Bench test the starter and make sure that starter operates properly before installing.

Starter Relay

The starter relay is mounted next to the battery.

1. Open the hood and locate the relay.

2. Disconnect the ground cable from the negative terminal of the battery.

3. Label all wires to the starter relay to assist in assembly.

4. Disconnect the wires from the starter relay.

5. Unbolt and remove the relay.

6. Install a new relay, using the same attaching point.

7. Clean all the electrical connectors with contact cleaner.

8. Attach all the electrical connectors and tighten the nuts securely.

9. Connect the ground cable to the negative terminal of the battery.

10. Check operation of the starter and relay.

WIRING DIAGRAMS

Wiring diagrams are located at the end of this book.

9

Table 1 BATTERY STATE OF CHARGE

Specific gravity	State of charge
1.110-1.130	Discharged
1.140-1.160	Almost discharged
1.170-1.190	One-quarter charged
1.200-1.220	One-half charged
1.230-1.250	Three-quarters charged
1.260-1.280	Fully charged

Table 2 TIGHTENING TORQUES

	N·m	ft.-lb.
Fan pulley, lower		
Air-cooled 431 cc engine		
(Z 440 1995-1997)	8-12	6-9
Fan pulley, upper		
Air-cooled 431 cc engine		
(Z 440 1995-1997)	25-40	18-30
Flywheel housing		
650cc Engine (1990-1991 El Tigre)	18-22	13-16
Flywheel nut		
650cc Engine (1990-1991 El Tigre)	90-110	66-81
Air-cooled 431 cc engine		
(Z 440 1995-1997)	70-90	52-66
435.8 cc engines	90-110	66-81
437.4 cc engine (1996-on ZR 440)	70-90	52-66
550 and 580 cc engines	69-90	51-65
Three-cylinder 594 cc engine	70-90	52-66
Magneto housing		
Three-cylinder 594 cc engine	18-22	13-16

Chapter Ten

Oil Injection System

The most desirable fuel/oil ratio for snowmobile engines depends upon engine speed and load. Without oil injection, oil must be hand-mixed with gasoline. Since the mixture of gasoline and oil does not change, oil must be mixed at the highest ratio necessary to ensure sufficient lubrication at all operating speeds and engine load conditions. This ratio contains more oil than required to lubricate the engine properly at idle speeds without load. The result is the spark plug is sometimes oil fouled due to excess.

With oil injection, the amount of oil injected varies to provide the optimum amount to lubricate the engine while it runs at varying speeds and load conditions.

All engines used in Arctic Cat snowmobiles are equipped with an oil injection system. The system consists of an external oil tank (reservoir), oil injection hoses, control cable and a mechanical gear-driven pump with variable control. The oil pump control cable is attached to the control lever of the pump and it is also joined to the throttle control cable so they operate simultaneously.

This chapter covers oil injection system service.

SYSTEM COMPONENTS

The oil injection pump (**Figure 1**, typical) is mounted on the lower crankcase half. The oil pump engages the end of the cross shaft driven by the crankshaft worm gear. An oil reservoir tank is mounted in the engine compartment (**Figure 2**, typical). Oil injection hoses connect the oil tank to the pump and connect the pump to the engine. A warning light on the dash indicates when oil in the reservoir becomes low.

OIL PUMP SERVICE

Oil Pump Bleeding

The oil lines and pump should always be filled with oil. Bleed air from the pump during pre-delivery service and whenever:

a. The oil tank was allowed to empty.
b. Any oil injection hose was disconnected.
c. The machine was on its side.

1. To ensure adequate lubrication when bleeding the pump, use a 50:1 pre-mix in the fuel tank. This gasoline/oil mixture will be used together with the oil supplied by the injection system.

NOTE
Do not continue to use a 50:1 pre-mix after bleeding the oil pump unless the snowmobile is operating in weather conditions where the ambient temperature is -26° C (-15° F) or colder. Under these temperature conditions, the 50:1 pre-mix together with the oil injection system will help to ensure sufficient engine lubrication. Continuing to use the pre-mix under normal conditions can lead to spark plug fouling and rapid buildup of carbon. Refer to Chapter Three for lubrication requirements.

2. Check that the oil tank is full (Chapter Three).
3. Check that all hoses are connected to the oil pump, engine and the oil reservoir tank.
4. *Main oil line*—To bleed the main oil supply line (line between the oil tank and pump):
   a. Remove the bleeder screw and washer (A, **Figure 1**).
   b. Allow oil to bleed from the open port until there are no air bubbles in the supply hose or oil leaking from the open port.
   c. Install and tighten the bleeder screw and sealing washer.

WARNING
***Never** lean into the snowmobile's engine compartment while wearing a scarf or other loose clothing when the engine is running or when the driver is attempting to start the engine. If the scarf or clothing should catch in the drive belt or clutch, severe injury or death could occur. Make sure the belt guard is in place.*

5. *Small oil lines*—To bleed the small oil lines (lines between the oil pump and intake), start the engine and allow it to idle. Hold the pump lever (B, **Figure 1**) in the fully open position. When there are no air bubbles in the hoses (**Figure 3**), release the pump lever and turn the engine off.

NOTE
*The carburetors and engine are removed in **Figure 3** for clarity. The engine shown is typical.*

COMPONENT REPLACEMENT

Oil Tank Removal/Installation

Refer to **Figure 2**, typical for this procedure.
1. Open the hood.
2. Label the hoses at the tank before removal.
3. Detach the wires from the oil level gauge or remove the gauge from the oil tank (**Figure 2**).
4. Remove the bolts attaching the oil tank to the frame.
5. Lift the oil tank up slightly and disconnect the hoses at the tank. Plug the outlet ports to prevent oil leakage.

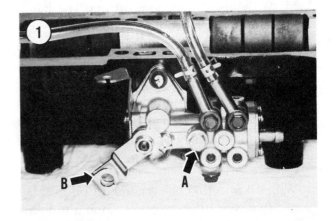

6. Installation is the reverse of the preceding steps.

7. Bleed the oil pump as described in this chapter.

Oil Level Gauge

Refer to Chapter Nine.

Oil Hoses

Install new fresh oil hoses whenever the old hoses become hard and brittle. When replacing damaged or worn oil hoses, make sure you install transparent hoses with the correct identification. Non-transparent hoses will not allow you to visually inspect the hoses for air pockets or other blockage that could cause engine seizure. When attaching hoses, secure each hose end with a clamp.

OIL PUMP

Removal

This procedure describes procedures to remove the oil pump and gear assembly. Refer to **Figure 4** when performing this procedure.

1. If the engine is installed in the frame, observe the following:

  a. Remove the carburetors as described in Chapter Six or the fuel injection unit as described in Chapter Seven.

  b. Disconnect the oil pump cable from the oil pump control lever.

  c. Detach the main oil hose at the oil pump and plug the hose to prevent leakage.

2. Detach the lines from the pump (**Figure 5** and A, **Figure 6**).

3. Remove the two screws (B, **Figure 6**) attaching the pump to the crankcase.

4. Pull the pump away from the crankcase.

NOTE
*You can remove the retainer (A, **Figure 7**) from the crankcase; however, do not remove the driveshaft (B, **Figure 5**) unless you disassembled the crankcase.*

5. If the gasket or O-ring seal is leaking between the retainer and the crankcase, withdraw the retainer (A, **Figure 7**) from the crankcase.

Inspection

1. The oil pump should not be disassembled. Individual parts are not available. If damaged, replace the entire oil pump assembly.

2. Outlet fittings (**Figure 6**) contain check valves which should permit oil to flow out, but not drain back. Check the valves for proper operation.

3. Check the oil hose fittings (**Figure 5** and **Figure 6**) for tightness.

4. Clean the banjo bolts with solvent and dry thoroughly before reassembly.

5. Move the oil pump arm (C, **Figure 6**) and check for tightness or other damage. Replace the oil pump, if necessary.

NOTE
*You can test oil pump operation by attaching a drill to the pump drive. The drill must rotate **counterclockwise** and the pump should always be supplied with oil. Do not rotate the pump dry. Oil should be pumped from the outlet fittings*

10

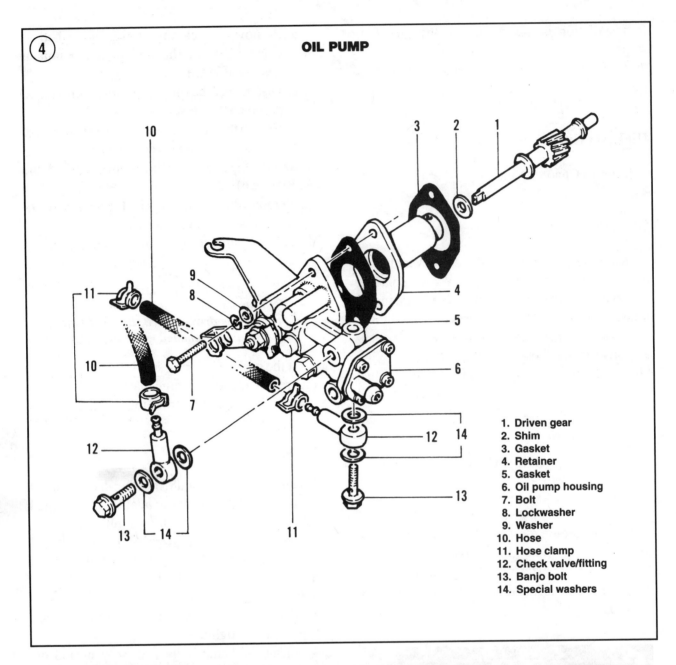

④ OIL PUMP

1. Driven gear
2. Shim
3. Gasket
4. Retainer
5. Gasket
6. Oil pump housing
7. Bolt
8. Lockwasher
9. Washer
10. Hose
11. Hose clamp
12. Check valve/fitting
13. Banjo bolt
14. Special washers

when the control lever is held in the maximum delivery position against spring pressure.

Assembly/Installation

1. If removed, install the retainer (A, **Figure 7**) using a new gasket or O-ring seal.

2. Install a new gasket or O-ring seal between the retainer and the oil pump.

3. Align the slot in the oil pump with the tang on the driveshaft. Install the pump and secure it with its mounting screws (B, **Figure 6**).

4. Attach the main supply hose and oil injection outlet lines to the pump. Install clamps on the hoses and place a washer on each side of the banjo bolts.

5. If the engine is installed in the frame, observe the following:

    a. Connect the main oil hose to the oil pump.

    b. Connect the oil pump cable to the oil pump.

    c. Bleed the oil pump as described in this chapter.

    d. Install the carburetors as described in Chapter Six or the fuel injection unit as described in Chapter Seven.

    e. If so equipped, synchronize the carburetors as described in Chapter Three.

    f. Adjust the oil pump as described in Chapter Three.

10

Chapter Eleven

Cooling Systems

FAN-COOLED MODELS

On Z 440 models, the engine is cooled by air passing over the engine's fins on the cylinders and cylinder heads. The air is circulated by a fan.

Fan Belt Removal/Installation

Refer to **Figure 1** during this procedure.
1. Remove the fan intake cover.
2. Remove the recoil starter assembly (A, **Figure 2**).
3. Remove the nut (B, **Figure 2**) and washers. Some of the flat washers may be adjusting shims.
4. Withdraw the outer pulley half. Do not lose shims which may be located between the pulley halves.
5. Lift the belt from the lower pulley (**Figure 3**).
6. Inspect the belt carefully. Install a new belt if its condition is questionable.
7. When installing, install the belt in the groove of the lower pulley and position the belt against the upper pulley inner half.

NOTE
If a new belt is installed, position all the shims between the pulley halves. If the old belt is installed, position the shims in the same place they were originally installed.

8. Install the outer pulley half.
9. Install any shims not needed between the pulley halves outside the pulley. These shims may be required for later adjustment.
10. Install the flat washer, lockwasher and pulley retaining nut. Tighten the nut to 25-40 N•m (18-30 ft.-lb.) torque.

NOTE
Turn the pulleys while tightening the retaining nut to prevent pinching the belt between the pulley halves.

11. Check the belt tension by pressing the belt (20, **Figure 1**) with your finger at about midpoint between the pulleys. The observed amount of deflection should be no more than 6 mm (1/4 in.).

12. Refer to *Checking/Adjusting Fan Belt Tension* in Chapter Three if the measured belt deflection is incorrect.

13. When the belt tension is correct, install the recoil starter and fan intake cover.

Cooling Fan Assembly

The procedure for removing and servicing the cooling fan, upper shaft and fan housing will depend upon the amount of other service required. Refer to **Figure 1**.

1. Remove the fan drive belt as described in this chapter.

2. Detach the wires from the CDI unit and ignition coil.

3. Remove the cylinder cowling or unbolt the fan housing from the cylinder cowling.

4. Remove the inner pulley half and Woodruff key from the shaft.

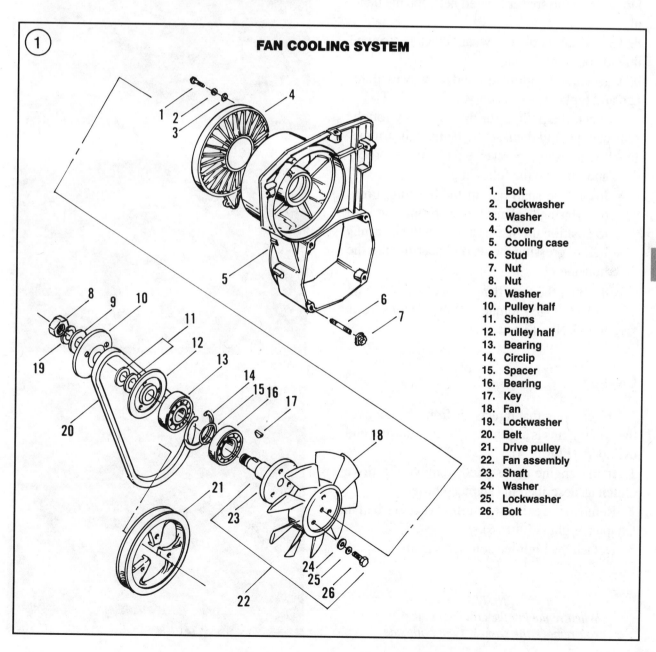

FAN COOLING SYSTEM

1. Bolt
2. Lockwasher
3. Washer
4. Cover
5. Cooling case
6. Stud
7. Nut
8. Nut
9. Washer
10. Pulley half
11. Shims
12. Pulley half
13. Bearing
14. Circlip
15. Spacer
16. Bearing
17. Key
18. Fan
19. Lockwasher
20. Belt
21. Drive pulley
22. Fan assembly
23. Shaft
24. Washer
25. Lockwasher
26. Bolt

11

5. Unbolt the fan housing from the engine and slide it from around the flywheel.

6. Unbolt and remove the fan from the shaft.

NOTE
Do not remove the bearings unless bearing replacement is required.

7. Check the bearings for roughness. If damaged, drive the bearings from the housing. A snap ring and spacer are located between the bearings. Do not lose the spacer located between the bearings.

8. Check all parts for wear, cracks, stripped threads or other damage.

9. Check the Woodruff key and keyway for damage and replace as necessary.

10. Check the pulleys for damage. Any roughness can quickly damage the belt and bearings.

11. When installing, reverse the removal procedure and observe the following.

    a. Install the snap ring in the housing. Press the bearings against the snap ring. Be sure to position the spacer between the bearings before pressing the second bearing into the housing.

    b. Tighten the four flange nuts to 18-22 N•m (13-16 ft.-lb.) torque and the 6 mm screws to 4-7 N•m (3-5 ft.-lb.).

Cowling

The cowling that directs air from the fan over the cooling fins is attached to the fan housing and cylinders (**Figure 4**).

1. If the engine is installed, remove the drive clutch as described in Chapter Thirteen.

2. Remove the exhaust manifold as described in Chapter Eight (**Figure 5**).

3. Detach the high-tension wires from the spark plugs.

NOTE
When removing the cowling, make sure you remove the gaskets from both sides

of the cowling around the exhaust ports and the intake ports.

4. Remove the screws, flat washers and lockwashers attaching the cowling and lift the top and exhaust cowling from the engine.

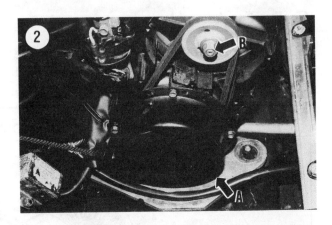

5. Remove the carburetors, shut off valves and intake adapters (**Figure 6**) as described in Chapter Six.

6. Clean the gasket material from around the exhaust and intake ports. Also, clean the cowling around the ports.

7. When installing the rear cowling around the intake ports, observe the following:

   a. Apply a thin coat of silicone sealer to both sides of all four intake port gaskets.

   b. Install one gasket on each intake port.

   c. Install the cowling on the intake side of the engine.

   d. Install the second gasket on each intake port outside the cowling.

   e. Position one intake adapter over each port and install the attaching screws (**Figure 7**).

   f. Apply Loctite to the threads of the retaining screws and tighten the screws securely.

   g. Attach the oil injection lines to the fittings on the adapters.

   h. Apply a thin coat of silicone sealer to the adapter plate. Install the shut off valves.

8. When installing the front cowling around the exhaust ports, observe the following:

   a. Apply a thin coat of high-temperature silicone to both sides of all four exhaust port gaskets.

   b. Install one gasket over the studs of each exhaust port with the metal side of the gasket toward the cylinder.

   c. Install the cowling on the exhaust side (front) of the engine over the exhaust studs.

   d. Install the top cowling and secure the cowling with the 14 screws, flat washers and lockwashers. Tighten the screws to 4-7 N•m (3-5 ft.-lb.) torque.

   e. Install the second gasket onto the exhaust studs outside the cowling with the metal side away from the cylinder.

   f. Position the exhaust manifold onto the studs. Tighten the retaining nuts to 18-22 N•m (13-16 ft.-lb.) torque.

9. Install the carburetors as described in Chapter Six.

LIQUID-COOLED MODELS

All models included in this book, except Z 440 models, are equipped with a liquid-cooling system to maintain the temperature of the engine. The liquid-cooling system is a closed system that consists of a pressure cap, coolant pump, coolant reservoir tank, heat exchanger and hoses. See

11

Figure 8 for a typical diagram. During operation the coolant heats and expands, thus pressurizing the system.

Cooling system flushing procedures are provided in Chapter Three.

> *WARNING*
> *Do not remove the filler cap (**Figure 9**) when the engine is hot. The coolant is very hot and is under pressure. Severe scalding could result if the coolant comes in contact with your skin. The cooling system must cool prior to removing any component from the system.*

Thermostat

The cooling system is equipped with a thermostat (**Figure 10**) located in an outlet housing that attaches to the cylinder heads. The thermostat reduces coolant flow from the engine when it is cold. As the engine warms up, the thermostat gradually opens, allowing coolant to circulate through the system, including the heat exchangers.

> *CAUTION*
> *Do not operate the engine without a thermostat. Removal of the thermostat may cause overcooling or in some cases may cause loss of coolant and overheating. The engine may be seriously damaged if it is operated while too hot or too cool. Be sure the correct thermostat is installed. Thermostats may appear to be similar, but may have entirely different operating characteristics.*

Removal

1. Open the hood.

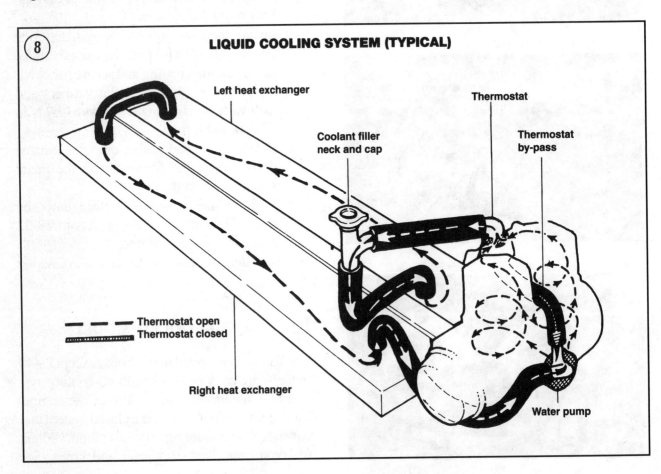

LIQUID COOLING SYSTEM (TYPICAL)

8

Left heat exchanger
Thermostat
Coolant filler neck and cap
Thermostat by-pass

--- --- Thermostat open
········· Thermostat closed

Right heat exchanger
Water pump

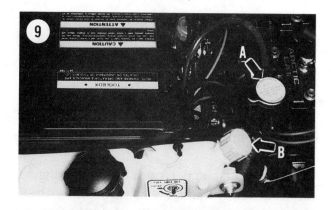

WARNING
Make sure the engine is cool before proceeding with Step 2. Severe scalding could result if hot coolant comes in contact with your skin.

2. Drain the cooling system as described in Chapter Three.

3. Locate the outlet housing (**Figure 11**) attached to the cylinder heads.

4. Loosen the clamp on the outlet hose and detach the hose from the outlet fitting.

5. Unbolt the thermostat housing (**Figure 11** and **12**) from the outlet housing and carefully separate the housings.

6. Remove the thermostat (**Figure 10**).

Testing

Test the thermostat to ensure proper operation. The thermostat should be replaced if it remains open at normal room temperature or stays closed after the specified temperature has been reached during the test procedure.

1. Pour some water into a container that can be heated. Submerge the thermostat in the water and suspend a thermometer as shown in **Figure 13**. Use a thermometer rated higher than the test temperature.

NOTE
Suspend the thermostat with wire so it does not touch the sides or bottom of the pan.

2. Heat the water until the thermostat starts to open. Check the water temperature with a thermometer. It should be approximately 107° F (42° C). If the thermostat valve did not start to open at the correct temperature, replace it.

3. Let the water cool to 10° *under* the thermostat's rated opening temperature. If the thermostat valve is not fully closed at this temperature, replace it.

4. Remove the thermostat from the water and let it cool to room temperature. Hold it close to a

light bulb and check for leakage. If light can be seen around the edge of the valve, the thermostat is defective and should be replaced.

Installation

1. If a new thermostat is being installed, test it as described in this chapter. Even new units can be faulty.
2. Place the thermostat into the cylinder head as shown in **Figure 10**. Install the thermostat housing.
3. Install the hoses and secure with the hose clamps.
4. Refill the cooling system as described in Chapter Three.

Coolant Pump (All Liquid-Cooled Models Except El Tigre)

The coolant pump impeller is mounted on the same shaft that drives the oil injection pump. The impeller is located under the cover (**Figure 14**) located on the front of the crankcase. The O-ring

seal (**Figure 15**) located on the cover can be replaced without disassembling the crankcase. If the internal seals are faulty, refer to Chapter Five for service procedures.

Coolant Pump (El Tigre Models)

The coolant pump, located behind the engine, is belt driven by a pulley attached to the flywheel. Coolant pump or pulley removal may be required for other engine service (**Figure 16**).

Removal

1. Remove the engine from the frame as described in Chapter Five.
2. Remove the screws attaching the coolant pump cover, then remove the cover (A, **Figure 17**).

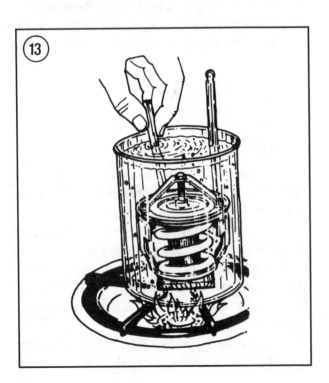

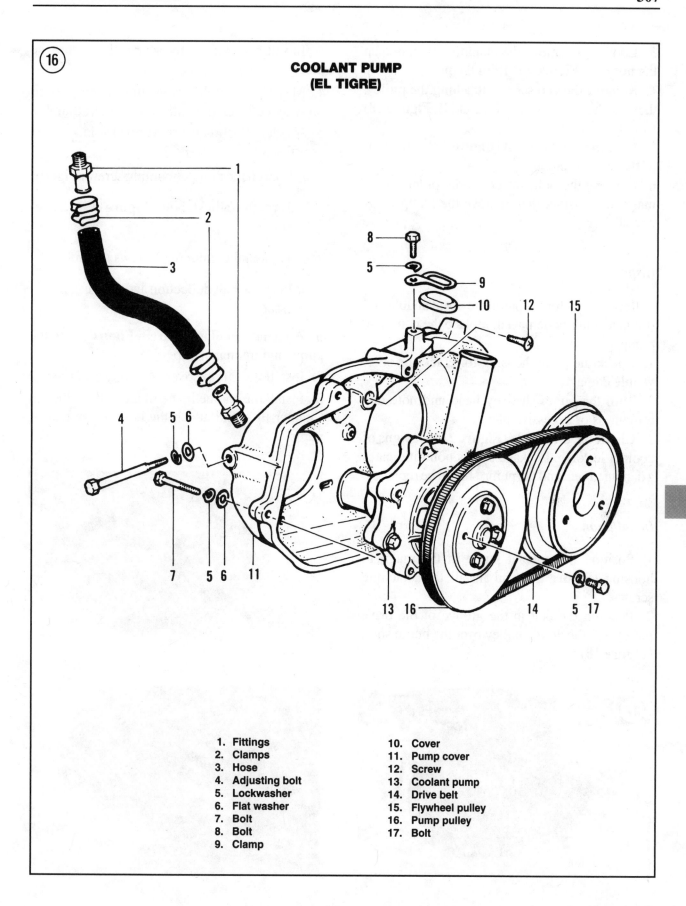

⑯

**COOLANT PUMP
(EL TIGRE)**

1. Fittings
2. Clamps
3. Hose
4. Adjusting bolt
5. Lockwasher
6. Flat washer
7. Bolt
8. Bolt
9. Clamp
10. Cover
11. Pump cover
12. Screw
13. Coolant pump
14. Drive belt
15. Flywheel pulley
16. Pump pulley
17. Bolt

11

3. Loosen or remove the clamp(s), then detach the hose (B, **Figure 17**) from the pump.

4. Remove the cap screws attaching the pulley, then lift the pulley and belt (A and B, **Figure 18**) from the engine.

5. Loosen the adjust bolt (**Figure 19**) at the rear of the coolant pump.

6. Remove the bolts attaching the pump to the magneto housing, then remove the pump (**Figure 20**).

Inspection

Repair parts for the pump are not available and if it is leaking or damaged, replace the complete pump.

1. Check the pump housing for cracks or other visible damage.

2. Turn the pump shaft by hand and note any roughness or excessive play.

3. Check the drain hole (**Figure 21**) for signs of coolant leakage. Leakage at this point indicates a damaged seal and the pump should be replaced.

Installation

1. Position the coolant pump in the magneto housing (**Figure 19**) and install the attaching screws.

2. Position the belt in the groove of the drive pulley and the driven pulley over the pump shaft (**Figure 18**).

3. Install, then tighten the screws that secure the pulley.

4. Measure the belt's deflection when pressed midway between the pulleys with your thumb.

5. If belt deflection is not 6 mm (1/4 in.), adjust as follows:

    a. Loosen the pump mounting screws slightly.

    b. Turn the adjust bolt (**Figure 19**), as required.

    c. Tighten the mounting screws securely.

    d. Recheck belt deflection and readjust, if necessary.

6. Attach the coolant hose (B, **Figure 17**) to the pump and tighten clamp.

7. Install the pump cover (A, **Figure 17**).

8. Install the engine in the frame as described in Chapter Five and attach the hose to the rear of pump.

Heat Exchangers

Inspection/Replacement

Inspect the cooling system if coolant leaks are found. Inspect the heat exchangers for damage and replace, if necessary. Different styles of heat exchangers have been used (**Figure 22** and **Figure 23**).

Hoses

Hoses deteriorate with age and should be replaced periodically or whenever they show cracking or leakage. Loss of coolant will cause the engine to overheat and result in severe damage.

Whenever any component of the cooling system is removed, inspect the hoses(s) and determine if replacement is necessary.

Inspection

1. Check all the cooling hoses for flexibility and softness after the engine has cooled. Replace a hose that is brittle or hard. Also check hoses for cracks, abrasions, cuts or other conditions that might cause a leak.

2. With the engine hot, examine the hoses for swelling along the entire hose length. Eventually a hose will rupture if softened by oil or heat.

3. Check clamps (**Figure 24**) and the condition of the hose around the hose clamps for possible leakage.

Replacement

Hose replacement should be performed when the engine is cool.

1. Drain the cooling system as described under *Coolant Change* in Chapter Three.

> *NOTE*
> *Note the routing and any clamps supported by the hoses. There may be some covers (**Figure 25**) that protect the hoses from being damaged by rubbing against another item. Make sure these guards are installed on the new hoses.*

2. Loosen the hose clamps from the hose to be replaced. Slide the clamps along the hose and out of the way.

3. Twist the hose end to break the seal and remove from the connecting joint. If the hose has been on for some time, it may be difficult to remove. If so, cut the hose parallel to the fitting connection with a knife or razor. Carefully pry the hose loose.

> *CAUTION*
> *Excessive force applied to the hose during removal could damage the fitting.*

4. Examine the fitting for cracks or other damage. Repair or replace parts as required. If the fitting is okay, remove rust with sandpaper.

11

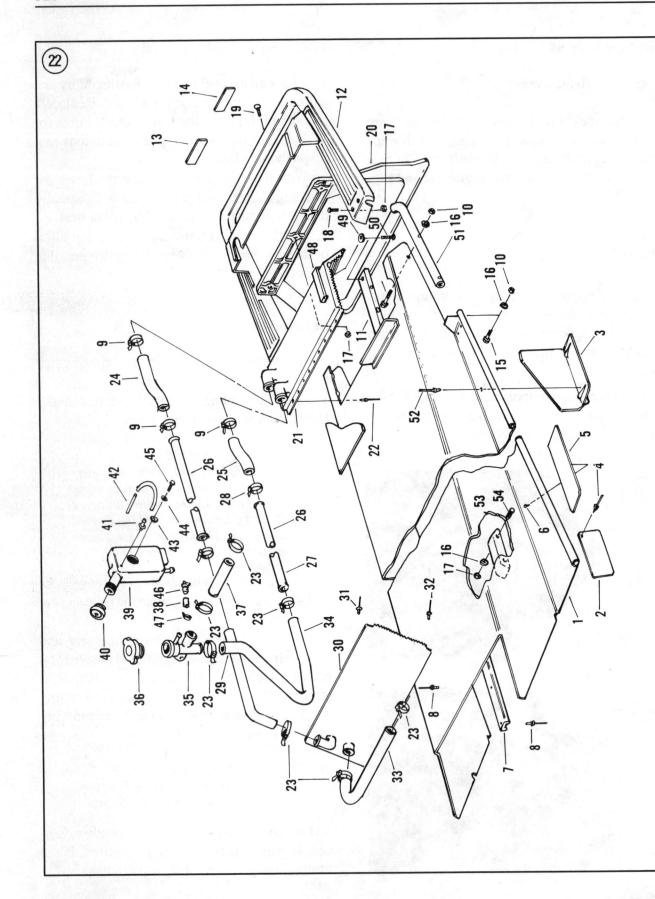

HEAT EXCHANGER
(1994 ZR 440/580 MODELS)

1. Tunnel
2. Plate
3. Bracket
4. Rivet
5. Safety pad
6. Screw
7. Tunnel wearstrip
8. Rivet
9. Clamp
10. Nut
11. Tunnel wearstrip
12. Bumper
13. Decal
14. Decal
15. Bolt
16. Washer
17. Locknut
18. Bolt
19. Screw
20. Snow flap
21. Heat exchanger
22. Rivet
23. Clamp
24. Hose
25. Hose
26. Hose
27. Hose

28. Clamp
29. Hose
30. Heat exchanger
31. Rivet
32. Rivet
33. Hose
34. Hose
35. Filler neck
36. Filler cap
37. Hose
38. Hose
39. Coolant reservoir
40. Reservoir cap
41. Vent
42. Vent hose
43. Nut
44. Washer
45. Bolt
46. Fitting
47. Clamp
48. Foam
49. Washer
50. Screw
51. Bumper insert
52. Rivet
53. Tunnel mounting
54. Bolt

11

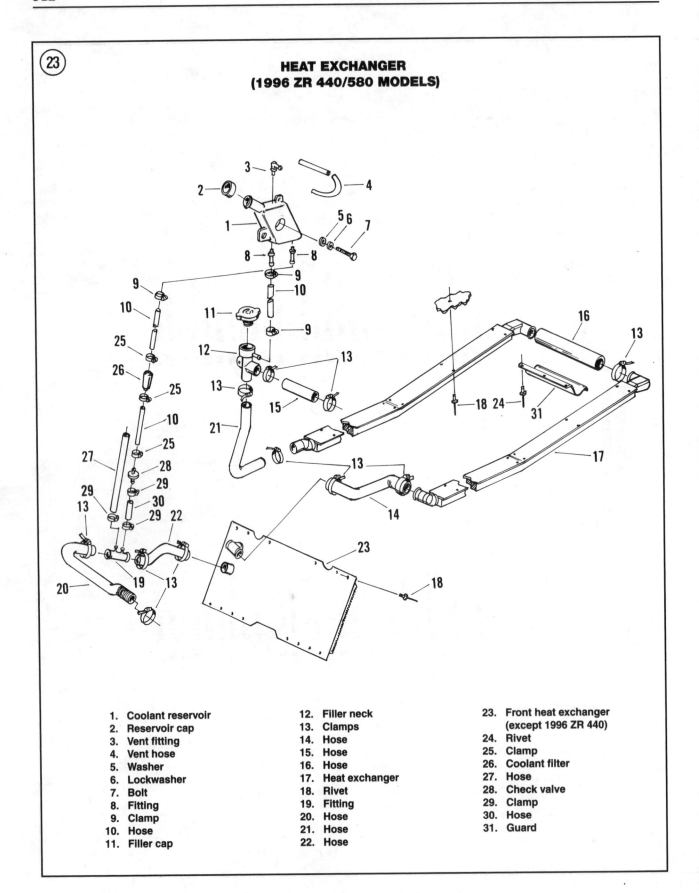

**HEAT EXCHANGER
(1996 ZR 440/580 MODELS)**

1. Coolant reservoir
2. Reservoir cap
3. Vent fitting
4. Vent hose
5. Washer
6. Lockwasher
7. Bolt
8. Fitting
9. Clamp
10. Hose
11. Filler cap

12. Filler neck
13. Clamps
14. Hose
15. Hose
16. Hose
17. Heat exchanger
18. Rivet
19. Fitting
20. Hose
21. Hose
22. Hose

23. Front heat exchanger
 (except 1996 ZR 440)
24. Rivet
25. Clamp
26. Coolant filter
27. Hose
28. Check valve
29. Clamp
30. Hose
31. Guard

5. Inspect the hose clamps and replace as necessary.

6. Slide the hose clamps over the outside of the hose and install hose fitting. Make sure the hose clears all obstructions and is routed properly.

NOTE
If it is difficult to install a hose on a fitting, soak the end of the hose in hot water for approximately two minutes.

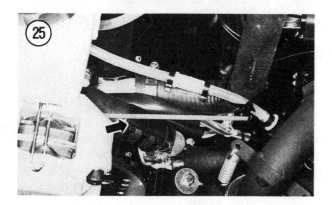

This will soften the hose and ease installation.

7. With the hose positioned correctly on the fitting, position the clamps slightly back away from the end of the hose. Tighten the clamps securely, but not so much that the hose is damaged (**Figure 24**).

8. Refill the cooling system as described under *Coolant Change* in Chapter Three. Start the engine and check for leaks. Tighten the hose clamps as necessary.

Coolant check valve and filter

Some models are equipped with a coolant filter (A, **Figure 26**) and check valve (B, **Figure 26**). The check valve must be installed so it will allow coolant to flow in the correct direction.

11

Chapter Twelve

Recoil Starter

All models are equipped with a rope-operated recoil starter. The starter is mounted in a housing bolted onto the engine next to the flywheel. Pulling the rope handle turns the starter sheave and moves the drive pawl out. The drive pawl engages the starter pulley attached to the flywheel and continued rotation of the starter sheave turns the engine. When the rope handle is released, the spring inside the assembly rewinds the sheave and wraps the rope around the sheave.

Rewind starters are relatively trouble-free. A broken or frayed rope is the most common malfunction. This chapter covers removal and installation of the starter assembly, starter pulley, rope and rewind spring.

Refer to Chapter Nine for service to the electric starter used on some models.

Starter Housing
Removal/Installation

1. Open the hood.
2. Remove the handle as follows.

a. Pull the starter handle out.
b. Slide the rope through the handle (**Figure 1**).

NOTE
If the starter is not broken, do not release the rope after removing the handle in substep 2c. After removing the handle, tie a knot in the end of the rope to temporarily stop the rope from retracting into the starter housing. Release the starter rope slowly until it is held by the temporary knot.

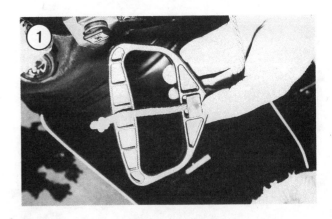

c. Untie the knot (**Figure 2**) and remove the handle.

3. Remove the screws attaching the starter housing to the engine, then remove the starter housing (**Figure 3**, typical).

4. Installation is the reverse of the preceding steps. Observe the following:

a. Position the starter housing with the rope exit correctly aligned toward the rear. Install the housing retaining screws and tighten securely.

b. Thread the starter rope back through its original path and out the hole in the cowl.

c. Untie the knot at the end of the rope and feed the rope through the handle (**Figure 4**).

d. Tie a knot in the end of the rope (**Figure 5**).

e. Operate the starter assembly to make sure it is working properly. Check the path of the rope through the engine compartment to make sure it is not kinked or interfering with any other component.

f. Close the hood.

Starter Pulley Removal/Installation

The starter pulley (13, **Figure 6**) is attached to the flywheel. You can remove the starter pulley with the engine installed in the frame. This procedure is shown with the engine removed for clarity.

1. Remove the hood assembly.

2. Remove the recoil starter assembly as described in this chapter.

3. Remove the screws and lockwashers attaching the starter pulley (**Figure 7**, typical) to the flywheel, then remove the starter pulley.

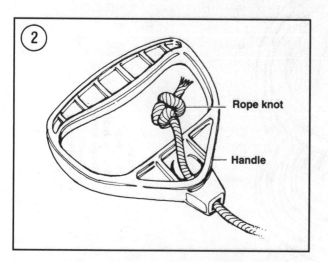

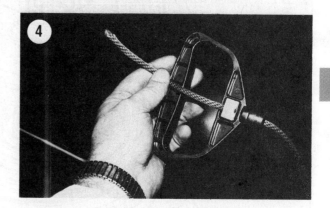

Rope knot

Handle

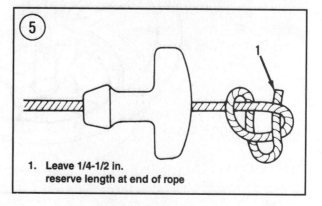

1. Leave 1/4-1/2 in. reserve length at end of rope

12

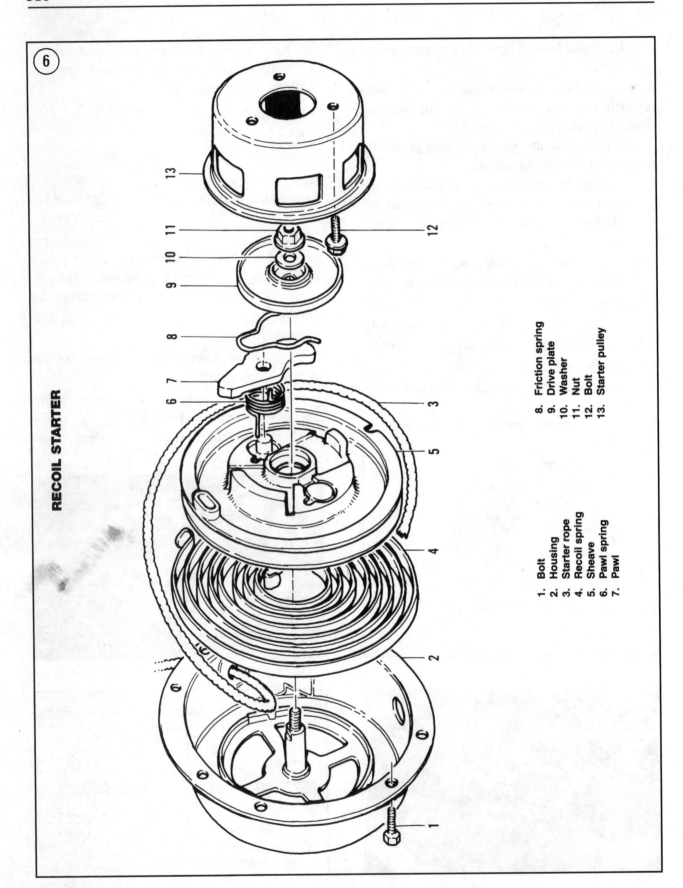

RECOIL STARTER

6

1. Bolt
2. Housing
3. Starter rope
4. Recoil spring
5. Sheave
6. Pawl spring
7. Pawl
8. Friction spring
9. Drive plate
10. Washer
11. Nut
12. Bolt
13. Starter pulley

NOTE
*The cooling pump pulley (**Figure 8**), fan drive pulley (**Figure 9**) or flywheel counterweight may be attached to the same screws as the starter pulley.*

4. Installation is the reverse of the preceding steps. Observe the following:

    a. Apply Loctite 271 (red) to the threads of the three retaining screws.

    b. Install the starter pulley (**Figure 7**), lockwashers and screws.

    c. Tighten the retaining screws evenly to 8-12 N•m (6-9 ft.-lb.) torque.

    d. Reinstall the recoil starter housing as described in this chapter.

Starter Housing Disassembly

This procedure describes complete disassembly of the recoil starter housing. Refer to **Figure 6** for this procedure.

WARNING
The rewind spring will usually remain in the cavity of the housing, but it may unwind suddenly and violently as the sheave is removed in Step 8. Wear safety glasses while disassembling the starter.

1. Remove the recoil starter housing as described in this chapter.

2. Hold the starter rope securely and remove the temporary knot tied in the rope during removal.

3. Hold the starter sheave (5, **Figure 6**) to keep it from turning, release the starter rope and allow the sheave to turn slowly until it stops.

4. Turn the starter assembly so that the sheave assembly faces up as shown in **Figure 10**.

5. Remove the nut (**Figure 10**). This nut was installed with (blue) Loctite.

6. Remove the drive plate and friction spring (**Figure 11**).

12

NOTE
Do not remove the friction spring (B,
Figure 11) *unless a new spring will be*
installed.

7. Remove the pawl (**Figure 12**) and pawl spring (**Figure 13**).

8. Remove the sheave (**Figure 14**) and rope assembly from the starter housing.

9. If the rope is being replaced, remove the rope from the sheave.

WARNING
Be careful if the rewind spring has re-
*mained in the cavity of the housing (**Fig-***
ure 15)*, because it may unwind suddenly*
and violently, causing serious injury.
Wear safety glasses and gloves while
removing and installing the spring.

10. Place the rewind assembly housing on the floor with the closed side up (**Figure 16**). Tap lightly on the top of the housing while holding it

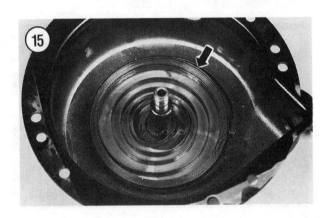

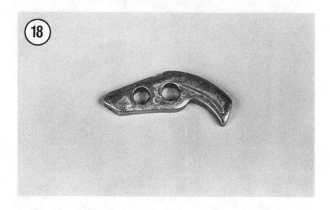

tightly against the floor and allow the spring to fall from the housing. When the spring has unwound completely, pick up the spring.

Starter Housing Inspection

> *NOTE*
> *Before cleaning plastic components, make sure the cleaning agent is compatible with plastic. Some types of solvents can permanently damage the plastic pieces.*

1. Clean all parts thoroughly and allow to dry.

2. Visually check the starter post (**Figure 17**) for cracks, deep scoring or excessive wear. Check the grooves in the post for damage. Replace the housing if the starter post is damaged.

3. Check the pawl (**Figure 18**) and pawl spring (**Figure 19**) for cracks or other damage. Replace damaged parts as required.

4. Check the sheave drum (**Figure 20**) for cracks or damage.

5. Be sure the friction spring (**Figure 21**) fits tightly in the drive plate. Do not remove the spring unless you are installing a new spring.

6. Check the recoil spring (**Figure 22**) for any signs of damage. Breakage often occurs near the attachment points at the ends of the spring. Install a new spring if cracked or broken. Reshaping ends or similar repairs are not recommended.

12

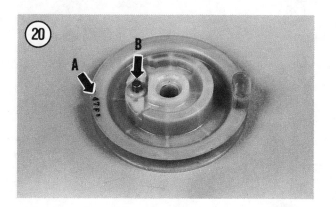

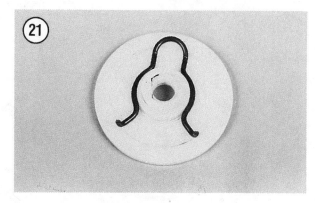

7. Check the starter rope for fraying, splitting or breakage. Measure the length and diameter of the old rope to determine the correct size of replacement.

8. If there is any doubt as to the condition of any part, replace it with a new one.

Starter Housing Assembly

Refer to **Figure 6** for this procedure.

> *WARNING*
> *Wear safety glasses and gloves while installing the recoil spring.*

1. Install the recoil spring (**Figure 22**) as follows:

   a. Lubricate the rewind spring and the cavity of the starter housing with a low-temperature grease.

   > *NOTE*
   > *Improper or insufficient lubrication will cause parts of the rewind starter, including the springs, to fail. The starter should be removed, cleaned and lubricated periodically as a part of regular maintenance.*

   b. Hook the outer spring loop over the notch in the housing (**Figure 23**).

   c. Wind the spring counterclockwise until the spring is completely installed in the cavity

of the housing. The spring should lie flat in the housing (**Figure 24**).

   d. Lubricate the starter post in the starter housing with a low temperature grease.

2. Attach the inner end of the starter rope to the sheave drum as follows:

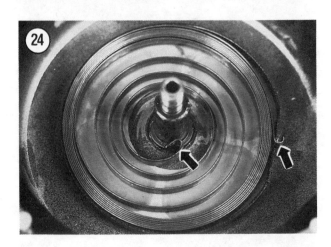

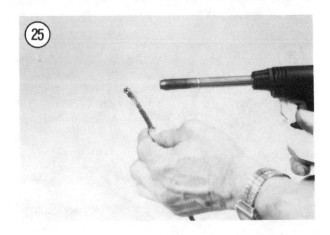

WARNING
Be extremely careful when heating the recoil rope. The hot melting rope can cause serious injury as well as the flame used to heat the rope.

a. Check the ends of the starter rope for fraying. To tighten the end of the rope, apply heat to melt the end (**Figure 25**).

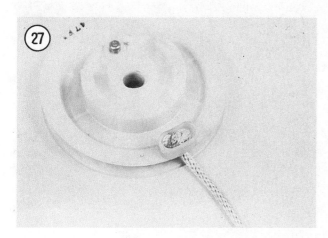

b. Push the end of the rope through the hole in the sheave drum past the window (**Figure 26**).

c. Tie a knot in the end of the rope. Pull the rope until the knot is tight in the pocket of the sheave (**Figure 27**).

d. Lay the sheave on the workbench with the open end up (**Figure 28**).

e. Wind the rope counterclockwise (**Figure 28**) tightly into the groove of the sheave.

NOTE
After the rope is wound into the groove, approximately 50 cm (20 in.) should remain free to install through the frame and body.

3. Align the inner hook of the recoil spring (**Figure 29**) with the notch in the sheave drum. Install the sheave drum. Twist the sheave drum slightly to make sure the drum and end of the spring are engaged.

4. Install the pawl spring (**Figure 30**).

5. Install the pawl (**Figure 31**). Make sure the spring engages the pawl.

6. If removed, install the friction spring on the drive plate (**Figure 21**).

7. Install the drive plate and friction spring (**Figure 32**) so the flat in the drive plate engages the flat on the center post.

12

8. Apply Loctite 242 (blue) on the threads of the nut. Install and tighten the nut (**Figure 33**) to 10 N.m (7 ft.-lb.) torque.

9. Preload the recoil spring as follows:

   a. Position the free end of the rope in the notch of the sheave (**Figure 33**).

   b. Wind the starter sheave counterclockwise while holding the free end of the rope in the notch.

   c. Remove the rope from the notch and allow the spring to wind the rope into the groove of the sheave.

NOTE
The rope should be too long to wind completely onto the sheave without binding in the housing. When the rope

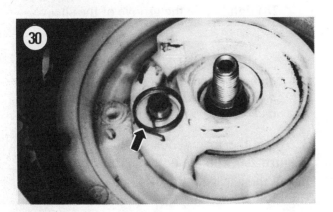

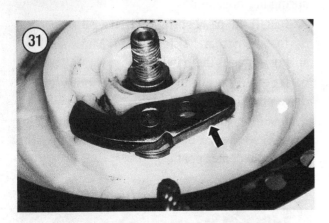

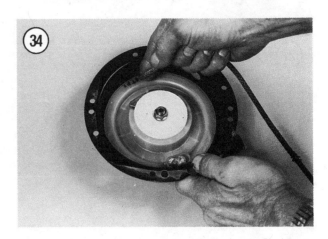

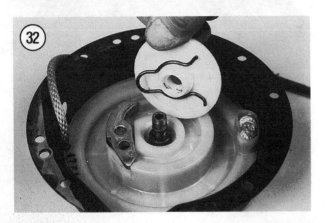

completely fills the sheave groove, there should be approximately 50 cm (20 in.) free to install through the frame and body.

d. Pull the rope several times to check for proper rewinding and binding. The rope should rewind completely, but should not cause the spring to bind before the rope is completely extended.

e. If necessary, position the rope in the notch of the sheave (**Figure 34**) and wind the spring or release tension on the spring as required for proper operation.

f. When the starter spring preload is correct, insert the rope through the opening and tie a temporary knot (**Figure 35**) to keep the rope partially extended until it is installed.

12

Chapter Thirteen

Drive System

The drive train consists of a drive pulley (sheave) mounted on the left end of the engine crankshaft, a driven pulley (sheave) mounted on the driven (chaincase input) shaft and a drive belt connecting the two pulleys. The chaincase contains a drive chain and reduction sprockets. A brake disc is also located near the right end of the driven shaft. The chaincase contains a speed reduction on all models. It also contains the reverse gears of models so equipped. A driveshaft fitted with track drive sprockets exits from the chaincase. This chapter describes complete procedures for the drive and driven pulley components. Service to the chaincase, driven shaft and brake are described in Chapter Fourteen.

General drive belt specifications are listed in **Table 1**. **Tables 1-8** are found at the end of this chapter.

WARNING
Never lean into a snowmobile's engine compartment while wearing a scarf or other loose clothing when the engine is running or when the driver is attempting to start the engine. If the scarf or clothing should catch in the drive system, severe injury or death could occur. Make sure the belt guard is always in place.

DRIVE UNIT

Torque is transferred from the engine crankshaft to the driven shaft by a centrifugally actuated, variable pulley type of transmission. The transmission or drive unit automatically changes the drive ratio to permit the machine to move from idle to maximum speed. The major components are the drive pulley assembly, driven pulley assembly and drive belt (**Figure 1**).

The drive and driven pulleys are basically two variable diameter pulleys that automatically vary the amount of reduction. Changes in the reduction ratio are possible by moving the sides of the pulleys closer together or further apart. Changing the gap between the sides of the pulley causes the belt to move up or down in the pulley groove, which changes the effective diameter of the pulley. These changes in pulley diameter adjust to correspond with the prevailing load and speed conditions (**Figure 2**).

The shift sequence is determined by a combination of engine torque and engine rpm. When track resistance, or load, increases, such as when going up a hill, the pulleys change the reduction ratio. Engine rpm will remain nearly the same but the vehicle's speed drops. When track resis-

tance decreases, the pulleys automatically shift toward a higher ratio. The engine rpm remains the same, but the vehicle's speed will increase.

DRIVE PULLEY ASSEMBLY

Major components of the drive pulley assembly are the sliding pulley half (sheave), fixed

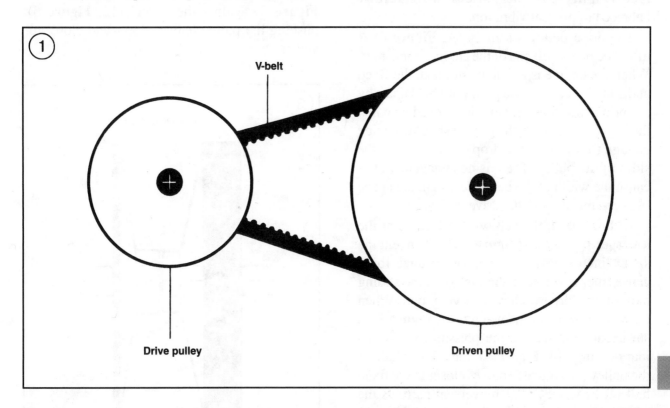

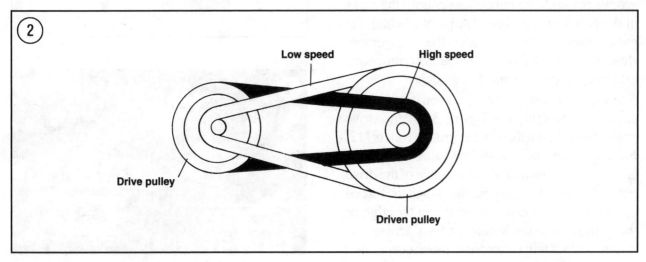

13

pulley half (sheave), weight levers, weight ramps, primary spring and V-belt. The V-belt connects the drive and driven pulleys.

Fixed and Sliding Pulley Halves

The tapered surfaces of the pulleys are precision machined to match the V-belt gripping surface (**Figure 3**). The pulleys are carefully balanced to prevent vibration.

The drive pulley assembly (A, **Figure 4**) is mounted on the left end of the engine crankshaft. When the engine is at idle or stopped, the fixed and sliding halves of the pulley are held apart by the primary spring. At slow idle speed or when the engine is stopped, the groove should be wide enough for the V-belt to drop down between the sides of the pulley. There is no engagement because the width of the belt is *less* than the space between the sides of the drive pulley.

At low speed, the belt will be located at the low-speed position (**Figure 2**). When engine speed increases from idle, centrifugal force causes the weight levers mounted on the sliding half of the drive pulley to swing out. When centrifugal force of the weights (7, **Figure 5**) is sufficient to overcome the pressure of the primary spring (14, **Figure 5**), the sliding half of the pulley (2, **Figure 5**) moves closer to the fixed half (1, **Figure 5**). This movement narrows the groove between the pulley halves until the sides of the pulley grip the belt. The point at which the pulley grips the belt is called the engagement rpm. Refer to **Table 3** for the recommended engagement rpm for specific models.

As engine rpm increases, centrifugal force causes the weights (7, **Figure 5**) of the drive pulley to swing further out against the rollers (12, **Figure 5**) and force the sliding half of the pulley closer to the fixed half. As the groove of the drive pulley becomes narrower, the V-belt is forced upward in the groove toward the outer edge of the pulley. Since the V-belt is a fixed length and width, the belt will be forced to move deeper into the groove of the driven pulley as indicated by the high-speed position of the belt in **Figure 2**.

Though not part of the drive pulley, it should be noted that the secondary spring of the driven pulley forces the sides of the pulley together. As the belt wedges against the sides of the driven (rear) pulley, it compresses the secondary spring in the driven pulley. As engine speed increases, centrifugal force forces the weight levers (7, **Figure 5**) against the rollers (12, **Figure 5**), pushing the pulley halves closer and closer together.

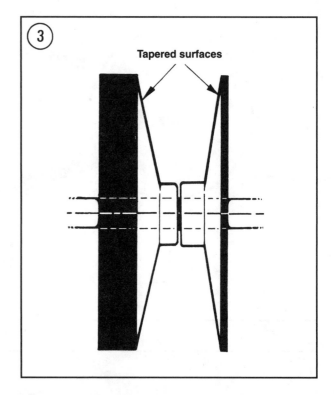

Tapered surfaces

Drive Pulley Spring

The clutch release spring (14, **Figure 5**) of the drive pulley controls engagement speed. If a lighter spring is installed, the belt will engage at a lower engine speed. If a heavier spring is installed, the engine speed (rpm) will have to be higher to overcome spring pressure and allow engagement.

Centrifugal Weight Levers

As previously noted, weighted levers (7, **Figure 5**) in the drive pulley react to engine speed and swing out. The levers press against rollers in the spider to move the sliding half of the drive pulley. Centrifugal force causes the weights to swing out as the speed of the engine increases. Movement of the weighted levers and the sliding

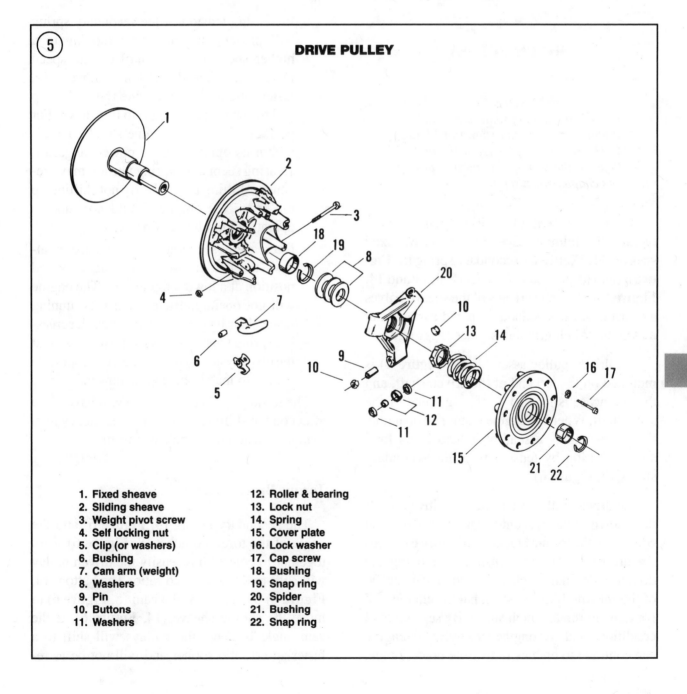

⑤   **DRIVE PULLEY**   13

1. Fixed sheave
2. Sliding sheave
3. Weight pivot screw
4. Self locking nut
5. Clip (or washers)
6. Bushing
7. Cam arm (weight)
8. Washers
9. Pin
10. Buttons
11. Washers
12. Roller & bearing
13. Lock nut
14. Spring
15. Cover plate
16. Lock washer
17. Cap screw
18. Bushing
19. Snap ring
20. Spider
21. Bushing
22. Snap ring

half of the pulley is opposed by the pressure of the spring. Until engine speed reaches the engagement rpm, the weights have not yet moved the sliding half of the pulley enough to engage the belt. The force exerted by the weighted levers is controlled by engine rpm. The faster the crankshaft rotates, the farther the weights pivot out. Movement of the sliding half of the drive pulley is controlled by the shape of the weight ramps.

DRIVEN PULLEY

NOTE
The driven pulley of some late models is slightly different than shown in **Figure 6**. *Operation of both types is similar. Refer to the appropriate paragraphs of this chapter when servicing.*

Major components of the driven pulley assembly are the sliding sheave (13, **Figure 6**), fixed sheave (11, **Figure 6**), secondary spring (5, **Figure 6**) and torque (cam) bracket (5, 8, 11 and 14, **Figure 6**). The belt surfaces of the sheave halves are machined to a smooth, tapered surface that match the V-belt gripping surface (**Figure 3**).

The driven pulley assembly (B, **Figure 4**) is mounted on the left end of the driven shaft, and the chaincase is located on the right end of the same shaft. When the engine is stopped or at idle, the driven pulley assembly is held in its low-speed position by tension from the secondary spring (5, **Figure 6**).

The driven pulley is a torque sensitive unit. If the snowmobile encounters an increased load condition, the torque bracket (8, **Figure 6**) forces the driven pulley to downshift by moving the driven pulley halves closer together. The speed of the snowmobile will slow, but the engine will continue to run at a high speed. By sensing load conditions and shifting accordingly, the engine can continue to operate in its peak power range.

Secondary Spring

The secondary spring (5, **Figure 6**) located in the driven pulley assembly helps determine the shifting pattern and keeps the torque bracket in contact with the slider buttons. Spring tension can be changed by installing a different spring or by repositioning the end of the spring in holes drilled in the torque bracket. Observe the following:

a. Increasing tension of the secondary spring will prevent the belt from moving to a higher speed position until engine speed increases. If the drive pulley moves to a faster ratio too soon, engine rpm will drop and the engine will begin to bog down. For peak efficiency, the engine should operate within its optimum peak power range. Increasing secondary spring tension may prevent upshifting too early. By not shifting up too soon, the engine should continue to operate within its peak power range.

b. Decreasing secondary spring tension allows the belt to move to a higher speed position at a lower engine rpm. The engine will not operate efficiently if it is running faster than its peak power range. Decreasing spring tension allows adjustment so that the drive system will shift into a higher ratio sooner to match the engine power.

The torque bracket cam angle will have more affect on the shifting sequence under heavy load than the tension of the release spring.

Torque Bracket Angle

The secondary spring (5, **Figure 6**) and the angle of the torque bracket (8, **Figure 6**) work together to control how easily the driven pulley will shift to a faster speed ratio. The buttons (4, **Figure 6**) push against the cam (8, **Figure 6**) to move the sliding sheave (14, **Figure 6**). If the cam angle is steep, the pulleys will shift to a faster speed ratio sooner and will not be as re-

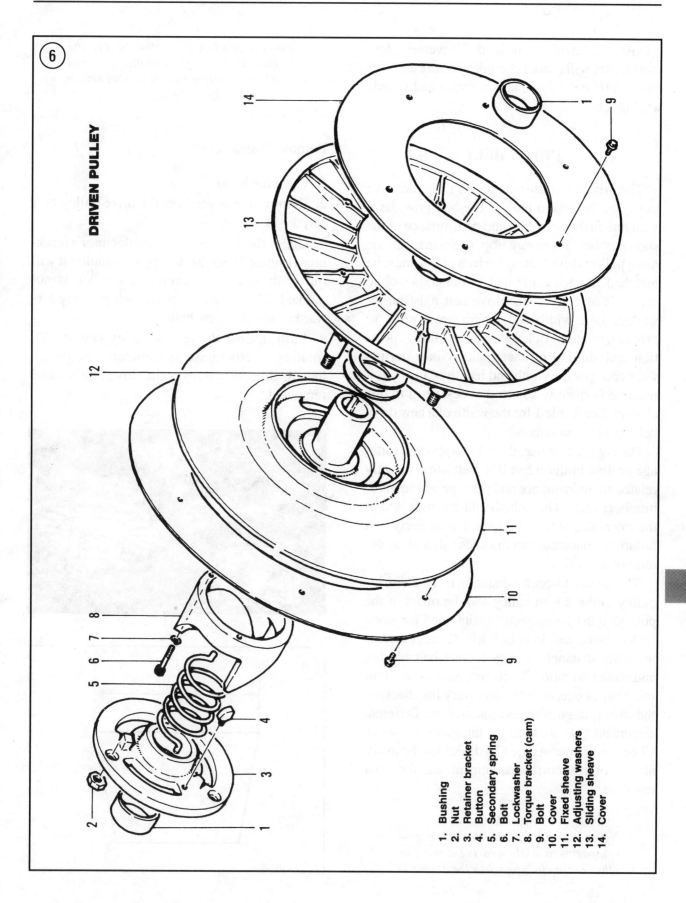

DRIVEN PULLEY

1. Bushing
2. Nut
3. Retainer bracket
4. Button
5. Secondary spring
6. Bolt
7. Lockwasher
8. Torque bracket (cam)
9. Bolt
10. Cover
11. Fixed sheave
12. Adjusting washers
13. Sliding sheave
14. Cover

13

sponsive to increases in load. Conversely, low cam angles will exert more side pressure and will slow shifts until the load is reduced and speeds are higher.

DRIVE BELT

The drive belt transmits power from the drive pulley to the driven pulley. The belt provides a vital link in the operation and performance of the snowmobile. To ensure top performance, the drive pulley, drive belt and driven pulley must be matched to each other and to the snowmobile model. The correct size drive belt must be installed. Belt width and length are critical to proper operation. Belt wear affects clutch operation and shifting characteristics. Since normal wear changes the width and length of the belt, it must be frequently adjusted as described in this chapter. See **Table 1** for the width of a new drive belt for your snowmobile.

During general use, there is no specific mileage or time limit on belt life. Belt life is directly related to maintenance and the type of snowmobile operation. The belt should be inspected at the intervals listed in Chapter Three. Early belt failure is abnormal and the cause should be determined.

The center-to-center distance from the drive pulley to the driven pulley and the offset of the pulleys must be correctly maintained for good performance and long belt life. Correct center-to-center distance ensures correct belt tension and reduction ratio. The correct Arctic Cat alignment bar or equivalent is necessary for checking the offset, alignment and parallelism. Different alignment bars are used for the various models. Check with your Arctic Cat dealer for the availability of the correct alignment bar for your machine.

> *WARNING*
> ***Never*** *lean into the snowmobile's engine compartment while wearing a scarf or other loose clothing when the engine is running or when attempting to start the engine. If the scarf or clothing should catch in the drive belt or clutch, severe injury or death could occur.*

Removal/Installation

1. Open the hood.
2. Remove the cover from the drive pulley, belt and driven pulley.
3. Check the drive belt for manufacturer's markings (**Figure 7**), so that during installation it will run in the correct direction. If the belt is not marked, draw an arrow on the belt pointing forward or install a new belt.
4. Push against the driven pulley (**Figure 7**), rotating it clockwise to separate the pulley halves. Roll the belt over the driven pulley and remove it.

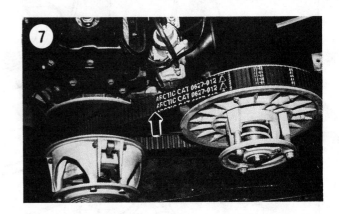

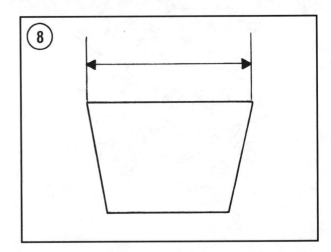

5. Inspect the drive belt as described in this chapter.

6. Perform the drive belt alignment procedure as described in this chapter.

7. Reverse Steps 1-4 and install the drive belt. If installing the original belt, make sure you install it so the manufacturer's marks on the belt, or those made before removal, all face forward. When installing a new belt, install it so that you can read the belt identification marks while standing on the left side of the machine and looking into the engine compartment (**Figure 7**).

Inspection

The belt should be inspected at the intervals listed in Chapter 3.

1. Remove the drive belt as described in this chapter.

2. Measure the width of the drive belt at its widest point (**Figure 8**). Replace the belt if the width is less than the minimum listed in **Table 1**.

3. Measure the circumference of the drive belt with a tape measure (**Figure 9**). Replace the belt if the outside circumference is not within the limits listed in **Table 1**.

4. Visually inspect the belt for the following conditions:

   a. *Frayed edge*—Check the sides of the belt for a frayed edge cord (**Figure 10**). This indicates drive belt misalignment. Drive belt misalignment can be caused by incorrect pulley alignment and loose engine mounting bolts.

   b. *Worn narrow in one section*—Examine the belt for a section worn narrower (**Figure 11**) than the rest of the belt. This condition is caused by excessive belt slippage due to a stuck track or to abnormally high engine idle speed.

   c. *Belt disintegration*—Drive belt disintegration (**Figure 12**) is caused by severe belt wear or misalignment. Disintegration can also be caused by the use of an incorrect belt.

   d. *Sheared cogs*—Sheared cogs (**Figure 13**) are usually caused by violent drive pulley engagement. This is an indication of a defective or improperly installed drive pulley.

5. Replace a worn or damaged belt immediately. Always carry a spare belt on your snowmobile for emergency purposes.

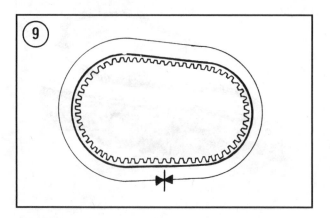

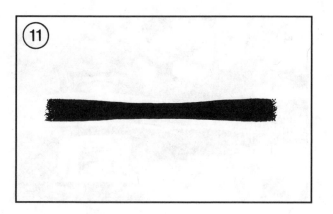

13

Drive Belt Deflection

Perform this procedure whenever a new drive belt is installed.

1. Open and secure the hood.
2. Remove the belt guard.
3. Check that the drive belt is resting at the top of the driven pulley (**Figure 14**).
4. Place a straightedge across the drive belt and compress the belt with a ruler placed midway between the pulleys.
5. Press the ruler down (**Figure 15**) until the slack is just removed. Do not press the belt hard enough to push the belt into the pulley groove.
6. Read the belt deflection at the bottom of the straightedge (**Figure 15**).
7. The belt deflection measured in Step 6 should be within the limits listed in **Table 2**.
8A. On all except some 1997 and later models, adjust the belt deflection as follows:

   a. Remove the belt and driven pulley as described in this chapter.
   b. Separate the pulley halves as described in this chapter.
   c. Change the thickness of adjust washers (12, **Figure 6**), as necessary, to provide the correct belt deflection. The adjust washers are located between the driven pulley sheaves.
   d. Reassemble and install the driven pulley as described in this chapter.

8B. Belt deflection of 1997 ZR 580 EFI and some other late models is externally adjusted as follows.

   a. Squeeze the adjustment arms together until they release from their locking pockets.
   b. Turn the adjustment arms and plate as necessary to provide the correct belt deflection.
   c. Release the adjustment arms and make sure they correctly latch into the locking pockets. The latching pockets are located every 90°.

9. After making any adjustment, rotate the driven pulley to relocate the belt in the pulley grooves. Recheck adjustment.

Drive Belt Alignment

The offset and parallelism of the drive pulley to the driven pulley must be correctly maintained for good performance and long belt life. It is necessary to use the correct Arctic Cat alignment bar for checking the alignment and parallelism. Different alignment bars are used for various

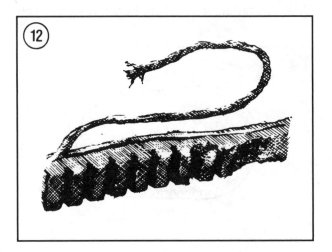

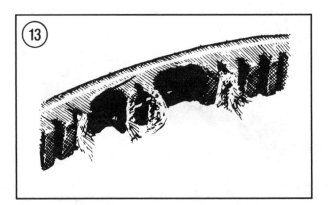

models. Check with your Arctic Cat dealer for the availability of the correct alignment bar for your machine.

1. Remove the drive belt as described in this chapter.

2. To check offset, place the alignment bar so that it rests over the center of the drive pulley and against the side of the driven pulley sheave (**Figure 16**).

3. Make sure the alignment bar is against the driven pulley sheave (A and B, **Figure 16**).

4. Measure the clearance between the bar and the inside edge of the drive pulley (C, **Figure 16**).

5. If there is no clearance (C, **Figure 16**) or the measured clearance is more than 1.5 mm (0.060 in.), correct the offset as follows:

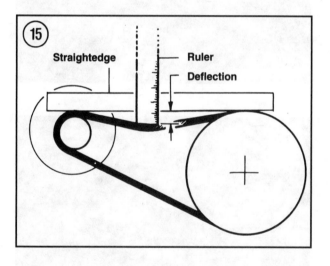

a. Remove the driven pulley as described in this chapter.

b. Increase or reduce the thickness of shims (**Figure 17**) located on the shaft, as necessary.

c. Install the driven pulley.

6. To check parallelism, make sure the alignment bar contacts the driven pulley sheave (A and B, **Figure 16**).

7. Measure the distance between the alignment bar and the rear edge of the drive pulley (D, **Figure 16**) and between the front of the pulley and the alignment bar (E, **Figure 16**).

8. The difference between the measurements at the front and rear of the drive pulley should be less than 1.6 mm (0.062 in.). Larger differences indicate the pulleys are not parallel.

9. The procedure to correct parallelism differs for different models. If the parallelism is incorrect, refer to the following.

   a. Before changing the engine alignment, make sure that the mounts are tight and in good condition.

   b. On most models, add or remove shims located on the left rear engine mount to alter engine crankshaft alignment.

   c. On air-cooled Z440 models, loosen the nuts on the torque link (**Figure 18**). Move the nuts, as required, to relocate the engine to correct parallelism.

13

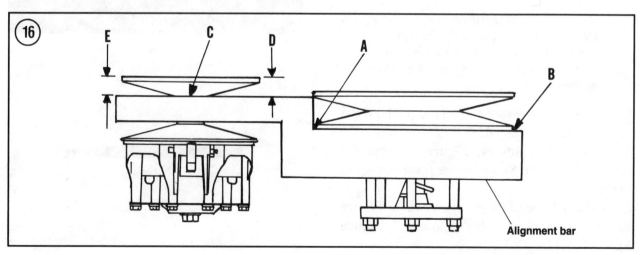

10. Reinstall the drive belt as described in this chapter.

NOTE
If offset or parallelism is adjusted, it is necessary to check drivebelt deflection.

DRIVE PULLEY SERVICE

The drive pulley is mounted on the left end of the engine crankshaft. It is necessary to use a special clutch puller (**Figure 19**) to remove the clutch from the crankshaft. Different pullers are used for various models. Check with your Arctic Cat dealer for the availability of the correct puller for your machine.

Cam Arm Removal

The weighted cam arms (7, **Figure 5**) located in the drive pulley govern the engagement and shifting of the drive clutch. The following procedure can be used to remove and install the cam arms without removing the drive pulley.

1. Remove the drive belt as described in this chapter.
2. Compress the movable sheave and cover (2 and 15, **Figure 5**) toward the engine about 2.5 cm (1 in.).
3. Insert a bar between the movable sheave and the spider (2 and 20, **Figure 5**).

WARNING
Do not run the engine with the belt removed or with the bar temporarily located between the spider and the movable sheave.

4. Release the pressure and let the bar hold the clutch partially engaged.
5. Remove the nuts (4, **Figure 5**) from the screws (3, **Figure 5**). Leave the pivot screws in place.
6. Withdraw one of the pivot screws (3, **Figure 5**) and its weight assembly (5, 6 and 7, **Figure 5**).

7. Install the new weight assembly (5, 6 and 7, **Figure 5**) and its pivot screw. The head of the pivot screw must be toward the direction of rotation.

NOTE
*Always install a new nut (4, **Figure 5**) when assembling. Be sure the head of the pivot screw is in the direction of rotation as shown.*

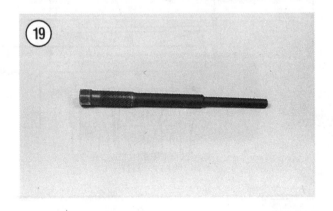

8. Install the nut on the newly installed screw and tighten until it just contacts the shoulder of the cam arm pivot screw (3, **Figure 5**), then tighten the nut an additional 1/8 turn.

9. Repeat Steps 6-8 for the remaining weight assemblies and pivot screws (3, 5, 6 and 7, **Figure 5**).

10. Compress the movable sheave and cover (2 and 15, **Figure 5**) toward the engine and remove

the bar, which is temporarily located between the movable sheave and the spider.

Removal

A special puller will be required to pull the drive pulley from the crankshaft and a special wrench is also available to hold the clutch while removing and installing the drive pulley.

1. Remove the drive belt as described in this chapter.

2. Remove the pulley retaining bolt and lockwasher from the center of the pulley cover.

3. Remove the plug (**Figure 20**) from the side of the body.

4. Oil the threads and apply grease to the end of the puller tool and insert the tool (**Figure 21**) through the plug hole in the body.

5. Thread the puller tool into the end of the drive pulley. Make sure the threads fully engage the threads in the pulley sheave.

6. Use a strap wrench, the special clutch holding wrench or an equivalent tool to hold the drive pulley and tighten the puller with an impact wrench (**Figure 22**) or breaker bar.

7. Tighten the puller tool to break the drive pulley loose from the crankshaft taper.

NOTE
It may be necessary to rap sharply on the head of the puller to shock the drive pulley loose from the crankshaft.

8. When the drive pulley is loose, remove the puller tool.

9. Remove the drive pulley assembly.

10. Account for the aluminum and then the urethane spacers inside the fixed sheave hub.

Disassembly

WARNING
The drive pulley is under spring pressure. Attempting to disassemble or reassemble the drive pulley without the use

13

of special tools may cause severe personal injury. If you do not have access to the necessary tools, have the service performed by a dealer or qualified snowmobile mechanic.

1A. On models with six screws retaining the cover, use a felt-tip pen to mark the cover, spider and the sliding sheave (**Figure 23**). Mark each component to identify correct alignment when assembling.

1B. On models with nine screws retaining the cover, the cover, spider and sliding sheave should have marks (**Figure 24**). If marks are not visible, mark the cover, spider and sliding sheave (**Figure 23**).

WARNING
The cover plate is spring-loaded. To prevent it from flying off during removal, the plate must be held as described in Step 2. In addition to physical injury, parts may be damaged by improper disassembly procedures.

2. Remove the cover as follows.

   a. Loosen all the screws attaching the cover.

   b. Remove every other screw attaching the cover. On covers attached with nine screws remove only five of the screws.

   c. Hold the cover down tightly and remove the remaining screws.

   d. Slowly release the cover after all of the attaching screws are removed (**Figure 25**).

   e. Lift the cover and spring from the pulley assembly.

NOTE
Special tools are available to hold the drive pulley, turn the jam nut and turn the spider while disassembling and assembling.

3. Remove the spider as follows.

   a. Bolt the clutch holding fixture (part No. 0644-058 or equivalent) to a workbench or stand so it is secure (**Figure 26**).

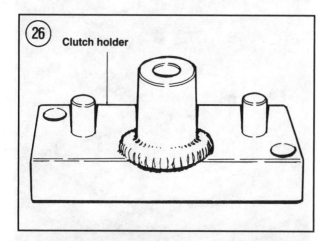

26 Clutch holder

27

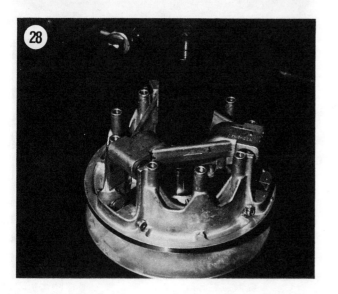

28

   b. Position the fixed sheave onto the clutch holder fixture and secure the sheave assembly with the retaining nut and washer.

   c. Use a torch to heat the jam nut to soften the Loctite bond (**Figure 27**).

   d. Use the special deep socket (part No. 0644-138 or equivalent) to remove the lock nut *counterclockwise* (**Figure 28**).

   e. Use a torch to heat the threaded center of the spider to soften the Loctite bond (**Figure 29**).

   f. Use the special removal tool (part No. 0644-085 or equivalent) to turn the spider *counterclockwise* (**Figure 30**).

   g. Remove the bolt and washer holding the assembly to the special clutch holding fixture.

   h. Lift the spider from the drive pulley assembly.

NOTE
*Do not lose, damage or mix washers shown in **Figure 31** with other washers.*

4. Remove the washers (**Figure 31**). Lift the sliding sheave from the pulley.

5. Disassemble the spider roller and bushing assembly (**Figure 32**) from each arm of the spider as follows.

   a. Use pliers to pull the buttons from each side of one roller.

   b. Use a punch to drive the pin from the roller.

13

29

NOTE
*When removing the roller, be sure that all parts are removed from the spider and are not lost. On some models, there will be a washer at each side of the roller; while on other models, a clip (**Figure 32**) is used instead.*

c. Remove the roller and washers or clip.

NOTE
Keep the parts for each assembly separate from the other similar roller assemblies.

d. Repeat substeps 5a-c for the other roller assemblies.

6. Remove the cam arm weight assemblies as follows.

a. Remove the nut (**Figure 33**) from one pivot screw.

b. Remove the pivot screw, weight and washers (or clip) (**Figure 34**).

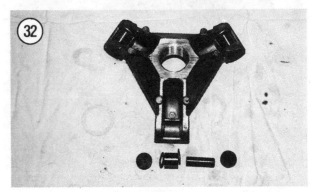

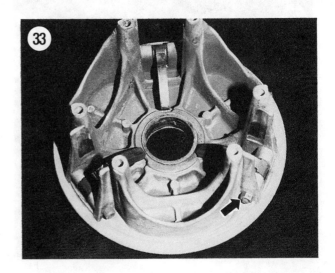

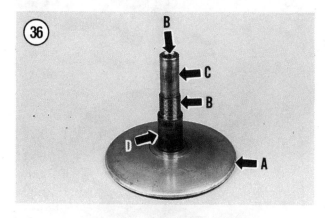

NOTE
Keep the parts for each assembly separate from the other similar weight assemblies.

c. Repeat substeps 6a-b for the other weight assemblies.

Inspection

CAUTION
Do not scratch parts by cleaning with steel wool or a wire brush. Clean parts with a suitable cleaning solvent only.

1. Clean all parts thoroughly and dry with compressed air.
2. Remove all Loctite residue from all threads.
3. Check all parts carefully for cracks or damage. Do not install any parts that are cracked.
4. Check the drive belt surfaces (**Figure 35**) of the sheaves for corrosion, burrs, nicks or any buildup of rubber. For proper operation, the surfaces must be *clean* and smooth.
5. Check the threads (B, **Figure 36**) in the fixed sheave for damage. A machine shop may be able to repair damaged threads.
6. Visually inspect the bushing surfaces (C and D, **Figure 36**) of the fixed sheave. Damage to these areas may cause the clutch to operate improperly. Make sure the cover and the sliding sheave slide easily on the hub of the fixed sheave.
7. Use a micrometer to measure the outside diameter of both bushing surfaces (C and D, **Figure 36**) on the fixed sheave. Record these diameters (**Figure 37**).
8. Measure the inside diameter of the bushing in the cover (**Figure 38**, typical). Record this diameter.
9. Subtract the journal diameter (C, **Figure 36**) from the bushing diameter (**Figure 38**) to determine the clearance.
10A. On models with six bolts retaining the cover, the clearance should not exceed 0.76 mm (0.030 in.). Install a new bushing and/or fixed sheave to reduce clearance.

13

10B. On models with nine bolts retaining the cover, the clearance should not exceed 0.20 mm (0.008 in.). Install a new bushing and/or fixed sheave to reduce clearance. The bushing can be pressed from the cover after removing the snap ring (22, **Figure 5**).

11. Measure the inside diameter of the bushing in the sliding sheave (**Figure 39**, typical). Record this diameter.

12. Subtract the journal diameter (D, **Figure 36**), measured and recorded in Step 7, from the bushing diameter (**Figure 39**).

13A. On models with six bolts retaining the cover, the clearance should not exceed 0.76 mm (0.030 in.). Install a new sliding sheave and/or fixed sheave to reduce the clearance.

13B. On models with nine bolts retaining the cover, the clearance should not exceed 0.20 mm (0.008 in.). Install a new bushing and/or fixed sheave to reduce clearance. The bushing can be pressed from the sliding sheave after removing the snap ring (19, **Figure 5**).

14. Visually check each of the cam arm weights for wear or damage. The bushings (B, **Figure 40**) in the cam arms can be replaced, but the weight should be replaced if the cam surface (C, **Figure 40**) is damaged.

NOTE
The weights may have been changed to tailor clutch operation for a specific application, but all three cam arm weights should be exactly the same. Differences will cause the unit to be out of balance.

15. The weight and shape of the cam arm weights (**Figure 40**) determine the clutch engagement and the pattern of the speed ratio change. Refer to **Table 7** for the part number and weight originally installed.

16. Check the drive pulley spring as follows:

a. Inspect the spring for cracks or distortion.

NOTE
A spring other than the one originally installed may have been installed for a specific application. If difficulties or im-

proper shifting occur, the list of springs originally installed may be helpful when searching for the correct replacement.

b. Compare the identifying color with the color of the original spring listed in **Table 4**.

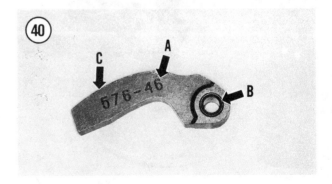

c. Use a spring tester (**Figure 41**) to check the spring pressure at specified compressed height as listed in **Table 5**.

17. Inspect the buttons (A, **Figure 42**) and the area of the sliding sheave where the buttons rub (B, **Figure 42**). Replace the parts, as necessary. The buttons should be replaced in sets of six.

Assembly

Refer to **Figure 43** for this procedure.

1. Install the cam arm weights as follows:

NOTE
The three pivot screws that secure the cam arm weights must be installed so the heads of the screws are toward the direction of rotation. See Figure 44.

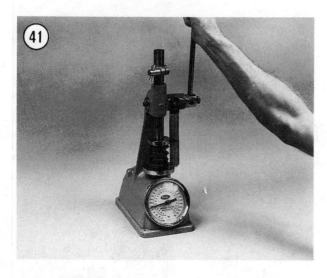

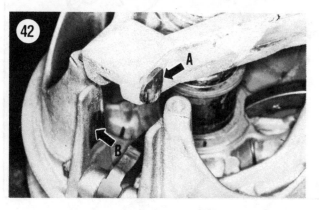

a. Insert a pivot screw (A, **Figure 44**) through the attaching lug from the direction shown.

b. If equipped with two washers, install one of the washers on the edge of the screw (B, **Figure 44**), then position the cam arm weight and second washer between the mounting lugs and push through the pivot screw.

c. If equipped with the clip shown in **Figure 34**, position the clip around the weight. Position the clip and weight between the mounting lugs and push through the pivot screw.

CAUTION
Always install new self-locking nuts as described in substep 1d. Do not install the old nuts.

d. Apply Loctite 271 (red) on the threads of a *new* locknut. Tighten the locknut until it bottoms against the mounting lug, but do not overtighten (**Figure 45**).

e. Pivot the weight back and forth to make sure the weight moves easily and smoothly. If the locknut is too tight, it will cause the weight to bind and stick.

f. Repeat substeps 1a-e and install the other weight assemblies.

2. Assemble the roller and bearing assembly (**Figure 32**) in the spider as follows:

a. Insert a pin partway through the spider (**Figure 46**).

NOTE
The washers (11, Figure 43) installed in substeps 2b and 2d may have one metal side and one fiber side. If so, install with the fiber side against the roller and the metal side against the spider.

b. Install one of the washers on the edge of the pin (**Figure 46**).

c. Position the roller and bearing assembly between the sides of the spider and push the pin in far enough to hold the roller assembly in place.

13

d. Insert the last washer between the roller and the spider (**Figure 47**) and push the pin into the arms of the spider. The pin must be centered in the spider.

e. Repeat substeps 2a-2d and install the other roller assemblies.

NOTE
The spider must move easily between the arms of the sliding pulley without play. If the buttons have alignment marks, install so the two dots on the face of the

button are aligned vertically as shown in ***Figure 48***. *If the buttons are not correctly installed, the spider will bind.*

f. Insert the six guide buttons in the bores at the ends of the roller pin. The buttons should fit tightly and should not be deformed.

3. Install the sliding sheave onto the fixed sheave (**Figure 49**).

4. Install the washers (8, **Figure 43**) onto the hub of the fixed sheave (A, **Figure 50**).

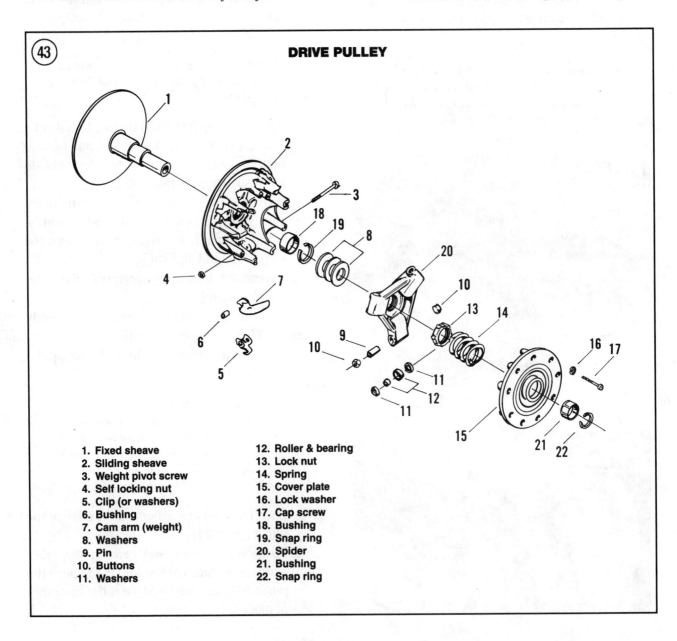

43   **DRIVE PULLEY**

1. **Fixed sheave**	12. **Roller & bearing**
2. **Sliding sheave**	13. **Lock nut**
3. **Weight pivot screw**	14. **Spring**
4. **Self locking nut**	15. **Cover plate**
5. **Clip (or washers)**	16. **Lock washer**
6. **Bushing**	17. **Cap screw**
7. **Cam arm (weight)**	18. **Bushing**
8. **Washers**	19. **Snap ring**
9. **Pin**	20. **Spider**
10. **Buttons**	21. **Bushing**
11. **Washers**	22. **Snap ring**

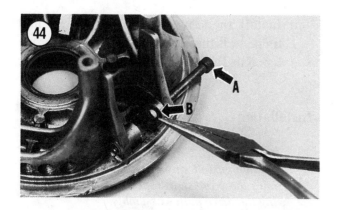

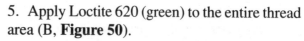

5. Apply Loctite 620 (green) to the entire thread area (B, **Figure 50**).

6. Secure the fixed sheave onto the clutch holding fixture (part No. 0644-058 or equivalent) so the fixed sheave will not move.

CAUTION
The drive pulley is balanced as a unit. The spider, sliding sheave and cover must be assembled as they were originally assembled to maintain that bal-

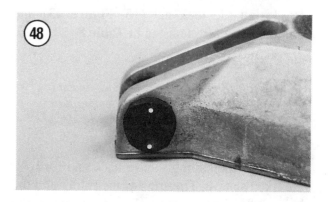

13

*ance. On models with a six-bolt cover, the parts must be marked as shown in **Figure 23** before disassembling. Later units with nine-bolt covers are equipped with marks (**Figure 51**).*

7. Install the spider, aligning the marks on the spider and sliding sheave.

8. Use the special tool to tighten the spider (**Figure 30**) to the torque listed in **Table 8**.

9. Apply Loctite 620 (green) to the thread area above the spider.

10. Install the lock nut (13, **Figure 43**) and tighten to the torque listed in **Table 8**.

> *NOTE*
> *Allow the Loctite on the spider and spider lock nut to cure at room temperature for 24 hours before installing the drive pulley assembly.*

11. Move the sliding sheave back and forth on the fixed sheave. The arms of the spider and the hub of the fixed sheave should not cause the sliding sheave to bind. If operation is not smooth, determine the cause and correct it before continuing.

12. Install the spring (**Figure 52**).

13. Install the cover as follows:

   a. Position the cover onto the spring.

> *CAUTION*
> *On models equipped with a six-bolt cover, the parts must be marked (**Figure 23**) before disassembling. Later units with a nine-bolt cover are equipped with marks (**Figure 53**).*

   b. Compress the cover against the spring, aligning the marks on the cover with those on the spider and sliding sheave. Hold the cover against the sliding sheave while installing the screws.

   c. On models with six screws retaining the cover, coat the threads of the retaining screws with Loctite 242 (blue).

   d. Install the cover retaining screws and tighten all the screws evenly to the torque listed in **Table 8** before releasing the cover.

Installation

> *CAUTION*
> *Do not install any antiseize lubricant onto the crankshaft taper when installing the drive pulley assembly.*

1. Clean the crankshaft taper with lacquer thinner or electrical contact cleaner.

2. Slide the drive pulley (**Figure 54**) onto the crankshaft.

3. Install the urethane spacer and then the aluminum spacer into the hub of the fixed sheave.

> *CAUTION*
> *Use only hand tools when installing and tightening the pulley retaining bolt.*

Never use an impact wrench to install this bolt.

4. Install the retaining bolt and lockwasher.

5. Tighten the drive pulley retaining bolt to the torque listed in **Table 8**.

6. Check the pulley offset and parallelism as described in this chapter. Make any necessary adjustments.

7. Install the drive belt as described in this chapter.

DRIVEN PULLEY SERVICE

The driven pulley is mounted on the left end of the chaincase input shaft. Refer to **Figure 55**

or **Figure 56** when performing procedures in this section.

Removal

1. Remove the drive belt as described in this chapter.

2. Apply the parking brake to lock the jackshaft.

3. Loosen and remove the driven pulley bolt (**Figure 57**). Do not lose the shims from the end of the bolt.

4. Separate the driven sheaves slightly and remove the stub shaft (**Figure 58**).

5. Pull the driven pulley from the shaft. If necessary, use the special puller (part No. 0644-110).

6. Remove the key (A, **Figure 59**).

> *NOTE*
> *The shim(s) installed on the shaft behind the driven pulley (**Figure 60**) are used to adjust pulley offset. Be sure to install the same shims before installing the driven pulley.*

Installation

1. Make sure the offset adjusting shims are installed on the shaft (**Figure 60**).

2. Install the key in the keyway.

3. Apply a small amount of antiseize to the driven shaft and key.

4. Position the stub shaft in the pulley, then slide the driven pulley onto the driven shaft.

5. Install the driven pulley bolt and the original number of shims (**Figure 57**). Tighten the bolt to the torque listed in **Table 8**.

6. Check the pulley offset and parallelism as described in this chapter and adjust if necessary.

7. Check the driven pulley free play on the shaft. The pulley should be able to float on the shaft, but it should not have more than 1.5 mm (0.060 in.) play. If play is not correct, adjust as follows.

13

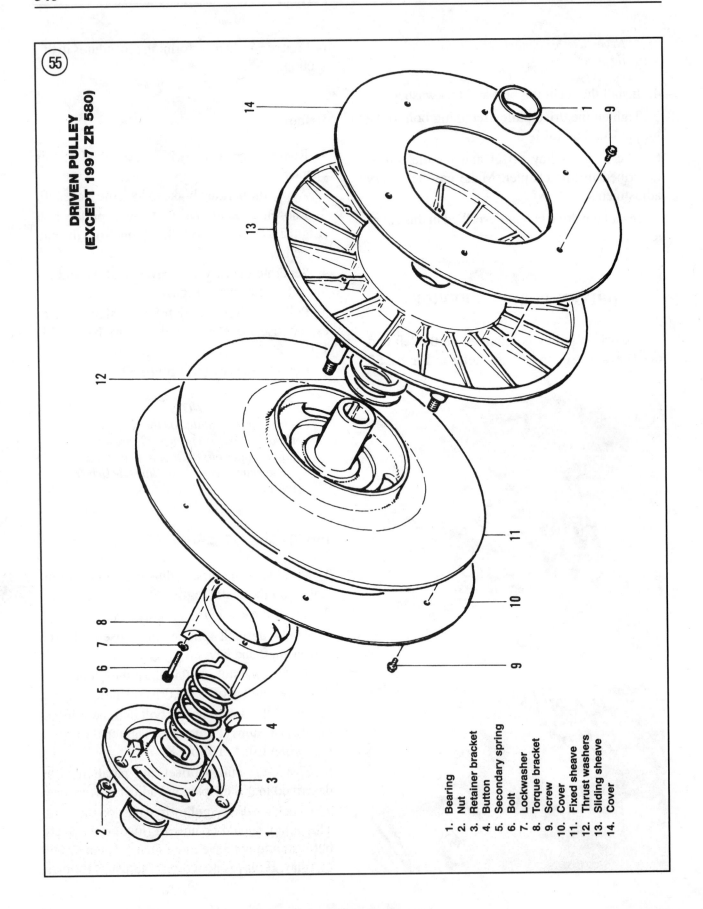

55

DRIVEN PULLEY
(EXCEPT 1997 ZR 580)

1. Bearing
2. Nut
3. Retainer bracket
4. Button
5. Secondary spring
6. Bolt
7. Lockwasher
8. Torque bracket
9. Screw
10. Cover
11. Fixed sheave
12. Thrust washers
13. Sliding sheave
14. Cover

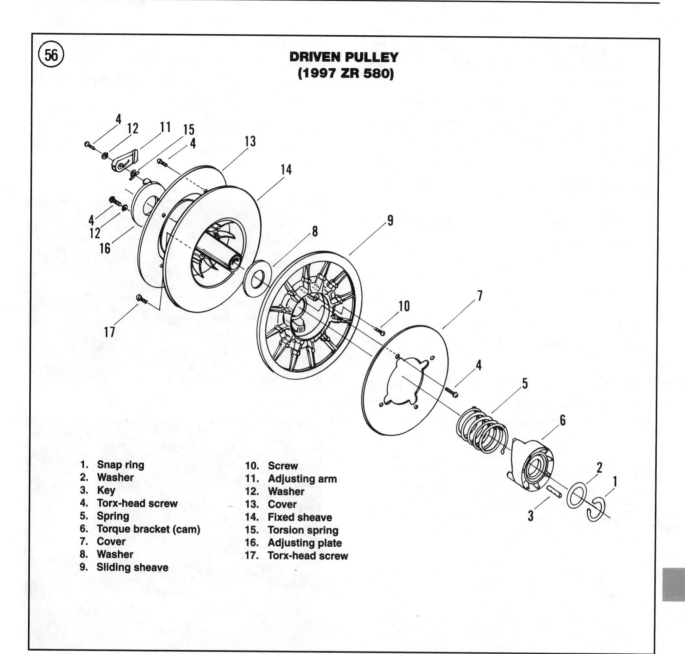

**DRIVEN PULLEY
(1997 ZR 580)**

1. Snap ring
2. Washer
3. Key
4. Torx-head screw
5. Spring
6. Torque bracket (cam)
7. Cover
8. Washer
9. Sliding sheave
10. Screw
11. Adjusting arm
12. Washer
13. Cover
14. Fixed sheave
15. Torsion spring
16. Adjusting plate
17. Torx-head screw

13

a. If there is too much play, remove the shims from the retaining bolt (**Figure 57**) outside the pulley.

b. If the pulley is tight on the shaft, add shims under the retaining bolt (**Figure 57**) as required to provide slight play.

8. Inspect the belt as described in this chapter. Install the drive belt if it is in good condition or replace the belt.

9. Check the belt tension as described in·this chapter.

Disassembly (Except 1997 ZR 580)

Refer to **Figure 55** when performing the following procedures for the driven pulley used on these models.

1. Before disassembling, use a felt tip pen to mark all of the components to identify correct alignment when assembling (**Figure 61**).

NOTE
*The retainer bracket is equipped with five holes for the spring adjustment (B, **Figure 61**). Identify the hole used when disassembling and record or mark it before removing the retainer bracket in Step 2.*

CAUTION
The retainer bracket is under spring pressure. Remove the nuts securing the bracket evenly to prevent damage. Hold the bracket to prevent it from flying off.

2. Hold the retainer bracket with one hand and loosen all three of the nuts retaining the bracket evenly. Continue to hold the retainer until all three nuts are removed.

3. Slowly release pressure on the retainer bracket until spring pressure is released, then remove the bracket (**Figure 62**).

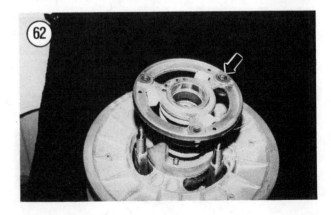

4. Remove the spring (A, **Figure 63**).

5. Remove the three screws (B, **Figure 63**) attaching the torque bracket (cam), then remove the torque bracket.

6. Separate the sliding and fixed sheaves (**Figure 64**).

> *NOTE*
> *Do not lose or damage the washers located between the sheaves. These are used to adjust belt deflection. If you are installing a new belt, check and adjust the drive belt deflection as described in this chapter.*

7. Remove the washers from between the sheaves (**Figure 65**).

8. If necessary, the covers can be removed from the sheaves after removing the screws. Covers are not used on 1996 and 1997 ZR 440 models.

9. To disassemble roller assembly on 1996 and 1997 ZR 440 models, remove the screws securing each roller assembly to the retainer plate.

10. To disassemble roller assembly on 1998 models, drive out the roll pin, then remove pin, washer and roller.

> *NOTE*
> *Keep the parts for each assembly separate.*

Inspection (Except 1997 ZR 580)

> *CAUTION*
> *Do not scratch parts by cleaning with steel wool or a wire brush. Clean parts with a suitable cleaning solvent only.*

1. Clean all parts thoroughly and dry with compressed air.

2. Check all parts carefully for cracks or damage. Do not install any parts that are cracked.

3. Check the drive belt surfaces (**Figure 66**) of the sheaves for corrosion, burrs, nicks or any buildup of rubber. For proper operation, the surfaces must be *clean* and smooth.

4. Check the torque bracket ramps (**Figure 67**) for wear, scoring, gouging or other signs of damage. If damage is not too severe, you can smooth the surface with No. 400 sandpaper. Refer to **Table 6** for original application.

13

5A. If the retainer bracket is equipped with buttons (**Figure 68**), inspect and service as follows:

   a. Inspect the buttons for wear.

   b. Slight scratching can be smoothed with emery cloth. Do not use a file.

   c. If any button is severely damaged, install a new set of three buttons.

   d. Buttons can be pulled from their locating holes with pliers.

   e. Press new buttons into the retainer (**Figure 68**).

5B. If the retainer bracket is equipped with rollers (**Figure 69**), inspect and service as follows.

   a. Check the rollers for freedom of rotation and any other damage.

   b. If it is necessary to remove a roller assembly, remove the screw (**Figure 69**), lift the shaft and roller from the retainer bracket.

   c. Install new parts as necessary. If a roller is damaged, check the condition of the ramps on the torque bracket.

6. Check the condition and measure the inside diameter of the bushing (**Figure 70**) in the retainer bracket. Record the measured diameter.

7. Check the condition and measure the outside diameter of the hub on the fixed sheave (**Figure 71**).

8. Subtract the hub outside diameter measured in Step 7 from the bushing inside diameter measured in Step 6. The difference (clearance) should not exceed 0.5 mm (0.020 in.), but the retainer should move easily on the hub.

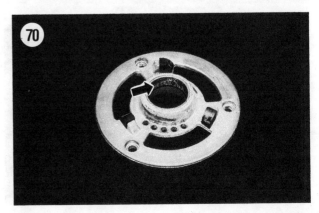

9. If necessary, the bushing can be replaced. Use the proper size driver to remove and install the bushing. Coat the outer surface of the bushing with Loctite 271 before pressing it into position. Check the fit of the new bushing to the hub.

10. Check the condition and measure the inside diameter of the bushing (**Figure 72**) in the sliding sheave. Record the measured diameter.

11. Check the condition and measure the outside diameter of the hub on the belt side of the fixed sheave (**Figure 73**).

12. Subtract the hub outside diameter measured in Step 11 from the bushing inside diameter measured in Step 10. The difference (clearance) should not exceed 0.5 mm (0.020 in.), but the installed bushing should move easily on the hub.

13. If necessary, the bushing can be replaced. Use the proper size driver to remove and install the bushing. Coat the outer surface of the bushing with Loctite 271 before pressing it into position. Check the fit of the new bushing to the hub.

14. Inspect the spring (**Figure 74**) for cracks or distortion. Install a new spring if necessary. Refer to **Table 6** for original application.

NOTE
Spring failure is usually caused by the constant twisting action that occurs during normal clutch operation. As the spring in the driven pulley weakens, it will allow the driven sheaves to separate quicker. This condition can be noticed when riding up steep grades or in deep snow. The machine will be slower and have less pulling power.

Assembly (Except 1997 ZR 580)

1. To install roller assembly on 1996 and 1997 ZR 440 models, proceed as follows:

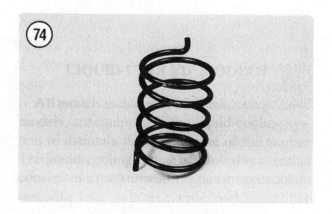

13

a. Position the roller pin and washer in retainer bracket. The washer must be on outer side of the roller.

b. Secure the pin in place with taper-head screw.

2. To install roller assembly on 1998 models, proceed as follows:

a. Position the roller, pin and washer in retainer bracket. The washer must be on outer side of roller.

b. Secure the pin in place with roll pin. Drive in the roll pin until it is flush with surface of the retainer bracket.

3. Install the sheave covers if they were removed. Coat the threads of the attaching screws with Loctite 242 (blue) before installing.

4. Place the fixed sheave on the workbench so the belt surface faces down.

5. Position the torque bracket on the fixed sheave with the previously affixed marks on the two parts aligned.

NOTE
If marks are not present, align the degree mark on the torque bracket with the part number on the fixed sheave.

6. Install, but do not tighten, the three Allen head screws (B, **Figure 63**) securing the torque bracket to the sheave.

7. Turn the fixed sheave assembly over and install the adjusting washers (12, **Figure 55**) that were previously used. These washers (**Figure 65**) adjust belt tension and may require changes later.

8. Install the sliding sheave over the fixed sheave, with the previously affixed marks aligned.

NOTE
The pulley can be held in Step 7 by placing the assembly on a roll of duct tape.

9. Position the assembly with the torque bracket side of the fixed sheave up.

10. Place the spring (A, **Figure 63**) over the fixed sheave hub and hook the end of the spring into the hole in the stationary sheave.

11. Hook the upper end of the spring in the center (3rd) hole of the retainer (**Figure 75**).

12. Install the retainer bracket as follows:

a. Hold the sheaves to prevent them from moving.

b. Twist the retainer bracket approximately 120° clockwise (**Figure 76**).

NOTE
If the holes in the retainer bracket are not aligned with the studs, it may be necessary to relocate the end of the spring (A, Figure 63). Check the previously affixed alignment marks (Figure 61) on the retainer bracket and pulley sheaves.

c. Push the retainer plate onto the studs and install the three locknuts. Tighten the nuts to the torque listed in **Table 8**.

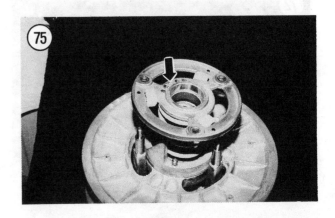

13. Finish installing the torque bracket as follows:

   a. Move the torque bracket, as necessary, until it contacts all buttons or rollers of the retainer plate.

   b. Tighten the three torque bracket retaining screws securely (**Figure 77**).

Disassembly/Inspection/Assembly (1997 ZR 580)

Refer to **Figure 78** when performing the following procedures for the driven pulley.

1. Before disassembling, use a felt-tip pen to mark across all the components to identify correct alignment when assembling.

2. Push down on the torque bracket and remove the snap ring (1, **Figure 78**).

NOTE
Identify the location of the spring end in the cam. The cam has four holes and the standard position is in the second hole from the left.

3. Remove the washer (2, **Figure 78**) torque bracket (6, **Figure 78**) and key (3, **Figure 78**).

4. Remove the spring (5, **Figure 78**).

5. Separate the sliding and fixed sheaves (9 and 14, **Figure 78**).

6. Loosen and remove the Torx-head screws (4, **Figure 78**), then remove the adjusting plate (16, **Figure 78**).

7. Remove the three adjusting pins.

8. If necessary, remove the screws attaching the covers to the stationary and fixed sheaves.

9. Clean all parts thoroughly and dry with compressed air.

10. Check all parts carefully for cracks or damage. Do not install any parts that are cracked.

11. Check the drive belt surfaces of the sheaves for corrosion, burrs, nicks or any buildup of rubber. For proper operation, the surfaces must be *clean* and smooth.

12. Check the ramps of the torque bracket (6, **Figure 78**) for wear, scoring, gouging or other signs of damage. If damage is not too severe, the surface can be smoothed with No. 400 sandpaper. Refer to **Table 6** for original application.

13. Inspect and service the buttons, as follows:

   a. Inspect the buttons for wear.

   b. Slight scratching can be smoothed with emery cloth. Do not file the buttons.

   c. If any button is severely damaged, install a new set of 3 buttons.

   d. You can drive the buttons from their locating holes using a hammer and punch and working from the outside of the sheave.

   e. Press new buttons into the retaining holes.

14. If necessary, remove and install the large bearing as follows:

   a. Remove the Torx-head screws and washers retaining the bearing.

   b. Carefully pry the bearing from its bore.

   c. Clean the bearing bore.

   d. Apply Loctite High-Temperature Super Bond to the bearing bore.

   e. Use a piloted driver of the proper size and drive the bearing into the bore.

   f. Remove any excess bonding material using acetone.

13

g. Allow the bonding material to cure at room temperature for 24 hours.

15. If necessary, remove and install the small bearing as follows:

    a. Remove the snap ring.

b. Use the proper size driver and drive the bearing from the sliding sheave.

c. Use a piloted driver of the proper size and drive the bearing into the bore.

d. Install the snap ring.

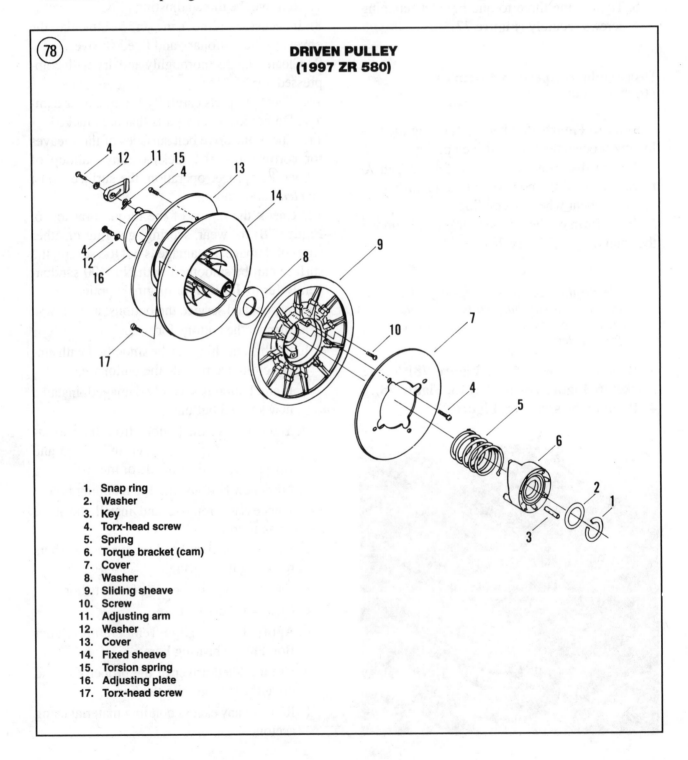

⑦⑧

DRIVEN PULLEY
(1997 ZR 580)

1. Snap ring
2. Washer
3. Key
4. Torx-head screw
5. Spring
6. Torque bracket (cam)
7. Cover
8. Washer
9. Sliding sheave
10. Screw
11. Adjusting arm
12. Washer
13. Cover
14. Fixed sheave
15. Torsion spring
16. Adjusting plate
17. Torx-head screw

16. To assemble the driven pulley, reverse the disassembly procedure while noting the following:

   a. Apply Loctite 242 (blue) to all screw threads.

   b. To properly install the torque bracket (6, **Figure 78**), first install the key (3, **Figure 78**). Place the torque bracket on the spring with the outer end of the spring inserted into the middle hole in the cam. While holding the torque bracket, turn the movable sheave counterclockwise approximately 120° to tension the spring. Push down the torque bracket so it bottoms on the buttons. Install the washer and snap ring.

NOTE
Install the snap ring so the sharp side is out, away from the washer.

   c. Be sure alignment marks are aligned.

Table 1 DRIVE BELT SPECIFICATIONS

Model	Part No.	Width mm (in.)	Circumference cm (in.)
1990			
Prowler, El Tigre EXT	0227-032	34.1-35.7 (1.344-1.406)	110.5-111.1 (43.50-43.74)
1991-1992			
Prowler, Cougar, El Tigre EXT	0227-032	34.1-35.7 (1.344-1.406)	110.5-111.1 (43.50-43.74)
1993			
Prowler, Cougar	0227-032	34.1-35.7 (1.344-1.406)	110.5-111.1 (43.50-43.74)
440 ZR	0627-009	34-36 (1.339-1.417)	120-121 (47.24-47.64)
EXT 550, EXT 580	0627-012	34-36 (1.339-1.417)	120-121 (47.24-47.64)
580 ZR	0627-009	34-36 (1.339-1.417)	120-121 (47.24-47.64)
1994			
Cougar, Prowler	0227-103	34-36 (1.339-1.417)	110.3-111.1 (43.43-43.74)
ZR 440, EXT 580, ZR 580	0627-012	34-36 (1.339-1.417)	120-121 (47.24-47.64)
1995			
Cougar, Prowler 2-Up	0627-012	34-36 (1.339-1.417)	120.8-121.3 (47.56-47.76)
Z 440	0627-012	34-36 (1.339-1.417)	120.8-121.7 (47.56-47.91)
ZR 440, EXT 580, EXT 580 EFI, ZR 580, ZR 580 EFI	0627-012	34-36 (1.339-1.417)	120-121 (47.24-47.64)

(continued)

13

Table 1 DRIVE BELT SPECIFICATIONS (continued)

Model	Part No.	Width mm (in.)	Circumference cm (in.)
1996			
Cougar	0627-012	34-36 (1.339-1.417)	120-121 (47.24-47.64)
Z 440	0627-012	34-36 (1.339-1.417)	120.8-121.7 (47.56-47.91)
ZR 440, ZRT 600	0627-010	34-36 (1.339-1.417)	120-121 (47.24-47.64)
EXT 580, EXT 580 EFI, ZR 580	0627-012	34-36 (1.339-1.417)	120-121 (47.24-47.64)
1997			
Z 440	0627-012	34-36 (1.339-1.417)	120-121 (47.24-47.64)
ZL 440	0627-012	34-36 (1.339-1.417)	120-121 (47.24-47.64)
ZR 440	0627-010	34-36 (1.339-1.417)	120-121 (47.24-47.64)
Panther 440	0627-012	34-36 (1.339-1.417)	120-121 (47.24-47.64)
Cougar	0627-012	34-36 (1.339-1.417)	120-121 (47.24-47.64)
Panther 550	0627-012	34-36 (1.339-1.417)	120-121 (47.24-47.64)
Pantera	0627-012	34-36 (1.339-1.417)	120-121 (47.24-47.64)
EXT 580 EFI	0627-012	34-36 (1.339-1.417)	120-121 (47.24-47.64)
Powder Special EFI	0627-012	34-36 (1.339-1.417)	120-121 (47.24-47.64)
ZR 580 EFI	0627-010	34-36 (1.339-1.417)	120-121 (47.24-47.64)
EXT 600	0627-010	34-36 (1.339-1.417)	120-121 (47.24-47.64)
ZRT 600	0627-010	34-36 (1.339-1.417)	120-121 (47.24-47.64)
Powder Extreme	0627-010	34-36 (1.339-1.417)	120-121 (47.24-47.64)
1998			
Z 440	0627-012	34-36 (1.339-1.417)	120-121 (47.24-47.64)
ZL 440	0627-021	34-36 (1.339-1.417)	120-121 (47.24-47.64)
ZR 440	0627-020	34-36 (1.339-1.417)	120-121 (47.24-47.64)
Panther 440	0627-021	34-36 (1.339-1.417)	120-121 (47.24-47.64)
ZL 500	0627-020	34-36 (1.339-1.417)	120-121 (47.24-47.64)
Cougar	0627-021	34-36 (1.339-1.417)	120-121 (47.24-47.64)
Panther 550	0627-021	34-36 (1.339-1.417)	120-121 (47.24-47.64)

(continued)

Table 1 DRIVE BELT SPECIFICATIONS (continued)

Model	Part No.	Width mm (in.)	Circumference cm (in.)
1998			
Pantera	0627-021	34-36 (1.339-1.417)	120-121 (47.24-47.64)
EXT 580 EFI	0627-021	34-36 (1.339-1.417)	120-121 (47.24-47.64)
Powder Special EFI	0627-020	34-36 (1.339-1.417)	120-121 (47.24-47.64)
ZR 600	0627-020	34-36 (1.339-1.417)	120-121 (47.24-47.64)
EXT 600	0627-020	34-36 (1.339-1.417)	120-121 (47.24-47.64)
ZRT 600	0627-020	34-36 (1.339-1.417)	120-121 (47.24-47.64)
Powder Extreme	0627-020	34-36 (1.339-1.417)	120-121 (47.24-47.64)

Table 2 DRIVE SYSTEM SPECIFICATIONS

Model	Belt deflection mm (in.)	Pulley center to center cm (in.)	Pulley offset mm (in.)
1990			
Prowler, El Tigre EXT	25.4-31.8 (1-1 1/4)	25.9 (10.2)	34.7 (1.366)
1991-1992			
Prowler, Cougar, El Tigre EXT	25.4-31.8 (1-1 1/4)	25.9 (10.2)	34.7 (1.366)
1993			
Prowler, Cougar	25.4-31.8 (1-1 1/4)	25.9 (10.2)	34.7 (1.366)
440 ZR	25.4-31.8 (1-1 1/4)	30.9 (12.2)	34.67 (1.365)
EXT 550, EXT 580, 580 ZR	25.4-31.8 (1-1 1/4)	30.9 (12.2)	34.67 (1.365)
1994			
Prowler, Cougar	25.4-31.8 (1-1 1/4)	25.9 (10.2)	34.7 (1.366)
ZR 440	25.4-31.8 (1-1 1/4)	30.9 (12.2)	34.67 (1.365)
EXT 580, EXT 580 EFI, ZR 580	25.4-31.8 (1-1 1/4)	30.9 (12.2)	34.67 (1.365)
1995			
Cougar, Prowler, Z 440, ZR 440	25.4-31.8 (1-1 1/4)	30.9 (12.2)	34.67 (1.365)
EXT 580, EXT 580 EFI	25.4-31.8 (1-1 1/4)	30.9 (12.2)	34.67 (1.365)
ZR 580, ZR 580 EFI	25.4-31.8 (1-1 1/4)	30.9 (12.2)	34.67 (1.365)

(continued)

13

Table 2 DRIVE SYSTEM SPECIFICATIONS (continued)

Model	Belt deflection mm (in.)	Pulley center to center cm (in.)	Pulley offset mm (in.)
1996			
Cougar, Z 440, ZR 440	25.4-31.8 (1-1 1/4)	30.9 (12.2)	34.67 (1.365)
EXT 580, EXT 580 EFI, ZR 580	25.4-31.8 (1-1 1/4)	30.9 (12.2)	34.67 (1.365)
ZRT 600	25.4-31.8 (1-1 1/4)	30.9 (12.2)	34.67 (1.365)
1997			
All Models	25.4-31.8 (1-1 1/4)	30.9 (12.2)	34.67 (1.365)
1998			
All Models	25.4-31.8 (1-1 1/4)	30.9 (12.2)	34.67 (1.365)

Table 3 ENGINE SPEEDS

Model	Engagement speed rpm	Peak rpm range
1990		
Prowler	–	–
El Tigre EXT	3200-3600	7250
1991		
Prowler	–	–
Prowler Special	–	–
Cougar	–	–
El Tigre EXT	–	–
1992		
Prowler	3400-3600	7800-8200
Cougar	–	–
El Tigre EXT	–	–
1993		
Prowler	–	–
Prowler Special	–	–
Cougar	–	–
440 ZR	4900-5100	8500-8750
EXT 550	–	–
580 ZR	3200-3600	8000-8200
EXT 580	–	–
1994		
Cougar	3200-3600	7800-8200
Prowler	–	–
Prowler II	–	–
ZR 440	5000	8400-8500
EXT 580	3200-3600	8200
EXT 580 Mountain Cat	–	–
EXT 580 EFI	–	–
ZR 580	4500	8400-8500

(continued)

Table 3 ENGINE SPEEDS (continued)

Model	Engagement speed rpm	Peak rpm range
1995		
Cougar, Prowler	3500-3800	7800-8000
Z 440	3200-3600	7000-7200
ZR 440	5000	8400-8500
EXT 580	–	–
EXT 580 EFI	3500-3800	8200-8300
ZR 580	–	–
ZR 580 EFI	3500-3800	8200-8300
1996		
Z 440	–	–
ZR 440	5000	8300-8500
Cougar	–	–
EXT 580	–	–
EXT 580 EFI	–	–
EXT 580 EFI Mountain Cat	–	–
EXT 580 Powder Special	–	–
EXT 580 EFI Deluxe	–	–
ZR 580	–	–
ZRT 600	4000-4200	8100-8300
1997		
Z 440	3400–3600	7000-7200
ZL 440	4500	8200-8300
ZR 440	5000	8500-8600
Panther 440	3500	7200
Cougar	3400-3800	7800-8000
Panther 550	3400-3800	7800-8000
Pantera	5000	8500-8600
EXT 580 EFI	3400-3800	8000-8250
Powder Spl. EFI	3500-3800	8000-8200
ZR 580 EFI	4500	8500-8600
EXT 600	4500-4900	8400-8500
ZRT 600	4500-4900	8400-8500
Powder Extreme	4500-4900	8400-8500
1998		
Z 440	3400-3600	7000-7200
ZL 440	4500	7800-8000
ZR 440	5000	8500-8600
Panther 440	3500	7200
ZL 500	4800	8500-8700
Cougar	3500	8000
Panther 550	3500	8000
Pantera	3500	8000-8200
EXT EFI	4500	8400-8500
EXT EFI Deluxe	3500	8000-8200
Powder Spl.	4500	8500-8700
ZR 580 EFI	4500	8500-8600
EXT 600	4500	8300-8400
ZRT 600	4500	8300-8400
Powder Extreme	4500	8200

13

Table 4 DRIVE PULLEY CLUTCH SPRING APPLICATION

Model	Part No.	Color
1990		
Prowler	0146-526	Yellow/green
El Tigre EXT	0725-069	Blue/red
1991		
Prowler, Cougar	0146-526	Yellow/green
El Tigre EXT	0725-069	Blue/red
1992		
Prowler, Cougar	0146-526	Yellow/green
El Tigre EXT	0725-069	Blue/red
1993		
Prowler, Cougar	0146-526	Yellow/green
440 ZR	0146-526	Yellow/green
EXT 550	–	–
580 ZR		
0-4000 ft.	0646-083	Red
Above 4000 ft.	0146-526	Yellow/green
EXT 580	–	–
1994		
Cougar, Cougar Mountain Cat	0146-526	Yellow/green
Prowler, ZR 440	0146-526	Yellow/green
EXT 580		
0-4000 ft.	0646-083	Red
Above 4000 ft.	0146-526	Yellow/green
EXT 580 EFI		
0-4000 ft.	0646-083	Red
Above 4000 ft.	0146-526	Yellow/green
ZR 580		
0-4000 ft.	0646-083	Red
Above 4000 ft.	0146-526	Yellow/green
1995		
Cougar, Cougar Mountain Cat,		
Prowler 2-Up		
0-4000 ft.	0646-083	Red
Above 4000 ft.	0146-526	Yellow/green
Z 440	0646-083	Red
ZR 440	0146-526	Yellow/green
EXT 580, EXT 580 EFI, ZR 580		
0-4000 ft.	0646-083	Red
Above 4000 ft.	0146-526	Yellow/green
1996		
Z 440	0646-083	Red
ZR 440	0146-526	Yellow/green
Cougar	–	–
Cougar Mountain Cat	–	–
Cougar 2-Up	–	–
EXT 580, EXT 580 EFI, ZR 580		
0-4000 ft.	0646-083	Red
Above 4000 ft.	0146-526	Yellow/green
EXT 580 Powder Special	0646-149	Red
ZRT 600	0646-147	Yellow/green
1997		
Z 440	0646-149	Red
ZL 440	0646-147	Yellow/green

(continued)

Table 4 DRIVE PULLEY CLUTCH SPRING APPLICATION (continued)

Model	Part No.	Color
1997		
ZR 440	0646-229	Yellow/white
Panther 440	0646-149	Red
Cougar	0646-149	Red
Panther 550	0646-149	Red
EXT 580 EFI	0646-149	Red
Powder Special	0646-149	Red
ZR 580 EFI	0646-147	Yellow/green
EXT 600	0646-147	Yellow/green
ZRT 600	0646-229	Yellow/white
Powder Extreme	0646-147	Yellow/green
1998		
Z 440	0646-149	Red
ZL 440	0646-147	Yellow/green
ZR 440	0646-229	Yellow/white
Panther 440	0646-149	Red
ZL 500	0646-229	Yellow/white
Cougar	0646-149	Red
Panther 550	0646-149	Red
EXT EFI Deluxe	0646-149	Red
Pantera	0646-149	Red
Powder Special	0646-229	Yellow/white
EXT 600	0646-147	Yellow/green
ZRT 600	0646-147	Yellow/green
Powder Extreme	0646-147	Yellow/green

Table 5 DRIVE PULLEY SPRING SPECIFICATIONS

Spring part No. and color	Pressure @ kg @ 60 mm (lb. @ 2 3/8 in.)	Pressure @ kg @ 35 mm (lb. @ 1 3/8 in.)
0646-150 Silver	38.4 (85)	76.4 (169)
0646-084 White	35.3 (78)	80.5 (178)
0646-148 Red/blue	24 (53)	89.1 (197)
0646-097 Blue/red	30.7 (68)	89.1 (197)
0725-069 Blue/red	41.6 (92)	–
0646-149 Red	33.5 (74)	100.4 (222)
0646-083 Red	41.6 (92)	100.4 (222)
0646-154 Purple	61.5 (136)	114.9 (254)
0646-155 Purple	61.5 (136)	114.9 (254)
0646-147 Yellow/Green	51.5 (114)	119.4 (264)
0146-526 Yellow/Green	60.6 (134)	119.4 (264)
0646-192 Orange	54.3 (120)	122.1 (270)
0646-229 Yellow/white	55.2 (122)	128.9 (285)
0646-248 Orange/white	64.7 (143)	131.1 (290)

13

Table 6 DRIVEN PULLEY TORQUE BRACKET (CAM) AND SPRING APPLICATION

Model	Spring part No./color	Torque bracket part No. (angle degrees)
1990		
Prowler	0648-012/blue	0648-011 (48-44°)
El Tigre EXT	–/yellow	0648-002 (53°)
1991		
Prowler, Cougar	0648-012/blue	0648-011 (48-44°)
El Tigre EXT	–/yellow	0648-002 (53°)
1992		
Prowler, Cougar	0648-012/blue	0648-011 (48-44°)
El Tigre EXT	–/yellow	0648-002 (53°)
1993		
Prowler, Cougar	0648-012/blue	0648-011 (48-44°)
440 ZR	0148-227/yellow	0648-001 (52-44°)
EXT 550	–	–
580 ZR	0148-227/yellow	0648-014 (49°)
EXT 580	–	–
1994		
Cougar, Prowler	0648-012/blue	0648-011 (48-44°)
ZR 440		
0-8000 ft.	0148-227/yellow	0648-002 (53°)
8000-10,000 ft.	0148-227/yellow	0648-014 (49°)
Above 10,000 ft.	0148-227/yellow	0648-011 (48-44°)
EXT 580, EXT 580 EFI		
0-10,000 ft.	0148-404/yellow	0648-014 (49°)
10,000 ft.	0148-404/yellow	0648-011 (48-44°)
ZR 580		
0-4000 ft.	0148-227/yellow	0648-002 (53°)
4000-8000 ft.	0148-227/yellow	0148-222 (51°)
Above 8000 ft.	0148-227/yellow	0648-014 (49°)
1995		
Cougar, Cougar Mountain Cat, Prowler 2-Up		
0-8000 ft.	0648-012/blue	0648-014 (49°)
8000-10,000 ft.	0648-012/blue	0648-011 (48-44°)
Above 10,000 ft.	0148-227/yellow	0648-011 (48-44°)
Z 440	0648-012/blue	0648-002 (53°)
ZR 440		
0-8000 ft.	0148-227/yellow	0648-024 (55-53°)
8000-10,000 ft.	0148-227/yellow	0148-222 (49°)
Above 10,000 ft.	0148-227/yellow	0648-011 (48-44°)
EXT 580, EXT 580 EFI, EXT 580 Powder Special, ZR 580		
0-8000 ft.	0148-227/yellow	0648-002 (51°)
8000-10,000 ft.	0148-227/yellow	0148-222 (49°)
Above 10,000 ft.	0148-227/yellow	0648-014 (47°)
1996		
Z 440	0648-012/blue	0648-002 (53°)
ZR 440	0148-227/yellow	0648-002 (53°)
Cougar	–	–
Cougar Mountain Cat	–	–
Cougar 2-Up	–	–

(continued)

Table 6 DRIVEN PULLEY TORQUE BRACKET (CAM) AND SPRING APPLICATION (continued)

Model	Spring part No./color	Torque bracket part No. (angle degrees)
1996		
EXT 580	–	–
EXT 580 EFI	–	–
EXT 580 EFI Mountain Cat	–	–
EXT 580 Powder Special	–	–
EXT 580 EFI Deluxe	–	–
ZR 580		
0-4000 ft.	0648-037/red	0648-058 (42-34°)
4000-10,000 ft.	0648-060/blue	0648-058 (42-34°)
Above 10,000 ft.	0648-060/blue	0648-038 (34°)
ZRT 600		
0-4000 ft.	0148-227/yellow	0648-005 (55°)
Above 4000 ft.	0148-227/yellow	0648-002 (53°)
1997		
Z 440	0648-012/blue	0648-002 (53°)
ZL 440	0648-012/blue	0648-014 (49°)
ZR 440	0148-227/yellow	0648-002 (53°)
Panther 440	0648-012/blue	0648-002 (53°)
Cougar	0148-227/yellow	0648-014 (49°)
Panther	0148-227/yellow	0648-014 (49°)
EXT 580 EFI	0148-227/yellow	0148-222 (51°)
Pantera	0148-227/yellow	0148-222 (51°)
Powder Special	0148-227/yellow	0648-002 (53°)
ZR 580 EFI	0648-076/green	0648-058 (42-34°)
EXT 600	0148-227/yellow	0648-005 (55°)
ZRT 600	0148-227/yellow	0648-005 (55°)
Powder Extreme	0148-227/yellow	0648-005 (55°)
1998		
Z 440	0648-012/blue	0648-002 (53°)
ZL 440	0148-227/yellow	0648-002 (53°)
ZR 440		
0-5000 ft.	0148-227/yellow	0648-005 (55°)
5000-9000 ft.	0148-227/yellow	0648-002 (53°)
Above 9000 ft.	0148-227/yellow	0648-025 (47°)
Panther 440	0648-012/blue	0648-002 (53°)
ZL 500	0148-227/yellow	0648-222 (51°)
Cougar	0148-227/yellow	0648-014 (49°)
Panther	0148-227/yellow	0648-014 (49°)
EXT EFI	0148-227/yellow	0648-002 (53°)
EXT EFI Deluxe	0148-227/yellow	0648-014 (49°)
EXT Triple Touring	0148-227/yellow	0648-005 (55°)
Pantera	0148-227/yellow	0648-014 (49°)
Powder Special	0148-227/yellow	0648-002 (53°)
ZR 580 EFI	0648-076/green	0648-058 (42-34°)
EXT 600	0148-227/yellow	0648-005 (55°)
ZRT 600	0148-227/yellow	0648-005 (55°)
Powder Extreme	0148-227/yellow	0648-005 (55°)

13

Table 7 CAM ARM SPECIFICATIONS

Model	Part No.	Weight (grams)
1990		
Prowler		
0-4000 ft.	0646-115	47.0
4000-8000 ft.	0146-530	44.5
8000-10,000 ft.	0646-018	43.5
Above 10,000 ft.	0646-019	42.0
El Tigre EXT		
0-4000 ft.	0646-098	54.5
4000-8000 ft.	0646-099	54.0
Above 8000 ft.	0646-102	50.5
1991		
Prowler, Cougar		
0-4000 ft.	0646-115	47.0
4000-8000 ft.	0146-530	44.5
8000-10,000 ft.	0646-018	43.5
Above 10,000 ft.	0646-019	42.0
El Tigre EXT		
0-4000 ft.	0646-098	54.5
4000-8000 ft.	0646-099	54.0
Above 8000 ft.	0646-102	50.5
1992		
Prowler, Cougar		
0-4000 ft.	0646-115	47.0
4000-8000 ft.	0146-530	44.5
8000-10,000 ft.	0646-018	43.5
Above 10,000 ft.	0646-019	42.0
El Tigre EXT		
0-4000 ft.	0646-098	54
4000-8000 ft.	0646-099	54
Above 8000 ft.	0646-102	50.5
1993		
Prowler, Cougar		
0-4000 ft.	0646-115	47.0
4000-8000 ft.	0146-530	44.5
8000-10,000 ft.	0646-018	43.5
Above 10,000 ft.	0646-019	42.0
440 ZR		
0-4000 ft.	0646-157	46.5
4000-8000 ft.	0646-156	45.0
8000-10,000 ft.	0646-018	43.5
Above 10,000 ft.	0646-019	42.0
EXT 550		
0-4000 ft.	0646-102	50.5
4000-8000 ft.	0646-080	48.5
Above 8000 ft.	0646-115	47.0
580 ZR		
0-4000 ft.	0646-102	50.5
4000-8000 ft.	0646-080	48.5
8000-10,000 ft.	0646-115	47.0
Above 10,000 ft.	0646-027	44.5
EXT 580		
0-4000 ft.	0646-102	50.5
4000-8000 ft.	0646-080	48.5

(continued)

Table 7 CAM ARM SPECIFICATIONS (continued)

Model	Part No.	Weight (grams)
1993		
EXT 580		
8000-10,000 ft.	0646-115	47.0
Above 10,000 ft.	0646-027	44.5
1994		
Cougar, Prowler		
0-4000 ft.	0646-115	47.0
4000-8000 ft.	0146-530	44.5
8000-10,000 ft.	0646-018	43.5
Above 10,000 ft.	0646-019	42.0
ZR 440		
0-4000 ft.	0646-102	50.5
Above 4,000 ft.	0646-166	39.5
EXT 580, EXT 580 EFI		
0-4000 ft.	0646-102	50.5
4000-8000 ft.	0646-080	48.5
8000-10,000 ft.	0646-115	47.0
Above 10,000 ft.	0646-027	44.5
ZR 580		
0-4000 ft.	0646-157	46.5
4000-10,000 ft.	0646-156	45.0
Above 10,000 ft.	0646-162	
1995		
Cougar		
0-4000 ft.	0646-102	50.5
4000-8000 ft.	0646-080	48.5
Above 8000 ft.	0646-115	47.0
Z 440		
0-4000 ft.	0646-080	48.5
4000-8000 ft.	0146-530	44.5
Above 8000 ft.	0646-079	43.5
ZR 440		
0-4000 ft.	0646-199	46.5
Above 4000 ft.	0646-166	39.5
EXT 580		
0-4000 ft.	0646-102	50.5
4000-8000 ft.	0646-080	48.5
8000-10,000 ft.	0646-115	47.0
Above 10,000 ft.	0646-027	44.5
EXT 580 EFI		
0-4000 ft.	0646-164	49.0
Above 4000 ft.	0646-156	45.0
ZR 580		
0-4000 ft.	0646-164	49.0
4000-8000 ft.	0646-157	46.5
Above 8000 ft.	0646-156	45.0
Powder Special		
0-4000 ft.	0646-164	49.0
4000-10,000 ft.	0646-157	46.5
Above 10,000 ft.	0646-156	45.0
ZR 580 EFI		
0-4000 ft.	0646-164	49.0
Above 4000 ft.	0646-156	45.0

(continued)

13

Table 7 CAM ARM SPECIFICATIONS (continued)

Model	Part No.	Weight (grams)
1996		
Z 440		
0-4000 ft.	0646-080	48.5
4000-8000 ft.	0146-530	44.5
Above 8000 ft.	0646-079	43.5
ZR 440	0646-250	44.5
Cougar		
0-4000 ft.	0646-102	50.5
4000-8000 ft.	0646-080	48.5
Above 8000 ft.	0646-115	47.0
EXT 580		
0-4000 ft.	0646-102	50.5
4000-8000 ft.	0646-080	48.5
8000-10,000 ft.	0646-115	47.0
Above 10,000 ft.	0646-027	44.5
EXT 580 EFI		
0-4000 ft.	0646-164	49.0
Above 4000 ft.	0646-156	45.0
EXT 580 Powder Special		
0-4000 ft.	0646-164	49.0
4000-10,000 ft.	0646-157	46.5
Above 10,000 ft.	0646-156	45.0
ZR 580		
0-4000 ft.	0646-249	–
4000-10,000 ft.	0646-235	–
Above 10,000 ft.	0646-234	–
ZRT 600		
0-4000 ft.	0746-500	54.0
4000-10,000 ft.	0746-547	50.0
Above 10,000 ft.	0746-546	48.0
1997		
Z 440		
0-5000 ft.	0746-527	50.5
5000-9000 ft.	0746-531	44.5
Above 9000 ft.	0746-525	44.0
ZL 440		
0-5000 ft.	0746-524	48.5
5000-9000 ft.	0746-563	44.5
Above 9000 ft.	0746-562	42.0
ZR 440	0746-576	46.0
Panther 440		
0-4000 ft.	0746-527	50.5
4000-10,000 ft.	0746-531	44.5
Above 10,000 ft.	0746-525	44.0
Cougar		
0-5000 ft.	0746-527	50.5
5000-9000 ft.	0746-524	48.5
Above 9000 ft.	0746-523	47.0
Panther 550		
0-5000 ft.	0746-527	50.5
5000-9000 ft.	0746-524	48.5
Above 9000 ft.	0746-523	47.0

(continued)

Table 7 CAM ARM SPECIFICATIONS (continued)

Model	Part No.	Weight (grams)
1997		
EXT 580 EFI, EXT Deluxe		
0-5000 ft.	0746-527	50.5
5000-9000 ft.	0746-524	48.5
Above 9000 ft.	0746-502	44.5
Pantera		
0-5000 ft.	0746-527	50.5
5000-9000 ft.	0746-524	48.5
Above 9000 ft.	0746-502	44.5
Powder Special (carbureted)		
0-5000 ft.	0746-529	49.5
5000-9000 ft.	0746-566	48.0
Above 9000 ft.	0746-549	46
Powder Special EFI		
0-5000 ft.	0746-527	50.5
5000-9000 ft.	0746-566	48.0
Above 9000 ft.	0746-567	46.0
ZR 580 EFI		
0-5000 ft.	0746-574	48.5
5000-9000 ft.	0746-564	45.0
Above 9000 ft.	0746-565	43.5
EXT 600		
0-5000 ft.	0746-560	55.0
5000-9000 ft.	0746-568	50.0
Above 9000 ft.	0746-570	47.0
ZRT 600		
0-5000 ft.	0746-560	55.0
5000-9000 ft.	0746-568	50.0
Above 9000 ft.	0746-570	47.0
Powder Extreme		
0-5000 ft.	0746-560	55.0
5000-9000 ft.	0746-568	50.0
Above 9000 ft.	0746-570	47.0
1998		
Z 440		
0-5000 ft.	0746-527	50.5
5000-9000 ft.	0746-525	44.0
Above 9000 ft.	0746-526	42.0
ZL 440		
0-5000 ft.	0746-583	46.5
5000-9000 ft.	0746-594	44.5
Above 9000 ft.	0746-562	42.0
ZR 440		
0-5000 ft.	0746-576	45.0
5000-9000 ft.	0746-595	41.5
Above 9000 ft.	0746-590	40.5
ZL 500		
0-5000 ft.	0746-579	46.5
5000-9000 ft.	0746-598	44.0
Above 9000 ft.	0746-590	40.5
Panther 440		
0-9000 ft.	0746-527	50.5
Above 9000 ft.	0746-523	47.0

(continued)

13

Table 7 CAM ARM SPECIFICATIONS (continued)

Model	Part No.	Weight (grams)
1998		
Cougar		
0-5000 ft.	0746-527	50.5
5000-9000 ft.	0746-524	48.5
Above 9000 ft.	0746-523	47.0
Panther 550		
0-5000 ft.	0746-527	50.5
5000-9000 ft.	0746-524	48.5
Above 9000 ft.	0746-523	47.0
EXT EFI		
0-5000 ft.	0746-501	48.5
5000-9000 ft.	0746-583	46.5
Above 9000 ft.	0746-591	44.0
EXT EFI DELUXE		
0-5000 ft.	0746-527	50.5
5000-9000 ft.	0746-524	48.5
Above 9000 ft.	0746-591	44.0
Pantera		
0-5000 ft.	0746-527	50.5
5000-9000 ft.	0746-524	48.5
Above 9000 ft.	0746-591	44.0
Powder Special (carbureted)		
0-5000 ft.	0746-587	50.0
5000-9000 ft.	0746-584	45
Above 9000 ft.	0746-602	42.5
Powder Special EFI		
0-5000 ft.	0746-587	50.0
5000-9000 ft.	0746-584	45
Above 9000 ft.	0746-602	42.5
ZR 600 EFI		
0-5000 ft.	0746-585	49
5000-9000 ft.	0746-593	45.5
Above 9000 ft.	0746-597	43.5
EXT 600		
0-5000 ft.	0746-582	48.5
5000-9000 ft.	0746-582	48.5
Above 9000 ft.	0746-589	45.0
EXT Triple Touring		
0-5000 ft.	0746-582	48.5
5000-9000 ft.	0746-583	46.5
Above 9000 ft.	0746-591	44.0
ZRT 600		
0-5000 ft.	0746-582	48.5
5000-9000 ft.	0746-582	48.5
Above 9000 ft.	0746-589	45.0
Powder Extreme		
0-5000 ft.	0746-581	52.5
5000-9000 ft.	0746-583	46.5
Above 9000 ft.	0746-596	44.5

Table 8 TIGHTENING TORQUES

	N·m	(ft.-lb.)
Drive pulley		
Retainer bolt		
Models w/6 bolt cover	65-69	48-51
Models w/9 bolt cover	69-76	51-56
Spider		
Models w/6 bolt cover	172.5	127
Models w/9 bolt cover	345	254
Spider locknut		
Models w/6 bolt cover	42-48	31-35
Models w/9 bolt cover	118	87
Cover screws		
6 bolt cover	10	7
9 bolt cover	14	10
Driven pulley		
Retainer bolt	26-33	19-24
Retainer bracket nuts		
1997 Powder Special	19-22	14-16
Other models so equipped	15-18	11-13

13

Chapter Fourteen

Brake, Driven Shaft, Dropcase And Driveshaft

This chapter describes service procedures for the brake, driven shaft (input shaft), dropcase (chaincase) and driveshaft. **Tables 1-3** are found at the end of the chapter.

DRIVE CHAIN AND SPROCKETS (MODELS WITHOUT REVERSE)

Removal

Refer to **Figure 1** for this procedure.

1. Open the hood.
2. Remove the drain plug (5, **Figure 1**). On some models the drain plug may be located in the cover.
3. Place shops rags under the dropcase cover to absorb any spilled oil.

> *NOTE*
> *The dropcase is filled with oil that will spill when the dropcase cover is removed. Use rags to absorb as much spilled oil as possible.*

4. Remove the screws retaining the cover (9, **Figure 1**).
5. Remove the cover (**Figure 2**) and gasket. Discard the gasket.
6. Clean up as much oil as possible before proceeding with the removal.
7. On models with mechanical tension adjustment, loosen chain tension as follows:
   a. Loosen the locknut (A, **Figure 3**).
   b. Turn the adjuster bolt (B, **Figure 3**) counterclockwise until the chain is completely loose.
8. Remove the cotter pins and washers retaining the tension spring (C, **Figure 3**), then remove the tension spring assembly.
9. On models with automatic tension adjustment, remove the self-locking nut (**Figure 4**), then remove the roller and cage assembly.

> *NOTE*
> *On some models, the sprocket may be retained by a bolt instead of a nut.*

10. Set the brake and remove sprocket retaining nuts (A and B, **Figure 5**).

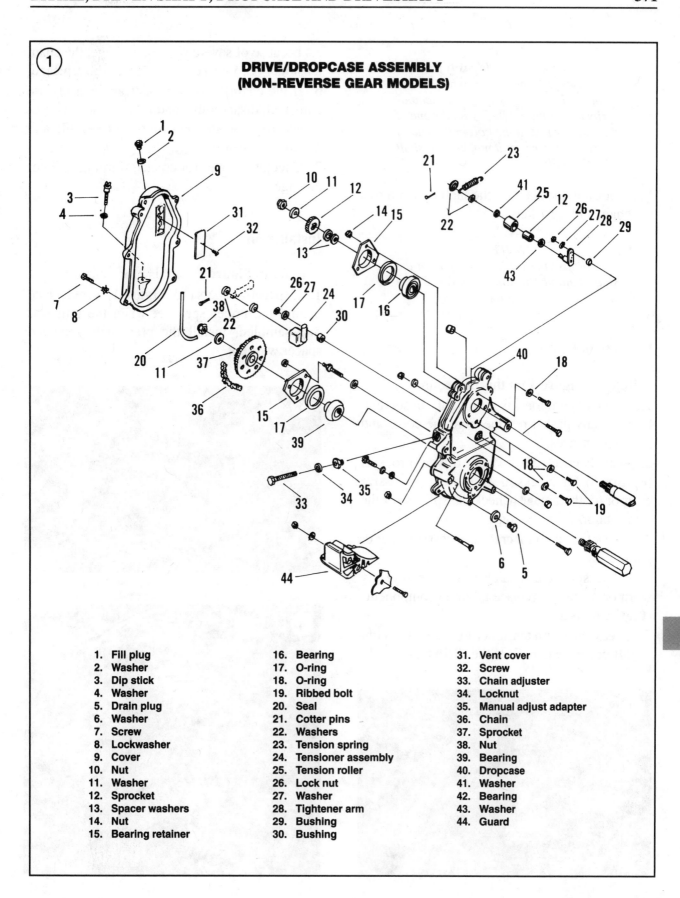

① **DRIVE/DROPCASE ASSEMBLY (NON-REVERSE GEAR MODELS)**

1. Fill plug	16. Bearing	31. Vent cover
2. Washer	17. O-ring	32. Screw
3. Dip stick	18. O-ring	33. Chain adjuster
4. Washer	19. Ribbed bolt	34. Locknut
5. Drain plug	20. Seal	35. Manual adjust adapter
6. Washer	21. Cotter pins	36. Chain
7. Screw	22. Washers	37. Sprocket
8. Lockwasher	23. Tension spring	38. Nut
9. Cover	24. Tensioner assembly	39. Bearing
10. Nut	25. Tension roller	40. Dropcase
11. Washer	26. Lock nut	41. Washer
12. Sprocket	27. Washer	42. Bearing
13. Spacer washers	28. Tightener arm	43. Washer
14. Nut	29. Bushing	44. Guard
15. Bearing retainer	30. Bushing	

NOTE
If a sprocket will not slide easily from the shaft, use a suitable puller to remove the sprocket. Before using the puller, temporarily install the nut flush with the end of the shaft or install the bolt in the end of the shaft to prevent damaging the shaft with the puller.

11. Slide the sprockets off the shafts and remove the chain and sprockets.

NOTE
Do not lose the washers located on the shaft behind the top sprocket. These washers align the sprockets.

Inspection

Refer to **Figure 1** for this procedure.
1. Clean all components thoroughly in solvent. Remove any gasket residue from the cover and housing surfaces.
2. Visually check the drive and driven sprockets (**Figure 6**) for cracks, deep scoring, excessive wear or tooth damage. Check the splines for the same abnormal conditions.
3. Check the chain for cracks, excessive wear or pin breakage.
4. If the sprockets and/or chain are severely worn or damaged, replace all three components (**Figure 6**) as a set.
5. Check the chain tensioner for wear and damage. If you have to replace the chain and sprock-

ets because of severe wear or damage, the chain tensioner (C, **Figure 5**) should also be replaced.
6. If the chain tensioner roller and bearing are damaged, disassemble and replace parts as necessary. Reverse the procedure to assemble and install the tensioner.
7. Check the cover for cracks, warping or other damage.

Installation

Refer to **Figure 1** for this procedure.
1. If spacer washers (13, **Figure 1**) were located behind the upper sprocket when the unit was disassembled, install the previously removed spacer washers.

NOTE
When installing the sprockets in Steps 2 and 3, fit the sprockets onto the drive chain so that the stamped sprocket numbers face out.

2. Determine the correct number and thickness of spacer washers necessary to align the sprockets as follows:

a. Install the upper sprocket (12, **Figure 1**), washer (11, **Figure 1**) and nut (10, **Figure**

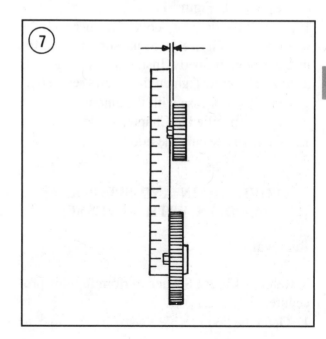

1). Temporarily tighten the nut until the sprocket is fully seated.

b. Install the lower sprocket (37, **Figure 1**), washer (11, **Figure 1**) and retaining screw or nut (38, **Figure 1**). Temporarily tighten the nut or retaining screw until the sprocket is fully seated.

c. Place a straightedge across the sides of both sprockets and measure any offset (**Figure 7**). The sprockets should be aligned within 0.8 mm (0.031 in.).

d. If the sprockets are not aligned, change the thickness of the spacer washers (13, **Figure 1**) behind the upper sprocket to align the sprockets.

e. When alignment is correct, remove the sprocket retaining nuts or bolts, washers and sprockets. Leave the selected spacer washers (13, **Figure 1**) on the shaft.

3. Install the chain and sprockets (**Figure 6**) as an assembly.

4. Coat the threads of the shafts for retaining nuts (A and B, **Figure 5**) or the threads of the retaining bolts with Loctite 271 (red).

14

NOTE
Engage the brake to hold the shafts from turning when tightening the retaining nuts or screws in Step 5.

5. Install the washers and retaining nuts (A and B, **Figure 5**) or bolts. Tighten to the torque listed in **Table 2**.

6A. On models with manual tension adjustment, install and adjust the chain tensioner assembly as follows:

    a. Install the tensioner assembly (24, **Figure 1**) and tighten the self-locking nut (26, **Figure 1**).

    b. Turn the adjusting screw (33, **Figure 1**) in finger-tight. Lock the position by tightening the locknut (34, **Figure 1**).

6B. On models with automatic chain adjustment, install the chain tensioner at the rear (24, **Figure 1**). On these models, the unit is similar to the front unit (25, 26, 27, 28, 29, 41, 42 and 43, **Figure 1**).

7. Install the front roller assembly (25, 26, 27, 28, 29, 41, 42 and 43, **Figure 1**).

8. Install the inner washers (22, **Figure 1**).

9. Attach the spring tensioner (C, **Figure 3**). Install the outer washers (22, **Figure 1**) and cotter pins (21, **Figure 1**).

10. Install the dropcase cover together with the seal ring (20, **Figure 1**). Make sure the seal fits in the groove properly. Install the cover and its attaching screws. Tighten the screws securely.

11. Fill the dropcase with the amount and type of gear oil specified in Chapter Three.

12. Close and secure the hood.

DRIVE CHAIN AND SPROCKETS (MODELS WITH REVERSE)

Removal

Refer to **Figure 8** when performing this procedure.

1. Open the hood.

2. Disconnect the shift linkage from the shift fork shaft on the dropcase.

3. Remove the screw (25, **Figure 8**) from the center of the dropcase cover.

4. Remove the drain plug (75, **Figure 8**). On some models, the drain plug may be located in the cover.

5. Place shop rags under the dropcase cover to absorb any spilled oil.

NOTE
The dropcase is filled with oil that will spill when the dropcase cover is removed. Use rags to absorb as much spilled oil as possible.

6. Remove the screws securing the cover (8, **Figure 8**).

7. Remove the cover and gasket (3 and 16, **Figure 8**). Discard the gasket. Pull the cover up as it is being removed so the shift fork will clear the internal mechanism.

8. Clean up as much oil as possible before proceeding with the removal.

9. Remove the spacer washer (27, **Figure 8**) from the idler sprocket shaft.

10A. On models with an external chain tensioner (**Figure 9**), proceed as follows:

    a. Remove screw (8, **Figure 9**) and install a setscrew in place of the original screw. Tighten the setscrew sufficiently to hold the adjuster shaft in position.

    b. Remove the adjuster assembly by turning the housing (7, **Figure 9**) counterclockwise using a 3/4-inch wrench.

10B. On models with an internal chain tensioner, lift the chain tensioner off the ratchet block (90, **Figure 8**) and hold it against the chaincase with locking pliers (**Figure 10**).

11. Engage the brake to hold the shaft, then remove the nut and lockwasher (17 and 18, **Figure 8**) from the top shaft.

NOTE
The lower sprocket bolt and washer are spring loaded. Hold the bolt and washer

during removal in Step 12 to prevent parts from flying off.

12. Loosen the bolt (46, **Figure 8**) securing the lower sprocket. Carefully remove the bolt, lockwasher, retainer and spring.

13. Remove the reverse gear (**Figure 11**) from the driveshaft extension.

14. Remove the upper sprocket, drive chain and idler gears. Be sure the alignment pin (30, **Figure 8**), located between the two idler gears, is not lost.

15. Remove the driveshaft extension, lower sprocket and spacer washer (54, 56 and 63, **Figure 8**).

16A. On models with an external chain tensioner (**Figure 9**), unscrew the shoulder nut (19, **Figure 9**) and remove the tensioner arm assembly (12, **Figure 9**).

16B. On models with an internal chain tensioner, release the locking pliers from the tensioner assembly and remove the tensioner assembly as follows.

  a. Use needlenose pliers to unhook the spring (88, **Figure 8**).

  b. Remove the shoulder nut (84, **Figure 8**), then remove the tension roller assembly.

  c. If necessary, remove the nut (81, **Figure 8**) and disassemble the roller assembly.

Inspection

Refer to **Figure 8** for this procedure.

1. Clean all components thoroughly in solvent. Remove any gasket residue from the cover and housing surfaces.

2. Inspect the upper and lower sprockets, idler gears and reverse gear for cracks, deep scoring, excessive wear or tooth damage.

3. Inspect the shaft splines for damage.

4. Check the lower sprocket drive pins for rounding, scoring or excessive wear. The pins are spring-loaded and must move without any sign of binding or roughness. Check pin movement by pressing the pins by hand.

5. Check all bearings by turning the race by hand. Bearings should operate smoothly.

6. Inspect the reverse gear (53, **Figure 8**) as follows:

  a. Remove the snap ring (50, **Figure 8**), outer washer (51, **Figure 8**), bearing (52, **Figure 8**) and inner washer (51, **Figure 8**) from the reverse gear. Check the washers and bearing for roughness or excessive wear. Install the bearing and washers as an assembly.

  b. Check the reverse gear pin holes for chipping, rounding or other wear. Install a new reverse gear, if necessary.

7. Assemble the reverse gear as follows:

  a. Oil the bearing and washers before assembling.

  b. Install the inner washer, followed by the bearing and outer washer.

  c. Install the snap ring making sure it seats firmly in the gear.

8A. On models equipped with an external chain tensioner (**Figure 9**), turn the chain tension roller (14, **Figure 9**) and check the condition of the roller and the bearing for smoothness.

8B. Check the internal chain tensioner on models so equipped as follows:

  a. Turn the chain tension roller (79, **Figure 8**) and check the condition of the roller and the bearing for smoothness.

  b. Check the ratchet block (90, **Figure 8**) for damage and replace as necessary.

  c. Check the brackets and spring for signs of damage and replace as necessary.

  d. Disassemble and replace parts as necessary.

9. Check the shift fork for wear or damage at the tips of the fork. Replace the shift fork, if it is damaged.

10. Check the shift fork shaft movement. If the shaft binds or is damaged, remove the roll pin (12, **Figure 8**) securing the fork and separate the parts.

14

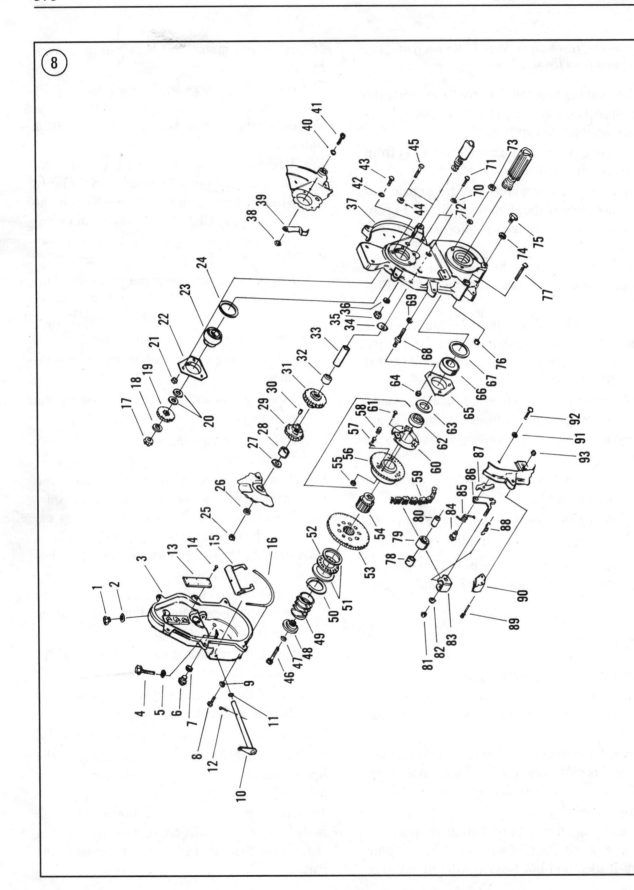

DRIVE/DROPCASE ASSEMBLY
REVERSE GEAR MODELS

1. Plug
2. Fiber washer
3. Cover
4. Dipstick
5. Washer
6. Plug
7. Washer
8. Bolt
9. Washer
10. Shift fork shaft
11. O-ring
12. Spring pin
13. Vent cover
14. Screw
15. Shift fork
16. Seal
17. Locknut
18. Washer
19. Sprocket
20. Spacer washers
21. Locknut
22. Bearing retainer
23. Bearing
24. Seal

25. Nut
26. Washer
27. Spacer
28. Bearing
29. Idler gear
30. Alignment pin
31. Idler gear
32. Bearing
33. Shaft
34. Washer
35. Locknut
36. Washer
37. Dropcase
38. Locknut
39. Bracket
40. O-ring
41. Ribbed bolt
42. O-ring
43. Ribbed bolt
44. O-ring
45. Ribbed bolt
46. Bolt
47. Lockwasher

48. Retainer
49. Spring
50. Snap ring
51. Washer
52. Bearing
53. Reverse gear
54. Driveshaft extension
55. Locknut
56. Sprocket
57. Pin
58. Spring
59. Chain
60. Spring retainer
61. Bolt
62. Bearing
63. Spacer
64. Locknut
65. Bearing retainer
66. Bearing
67. Seal
68. Stud
69. O-ring
70. O-ring

71. Ribbed bolt
72. Washer
73. Nut
74. Fiber washer
75. Drain plug
76. Nut
77. Bolt
78. Bearing
79. Roller
80. Shaft
81. Nut
82. Washer
83. Bracket
84. Shoulder nut
85. Spring
86. Link pin
87. Spring bracket
88. Spring
89. Bolt
90. Ratchet block
91. O-ring
92. Ribbed bolt
93. Locknut

14

Installation

Refer to **Figure 8** for this procedure.

1A. On models equipped with an external chain tensioner, install the tensioner arm assembly (**Figure 9**). Apply Loctite 242 (blue) to the threads of the stud in the drop case housing. Tighten the shoulder nut to 6-7 N•m (4-5 ft.-lb.).

1B. On models equipped with an internal chain tensioner, install the chain tensioner assembly by reversing the removal procedure. Apply Loctite 242 (blue) to the threads of the stud in the drop case housing. Tighten the shoulder nut to 6-7 N•m (4-5 ft.-lb.).

2. On models equipped with an internal chain tensioner, lift the chain tensioner off the ratchet block (90, **Figure 8**) and use locking pliers to hold it against the chaincase. See **Figure 10**.

3. Install the spacer washer (63, **Figure 8**) on the driveshaft.

4. Place the chain around the upper and lower sprockets. Install both sprockets and the chain. The drive pins of the lower sprocket should face out.

5. Install the idler gears as follows:
   a. Lubricate bearings in the idler gears (29 and 31, **Figure 8**) with oil before installation.
   b. Pull the lower sprocket and chain out slightly and slide the inner idler gear (31, **Figure 8**) onto the idler gear shaft while engaging the idler gear with the chain.
   c. Insert the alignment pin (30, **Figure 8**) in the hole of the inner idler.
   d. Align the hole in the outer idler (29, **Figure 8**) with the alignment pin already installed in the inner idler. Install the outer idler.

NOTE
If a new chain has been installed, it may be difficult to install the driveshaft extension (54, Figure 8) in Step 6. If necessary, remove the drive belt, driven pulley

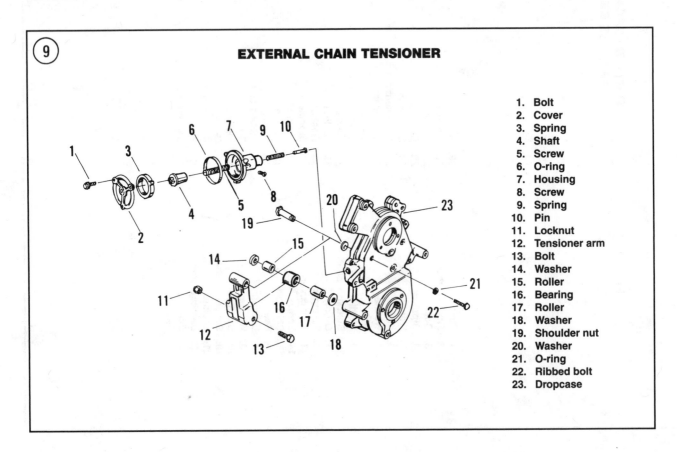

⑨ **EXTERNAL CHAIN TENSIONER**

1. Bolt
2. Cover
3. Spring
4. Shaft
5. Screw
6. O-ring
7. Housing
8. Screw
9. Spring
10. Pin
11. Locknut
12. Tensioner arm
13. Bolt
14. Washer
15. Roller
16. Bearing
17. Roller
18. Washer
19. Shoulder nut
20. Washer
21. O-ring
22. Ribbed bolt
23. Dropcase

*and bearing flange (**Figure 12**). Remove the bearing from the flange. Lift the driven shaft to obtain enough slack in the chain to install the extension.*

6. Oil the splines of the inner driveshaft extension and slide the extension onto the driveshaft. Engage the splines.

7. Install the reverse gear onto the driveshaft extension. The holes must face the pins in the lower sprocket (**Figure 8**).

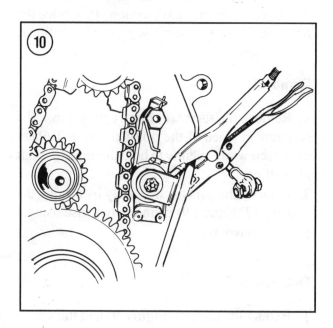

8. Install the spring (49, **Figure 8**) into the reverse gear. Install the retainer (48, **Figure 8**), washer (47, **Figure 8**) and bolt (46, **Figure 8**).

9. Tighten the reverse gear bolt to the torque listed in **Table 2**.

10. Coat the threads of the upper sprocket retaining nut with Loctite 271. Install the retaining nut. Tighten to the torque listed in **Table 2**.

11. On models equipped with an internal chain tensioner, release the locking pliers (**Figure 10**). Check to be sure the tensioner engages the ratchet block correctly.

12. If the driven shaft bearing flange was removed to install the driveshaft extension (Step 6), install the bearing and flange. Refer to **Table 2** for tightening torque.

13. Install the dropcase cover as follows:

    a. Install the seal ring in the dropcase housing.

    b. Position the cover with the fingers of the shift fork behind the large washer and bearing of the reverse gear. The cover must be lowered into position to properly locate the shift fork.

    c. Apply Loctite 290 on the threads of the reverse idler shaft screw (25, **Figure 8**).

    d. Install the reverse idler shaft screw (25, **Figure 8**). Tighten the screw securely.

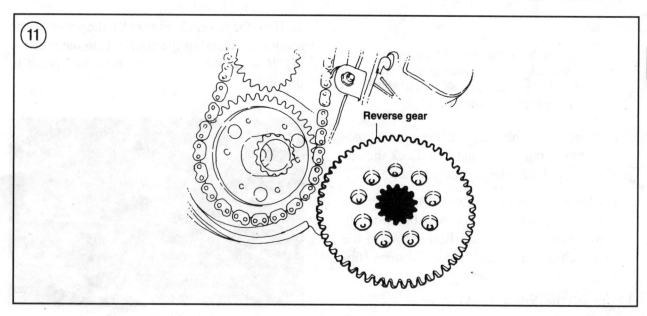

Reverse gear

14

e. Install the dropcase cover retaining screws and tighten to the torque listed in **Table 2**.

14. On models equipped with an external chain tensioner, proceed as follows:

  a. Install the chain tensioner housing assembly (7, **Figure 9**) in the side of the dropcase. Tighten the tensioner housing securely.

  b. Unscrew the temporarily installed setscrew in the side of the tensioner housing.

  c. Reinstall the original capscrew (8, **Figure 9**).

15. Fill the dropcase with the amount and type of gear oil specified in Chapter Three.

16. Adjust the shift linkage as follows:

  a. If not previously removed, remove the drive belt as described in Chapter Thirteen.

  b. Rotate the driven pulley while turning the shift fork arm toward the dropcase. Make sure the transmission is fully in reverse.

  c. With the transmission in reverse, rotate the adjustment rod of the shift linkage until the ball joint hole aligns with the hole in the shift fork shaft arm.

  d. Install and tighten the retaining screw and locknut securely.

NOTE
Be careful. If the linkage is too short, the shift fork shaft can be damaged. If the linkage is too long, the gears will not shift completely into reverse.

  e. Shorten the linkage by rotating the adjustment rod one additional turn. Lock the adjustment by tightening the jam nut.

  f. Check the shifting. With the shift lever in reverse, it should not be possible to rotate the shift fork shaft arm further toward the dropcase. If necessary, repeat substeps 16b-e.

17. Install the drive belt and cover.

EXTERNAL CHAIN TENSIONER

Some models are equipped with an external chain tensioner (**Figure 9**). The coil spring (3, **Figure 9**) rotates an adjuster shaft (4), which rotates the adjuster screw (5). The adjuster screw contacts the tensioner spring (9), which forces the pin (10) against the tensioner arm (12), thereby maintaining chain tension.

To service the internal components of the chain tensioner, remove the dropcase cover as discussed in the previous section. To service the tensioner housing assembly, proceed as follows.

Removal

1. Remove the screw (8, **Figure 9**) and install a setscrew in place of the original screw. Tighten the setscrew sufficiently to hold the adjuster shaft in position.

2. Remove the adjuster assembly by turning the housing (7, **Figure 9**) counterclockwise using a 3/4-inch wrench.

Disassembly

1. Extract the pin (10, **Figure 9**) and the spring (9) from the housing.

2. Hold the cover (2, **Figure 9**), then remove the screws (1) securing the cover (2) to the housing (7). Release the cover and allow the spring to unwind.

3. Carefully lift the cover (2, **Figure 9**) while disengaging the cover from the end of the coil spring (3).

4. Carefully lift out the coil spring (3, **Figure 9**) without letting it uncoil. Use a tie wrap to prevent the coil spring from uncoiling.

5. Unscrew the temporary setscrew in the housing.

6. Extract the adjuster shaft (4, **Figure 9**).

7. Unscrew the adjuster screw (5, **Figure 9**).

Assembly

1. Lightly lubricate the adjuster screw (5, **Figure 9**) with oil. Install the screw in the housing (7). Rotate the screw a few turns.

2. Note the flat on the side of the adjuster shaft (4, **Figure 9**). Install the adjuster shaft (4, **Figure 9**) around the adjuster screw (5) so the flat aligns with the threaded hole on the outside of the housing (7). Push the shaft down until it bottoms in the housing.

3. Install an 8mm-32mm setscrew in the threaded hole in the side of the housing.

4. Install the coil spring (3, **Figure 9**) by engaging the inner end in the slot on the adjuster shaft (4). Install the coil spring so the coils are wound in a clockwise direction from the inner end.

5. Install the O-ring (6, **Figure 9**) in the groove in the housing (7).

6. Install the cover (2, **Figure 9**) while engaging the tab with the outer end of the coil spring (3).

7. Note the socket hole in the center of the cover (2, **Figure 9**). Insert an Allen wrench into the cover, then rotate the cover 20 turns clockwise to apply tension to the coil spring. Hold the cover and install the three screws that secure the cover.

8. Lightly lubricate the spring (9, **Figure 9**) with grease. Insert the spring and pin (10) into the adjuster screw (5).

9. Install the adjuster in the dropcase and tighten securely.

10. Remove the setscrew and install the capscrew (8, **Figure 9**).

DRIVEN SHAFT

The driven pulley is attached to the left end of the driven shaft and the upper sprocket is attached to the right end of the shaft in the dropcase (**Figure 13**). Note that the brake disc (2, **Figure 13**) may be mounted on the inboard or outboard side of the brake hub (3) depending on the model.

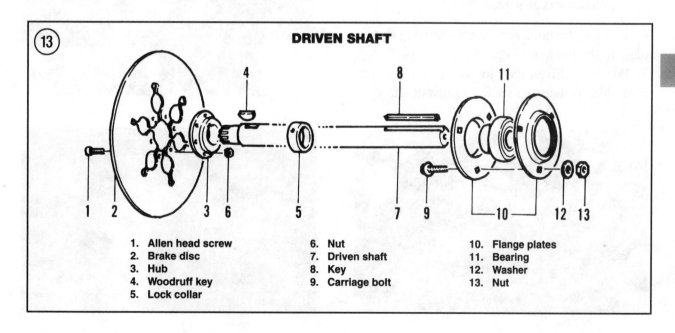

DRIVEN SHAFT

1. Allen head screw	6. Nut	10. Flange plates
2. Brake disc	7. Driven shaft	11. Bearing
3. Hub	8. Key	12. Washer
4. Woodruff key	9. Carriage bolt	13. Nut
5. Lock collar		

14

Removal

1. Refer to the appropriate section in this chapter and remove the chain and upper sprocket from the dropcase. Refer to the proper procedure for the models with reverse or for models without reverse.

2. Remove the driven pulley as described in Chapter Thirteen.

> *NOTE*
> *Some of the following procedures are shown with the dropcase removed for clarity. It is not necessary to remove the dropcase when removing the driven shaft bearings.*

3. Remove the three nuts (**Figure 14**) securing the bearing flange to the dropcase, then remove the bearing and flange.

4. Locate the lock collar on the left end of the driven shaft and loosen the setscrew (**Figure 15**).

5. Use a punch to turn the lock collar (**Figure 16**) opposite of shaft rotation (clockwise) to loosen it from the shaft.

> *NOTE*
> *It may be necessary to remove the air intake silencer while accomplishing the procedure in Step 6 and Step 7.*

6. Remove the bolts securing the bearing flange plate to the left side (**Figure 17**).

7. Force the driven shaft toward the left (engine pto) side. Rotate the shaft to prevent the disc brake from binding on the shaft. Do not lose the key that locates the disc brake hub on the shaft.

8. Continue pushing the driven shaft out toward the left side (**Figure 18**).

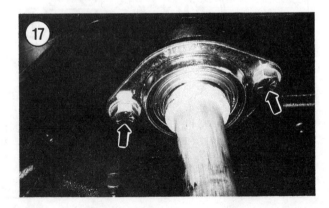

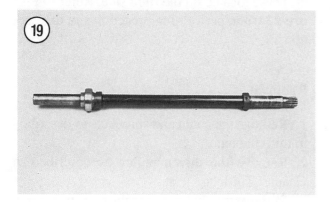

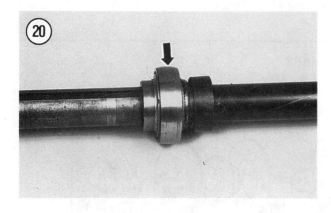

Driven Shaft Inspection

Refer to **Figure 13** for this procedure.

1. Clean the driven shaft in solvent and thoroughly dry.

2. Check the driven shaft (**Figure 19**) for straightness.

3. Turn the bearing (**Figure 20**) and check for excessive noise or roughness. Replace the bearing if worn or damaged.

4. Inspect both ends of the driven shaft for cracks, deep scoring or excessive wear (**Figure 19**). Smooth the area of the shaft damaged by the lock collar setscrew.

5. If the condition of the driven shaft is in question, repair or replace it.

Brake Disc Inspection

1. If it is necessary to remove the hub and brake disc (A and B, **Figure 21**), first remove the caliper assembly.

2. To separate the brake hub and disc, remove the Allen head screws and nuts holding the hub to the disc.

3. Visually check the brake disc (B, **Figure 21**) for cracks, deep scoring or excessive wear.

4. Install a new brake disc if necessary. Tighten the disc-to-hub screws to the torque listed in **Table 2**.

> *CAUTION*
> *Do not resurface the brake disc. If the brake disc surface is damaged or worn, replace the brake disc.*

Driven Shaft Installation

1. If removed, install the lower driveshaft before installing the driven shaft.

2. Position the brake disc and hub between the brake pads.

3. Insert the driven shaft into the frame partway so the splined end is toward the right side.

14

4. Install the bearing (**Figure 20**) on the left (engine PTO) end of the driven shaft.

5. Insert the driven shaft through the brake disc hub, engaging the key with the keyway in the hub.

6. Check that the driven shaft is centered, then install the flange plates against the side pan (**Figure 12** or **Figure 17**). Tighten the retaining bolts to the torque listed in **Table 2**.

7. Slide the lock collar toward the bearing, but do not lock it.

8. Apply Scotch Bond Adhesive 4174 to the bearing seating area adjacent to the shaft splines.

9. Install the bearing, seal and flange plate on the dropcase housing side. Tighten the flange plate retaining nuts to the torque listed in **Table 2**.

10. Slide the lock collar against the bearing and turn the collar in the direction of rotation (opposite the direction shown in **Figure 16**) to lock the collar.

11. Tighten the setscrew (**Figure 15**) in the lock collar.

12. Install the driven pulley as described in Chapter Thirteen. Align the pulleys and set the belt deflection as necessary.

13. Install the sprockets and chain as described in this chapter.

14. Install the drive belt and covers.

DRIVESHAFT

The driveshaft is driven by the chain in the dropcase located on the right side. Refer to **Figure 22** when performing procedures in this section.

Removal

1. Remove the chain and sprockets as described in this chapter.

2. Remove the driven pulley as described in Chapter Thirteen.

3. Remove the skid frame of the rear suspension from the tunnel as described in Chapter Sixteen.

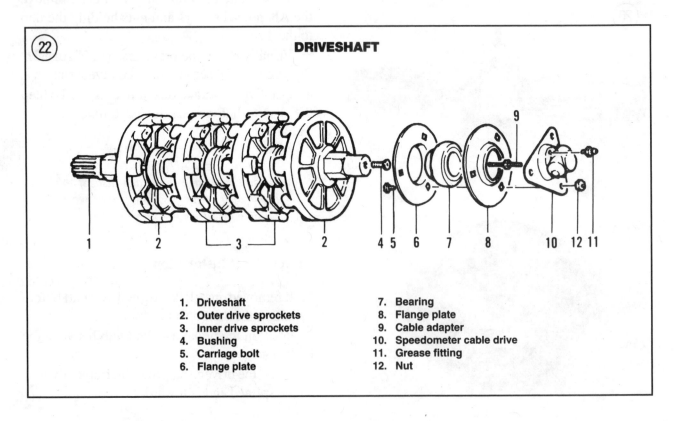

DRIVESHAFT

1. Driveshaft
2. Outer drive sprockets
3. Inner drive sprockets
4. Bushing
5. Carriage bolt
6. Flange plate
7. Bearing
8. Flange plate
9. Cable adapter
10. Speedometer cable drive
11. Grease fitting
12. Nut

4. Disconnect the speedometer cable from the speedometer adapter.

5. Remove the three locknuts and carriage bolts attaching the speedometer adapter and bearing flange plate to the left (engine PTO) side of the tunnel.

6. Remove the speedometer adapter (**Figure 23**) and flange plate.

7. Remove the bearing from the right (MAG) end of the driveshaft as follows.

   a. Remove the three screws attaching the bearing flange plate to the dropcase (**Figure 24**, typical), then remove the flange plate and seal ring.

   b. Use a soft-faced hammer to bump the driveshaft toward the right to unseat the bearing at the dropcase end.

   c. Remove the bearing from the right end of the driveshaft.

   d. Slide the driveshaft toward the right until the left end of the driveshaft and the bearing are outside the mounting hole.

   e. Tilt the driveshaft, then withdraw it from the tunnel. The track can be removed, if desired.

8. Remove the bearing from the left end of the driveshaft as follows:

   a. Remove the outer flange plate and slide the inner flange plate toward the drive sprocket to expose the locking collar.

   b. Loosen the locking collar setscrew (**Figure 25**).

   c. Insert a punch into the locking collar and drive the collar clockwise to loosen it from the shaft (**Figure 26**).

   d. Remove the bearing, locking collar and flange plate.

14

Inspection

Refer to **Figure 22**.

1. Check the bearings by holding the outer race and spinning the inner race by hand. If any roughness or excessive noise is noticed, replace the bearing.

2. Check the bearing seals for damage and replace as necessary.

3. Check the driveshaft (**Figure 27**) for straightness.

4. Check the driveshaft splines for damage.

5. Visually inspect the sprocket wheels for excessive wear, cracks, distortion or other damage. If necessary, replace drive sprockets and idler wheels on the driveshaft as described in this chapter.

Drive Sprockets and Idler Wheel Replacement

A press is required to remove and install the sprockets and idler wheels. Make sure any parts that will be replaced are available before pressing old parts from the driveshaft (**Figure 22**).

> *NOTE*
> *The drive sprockets have a mark molded into one of the lugs (**Figure 28**) to time the sprocket's drive lugs with the lugs of the track. Alignment marks installed in Step 1 establish the lateral position on the driveshaft that should align with the proper location on the track.*

1. Scribe a mark on the driveshaft along both sides of the drive sprockets and idler wheels to identify their position on the driveshaft to facilitate installation.

2. Place the assembly in a press and press each idler wheel and drive sprocket from the driveshaft.

3. Clean the driveshaft thoroughly and remove nicks with a file.

4. Observe the following when installing the drive sprockets and idler wheels.

a. Each drive sprocket has an index mark molded into one of the drive lugs (**Figure 28**). After installing the first drive sprocket, make sure marks on other sprockets align with the one on the first. All of the molded index marks must be aligned.

b. Press the drive sprockets and idler wheels onto the driveshaft with the sides of the sprockets and wheels between previously affixed marks (Step 1). The lateral position of the drive sprockets and idler wheels must be in line with the correct path of the track (**Figure 29**).

Installation

1. Install the bearing assembly on the left (engine PTO) end of the driveshaft as follows:

a. Install the bearing inner flange plate and lock collar onto the driveshaft.

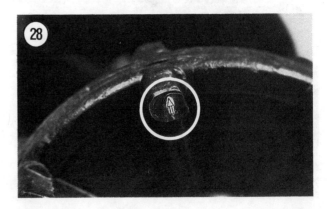

b. Slide the bearing onto the driveshaft with the shoulder side toward the inside.

c. Align the bearing with the end of the shaft (**Figure 30**).

d. Hold the bearing in position and slide the locking collar against the bearing inner shoulder.

e. Turn the locking collar counterclockwise to hold it in position on the shaft.

f. Drive the locking collar counterclockwise using a punch to lock it firmly to the shaft.

g. Tighten the setscrew (**Figure 25**) to hold the collar in this position.

2. If removed, install the track in the tunnel.

3. Install the outer flange plate (8, **Figure 22**) over the bearing, aligning the holes in both flanges.

4. Install the drive axle by reversing the removal procedure. Insert the splined end into the dropcase, then tip the other end up. Insert the bearing into the bore in the tunnel.

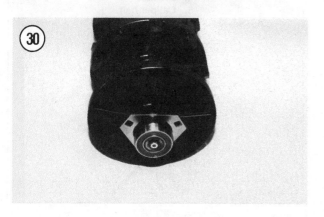

5. Align the holes in the flange plate with the holes in the tunnel. Position the speedometer adapter against the tunnel (**Figure 23**).

6. Align the holes in the bearing flanges, tunnel and speedometer adapter, then insert the three retaining carriage bolts from inside the tunnel. Install and tighten the nuts to the torque listed in **Table 2**.

7. Install the bearing assembly on the right (MAG) end of the driveshaft as follows:

a. Slide the bearing onto the driveshaft so the bearing shoulder is toward the outside.

b. Install the bearing seal ring.

c. Install the bearing flange plate over the mounting studs.

d. Install the mounting nuts and tighten to the torque listed in **Table 2**.

8. Install the chain and sprocket assembly, as described in this chapter.

9. Install the skid frame of the rear suspension as described in Chapter Sixteen.

10. Install the driven pulley and drive belt as described in Chapter Thirteen.

MECHANICAL BRAKE SYSTEM

The disc brake installed on some models is actuated by a cable attached to the handlebar mounted control lever. The caliper unit grips a disc mounted on the right end of the driven shaft. Service to the hydraulic brakes used on other models is described elsewhere in this chapter.

WARNING
The brake system is an important part of machine safety. If you are unsure about the condition of any brake component or assembly, have it checked by a qualified snowmobile mechanic.

Removal/Disassembly (1994 and Earlier Models)

1. Open and secure the hood.

14

2. Loosen the brake cable flange nut (A, **Figure 31**). Detach the cable from the bracket.

3. Detach the brake return spring (B, **Figure 31**).

4. Disconnect the brake cable from the caliper.

5. Remove the two bolts (B, **Figure 32**) attaching the brake bracket to the dropcase. Do not lose the spacers.

6. Remove the caliper assembly from the bracket. Do not lose the spacers.

7. Remove the brake pad and pad spring (6 and 7, **Figure 33**) from the movable half (14, **Figure 33**).

NOTE
*Do not remove the stationary brake pad from the caliper half (5, **Figure 33**) unless the pad requires replacement.*

8. Twist the actuator lever to remove the pad from the caliper (**Figure 34**).

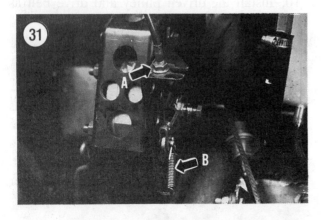

Removal/Disassembly (1995 and Later Models)

1. Open and secure the hood.

2. Loosen the brake cable flange nut (A, **Figure 35**) and detach the cable from the bracket.

3. Disconnect the brake cable from the caliper.

4. Pull the recoil starter rope out about 2 ft. (61 cm), tie a knot in the rope so it will not rewind.

5. Remove the handle from the recoil starter.

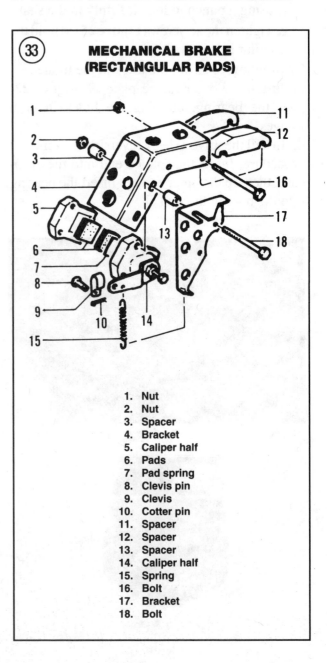

MECHANICAL BRAKE (RECTANGULAR PADS)

1. Nut
2. Nut
3. Spacer
4. Bracket
5. Caliper half
6. Pads
7. Pad spring
8. Clevis pin
9. Clevis
10. Cotter pin
11. Spacer
12. Spacer
13. Spacer
14. Caliper half
15. Spring
16. Bolt
17. Bracket
18. Bolt

6. Remove the rope from the rope guide attached to the brake bracket.

7. Remove the two bolts (**Figure 36**) attaching the caliper to the dropcase. Do not lose the alignment ball in the front bolt location.

8. Remove the snap ring (**Figure 37**), then remove the support plate and stationary pad (**Figure 38**).

9. Remove the movable pad and piston (**Figure 39**).

10. Detach the return spring.

11. Unbolt and remove the cable bracket.

12. Remove the actuator arm (**Figure 40**).

13. Pull the adjuster knob out and turn counterclockwise to remove the adjuster from the actuator arm.

14. Remove the jam nut, washer, spring and alignment ball (**Figure 41**).

Inspection

Clean all parts and replace any that are cracked, worn or otherwise damaged. Measure the thickness of the brake pads. If the measured thickness is less than the minimum thickness listed in **Table 3**, install new pads. Always install new pads as a set.

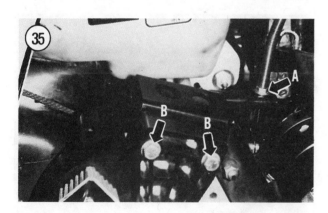

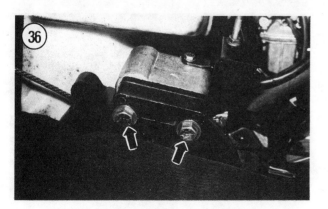

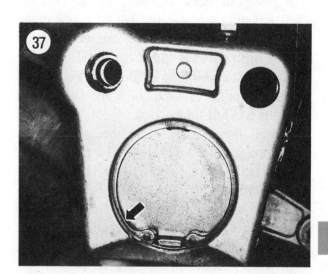

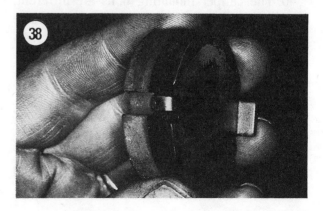

14

On 1994 and earlier models, the stationary pad is bonded to the caliper, but can be removed by inserting a punch through the hole (**Figure 42**) in the caliper. Install the stationary pad of these early models using Loctite Superbonder Adhesive or equivalent.

Assembly/Installation (1994 and Earlier Models)

1. Assemble the actuator in the caliper as follows:
   a. Install the locknut and locking tab onto the adjusting screw (**Figure 34**).
   b. Insert the spiral into the caliper and turn it until it bottoms.
   c. Install the brake actuator arm onto the spiral so it is positioned vertically (**Figure 43**).
   d. Install the locknut and lockwasher on the adjusting screw and install the screw in the spiral. Turn the screw until the threaded end is flush with the end of the spiral.
   e. Place the tab of the locking tab (**Figure 44**) in the notch of the actuator arm and tighten the locknut finger-tight.
2. Install the pad spring in the caliper, then install the plate and movable brake pad.
3. Assemble the brake/caliper halves and bracket (**Figure 33**). Observe the following.
   a. The spacers installed at the top of the bracket are different. Install the thicker spacer on the side that faces the engine, when installed in the snowmobile.
   b. The caliper mounting bolts are different. The bolt head of the front bolt may have been machined to provide additional clearance for the brake actuator lever.
   c. Install the caliper mounting bolts so the heads are toward the engine.
   d. Tighten the caliper bolts to the torque listed in **Table 2**.
4. Connect the brake actuating cable as follows:
   a. Place the clevis (9, **Figure 33**) over the end of the brake cable. Align the hole in the

clevis with the hole in the brake actuator arm and install the clevis pin (8, **Figure 33**).

b. Secure the clevis pin (8, **Figure 33**) with a *new* cotter pin.

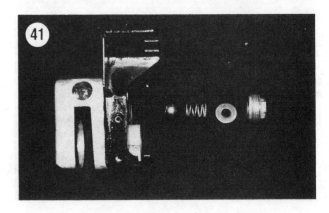

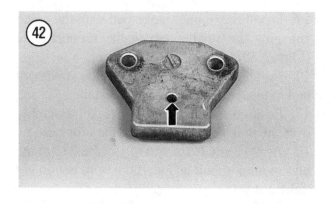

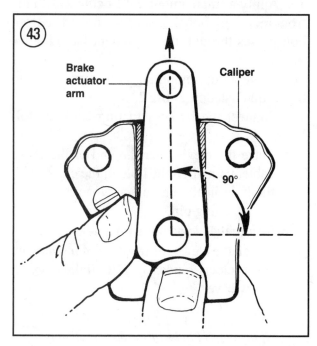

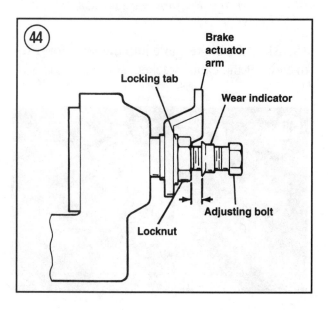

c. Check the clevis for freedom of movement. If the clevis binds, open it slightly with a screwdriver.

> *WARNING*
> *If the clevis binds, brake operation may be erratic. Be sure the clevis moves freely.*

5. Slide the brake cable into the slot of the cable bracket. A flange nut (A, **Figure 31**) must be on both sides of the bracket.

6. Center the cable. Make sure the cable does not bind and is not kinked, then tighten the flange nuts securely.

7. Attach the brake return spring (B, **Figure 31**) to the actuator arm and the bracket.

> *NOTE*
> *If the bolts (16, **Figure 33**) attaching the bracket are not the same length, the longer screw should be installed at the front.*

8. Position the brake and bracket assembly on the dropcase, install the spacers, screws and locknuts (**Figure 33**). Tighten the attaching locknuts to the torque listed in **Table 2**.

9. Adjust the brake as described in Chapter Three.

10. Test the operation of the brake before riding.

> *WARNING*
> *Make sure the brake is operating properly before riding. Brake failure can result in loss of control and injury.*

Assembly/Installation (1995 and later Models)

1. Assemble the alignment ball, spring, washer and jam nut (**Figure 41**) as follows:

   a. Temporarily install a mounting screw in the rear mounting location.

   b. Apply a small amount of grease to the alignment ball and install over the temporarily installed screw.

14

c. Install the spring and washer (**Figure 41**) over the temporarily installed mounting screw.

d. Install the jam nut, tightening the nut until slight spring pressure is felt. The spring pressure should be sufficient to hold the alignment bushing when the screw is removed.

e. Remove the temporarily installed mounting screw.

2. Assemble the adjuster in the actuator as follows:

a. Apply a small amount of Molylube Silicone Anti-Seize to the threads of the adjusting screw (**Figure 40**).

b. Insert the adjusting screw and spring into the quick-adjust knob. Install the assembly in the actuating arm. Turn the adjusting screw a couple of turns.

3. Apply Molylube Silicone Anti-Seize to the threads of the actuator shaft.

4. Start the actuator arm in the 11 o'clock position (**Figure 45**) and screw the arm into the caliper.

5. Install the brake cable bracket.

6. Attach the return spring to the bracket and the actuating arm.

7. Install the brake piston. The notch must engage the roll pin in the caliper.

8. Install the thicker (movable) brake pad, making sure the notch engages the roll pin.

WARNING
Make sure the snap ring installed in Step 9 is properly seated before continuing. Failure to seat the snap ring can result in injury.

9. Install the snap ring (**Figure 37**) with the sharp edge facing out. The opening in the snap ring should be down as shown.

10. Install the pad support plate with the longer tab (**Figure 38**) located in the opening of the snap ring.

11. Install the thinner brake pad with the notch engaging the smaller tab of the support plate (**Figure 38**).

12. Install a rubber band to hold the stationary pad in place until the caliper is installed.

13. Position the caliper and bracket assembly over the brake disc and against the dropcase.

14. Apply a small amount of Loctite 271 to the rear mounting bolt and start the bolt, but do not tighten it yet.

15. Apply a small amount of Loctite 271 to the front mounting bolt and start the bolt. The front bolt passes through the alignment ball (**Figure 41**).

16. Tighten both mounting bolts evenly and to the torque listed in **Table 2**.

17. Connect the brake actuating cable as follows.

a. Place the clevis over the end of the brake cable, then align the hole in the clevis with the hole in the brake actuator arm. Install the attaching pin.

b. Secure the clevis pin with a *new* cotter pin.

c. Check the clevis for freedom of movement. If the clevis binds, open it slightly with a screwdriver.

WARNING
If the clevis binds, brake operation may be erratic. Be sure the clevis moves freely.

18. Slide the brake cable into the rear slot (**Figure 46**) of the cable bracket.

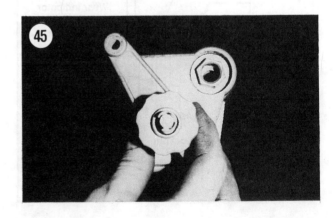

19. Center the cable. Make sure the cable does not bind and is not kinked. Tighten the flange nut securely.

NOTE
*Turn the adjustment knob (**Figure 45**) clockwise to tighten the brake.*

20. Pull the adjustment knob out. Turn the knob to adjust the free play of the handlebar lever.

21. Set the parking brake. Tighten the jam nut (**Figure 41**) on the rear mounting bolt.

22. Release the parking brake. Recheck the handlebar lever free play. Adjust the brake as described in Chapter Three, if necessary.

23. Route the starter rope through the guide attached to the brake bracket. Attach the handle to the starter rope.

24. Test the operation of the brake before riding.

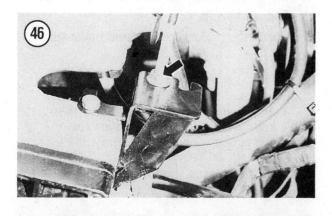

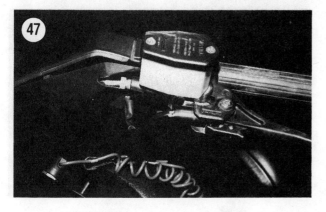

WARNING
Make sure the brake is operating properly before riding. Brake failure can result in loss of control and injury.

HYDRAULIC BRAKE SYSTEM

The disc brake installed on some models is actuated by a handlebar-mounted master cylinder and control lever. The hydraulic brake caliper unit, attached to the top of the dropcase, grips a disc mounted on the right end of the driven shaft.

Use only Arctic Cat Hi-Temp Brake fluid (part No. 0638-315) in the hydraulic brake system. Do not substitute a different fluid or mix different types of fluid.

Service to cable-operated, mechanical brakes used on other models is described elsewhere in this chapter.

WARNING
The brake system is an important part of machine safety. If you are unsure about the condition of any brake component or assembly, have it checked by a qualified snowmobile mechanic.

Bleeding

Air should be bled from the hydraulic brake system if the brake feels spongy, if there is a leak in the system, if any component of the system has been removed or if the fluid has been rechanged.

CAUTION
Immediately clean any spilled brake fluid. Wash spilled brake fluid from painted surfaces immediately because it will damage the finish. Use soapy water and rinse with clean water.

1. Clean all dirt and foreign material from the top of the master cylinder. Remove the cover (**Figure 47**) from the master cylinder and fill to the upper level mark with brake fluid.

14

2. If the master cylinder was allowed to run dry, bleed as follows:

    a. Pump the brake lever several times, then hold the lever in.

    b. Loosen the hose attached to the master cylinder and allow some fluid and air to seep out, then tighten the hose connection. Do not attempt to reuse any brake fluid. Discard any fluid bled from the system.

    c. Repeat substeps a and b several times until air is removed from the master cylinder.

    d. Refill the reservoir. Make sure that it does not run dry during the bleeding process.

3. Connect a length of clear tubing to the bleeder valve (A, **Figure 48**, typical). Place the other end of the tube into a clean container. Add enough brake fluid to the container to keep the end of the hose submerged, which prevents air from being drawn in during the bleeding procedure.

4. Pump the brake lever several times, then hold the lever in.

5. Loosen the bleeder valve slowly and allow fluid and air to escape from the hose. Tighten the bleeder valve before releasing the brake lever.

6. Check the reservoir frequently to make sure that it does not run dry during the bleeding process. Air will be pumped into the system if the reservoir is emptied while bleeding.

7. Repeat Steps 4 and 5 several times until fluid without air bubbles is expelled from the bleeder tube.

8. Fill the reservoir and clean any spilled fluid.

Brake Pads

1. Remove the pin (B, **Figure 48**). On some models, a cotter pin will be located in a similar location.

2. Use a suitable tool to push the pistons and brake pads away from the disc.

3. Pull the brake pads (**Figure 49**) from the caliper.

4. Inspect the brake pads and disc (rotor). Brake pads must be replaced as a set.

5. Install the brake pads and retaining pins by reversing the removal procedure. If new pads are installed, it will be necessary to push both brake pistons completely into the caliper.

NOTE
On some models, a cotter pin is used as the retaining pin. If a cotter pin is used, use a new pin. Bend the ends out to hold it in place after installing.

6. Install the retaining pin (B, **Figure 48**, typical). Make sure the retaining pin is completely and correctly installed.

7. Pump the brake several times to position the new brake pads. If the brake does not feel firm, it may be necessary to bleed the brakes as described in this chapter.

8. Check the brake reservoir and make sure it is full of fluid.

WARNING
Make sure the brake is operating properly before riding. Brake failure can result in loss of control and injury.

9. New brake pads should be bedded/seated as follows.

a. Drive the snowmobile slowly and compress the brake lever several times until they just start to heat up.

b. Stop the snowmobile and allow the brakes to cool. This process will stabilize and extend the life of the pads.

Caliper Assembly

Make sure repair parts are available before disassembling the caliper. Some models are equipped with brake calipers that have one piston and movable pad.

1. Remove the caliper as follows.

a. Attach a hose to the bleeder valve (A, **Figure 48**). Insert the hose into a container and open the bleeder valve.

b. Allow the brake fluid to drain.

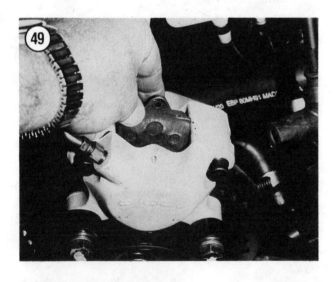

c. Operate the brake lever several times, then close the bleeder valve when the system has drained. Discard the drained fluid. Do not attempt to reuse any brake fluid.

d. Remove the brake pads as described in this chapter.

e. Disconnect the brake line from the fitting (C, **Figure 48**).

> *CAUTION*
> *Immediately clean any spilled brake fluid. Wash spilled brake fluid from painted surfaces immediately because it will damage the finish. Use soapy water and rinse with clean water.*

> *WARNING*
> *Be careful when using compressed air in steps 2A or 2B. The piston can fly from the caliper causing injury.*

2A. For models with a single piston, proceed as follows:

a. Remove the two upper Allen head bolts that attach the caliper to the dropcase.

b. Loosen the two brake studs evenly until the caliper can be lifted from the bracket.

c. Remove the brake studs.

d. Use compressed air to remove the piston from the caliper. Catch the piston in shop cloths.

e. Remove the O-ring from the caliper bore.

2B. For models with dual pistons, proceed as follows:

a. Remove the two mounting bolts (**Figure 50**) and lift the caliper from the snowmobile.

b. Remove the two Allen head bolts (**Figure 51**).

c. Separate the halves of the caliper and remove the small O-ring (A, **Figure 52**).

d. Use compressed air to remove the pistons from the caliper halves. Catch the pistons in shop cloths.

e. Remove the O-rings (B, **Figure 52**) from each caliper bore.

14

3. Clean the brake caliper assembly with a brake parts cleaner and dry with compressed air.

4. Inspect all parts for scratches, gouges, cracks, pitting or corrosion. Replace any damaged parts.

5. On models with a single piston and one movable pad, inspect the brake studs and bushings for damage or wear. Install new parts, as necessary.

6. Apply brake fluid to the O-ring seal and install in the groove in the caliper bore. Make sure the sealing ring is not twisted or cut while installing.

7. Coat the piston with brake fluid.

8. Use a twisting motion to insert the piston in the bore with the open side out.

9A. On models with a single piston and one movable pad, proceed as follows:

    a. Install the brake studs in the caliper.

    b. Assemble the caliper halves and install, but do not tighten, the two Allen head bolts.

    c. Attach the caliper to the dropcase. Tighten the two studs and two Allen head mounting bolts to the torque listed in **Table 2**.

9B. On models with dual pistons, proceed as follows:

    a. Repeat Steps 6-8 to assemble the second piston.

    b. Position the small O-ring (A, **Figure 52**) as shown, then assemble the two halves of the caliper.

    c. Hold the caliper halves together and install the Allen head bolts (**Figure 51**). Tighten the Allen head bolts only enough to hold the caliper halves together.

    d. Attach the caliper to the dropcase and tighten the mounting bolts to the torque listed in **Table 2**.

    e. Tighten the two Allen head bolts (**Figure 51**) to the torque listed in **Table 2**.

10. Attach the brake line to the caliper. Tighten the fitting securely.

11. Install the brake pads and secure with the retaining pin as described in this chapter.

12. Fill the system with approved brake fluid and bleed the system as described in this chapter.

Master Cylinder

Repair parts for the master cylinder are not available. Service to the master cylinder is limited to removal of the old part and installation of a new part. The brake light switch, hand lever and clamp parts are available.

1. Drain the master cylinder as follows:

    a. Attach a hose to the brake caliper bleeder valve (A, **Figure 48**, typical).

    b. Place the open end of the hose in a clean container.

    c. Open the bleed valve and operate the brake lever to drain all fluid from the master cylinder reservoir.

    d. Close the bleeder valve and remove the drain hose.

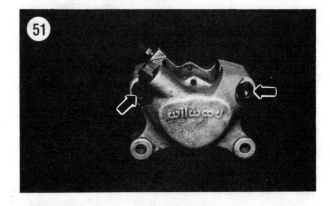

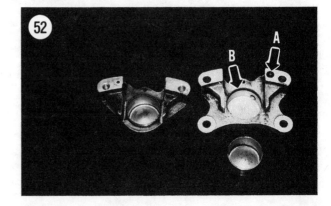

e. Discard the drained fluid. Do not attempt to reuse any brake fluid.

2. Disconnect wires from the brake light switch.

3. Detach the hose from the master cylinder, then cover the openings to prevent the entrance of dirt.

4. Remove the clamping bolts and clamp attaching the master cylinder to the handlebar. Remove the master cylinder.

5. Install the master cylinder by reversing the removal procedure.

6. Fill the reservoir with brake fluid and bleed the system as described in this chapter.

WARNING
Do not operate the snowmobile until the brake is operating properly.

Table 1 SPROCKET SPECIFICATIONS

Model	Upper sprocket (number of teeth)	Lower sprocket (number of teeth)
1990		
Prowler	–	–
El Tigre EXT		
Models without reverse	20	35
Models with reverse	24	39
1991		
Prowler, Cougar		
0-4000 ft.	20	39
Above 4000 ft.	18	40
El Tigre EXT		
Models without reverse	20	35
Models with reverse	24	39
1992		
Prowler, Cougar		
0-4000 ft.	20	39
Above 4000 ft.	18	40
El Tigre EXT		
Models without reverse	20	35
Models with reverse	24	39
1993		
Prowler, Cougar		
0-4000 ft.	20	39
Above 4000 ft.	18	40
440 ZR		
0-4000 ft.	20	39
Above 4000 ft.	19	39
EXT 550	19	39
580 ZR, EXT 580	20	39

(continued)

14

Table 1 SPROCKET SPECIFICATIONS (continued)

Model	Upper sprocket (number of teeth)	Lower sprocket (number of teeth)
1994		
Cougar, Cougar Mountain Cat		
0-4000 ft.	20	39
Above 4000 ft.	18	40
Prowler		
0-4000 ft.	20	39
Above 4000 ft.	18	40
ZR 440, ZR 580	20	39
EXT 580	20	39
1995		
Cougar, Cougar Mountain Cat	20	39
Prowler 2-Up	19	39
Z 440		
0-10,000 ft.	20	39
over 10,000 ft.	18	40
ZR 440	20	39
EXT 580, EXT 580 EFI	20	39
ZR 580, ZR 580 EFI	20	39
1996		
Z 440		
0-10,000 ft.	20	39
over 10,000 ft.	18	40
ZR 440	20	39
Cougar, Cougar Mountain Cat	20	39
Cougar 2-Up	19	39
EXT 580, EXT 580 EFI	20	39
EXT 580 EFI Mountain Cat, EXT 580 Powder Special		
0-5000 ft.	20	39
Above 5000 ft.	19	40
ZR 580	20	39
ZRT 600	23	40
1997		
Z 440		
0-5000 ft.	20	39
Above 5000 ft.	19	40
ZL 440, ZR 440	20	39
Panther 440		
0-5000 ft.	19	39
Above 5000 ft.	18	40
Cougar, Cougar Mountain Cat	20	39
Panther 550	20	39
EXT 580 EFI		
0-5000 ft.	20	39
Above 5000 ft.	19	40
ZR 580 EFI, Powder Special EFI		
0-5000 ft.	20	39
Above 5000 ft.	19	40
Pantera		
0-5000 ft.	19	39
5000-9000 ft.	19	40
Above 9000 ft.	19	39

(continued)

Table 1 SPROCKET SPECIFICATIONS (continued)

Model	Upper sprocket (number of teeth)	Lower sprocket (number of teeth)
1997		
EXT 600		
0-5000 ft.	23	40
Above 5000 ft.	20	39
ZRT 600		
0-5000 ft.	23	40
Above 5000 ft.	20	39
Powder Extreme		
0-5000 ft.	23	40
Above 5000 ft.	20	39
1998		
Z 440, ZL 440		
0-5000 ft.	20	39
Above 5000 ft.	19	40
ZR 440	19	40
Panther 440		
0-5000 ft.	19	39
Above 5000 ft.	18	40
ZL 500		
0-5000 ft.	20	39
Above 5000 ft.	19	40
Cougar, Cougar Mountain Cat	20	39
Cougar Deluxe	19	39
Panther 550	19	39
EXT EFI		
0-5000 ft.	20	39
Above 5000 ft.	19	40
EXT EFI Deluxe	19	39
ZR 600 EFI	19	39
Powder Special (carbureted)	19	40
Powder Special EFI	19	40
Pantera	19	39
EXT 600		
0-5000 ft.	23	40
Above 5000 ft.	20	39
EXT Triple Touring		
0-5000 ft.	23	40
Above 5000 ft.	19	39
ZRT 600		
0-5000 ft.	23	40
Above 5000 ft.	20	39
Powder Extreme	20	39

Table 2 TIGHTENING TORQUE

	N·m	ft.-lb.
Mechanical brake (1994 and earlier)		
Bracket to dropcase	32	24
Brake disc to hub	4	35 in.-lb.
Caliper to bracket	35	26
(continued)		

14

Table 2 TIGHTENING TORQUE (continued)

	N·m	ft.-lb.
Mechanical brake (1995 and later)		
Brake disc to hub	4	35 in.-lb.
Caliper mounting nuts	83-97	61-72
Caliper brake w/one piston		
Brake studs	35	26
Allen head mounting bolts	50	37
Caliper brake w/two pistons		
Allen head bolts	50	37
Mounting bolts	42	31
Models without reverse		
Drain plug (on dropcase housing)	48	35
Drive and driven shafts		
Bearing flange plate nuts	22-25	16-18
Driven pulley	26-33	19-24
Drive shaft lock collar	4	35 in.-lb.
Dropcase cover bolts	17-21	13-15
Lower sprocket bolts	26-33	19-24
Upper and lower sprocket nuts	48-55	35-40
Models with reverse		
Chain tensioner nut	6-7	4-5
Drain plug (on dropcase housing)	48	35
Drive and driven shafts		
Bearing flange plate nuts	22-25	16-18
Driven pulley	26-33	19-24
Dropcase cover bolts	17-21	13-15
Reverse gear bolt	26-33	19-24
Upper sprocket nut	26-33	19-24

Table 3 BRAKE SPECIFICATIONS

Free play at handlebar lever	
Mechanical brakes	6-13 mm (1/4-1/2 in.)
Brake pad *minimum* thickness	
Mechanical 1994 and earlier	
Both rectangular pads	6.2 mm (0.244 in.)
Mechanical 1995 and later	
Stationary round pad	6.22 mm (0.2449 in.)
Movable round pad	12.7 mm (0.500 in.)
Hydraulic caliper w/one piston	
Both pads	3.8 mm (0.150 in.)
Hydraulic caliper w/two pistons	
Both pads	3.2 mm (0.126 in.)

Chapter Fifteen

Front Suspension And Steering

Early models are equipped with the suspension shown in **Figure 1** and later models with a double wishbone suspension similar to that shown in **Figure 2-4**. This chapter describes service to the skis, handlebar, steering assembly, steering column and tie rods of both systems. Ski alignment is described in Chapter Three.

Table 1 and **Table 2** are located at the end of this chapter.

SKIS

The skis are equipped with wear bars, or skags, that aid in turning the machine and protect the bottoms of the skis from wear and damage caused by road crossings and bare terrain. The skags are expendable and should be checked for wear and damage at periodic intervals and replaced when they are worn to the point they no longer protect the skis or aid in turning.

Removal/Installation

Refer to **Figure 1-4** for this procedure.

1. Support the front of the machine so both skis are off the ground.

> *NOTE*
> *Mark the skis with a L (left) or R (right). The skis should be installed on their original mounting side.*

2. Remove the cotter pin from the end of the ski pivot bolt. Loosen and remove the nut, bolt and ski (**Figure 5**, typical).

> *NOTE*
> *Do not lose the washers from the sides of the ski pivot bolt (23, **Figure 2**) or the rubber ski damper (19, **Figure 2**).*

3. Inspect the skis and hardware and replace as necessary.

4. Installation is the reverse of the preceding steps. Observe the following:

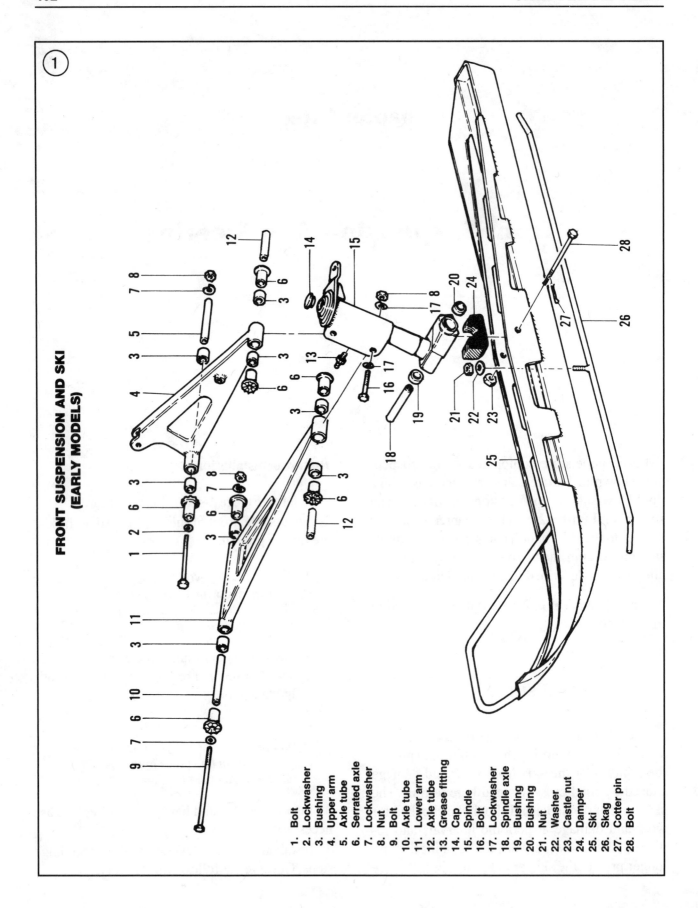

FRONT SUSPENSION AND SKI
(EARLY MODELS)

1. Bolt
2. Lockwasher
3. Bushing
4. Upper arm
5. Axle tube
6. Serrated axle
7. Lockwasher
8. Nut
9. Bolt
10. Axle tube
11. Lower arm
12. Axle tube
13. Grease fitting
14. Cap
15. Spindle
16. Bolt
17. Lockwasher
18. Spindle axle
19. Bushing
20. Bushing
21. Nut
22. Washer
23. Castle nut
24. Damper
25. Ski
26. Skag
27. Cotter pin
28. Bolt

a. Clean all the old grease from the pivot bolt, bushing and washers.

b. When installing the skis, refer to the alignment marks made before removal. Skis should be reinstalled on the same side as originally installed.

c. Coat the nonthreaded part of the pivot bolt and bushing with a low-temperature grease before installation.

d. Hold the ski in place, then position the spindle, bushings and rubber damper.

e. Insert the pivot bolt through the ski and spindle with the bolt head toward the outside.

f. Coat the threads of the installed ski pivot bolt with Loctite 271 (red). Install and tighten the nut to the torque specified in **Table 1**.

g. Check that the ski pivots up and down with slight resistance.

h. Lock the pivot bolt by inserting a new cotter pin through the nut and bolt. Bend the ends of the cotter pin over the edges of the nut.

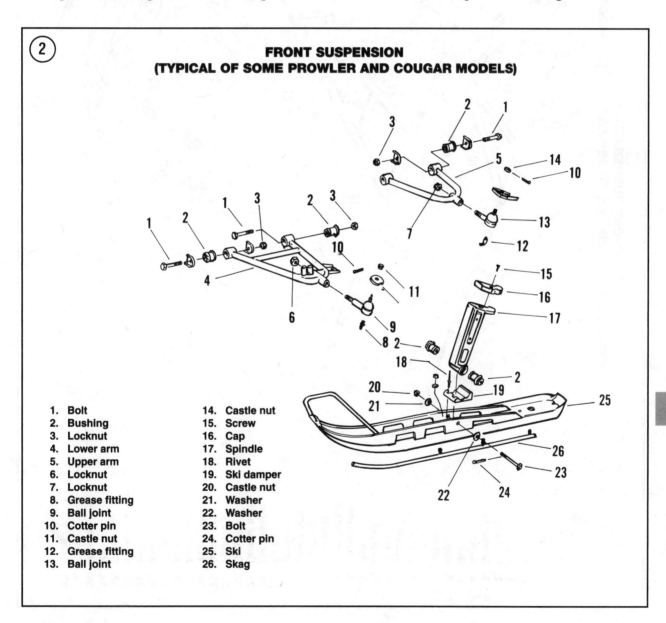

FRONT SUSPENSION (TYPICAL OF SOME PROWLER AND COUGAR MODELS)

1. Bolt
2. Bushing
3. Locknut
4. Lower arm
5. Upper arm
6. Locknut
7. Locknut
8. Grease fitting
9. Ball joint
10. Cotter pin
11. Castle nut
12. Grease fitting
13. Ball joint
14. Castle nut
15. Screw
16. Cap
17. Spindle
18. Rivet
19. Ski damper
20. Castle nut
21. Washer
22. Washer
23. Bolt
24. Cotter pin
25. Ski
26. Skag

15

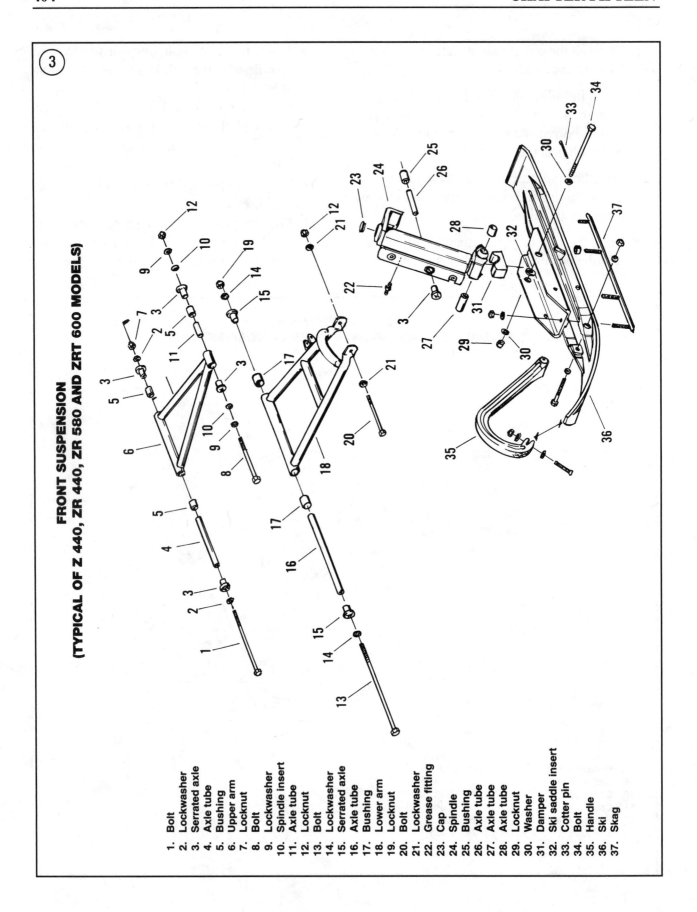

FRONT SUSPENSION
(TYPICAL OF Z 440, ZR 440, ZR 580 AND ZRT 600 MODELS)

1. Bolt
2. Lockwasher
3. Serrated axle
4. Axle tube
5. Bushing
6. Upper arm
7. Locknut
8. Bolt
9. Lockwasher
10. Spindle insert
11. Axle tube
12. Locknut
13. Bolt
14. Lockwasher
15. Serrated axle
16. Axle tube
17. Bushing
18. Lower arm
19. Locknut
20. Bolt
21. Lockwasher
22. Grease fitting
23. Cap
24. Spindle
25. Bushing
26. Axle tube
27. Axle tube
28. Axle tube
29. Locknut
30. Washer
31. Damper
32. Ski saddle insert
33. Cotter pin
34. Bolt
35. Handle
36. Ski
37. Skag

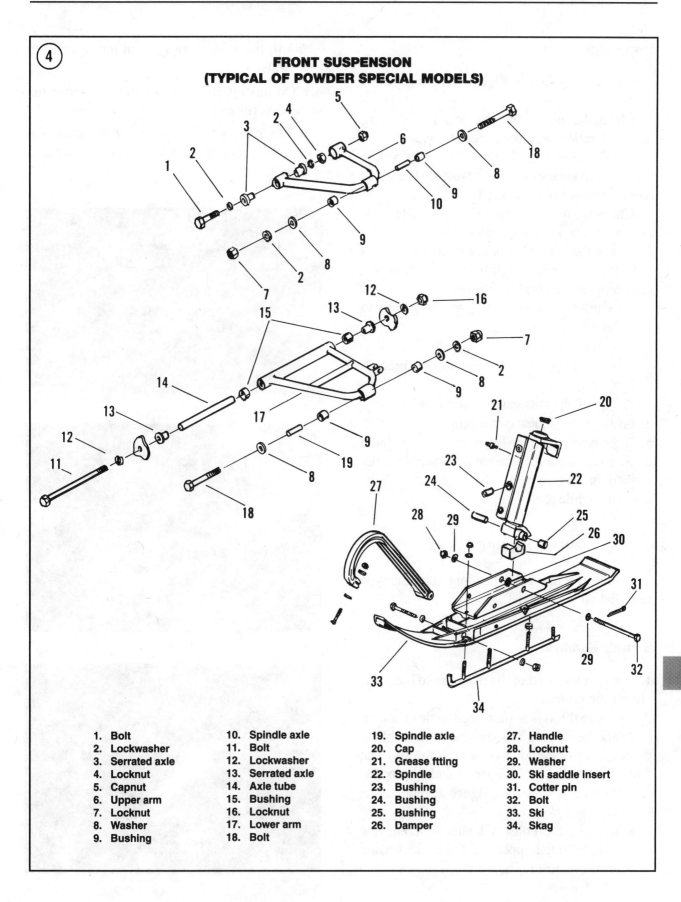

**FRONT SUSPENSION
(TYPICAL OF POWDER SPECIAL MODELS)**

1. Bolt	10. Spindle axle	19. Spindle axle	27. Handle
2. Lockwasher	11. Bolt	20. Cap	28. Locknut
3. Serrated axle	12. Lockwasher	21. Grease ftting	29. Washer
4. Locknut	13. Serrated axle	22. Spindle	30. Ski saddle insert
5. Capnut	14. Axle tube	23. Bushing	31. Cotter pin
6. Upper arm	15. Bushing	24. Bushing	32. Bolt
7. Locknut	16. Locknut	25. Bushing	33. Ski
8. Washer	17. Lower arm	26. Damper	34. Skag
9. Bushing	18. Bolt		

15

Inspection

Refer to **Figure 3** or **Figure 4** for this procedure.

1. Check the rubber stoppers for wear, cracking or deterioration. Replace if necessary.

2. Check the skis for fatigue cracks, distortion, bends, deep scrapes or other damage. Repair or replace the ski(s) as required.

3. Check the rubber damper for any visible damage, wear, cracking or deterioration.

4. Check the wear bars, or skags, on the bottom of the skis for severe wear or damage. If necessary, replace the skags as follows:

    a. Remove the nuts holding the wear bars to the ski.

    b. Remove the skag.

    c. Install a new skag by reversing the preceding steps.

    d. Tighten the nuts securing the skag securely.

5. Always install new cotter pins.

6. If the bushings in the lower end of the spindle require replacement, remove the spindle as described in this chapter. The bushings will be damaged while removing.

FRONT SUSPENSION

Refer to **Figure 1-4** depending upon the type installed on your model.

Spindle Removal

1. Support the front of the machine so both skis are off the ground.

2. Remove the skis as described in this chapter.

3. Mark the steering arm with the location of the tie rod/drag link end, then detach the rod end from the steering arm (**Figure 6** and **Figure 7**).

4A. On models shown in **Figure 1**, remove the spindle as follows:

    a. Remove the bolts and nuts attaching the spindle to the upper and lower suspension arms (4 and 11, **Figure 1**).

    b. Lift the spindle away from the suspension arms.

4B. On models shown in **Figure 2**, remove the spindle as follows:

    a. Remove the bolt (A, **Figure 8**) attaching the shock absorber to the lower suspension arm.

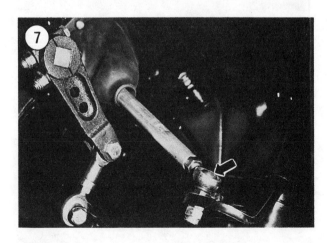

b. Remove the screw attaching the cover to the top of the spindle, then remove the cover (B, **Figure 8**).

c. Remove the two cotter pins and castle nuts attaching the ball joints to the spindle.

d. Raise the spindle until the suspension arms are parallel to the floor. Support the spindle in this position.

NOTE
The suspension arms must be parallel to the floor to allow use of the tie rod/ball joint tool.

WARNING
Do not strike the ball joint when attempting to separate the ball joint from the spindle. The ball joint will be damaged and separation will probably still require the tie rod/ball joint tool.

e. Use a tie rod/ball joint fork (part No. 0644-098 or equivalent) to separate the ball joint from the spindle.

f. Inspect the ball joints for damage and install new parts as required. If it is necessary to remove the ball joints, first remove the suspension arm.

NOTE
The ball joints are pressed into the suspension arms. Loctite is applied to the threads of the retaining nuts. It may be necessary to heat the nuts to soften the Loctite before removing the nuts.

4C. On models shown in **Figure 3** or **4**, remove the spindle as follows:

a. Remove the bolt attaching the lower end of the shock absorber to the spindle.

NOTE
*The bolts attaching the suspension arms to the spindle should be installed in the direction originally installed. Use paint or a marker to identify the original location of the bolt head, before removing the attaching bolts. The bolt heads shown in **Figure 9** are for one model, but the heads may be located differently for other models.*

b. Mark the location, either front or rear, of the heads of bolts attaching the spindle to the upper and lower suspension arms, then remove the bolts and nuts.

c. Withdraw the spindle from the suspension arms.

15

Inspection

1. Clean all components thoroughly in solvent. Remove all dirt and other residue from all surfaces.

2. If so equipped, remove the spindle/suspension arm bushing assembly from the arm or spindle (**Figure 1, 3** or **4**). Inspect all parts of the

bushing for wear or damage and replace as necessary.

NOTE
If paint has been removed from parts during cleaning, touch up areas, as required, before assembly or installation.

3. Visually check the steering arm (A, **Figure 10**) for bends, cracks or other damage.

4. Check the bushings (B, **Figure 10**) for wear, cracks or other damage. If the bushings require replacement, observe the following:

CAUTION
The ski bolt bushings will be damaged when removing from the spindle in substep 3a; however, use extreme care to prevent damaging the spindle while removing the bushings.

a. Press the bushings from the spindle.

b. Clean the bushing bore thoroughly. Remove all grease and other residue.

c. Inspect the spindle to make sure it is not damaged.

d. Paint the spindle if paint was removed while removing the bushings.

e. Press new bushings into the bore in the spindle.

5A. On all models without ball joints, secure the spindle in a vise, then turn the spindle arm. The spindle should move smoothly without binding or excessive looseness. Replace the spindle assembly if damaged.

5B. On models with ball joints (**Figure 2**), inspect the ball joints for damage. Install new parts, as required. If necessary, remove the ball joints as follows:

a. Remove the suspension arm.

b. Remove the retaining nut. Loctite is applied to the threads and it may be necessary to heat the nut before removing.

c. Press the ball joint from the suspension arm.

d. Press the new ball joint into the arm until bottomed.

e. Apply Loctite 271 to the threads and install the retaining nut.

f. Tighten the nut to the torque listed in **Table 2**.

6. Check the suspension arms for cracks, dents, twists, excessive wear or other damage.

7. Replace worn or damaged parts as required.

Spindle Installation

1. Except for models with ball joints, the suspension arms are equipped with axle bushing assemblies at the pivots (**Figure 11**). Service the axle bushings as follows:

a. Remove and separate parts of the axle bushings. Clean them thoroughly in solvent.

b. Coat each axle bushing with a low temperature grease.

c. Install the axle assemblies in the suspension arms or spindle (**Figure 1, 3** or **4**).

2. Attach the upper and lower arms to the spindle, observing the following:

a. Except for models with ball joints, the heads of the bolts should be the same direction as originally installed. Tighten the bolts to the torque listed in **Table 1**.

NOTE
*If the bolts in substep 2a were not marked before disassembling, check with your dealer or inspect a similar machine to determine correct direction of assembly. All models are not installed as shown in **Figure 9**.*

b. On models with ball joints, tighten the retaining castle nuts to the torque listed in **Table 1** and install new cotter pins.

3. If the shock absorber was detached or removed, install the attaching bolts and tighten to the torque listed in **Table 1**.

4. Attach the tie rod/drag link end to the steering arm. Tighten the retaining screw to the torque listed in **Table 1**.

WARNING
*The rod end should be attached to the same side of the steering arm as originally installed. If the original position is not known, check with your dealer or inspect a similar machine to determine correct assembly (**Figure 6** or **Figure 7**). Improper assembly will interfere with the steering and may result in damage or injury.*

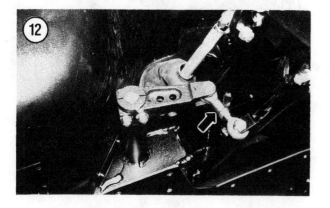

5. Install the ski as described in this chapter.

6. Check ski alignment as described in Chapter Three. Adjust as necessary.

Lower Suspension Arm Removal/Installation

Refer to **Figure 1-4** for this procedure.

1. Support the front of the machine so both skis are off the ground.

2. Open the hood.

NOTE
Bolts should be reinstalled with the heads in the same direction as the manufacturer originally installed them. Before removing the bolts, mark the location of the head with paint or a marker to facilitate assembly.

3. Remove the spindle as described in this chapter.

NOTE
If suspension arms will be removed from both sides, mark the arms L or R to indicate the side each was originally installed.

4. If a sway bar link (**Figure 12**, typical) is attached to the lower suspension arm, it must be detached.

5. On models with ball joints, detach the lower shock absorber mount from the lower suspension arm (**Figure 13**).

NOTE
On some models, the bolts that retain the inner end of the suspension arm may be located under the engine plate. If the bolts are not accessible through a panel or opening, it may be necessary to remove the engine to remove these bolts.

6. Remove the bolts that attach the lower control arm to the frame.

7. Remove the lower control arm.

15

8. Check parts as described in the following inspection procedure.

9. Installation is the reverse of removal. Observe the following:

    a. Assemble the bushings in the lower suspension arm and make sure the bushings operate properly.

    b. Lubricate the bushings with low temperature grease while assembling.

    c. Check the suspension for free movement at all stages of assembly. The suspension should not bind.

    d. Make sure the heads of all bolts are installed in the same direction as they were originally installed by the manufacturer.

NOTE
If the bolts were not marked before disassembling, check with your dealer or inspect a similar machine to determine the correct direction of assembly.

    e. Tighten bolts to the torque specification in **Table 1**.

Lower Suspension Arm Inspection

1. Clean the lower suspension arm in solvent and dry thoroughly.

2. If paint has been removed during cleaning or through use, touch up areas before installation.

CAUTION
Do not paint any radial ball joints (rod ends).

3. Check the lower suspension arm for cracks, twists, dents or other damage. The arm should be straight.

4. On models with ball joints (**Figure 2**), inspect the joints for damage. Install new parts as required. If necessary, remove the ball joint as follows:

    a. Remove the retaining nut (6, **Figure 2**). Loctite is applied to the threads and it may

be necessary to heat the nut before removing it.

    b. Press the ball joint from the suspension arm.

NOTE
Install the ball joint in the suspension arm straight with the arm. If the ball joint is not straight, remove it and reinstall correctly.

    c. Press the new ball joint into the arm until bottomed.

    d. Apply Loctite 271 to the threads and install the retaining nut.

    e. Tighten the nut to the torque listed in **Table 1**.

5. Pivot bearings and axles should be lubricated with low-temperature grease while installing.

Upper Suspension Arm Removal/Installation

Refer to **Figure 1-4** for this procedure.

1. Open the hood.

2. Remove the spindle as outlined in this chapter.

NOTE
If suspension arms will be removed from both sides, mark the arms L or R to indicate original location.

3. On models with shock absorbers inside the body, proceed as follows:

    a. Remove the exhaust pipes.

    b. Remove the bolt (**Figure 14**) attaching the shock absorber to the upper suspension arm.

    c. Unbolt the sway bar link from the upper suspension arm (**Figure 15**).

4. Remove the bolt(s) attaching the upper suspension arm to the frame.

5. Remove the upper suspension arm.

6. Check parts as described in the following Inspection procedure.

7. Installation is the reverse of removal. Observe the following:

    a. Assemble the bushings in the upper suspension arm and make sure the bushings operate properly.

    b. Lubricate bushings with low-temperature grease while assembling.

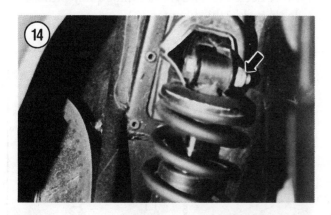

c. Check the suspension for free movement at all stages of assembly. The suspension should not bind.

d. Make sure the heads of all bolts are installed in the same direction as they were originally installed by the manufacturer.

NOTE
If the bolts were not marked before disassembling, check with your dealer or inspect a similar machine to determine the correct direction of assembly.

e. Tighten bolts to the torque specification in **Table 1**.

Upper Suspension Arm Inspection

1. Clean the upper suspension arm in solvent and dry thoroughly.

2. If paint has been removed during cleaning or through use, touch up areas before installation.

CAUTION
Do not paint the ball joints rod ends.

3. Check the upper suspension arm for cracks, twists, dents or other damage. The arm should be straight.

4. On models with ball joints (**Figure 2**), inspect the joints for damage and install new parts as required. If necessary, remove the ball joint as follows:

    a. Remove the retaining nut (7, **Figure 2**). Loctite is applied to the threads and it may be necessary to heat the nut before removing it.

    b. Press the ball joint from the suspension arm.

NOTE
Install the ball joint in the suspension arm straight with the arm. If the ball joint is not straight, remove it and reinstall correctly.

15

c. Press the new ball joint into the arm until bottomed.

d. Apply Loctite 271 to the threads and install the retaining nut.

e. Tighten the nut to the torque listed in **Table 1**.

5. Pivot bushings and axles should be lubricated with low-temperature grease while installing.

**Sway (Stabilizer) Bar
Removal/Installation**

Refer to **Figure 16** for this procedure.

1. Detach the linkage from both sway bar arms by removing the bolts (13, **Figure 16**).

2. Remove the pinch bolts and nuts (**Figure 17**) attaching the arm to one side, then slide the arm from the bar.

3. If equipped with a spacer (3, **Figure 16**), remove the spacer.

4. Repeat Steps 2 and 3 for the other side.

5. Pull the sway bar from either side.

6. Clean and inspect the linkage (7-11, **Figure 16**). Replace parts as necessary.

7. Inspect all parts for wear, cracks, twisting or other damage. Install new parts as necessary.

8. Position the sway bar in the snowmobile without the bushings.

9. Install a bushing (5, **Figure 16**) at each end of the sway bar. Seat the shoulder of the bushing against the frame.

10. Install the spacers (3, **Figure 16**), if so equipped.

11. Install both arms (2, **Figure 16**) on the sway bar with the bolt holes in the arms aligned with the notch in the bar. Make sure the arms are aligned the same on both sides.

12. Install the pinch bolts and nuts (**Figure 17**). Tighten to the torque listed in **Table 1**.

13. Connect the linkage (7-11, **Figure 16**) to each arm. Tighten the bolt to the torque listed in **Table 1**.

14. Check the sway bar linkage adjustment as described in this chapter.

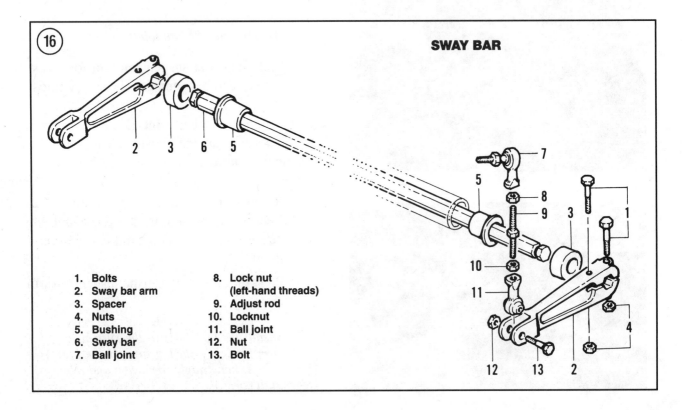

⑯   **SWAY BAR**

1. Bolts	8. Lock nut
2. Sway bar arm	(left-hand threads)
3. Spacer	9. Adjust rod
4. Nuts	10. Locknut
5. Bushing	11. Ball joint
6. Sway bar	12. Nut
7. Ball joint	13. Bolt

Sway Bar Linkage Adjustment

1. Lift and support the snowmobile so that the skis are off the ground.

2. Remove the bolt and nut (12 and 13, **Figure 16**) from one side.

3. The holes in the arm and ball joint (2 and 11, **Figure 16**) should remain aligned. If the holes are not aligned, proceed as follows:

   a. Make sure the suspension is not binding or restricted on either side.

   b. Loosen the locknuts (8 and 10, **Figure 16**) and adjust the length of the linkage until the holes are aligned.

   c. Measure the distance between the ends (7 and 11, **Figure 16**) for the linkage on both sides.

   d. If the linkage for one side is much longer than the linkage on the other, check for damage. Make sure the arms (2, **Figure 16**) are aligned on the sway bar.

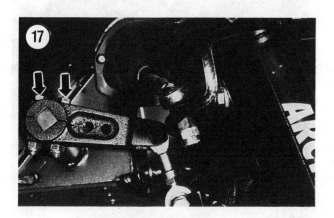

Shock Absorber Removal/Installation

Some models are equipped with rebuildable gas-filled shock absorbers, while the units on other models are sealed and must not be disassembled.

1. Support the front of the machine so both skis are off the ground.

2. Open the hood.

3A. For early models with shock absorbers inside the body, proceed as follows:

   a. Remove the exhaust pipes.

   b. Remove the bolt (**Figure 14**) attaching the top of the shock absorber to the upper suspension arm.

   c. Remove the bolt (**Figure 18**) attaching the lower end of the shock absorber.

3B. For models with the lower end of the shock absorber attached to the outer end of the suspension arm, proceed as follows:

   a. Before removing any bolts, mark the location of the bolt heads so they can be installed in the same locations.

   b. Remove the bolt (**Figure 19**, typical) attaching the lower end of the shock absorber to the suspension arm.

   c. If equipped with a reservoir (**Figure 20**), loosen the clamps and free the reservoir.

   d. Remove the bolt attaching the upper end of the shock absorber to the frame.

4. Remove the shock absorber.

15

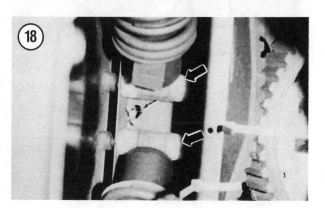

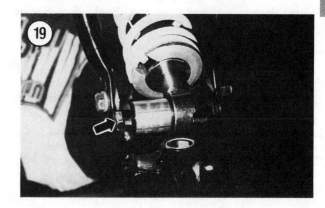

5. Check the shock absorber as described in *Shock Inspection* section in this chapter.

6. Installation is the reverse of the preceding steps. Tighten the shock absorber attaching bolts to the torque specified in **Table 1**.

Spring
Removal/Installation

The spring can be removed from all models, but the shock absorber of some models should not be disassembled.

> *WARNING*
> *Do not attempt to remove or install the shock spring without the use of a spring compressor tool (part No. 0644-057) or a suitable equivalent. Attempting to remove the spring without the use of a spring compressor may cause severe personal injury. If you do not have access to a spring compressor, refer spring removal to a dealer.*

1. Remove the shock absorber as described in this chapter.

2. Secure the bottom of the shock absorber in a vise with soft jaws.

3. Attach a suitable spring compressor to the shock absorber following the compressor manufacturer's instructions. Compress the spring with the tool, then remove the spring retainer (A, **Figure 21**, typical) from the shock.

4. Remove the spring.

5. Remove the spring from the compressor tool and the spring seat from the shock absorber as required.

> *CAUTION*
> *Do not attempt to disassemble the shock damper housing (4, **Figure 22**). The unit used on some models can be disassembled and serviced, but special tools and techniques are necessary for safe and successful repair. Refer to the appropriate paragraphs in this chapter for servicing rebuildable shock absorbers.*

6. Visually check the spring for cracks or damage. If the spring appears okay, compare the free length to that of a new spring. The free length of the springs for the two sides should be the same. Replace the springs if either has sagged significantly.

7. Check the spring retainer (11, **Figure 22**) for cracks, deep scoring or excessive wear. Replace if necessary.

8. Install the spring by reversing the removal steps. Make sure the spring retainer retains the spring securely.

9. Refer to **Table 2** for the standard spring settings for models with adjustable settings. The distance listed is the length of the exposed threads (B, **Figure 21**).

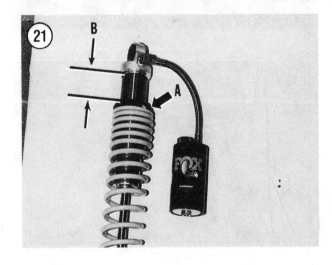

Shock Inspection

1. Remove the spring from the shock absorber as described in this chapter.

2. Clean all components thoroughly in solvent and allow to dry.

3. Check the damper assembly as follows:

   a. Check the damper housing for leakage. If the damper is leaking, replace it. Oil seeping from around the rod of rebuildable shock absorbers indicates leakage past the seal in the cap (23, **Figure 23** or 3, **Figure 24**).

   b. Check the damper rod for bending or other damage.

   c. Operate the damper rod by hand and check its operation. If the damper is operating correctly, a small amount of resistance should be felt on the compression stroke and a considerable amount of resistance felt on the return stroke.

   d. Replace the damper assembly, if necessary.

4. Check the damper housing for cracks, dents or other damage. Replace the damper housing, if damaged. Do not attempt to repair or straighten it.

5. On models with rebuildable and nitrogen-charged shock absorbers (**Figure 23** and **Figure 24**), refer to the Disassembly/Assembly procedures in this chapter.

Rebuildable Shock Absorbers Disassembly/Assembly/Charging

Some models are equipped with rebuildable gas-filled shock absorbers (**Figure 23** or **Figure 24**). The unit shown in **Figure 23** is equipped with a external reservoir (**Figure 21**). While these units are similar, service procedures are different. Refer to the appropriate following procedures for the type of shock absorber being serviced.

> *CAUTION*
> *The shock absorber is charged with nitrogen gas under high pressure. Wear eye protection and use extreme caution whenever you are working with high pressure gas. Do not attempt any service before releasing all pressure.*

Units with an external reservoir

Refer to **Figure 23** for these procedures.

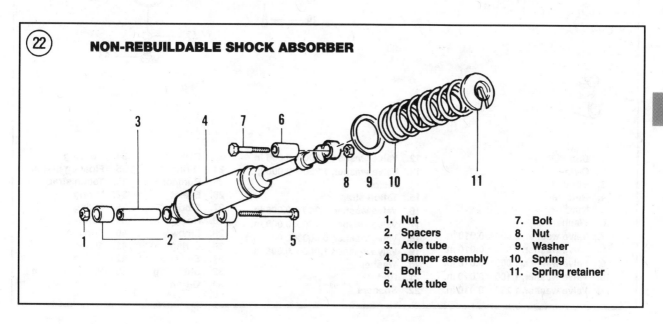

(22) NON-REBUILDABLE SHOCK ABSORBER

1. Nut
2. Spacers
3. Axle tube
4. Damper assembly
5. Bolt
6. Axle tube
7. Bolt
8. Nut
9. Washer
10. Spring
11. Spring retainer

15

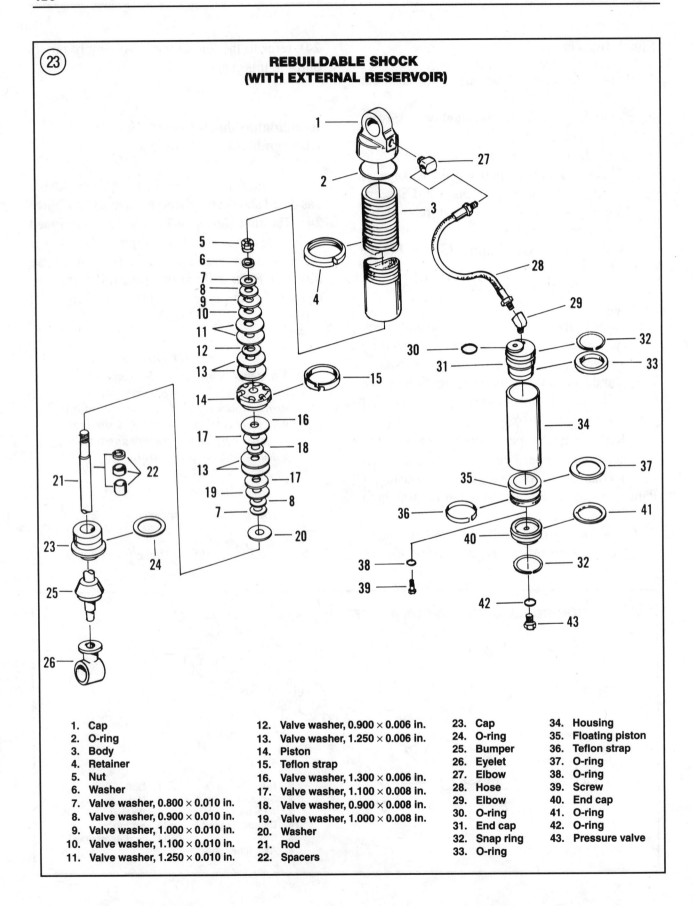

**REBUILDABLE SHOCK
(WITH EXTERNAL RESERVOIR)**

1. Cap
2. O-ring
3. Body
4. Retainer
5. Nut
6. Washer
7. Valve washer, 0.800 × 0.010 in.
8. Valve washer, 0.900 × 0.010 in.
9. Valve washer, 1.000 × 0.010 in.
10. Valve washer, 1.100 × 0.010 in.
11. Valve washer, 1.250 × 0.010 in.
12. Valve washer, 0.900 × 0.006 in.
13. Valve washer, 1.250 × 0.006 in.
14. Piston
15. Teflon strap
16. Valve washer, 1.300 × 0.006 in.
17. Valve washer, 1.100 × 0.008 in.
18. Valve washer, 0.900 × 0.008 in.
19. Valve washer, 1.000 × 0.008 in.
20. Washer
21. Rod
22. Spacers
23. Cap
24. O-ring
25. Bumper
26. Eyelet
27. Elbow
28. Hose
29. Elbow
30. O-ring
31. End cap
32. Snap ring
33. O-ring
34. Housing
35. Floating piston
36. Teflon strap
37. O-ring
38. O-ring
39. Screw
40. End cap
41. O-ring
42. O-ring
43. Pressure valve

CAUTION
Do not lay parts on a rag or other sur-
face where they can pick up lint that
would cause leakage. Even small imper-
fections can result in leakage.

1. Remove the screw and washer (43, **Figure 23**).

2. Release the pressurized nitrogen carefully using the special tool (part No. 0644-158) or equivalent.

3. If necessary, pull the eyelet to extend the rod (21, **Figure 23**).

4. Clamp the body (3, **Figure 23**) in a special holding fixture (part No. 0644-158) or equivalent.

5. Unscrew the cap (23, **Figure 23**), then lift the rod, cap and piston assembly from the body.

6. Loosen, but do not remove, the nut (5, **Figure 23**).

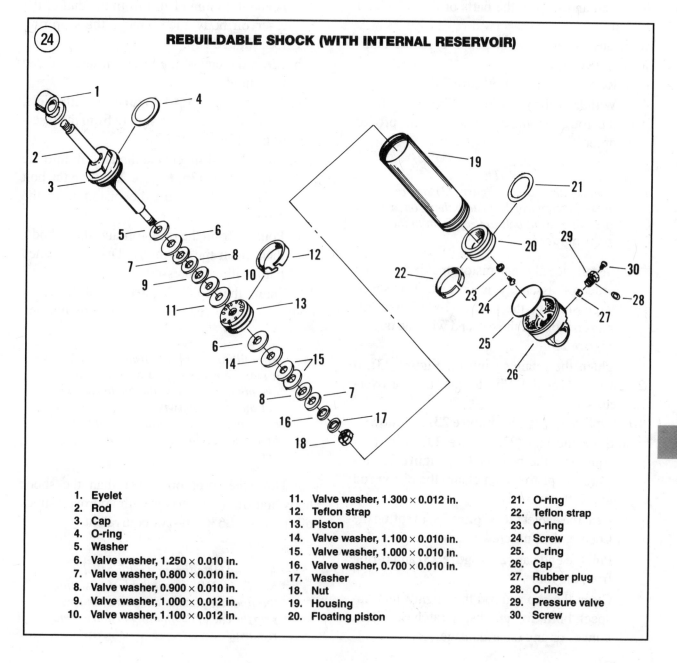

(24)   REBUILDABLE SHOCK (WITH INTERNAL RESERVOIR)

1. Eyelet	11. Valve washer, 1.300 × 0.012 in.	21. O-ring
2. Rod	12. Teflon strap	22. Teflon strap
3. Cap	13. Piston	23. O-ring
4. O-ring	14. Valve washer, 1.100 × 0.010 in.	24. Screw
5. Washer	15. Valve washer, 1.000 × 0.010 in.	25. O-ring
6. Valve washer, 1.250 × 0.010 in.	16. Valve washer, 0.700 × 0.010 in.	26. Cap
7. Valve washer, 0.800 × 0.010 in.	17. Washer	27. Rubber plug
8. Valve washer, 0.900 × 0.010 in.	18. Nut	28. O-ring
9. Valve washer, 1.000 × 0.012 in.	19. Housing	29. Pressure valve
10. Valve washer, 1.100 × 0.012 in.	20. Floating piston	30. Screw

15

NOTE
Do not mix the order of the valve plates (washers). The number, size and order of the valve plates (7-13 and 16-19, Figure 23) determines dampening action. The valve and piston can be cleaned and inspected after loosening the retaining nut, while leaving the valve and piston on the rod. If additional disassembly is required, keep these parts in the correct order to aid in reassembly.

7. Clean and inspect the parts of the valve and piston.

8. If any of the valve or piston parts are damaged, proceed as follows:

a. Remove the nut (5, **Figure 23**).

b. Withdraw the parts (6-20, **Figure 23**) from the rod, keeping the parts in the proper order.

NOTE
While parts (6-20, Figure 23) are removed, temporarily install them on a 5/16 in. × 3 in. bolt to keep them in the proper order.

c. Install the valve and piston, making sure the order of assembly is correct. The seven large slots in the piston (14, **Figure 23**) must be toward the rod end with the nut (5, **Figure 23**).

9. Tighten the retaining nut (5, **Figure 23**) to 21-28 N.m (15-21 ft.-lb.) torque. Do not overtighten.

10. Replace o-ring (24, **Figure 23**) as follows:

a. Slide the cap (23, **Figure 23**) and, if so equipped, the bumper (25, **Figure 23**) toward the piston, then clamp the piston rod in a soft-jawed vise.

b. Heat the eyelet (26, **Figure 23**) to soften the Loctite, then unscrew the eyelet.

c. Pull the end cap (23, **Figure 23**) and o-ring from the rod.

d. Clean the cap and rod thoroughly, then inspect both for cracks, scratches, nicks, gouges or any other damage.

e. Lubricate the O-ring in the cap with oil.

f. Slide the cap over the end of the rod. Be very careful not to damage the O-ring while installing.

g. Apply Loctite 271 on the threads of the rod, then install the eyelet. Tighten the eyelet securely.

11. Replace the piston ring (15, **Figure 23**).

12. Disassemble the reservoir as follows:

a. Press the end cap (40, **Figure 23**) in until it is about 25 mm (1 in.) from the end of the reservoir body, then remove the snap ring (32, **Figure 23**).

b. Clean the end of the reservoir and end cap thoroughly.

c. Grip the end cap (40, **Figure 23**) with pliers, then pull the end cap slowly from the reservoir.

d. Thread a 1/4 in. coarse thread bolt into the end of piston (35, **Figure 23**). Grip the bolt with pliers and pull the piston from the reservoir.

e. Pour oil from the reservoir and shock body, then clean the assembly. Dry the cleaned parts with compressed air.

13. Clamp the cap (1, **Figure 23**) of the shock body in a soft-jawed vise with the body upright.

NOTE
After filling the shock absorber with oil, it may be necessary to wait as long as five minutes to allow the air to rise. Do not shake or otherwise agitate the shock oil before or during filling. The installed fluid must be free of air bubbles before continuing.

14. Hold the reservoir lower than the shock body and fill the reservoir with approved shock oil (part No. 0636-664) or equivalent.

NOTE
A special installing and setting tool (part No. 0644-169) is available for setting the floating piston. The same tool will grip the end of the floating piston to help removal.

15. Coat the rings on the floating piston (35, **Figure 23**) with oil and insert the piston into the reservoir until it is located at the correct distance from the end (A, **Figure 25**). Refer to **Table 2** for the correct distance to position the floating piston.

16. Remove the bolt from the floating piston. Make sure the piston is still at the correct distance from the end of the reservoir.

17. Install a new O-ring (33, **Figure 23**) on the end cap, lubricate the O-ring, then install the cap.

18. Press the cap into the reservoir about 25 mm (1 in.). Do not move the floating piston.

19. Install the retaining snap ring (32, **Figure 23**), then pull the end cap back against the snap ring.

20. Fill the body with approved shock oil (part No. 0636-664) or equivalent until the oil is 1/4 in. (B, **Figure 25**) from the top of the body. Wait about five minutes for the bubbles to rise after filling. There should not be *any* air mixed with the oil.

21. Slide the cap (23, **Figure 23**) onto the rod until it is about 1/8-1/4 in. from the piston and valve assembly.

NOTE
Do not move the piston down into the body until the reservoir has been pressurized.

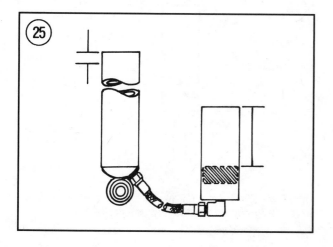

22. Compress the piston ring with your fingers and slowly move the piston into the shock body until the cap can be installed.

23. Install the cap (23, **Figure 23**) and tighten into position.

24. Grip the protrusion in the center of the end cap (40, **Figure 23**) with locking needlenose pliers, then clamp the pliers in a vise. This procedure will allow the filling valve to be pressed against the valve while filling.

NOTE
The system should be filled with dry nitrogen gas. Do not attempt to fill the shock with air.

25. Insert the inflation needle (part No. 0644-158) or equivalent into the valve. Open the fill valve, then slowly increase the regulated pressure to 200 psi.

26. When filled, close the filler valve, remove the inflation needle and reduce the regulated pressure to zero. Install and tighten the screw (43, **Figure 23**).

27. Test operation of the assembled shock as follows:

   a. Compress the shock fully.

   b. If spongy spots are felt while compressing, it indicates air is in the oil. Disassemble and fill with oil that does not contain any air bubbles.

   c. When released, the shock absorber rod should extend fully. Failure to extend indicates binding or pressure leakage.

   d. Submerge the shock in water to check for nitrogen leaks.

15

Units with integral reservoir

Refer to **Figure 24** for these procedures.

CAUTION
Do not lay parts on a rag or other surface where they can pick up lint that would cause leakage. Even small imperfections can result in leakage.

1. Remove the screw (30, **Figure 24**).

2. Carefully release the pressurized nitrogen using the special tool (part No. 0644-158) or equivalent.

3. If necessary, pull the eyelet to extend the rod (2, **Figure 24**).

CAUTION
Do not attempt to disassemble the unit without the proper holding fixture. Parts are easily damaged by improper holding procedures.

4. Clamp the housing (19, **Figure 24**) in a special holding fixture (part No. 0644-158) or equivalent with the cap (26, **Figure 24**) up.

5. Remove the valve (29, **Figure 24**).

6. Unscrew the cap (26, **Figure 24**) from the housing. Allow oil to drain from the housing.

7. Make sure the housing is still securely clamped in the holding fixture (part No. 0644-158) or equivalent and unscrew the cap (3, **Figure 24**).

8. Lift the rod, cap and piston assembly from the body.

9. Loosen, but do not remove, the nut (18, **Figure 24**).

NOTE
*Do not mix the order of the valve plates (washers). The number, size and order of the valve plates (6-11 and 14-16, **Figure 24**) determines dampening action. The valve and piston can be cleaned and inspected after loosening the retaining nut, while leaving the valve and piston on the rod. If additional disassembly is required, keep these parts in the correct order to aid in reassembly.*

10. Clean and inspect the parts of the valve and piston.

11. If any of the valve or piston parts are damaged, proceed as follows:

  a. Remove the nut (18, **Figure 24**).

  b. Withdraw the parts (5-17, **Figure 24**) from the rod, keeping the parts in the proper order.

NOTE
*While parts (5-17, **Figure 24**) are removed, they can be temporarily installed on a 5/16 in. × 3 in. bolt to keep them in the proper order.*

  c. Install the valve and piston, making sure the order of assembly is correct. The seven large slots in the piston (13, **Figure 24**) must be toward the rod end with the nut (18, **Figure 24**).

12. Tighten the retaining nut (18, **Figure 24**) to 21-28 N•m (15-21 ft.-lb.) torque. Do not over tighten.

13. Remove the cap (3, **Figure 24**) as follows:

  a. Slide the cap (3, **Figure 24**) toward the piston, then clamp the piston rod in a soft-jawed vise.

  b. Heat the eyelet (1, **Figure 24**) to soften the Loctite, then unscrew the eyelet.

  c. Remove the assembly from the vise, then pull the end cap (3, **Figure 24**) from the rod.

  d. Clean the cap and rod thoroughly. Inspect both for cracks, scratches, gouges or any other damage.

  e. Lubricate the O-ring in the cap with oil.

  f. Slide the cap over the end of the rod. Be very careful not to damage the O-ring while installing.

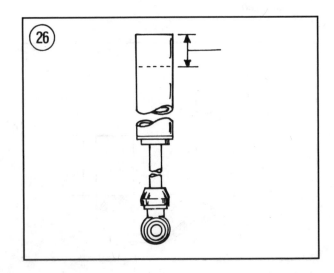

g. Apply Loctite 271 on the threads of the rod, then install the eyelet. Tighten the eyelet securely.

14. Replace the piston ring (12, **Figure 24**).

15. Use the proper size Allen wrench and remove the small screw and O-ring (23 and 24, **Figure 24**).

16. Grip the piston (20, **Figure 24**) with pliers, then pull the floating piston from the body.

17. Clean the shock body thoroughly, then blow dry with compressed air.

18. Clamp the housing (19, **Figure 24**) in the special holding fixture (part No. 0644-158) or equivalent.

19. Lubricate the piston ring and cap O-ring (4 and 12, **Figure 24**).

20. Compress the piston ring with your fingers and slowly move the piston into the shock body until the cap can be installed.

21. Install the cap (3, **Figure 24**) and tighten into position.

22. Reposition the shock housing with the open end upright.

23. Pull the rod out to its fully extended position. Fill the body with approved shock oil (part No. 0636-664) or equivalent until the oil is 1.5 in. from the top (**Figure 26**).

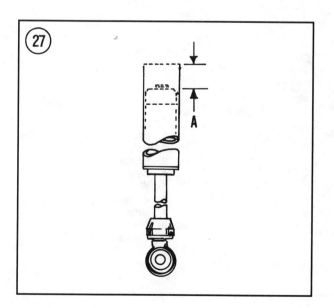

NOTE
After filling the shock absorber with oil, it may be necessary to wait as long as five minutes to allow the air to rise. Do not shake or otherwise agitate the shock oil before or during filling. The installed fluid must be free of air bubbles before continuing.

24. Move the shock rod slowly up and down a few times to remove any air trapped around the piston. Keep the piston below the level of the oil.

25. Check the oil level and make sure the oil level is still 1.5 in. from the top of the body.

26. Lubricate the floating piston and rings (20, 21 and 22, **Figure 24**) lightly with shock oil and insert the floating piston into the body.

NOTE
A special installing and setting tool (part No. 0644-169) is available for setting the floating piston. The same tool will grip the end of the floating piston to help removal.

27. Position the floating piston at the distance from the top of the body indicated in **Table 2** (**Figure 27**). Oil should be expelled from the hole in the piston.

NOTE
If oil is not expelled when positioning the floating piston in Step 27, there is not enough oil in the reservoir. Add oil and make sure that oil without bubbles flows from the orifice in the floating piston. If necessary, push the piston in, then pull the piston up, but do not pull the piston above the level of the oil.

28. Install the Allen head screw and O-ring in the floating piston. Hold the piston with a 9/16 in. wrench while tightening the Allen head screw.

29. Dump excess oil from the shock body.

30. Apply a light coat of Loctite 291 to the threads of the end cap. Install the cap on the shock body. Hold the body of the shock with special blocks (part No. 0644-142) and tighten the end cap securely.

15

31. Lubricate the O-ring (28, **Figure 24**) lightly with oil before installing the valve (29, **Figure 24**). Tighten the valve securely.

NOTE
The system should be filled with dry nitrogen gas. Do not attempt to fill the shock with air.

32. Insert the inflation needle (part No. 0644-158) or equivalent into the valve, open the fill valve, then slowly increase the regulated pressure to 200 psi.

33. When filled, close the filler valve, remove the inflation needle and reduce the regulated pressure to zero. Install and tighten the screw (29, **Figure 24**).

34. Test operation of the assembled shock as follows:
  a. Compress the shock fully.
  b. If spongy spots are felt while compressing, it indicates air in the oil. Disassemble and fill with oil that does not contain any air bubbles.
  c. When released, the shock absorber rod should extend fully. Failure to extend indicates binding or pressure leakage.
  d. Submerge the shock in water to check for nitrogen leaks.

STEERING ASSEMBLY

This section describes service to the handlebar, steering column, drag link and tie rods.

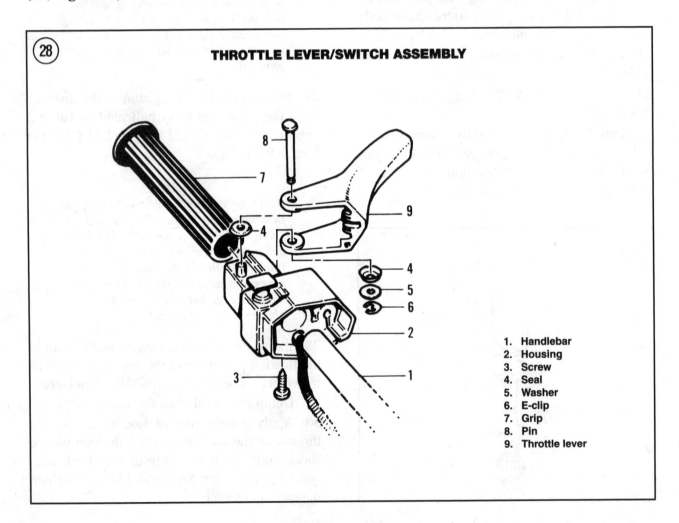

(28)   THROTTLE LEVER/SWITCH ASSEMBLY

1. Handlebar
2. Housing
3. Screw
4. Seal
5. Washer
6. E-clip
7. Grip
8. Pin
9. Throttle lever

Handlebar
Removal/Installation

If handlebar replacement is required, the hand grips will have to be removed to allow removal of the throttle and brake control housings. If the steering post will be removed, the handle bar assembly can be separated from the post and set aside without removing the throttle and brake controls.

1. Remove the steering pad assembly.

2. If required, remove the throttle and brake control housings from the handlebar (**Figure 28** and **Figure 29**).

3. Remove the steering clamp bolts and steering clamps (**Figure 30**), then remove the handlebar.

4. Install in reverse of the removal procedure, observing the following:

a. Install the handlebar, clamp and mounting bolts.

b. Position the handlebar and tighten the steering clamp bolts (**Figure 30**) in a crisscross pattern to the torque specification in **Table 1**. Make sure the gap between the steering clamp steering column support is equal on all four sides.

> *WARNING*
> *If the handlebar is positioned too high, the brake lever may contact the windshield while turning. Check the clearance between the handlebar and the windshield before riding the snowmobile. If necessary, adjust the position to permit full handlebar movement.*

c. Reinstall the steering pad assembly.

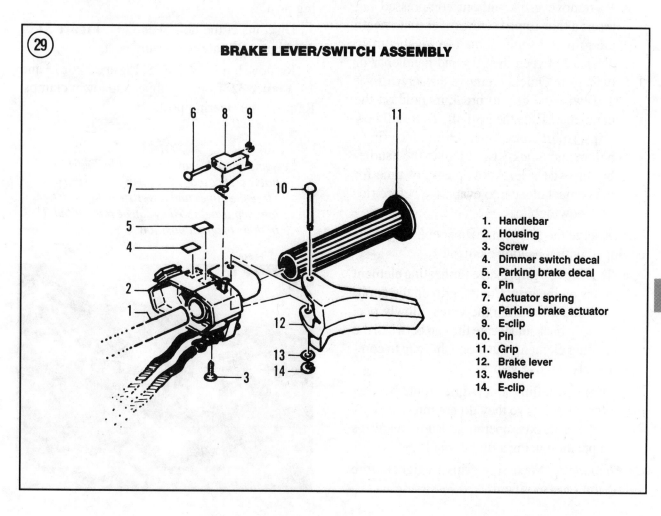

(29) **BRAKE LEVER/SWITCH ASSEMBLY**

1. Handlebar
2. Housing
3. Screw
4. Dimmer switch decal
5. Parking brake decal
6. Pin
7. Actuator spring
8. Parking brake actuator
9. E-clip
10. Pin
11. Grip
12. Brake lever
13. Washer
14. E-clip

15

d. Reinstall the housings for throttle and brake control. Make sure all controls operate properly.

Handlebar Grips
Removal/Installation

1A. Observe the following when replacing handlebar grips not equipped with a heating element:

a. Grips can be removed easily by blowing compressed air into the opposite handlebar end while covering the hole in the opposite grip with a finger. To install grips using compressed air, align the grip with the handlebar and direct air from the opposite side through the handlebar.

b. To remove grips without compressed air, insert a thin-tipped screwdriver underneath the grip and squirt some electrical contact cleaner between the grip and handlebar or twist grip. Quickly remove the screwdriver and twist the grip to break its hold on the handlebar; slide the grip off. To install new grips, squirt contact cleaner into the grip as before and quickly twist it onto the handlebar or twist grip. Allow plenty of time for the contact cleaner to evaporate before riding snowmobile.

1B. Observe the following when replacing grips equipped with a heating element:

a. To remove a grip, locate the heating element wires on the grip. Cut the grip on the opposite side away from the wires. Slowly peel the grip back and locate the gap between the heating element. Cut along this gap to completely remove grip.

b. When installing a new grip, route heating element wires so they do not interfere with brake or throttle operation. Bump the grips in position using a rubber mallet.

2. *All models*—Make sure grips are tight before riding the snowmobile.

WARNING
Do not use any type of grease, soap or other lubricant to install grips. Loose grips can cause you to crash. Always replace damaged or loose grips before riding.

Steering Post
Removal/Installation

NOTE
The following procedure is shown with the engine removed for clarity.

1. Remove the handlebar as described in this chapter.

2. If equipped with an adjustable shock absorber, unbolt the shock adjuster from the steering post.

3. Disconnect the tie rod end (31, **Figure 31** or 26, **Figure 32**) at the steering post.

4. Remove bolts (24 and 28, **Figure 31** or 13 and 14, **Figure 32**) from the upper and lower clamps. Remove the steering post.

NOTE
Some models have renewable bearing halves located in bearing housings. Store the upper and lower steering bushings separately so they can be reinstalled in their original position.

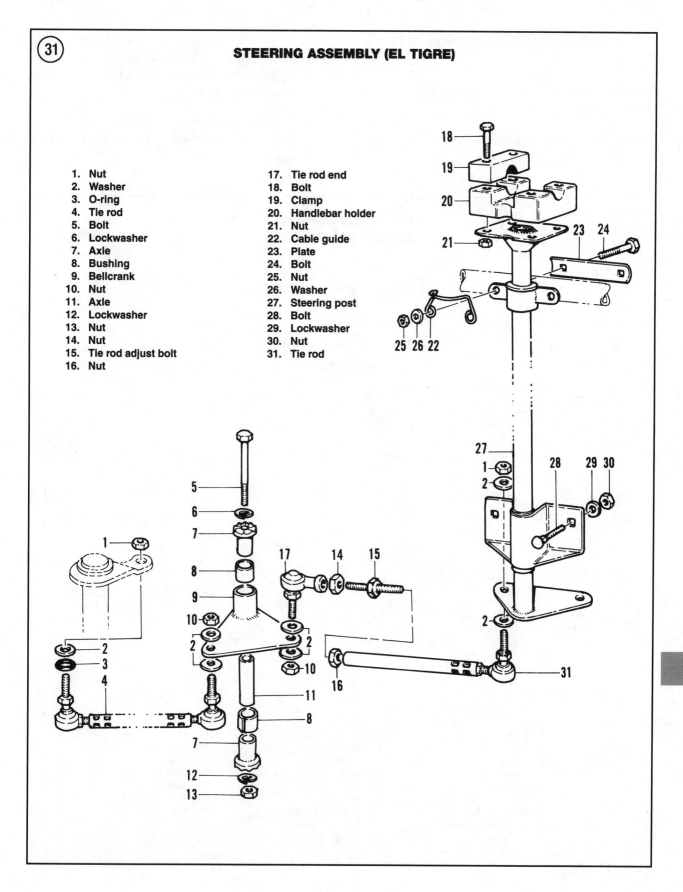

STEERING ASSEMBLY (EL TIGRE)

1. Nut
2. Washer
3. O-ring
4. Tie rod
5. Bolt
6. Lockwasher
7. Axle
8. Bushing
9. Bellcrank
10. Nut
11. Axle
12. Lockwasher
13. Nut
14. Nut
15. Tie rod adjust bolt
16. Nut

17. Tie rod end
18. Bolt
19. Clamp
20. Handlebar holder
21. Nut
22. Cable guide
23. Plate
24. Bolt
25. Nut
26. Washer
27. Steering post
28. Bolt
29. Lockwasher
30. Nut
31. Tie rod

15

5. Inspect the steering post as described in this chapter.

6. Install in the reverse of removal while observing the following:

   a. Apply a low-temperature grease to the bearing halves before assembly.

b. If the original bearings are reinstalled, install them in their original positions. Tighten the bolts to the torque specifications in **Table 1**.

c. If equipped with an adjustable shock absorber, attach the shock adjuster to the steering post.

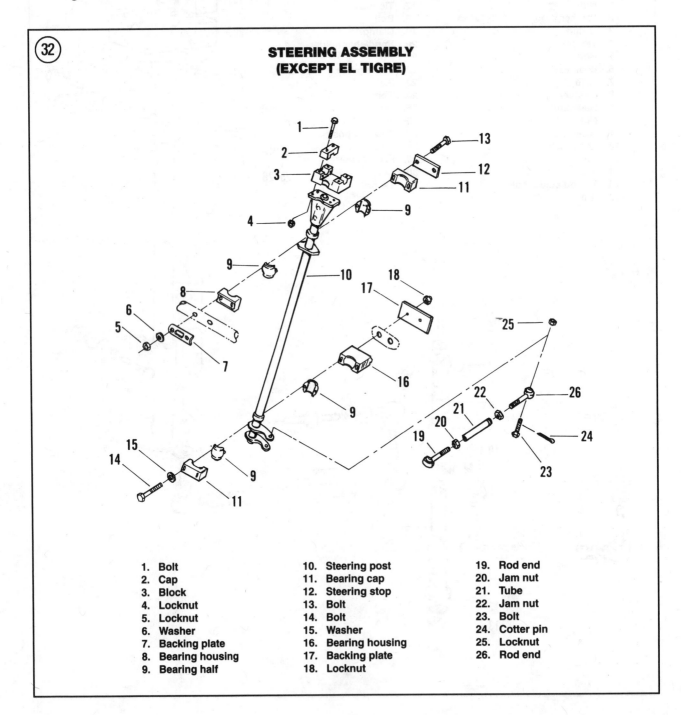

**STEERING ASSEMBLY
(EXCEPT EL TIGRE)**

1. Bolt	10. Steering post	19. Rod end
2. Cap	11. Bearing cap	20. Jam nut
3. Block	12. Steering stop	21. Tube
4. Locknut	13. Bolt	22. Jam nut
5. Locknut	14. Bolt	23. Bolt
6. Washer	15. Washer	24. Cotter pin
7. Backing plate	16. Bearing housing	25. Locknut
8. Bearing housing	17. Backing plate	26. Rod end
9. Bearing half	18. Locknut	

d. Check ski alignment as described in this chapter.

Steering Post Inspection

1. Clean all components thoroughly in solvent. Remove all grease residue from the bearing halves.
2. Visually check the steering post for cracks or deep scoring. Check the welds at the top and bottom of the shaft for cracks or damage.
3. Inspect the steering bearings for cracks, deep scoring or excessive wear.

Drag Link and Tie Rods Removal/Installation

On El Tigre models, two center tie rods (31, **Figure 31**) connect the steering post to bellcranks (9, **Figure 31**). Tie rods (4, **Figure 31**) connect the bellcrank to the steering arms located at the top of each ski leg.

Other models are equipped with short tie rods that connect the ends of a drag link to the steering arms at the top of each ski leg (**Figure 33** or **Figure 34**).

NOTE
The outer jam nuts on the tie rods have left-hand threads.

1. Remove the engine as described in Chapter Five.
2. Use a No. 10 drill to remove the rivets securing the rubber boots.
3. Detach the tie rods as required (**Figure 31**, **Figure 33** or **Figure 34**).
4. Refer to **Figure 31**, **Figure 33** or **Figure 34** to remove the bellcrank(s), idler arm, drag link and center tie rod.
5. Inspect each tie rod as described in the following procedure.
6. Installation is the reverse of the preceding steps. Note the following:
   a. After attaching the tie rods, check ski alignment as described in Chapter Three.
   b. When ski alignment is correct, tighten tie rod bolts to the torque specification in **Table 1**.

Tie Rod Inspection

1. Clean the tie rod in solvent and dry thoroughly.

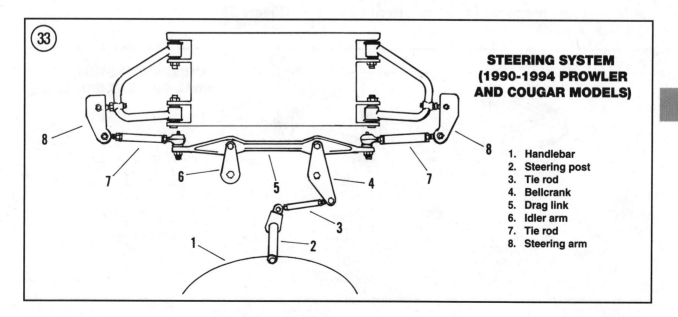

STEERING SYSTEM (1990-1994 PROWLER AND COUGAR MODELS)

1. Handlebar
2. Steering post
3. Tie rod
4. Bellcrank
5. Drag link
6. Idler arm
7. Tie rod
8. Steering arm

15

2. If paint has been removed from the tie rod during cleaning or through use, touch up areas before installation.

3. Visually check the tie rod for dents, bends, cracks or other damage. Check the ball joints for deep scoring or excessive wear. If a ball joint has been loose, threads in the tie rod may be damaged.

4. Check the ball joints for excessive wear or damage.

    a. If damaged, loosen the nut and unscrew the ball joint.

    b. Reverse to install. When installing new ball joints, turn the new ball joint into the tie rod at the same distance as the original.

    c. If a tie rod or ball joint was replaced, check *Steering Adjustment* as described in this chapter.

5. Replace worn or damaged parts as required.

6. If one or more ball joints were loosened or replaced, check steering adjustment as described in Chapter Three.

STEERING ADJUSTMENT

Incorrect ski alignment can cause difficult steering and result in lack of control. Accurate checks and adjustments are important. Steering adjustment includes centering the handlebars and ski alignment.

Handlebar Alignment

To adjust the center tie rod(s), the engine must be removed. (**Figure 31**, **Figure 33** or **Figure 34**).

1. Raise and support the snowmobile so that the skis are off the ground.

2. Turn the handlebar until both skis face forward.

3. Center the handlebars as follows:

    a. Measure from the end of one handlebar grip to a point at the back of the snowmobile (**Figure 35**). Record the length.

    b. Repeat measurement for opposite side (**Figure 35**). Make sure you use the same reference points. Record the length.

4. The distance recorded in substep a and b must be the same. If adjustment is required, adjust as described in Step 5A or 5B.

5A. On El Tigre models, proceed as follows:

NOTE
The outer jam nuts on the tie rods have left-hand threads.

    a. Loosen the two locknuts on each tie rod (**Figure 31**).

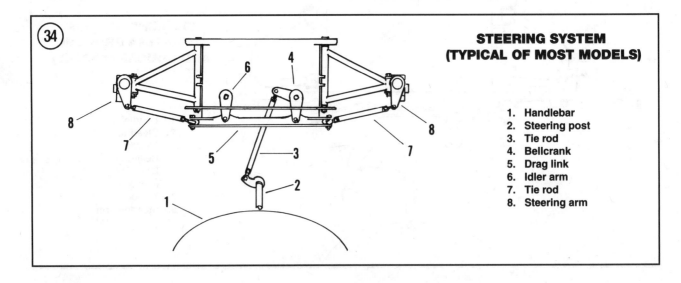

(34)

**STEERING SYSTEM
(TYPICAL OF MOST MODELS)**

1. Handlebar
2. Steering post
3. Tie rod
4. Bellcrank
5. Drag link
6. Idler arm
7. Tie rod
8. Steering arm

b. Determine from Step 3 which direction the skis have to be turned to correctly align the handlebar, then turn one tie rod to shorten its length and turn the opposite tie rod to lengthen it.

c. Make sure you turn both tie rods the *same* amount so that you do not change the ski alignment. Tighten locknuts and recheck adjustment.

5B. On models except El Tigre, refer to **Figure 33** or **Figure 34** and proceed as follows:

a. Check to be sure the drag link is centered in the frame when the handlebars are centered.

b. If the drag link is not centered, loosen the locknuts on the steering tie rod (**Figure 33** or **Figure 34**), then turn the tie rod to short-en or lengthen it. Check to be sure the handlebars and drag link are centered, then tighten the locknuts.

c. If the drag link was centered when checked in substep a, but the skis were not straight, loosen the locknuts and adjust the tie rods (**Figure 33** or **Figure 34**) as necessary.

NOTE
When adjusting the length of the tie rods, make sure the exposed thread lengths of both ball joints are the same. If the exposed threads of one is much longer than the other, detach the tie rod and adjust to make both ends the same length. Reattach the tie rod, then adjust the length by turning the tie rod.

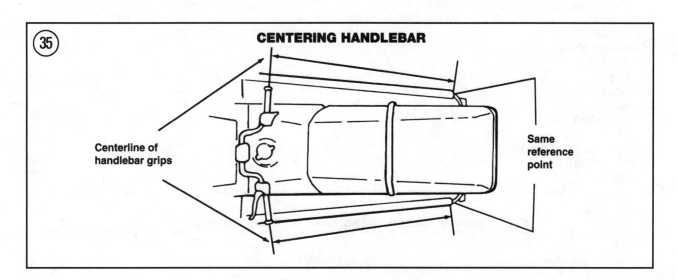

(35) **CENTERING HANDLEBAR**

Centerline of handlebar grips

Same reference point

Table 1 TIGHTENING TORQUE

	N·m	ft.-lb.
Spindle bolts		
El Tigre	29-36	21-27
Prowler, Cougar (1990-1994)		
Upper ball joint nut	83	61
Lower ball joint nut	138	102
Other models (1993-on)		
Both upper and lower	42	31
Ball joints to suspension arms		
Prowler, Cougar (1990-1994)		
Upper	125	92
Lower	240	177
	(continued)	

15

Table 1 TIGHTENING TORQUE (continued)

	N·m	ft.-lb.
Tie rod locknut		
Prior to 1997		
Inner	39	28
Outer	35	25
1997 and 1998		
Inner	28	21
Outer	35	26
Upper suspension arm		
El Tigre	32	24
Prowler, Cougar (1990-1994)	62-69	46-51
Cougar, Panther 550 (1995-1998)	39	28
Other models (1993-on)	46	34
Lower suspension arm		
El Tigre	32	24
Prowler, Cougar (1990-1994)	62-69	46-51
Other models (1993-on)	76	56
Sway bar pinch bolt	18	13
Shock absorber bolts		
1990-1996	32	24
1997-on	39	29
Handlebar	14	10
Steering column		
1990-1991		
Upper	14	10
Lower	25	18
1992-on	25	18
Ski pivot bolt		
El Tigre	29-36	21-27
Other models (1990-1995)	97-111	72-82
1996 models	69	51
1997-on	62	46

Table 2 SHOCK ABSORBER SPECIFICATIONS

1992	
Prowler (threads exposed)	19-25 mm (3/4-1 in.)
1993	
Prowler, Cougar, 440 ZR, 580 ZR	
Spring setting (threads exposed)	19-25 mm (3/4-1 in.)
EXT 550, EXT 580	–
1994	
Cougar, Prowler (threads exposed)	19-25 mm (3/4-1 in.)
ZR 440	
Spring setting (threads exposed)	–
Floating piston setting	61 mm (2.402 in.)
EXT 580 (threads exposed)	19-25 mm (3/4-1 in.)
ZR 580	
Spring setting (threads exposed)	–
Floating piston setting	19.4 mm (0.764 in.)
1995	
Cougar, Prowler 2-Up	
Spring setting (threads exposed)	19-24 mm (3/4-1 in.)

Table 2 SHOCK ABSORBER SPECIFICATIONS (continued)

1995	
Z 440 threads exposed	19-24 mm (3/4-1 in.)
ZR 440	
Spring setting (threads exposed)	31-38 mm (1 1/4-1 1/2 in.)
Floating piston setting	
External reservoir	3 mm (1/8 in.) from bottom
EXT 580	19-24 mm (3/4-1 in.)
ZR 580	
Spring setting (threads exposed)	31-38 mm (1 1/4-1 1/2 in.)
Floating piston setting	19.4 mm (0.764 in.)
ZR 580 EFI	–
1996	
Z 440 (threads exposed)	31-38 mm (1 1/4-1 1/2 in.)
ZR 440	
Spring setting (threads exposed)	31-38 mm (1 1/4-1 1/2 in.)
Floating piston setting	
External reservoir	3 mm (1/8 in.) from bottom
ZR 580, ZRT 600	
Spring setting (threads exposed)	31-38 mm (1 1/4-1 1/2 in.)
Floating piston setting	19.4 mm (0.764 in.)
EXT 580	19-24 mm (3/4-1 in.)
1997	
Z 440 (threads exposed)	19-25 mm (3/4-1 in.)
ZL 440	19-25 mm (3/4-1 in.)
ZR 440	
Spring setting (threads exposed)	38-48 mm (1 1/2-1 7/8 in.)
Floating piston setting	20.32 mm (0.800 in.)
Cougar	19-25 mm (3/4-1 in.)
Panther 550 (threads exposed)	19-25 mm (3/4-1 in.)
EXT 580 EFI	19-25 mm (3/4-1 in.)
Powder Extreme (threads exposed)	19-25 mm (3/4-1 in.)
Powder Special EFI (threads exposed)	31-38 mm (1 1/4-1 1/2 in.)
ZR 580 EFI	
Spring setting (threads exposed)	15.8 mm (5/8 in.)
Floating piston setting	20.32 mm (0.800 in.)
EXT 600	19-25 mm (3/4-1 in.)
ZRT 600	
Spring setting (threads exposed)	15.8 mm (5/8 in.)
Floating piston setting	20.32 mm (0.800 in.)
1998	
Z 440 (threads exposed)	12.5-25 mm (1/2-1 in.)
ZL 440 (threads exposed)	12.5-25 mm (1/2-1 in.)
ZR 440	
Spring setting (threads exposed)	38-48 mm (1 1/2-1 7/8 in.)
Floating piston setting	20.32 mm (0.800 in.)
Cougar	19-25 mm (3/4-1 in.)
Panther 550 (threads exposed)	19-25 mm (3/4-1 in.)
EXT EFI (eyelet to bottom of adjuster)	76-109 mm (3.0-4.3 in.)
EXT EFI Deluxe (threads exposed)	12.5-25 mm (1/2-1 in.)
Pantera	12.5-25 mm (1/2-1 in.)
Powder Extreme (threads exposed)	12.5-25 mm (1/2-1 in.)
Powder Special (eyelet to bottom of adjuster)	76-109 mm (3.0-4.3 in.)
EXT 600 (threads exposed)	12.5-25 mm (1/2-1 in.)
ZRT 600	
Spring setting (threads exposed)	13 mm (1/2 in.)
Floating piston setting	20.32 mm (0.800 in.)

15

Chapter Sixteen

Track And Rear Suspension

All models are equipped with a slide rail rear suspension. Refer to Chapter Four to adjust the rear suspension. Tightening torques are found in **Table 1**.

REAR SUSPENSION

Removal

NOTE
The front shock absorber of the rear suspension on some models is equipped with a remote adjuster located on the steering post. The remote adjuster on these models has a hose between the adjuster and the shock absorber. Before removing the rear suspension, detach the adjuster from the steering post and relocated near the suspension. The complete shock absorber and adjuster on these models should be removed from the suspension and serviced as an assembly.

1. Loosen the locknuts (A, **Figure 1**) on the track adjusting bolts and back the bolts out to relieve track tension.

2. Place a jack under the rear of the snowmobile and raise the rear of the snowmobile enough to remove tension from the track.

WARNING
Be careful when releasing the spring in Step 3. Injury or damage may occur even when using the proper tool.

3. Use a rear suspension spring tool (part No. 0144-311) or equivalent to release the short leg of the spring from the adjusting cam (**Figure 2**).

NOTE
Several mounting holes may be located in the snowmobile tunnel to allow the suspension to be adjusted for various riding conditions. Before removing the attaching bolts in Step 4, mark the original location with a marker or paint to facilitate assembly.

4. Remove the bolts from both sides attaching the rear suspension skid frame to the tunnel.

NOTE
Before turning the snowmobile on its side in Step 5, place a large piece of

cardboard next to the snowmobile to protect it from damage. Also, plug the oil injection reservoir cap and other vents to prevent leakage.

5. Tip the snowmobile on its side, then lift the suspension assembly from the track (**Figure 3**).

Inspection

1. Clean all bolts, nuts and threaded holes thoroughly with solvent to remove all Loctite residue.

2. Inspect the suspension attaching bolts for thread damage or breakage. Replace damaged bolts as required.

3. Visually inspect bolts for signs of wear, cracks, bends or other abnormal conditions. If there is any doubt about the condition of a bolt, replace it.

4. Clean the complete suspension assembly and check visually for obvious damage.

5. Inspect the wheels and slides for damage. Replace parts as required.

6. Check the suspension components and frame for obvious damage. Refer to the appropriate sections in this chapter for inspection of specific components.

Installation

NOTE
Attaching the rear suspension to different holes in the frame will change suspension characteristics. Follow the guidelines in Chapter Four, if necessary, to adjust the suspension for different riding conditions.

1. Pull the track away from the tunnel and open it (**Figure 4**) so that the suspension can be installed.

2. Install the rear suspension into the track, starting at the front and working toward the rear (**Figure 3**).

16

NOTE
When installing the rear suspension mounting bolts in the following steps, do not tighten any bolt until all the bolts are installed finger-tight. Wait until after the suspension is correctly attached and tightened before installing the springs onto the adjusting cams.

3. Install the rear suspension mounting bolts in the following order:

    a. Raise the front arm and align the bolt hole with the hole in the tunnel (**Figure 5**). Install the bolts and washers finger-tight.

    b. Turn the snowmobile onto its other side and repeat substep 3a for the other side.

    c. Align the pivot arm assembly with the appropriate hole in the tunnel, then attach with a bolt, flat washer and lockwasher.

    d. Turn the snowmobile onto its other side and repeat substep 3c for the other side.

4. After bolts have been installed, tighten all bolts to the torque listed in **Table 1**.

5. Use a rear suspension spring tool (part No. 0144-311) or equivalent to position the short leg of the spring on the adjusting cam.

6. Adjust track tension by turning the adjusting screws (**Figure 1**) on both sides. Refer to Chapter Three for adjusting procedure.

7. If the snowmobile was placed on its side, bleed the oil pump as described in Chapter Ten.

WEAR STRIPS

Inspection/Replacement

The wear strips are installed in the bottom of the runner and held in position with a single screw located near the front. The wear strips should be replaced when worn or otherwise damaged. If the wear strips show signs of unusual wear, check the slide rails for twists or other damage.

1. Remove the rear suspension as described in this chapter.

2. Visually inspect the slide rails for cracks or other damage. If a crack is found, replace the slide rail as described in this procedure.

3. Install new wear strips if the thickness is less than 10.7 mm (0.42 in.) thick.

NOTE
The wear strips must be replaced as a set.

4. Remove the wear strips as follows:

    a. Turn the rear suspension over and rest it upside down on the workbench.

    b. Remove the screws (**Figure 6**) from the front of each shoe.

NOTE
Some mechanics prefer to use a pipe wrench to roll the wear strip from a rail. If removed in this way, be careful not to damage the rail.

c. Working at the front of the slide shoe, drive the shoe to the rear of the runner (**Figure 7**).

> *CAUTION*
> *If necessary, use a block of wood and hammer to drive the wear strips toward the rear. Do not use a steel punch or the runner may become damaged.*

5. Inspect the slide rail as follows:

   a. Clean the slide rail with solvent and dry thoroughly.

   b. Place a straightedge along the side of the rail and check for bends. If a slide rail is bent, it must be straightened or replaced. If the bend is severe or if the rail is cracked or damaged, replace it.

   c. Check the slide rail for gouges or cracks along the path of the wear strip. Smooth any rough surfaces with a file or sandpaper.

6. Install the wear strips as follows:

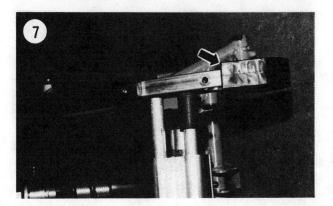

a. Grease the rail surface lightly to ease installation.

b. Working from the back of the runner, align the front of the wear strip (end with hole) with the rear of the rail. Push the wear strip onto the rail. A wooden block and hammer can be used during installation if necessary.

c. Continue to drive the wear strip onto the rail until the screw hole in the wear strip aligns with the hole in the rail.

d. Install the screw, lockwasher and nut, then tighten securely.

END CAPS

The end caps are attached to the front end of the slide rail with a bolt (**Figure 6**). Inspect the end caps for wear, cracks or other damage. Replace the end cap by removing the nut, bolt and washer. Reverse the procedure to install.

SHOCK ABSORBERS

One shock absorber is located at the front of the rear suspension; the other is located at the rear. Depending upon the application, the shock absorber may incorporate a spring, be charged with high pressure gas or may include a remote adjuster. The procedure for removal and service will be different for the various models.

Front Shock Removal/Installation

The procedure for removing the front shock absorber will depend upon construction. On most models, the shock absorber for the front arm of the rear suspension incorporates the spring and the spring pressure must be relieved before removing the shock absorber. On some early models, separate springs are located at the sides and the shock absorber is not spring-loaded.

16

1. Remove the rear suspension as described in this chapter.

NOTE
*On some models the shock absorber for the front arm of the rear suspension has a remote reservoir (**Figure 8**). Other models may have a remote reservoir and a cockpit adjuster that is attached to the steering post. On models so equipped, the remote reservoir and cockpit adjuster are attached to the shock absorber with hoses. The reservoir, cockpit adjuster and attaching hoses must be free before unbolting the shock from its mounts. The hose to the cockpit adjuster is provided with a coupling in its hose.*

2A. On models with a spring-loaded shock absorber, proceed as follows:

   a. Push the front arm down to relieve pressure from the limiter strap(s), then remove bolts (**Figure 9**) from the limiter strap(s).

   b. Release the pressure on the suspension front arm, allowing the shock to extend.

   c. Remove the bolt attaching the top of the front shock absorber to the arm.

   d. Remove the bolts (B, **Figure 10**) attaching the idler wheels to the cross shaft that is also the lower shock mount.

   e. Remove the front shock absorber from the rear suspension assembly.

2B. If a spring is not located on the shock absorber, both ends can be unbolted and the shock removed (**Figure 11**).

3. Remove the shock bushings and inspect them for wear or damage. Replace bushings if necessary.

4. Inspect the shock absorbers as described in this chapter.

5. Installation is the reverse of the removal steps. Observe the following:

   a. Coat the threads of bolts and nuts that are not self-locking with Loctite 271 before assembling.

   b. Reassemble using new self-locking nuts.

   c. Tighten the shock bolts to the tightening torque in **Table 1**.

   d. If equipped with a remote reservoir, attach the reservoir securely in the location provided. Make sure the hose is correctly routed and secured.

   e. If equipped with a cockpit adjuster, route the hose in its original path, then attach and secure the hose properly using tie straps.

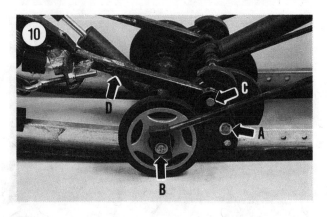

Rear Shock Absorber
Removal/Installation

WARNING
Be careful when releasing the spring in
Step 1. Injury or damage may occur even
when using the proper tool.

1. Release the short leg of the spring from the
adjusting cam using a rear suspension spring tool

(part No. 0144-311) or equivalent before unbolting the suspension.

NOTE
Several mounting holes may be provided
for mounting some of the components to
allow the suspension to be adjusted for
various riding conditions. Mark the
original location of bolts with a marker
or paint before removing the bolts to aid
in assembly.

2. Unbolt and remove the complete rear suspension as described in this chapter.

NOTE
Keep the washers, spacers and axles in
order as they are removed to aid in as-
sembly.

3. Remove the bolts (**Figure 12**) attaching the
rear idler wheel axles to the slide rails, then
remove the idler wheel assembly.
4. Remove the bolts (**Figure 13**) attaching the
spring slides to the rails on each side.
5. Bump the idler wheels, shaft and lower shock
mount toward the rear until it is clear of the
mounting bracket, then lift the assembly upward
out of the rails.
6. Remove the spacers, washers, idler wheels
and axle from the shock lower bracket. Keep the
parts in the correct order to aid in assembly.
7. Unbolt the shock absorber from the lower
bracket. Keep the parts in order to aid in assembly.
8. Unbolt the upper end of the shock absorber
and remove the shock.
9. Inspect the shock absorber and shock rods as
described in this chapter.
10. Apply a light coat of low-temperature grease
to all the bushings and axles.

NOTE
Bolt, washer, and spacer location and
assembly order may be different than
shown in **Figures 14-16.** *It is important*
to keep the parts in the correct order as
originally assembled.

16

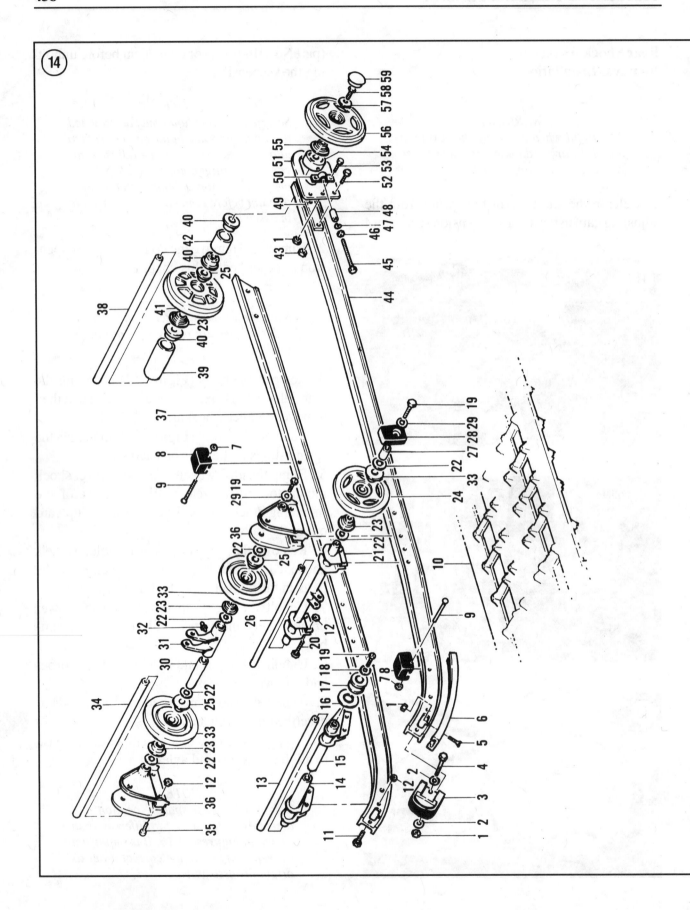

SLIDE RAIL (EARLY TYPE)

1. Nut
2. Washer
3. End cap
4. Bolt
5. Screw
6. Wear strip
7. Push nut
8. Shock pad
9. Solid rivet
10. Track
11. Bolt
12. Nut
13. Axle
14. Bracket
15. Bracket
16. Roller spacer
17. Spring roller
18. Washer
19. Bolt
20. Bolt
21. Crossbrace
22. Washer
23. Wheel insert
24. Idler wheel
25. Wheel insert
26. Axle
27. Spacer
28. Spring slide
29. Washer
30. Spacer

31. Shock pivot
32. Grease nipple
33. Idler wheel
34. Axle
35. Bolt
36. Bracket
37. Slide rail
38. Axle
39. Spacer
40. Spacer bushing
41. Idler wheel
42. Outer spacer
43. Nut
44. Slide rail
45. Bolt
46. Nut
47. Lockwasher
48. Spacer
49. Spacer
50. Track tension adjuster
51. Housing
52. Bolt
53. Bolt
54. Bushing
55. Wheel insert
56. Rear idler wheel
57. Washer
58. Bolt
59. Cap

16

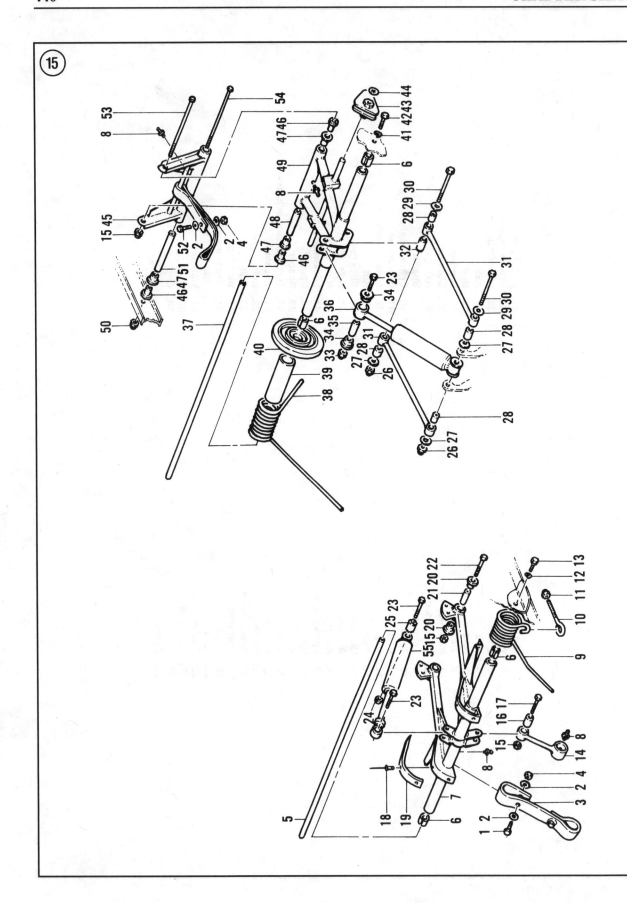

REAR SUSPENSION (EARLY TYPE)

1. Bolt
2. Flat washers
3. Limiter strap
4. Nut
5. Axle
6. Bearing
7. Front arm
8. Grease nipple
9. Spring
10. Eye bolt
11. Nut
12. Lockwasher
13. Bolt
14. Front shock link
15. Nut
16. Axle
17. Bolt
18. Rivet
19. Bumper
20. Bushing
21. Spacer
22. Bolt
23. Bolt
24. Nut
25. Axle
26. Nut
27. Washer

28. Link axle
29. Washer
30. Bolt
31. Rear shock link
32. Shock link spacer
33. Nut
34. Bushing
35. Sleeve
36. Rear shock absorber
37. Axle
38. Spring
39. Spring sleeve
40. Idler wheel
41. Lockwasher
42. Bolt
43. Spring adjuster block
44. Retaining ring
45. Lower arm
46. Axle
47. Bushing
48. Axle
49. Rear arm
50. Nut
51. Axle tube
52. Bolt
53. Bolt
54. Bolt
55. Front shock absorber

16

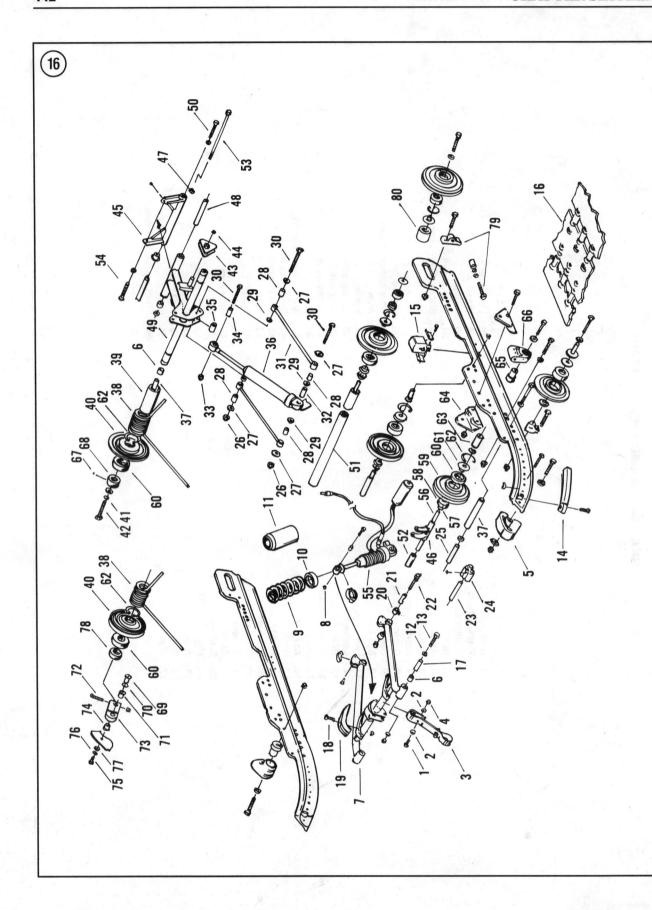

REAR SUSPENSION (LATER MODELS)

1. Bolt
2. Flat washers
3. Limiter strap
4. Nut
5. End cap
6. Bearing
7. Front arm
8. Nut
9. Spring
10. Retainer nut
11. Cover
12. Lockwasher
13. Bolt
14. Wear strip
15. Shock pad
16. Track
17. Axle
18. Bolt
19. Bumper
20. Bushing
21. Axle
22. Bolt
23. Crossbrace
24. Shock reservoir clamp
25. Shock mount axle
26. Nut
27. Washer
28. Link axle
29. Washer
30. Bolt
31. Rear shock link
32. Sleeve
33. Nut
34. Bushing
35. Spacer
36. Rear shock absorber
37. Spacer
38. Spring
39. Spring sleeve
40. Idler wheel

41. Lockwasher
42. Bolt
43. Spring adjuster block
44. Retaining ring
45. Lower arm
46. Shock link
47. Washer
48. Axle
49. Rear arm
50. Bolt
51. Axle
52. Spacer
53. Bolt
54. Bolt
55. Front shock absorber
56. Inner axle
57. Washer
58. Wheel insert
59. Idler wheel
60. Bearing
61. Wheel insert
62. Snap ring
63. Spacer
64. Front arm mounting bracket
65. Spacer
66. Spring slide
67. Allen screw
68. Lock collar
69. Axle
70. Washer
71. Bushing
72. Pinch bolt
73. Offset pivot
74. Bushing
75. Bolt
76. Lockwasher
77. Flat washer
78. Collar
79. Track tension adjuster
80. Adjuster bushing

16

11. Install the bushings, washers and wheels on the axle in the same order as originally installed.

> *NOTE*
> *Coat the threads of the bolts and nuts that are not self-locking with Loctite 271. Reassemble using new self locking nuts.*

12. Tighten the bolts to the torque specified in **Table 1**.

13. Install the short leg of the spring over the adjusting cam (**Figure 17**) using spring tool (part No. 0144-311) or equivalent.

Shock Inspection

1. If the shock absorber has a spring installed on the unit, remove the spring from the shock absorber as follows:

   a. Secure the bottom of the shock absorber in a vise with soft jaws.

   b. Attach a suitable spring compressor to the shock absorber following the compressor manufacturer's instructions. Compress the spring with the tool, then remove the spring retainer (**Figure 18**, typical) from the shock.

   c. Remove the spring.

   d. Remove the spring from the compressor tool and the spring seat from the shock absorber as required.

> *CAUTION*
> *Do not attempt to disassemble the shock damper housing. The unit used on some models can be disassembled and serviced, but special tools and techniques are necessary for safe and successful repair. Refer to the appropriate paragraphs in this chapter for servicing rebuildable shock absorbers.*

2. Clean all components thoroughly in solvent and allow to dry.

3. If a spring was removed from the shock absorber, inspect the spring and retainer as follows:

   a. Visually check the spring for cracks or damage. If the spring appears okay, compare the free length to that of a new spring. Replace the spring if it has sagged significantly.

   b. Check the spring retainers for cracks, deep scoring or excessive wear. Replace if necessary.

4. Check the damper assembly as follows:

   a. Inspect the damper housing for cracks, dents or other damage. Replace the damper housing if damaged. Do not attempt to repair or straighten it.

   b. Check the damper housing for leakage. If the damper is leaking, replace it. Oil seeping from around the rod of rebuildable shock absorbers indicates the seal is leaking.

   c. Check the damper rod for bending or other damage. Check the damper housing for dents or other damage.

   d. Operate the damper rod by hand and check its operation. If the damper is operating correctly, a small amount of resistance should be felt on the compression stroke and a considerable amount of resistance felt on the return stroke.

   e. Replace the damper assembly if necessary.

5. On models with rebuildable gas-filled shock absorbers (**Figures 19-21**), refer to the Disassembly/Assembly procedures in this chapter.

Rebuildable Shock Absorbers
Disassembly/Assembly/Charging

Some models are equipped with rebuildable gas-filled shock absorbers (**Figures 19-21**). The unit shown in **Figure 19** is equipped with an external reservoir. The unit shown in **Figure 20** is equipped with an external reservoir and cockpit control. The units shown in **Figure 19** and **Figure 20** are used in the forward position of the rear suspension on certain models. The unit shown in **Figure 21** is equipped with an integral reservoir. While these units are similar, service procedures are different. Refer to the appropriate following procedures for the type of shock absorber being serviced.

CAUTION
The shock absorber is charged with nitrogen gas under high pressure. Wear eye protection and use extreme caution whenever you are working with high pressure gas. Do not attempt any service before releasing all pressure.

Units with external reservoir only

Refer to **Figure 19** for this procedure.

1. Remove the screw and washer (43, **Figure 19**).

2. Release the pressurized nitrogen carefully using the special tool (part No. 0644-158) or equivalent.

3. If necessary, pull the eyelet to extend the rod (21, **Figure 19**).

4. Clamp the body (34, **Figure 19**) in a special holding fixture (part No. 0644-158) or equivalent.

5. Unscrew the cap (23, **Figure 19**), then lift the rod, cap and piston assembly from the body.

6. Loosen, but do not remove, the nut (5, **Figure 19**).

NOTE
Do not mix the order of the valve plates (washers). The number, size and order of the valve plates determines dampening action. The valve and piston can be cleaned and inspected after loosening the retaining nut, while leaving the valve and piston on the rod. If additional disassembly is required, keep these parts in the correct order to aid in reassembly.

7. Clean and inspect the parts of the valve plates and piston.

8. If any of the valve plates or piston parts are damaged, proceed as follows:

   a. Remove the nut (5, **Figure 19**).

   b. Withdraw the parts (6-20, **Figure 19**) from the rod, keeping the parts in the proper order.

NOTE
*When parts (6-20, **Figure 19**) are removed, they can be temporarily installed on a 5/16 in. × 3 in. bolt to keep them from becoming mixed up. The parts*

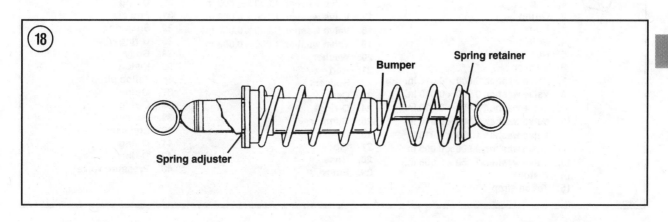

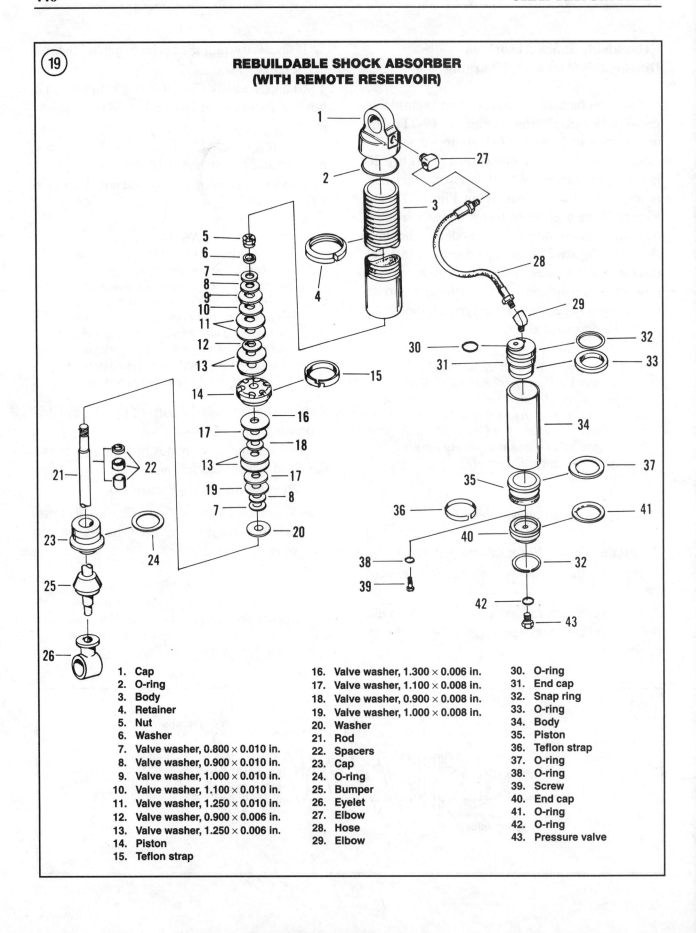

**REBUILDABLE SHOCK ABSORBER
(WITH REMOTE RESERVOIR)**

1. Cap
2. O-ring
3. Body
4. Retainer
5. Nut
6. Washer
7. Valve washer, 0.800 × 0.010 in.
8. Valve washer, 0.900 × 0.010 in.
9. Valve washer, 1.000 × 0.010 in.
10. Valve washer, 1.100 × 0.010 in.
11. Valve washer, 1.250 × 0.010 in.
12. Valve washer, 0.900 × 0.006 in.
13. Valve washer, 1.250 × 0.006 in.
14. Piston
15. Teflon strap

16. Valve washer, 1.300 × 0.006 in.
17. Valve washer, 1.100 × 0.008 in.
18. Valve washer, 0.900 × 0.008 in.
19. Valve washer, 1.000 × 0.008 in.
20. Washer
21. Rod
22. Spacers
23. Cap
24. O-ring
25. Bumper
26. Eyelet
27. Elbow
28. Hose
29. Elbow

30. O-ring
31. End cap
32. Snap ring
33. O-ring
34. Body
35. Piston
36. Teflon strap
37. O-ring
38. O-ring
39. Screw
40. End cap
41. O-ring
42. O-ring
43. Pressure valve

REBUILDABLE SHOCK ABSORBER
(WITH EXTERNAL RESERVOIR AND COCKPIT CONTROL)

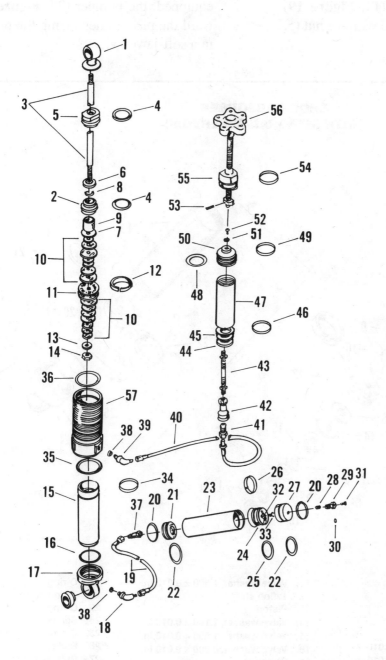

1. Eyelet
2. Separator piston
3. Rod
4. O-ring
5. Cap
6. Spacer
7. Washer
8. Seal
9. Spacer
10. Valve plates
11. Piston
12. Piston ring
13. Backup washer
14. Lock nut
15. Body
16. O-ring
17. End cap
18. Fitting
19. Hose
20. Snap rings
21. Reservoir end cap
22. O-rings
23. Reservoir body
24. Floating piston
25. O-ring
26. Piston ring
27. Reservoir end cap
28. Rubber plug
29. Pressure valve
30. O-ring
31. Valve screw
32. Relief screw
33. O-ring
34. Spiral ring
35. O-ring
36. O-ring
37. Fitting
38. O-ring
39. Fitting
40. Hose
41. Male coupling
42. Female coupling
43. Hose
44. Snap ring
45. Adjuster end cap
46. O-ring
47. Adjuster body
48. O-ring
49. Piston ring
50. Adjuster piston
51. O-ring
52. Relief screw
53. Split ring
54. O-ring
55. End cap
56. Adjuster knob
57. Threaded sleeve

16

should be installed on the bolt in the order they are removed.

c. Install the valve and piston, making sure the order of assembly is correct. The seven large slots in the piston (14, **Figure 19**) must be toward the rod end with the nut (5, **Figure 19**).

9. Tighten the retaining nut (5, **Figure 19**) to 21-28 N·m (15-21 ft.-lb.) torque. Do not over-tighten.

10. Replace the seal (6, **Figure 19**) as follows:

a. Slide the cap (23, **Figure 19**) and, if so equipped, the bumper (25, **Figure 19**) toward the piston, then clamp the piston rod in a soft-jawed vise.

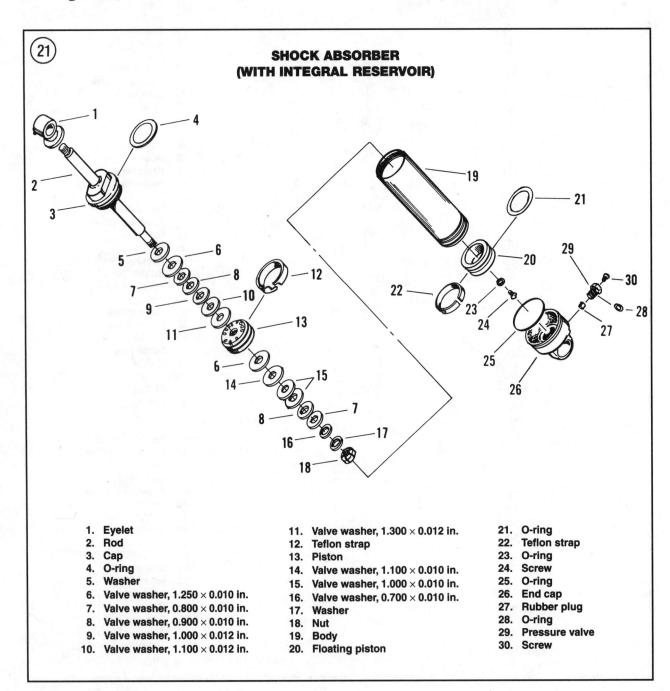

(21)

SHOCK ABSORBER
(WITH INTEGRAL RESERVOIR)

1. Eyelet	11. Valve washer, 1.300 × 0.012 in.	21. O-ring
2. Rod	12. Teflon strap	22. Teflon strap
3. Cap	13. Piston	23. O-ring
4. O-ring	14. Valve washer, 1.100 × 0.010 in.	24. Screw
5. Washer	15. Valve washer, 1.000 × 0.010 in.	25. O-ring
6. Valve washer, 1.250 × 0.010 in.	16. Valve washer, 0.700 × 0.010 in.	26. End cap
7. Valve washer, 0.800 × 0.010 in.	17. Washer	27. Rubber plug
8. Valve washer, 0.900 × 0.010 in.	18. Nut	28. O-ring
9. Valve washer, 1.000 × 0.012 in.	19. Body	29. Pressure valve
10. Valve washer, 1.100 × 0.012 in.	20. Floating piston	30. Screw

b. Heat the eyelet (26, **Figure 19**) to soften the Loctite, then unscrew the eyelet.

c. Pull the end cap (23, **Figure 19**) and seal from the rod.

WARNING
Do not damage the end cap by scratching or gouging while removing or installing the rod seal. Do not lay parts on a rag or other surface where they can pick up lint that would cause leakage. Very small imperfections can result in leakage.

d. Remove the plastic wiper, rubber wiper and O-ring (22, **Figure 19**) from the removed end cap.

e. Clean the cap and rod thoroughly. Inspect both for cracks, scratches, gouges or any other damage.

f. Install the O-ring, rubber wiper and plastic wiper in the cap, then coat the installed seal with oil.

g. Slide the cap with the installed seal over the end of the rod. Be very careful not to damage the seal while installing.

h. Apply Loctite 271 on the threads of the rod, then install the eyelet. Tighten the eyelet securely.

11. Replace the piston ring (24, **Figure 19**).

12. Disassemble the reservoir as follows:

a. Press the end cap (31, **Figure 19**) in until it is about 25 mm (1 in.) from the end of the reservoir body, then remove the snap ring (32, **Figure 19**).

b. Clean the end of the reservoir and end cap thoroughly.

c. Grip the end cap (31, **Figure 19**) with pliers, then pull the end cap slowly from the reservoir.

d. Thread a 1/4 in. coarse-thread bolt into the end of piston (35, **Figure 19**), then grip the bolt with pliers and pull the piston from the reservoir.

e. Pour oil from the reservoir and shock body, then clean the assembly. Dry the cleaned parts with compressed air.

13. Clamp the cap (1, **Figure 19**) of the shock body in a soft-jawed vise with the body upright.

NOTE
After filling the shock absorber with oil, it may be necessary to wait as long as five minutes to allow the air to rise. Do not shake or otherwise agitate the shock oil before or during filling. The installed fluid must be free of air bubbles before continuing.

14. Hold the reservoir lower than the shock body and fill the reservoir with approved shock oil (part No. 0636-664) or equivalent.

NOTE
*A special installing and setting tool (part No. 0644-169) is available for setting the floating piston. The same tool will grip the end of the floating piston to help removal. Make sure the valve (43, **Figure 19**) is removed while installing the floating piston in Step 15.*

15. Coat the rings on the floating piston (35, **Figure 19**) with oil and insert the piston into the reservoir until it is located at the correct distance from the end (A, **Figure 22**). Refer to **Table 2** for the correct distance to position the floating piston.

16. Remove the bolt from the floating piston. Make sure the piston is still the correct distance from the end of the reservoir.

16

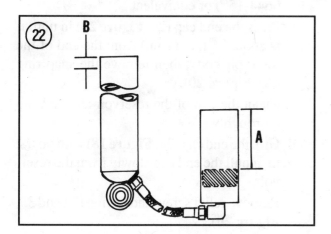

17. Install a new O-ring (41, **Figure 19**) on the end cap, lubricate the O-ring, then install the cap.

18. Press the cap into the reservoir about 25 mm (1 in.). Do not move the floating piston.

19. Install the retaining snap ring (32, **Figure 19**), then pull the end cap back against the snap ring.

20. Fill the body with approved shock oil (part No. 0636-664) or equivalent until the oil is 1/4 in. (B, **Figure 22**) from the top of the body. Wait about five minutes for the bubbles to rise after filling. There should not be **any** air mixed with the oil.

21. Slide the cap (23, **Figure 19**) on the rod until it is about 1/8-1/4 in. from the piston and valve assembly.

NOTE
After assembling the piston and bearing cap in Step 22 and 23, do not move the piston in the body until assembly is complete and the reservoir has been pressurized.

22. Compress the piston ring with your fingers and slowly slide the piston into the shock body until the bearing cap can just be installed. Do not move the piston into the body further than necessary.

23. Install the cap (23, **Figure 19**) using a new O-ring (24, **Figure 19**) and tighten into position.

24. Install the valve (43, **Figure 19**) using a new O-ring (42, **Figure 19**).

25. Grip the protrusion in the center of the end cap (40, **Figure 19**) with locking needlenose pliers, then clamp the pliers in a vise. This procedure will allow the filling valve to be pressed against the valve while filling.

NOTE
Fill the system with nitrogen gas. Do not attempt to fill the shock with air.

26. Insert the inflation needle (part No. 0644-158) or equivalent into the valve, open the fill valve, then slowly increase the regulated pressure to 200 psi.

27. When filled, close the filler valve, remove the inflation needle and reduce the regulated pressure to zero. Install and tighten the screw (39, **Figure 19**).

28. Test operation of the assembled shock as follows:

a. Compress the shock fully.

b. If spongy spots are felt while compressing, it indicates air in the oil. Disassemble and fill with oil that does not contain any air bubbles.

c. When released, the shock absorber rod should extend fully. Failure to extend indicates binding or pressure leakage.

d. Submerge the shock in water to check for nitrogen leaks.

Units with cockpit control

Refer to **Figure 20** for this procedure.

1. Remove the screw and washer (31, **Figure 20**).

2. Release the pressurized nitrogen carefully using the special tool (part No. 0644-158) or equivalent.

3. If not already done, separate the coupler (41 and 42, **Figure 20**), then release pressure in the hose.

4. Disassemble the reservoir as follows:

a. Clamp the remote reservoir body (23, **Figure 20**) in a special holding fixture (part No. 0644-158) or equivalent.

b. Press the end cap (27, **Figure 20**) in until it is about 25 mm (1 in.) from the end of the reservoir body, then remove the snap ring (20, **Figure 20**).

c. Clean the end of the reservoir and end cap thoroughly.

d. Grip the end cap (27, **Figure 18**) with pliers, then pull the end cap slowly from the reservoir.

e. Remove relief screw and O-ring (32 and 33, **Figure 20**).

NOTE
*Use the special removing/installing/setting tool (part No. 0644-169) or a long bolt with 1/4-20 thread to grip the piston (24, **Figure 20**).*

f. Pull the piston (24, **Figure 20**) from the reservoir.

g. Pour oil from the reservoir and shock body, then clean the assembly. Blow dry the cleaned parts with compressed air.

5. Clamp the shock absorber end cap (17, **Figure 20**) in a vise and remove the end cap (5, **Figure 20**).

6. Lift the rod, cap and piston assembly from the body. Clean and inspect the removed assembly as follows:

a. Loosen, but do not remove, the nut (14, **Figure 20**).

NOTE
*Do not mix the order of the valve plates (washers). The number, size and order of the valve plates (10, **Figure 20**) determines dampening action. The valve and piston can be cleaned and inspected after loosening the retaining nut, while leaving the valve and piston on the rod. If additional disassembly is required, keep these parts in the correct order to facilitate reassembly.*

b. Clean and inspect the parts of the valve and piston.

7. If any of the valve or piston parts (10-11, **Figure 20**) are damaged, proceed as follows:

a. Remove the nut (14, **Figure 20**).

b. Withdraw the parts (6-13, **Figure 20**) from the rod, keeping the parts in the proper order.

NOTE
*When parts (6-13, **Figure 20**) are removed, they can be temporarily installed on a 5/16 in. × 3 in. bolt to keep them from becoming mixed up. The parts should be installed on the bolt in the order they are removed.*

c. Install the valve and piston, making sure the order of assembly is correct. The seven large slots in the piston (11, **Figure 20**) must be toward the rod end with the nut (14, **Figure 20**).

8. Tighten the retaining nut (14, **Figure 20**) to 21-28 N•m (15-21 ft.-lb.) torque. Do not overtighten.

9. Replace the seal (8, **Figure 20**) as follows:

a. Slide the cap (5, **Figure 20**) toward the piston. Clamp the piston rod in a soft-jawed vise.

b. Heat the eyelet (1, **Figure 20**) to soften the Loctite, then unscrew the eyelet.

c. Pull the end cap and the separator (2 and 3, **Figure 20**) assemblies from the rod.

WARNING
Do not damage the parts by scratching or gouging while removing or installing the rod seal. Do not lay parts on a rag or other surface where they can pick up lint that would cause leakage. Even small imperfections can result in leakage.

d. Remove the seal (8, **Figure 20**).

e. Clean the cap, separator and rod thoroughly, then inspect each for cracks, scratches, gouges or any other damage.

f. Install the seal, then coat the installed seal with oil.

g. Slide spacers, separator and end cap carefully over the end of the rod. Be very careful not to damage the seal while installing.

h. Apply Loctite 271 on the threads of the rod, then install the eyelet (1, **Figure 20**). Tighten the eyelet securely.

10. Replace the piston ring (12, **Figure 20**).

11. Remove the spiral retaining ring (34, **Figure 20**), then lift the outer threaded sleeve (57, **Figure 20**) from the shock absorber body.

12. Disassemble the cockpit adjuster as follows:

a. Clamp the adjuster body (47, **Figure 20**) in a special holding fixture (part No. 0644-158) or equivalent.

b. Unscrew cap (55, **Figure 20**) from the body.

16

c. Remove the relief screw and O-ring (51 and 52, **Figure 20**).

> *NOTE*
> *Use the special removing/installing/setting tool (part No. 0644-169) or a long bolt with 1/4-20 thread to grip the piston (50, Figure 20).*

d. Pull the piston (50, **Figure 20**) from the body.

e. Pour oil from the body, then clean the assembly. Dry the cleaned parts with compressed air.

> *NOTE*
> *The shock absorber should be assembled using new O-rings. After parts are cleaned, be careful that parts do not pick up lint, such as from a rag, or any other material before it is assembled. Very small imperfections can result in leakage.*

13. Assemble and bleed the cockpit adjuster as follows:

a. Pour approved shock oil (part No. 0636-664) or equivalent into the body until it reaches the bottom of the threads.

b. Allow a few minutes for air bubbles to come to the top and dissipate.

c. Lubricate the adjuster piston and rings (48-50, **Figure 20**) lightly with shock oil and insert the adjuster piston into the body.

> *NOTE*
> *A special installing and setting tool (part No. 0644-169) is available for setting the floating piston. The same tool will grip the end of the floating piston to help removal.*

d. Position the adjuster piston at the distance from the top of the body indicated in **Table 2** (similar to measurement A, **Figure 22**). Oil should be expelled from the hole in the piston when installing.

> *NOTE*
> *If oil is not expelled when positioning the piston in substep 13d, there is not enough oil in the body. Add oil and make sure that oil without bubbles flows from the orifice in the piston. If necessary, push the piston in, then pull the piston up, but do not pull the piston above the level of the oil.*

e. Install the relief screw and O-ring (51 and 52, **Figure 20**) in the adjuster piston.

f. Dump excess oil from the adjuster body. Oil without air should be below the adjuster piston and air should be above the piston.

g. Turn the adjuster knob (56, **Figure 20**) counterclockwise all the way out.

h. Install the cap and adjuster assembly (53-56, **Figure 20**). Tighten the cap securely.

> *NOTE*
> *Make sure the adjuster knob has 1/4-1/2 turn free play before contacting the piston. If free play is not correct, the position of the piston may not be correct.*

14. If detached, attach the hose and fittings to the remote reservoir (23, **Figure 20**). The hose (40, **Figure 20**) to the cockpit adjuster should remain removed until Step 19.

15. Begin filling the shock absorber with oil and bleed air from the system as follows: Use only approved shock oil (part No. 0636-664) or equivalent.

a. Clamp the end cap (17, **Figure 20**) in a vise with the shock body (15, **Figure 20**) up.

b. Hold the remote reservoir above the shock body and add oil to the reservoir until *oil without bubbles* flows into the shock body.

c. Lower the reservoir while filling the reservoir with oil. Oil should remain in the body of the shock absorber and be near the top of the reservoir.

d. Let the oil stand a few minutes to allow any air bubbles to escape.

e. Insert the floating piston (24, **Figure 20**) in the reservoir, pushing the piston to the bottom of the reservoir.

16. Lubricate the O-rings (35 and 36, **Figure 20**) and the body of the shock absorber lightly with low-temperature grease, then install the threaded outer body (57, **Figure 20**).

NOTE
*The adjuster hose (40, **Figure 20**) should not be installed yet.*

17. Align the opening for the fitting (39, **Figure 20**) with the fitting (18, **Figure 20**), then install the spiral ring (34, **Figure 20**). Make sure the ring is fully seated in its groove.

18. Install the piston and rod (1-14, **Figure 20**) assembly as follows:

a. Coat the threads at the top of the shock absorber body (15, **Figure 20**), O-ring (4, **Figure 20**) and separator piston (2, **Figure 20**) with low-temperature grease.

b. Push the separator piston (2, **Figure 20**) against the piston (11, **Figure 20**), but hold the end cap (5, **Figure 20**) against the eyelet (1, **Figure 20**).

c. Turn the piston ring (12, **Figure 20**) until the gap is aligned with the low-speed orifice cut-away.

NOTE
*When installing the shock valve and piston in substep 18d, push only on the separator piston (2, **Figure 20**). Do not push on the shock eyelet or rod (1 or 3, **Figure 20**).*

d. Insert the valve and piston into the bore of the body slowly, while allowing air to escape. Continue to push the piston into position until the separator piston (2, **Figure 20**) is past the orifices in the shock absorber body.

19. Fill the hose (40, **Figure 20**) with oil, then attach fitting and hose (39 and 40, **Figure 20**) to the threaded sleeve. Make sure all air is removed from the hose.

NOTE
*Make sure the cockpit adjuster assembly (42-56, **Figure 20**) is assembled, filled and bled as described in Step 13, before continuing assembly in Step 20.*

20. Install the cap (5, **Figure 20**) and use the cockpit adjuster to bleed air from the shock absorber as follows:

a. Pour approved shock oil into the open end of the body (15, **Figure 20**) until the body is full.

b. Attach the cockpit adjuster fittings (41 and 42, **Figure 20**).

c. Slide the end cap (5, **Figure 20**) down and begin to screw the cap into the threads of the shock body.

d. Turn the adjuster knob (56, **Figure 20**) clockwise a small amount and make sure that oil without bubbles flows from around the threads of the cap and shock body (5 and 15, **Figure 20**).

e. Tighten the cap (5, **Figure 20**) securely while continuing to turn the adjusting knob (56, **Figure 20**).

f. Disconnect the fittings (41 and 42, **Figure 20**) of the cockpit adjuster and cover the fittings to prevent the entrance of dirt.

NOTE
After using the cockpit adjuster to bleed the shock (Step 20), it is necessary to refill the cockpit adjuster (Step 21).

21. Fill the cockpit adjuster as follows:

a. Clamp the adjuster body (47, **Figure 20**) in a special holding fixture (part No. 0644-158) or equivalent.

b. Unscrew the cap (55, **Figure 20**) from the body.

c. Remove the relief screw and O-ring (51 and 52, **Figure 20**).

d. Pour approved shock oil (part No. 0636-664) or equivalent into the body until it reaches the bottom of the threads.

16

e. Allow a few minutes for air bubbles to come to the top and dissipate.

NOTE
A special installing and setting tool (part No. 0644-169) is available that will grip the end of the adjuster piston when setting the height of the adjuster piston.

f. Position the adjuster piston at the distance from the top of the body indicated in **Table 2**.

NOTE
If necessary, push the piston in, then pull the piston up, but do not pull the piston above the level of the oil.

g. Install the relief screw and O-ring (51 and 52, **Figure 20**) in the floating piston.

h. Dump excess oil from the adjuster body. Oil without air should be below the floating piston and air above the piston.

i. Turn the adjuster knob (56, **Figure 20**) counterclockwise all the way out.

j. Install the cap and adjuster assembly (53-56, **Figure 20**). Tighten the cap securely.

NOTE
Make sure the adjuster knob had 1/4-1/2 turn free play before contacting the piston. If free play is not correct, the position of the piston may not be correct.

Units with integral reservoir

Refer to **Figure 21** for these procedures.

1. Remove the screw (30, **Figure 21**) and O-ring.
2. Release the pressurized nitrogen carefully using the special tool (part No. 0644-158) or equivalent.
3. If necessary, pull the eyelet to extend the rod (2, **Figure 21**).

CAUTION
Do not attempt to disassemble the unit without the proper holding fixture. Parts are easily damaged by improper holding procedures.

4. Clamp the body (19, **Figure 21**) in a special holding fixture (part No. 0644-158) or equivalent with the cap (26, **Figure 21**) up.
5. Remove valve (29, **Figure 21**).
6. Unscrew cap (26, **Figure 21**) from the body. Allow oil to drain from the body.
7. Make sure the body is still securely clamped in the holding fixture (part No. 0644-158) or equivalent and unscrew the cap (3, **Figure 21**).
8. Lift the rod, cap and piston assembly from the body.
9. Loosen, but do not remove, the nut (18, **Figure 21**).

NOTE
Do not mix the order of the valve plates (washers). The number, size and order of the valve plates determines dampening action. The valve plates and piston can be cleaned and inspected after loosening the retaining nut, while leaving the valve and piston on the rod. If additional disassembly is required, keep these parts in the correct order to facilitate reassembly.

10. Clean and inspect the parts of the valve and piston.
11. If any of the valve or piston parts are damaged, proceed as follows:
    a. Remove the nut (14, **Figure 21**).
    b. Withdraw the parts (5-19, **Figure 21**) from the rod, keeping the parts in the proper order.

NOTE
*When parts (5-17, **Figure 21**) are removed, they can be temporarily installed on a 5/16 in. × 3 in. bolt to keep them from becoming mixed up. The parts should be installed on the bolt in the order they are removed.*

    c. Install the valve and piston, making sure the order of assembly is correct. The seven large slots in the piston (13, **Figure 21**) must be toward the rod end with nut (18, **Figure 21**).

12. Tighten the retaining nut (18, **Figure 21**) to 21-28 N•m (15-21 ft.-lb.) torque. Do not over-tighten.

13. Replace the O-ring (4, **Figure 21**) as follows:

  a. Slide the cap (3, **Figure 21**) toward the piston, then clamp the piston rod in a soft-jawed vise.

  b. Heat the eyelet (1, **Figure 21**) to soften the Loctite, then unscrew the eyelet.

  c. Remove the assembly from the vise, then pull the end cap (3, **Figure 21**) and O-ring from the rod.

WARNING
Do not damage the end cap by scratching or gouging while removing or installing the rod seal. Do not lay parts on a rag or other surface where they can pick up lint that would cause leakage. Even small imperfections can result in leakage.

  d. Clean the cap and rod thoroughly. Inspect both for cracks, scratches, gouges or any other damage.

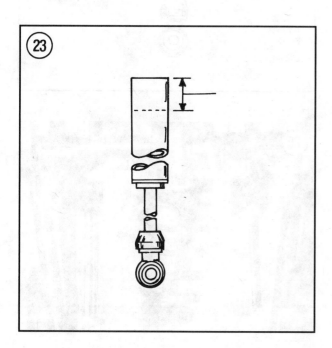

  e. Install the O-ring in the cap. Coat the installed seal with oil.

  f. Slide the cap with the installed seal over the end of the rod. Be very careful not to damage the seal while installing.

  g. Apply Loctite 271 on the threads of the rod, then install the eyelet. Tighten the eyelet securely.

14. Replace the piston ring (12, **Figure 21**).

15. Use the proper size Allen wrench and remove the small screw and O-ring (23 and 24, **Figure 21**) from the floating piston.

16. Grip the center of piston (20, **Figure 21**) with pliers or the special holding/setting tool (part No. 0644-169), then pull the floating piston from the body.

17. Clean the shock body thoroughly. Blow dry with compressed air.

18. Clamp the body (19, **Figure 21**) in the special holding fixture (part No. 0644-158) or equivalent.

19. Lubricate the piston ring and cap O-ring (22 and 25, **Figure 21**).

20. Compress the piston ring with your fingers and slowly slide the piston into the shock body until the cap can just be installed.

21. Install the cap (3, **Figure 21**) and tighten into position.

22. Reposition the shock body with the open end upright.

23. Pull the rod out to its fully extended position. Fill the body with approved shock oil (part No. 0636-664) or equivalent until the oil is 1.5 in. from the top (**Figure 23**).

16

NOTE
After filling the shock absorber with oil, it may be necessary to wait as long as five minutes to allow the air to rise. Do not shake or otherwise agitate the shock oil before or during filling. The installed fluid must be free of air bubbles before continuing.

24. Move the shock rod slowly up and down a few times to remove any air trapped around the piston. Keep the piston below the level of the oil.

25. Check the oil level and make sure the oil level is still 1.5 in. from the top of the body.

26. Lubricate the floating piston and rings (20-21, **Figure 21**) lightly with shock oil and insert the floating piston into the body.

NOTE
A special installing and setting tool (part No. 0644-169) is available for setting the floating piston. The same tool will grip the end of the floating piston to help removal.

27. Position the floating piston at the distance from the top of the body indicated in **Table 2** (**Figure 24**). Oil should be expelled from the hole in the piston when installing.

NOTE
If oil is not expelled when positioning the floating piston in Step 27, there is not enough oil in the reservoir. Add oil and make sure oil without bubbles flows from the orifice in the floating piston. If necessary, push the piston in, then pull the piston up, but do not pull the piston above the level of the oil.

28. Install the Allen head screw and O-ring in the floating piston. Hold the piston with a 9/16 in. wrench while tightening the Allen head screw.

29. Dump excess oil from the shock body. Oil without air should be below the floating piston and air should be above the piston.

30. Apply a light coat of Loctite 271 to the threads of the end cap. Install the cap on the shock body. Hold the body of the shock with special blocks (part No. 0644-142) and tighten the end cap securely.

31. Lubricate the O-ring (25, **Figure 21**) lightly with oil before installing the valve and plug (29 and 27, **Figure 21**). Tighten the valve securely.

NOTE
Fill the system with nitrogen gas. Do not attempt to fill the shock with air.

32. Insert the inflation needle (part No. 0644-158) or equivalent into the valve, open the fill valve, then slowly increase the regulated pressure to 200 psi.

33. When filled, close the filler valve, remove the inflation needle and reduce the regulated pressure to zero. Install and tighten the screw (30, **Figure 21**).

34. Test operation of the assembled shock as follows:

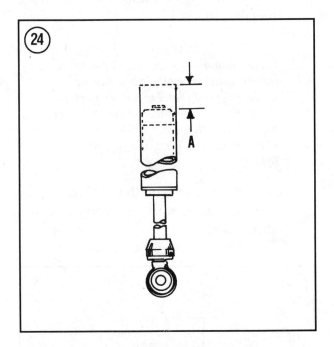

a. Compress the shock fully.

b. If spongy spots are felt while compressing, it indicates air in the oil. Disassemble and fill with oil that does not contain any air bubbles.

c. When released, the shock absorber rod should extend fully. Failure to extend indicates binding or pressure leakage.

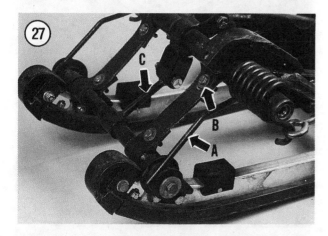

d. Submerge the shock in water to check for nitrogen leaks.

FRONT ARM SPRING

Removal/Installation

On most models, the spring for the front arm of the rear suspension is located on the shock absorber (**Figure 25** or **Figure 26**). The spring can be removed as described in the removal and service instructions for the front shock absorber in this chapter.

On some early models, the spring for the front arm of the rear suspension is located as shown in **Figure 27**. Refer to the following removal procedure.

1. Remove the front suspension as described in this chapter.

2. Remove the self-locking nut (**Figure 28**) from the eyebolt.

3. Unhook the spring from the eyebolt and remove the spring (A, **Figure 27**).

4. Inspect the spring for damage. If one spring is damaged, both front springs should be replaced.

5. Installation is the reverse of removal. A new self-locking nut (**Figure 28**) should be installed.

REAR SPRING

1. Remove the rear suspension as described in this chapter.

2. Remove the bolt and washer attaching the spring slide (B, **Figure 10**). On some models the spring slide is bolted to the rail (**Figure 29**).

16

NOTE
The rear upper idler wheels must be removed from some models before the rear springs can be removed. If the idler wheel must be removed, refer to the procedures described in Step 3 and Step 4.

3A. If a collar is located as shown in **Figure 30**, loosen the set screw and remove the collar.

3B. If an offset pivot lever is located as shown in **Figure 31**, remove the lever as follows:

> *NOTE*
> *It is important to mark the position of the lever in substep a before removing it to aid in assembly.*

   a. Mark the shaft in line with the slots in the lever.
   b. Remove the pinch bolts that clamp the lever to the shaft.

> *CAUTION*
> *The shaft can be damaged if the offset pivot is pulled from the shaft splines in substep c without removing the pinch bolts. The axle is notched to allow clearance for the pinch bolts.*

   c. Pull the lever from the shaft. Be careful not to lose the pivot shaft and axle (**Figure 32**).

4. Attach a suitable puller (**Figure 33**) and pull the wheel from the pivot shaft.

5. Installation is the reverse of removal, observing the following:

   a. Install the spring and spring sleeve (38 and 39, **Figure 16**). Install the spring slide (B, **Figure 10** or **Figure 29**).
   b. Tighten the bolt attaching the spring slide to the torque listed in **Table 1**.
   c. Use a driver **Figure 34** that contacts only the inner race of the bearing to install the idler wheel. Make sure the bearing is seated.
   d. Install spacers and thrust washers, as required. A spacer and thrust washer may be located between the idler wheel and the collar (**Figure 30**) or offset pivot (**Figure 31**) on some models.
   e. If so equipped, install the axle and washer in the offset pivot (**Figure 35**). The notched side of the offset pivot should be toward the inside.
   f. If equipped with the offset pivot, align the split with the alignment marks made on the

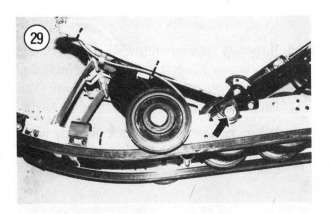

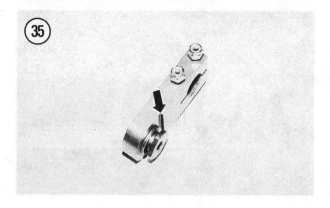

axle (substep 3Ba) before removing the pivot (**Figure 31**). Tighten the pinch bolts to the torque listed in **Table 1**.

FRONT ARM

Removal/Installation

Refer to **Figure 15** or **Figure 16** for this procedure.

1. Remove the rear suspension as described in this chapter.

2. Remove or detach the shock absorber for the front arm as described in this chapter.

3. If equipped with the springs for the front arm (**Figure 27**), remove the springs as described in this chapter.

4. If the limit straps were not detached during shock absorber removal, remove the bolts (**Figure 9**) from the limit straps.

5. On early models, remove the bolt attaching the shock link (C, **Figure 27**) to the front arm.

6. Remove the bolts (C, **Figure 10**, typical) attaching the front arms to the slide rail brackets.

7. Lift the front arms from the rear suspension unit. Do not lose the bushings (20, **Figure 16**) from the front arms.

> *WARNING*
> *Do not unbolt any brackets from the slide rails until the original mounting hole location is clearly marked. The mounting locations affect suspension action and machine handling. If there is any question regarding the correct mounting location of any part of the suspension, contact an Arctic Cat dealer or compare mounting location of similar machines. A poorly handling machine is dangerous.*

8. Inspect the front arms for cracks, twists or other damage.

9. Lubricate all bushings with low-temperature grease when assembling.

16

NOTE
Coat threads of bolts and nuts that are not self-locking with Loctite 271. Reassemble using new self-locking nuts.

10. Tighten bolts to the torques listed in **Table 1**.

11. Secure the limit straps with a bolt, two large flat washers and a nut (**Figure 9**).

REAR ARM AND LOWER ARM

Removal/Installation

Refer to **Figure 15** or **Figure 16** when performing this procedure.

1. Remove the rear suspension as described in this chapter.

2. Remove the rear shock absorber as described in this chapter.

3. Remove the rear springs as described in this chapter.

4. Remove the pivot bolt(s) (**Figure 36**) and remove the rear arm (49, **Figure 15** or **Figure 16**).

WARNING
Do not unbolt any brackets from the slide rails until the original mounting hole location is clearly marked. The mounting locations affect suspension action and machine handling. If there is any question regarding the correct mounting location of any part of the suspension, contact an Arctic Cat dealer or compare mounting location of similar machines. A poorly handling machine is dangerous.

5. Mark the side rails with the location of the mounting bolts (**Figure 37**).

6. Lift the lower arm (45, **Figure 15** or **Figure 16**) from the rails.

7. Inspect the rear arm, lower arm and slide rails for cracks, twists, or other damage and replace as necessary.

8. Lubricate all bushings with low-temperature grease when assembling.

9. Assemble by reversing the removal procedure.

NOTE
Coat threads of bolts and nuts that are not self-locking with Loctite 271. Reassemble using new self-locking nuts.

10. Tighten bolts to the torques listed in **Table 1**.

IDLER WHEELS

Inspection

1. Remove the rear suspension as described in this chapter.

2. Spin each of the idler (guide) wheels while checking for any roughness, noise or other damage that would indicate bearing damage.

3. Check the wheel surface for cracks, deep scoring or excessive wear.

4. If the bearing is damaged, it can be removed and replaced as described in this chapter.

REAR AXLE

Removal/Installation

1. Remove the rear suspension as described in this chapter.

2. Remove the screw (**Figure 38**) and washer from the center of both outside guide wheels.

3. Remove both outside guide wheels (A, **Figure 39**).

4. Remove the adjusting bushings (B, **Figure 39**).

5. Withdraw the rear axle, spacers and inner guide wheels.

6. Clean all components thoroughly in solvent.

7. Check the rear axle for wear, cracks or other damage.

8. Check the inner spacers for cracks or damage.

9. Check the outer spacers (adjust bushings) for cracks or damage. Check around the adjust bolt hole in the spacer for damage.

10. If there is any doubt as to the condition of any part, repair or replace it as required.

11. Apply a low-temperature grease to all pivot shafts and bushings.

12. Installation is the reverse of the preceding steps. Observe the following:

   a. Install the adjusting bushing so that the hole faces toward the front and engages the adjuster bolt (C, **Figure 39**).

   b. Tighten the idler wheel bolts to the torque specified in **Table 1**.

Wheel Bearing Replacement

1. Remove the wheel as described in this chapter. Some wheels are pressed on the axle and will require a puller (**Figure 33**).

2. Remove the snap ring (**Figure 40**), *then pull the bearing from the wheel.*

3. Inspect the wheel carefully and if it is found to be in good condition, press a new bearing into the wheel until seated.

16

4. Install the retaining snap ring (**Figure 40**). Make sure the snap ring is fully seated.

5. Spin the wheel and check to be sure the wheel rotates straight and smoothly. If the wheel wobbles, the bearing may not be installed properly.

6. Spin the wheel and check for smoothness after installing.

TRACK

Removal/Installation

1. Remove the rear suspension as described in this chapter.

2. Remove the driveshaft (**Figure 41**) as described in Chapter Fourteen.

3. Remove the track.

4. Installation is the reverse of the preceding steps. Observe the following step.

5. When installing the track, orient the track lugs to run in the direction shown in **Figure 42**.

Inspection

1. Check for missing or damaged track cleats. Replace cleats as described in this chapter.

2. Visually inspect the track for the following conditions:

    a. *Obstruction damage*—Cuts, slashes and gouges in the track surface are caused by hitting obstructions. These could include

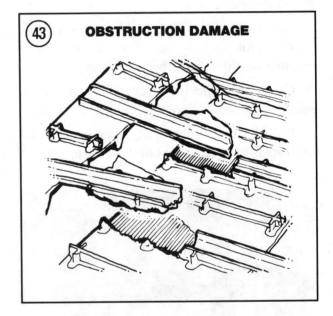

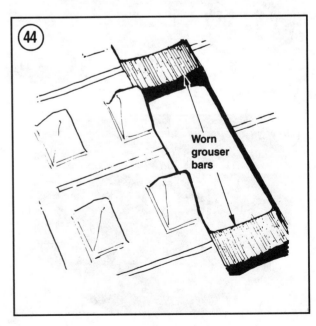

LUG DAMAGE

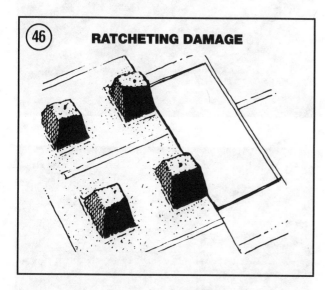

RATCHETING DAMAGE

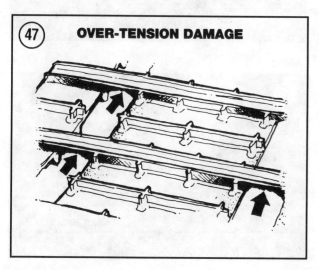

OVER-TENSION DAMAGE

broken glass, sharp rocks or buried steel (**Figure 43**).

b. *Worn grouser bars*—Excessively worn grouser bars are caused by snowmobile operation over rough and non-snow covered terrain such as gravel roads and highway roadsides (**Figure 44**).

c. *Lug damage*—The lug damage shown in **Figure 45** is caused by lack of snow lubrication.

d. *Ratcheting damage*— Insufficient track tension is a major cause of ratcheting damage to the top of the lugs (**Figure 46**). Ratcheting can also be caused by too great a load and constant jack-rabbit starts.

e. *Over-tension damage*—Excessive track tension can cause too much friction on the wear bars. This friction causes the wear bars to melt and adhere to the track grouser bars (**Figure 47**). An indication of this condition is a sticky track that has a tendency to lock up.

f. *Loose track damage*—A track adjusted too loosely can cause the outer edge to flex excessively. This results in the type of damage shown in **Figure 48**. Excessive weight can also contribute to the damage.

g. *Impact damage*—Impact damage (**Figure 49**) causes the track rubber to open and

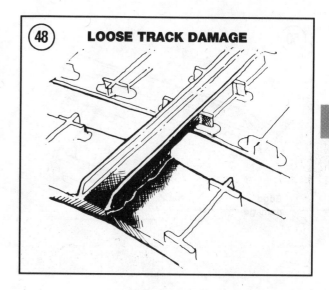

LOOSE TRACK DAMAGE

16

expose the cord. This frequently happens in more than one place. Impact damage is usually caused by riding on rough or frozen ground or ice. Also, insufficient track tension can allow the track to pound against the track stabilizers inside the tunnel.

h. *Edge damage*—Edge damage (**Figure 50**) is usually caused by tipping the snowmobile on its side to clear the track and allowing the track edge to contact an abrasive surface.

Cleat Replacement

Follow the same cleat pattern when installing new cleats.

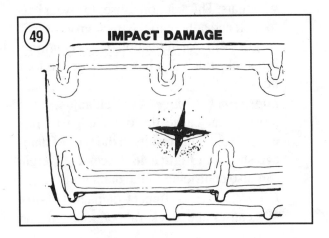

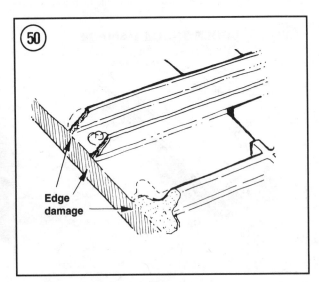

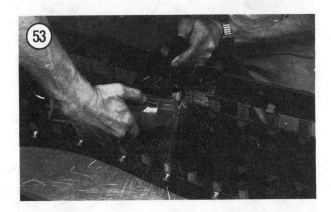

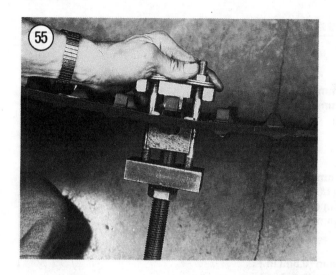

You need a hand grinder, safety glasses and a universal track clip installer to remove and install new cleats (**Figure 51**).

WARNING
Wear safety glasses when using a hand grinder to remove cleats.

1. Using a hand grinder (**Figure 52**), grind a slit in the corner of the cleat (**Figure 53**).
2. Pry the cleat off the track (**Figure 54**).
3. Align the new cleat onto the track. Install the cleat with the cleat installation tool (**Figure 55**). Check the cleat to make sure it is tight.

Table 1 TIGHTENING TORQUES

	N·m	ft.-lb.
End caps	15	11
Front arm mounting bracket to slide rail	32	24
Front shock absorber to slide rail	42	31
Idler wheel	32	24
Offset pivot arm pinch bolts	26	19
Rail supports (front)	24	18
Rear arm to slide rail	32	24
Skid frame mounting screws	32	24
Spring slide blocks to slide rail	32	24
Track adjuster to slide rail	15	11
Wear strips	15	11

Table 2 SHOCK ABSORBER SPECIFICATIONS

1993	
ZR 440	
Floating piston setting	
Front arm integral reservoir	15.24 mm (0.600 in.)
Rear arm	20.32 mm (0.800 in.)
1994	
ZR 440	
Floating piston setting	
Front arm	
Integral reservoir	15.24 mm (0.600 in.)
External reservoir	61 mm (2.402 in.)
Cockpit adjustment	13.2 mm (0.520 in.)
Rear arm	20.32 mm (0.800 in.)
	(continued)

16

Table 2 SHOCK ABSORBER SPECIFICATIONS (continued)

1994	
ZR 580	
Floating piston setting	
Front arm	15.24 mm (0.600 in.)
Rear arm	20.32 mm (0.800 in.)
1995	
ZR 440	
Floating piston setting	
Front arm	
With integral reservoir	15.24 mm (0.600 in.)
External reservoir	3 mm (1/8 in.) from bottom
Cockpit adjustment	13.2 mm (0.520 in.)
Rear arm	20.32 mm (0.800 in.)
ZR 580	
Floating piston setting	
Front arm	15.24 mm (0.600 in.)
Rear arm	20.32 mm (0.800 in.)
1996	
ZR 440, ZR 580, ZRT 600	
Floating piston setting	
Front arm	
With integral reservoir	15.24 mm (0.600 in.)
External reservoir	3 mm (1/8 in.) from bottom
Cockpit adjustment	13.2 mm (0.520 in.)
Rear arm	18.29 mm (0.720 in.)
1997	
ZR 440	
Floating piston setting	
Front shock	76.2-88.9 mm (3.0-3.5 in.)
Rear shock	18.29 mm (0.720 in.)
ZR 580 EFI	
Floating piston setting	
Front shock	15.24 mm (0.600 in.)
Rear shock	18.29 mm (0.720 in.)
ZRT 600	
Floating piston setting	
Front shock	15.24 mm (0.600 in.)
Rear shock	18.29 mm (0.720 in.)
1998	
ZR 440	
Floating piston setting	
Front shock	76.2-88.9 mm (3.0-3.5 in.)
Rear shock	18.29 mm (0.720 in.)
ZRT 600	
Floating piston setting	
Front shock	15.24 mm (0.600 in.)
Rear shock	18.29 mm (0.720 in.)

Chapter Seventeen

Off-season Storage

One of the most critical aspects of snowmobile maintenance is off-season storage. Proper storage will prevent engine and suspension damage and fuel system contamination. Improper storage will cause various degrees of deterioration and damage.

Preparation for Storage

Careful preparation will minimize deterioration and make it easier to restore the snowmobile to service later. When performing the following procedure, make a list of replacement or damaged parts, so that they can be ordered and installed before next season.

1. Remove the seat and clean the area underneath the seat thoroughly. Wipe the seat off with a damp cloth and wipe a preservative over the seat to keep it from drying out. If you are concerned about the seat during storage, store it away from the snowmobile in a safe place.

2. Flush the cooling system as described in Chapter Three. Before refilling the cooling system, check all of the hoses for cracks or deterioration. Replace hoses as described in Chapter Eleven. Make sure all hose clamps are tight. Replace questionable hose clamps as required.

3. Change the chaincase oil as described in Chapter Three.

CAUTION
Do not allow water to enter the engine when performing Step 4.

4. Clean the snowmobile from front to back. Remove all dirt and other debris from the pan and tunnel. Clean out debris caught in the track.

5. Check the frame, skis and other metal parts for cracks or other damage. Apply paint to all bare metal surfaces.

6. Check all fasteners for looseness and tighten, as required. Replace loose or damaged rivets.

NOTE
Refer to the appropriate chapter for the specified tightening torque as required.

17

7. Lubricate all pivot points with a low-temperature grease as described in Chapter Three.

8. Unplug all electrical connectors and clean both connector halves with electrical contact cleaner. Check the electrical contact pins for damage or looseness. Repair connectors as required. After the contact cleaner evaporates, apply a dielectric grease to one connector half and reconnect the connectors.

> *CAUTION*
> *Dielectric grease is formulated for electrical use. Do not use a regular type grease on electrical connectors.*

9. To protect the engine from rust buildup during storage, perform the following procedure:

   a. Jack up the snowmobile so that the track clears the ground.

   b. Start the engine and allow it to warm to normal operating temperature.

> *WARNING*
> *The exhaust gases are poisonous. Do not run the engine in a closed area. Make sure there is plenty of ventilation.*

> *NOTE*
> *A cloud of smoke will develop in substep 9c. This is normal.*

   c. Open the hood and remove the boots (**Figure 1**, typical) at the back of the carburetors.

   d. Spray engine preservative (storage oil) into both carburetors until the engine smokes heavily or begins to stall.

   e. Turn all switches OFF.

   f. Attach the boots (**Figure 1**) to the back of the carburetors.

> *CAUTION*
> *To prevent expensive engine damage, clean the area around the spark plug holes before removing the spark plugs.*

   g. Remove the spark plugs (**Figure 2**). Reconnect the spark plugs at their plug caps to ground them.

   h. Pour 30 cc (1 fl. oz.) of SAE 30 engine oil into each spark plug hole.

   i. Pull the recoil starter handle several times to distribute the oil around the cylinder walls.

   j. Wipe a film of oil onto the spark plug threads and reinstall the spark plugs. Reconnect the spark plug caps to the plugs.

> *CAUTION*
> *During the storage period, do not run the engine.*

10. *Electric start models*—Remove the battery and coat the cable terminals with petroleum jelly. See Chapter Nine. Check the electrolyte level and refill with distilled water if it is low. Store the battery in an area where it will not freeze and recharge it once each month.

11. Plug the end of the muffler with a rag to prevent moisture from entering. Tag the machine

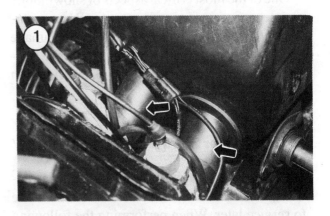

with a note to remind you to remove the rag before restarting the engine next season.

12. Remove the drive belt (**Figure 3**) and store it on a flat surface.

13. Remove and service the primary and secondary sheaves as described in Chapter Thirteen. Replace worn or damaged parts as required.

14. Clean the driven shaft (jackshaft) thoroughly.

15. Reinstall the primary and secondary sheaves. Tighten the bolts to the torque specification listed in Chapter Thirteen.

16. Install and secure the belt shield.

WARNING
Some fuel may spill in the following procedure. Work in a well-ventilated area at least 50 feet from any sparks or flames, including gas appliance pilot lights. Do not smoke in the area. Keep a fire extinguisher handy.

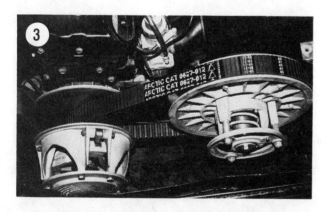

17. Using a suitable siphon tool, siphon fuel out of the fuel tank and into a gasoline storage tank.

18. When the fuel tank is empty, remove the drain plug (**Figure 4**) on each carburetor and drain the carburetors. Wipe up spilled gasoline immediately.

19. Protect all glossy surfaces on the chassis, hood and dash with an automotive type wax.

20. Raise the track off the ground with wooden blocks. Make sure the snowmobile is secure.

21. Cover the snowmobile with a heavy cover that will provide adequate protection from dust and damage. Do not cover the snowmobile with plastic as moisture can collect and cause rusting. If the snowmobile has to be stored outside, place the entire vehicle off the ground on blocks.

Removal From Storage

Preparing the snowmobile for use after storage should be relatively easy, if proper storage procedures were followed.

1. Remove the plug from the end of the muffler.

2. Adjust track tension as described in Chapter Three.

3. Inspect the drive belt for cracks or other abnormal conditions. Reinstall the drive belt as described in Chapter Thirteen.

4. Check the chaincase oil level. Refill as described in Chapter Three. If the oil was not changed before storage, change the oil as described in Chapter Three.

5. Check and adjust drive belt tension.

6. Check the coolant level and refill if necessary.

7. Check all of the control cables for proper operation. Adjust as described in Chapter Three.

8. Fill the oil injection tank. If the tank was dry or if a hose was disconnected, bleed the oil pump as described in Chapter Ten.

9. *Electric start models*—Check the battery electrolyte level and fill with distilled water as necessary. Make sure the battery has a full charge. Recharge if necessary. Clean the battery terminals and install the battery. Connect the

17

cable to the positive terminal first, then the ground cable to the negative terminal of the battery. Apply petroleum jelly to the battery terminals.

10. Perform an engine tune-up as described in Chapter Three.

11. Check the fuel system. Refill the tank with a 50:1 fuel/oil mixture as described in Chapter Three. Replace the fuel filter, as described in Chapter Three, if it is clogged.

CAUTION
Use a 50:1 fuel/oil ratio initially whenever the snowmobile is removed from an extended storage period. After running through the first tank of gas, it is unnecessary to continue with the 50:1 mixture unless the snowmobile is going to be run in extreme weather conditions. Refer to Chapter Three for additional information.

12. Make a thorough check of the snowmobile for loose or missing nuts, bolts or screws.

13. Start the engine and check for fuel or exhaust leaks. Make sure the lights and all switches work properly. Turn the engine off.

WARNING
The exhaust gases are poisonous. Do not run the engine in a closed area. Make sure there is plenty of ventilation.

14. After the engine has been initially run for a period of time, install new spark plugs as described in Chapter Three.

Index

18

WIRING
DIAGRAMS

MAIN HARNESS 1992 PROWLER

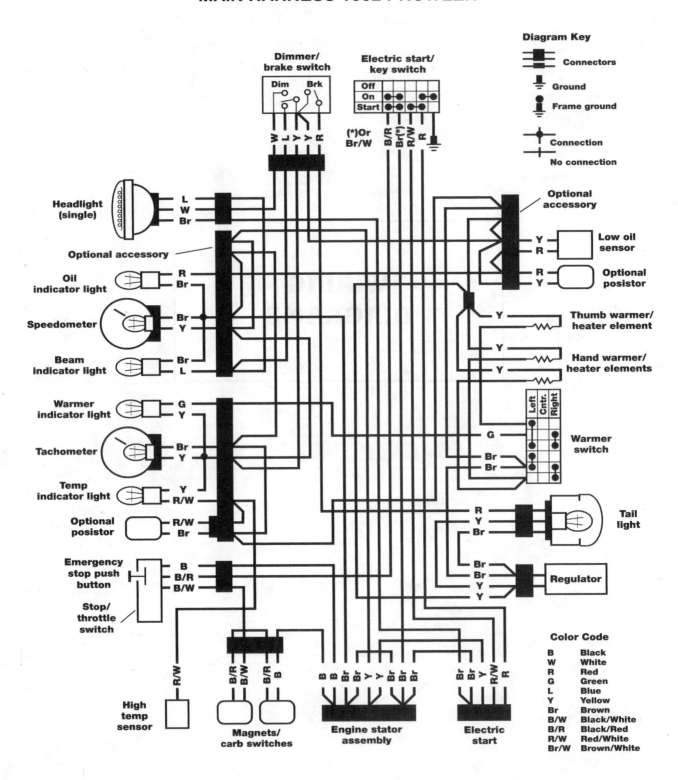

MAIN HARNESS 1993 440 ZR AND 580 ZR, 1995 ZR 440 AND ZR 580, 1995 Z 440 AND Z 580

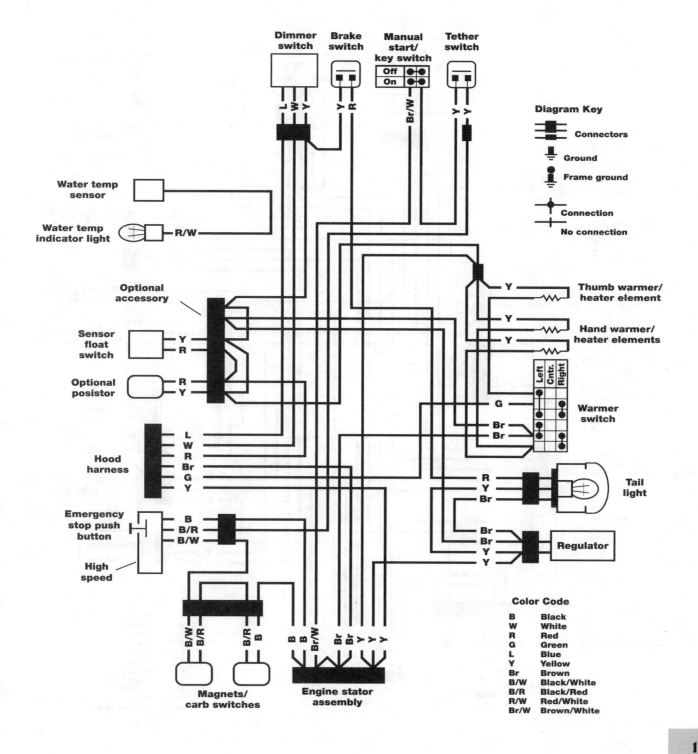

MAIN HARNESS 1993 440 ZR AND 580 ZR, 1995 ZR 440 AND ZR 580, 1995 Z 440 AND Z 580

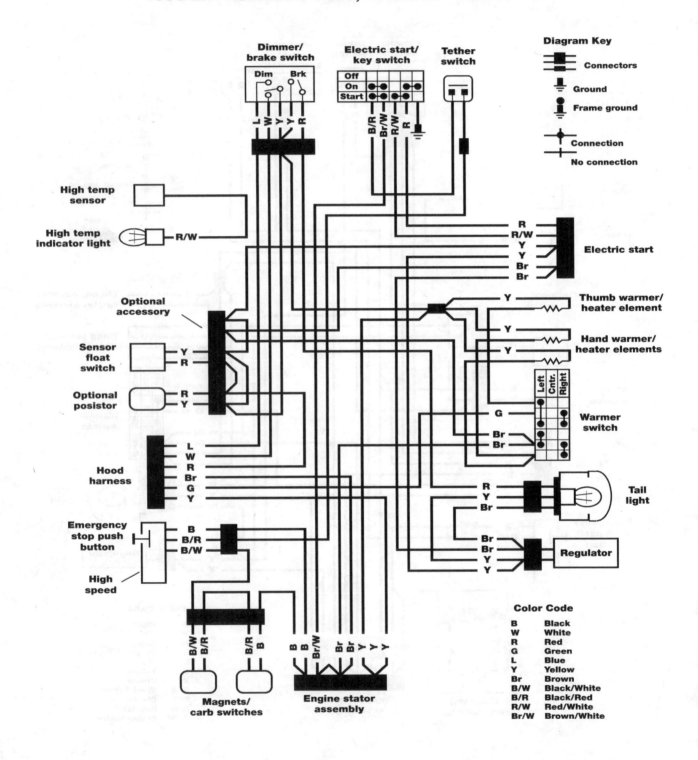

MAIN HARNESS 1995 AND 1996 ZR 440

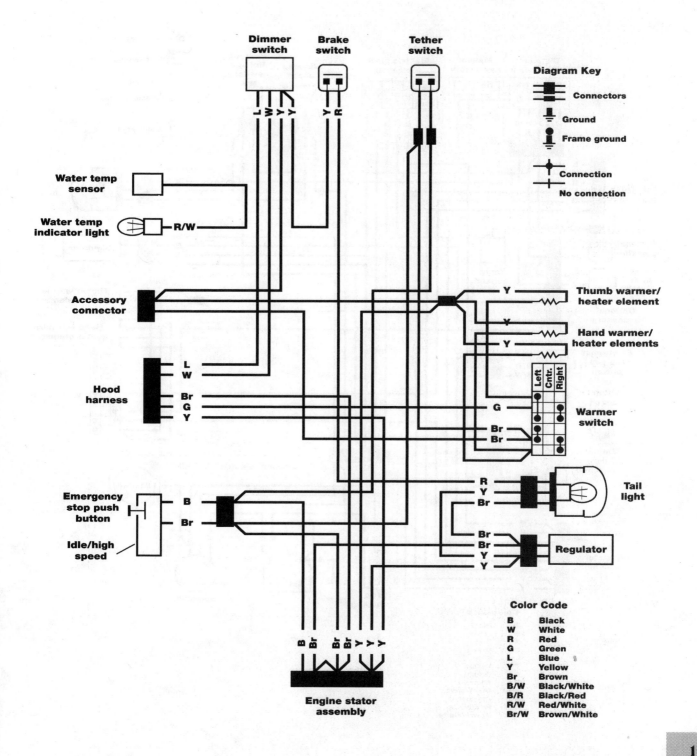

Color Code

B	Black
W	White
R	Red
G	Green
L	Blue
Y	Yellow
Br	Brown
B/W	Black/White
B/R	Black/Red
R/W	Red/White
Br/W	Brown/White

MAIN HARNESS 1995 PROWLER 2-UP, COUGAR (SIMILAR)

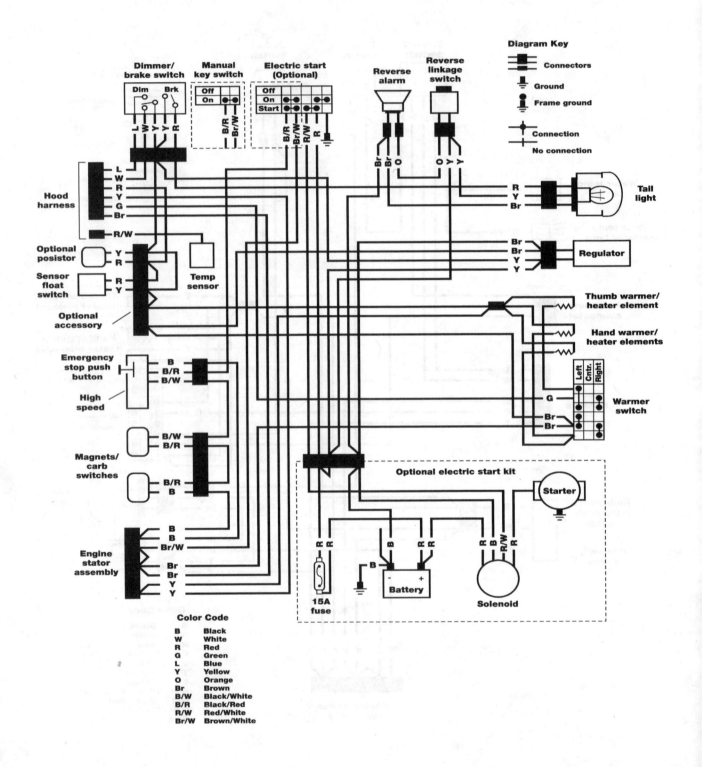

MAIN HARNESS 1995 PANTERA,
EXT 580 EFI (SIMILAR), ZR 580 EFI (SIMILAR)

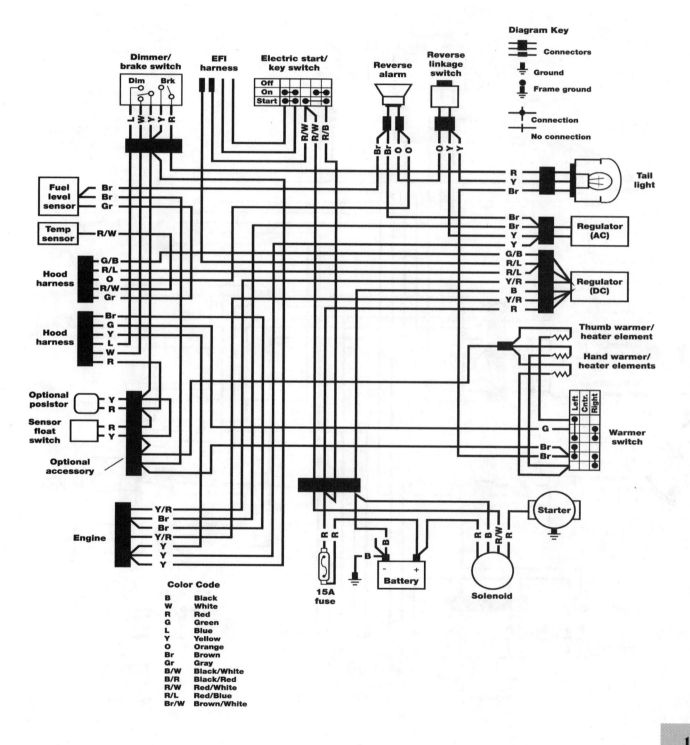

Diagram Key
- Connectors
- Ground
- Frame ground
- Connection
- No connection

Color Code

B	Black
W	White
R	Red
G	Green
L	Blue
Y	Yellow
O	Orange
Br	Brown
Gr	Gray
B/W	Black/White
B/R	Black/Red
R/W	Red/White
R/L	Red/Blue
Br/W	Brown/White

MAIN HARNESS 1996 ZRT 600, 1997 ZRT 600, EXT 600, POWDER EXTREME

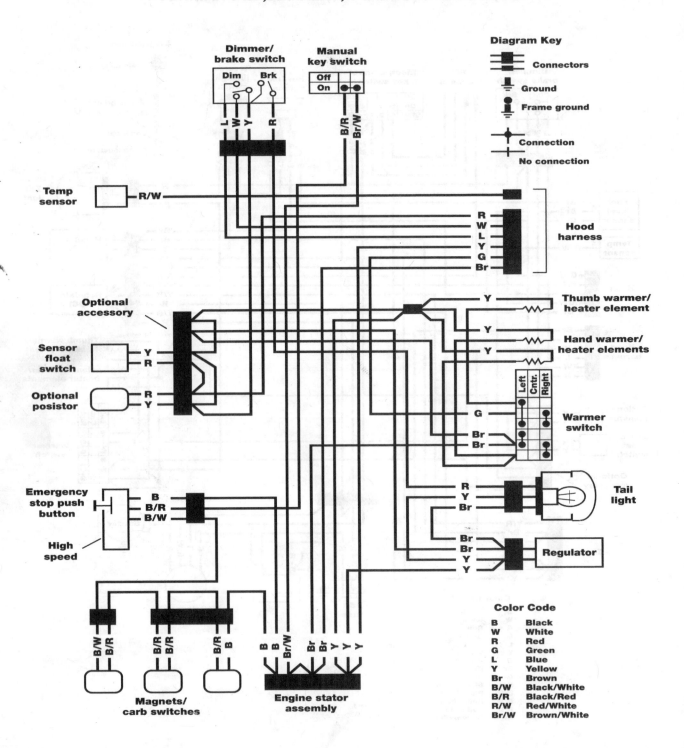

MAIN HARNESS 1996 AND 1997 ZR 580 EFI

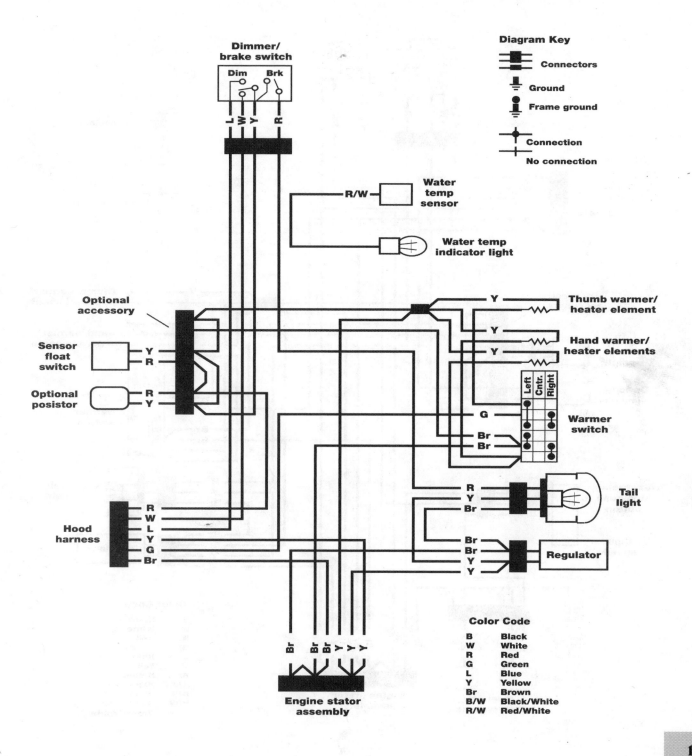

Diagram Key

- Connectors
- Ground
- Frame ground
- Connection
- No connection

Color Code

B	Black
W	White
R	Red
G	Green
L	Blue
Y	Yellow
Br	Brown
B/W	Black/White
R/W	Red/White

19

MAIN HARNESS 1997 Z 440

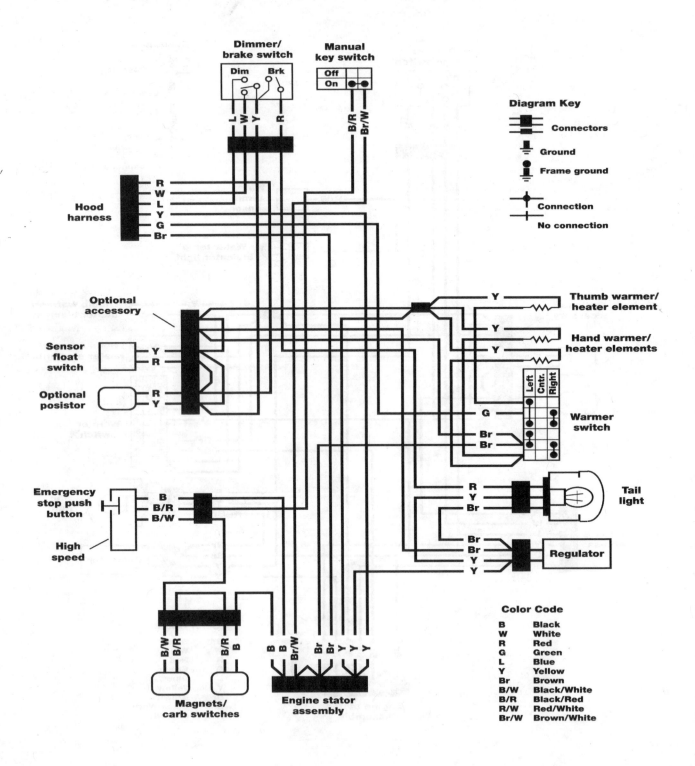

MAIN HARNESS 1997 ZL 440, PANTHER 550 COUGAR (SIMILAR), COUGAR MOUNTAIN CAT, 1998 ZL 440 (SIMILAR)

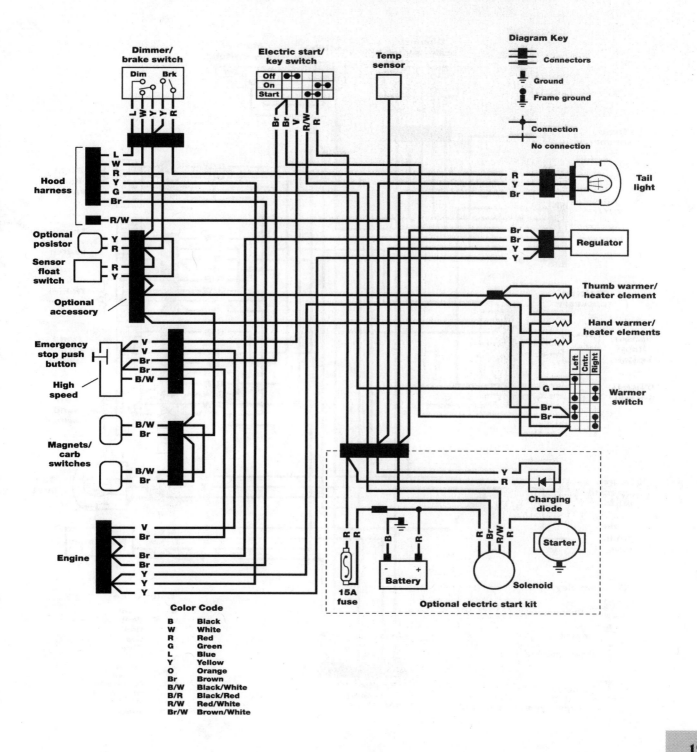

MAIN HARNESS 1997 ZR 440 (SIMILAR), 1998 ZR 440

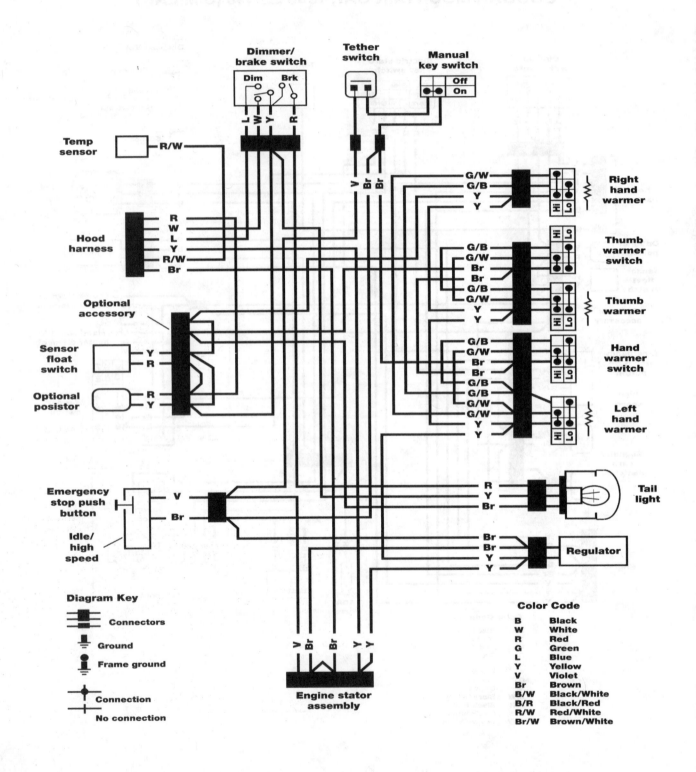

MAIN HARNESS 1997 PANTERA, EXT 580 EFI (SIMILAR), EXT 580 EFI DELUXE (SIMILAR)

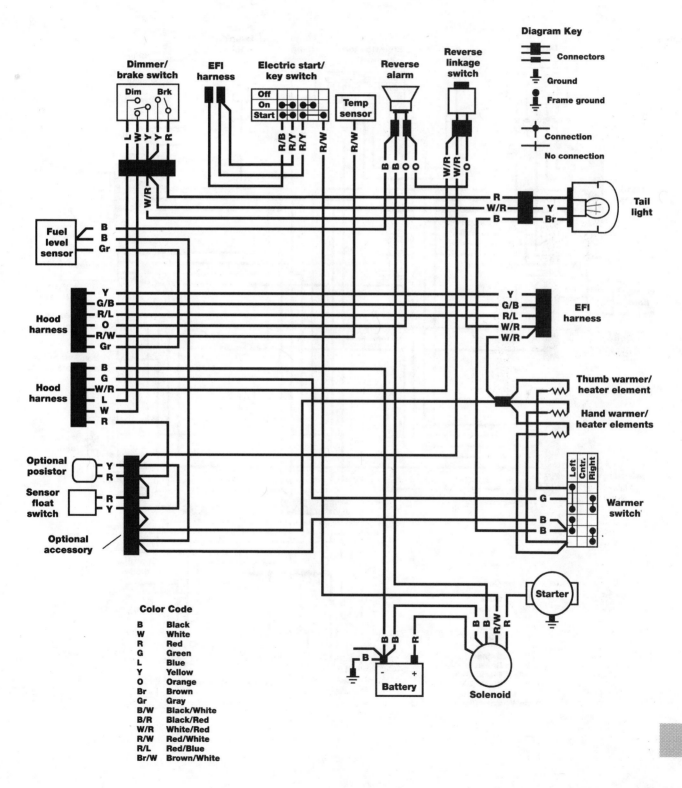

Color Code

B	Black
W	White
R	Red
G	Green
L	Blue
Y	Yellow
O	Orange
Br	Brown
Gr	Gray
B/W	Black/White
B/R	Black/Red
W/R	White/Red
R/W	Red/White
R/L	Red/Blue
Br/W	Brown/White

MAIN HARNESS 1997 POWDER SPECIAL EFI

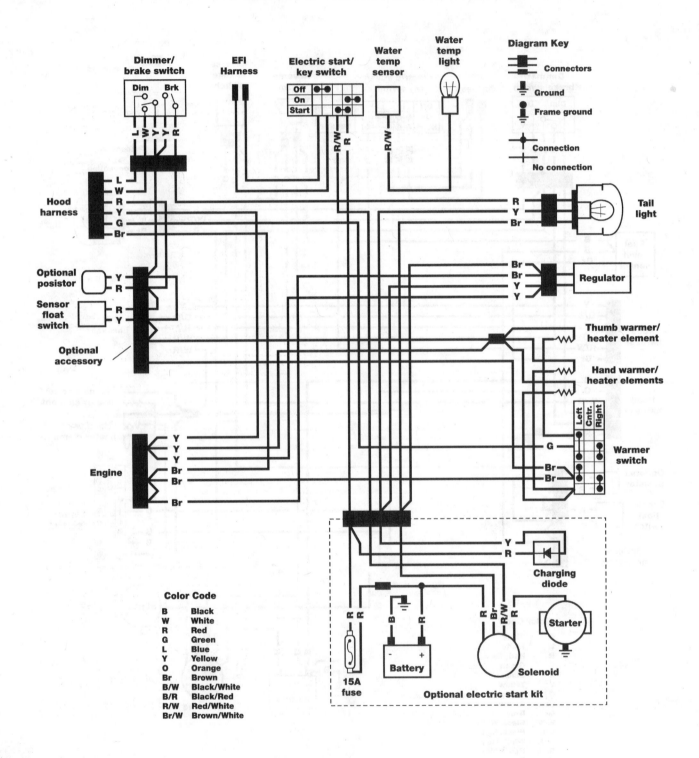

MAIN HARNESS 1998 Z 440 (SIMILAR), ZL 500, COUGAR, COUGAR MOUNTAIN CAT, EXT 600 TRIPLE, EXT TRIPLE TOUR, ZRT 600, POWDER EXTREME, POWDER SPECIAL (CARBURETED)

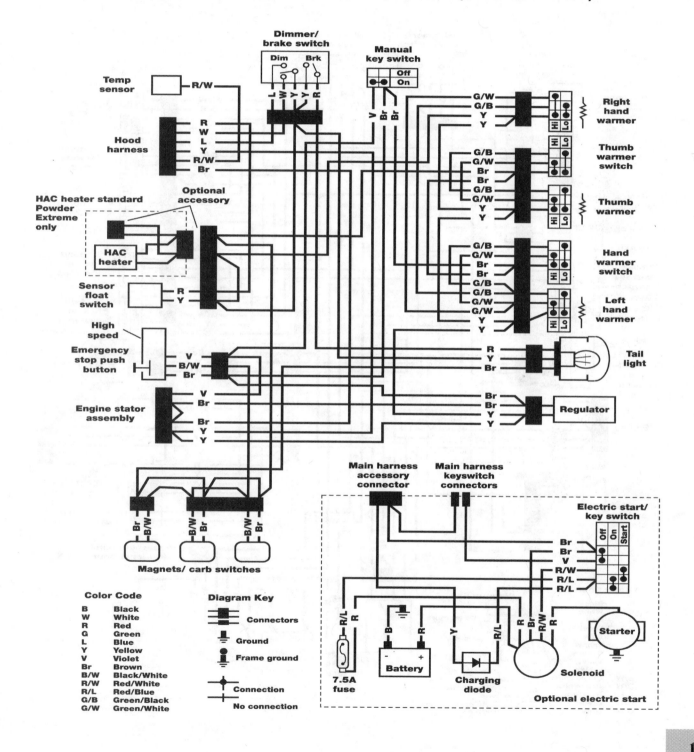

MAIN HARNESS 1998 PANTHER 550 AND COUGAR DELUXE

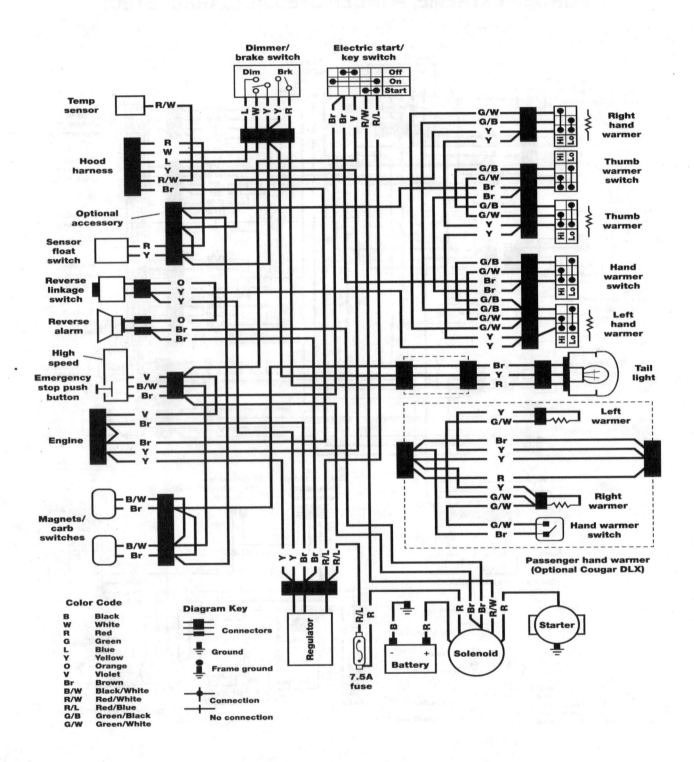

Color Code

B	Black
W	White
R	Red
G	Green
L	Blue
Y	Yellow
O	Orange
V	Violet
Br	Brown
B/W	Black/White
R/W	Red/White
R/L	Red/Blue
G/B	Green/Black
G/W	Green/White

Diagram Key

- Connectors
- Ground
- Frame ground
- Connection
- No connection

MAIN HARNESS 1998 EXT EFI

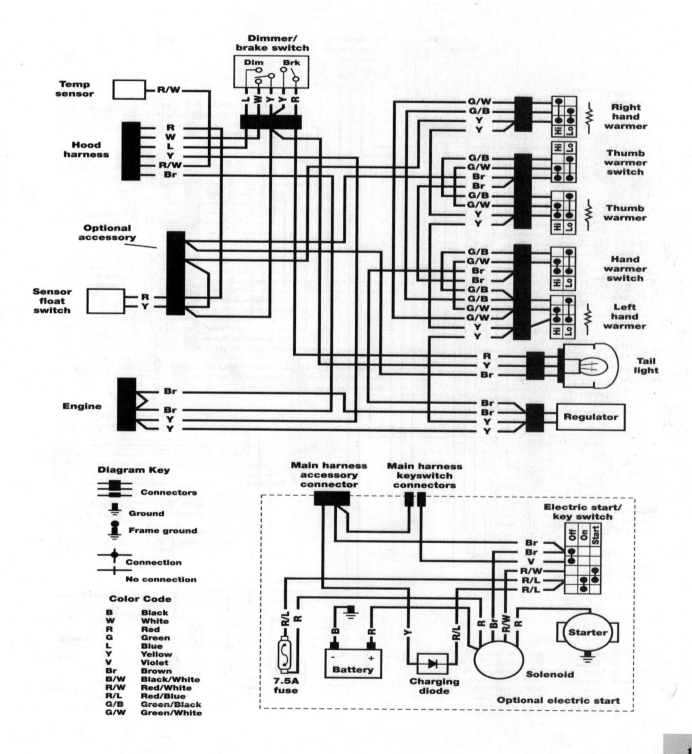

MAIN HARNESS 1998 PANTERA AND EXT EFI DLX

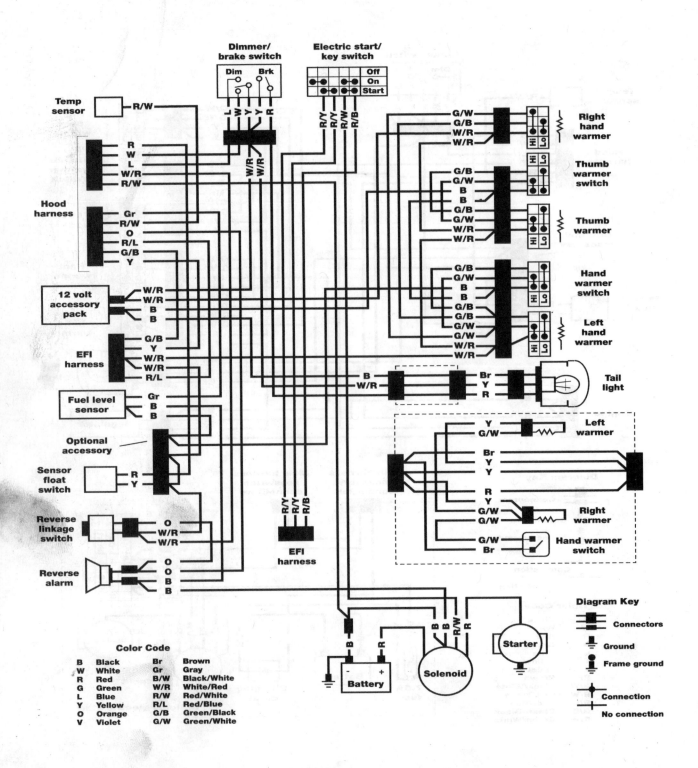